50% OFF HiSET Test Prep Course!

Dear Customer,

Thank you for your purchase of this HiSET Study Guide. Included with your purchase is **discounted access to our online HiSET Prep Course.** Many High School Equivalency Test courses are needlessly expensive and don't deliver enough value. Our course provides the best HiSET prep material, and with discounted access, you only pay half price.

We have structured our online course to perfectly complement your printed study guide. The HiSET Test Prep Course contains **in-depth lessons** that cover all the most important topics, over **1,950 practice questions** to ensure you feel prepared, more than **1,200 flashcards** for studying on the go, and over **400 instructional videos**.

Online HiSET Prep Course

Topics Covered:

- Language Arts - Reading
  - Informational Texts
  - Literary Texts
- Language Arts - Writing
  - Development of Central Position or Claim
  - Organization of Ideas
  - Conventions and Language Facility
- Mathematics
  - Numbers and Operations on Numbers
  - Measurement and Geometry
  - Data Analysis, Probability, and Statistics
- Social Studies
  - American History
  - World History
  - Civics and Government

Course Features:

- HiSET Study Guide
  - Get access to content from the best reviewed study guide available.
- Track Your Progress
  - Our customized course allows you to check off content you have studied or feel confident with.
- 5 Full-Length Practice Tests
  - With 1,950+ practice questions and lesson reviews, you can test yourself again and again to build confidence.
- HiSET Flashcards
  - Our course includes a flashcard mode consisting of over 1,200 content cards to help you study.

To lock in your discounted access, visit www.mometrix.com/university/hiset or simply scan this QR code with your smartphone. At the checkout page, enter the discount code: **HISET50OFF**

If you have any questions or concerns, please contact us at support@mometrix.com.

Access Your Online Resources

Don't miss out on the Online Resources included with your purchase!

Your purchase of this product unlocks access to our Online Resources page. Elevate your study experience with our **interactive practice test interface**, along with all of the additional resources that we couldn't include in this book.

Flip to the Online Resources section at the end of this book to find the link and a QR code to get started!

HiSET®

Prep Book 2026-2027 All Subjects

Secrets Study Guide for the High School Equivalency Test

3 Full-Length Practice Test

350+ Online Video Tutorials

4th Edition

Written and edited by Matthew Bowling

Printed in the United States of America

This paper meets the requirements of ANSI/NISO Z39.48-1992 (Permanence of Paper).

Paperback
ISBN 13: 978-1-5167-2733-9
ISBN 10: 1-5167-2733-9

DEAR FUTURE EXAM SUCCESS STORY

First of all, **THANK YOU** for purchasing Mometrix study materials!

Second, congratulations! You are one of the few determined test-takers who are committed to doing whatever it takes to excel on your exam. **You have come to the right place.** We developed these study materials with one goal in mind: to deliver you the information you need in a format that's concise and easy to use.

In addition to optimizing your guide for the content of the test, we've outlined our recommended steps for breaking down the preparation process into small, attainable goals so you can make sure you stay on track.

We've also analyzed the entire test-taking process, identifying the most common pitfalls and showing how you can overcome them and be ready for any curveball the test throws you.

Standardized testing is one of the biggest obstacles on your road to success, which only increases the importance of doing well in the high-pressure, high-stakes environment of test day. Your results on this test could have a significant impact on your future, and this guide provides the information and practical advice to help you achieve your full potential on test day.

Your success is our success

We would love to hear from you! If you would like to share the story of your exam success or if you have any questions or comments in regard to our products, please contact us at **800-673-8175** or **support@mometrix.com**.

Thanks again for your business and we wish you continued success!

Sincerely,
The Mometrix Test Preparation Team

Need more help? Check out our flashcards at:
http://MometrixFlashcards.com/HiSET

TABLE OF CONTENTS

Introduction

Thank you for purchasing this resource! You have made the choice to prepare yourself for a test that could have a huge impact on your future, and this guide is designed to help you be fully ready for test day. Obviously, it's important to have a solid understanding of the test material, but you also need to be prepared for the unique environment and stressors of the test, so that you can perform to the best of your abilities.

For this purpose, the first section that appears in this guide is the **Secret Keys**. We've devoted countless hours to meticulously researching what works and what doesn't, and we've boiled down our findings to the five most impactful steps you can take to improve your performance on the test. We start at the beginning with study planning and move through the preparation process, all the way to the testing strategies that will help you get the most out of what you know when you're finally sitting in front of the test.

We recommend that you start preparing for your test as far in advance as possible. However, if you've bought this guide as a last-minute study resource and only have a few days before your test, we recommend that you skip over the first two Secret Keys since they address a long-term study plan.

If you struggle with **test anxiety**, we strongly encourage you to check out our recommendations for how you can overcome it. Test anxiety is a formidable foe, but it can be beaten, and we want to make sure you have the tools you need to defeat it.

Review Video Directory

As you work your way through this guide, you will see numerous review video links interspersed with the written content. If you would like to access all of these review videos in one place, click on the video directory link found on the online resources page: **mometrix.com/resources719/hiset-27339**

Secret Key #1 – Plan Big, Study Small

There's a lot riding on your performance. If you want to ace this test, you're going to need to keep your skills sharp and the material fresh in your mind. You need a plan that lets you review everything you need to know while still fitting in your schedule. We'll break this strategy down into three categories.

Information Organization

Start with the information you already have: the official test outline. From this, you can make a complete list of all the concepts you need to cover before the test. Organize these concepts into groups that can be studied together, and create a list of any related vocabulary you need to learn so you can brush up on any difficult terms. You'll want to keep this vocabulary list handy once you actually start studying since you may need to add to it along the way.

Time Management

Once you have your set of study concepts, decide how to spread them out over the time you have left before the test. Break your study plan into small, clear goals so you have a manageable task for each day and know exactly what you're doing. Then just focus on one small step at a time. When you manage your time this way, you don't need to spend hours at a time studying. Studying a small block of content for a short period each day helps you retain information better and avoid stressing over how much you have left to do. You can relax knowing that you have a plan to cover everything in time. In order for this strategy to be effective though, you have to start studying early and stick to your schedule. Avoid the exhaustion and futility that comes from last-minute cramming!

Study Environment

The environment you study in has a big impact on your learning. Studying in a coffee shop, while probably more enjoyable, is not likely to be as fruitful as studying in a quiet room. It's important to keep distractions to a minimum. You're only planning to study for a short block of time, so make the most of it. Don't pause to check your phone or get up to find a snack. It's also important to **avoid multitasking**. Research has consistently shown that multitasking will make your studying dramatically less effective. Your study area should also be comfortable and well-lit so you don't have the distraction of straining your eyes or sitting on an uncomfortable chair.

The time of day you study is also important. You want to be rested and alert. Don't wait until just before bedtime. Study when you'll be most likely to comprehend and remember. Even better, if you know what time of day your test will be, set that time aside for study. That way your brain will be used to working on that subject at that specific time and you'll have a better chance of recalling information.

Finally, it can be helpful to team up with others who are studying for the same test. Your actual studying should be done in as isolated an environment as possible, but the work of organizing the information and setting up the study plan can be divided up. In between study sessions, you can discuss with your teammates the concepts that you're all studying and quiz each other on the details. Just be sure that your teammates are as serious about the test as you are. If you find that your study time is being replaced with social time, you might need to find a new team.

Secret Key #2 – Make Your Studying Count

You're devoting a lot of time and effort to preparing for this test, so you want to be absolutely certain it will pay off. This means doing more than just reading the content and hoping you can remember it on test day. It's important to make every minute of study count. There are two main areas you can focus on to make your studying count.

Retention

It doesn't matter how much time you study if you can't remember the material. You need to make sure you are retaining the concepts. To check your retention of the information you're learning, try recalling it at later times with minimal prompting. Try carrying around flashcards and glance at one or two from time to time or ask a friend who's also studying for the test to quiz you.

To enhance your retention, look for ways to put the information into practice so that you can apply it rather than simply recalling it. If you're using the information in practical ways, it will be much easier to remember. Similarly, it helps to solidify a concept in your mind if you're not only reading it to yourself but also explaining it to someone else. Ask a friend to let you teach them about a concept you're a little shaky on (or speak aloud to an imaginary audience if necessary). As you try to summarize, define, give examples, and answer your friend's questions, you'll understand the concepts better and they will stay with you longer. Finally, step back for a big picture view and ask yourself how each piece of information fits with the whole subject. When you link the different concepts together and see them working together as a whole, it's easier to remember the individual components.

Finally, practice showing your work on any multi-step problems, even if you're just studying. Writing out each step you take to solve a problem will help solidify the process in your mind, and you'll be more likely to remember it during the test.

Modality

Modality simply refers to the means or method by which you study. Choosing a study modality that fits your own individual learning style is crucial. No two people learn best in exactly the same way, so it's important to know your strengths and use them to your advantage.

For example, if you learn best by visualization, focus on visualizing a concept in your mind and draw an image or a diagram. Try color-coding your notes, illustrating them, or creating symbols that will trigger your mind to recall a learned concept. If you learn best by hearing or discussing information, find a study partner who learns the same way or read aloud to yourself. Think about how to put the information in your own words. Imagine that you are giving a lecture on the topic and record yourself so you can listen to it later.

For any learning style, flashcards can be helpful. Organize the information so you can take advantage of spare moments to review. Underline key words or phrases. Use different colors for different categories. Mnemonic devices (such as creating a short list in which every item starts with the same letter) can also help with retention. Find what works best for you and use it to store the information in your mind most effectively and easily.

Secret Key #3 – Practice the Right Way

Your success on test day depends not only on how many hours you put into preparing, but also on whether you prepared the right way. It's good to check along the way to see if your studying is paying off. One of the most effective ways to do this is by taking practice tests to evaluate your progress. Practice tests are useful because they show exactly where you need to improve. Every time you take a practice test, pay special attention to these three groups of questions:

- The questions you got wrong
- The questions you had to guess on, even if you guessed right
- The questions you found difficult or slow to work through

This will show you exactly what your weak areas are, and where you need to devote more study time. Ask yourself why each of these questions gave you trouble. Was it because you didn't understand the material? Was it because you didn't remember the vocabulary? Do you need more repetitions on this type of question to build speed and confidence? Dig into those questions and figure out how you can strengthen your weak areas as you go back to review the material.

Additionally, many practice tests have a section explaining the answer choices. It can be tempting to read the explanation and think that you now have a good understanding of the concept. However, an explanation likely only covers part of the question's broader context. Even if the explanation makes perfect sense, **go back and investigate** every concept related to the question until you're positive you have a thorough understanding.

As you go along, keep in mind that the practice test is just that: practice. Memorizing these questions and answers will not be very helpful on the actual test because it is unlikely to have any of the same exact questions. If you only know the right answers to the sample questions, you won't be prepared for the real thing. **Study the concepts** until you understand them fully, and then you'll be able to answer any question that shows up on the test.

It's important to wait on the practice tests until you're ready. If you take a test on your first day of study, you may be overwhelmed by the amount of material covered and how much you need to learn. Work up to it gradually.

On test day, you'll need to be prepared for answering questions, managing your time, and using the test-taking strategies you've learned. It's a lot to balance, like a mental marathon that will have a big impact on your future. Like training for a marathon, you'll need to start slowly and work your way up. When test day arrives, you'll be ready.

Start with the strategies you've read in the first two Secret Keys—plan your course and study in the way that works best for you. If you have time, consider using multiple study resources to get different approaches to the same concepts. It can be helpful to see difficult concepts from more than one angle. Then find a good source for practice tests. Many times, the test website will suggest potential study resources or provide sample tests.

Practice Test Strategy

If you're able to find at least three practice tests, we recommend this strategy:

Untimed and Open-Book Practice

Take the first test with no time constraints and with your notes and study guide handy. Take your time and focus on applying the strategies you've learned.

Timed and Open-Book Practice

Take the second practice test open-book as well, but set a timer and practice pacing yourself to finish in time.

Timed and Closed-Book Practice

Take any other practice tests as if it were test day. Set a timer and put away your study materials. Sit at a table or desk in a quiet room, imagine yourself at the testing center, and answer questions as quickly and accurately as possible.

Keep repeating timed and closed-book tests on a regular basis until you run out of practice tests or it's time for the actual test. Your mind will be ready for the schedule and stress of test day, and you'll be able to focus on recalling the material you've learned.

Secret Key #4 – Pace Yourself

Once you're fully prepared for the material on the test, your biggest challenge on test day will be managing your time. Just knowing that the clock is ticking can make you panic even if you have plenty of time left. Work on pacing yourself so you can build confidence against the time constraints of the exam. Pacing is a difficult skill to master, especially in a high-pressure environment, so **practice is vital**.

Set time expectations for your pace based on how much time is available. For example, if a section has 60 questions and the time limit is 30 minutes, you know you have to average 30 seconds or less per question in order to answer them all. Although 30 seconds is the hard limit, set 25 seconds per question as your goal, so you reserve extra time to spend on harder questions. When you budget extra time for the harder questions, you no longer have any reason to stress when those questions take longer to answer.

Don't let this time expectation distract you from working through the test at a calm, steady pace, but keep it in mind so you don't spend too much time on any one question. Recognize that taking extra time on one question you don't understand may keep you from answering two that you do understand later in the test. If your time limit for a question is up and you're still not sure of the answer, mark it and move on, and come back to it later if the time and the test format allow. If the testing format doesn't allow you to return to earlier questions, just make an educated guess; then put it out of your mind and move on.

On the easier questions, be careful not to rush. It may seem wise to hurry through them so you have more time for the challenging ones, but it's not worth missing one if you know the concept and just didn't take the time to read the question fully. Work efficiently but make sure you understand the question and have looked at all of the answer choices, since more than one may seem right at first.

Even if you're paying attention to the time, you may find yourself a little behind at some point. You should speed up to get back on track, but do so wisely. Don't panic; just take a few seconds less on each question until you're caught up. Don't guess without thinking, but do look through the answer choices and eliminate any you know are wrong. If you can get down to two choices, it is often worthwhile to guess from those. Once you've chosen an answer, move on and don't dwell on any that you skipped or had to hurry through. If a question was taking too long, chances are it was one of the harder ones, so you weren't as likely to get it right anyway.

On the other hand, if you find yourself getting ahead of schedule, it may be beneficial to slow down a little. The more quickly you work, the more likely you are to make a careless mistake that will affect your score. You've budgeted time for each question, so don't be afraid to spend that time. Practice an efficient but careful pace to get the most out of the time you have.

Secret Key #5 – Have a Plan for Guessing

When you're taking the test, you may find yourself stuck on a question. Some of the answer choices seem better than others, but you don't see the one answer choice that is obviously correct. What do you do?

The scenario described above is very common, yet most test takers have not effectively prepared for it. Developing and practicing a plan for guessing may be one of the single most effective uses of your time as you get ready for the exam.

In developing your plan for guessing, there are three questions to address:

- When should you start the guessing process?
- How should you narrow down the choices?
- Which answer should you choose?

When to Start the Guessing Process

Unless your plan for guessing is to select C every time (which, despite its merits, is not what we recommend), you need to leave yourself enough time to apply your answer elimination strategies. Since you have a limited amount of time for each question, that means that if you're going to give yourself the best shot at guessing correctly, you have to decide quickly whether or not you will guess.

Of course, the best-case scenario is that you don't have to guess at all, so first, see if you can answer the question based on your knowledge of the subject and basic reasoning skills. Focus on the key words in the question and try to jog your memory of related topics. Give yourself a chance to bring the knowledge to mind, but once you realize that you don't have (or you can't access) the knowledge you need to answer the question, it's time to start the guessing process.

It's almost always better to start the guessing process too early than too late. It only takes a few seconds to remember something and answer the question from knowledge. Carefully eliminating wrong answer choices takes longer. Plus, going through the process of eliminating answer choices can actually help jog your memory.

Summary: Start the guessing process as soon as you decide that you can't answer the question based on your knowledge.

How to Narrow Down the Choices

The next chapter in this book (**Test-Taking Strategies**) includes a wide range of strategies for how to approach questions and how to look for answer choices to eliminate. You will definitely want to read those carefully, practice them, and figure out which ones work best for you. Here though, we're going to address a mindset rather than a particular strategy.

Your odds of guessing an answer correctly depend on how many options you are choosing from.

Number of options left	5	4	3	2	1
Odds of guessing correctly	20%	25%	33%	50%	100%

You can see from this chart just how valuable it is to be able to eliminate incorrect answers and make an educated guess, but there are two things that many test takers do that cause them to miss out on the benefits of guessing:

- Accidentally eliminating the correct answer
- Selecting an answer based on an impression

We'll look at the first one here, and the second one in the next section.

To avoid accidentally eliminating the correct answer, we recommend a thought exercise called **the $5 challenge**. In this challenge, you only eliminate an answer choice from contention if you are willing to bet $5 on it being wrong. Why $5? Five dollars is a small but not insignificant amount of money. It's an amount you could afford to lose but wouldn't want to throw away. And while losing $5 once might not hurt too much, doing it twenty times will set you back $100. In the same way, each small decision you make—eliminating a choice here, guessing on a question there—won't by itself impact your score very much, but when you put them all together, they can make a big difference. By holding each answer choice elimination decision to a higher standard, you can reduce the risk of accidentally eliminating the correct answer.

The $5 challenge can also be applied in a positive sense: If you are willing to bet $5 that an answer choice *is* correct, go ahead and mark it as correct.

Summary: Only eliminate an answer choice if you are willing to bet $5 that it is wrong.

Which Answer to Choose

You're taking the test. You've run into a hard question and decided you'll have to guess. You've eliminated all the answer choices you're willing to bet $5 on. Now you have to pick an answer. Why do we even need to talk about this? Why can't you just pick whichever one you feel like when the time comes?

The answer to these questions is that if you don't come into the test with a plan, you'll rely on your impression to select an answer choice, and if you do that, you risk falling into a trap. The test writers know that everyone who takes their test will be guessing on some of the questions, so they intentionally write wrong answer choices to seem plausible. You still have to pick an answer though, and if the wrong answer choices are designed to look right, how can you ever be sure that you're not falling for their trap? The best solution we've found to this dilemma is to take the decision out of your hands entirely. Here is the process we recommend:

Once you've eliminated any choices that you are confident (willing to bet $5) are wrong, select the first remaining choice as your answer.

Whether you choose to select the first remaining choice, the second, or the last, the important thing is that you use some preselected standard. Using this approach guarantees that you will not be enticed into selecting an answer choice that looks right, because you are not basing your decision on how the answer choices look.

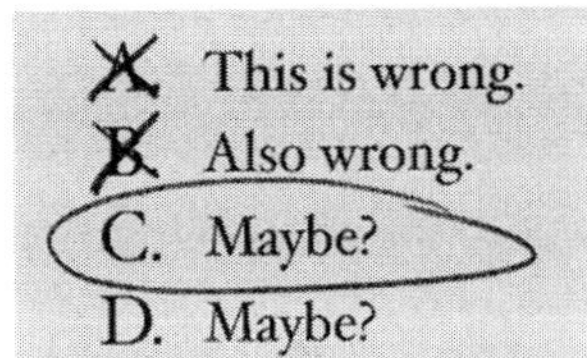

This is not meant to make you question your knowledge. Instead, it is to help you recognize the difference between your knowledge and your impressions. There's a huge difference between thinking an answer is right because of what you know, and thinking an answer is right because it looks or sounds like it should be right.

Summary: To ensure that your selection is appropriately random, make a predetermined selection from among all answer choices you have not eliminated.

Test-Taking Strategies

This section contains a list of test-taking strategies that you may find helpful as you work through the test. By taking what you know and applying logical thought, you can maximize your chances of answering any question correctly!

It is very important to realize that every question is different and every person is different: no single strategy will work on every question, and no single strategy will work for every person. That's why we've included all of them here, so you can try them out and determine which ones work best for different types of questions and which ones work best for you.

Question Strategies

⊘ Read Carefully

Read the question and the answer choices carefully. Don't miss the question because you misread the terms. You have plenty of time to read each question thoroughly and make sure you understand what is being asked. Yet a happy medium must be attained, so don't waste too much time. You must read carefully and efficiently.

⊘ Contextual Clues

Look for contextual clues. If the question includes a word you are not familiar with, look at the immediate context for some indication of what the word might mean. Contextual clues can often give you all the information you need to decipher the meaning of an unfamiliar word. Even if you can't determine the meaning, you may be able to narrow down the possibilities enough to make a solid guess at the answer to the question.

⊘ Prefixes

If you're having trouble with a word in the question or answer choices, try dissecting it. Take advantage of every clue that the word might include. Prefixes can be a huge help. Usually, they allow you to determine a basic meaning. *Pre-* means before, *post-* means after, *pro-* is positive, *de-* is negative. From prefixes, you can get an idea of the general meaning of the word and try to put it into context.

⊘ Hedge Words

Watch out for critical hedge words, such as *likely, may, can, often, almost, mostly, usually, generally, rarely*, and *sometimes*. Question writers insert these hedge phrases to cover every possibility. Often an answer choice will be wrong simply because it leaves no room for exception. Be on guard for answer choices that have definitive words such as *exactly* and *always*.

⊘ Switchback Words

Stay alert for *switchbacks*. These are the words and phrases frequently used to alert you to shifts in thought. The most common switchback words are *but, although*, and *however*. Others include *nevertheless, on the other hand, even though, while, in spite of, despite*, and *regardless of*. Switchback words are important to catch because they can change the direction of the question or an answer choice.

⊘ Face Value

When in doubt, use common sense. Accept the situation in the problem at face value. Don't read too much into it. These problems will not require you to make wild assumptions. If you have to go beyond creativity and warp time or space in order to have an answer choice fit the question, then you should move on and consider the other answer choices. These are normal problems rooted in reality. The applicable relationship or explanation may not be readily apparent, but it is there for you to figure out. Use your common sense to interpret anything that isn't clear.

Answer Choice Strategies

⊘ Answer Selection

The most thorough way to pick an answer choice is to identify and eliminate wrong answers until only one is left, then confirm it is the correct answer. Sometimes an answer choice may immediately seem right, but be careful. The test writers will usually put more than one reasonable answer choice on each question, so take a second to read all of them and make sure that the other choices are not equally obvious. As long as you have time left, it is better to read every answer choice than to pick the first one that looks right without checking the others.

⊘ Answer Choice Families

An answer choice family consists of two (in rare cases, three) answer choices that are very similar in construction and cannot all be true at the same time. If you see two answer choices that are direct opposites or parallels, one of them is usually the correct answer. For instance, if one answer choice says that quantity *x* increases and another either says that quantity *x* decreases (opposite) or says that quantity *y* increases (parallel), then those answer choices would fall into the same family. An answer choice that doesn't match the construction of the answer choice family is more likely to be incorrect. Most questions will not have answer choice families, but when they do appear, you should be prepared to recognize them.

⊘ Eliminate Answers

Eliminate answer choices as soon as you realize they are wrong, but make sure you consider all possibilities. If you are eliminating answer choices and realize that the last one you are left with is also wrong, don't panic. Start over and consider each choice again. There may be something you missed the first time that you will realize on the second pass.

⊘ Avoid Fact Traps

Don't be distracted by an answer choice that is factually true but doesn't answer the question. You are looking for the choice that answers the question. Stay focused on what the question is asking for so you don't accidentally pick an answer that is true but incorrect. Always go back to the question and make sure the answer choice you've selected actually answers the question and is not merely a true statement.

⊘ Extreme Statements

In general, you should avoid answers that put forth extreme actions as standard practice or proclaim controversial ideas as established fact. An answer choice that states the "process should be used in certain situations, if..." is much more likely to be correct than one that states the "process should be discontinued completely." The first is a calm rational statement and doesn't even make a definitive, uncompromising stance, using a hedge word *if* to provide wiggle room, whereas the second choice is far more extreme.

⊘ Benchmark

As you read through the answer choices and you come across one that seems to answer the question well, mentally select that answer choice. This is not your final answer, but it's the one that will help you evaluate the other answer choices. The one that you selected is your benchmark or standard for judging each of the other answer choices. Every other answer choice must be compared to your benchmark. That choice is correct until proven otherwise by another answer choice beating it. If you find a better answer, then that one becomes your new benchmark. Once you've decided that no other choice answers the question as well as your benchmark, you have your final answer.

⊘ Predict the Answer

Before you even start looking at the answer choices, it is often best to try to predict the answer. When you come up with the answer on your own, it is easier to avoid distractions and traps because you will know exactly what to look for. The right answer choice is unlikely to be word-for-word what you came up with, but it should be a close match. Even if you are confident that you have the right answer, you should still take the time to read each option before moving on.

General Strategies

⊘ Tough Questions

If you are stumped on a problem or it appears too hard or too difficult, don't waste time. Move on! Remember though, if you can quickly check for obviously incorrect answer choices, your chances of guessing correctly are greatly improved. Before you completely give up, at least try to knock out a couple of possible answers. Eliminate what you can and then guess at the remaining answer choices before moving on.

⊘ Check Your Work

Since you will probably not know every term listed and the answer to every question, it is important that you get credit for the ones that you do know. Don't miss any questions through careless mistakes. If at all possible, try to take a second to look back over your answer selection and make sure you've selected the correct answer choice and haven't made a costly careless mistake (such as marking an answer choice that you didn't mean to mark). This quick double check should more than pay for itself in caught mistakes for the time it costs.

⊘ Pace Yourself

It's easy to be overwhelmed when you're looking at a page full of questions; your mind is confused and full of random thoughts, and the clock is ticking down faster than you would like. Calm down and maintain the pace that you have set for yourself. Especially as you get down to the last few minutes of the test, don't let the small numbers on the clock make you panic. As long as you are on track by monitoring your pace, you are guaranteed to have time for each question.

⊘ Don't Rush

It is very easy to make errors when you are in a hurry. Maintaining a fast pace in answering questions is pointless if it makes you miss questions that you would have gotten right otherwise. Test writers like to include distracting information and wrong answers that seem right. Taking a little extra time to avoid careless mistakes can make all the difference in your test score. Find a pace that allows you to be confident in the answers that you select.

⊘ Keep Moving

Panicking will not help you pass the test, so do your best to stay calm and keep moving. Taking deep breaths and going through the answer elimination steps you practiced can help to break through a stress barrier and keep your pace.

Final Notes

The combination of a solid foundation of content knowledge and the confidence that comes from practicing your plan for applying that knowledge is the key to maximizing your performance on test day. As your foundation of content knowledge is built up and strengthened, you'll find that the strategies included in this chapter become more and more effective in helping you quickly sift through the distractions and traps of the test to isolate the correct answer.

Now that you're preparing to move forward into the test content chapters of this book, be sure to keep your goal in mind. As you read, think about how you will be able to apply this information on the test. If you've already seen sample questions for the test and you have an idea of the question format and style, try to come up with questions of your own that you can answer based on what you're reading. This will give you valuable practice applying your knowledge in the same ways you can expect to on test day.

Good luck and good studying!

Language Arts—Reading

Informational Texts

Main Ideas and Supporting Details

Identifying Topics and Main Ideas

One of the most important skills in reading comprehension is the identification of **topics** and **main ideas**. There is a subtle difference between these two features. The topic is the subject of a text (i.e., what the text is all about). The main idea, on the other hand, is the most important point being made by the author. The topic is usually expressed in a few words at the most while the main idea often needs a full sentence to be completely defined. As an example, a short passage might be written on the topic of penguins, and the main idea could be written as *Penguins are different from other birds in many ways.* In most nonfiction writing, the topic and the main idea will be **stated directly** and often appear in a sentence at the very beginning or end of the text. When being tested on an understanding of the author's topic, you may be able to skim the passage for the general idea by reading only the first sentence of each paragraph. A body paragraph's first sentence is often—but not always—the main **topic sentence** which gives you a summary of the content in the paragraph.

However, there are cases in which the reader must figure out an **unstated** topic or main idea. In these instances, you must read every sentence of the text and try to come up with an overarching idea that is supported by each of those sentences.

Note: The main idea should not be confused with the thesis statement. While the main idea gives a brief, general summary of a text, the thesis statement provides a **specific perspective** on an issue that the author supports with evidence.

Review Video: Topics and Main Ideas
Visit mometrix.com/academy and enter code: 407801

Supporting Details

Supporting details are smaller pieces of evidence that provide backing for the main point. In order to show that a main idea is correct or valid, an author must add details that prove their point. All texts contain details, but they are only classified as supporting details when they serve to reinforce some larger point. Supporting details are most commonly found in informative and persuasive texts. In some cases, they will be clearly indicated with terms like *for example* or *for instance*, or they will be enumerated with terms like *first, second,* and *last.* However, you need to be prepared for texts that do not contain those indicators. As a reader, you should consider whether the author's supporting details really back up his or her main point. Details can be factual and correct, yet they may not be **relevant** to the author's point. Conversely, details can be relevant, but be ineffective because they are based on opinion or assertions that cannot be proven.

Review Video: Supporting Details
Visit mometrix.com/academy and enter code: 396297

AUTHOR'S PURPOSE

AUTHOR'S PURPOSE

Usually, identifying the author's **purpose** is easier than identifying his or her **position**. In most cases, the author has no interest in hiding his or her purpose. A text that is meant to entertain, for instance, should be written to please the reader. Most narratives, or stories, are written to entertain, though they may also inform or persuade. Informative texts are easy to identify, while the most difficult purpose of a text to identify is persuasion because the author has an interest in making this purpose hard to detect. When a reader discovers that the author is trying to persuade, he or she should be skeptical of the argument. For this reason, persuasive texts often try to establish an entertaining tone and hope to amuse the reader into agreement. On the other hand, an informative tone may be implemented to create an appearance of authority and objectivity.

An author's purpose is evident often in the **organization** of the text (e.g., section headings in bold font points to an informative text). However, you may not have such organization available to you in your exam. Instead, if the author makes his or her main idea clear from the beginning, then the likely purpose of the text is to **inform**. If the author begins by making a claim and provides various arguments to support that claim, then the purpose is probably to **persuade**. If the author tells a story or wants to gain the reader's attention more than to push a particular point or deliver information, then his or her purpose is most likely to **entertain**. As a reader, you must judge authors on how well they accomplish their purpose. In other words, you need to consider the type of passage (e.g., technical, persuasive, etc.) that the author has written and if the author has followed the requirements of the passage type.

Review Video: Understanding the Author's Intent
Visit mometrix.com/academy and enter code: 511819

INFORMATIONAL TEXTS

An **informational text** is written to educate and enlighten readers. Informational texts are almost always nonfiction and are rarely structured as a story. The intention of an informational text is to deliver information in the most comprehensible way. So, look for the structure of the text to be very clear. In an informational text, the thesis statement is one or two sentences that normally appears at the end of the first paragraph. The author may use some colorful language, but he or she is likely to put more emphasis on clarity and precision. Informational essays do not typically appeal to the emotions. They often contain facts and figures and rarely include the opinion of the author; however, readers should remain aware of the possibility for bias as those facts are presented. Sometimes a persuasive essay can resemble an informative essay, especially if the author maintains an even tone and presents his or her views as if they were established fact.

Review Video: Informational Text
Visit mometrix.com/academy and enter code: 924964

PERSUASIVE WRITING

In a persuasive essay, the author is attempting to change the reader's mind or **convince** him or her of something that he or she did not believe previously. There are several identifying characteristics of **persuasive writing**. One is **opinion presented as fact**. When authors attempt to persuade readers, they often present their opinions as if they were fact. Readers must be on guard for statements that sound factual but which cannot be subjected to research, observation, or experiment. Another characteristic of persuasive writing is **emotional language**. An author will often try to play on the emotions of readers by appealing to their sympathy or sense of morality. When an author uses colorful or evocative language with the intent of arousing the reader's passions, then the author may be attempting to persuade. Finally, in many cases, a persuasive text will give an **unfair explanation of opposing positions**, if these positions are mentioned at all.

ENTERTAINING TEXTS

The success or failure of an author's intent to **entertain** is determined by those who read the author's work. Entertaining texts may be either fiction or nonfiction, and they may describe real or imagined people, places, and events. Entertaining texts are often narratives or poems. A text that is written to entertain is likely to contain **colorful language** that engages the imagination and the emotions. Such writing often features a great deal of figurative language, which typically enlivens the subject matter with images and analogies.

Though an entertaining text is not usually written to persuade or inform, authors may accomplish both of these tasks in their work. An entertaining text may *appeal to the reader's emotions* and cause him or her to think differently about a particular subject. In any case, entertaining texts tend to showcase the personality of the author more than other types of writing.

Descriptive Text

In a sense, almost all writing is descriptive, insofar as an author seeks to describe events, ideas, or people to the reader. Some texts, however, are primarily concerned with **description**. A descriptive text focuses on a particular subject and attempts to depict the subject in a way that will be clear to readers. Descriptive texts contain many adjectives and adverbs (i.e., words that give shades of meaning and create a more detailed mental picture for the reader). A descriptive text fails when it is unclear to the reader. A descriptive text will certainly be informative and may be persuasive and entertaining as well.

Review Video: Descriptive Texts
Visit mometrix.com/academy and enter code: 174903

Expression of Feelings

When an author intends to **express feelings**, he or she may use **expressive and bold language**. An author may write with emotion for any number of reasons. Sometimes, authors will express feelings because they are describing a personal situation of great pain or happiness. In other situations, authors will attempt to persuade the reader and will use emotion to stir up the passions. This kind of expression is easy to identify when the writer uses phrases like *I felt* and *I sense*. However, readers may find that the author will simply describe feelings without introducing them. As a reader, you must know the importance of recognizing when an author is expressing emotion and not to become overwhelmed by sympathy or passion. Readers should maintain some **detachment** so that they can still evaluate the strength of the author's argument or the quality of the writing.

Review Video: Emotional Language in Literature
Visit mometrix.com/academy and enter code: 759390

Expository Passage

An **expository** passage aims to **inform** and enlighten readers. Expository passages are nonfiction and usually center around a simple, easily defined topic. Since the goal of exposition is to teach, such a passage should be as clear as possible. Often, an expository passage contains helpful organizing words, like *first*, *next*, *for example*, and *therefore*. These words keep the reader **oriented** in the text. Although expository passages do not need to feature colorful language and artful writing, they are often more effective with these features. For a reader, the challenge of expository passages is to maintain steady attention. Expository passages are not always about subjects that will naturally interest a reader, so the writer is often more concerned with **clarity** and **comprehensibility** than with engaging the reader. By reading actively, you can ensure a good habit of focus when reading an expository passage.

Review Video: Expository Passages
Visit mometrix.com/academy and enter code: 256515

Narrative Passage

A **narrative** passage is a story that can be fiction or nonfiction. However, there are a few elements that a text must have in order to be classified as a narrative. First, the text must have a **plot** (i.e., a series of events). Narratives often proceed in a clear sequence, but this is not a requirement. If the narrative is good, then these events will be interesting to readers. Second, a narrative has **characters**. These characters could be people, animals, or even inanimate objects—so long as they participate in the plot. Third, a narrative passage often contains **figurative language** which is meant to stimulate the imagination of readers by making comparisons and observations. For instance, a *metaphor*, a common piece of figurative language, is a description of one thing in terms of another. *The moon was a frosty snowball* is an example of a metaphor. In the literal sense this is obviously untrue, but the comparison suggests a certain mood for the reader.

TECHNICAL PASSAGE

A **technical** passage is written to *describe* a complex object or process. Technical writing is common in medical and technological fields, in which complex ideas of mathematics, science, and engineering need to be explained *simply* and *clearly*. To ease comprehension, a technical passage usually proceeds in a very logical order. Technical passages often have clear headings and subheadings, which are used to keep the reader oriented in the text. Additionally, you will find that these passages divide sections up with numbers or letters. Many technical passages look more like an outline than a piece of prose. The amount of **jargon** or difficult vocabulary will vary in a technical passage depending on the intended audience. As much as possible, technical passages try to avoid language that the reader will have to research in order to understand the message, yet readers will find that jargon cannot always be avoided.

> **Review Video: Technical Passages**
> Visit mometrix.com/academy and enter code: 478923

COMMON ORGANIZATIONS OF TEXTS

ORGANIZATION OF THE TEXT

The way a text is organized can help readers understand the author's intent and his or her conclusions. There are various ways to organize a text, and each one has a purpose and use. Usually, authors will organize information logically in a passage so the reader can follow and locate the information within the text. However, since not all passages are written with the same logical structure, you need to be familiar with several different types of passage structure.

> **Review Video: Sequence of Events in a Story**
> Visit mometrix.com/academy and enter code: 807512

CHRONOLOGICAL

When using **chronological** order, the author presents information in the order that it happened. For example, biographies are typically written in chronological order. The subject's birth and childhood are presented first, followed by their adult life, and lastly the events leading up to the person's death.

CAUSE AND EFFECT

One of the most common text structures is **cause and effect**. A **cause** is an act or event that makes something happen, and an **effect** is the thing that happens as a result of the cause. A cause-and-effect relationship is not always explicit, but there are some terms in English that signal causes, such as *since*, *because*, and *due to*. Furthermore, terms that signal effects include *consequently, therefore, this leads to*. As an example, consider the sentence *Because the sky was clear, Ron did not bring an umbrella*. The cause is the clear sky, and the effect is that Ron did not bring an umbrella. However, readers may find that sometimes the cause-and-effect relationship will not be clearly noted. For instance, the sentence *He was late and missed the meeting* does not contain any signaling words, but the sentence still contains a cause (he was late) and an effect (he missed the meeting).

> **Review Video: Cause and Effect**
> Visit mometrix.com/academy and enter code: 868099

Review Video: Rhetorical Strategy of Cause and Effect Analysis
Visit mometrix.com/academy and enter code: 725944

Multiple Effects

Be aware of the possibility for a single cause to have **multiple effects.** (e.g., *Single cause*: Because you left your homework on the table, your dog engulfed the assignment. *Multiple effects*: As a result, you receive a failing grade, your parents do not allow you to go out with your friends, you miss out on the new movie, and one of your classmates spoils it for you before you have another chance to watch it).

Multiple Causes

Also, there is the possibility for a single effect to have **multiple causes.** (e.g., *Single effect*: Alan has a fever. *Multiple causes*: An unexpected cold front came through the area, and Alan forgot to take his multi-vitamin to avoid getting sick.) Additionally, an effect can in turn be the cause of another effect, in what is known as a cause-and-effect chain. (e.g., As a result of her disdain for procrastination, Lynn prepared for her exam. This led to her passing her test with high marks. Hence, her resume was accepted and her application was approved.)

Cause and Effect in Persuasive Essays

Persuasive essays, in which an author tries to make a convincing argument and change the minds of readers, usually include cause-and-effect relationships. However, these relationships should not always be taken at face value. Frequently, an author will assume a cause or take an effect for granted. To read a persuasive essay effectively, readers need to judge the cause-and-effect relationships that the author is presenting. For instance, imagine an author wrote the following: *The parking deck has been unprofitable because people would prefer to ride their bikes.* The relationship is clear: the cause is that people prefer to ride their bikes, and the effect is that the parking deck has been unprofitable. However, readers should consider whether this argument is conclusive. Perhaps there are other reasons for the failure of the parking deck: a down economy, excessive fees, etc. Too often, authors present causal relationships as if they are fact rather than opinion. Readers should be on the alert for these dubious claims.

Problem-Solution

Some nonfiction texts are organized to **present a problem** followed by a solution. For this type of text, the problem is often explained before the solution is offered. In some cases, as when the problem is well known, the solution may be introduced briefly at the beginning. Other passages may focus on the solution, and the problem will be referenced only occasionally. Some texts will outline multiple solutions to a problem, leaving readers to choose among them. If the author has an interest or an allegiance to one solution, he or she may fail to mention or describe accurately some of the other solutions. Readers should be careful of the author's agenda when reading a problem-solution text. Only by understanding the author's perspective and interests can one develop a proper judgment of the proposed solution.

Compare and Contrast

Many texts follow the **compare-and-contrast** model in which the similarities and differences between two ideas or things are explored. Analysis of the similarities between ideas is called **comparison**. In an ideal comparison, the author places ideas or things in an equivalent structure, i.e., the author presents the ideas in the same way. If an author wants to show the similarities between cricket and baseball, then he or she may do so by summarizing the equipment and rules for each game. Be mindful of the similarities as they appear in the passage and take note of any differences that are mentioned. Often, these small differences will only reinforce the more general similarity.

Review Video: Compare and Contrast
Visit mometrix.com/academy and enter code: 798319

Thinking critically about ideas and conclusions can seem like a daunting task. One way to ease this task is to understand the basic elements of ideas and writing techniques. Looking at the ways different ideas relate to each other can be a good way for readers to begin their analysis. For instance, sometimes authors will write about two ideas that are in opposition to each other. Or, one author will provide his or her ideas on a topic, and another author may respond in opposition. The analysis of these opposing ideas is known as **contrast**. Contrast is often marred by the author's obvious partiality to one of the ideas. A discerning reader will be put off by an author who does not engage in a fair fight. In an analysis of opposing ideas, both ideas should be presented in clear and reasonable terms. If the author does prefer a side, you need to read carefully to determine the areas where the author shows or avoids this preference. In an analysis of opposing ideas, you should proceed through the passage by marking the major differences point by point with an eye that is looking for an explanation of each side's view. For instance, in an analysis of capitalism and communism, there is an importance in outlining each side's view on labor, markets, prices, personal responsibility, etc. Additionally, as you read through the passages, you should note whether the opposing views present each side in a similar manner.

SEQUENCE

Readers must be able to identify a text's **sequence**, or the order in which things happen. Often, when the sequence is very important to the author, the text is indicated with signal words like *first*, *then*, *next*, and *last*. However, a sequence can be merely implied and must be noted by the reader. Consider the sentence *He walked through the garden and gave water and fertilizer to the plants.* Clearly, the man did not walk through the garden before he collected water and fertilizer for the plants. So, the implied sequence is that he first collected water, then he collected fertilizer, next he walked through the garden, and last he gave water or fertilizer as necessary to the plants. Texts do not always proceed in an orderly sequence from first to last. Sometimes they begin at the end and start over at the beginning. As a reader, you can enhance your understanding of the passage by taking brief notes to clarify the sequence.

Review Video: Sequence
Visit mometrix.com/academy and enter code: 489027

MAKING AND EVALUATING PREDICTIONS

MAKING PREDICTIONS

When we read literature, **making predictions** about what will happen in the writing reinforces our purpose for reading and prepares us mentally. A **prediction** is a guess about what will happen next. Readers constantly make predictions based on what they have read and what they already know. We can make predictions before we begin reading and during our reading. Consider the following sentence: *Staring at the computer screen in shock, Kim blindly reached over for the brimming glass of water on the shelf to her side.* The sentence suggests that Kim is distracted, and that she is not looking at the glass that she is going to pick up. So, a reader might predict that Kim is going to knock over the glass. Of course, not every prediction will be accurate: perhaps Kim will pick the glass up cleanly. Nevertheless, the author has certainly created the expectation that the water might be spilled.

As we read on, we can test the accuracy of our predictions, revise them in light of additional reading, and confirm or refute our predictions. Predictions are always subject to revision as the reader acquires more information. A reader can make predictions by observing the title and illustrations; noting the structure, characters, and subject; drawing on existing knowledge relative to the subject; and asking "why" and "who" questions. Connecting reading to what we already know enables us to learn new information and construct meaning. For example, before third-graders read a book about Johnny Appleseed, they may start a KWL chart—a list of what they *Know*, what they *Want* to know or learn, and what they have *Learned* after reading.

Activating existing background knowledge and thinking about the text before reading improves comprehension.

> **Review Video: Predictive Reading**
> Visit mometrix.com/academy and enter code: 437248

Test-taking tip: To respond to questions requiring future predictions, your answers should be based on evidence of past or present behavior and events.

Evaluating Predictions

When making predictions, readers should be able to explain how they developed their prediction. One way readers can defend their thought process is by citing textual evidence. Textual evidence to evaluate reader predictions about literature includes specific synopses of the work, paraphrases of the work or parts of it, and direct quotations from the work. These references to the text must support the prediction by indicating, clearly or unclearly, what will happen later in the story. A text may provide these indications through literary devices such as foreshadowing. Foreshadowing is anything in a text that gives the reader a hint about what is to come by emphasizing the likelihood of an event or development. Foreshadowing can occur through descriptions, exposition, and dialogue. Foreshadowing in dialogue usually occurs when a character gives a warning or expresses a strong feeling that a certain event will occur. Foreshadowing can also occur through irony. However, unlike other forms of foreshadowing, the events that seem the most likely are the opposite of what actually happens. Instances of foreshadowing and irony can be summarized, paraphrased, or quoted to defend a reader's prediction.

> **Review Video: Textual Evidence for Predictions**
> Visit mometrix.com/academy and enter code: 261070

Making Inferences and Drawing Conclusions

Inferences are logical conclusions that readers make based on their observations and previous knowledge. An inference is based on both what is found in a passage or a story and what is known from personal experience. For instance, a story may say that a character is frightened and can hear howling in the distance. Based on both what is in the text and personal knowledge, it is a logical conclusion that the character is frightened because he hears the sound of wolves. A good inference is supported by the information in a passage.

Implicit and Explicit Information

By inferring, readers construct meanings from text that are personally relevant. By combining their own schemas or concepts and their background information pertinent to the text with what they read, readers interpret it according to both what the author has conveyed and their own unique perspectives. Inferences are different from **explicit information**, which is clearly stated in a passage. Authors do not always explicitly spell out every meaning in what they write; many meanings are implicit. Through inference, readers can comprehend implied meanings in the text, and also derive personal significance from it, making the text meaningful and memorable to them. Inference is a natural process in everyday life. When readers infer, they can draw conclusions about what the author is saying, predict what may reasonably follow, amend these predictions as they continue to read, interpret the import of themes, and analyze the characters' feelings and motivations through their actions.

Example of Drawing Conclusions from Inferences

Read the excerpt and decide why Jana finally relaxed.

> Jana loved her job, but the work was very demanding. She had trouble relaxing. She called a friend, but she still thought about work. She ordered a pizza, but eating it did not help. Then, her kitten jumped on her lap and began to purr. Jana leaned back and began to hum a little tune. She felt better.

You can draw the conclusion that Jana relaxed because her kitten jumped on her lap. The kitten purred, and Jana leaned back and hummed a tune. Then she felt better. The excerpt does not explicitly say that this is the reason why she was able to relax. The text leaves the matter unclear, but the reader can infer or make a "best guess" that this is the reason she is relaxing. This is a logical conclusion based on the information in the passage. It is the best conclusion a reader can make based on the information he or she has read. Inferences are based on the information in a passage, but they are not directly stated in the passage.

Test-taking tip: While being tested on your ability to make correct inferences, you must look for **contextual clues**. An answer can be true, but not the best or most correct answer. The contextual clues will help you find the answer that is the **best answer** out of the given choices. Be careful in your reading to understand the context in which a phrase is stated. When asked for the implied meaning of a statement made in the passage, you should immediately locate the statement and read the **context** in which the statement was made. Also, look for an answer choice that has a similar phrase to the statement in question.

Review Video: Inference
Visit mometrix.com/academy and enter code: 379203

Review Video: How to Support a Conclusion
Visit mometrix.com/academy and enter code: 281653

Reading Comprehension and Connecting with Texts

Comparing Two Stories

When presented with two different stories, there will be **similarities** and **differences** between the two. A reader needs to make a list, or other graphic organizer, of the points presented in each story. Once the reader has written down the main point and supporting points for each story, the two sets of ideas can be compared. The reader can then present each idea and show how it is the same or different in the other story. This is called **comparing and contrasting ideas**.

The reader can compare ideas by stating, for example: "In Story 1, the author believes that humankind will one day land on Mars, whereas in Story 2, the author believes that Mars is too far away for humans to ever step foot on." Note that the two viewpoints are different in each story that the reader is comparing. A reader may state that: "Both stories discussed the likelihood of humankind landing on Mars." This statement shows how the viewpoint presented in both stories is based on the same topic, rather than how each viewpoint is different. The reader will complete a comparison of two stories with a conclusion.

Review Video: How to Compare and Contrast
Visit mometrix.com/academy and enter code: 833765

Outlining a Passage

As an aid to drawing conclusions, **outlining** the information contained in the passage should be a familiar skill to readers. An effective outline will reveal the structure of the passage and will lead to solid conclusions. An effective outline will have a title that refers to the basic subject of the text, though the title does not need to restate the main idea. In most outlines, the main idea will be the first major section. Each major idea in the passage will be established as the head of a category. For instance, the most common outline format calls for the main ideas of the passage to be indicated with Roman numerals. In an effective outline of this kind, each of the main ideas will be represented by a Roman numeral and none of the Roman numerals will designate minor details or secondary ideas. Moreover, all supporting ideas and details should be placed in the appropriate place on the outline. An outline does not need to include every detail listed in the text, but it should feature all of those that are central to the argument or message. Each of these details should be listed under the corresponding main idea.

Review Video: Outlining as an Aid to Drawing Conclusions
Visit mometrix.com/academy and enter code: 584445

Using Graphic Organizers

Ideas from a text can also be organized using **graphic organizers**. A graphic organizer is a way to simplify information and take key points from the text. A graphic organizer such as a timeline may have an event listed for a corresponding date on the timeline, while an outline may have an event listed under a key point that occurs in the text. Each reader needs to create the type of graphic organizer that works the best for him or her in terms of being able to recall information from a story. Examples include a spider-map, which takes a main idea from the story and places it in a bubble with supporting points branching off the main idea. An outline is useful for diagramming the main and supporting points of the entire story, and a Venn diagram compares and contrasts characteristics of two or more ideas.

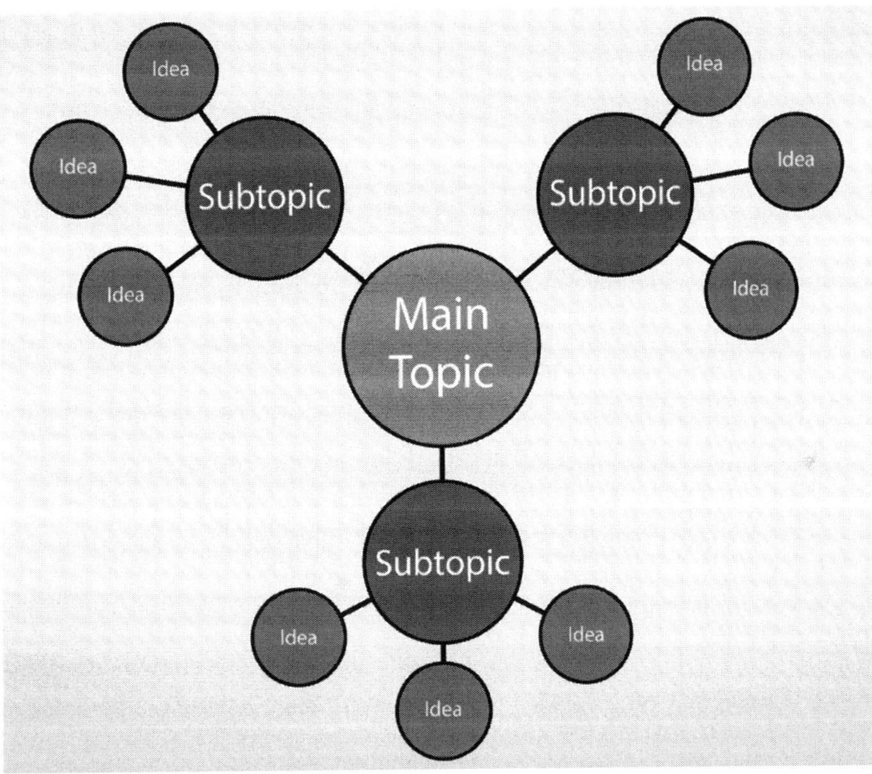

Review Video: Graphic Organizers
Visit mometrix.com/academy and enter code: 665513

Making Logical Conclusions about a Passage

A reader should always be drawing conclusions from the text. Sometimes conclusions are **implied** from written information, and other times the information is **stated directly** within the passage. One should always aim to draw conclusions from information stated within a passage, rather than to draw them from mere implications. At times an author may provide some information and then describe a counterargument. Readers should be alert for direct statements that are subsequently rejected or weakened by the author. Furthermore, you should always read through the entire passage before drawing conclusions. Many readers are trained to expect the author's conclusions at either the beginning or the end of the passage, but many texts do not adhere to this format.

Drawing conclusions from information implied within a passage requires confidence on the part of the reader. **Implications** are things that the author does not state directly, but readers can assume based on what the author does say. Consider the following passage: *I stepped outside and opened my umbrella. By the time I got to work, the cuffs of my pants were soaked.* The author never states that it is raining, but this fact is clearly implied. Conclusions based on implication must be well supported by the text. In order to draw a solid conclusion, readers should have **multiple pieces of evidence**. If readers have only one piece, they must be assured that there is no other possible explanation than their conclusion. A good reader will be able to draw many conclusions from information implied by the text, which will be a great help on the exam.

DRAWING CONCLUSIONS

A common type of inference that a reader has to make is **drawing a conclusion**. The reader makes this conclusion based on the information provided within a text. Certain facts are included to help a reader come to a specific conclusion. For example, a story may open with a man trudging through the snow on a cold winter day, dragging a sled behind him. The reader can logically **infer** from the setting of the story that the man is wearing heavy winter clothes in order to stay warm. Information is implied based on the setting of a story, which is why **setting** is an important element of the text. If the same man in the example was trudging down a beach on a hot summer day, dragging a surf board behind him, the reader would assume that the man is not wearing heavy clothes. The reader makes inferences based on their own experiences and the information presented to them in the story.

Test-taking tip: When asked to identify a conclusion that may be drawn, look for critical "hedge" phrases, such as *likely*, *may*, *can*, and *will often*, among many others. When you are being tested on this knowledge, remember the question that writers insert into these hedge phrases to cover every possibility. Often an answer will be wrong simply because there is no room for exception. Extreme positive or negative answers (such as always or never) are usually not correct. When answering these questions, the reader **should not** use any outside knowledge that is not gathered directly or reasonably inferred from the passage. Correct answers can be derived straight from the passage.

EXAMPLE

Read the following sentence from *Little Women* by Louisa May Alcott and draw a conclusion based upon the information presented:

> *You know the reason Mother proposed not having any presents this Christmas was because it is going to be a hard winter for everyone; and she thinks we ought not to spend money for pleasure, when our men are suffering so in the army.*

Based on the information in the sentence, the reader can conclude, or **infer**, that the men are away at war while the women are still at home. The pronoun *our* gives a clue to the reader that the character is speaking about men she knows. In addition, the reader can assume that the character is speaking to a brother or sister, since the term "Mother" is used by the character while speaking to another person. The reader can also come to the conclusion that the characters celebrate Christmas, since it is mentioned in the **context** of the sentence. In the sentence, the mother is presented as an unselfish character who is opinionated and thinks about the wellbeing of other people.

SUMMARIZING

A helpful tool is the ability to **summarize** the information that you have read in a paragraph or passage format. This process is similar to creating an effective outline. First, a summary should accurately define the main idea of the passage, though the summary does not need to explain this main idea in exhaustive detail. The summary should continue by laying out the most important supporting details or arguments from the passage. All of the significant supporting details should be included, and none of the details included should be irrelevant or insignificant. Also, the summary should accurately report all of these details. Too often, the desire for brevity in a summary leads to the sacrifice of clarity or accuracy. Summaries are often difficult to read because they omit all of the graceful language, digressions, and asides that distinguish great writing. However, an effective summary should communicate the same overall message as the original text.

Review Video: Summarizing Text
Visit mometrix.com/academy and enter code: 172903

Paraphrasing

Paraphrasing is another method that the reader can use to aid in comprehension. When paraphrasing, one puts what they have read into their own words by rephrasing what the author has written, or one "translates" all of what the author shared into their own words by including as many details as they can.

Evaluating a Passage

It is important to understand the logical conclusion of the ideas presented in an informational text. **Identifying a logical conclusion** can help you determine whether you agree with the writer or not. Coming to this conclusion is much like making an inference: the approach requires you to combine the information given by the text with what you already know and make a logical conclusion. If the author intended for the reader to draw a certain conclusion, then you can expect the author's argumentation and detail to be leading in that direction.

One way to approach the task of drawing conclusions is to make brief **notes** of all the points made by the author. When the notes are arranged on paper, they may clarify the logical conclusion. Another way to approach conclusions is to consider whether the reasoning of the author raises any pertinent questions. Sometimes you will be able to draw several conclusions from a passage. On occasion these will be conclusions that were never imagined by the author. Therefore, be aware that these conclusions must be **supported directly by the text**.

Evaluation of Summaries

A summary of a literary passage is a condensation in the reader's own words of the passage's main points. Several guidelines can be used in evaluating a summary. The summary should be complete yet concise. It should be accurate, balanced, fair, neutral, and objective, excluding the reader's own opinions or reactions. It should reflect in similar proportion how much each point summarized was covered in the original passage. Summary writers should include tags of attribution, like "Macaulay argues that" to reference the original author whose ideas are represented in the summary. Summary writers should not overuse quotations; they should only quote central concepts or phrases they cannot precisely convey in words other than those of the original author. Another aspect of evaluating a summary is considering whether it can stand alone as a coherent, unified composition. In addition, evaluation of a summary should include whether its writer has cited the original source of the passage they have summarized so that readers can find it.

Making Connections to Enhance Comprehension

Reading involves thinking. For good comprehension, readers make **text-to-self**, **text-to-text**, and **text-to-world connections**. Making connections helps readers understand text better and predict what might occur next based on what they already know, such as how characters in the story feel or what happened in another text. Text-to-self connections with the reader's life and experiences make literature more personally relevant and meaningful to readers. Readers can make connections before, during, and after reading—including whenever the text reminds them of something similar they have encountered in life or other texts. The genre, setting, characters, plot elements, literary structure and devices, and themes an author uses allow a reader to make connections to other works of literature or to people and events in their own lives. Venn diagrams and other graphic organizers help visualize connections. Readers can also make double-entry notes: key content, ideas, events, words, and quotations on one side, and the connections with these on the other.

Reading Informational Texts

Language Use

Literal and Figurative Language

As in fictional literature, informational text also uses both **literal language**, which means just what it says, and **figurative language**, which imparts more than literal meaning. For example, an informational text author might use a simile or direct comparison, such as writing that a racehorse "ran like the wind." Informational text authors also use metaphors or implied comparisons, such as "the cloud of the Great Depression." Imagery may also appear in informational texts to increase the reader's understanding of ideas and concepts discussed in the text.

> **Review Video: Figurative Language**
> Visit mometrix.com/academy and enter code: 584902

Explicit and Implicit Information

When informational text states something explicitly, the reader is told by the author exactly what is meant, which can include the author's interpretation or perspective of events. For example, a professor writes, "I have seen students go into an absolute panic just because they weren't able to complete the exam in the time they were allotted." This explicitly tells the reader that the students were afraid, and by using the words "just because," the writer indicates their fear was exaggerated out of proportion relative to what happened. However, another professor writes, "I have had students come to me, their faces drained of all color, saying 'We weren't able to finish the exam.'" This is an example of implicit meaning: the second writer did not state explicitly that the students were panicked. Instead, he wrote a description of their faces being "drained of all color." From this description, the reader can infer that the students were so frightened that their faces paled.

> **Review Video: Explicit and Implicit Information**
> Visit mometrix.com/academy and enter code: 735771

Making Inferences About Informational Text

With informational text, reader comprehension depends not only on recalling important statements and details, but also on reader inferences based on examples and details. Readers add information from the text to what they already know to draw inferences about the text. These inferences help the readers to fill in the information that the text does not explicitly state, enabling them to understand the text better. When reading a nonfictional autobiography or biography, for example, the most appropriate inferences might concern the events in the book, the actions of the subject of the autobiography or biography, and the message the author means to convey. When reading a nonfictional expository (informational) text, the reader would best draw inferences about problems and their solutions, and causes and their effects. When reading a nonfictional persuasive text, the reader will want to infer ideas supporting the author's message and intent.

Structures or Organizational Patterns in Informational Texts

Informational text can be **descriptive**, appealing to the five senses and answering the questions what, who, when, where, and why. Another method of structuring informational text is sequence and order. **Chronological** texts relate events in the sequence that they occurred, from start to finish, while how-to texts organize information into a series of instructions in the sequence in which the steps should be followed. **Comparison-contrast** structures of informational text describe various ideas to their readers by pointing out how things or ideas are similar and how they are different. **Cause and effect** structures of informational text describe events that occurred and identify the causes or reasons that those events occurred. **Problem and solution** structures of informational texts introduce and describe problems and offer one or more solutions for each problem described.

Determining an Informational Author's Purpose

Informational authors' purposes are why they write texts. Readers must determine authors' motivations and goals. Readers gain greater insight into a text by considering the author's motivation. This develops critical reading skills. Readers perceive writing as a person's voice, not simply printed words. Uncovering author motivations and purposes empowers readers to know what to expect from the text, read for relevant details, evaluate authors and their work critically, and respond effectively to the motivations and persuasions of the text. The main idea of a text is what the reader is supposed to understand from reading it; the purpose of the text is why the author has written it and what the author wants readers to do with its information. Authors state some purposes clearly, while other purposes may be unstated but equally significant. When stated purposes contradict other parts of a text, the author may have a hidden agenda. Readers can better evaluate a text's effectiveness, whether they agree or disagree with it, and why they agree or disagree through identifying unstated author purposes.

Identifying Author's Point of View or Purpose

In some informational texts, readers find it easy to identify the author's point of view and purpose, such as when the author explicitly states his or her position and reason for writing. But other texts are more difficult, either because of the content or because the authors give neutral or balanced viewpoints. This is particularly true in scientific texts, in which authors may state the purpose of their research in the report, but never state their point of view except by interpreting evidence or data.

To analyze text and identify point of view or purpose, readers should ask themselves the following four questions:

1. With what main point or idea does this author want to persuade readers to agree?
2. How does this author's word choice affect the way that readers consider this subject?
3. How do this author's choices of examples and facts affect the way that readers consider this subject?
4. What is it that this author wants to accomplish by writing this text?

Review Video: Understanding the Author's Intent
Visit mometrix.com/academy and enter code: 511819

Review Video: Author's Position
Visit mometrix.com/academy and enter code: 827954

Evaluating Arguments Made by Informational Text Writers

When evaluating an informational text, the first step is to identify the argument's conclusion. Then identify the author's premises that support the conclusion. Try to paraphrase premises for clarification and make the conclusion and premises fit. List all premises first, sequentially numbered, then finish with the conclusion. Identify any premises or assumptions not stated by the author but required for the stated premises to support the conclusion. Read word assumptions sympathetically, as the author might. Evaluate whether premises reasonably support the conclusion. For inductive reasoning, the reader should ask if the premises are true, if they support the conclusion, and if so, how strongly. For deductive reasoning, the reader should ask if the argument is valid or invalid. If all premises are true, then the argument is valid unless the conclusion can be false. If it can, then the argument is invalid. An invalid argument can be made valid through alterations such as the addition of needed premises.

Use of Rhetoric in Informational Texts

There are many ways authors can support their claims, arguments, beliefs, ideas, and reasons for writing in informational texts. For example, authors can appeal to readers' sense of **logic** by communicating their reasoning through a carefully sequenced series of logical steps to help "prove" the points made. Authors can appeal to readers' **emotions** by using descriptions and words that evoke feelings of sympathy, sadness, anger, righteous indignation, hope, happiness, or any other emotion to reinforce what they express and share with their audience. Authors may appeal to the **moral** or **ethical values** of readers by using words and descriptions that can convince readers that something is right or wrong. By relating personal anecdotes, authors can supply readers with more accessible, realistic examples of points they make, as well as appealing to their emotions. They can provide supporting evidence by reporting case studies. They can also illustrate their points by making analogies to which readers can better relate.

ORGANIZATIONAL FEATURES IN TEXTS

TEXT FEATURES IN INFORMATIONAL TEXTS

- The **title of a text** gives readers some idea of its content.
- The **table of contents** is a list near the beginning of a text, showing the book's sections and chapters and their coinciding page numbers. This gives readers an overview of the whole text and helps them find specific chapters easily.
- An **appendix**, at the back of the book or document, includes important information that is not present in the main text.
- Also at the back, an **index** lists the book's important topics alphabetically with their page numbers to help readers find them easily.
- **Glossaries**, usually found at the backs of books, list technical terms alphabetically with their definitions to aid vocabulary learning and comprehension. Boldface print is used to emphasize certain words, often identifying words included in the text's glossary where readers can look up their definitions.
- **Headings** separate sections of text and show the topic of each.
- **Subheadings** divide subject headings into smaller, more specific categories to help readers organize information.
- **Footnotes**, at the bottom of the page, give readers more information, such as citations or links.
- **Bullet points** list items separately, making facts and ideas easier to see and understand.
- A **sidebar** is a box of information to one side of the main text giving additional information, often on a more focused or in-depth example of a topic.

VISUAL FEATURES IN TEXTS

- **Illustrations** and **photographs** are pictures that visually emphasize important points in text.
- The **captions** below the illustrations explain what those images show.
- **Charts** and **tables** are visual forms of information that make something easier to understand quickly.
- **Diagrams** are drawings that show relationships or explain a process.
- **Graphs** visually show the relationships among multiple sets of information plotted along vertical and horizontal axes.
- **Maps** show geographical information visually to help readers understand the relative locations of places covered in the text.
- **Timelines** are visual graphics that show historical events in chronological order to help readers see their sequence.

Review Video: Informational Text
Visit mometrix.com/academy and enter code: 924964

Technical Language

Technical Language

Technical language is more impersonal than literary and vernacular language. Passive voice makes the tone impersonal. For example, instead of writing, "We found this a central component of protein metabolism," scientists write, "This was found a central component of protein metabolism." While science professors have traditionally instructed students to avoid active voice because it leads to first-person ("I" and "we") usage, science editors today find passive voice dull and weak. Many journal articles combine both. Tone in technical science writing should be detached, concise, and professional. While one may normally write, "This chemical has to be available for proteins to be digested," professionals write technically, "The presence of this chemical is required for the enzyme to break the covalent bonds of proteins." The use of technical language appeals to both technical and non-technical audiences by displaying the author or speaker's understanding of the subject and suggesting their credibility regarding the message they are communicating.

Technical Material for Non-Technical Readers

Writing about **technical subjects** for **non-technical readers** differs from writing for colleagues because authors place more importance on delivering a critical message than on imparting the maximum technical content possible. Technical authors also must assume that non-technical audiences do not have the expertise to comprehend extremely scientific or technical messages, concepts, and terminology. They must resist the temptation to impress audiences with their scientific knowledge and expertise and remember that their primary purpose is to communicate a message that non-technical readers will understand, feel, and respond to. Non-technical and technical styles include similarities. Both should formally cite any references or other authors' work utilized in the text. Both must follow intellectual property and copyright regulations. This includes the author's protecting his or her own rights, or a public domain statement, as he or she chooses.

Review Video: Technical Passages
Visit mometrix.com/academy and enter code: 478923

Non-Technical Audiences

Writers of technical or scientific material may need to write for many non-technical audiences. Some readers have no technical or scientific background, and those who do may not be in the same field as the authors. Government and corporate policymakers and budget managers need technical information they can understand for decision-making. Citizens affected by technology or science are a different audience. Non-governmental organizations can encompass many of the preceding groups. Elementary and secondary school programs also need non-technical language for presenting technical subject matter. Additionally, technical authors will need to use non-technical language when collecting consumer responses to surveys, presenting scientific or para-scientific material to the public, writing about the history of science, and writing about science and technology in developing countries.

Use of Everyday Language

Authors of technical information sometimes must write using non-technical language that readers outside their disciplinary fields can comprehend. They should use not only non-technical terms, but also normal, everyday language to accommodate readers whose native language is different than the language the text is written in. For example, instead of writing that "eustatic changes like thermal expansion are causing hazardous conditions in the littoral zone," an author would do better to write that "a rising sea level is threatening the coast." When technical terms cannot be avoided, authors should also define or explain them using non-technical language. Although authors must cite references and acknowledge their use of others' work, they should avoid the kinds of references or citations that they would use in scientific journals—unless they reinforce author messages. They should not use endnotes, footnotes, or any other complicated referential techniques because non-technical journal publishers usually do not accept them. Including high-resolution illustrations, photos, maps, or satellite images and incorporating multimedia into digital publications will enhance non-technical writing about technical subjects. Technical authors may publish using non-technical language in e-journals, trade journals, specialty newsletters, and daily newspapers.

Types of Technical Writing

Types of Printed Communication

Memo

A memo (short for *memorandum*) is a common form of written communication. There is a standard format for these documents. It is typical for there to be a **heading** at the top indicating the author, date, and recipient. In some cases, this heading will also include the author's title and the name of his or her institution. Below this information will be the **body** of the memo. These documents are typically written by and for members of the same organization. They usually contain a plan of action, a request for information on a specific topic, or a response to such a request. Memos are considered to be official documents, so they are usually written in a **formal** style. Many memos are organized with numbers or bullet points, which make it easier for the reader to identify key ideas.

Posted Announcement

People post **announcements** for all sorts of occasions. Many people are familiar with notices for lost pets, yard sales, and landscaping services. In order to be effective, these announcements need to *contain all of the information* the reader requires to act on the message. For instance, a lost pet announcement needs to include a good description of the animal and a contact number for the owner. A yard sale notice should include the address, date, and hours of the sale, as well as a brief description of the products that will be available there. When composing an announcement, it is important to consider the perspective of the **audience**—what will they need to know in order to respond to the message? Although a posted announcement can have color and decoration to attract the eye of the passerby, it must also convey the necessary information clearly.

Classified Advertisement

Classified advertisements, or **ads**, are used to sell or buy goods, to attract business, to make romantic connections, and to do countless other things. They are an inexpensive, and sometimes free, way to make a brief **pitch**. Classified ads used to be found only in newspapers or special advertising circulars, but there are now online listings as well. The style of these ads has remained basically the same. An ad usually begins with a word or phrase indicating what is being **sold** or **sought**. Then, the listing will give a brief **description** of the product or service. Because space is limited and costly in newspapers, classified ads there will often contain abbreviations for common attributes. For instance, two common abbreviations are *bk* for *black*, and *obo* for *or best offer*. Classified ads will then usually conclude by listing the **price** (or the amount the seeker is willing to pay), followed by **contact information** like a telephone number or email address.

Scale Readings of Standard Measurement Instruments

The scales used on **standard measurement instruments** are fairly easy to read with a little practice. Take the **ruler** as an example. A typical ruler has different units along each long edge. One side measures inches, and the other measures centimeters. The units are specified close to the zero reading for the ruler. Note that the ruler does not begin measuring from its outermost edge. The zero reading is a black line a tiny distance inside of the edge. On the inches side, each inch is indicated with a long black line and a number. Each half-inch is noted with a slightly shorter line. Quarter-inches are noted with still shorter lines, eighth-inches are noted with even shorter lines, and sixteenth-inches are noted with the shortest lines of all. On the centimeter side, the second-largest black lines indicate half-centimeters, and the smaller lines indicate tenths of centimeters, otherwise known as millimeters.

Visual Information in Informational Texts

Charts, Graphs, and Visuals

Tables

Tables are presented in a standard format so they will be easy to read and understand. A title is at the top, a short phrase indicating the information the table or graph intends to convey. The title of a table could be something like "Median Income for Various Education Levels" or "Price of Milk Compared to Demand." A table is composed of information laid out in vertical columns and horizontal rows. Typically, each column will have a label. If "Median Income for Various Education Levels" was placed in a table format, the two columns could be labeled "Education Level" and "Median Annual Salary." Each location on the table is called a cell, which holds a piece of information. Cells are defined by their column and row (e.g., second column, fifth row).

Median Annual Salary for Various Education Levels

Education Level	Median Annual Salary
Associate degree	$52,260
Bachelor's degree	$74,464
Master's degree	$86,372
Professional degree	$108,160
Doctoral degree	$108,316

GRAPHS

Like a table, a graph typically has a title at the top. This title may simply state the identities of the two axes: e.g., "Income vs. Education." However, the title may also be something more descriptive, like "A comparison of average income with level of education." In any case, bar and line graphs are laid out along two perpendicular lines, or axes. The vertical axis is called the *y*-axis, and the horizontal axis is called the *x*-axis. It is typical for the *x*-axis to be the independent variable and the *y*-axis to be the dependent variable. The independent variable is the one manipulated by the researcher or creator of the graph. In the above example, the independent variable would be "education level," since the maker of the graph will define these values (associate degree, bachelor's degree, master's degree, etc.). The dependent value is not controlled by the researcher.

When selecting a graph format, it is important to consider the intention and the structure of the presentation. A bar graph is appropriate for displaying the relations between a series of distinct quantities that are on the same scale. For instance, if one wanted to display the amount of money spent on groceries during the months of a year, a bar graph would be appropriate. The vertical axis would represent values of money, and the horizontal axis would identify each month. A line graph also requires data expressed in common units, but it is better for demonstrating the general trend in that data. If the grocery expenses were plotted on a line graph instead of a bar graph, there would be more emphasis on whether the amount of money spent rose or fell over the course of the year. Whereas a bar graph is good for showing the relationships between the different values plotted, the line graph is good for showing whether the values tended to increase, decrease, or remain stable.

PIE CHART

A pie chart, also known as a circle graph, is useful for depicting how a single unit or category is divided. The standard pie chart is a circle with designated wedges. Each wedge is **proportional** in size to a part of the whole. For instance, consider Shawna, a student at City College, who uses a pie chart to represent her budget. If she spends half of her money on rent, then the pie chart will represent that amount with a line through the center of the pie. If she spends a quarter of her money on food, there will be a line extending from the edge of the circle to the center at a right angle to the line depicting rent. This illustration would make it clear that the student spends twice the amount of money on rent as she does on food.

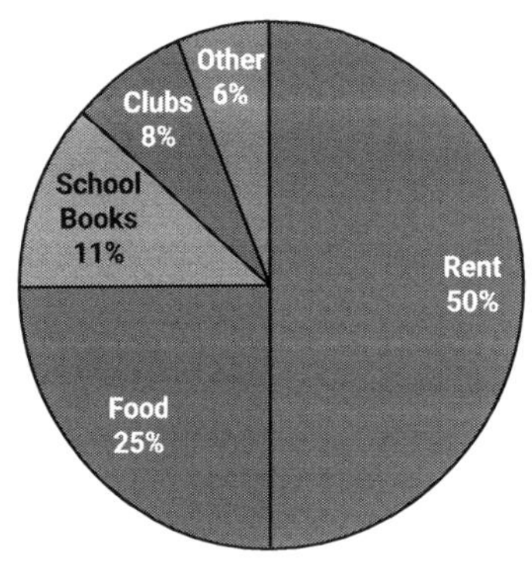

A pie chart is effective at showing how a single entity is divided into parts. They are not effective at demonstrating the relationships between parts of different wholes. For example, an unhelpful use of a pie chart would be to compare the respective amounts of state and federal spending devoted to infrastructure since these values are only meaningful in the context of the entire budget.

Bar Graph

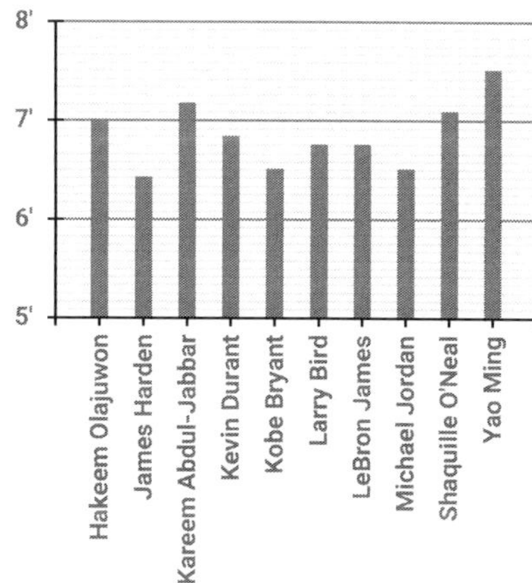

The bar graph is one of the most common visual representations of information. **Bar graphs** are used to illustrate sets of numerical **data**. The graph has a vertical axis (along which numbers are listed) and a horizontal axis (along which categories, words, or some other indicators are placed). One example of a bar graph is a depiction of the respective heights of famous basketball players: the vertical axis would contain numbers ranging from five to eight feet, and the horizontal axis would contain the names of the players. The length of the bar above the player's name would illustrate his height, and the top of the bar would stop perpendicular to the height listed along the left side. In this representation, one would see that Yao Ming is taller than Michael Jordan because Yao's bar would be higher.

Line Graph

A line graph is a type of graph that is typically used for measuring trends over time. The graph is set up along a vertical and a horizontal **axis**. The variables being measured are listed along the left side and the bottom side of the axes. Points are then plotted along the graph as they correspond with their values for each variable. For instance, consider a line graph measuring a person's income for each month of the year. If the person earned $1500 in January, there should be a point directly above January (perpendicular to the horizontal axis) and directly to the right of $1500 (perpendicular to the vertical axis). Once all of the lines are plotted, they are connected with a line from left to right. This line provides a nice visual illustration of the general **trends** of the data, if they exist. For instance, using the earlier example, if the line sloped up, then one would see that the person's income had increased over the course of the year.

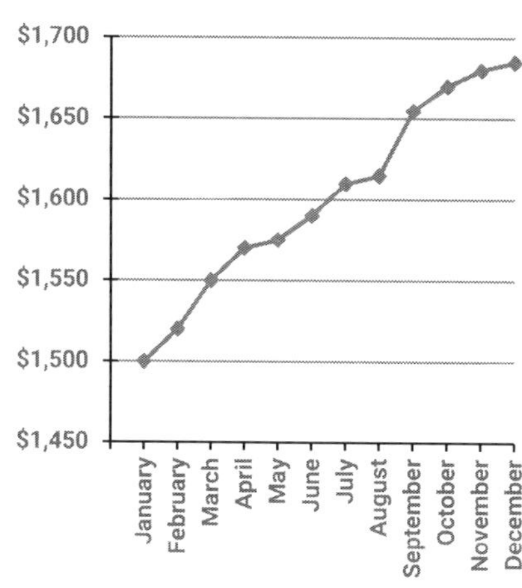

Pictographs

A **pictograph** is a graph, generally in the horizontal orientation, that uses pictures or symbols to represent the data. Each pictograph must have a key that defines the picture or symbol and gives the quantity each picture or symbol represents. Pictures or symbols on a pictograph are not always shown as whole elements. In this case, the fraction of the picture or symbol shown represents the same fraction of the quantity a whole picture or symbol stands for.

> **Review Video: Pictographs**
> Visit mometrix.com/academy and enter code: 147860

Media Types

Media and Format Choices

Effective communication depends on choosing the correct method. Media and format choices are influenced by the target audience, the budget, and the needs of the audience.

Instructional Videos

Instructional videos have potential for excellent two-way communication because questions and feedback can be built in. Videos can be targeted to particular audiences, and they can be paused for discussion or replayed to reinforce concepts. Viewers can see processes, including "before," "during," and "after" phases. Videos are accessible because most communities have at least one DVD player or computer. Moreover, video players and computers are continually becoming less expensive to buy and use. Disadvantages include the necessity of editing software and equipment in some cases, as well as the need for support from other print materials. There is also danger of overuse, if other media or methods are more appropriate, and higher up-front costs. Producers of instructional videos must account for the costs of script development and hiring local performers as needed.

DVDs and CDs

Interactive DVDs and CDs, such as games, give viewers the opportunity to actively participate as they learn information. Additionally, videos are considered to be a professional method of sharing information. Compared to many other media formats, discs are comparatively inexpensive to make and are easy to transport due to their small size and weight. They are more resistant to damage and aging than older videotape technology, making them more durable. Some disadvantages include needing access to technology to play what is stored on the disc and access to certain software programs to add new content to a disc, especially if the producer wants to include video animation or audio commentary. Producers must also consider expenses concerning paid staff and production and labeling expenses. Content that would appear on DVDs and CDs can alternatively be shared through streaming services or digital files stored on a computer or other compatible device.

Television and Radio

Both television and radio are forms of mass media that reach many people. TV has the broadest reach and can market to the general public or be customized for target audiences, while radio only tends to reach specific target audiences. TV has the advantage of video plus audio, while radio broadcasts only feature audio. However, access to television programs is more expensive than access to radio broadcasts. A shared disadvantage is that TV and radio audiences can only interact directly during call-in programs. Additionally, programming times may be inconvenient, but tape, digital sound, and digital video recording (DVR) can remedy this. Many streaming services also provide access to these programs. Both television and radio are useful for communicating simple slogans and messages, and both can generate awareness, interest, and excitement.

Newspapers

Except for the occasional community columns, news releases, and letters to the editor, newspaper pages and features afford little opportunity for audience input or participation. However, they do reach and appeal to the general public. Cost is an advantage: hiring a PR writer and paying for a news advertisement costs much less than a radio or TV spot. Additionally, newspaper features are high-status, and audiences can reread and review them as often as they like. However, newspaper ads may have difficulty affecting the reader as deeply without audio or video, and they require a literate audience. Their publication is also subject to editors' whims and biases. Newspaper pieces combining advertising and editorial content—"advertorials"—provide inclusion of paid material, but are viewed as medium-status and cost more.

Websites, Blogs, Mobile Phones, and Text Messaging

Computer literacy is required for online material, but participation potential is high via websites, e-networking, and blogging. Mobile phones and text messaging are used for enormous direct, public, two-way and one-on-one communication, with timely information and reminders. Web media need a literate public and can be tailored for specific audiences. They afford global information, are accessible by increasingly technology-literate populations, and are high-status. Web media disadvantages include the necessity of computers and people to design, manage, and supply content, as well as to provide technical support. Mobile and text media are globally popular, but appeal especially to certain demographics like teens and young adults. They are increasingly available, especially in rural regions, and are decreasing in cost. Mobile and text media disadvantages include required brevity in texts and provider messaging charges. Links to related websites and pages within existing sites are also advantages of digital media.

Public Presentations and Slideshows

Public presentations have great potential for audience participation and can directly target various audiences. They can encourage the establishment of partnerships and groups, stimulate local ownership of issues and projects, and make information public. A drawback to public presentations is that they are limited to nights, weekends, or whenever audiences are available and do not always attract the intended audience.

Another method of presentation is to use **slideshows**. These presentations are best for sophisticated audiences like professionals, civil servants, and service organizations. Well-designed slideshows are good for stimulating audience interest, selling ideas, and marketing products. Also, they are accessible online as well as in-person so they can reach a broader audience. Slideshow disadvantages include the necessity of projectors and other equipment. They are also limited to communicating more general points, outlines, and summaries rather than conveying a multitude of information in more detail.

Posters and Brochures

Both **posters** and **brochures** can target audiences of the general public and more specific public sectors. Posters are better for communicating simple slogans and messages, while brochures can include more detail and are better for printing instructional information. Both can be inexpensive to produce, especially if printed only as needed and in-house. Posters can often be printed in-house without using outside printing companies. However, it is difficult to get feedback on both posters and brochures—unless they have been broadly tested, or if their publication is accompanied by workshops and other participatory events. A disadvantage of using posters is that they are designed to draw attention and communicate quickly, as they are mostly viewed in passing. This means that their messages must be simple and communicate efficiently. A disadvantage of using brochures is that they can only be distributed to a specific, limited group or area. Posters and brochures are also only understood when audiences are literate in both written language and visual elements.

Flyers and Fact Sheets

Flyers and fact sheets have one-way communication potential because readers cannot give feedback. Their target audiences are general. Some advantages of using this form of media include flexibility: people can distribute them at meetings or events, put them on car windshields in parking lots, leave them in stores or on bulletin boards at community agencies and schools, hand them out from booths and other displays, or mail them. When printed in black and white, they can be very inexpensive. They afford recipients the convenience of being able to review them at their leisure. Organizations and individuals can produce flyers and fact sheets in-house, or even at home with desktop publishing software. Disadvantages include their limitation to single facts or tips and specific information on specified topics.

Review Video: Different Types of Media
Visit mometrix.com/academy and enter code: 785859

Evaluating Media Information Sources

With the wealth of media in different formats available today, users are more likely to take media at face value. However, to understand the content of media, consumers must **critically evaluate each source**.

Users should ask themselves the following questions about media sources:

- Who is delivering this message and why?
- What methods do a media source's publishers employ to gain and maintain users' attention?
- Which points of view is the media source representing?
- What are the various ways this message could be interpreted?
- What information is missing from the message?
- Is the source scholarly, i.e., peer-reviewed?
- Does it include author names and their credentials as they relate to the topic?
- Who publishes it and why?
- Who is the target audience?
- Is the language technically specific or non-technical?
- Are sources cited, research claims documented, conclusions based on furnished evidence, and references provided?
- Is the publication current?

Other Considerations for the Validity of Sources

For books, consider whether information is **up-to-date** and whether **historical perspectives** apply. Content is more likely to be **scholarly** if publishers are universities, government, or professional organizations. Book reviews can also provide useful information. For articles, identify the author, publisher, frequency of the periodical's publication, and what kind of advertising, if any, is included. Looking for book reviews also informs users. For articles, look for biographical author information, publisher name, frequency of the periodical's publication, and whether advertising is included and, if so, whether it is for certain occupations or disciplines. For web pages, check their domain names, identify publishers or sponsors, look for the author or publisher's contact information, check dates of most recent page updates, be alert to biases, and verify the validity of the information on the webpage. The quality and accuracy of web pages located through search engines rather than library databases varies widely and requires careful user inspection. Web page recommendations from reliable sources like university faculties can help indicate quality and accuracy. Citations of websites by credible or scholarly sources also show reliability. Authors' names, relevant credentials, affiliations, and contact information support their authority. Site functionality, such as ease of navigation, ability to search, site maps, and indexes, is also a criterion to consider.

Persuasive Media

Advertising, public relations, and advocacy media all use **persuasion**. Advertisers use persuasion to sell goods and services. The public relations field uses persuasion to give good impressions of companies, governments, or organizations. Advocacy groups use persuasion to garner support or votes. Persuasion can come through commercials, public service announcements, speeches, websites, and newsletters, among other channels. Activists, lobbyists, government officials, and politicians use political rhetoric involving persuasive techniques. Basic techniques include using celebrity spokespersons, whom consumers admire or aspire to resemble, or conversely, "everyday people" (albeit often portrayed by actors) with whom consumers identify. Using expert testimonials lends credibility. Explicit claims of content, effectiveness, quality, and reliability—which often cannot be proven or disproven—are used to persuade. While news and advocacy messages mostly eschew humor for credibility's sake (except in political satire), advertising often persuades via humor, which gets consumer attention and associates its pleasure with advertised products and services. Qualifiers and other misleading terms, sometimes called "Weasel words," are often combined with exaggerated claims. Intensifiers, such as hyperboles, superlatives, repetitions, and sentimental appeals are also persuasive.

Intermediate Techniques

Dangerous propagandist Adolf Hitler said people suspect little lies more than big ones; hence the "Big Lie" is a persuasion method that cannot be identified without consumers' keen critical thinking. A related method is **charisma**, which can induce people to believe messages they would otherwise reject. **Euphemisms** substitute abstract, vague, or bland terms in place of more graphic, clear, and unpleasant ones. For example, the terms "layoffs" and "firing" are replaced by "downsizing," and "torture" is replaced with "intensive interrogation techniques." **Extrapolation** bases sweeping conclusions on small amounts of minor information to appeal to what consumers wish or hope. Flattery appeals to consumer self-esteem needs, such as L'Oréal's "You're worth it." Flattery is sometimes accomplished through contrast, like ads showing others' mistakes to make consumers feel superior and smarter. "Glittering generalities" refer to claims based on concepts such as beauty, love, health, democracy, freedom, and science. Persuaders use this tactic to gain consumer acceptance without consumers questioning what they mean. The opposite is name-calling to persuade consumers to reject someone or something.

American citizens love new ideas and technology. Persuaders exploit this by emphasizing the **newness** of products, services, and candidates. Conversely, they also use **nostalgia** to evoke consumers' happy memories, which they often remember more than unhappy ones. Citing "scientific evidence" is an intermediate version of the basic technique of expert testimonials. Consumers may accept this as proof, but some advertisers, politicians, and other persuaders may present inaccurate or misleading "evidence." Another intermediate technique is the "simple solution." Although the natures of people and life are complex, when consumers feel overwhelmed by complexity, persuaders exploit this by offering policies, products, or services they claim will solve complicated problems by simple means. Persuaders also use symbols, images, words, and names we associate with more general, emotional concepts like lifestyle, country, family, religion, and gender. While symbols have power, their significance also varies across individuals. For example, some consumers regard the Hummer SUV as a prestigious status symbol, while others regard it as environmentally harmful and irresponsible.

Advanced Techniques

Ad hominem, Latin for "against the man" attacks the person behind an idea rather than criticizing the idea itself. It operates by association: if a person is considered immoral or uneducated, then his or her ideas must be bad as well. **"Stacking the deck"** misleads by presenting only selected information that supports one position. **Apophasis**, or a false denial, allows the speaker or writer to indirectly bring attention to a flaw in an opponent's credibility. For example, a politician saying, "I won't mention my opponent's tax evasion issues" manages to mention them while seeming less accusatory. Persuaders may also use **majority belief**, making statements such as "Four out of five dentists recommend this brand" or "[insert number] people can't be wrong." In an intensified version, persuaders exploit group dynamics at rallies, speeches, and other live-audience events where people are vulnerable to surrounding crowd influences. **Scapegoating**, blaming one person or group for complex problems, is a form of the intermediate "simple solution" technique, a practice common in politics. **Timing** also persuades, like advertising flowers and candy in the weeks preceding Valentine's Day, ad campaigns preceding new technology rollouts, and politician speeches following big news events.

Visual Media

Some images have the power to communicate more information than an entire paragraph. Images can contain several elements and be interpreted different ways, making them an effective vessel for abstract and emotionally appealing ideas. Humans are also able to understand images before they fully acquire language, meaning that images can reach more people than language can at any time. Images are also more quickly comprehended than text, making them a highly efficient method of communication. People can remember or memorize images more easily than text, also. Historically, images have been used for propaganda and subliminal messaging. Images are also used by different companies as an effective technique to entice customers to buy their products. Though images do not always contain text, they can still convey explicit and implicit meanings. An image's explicit meaning would be the most recognizable shape or concept in the image. The implicit meaning may be obscured within the image through the use of negative space, background images, or out-of-focus shapes.

Interpreting and Evaluating Persuasive Media

Most messages can be interpreted in different ways. They can be interpreted explicitly, where the literal meaning of the words in the message creates the meaning of the message, and no context is considered. Alternatively, other contexts can be considered alongside the explicit meaning of the message. These create alternative, not clearly stated meanings called **implicit meanings**. Politics, current events, regional norms, and even emotions are examples of contexts that can add implicit meanings to a message. These implicit meanings can change the effect a message has on its recipient. Many products have slogans with both implicit and explicit meanings. These implicit meanings must be considered to fully interpret a message.

Messages come in different forms, and each form has a unique way of communicating both explicit and implicit meanings. Images can come with captions that communicate a message, but some images carry subliminal messages. This means that their implicit meaning is received by the viewer, but the viewer is not aware of it. The term **propaganda** describes messages that advocate for a specific opinion or way of thinking. Most propaganda is politically driven and has been used during historical periods, most notably World War II. Unlike messages with hidden or veiled implicit meanings, most propaganda aggressively communicates its entire meaning and is difficult to misinterpret. Documentaries are another prominent form of communication. Documentaries are informational videos that focus on a specific figure, subject, phenomenon, or time period. While documentaries are primarily fact based and contain excerpts from interviews and testimonials, documentaries feature a limited view of their subject and sometimes attempt to persuade viewers to take action or embrace their central message. While some documentaries communicate this clearly, some hide an implicit meaning through the way they present each piece of information.

Literary Texts

Critical Reading Skills

Opinions, Facts, and Fallacies

Critical thinking skills are mastered through understanding various types of writing and the different purposes authors can have for writing different passages. Every author writes for a purpose. When you understand their purpose and how they accomplish their goal, you will be able to analyze their writing and determine whether or not you agree with their conclusions.

Readers must always be aware of the difference between fact and opinion. A **fact** can be subjected to analysis and proven to be true. An **opinion**, on the other hand, is the author's personal thoughts or feelings and may not be altered by research or evidence. If the author writes that the distance from New York City to Boston is about two hundred miles, then he or she is stating a fact. If the author writes that New York City is too crowded, then he or she is giving an opinion because there is no objective standard for overpopulation. Opinions are often supported by facts. For instance, an author might use a comparison between the population density of New York City and that of other major American cities as evidence of an overcrowded population. An opinion supported by facts tends to be more convincing. On the other hand, when authors support their opinions with other opinions, readers should employ critical thinking and approach the argument with skepticism.

Review Video: Distinguishing Fact and Opinion
Visit mometrix.com/academy and enter code: 870899

Reliable Sources

When you read an argumentative passage, you need to be sure that facts are presented to the reader from **reliable sources**. An opinion is what the author thinks about a given topic. An opinion is not common knowledge or proven by expert sources, instead the information is the personal beliefs and thoughts of the author. To distinguish between fact and opinion, a reader needs to consider the type of source that is presenting information, the information that backs-up a claim, and the author's motivation to have a certain point-of-view on a given topic. For example, if a panel of scientists has conducted multiple studies on the effectiveness of taking a certain vitamin, then the results are more likely to be factual than those of a company that is selling a vitamin and simply claims that taking the vitamin can produce positive effects. The company is motivated to sell their product, and the scientists are using the scientific method to prove a theory. Remember, if you find sentences that contain phrases such as "I think...", then the statement is an opinion.

BIASES

In their attempts to persuade, writers often make mistakes in their thought processes and writing choices. These processes and choices are important to understand so you can make an informed decision about the author's credibility. Every author has a point of view, but authors demonstrate a **bias** when they ignore reasonable counterarguments or distort opposing viewpoints. A bias is evident whenever the author's claims are presented in a way that is unfair or inaccurate. Bias can be intentional or unintentional, but readers should be skeptical of the author's argument in either case. Remember that a biased author may still be correct. However, the author will be correct in spite of, not because of, his or her bias.

A **stereotype** is a bias applied specifically to a group of people or a place. Stereotyping is considered to be particularly abhorrent because it promotes negative, misleading generalizations about people. Readers should be very cautious of authors who use stereotypes in their writing. These faulty assumptions typically reveal the author's ignorance and lack of curiosity.

Review Video: Bias and Stereotype
Visit mometrix.com/academy and enter code: 644829

PERSUASION AND RHETORIC

PERSUASIVE TECHNIQUES

To **appeal using reason**, writers present logical arguments, such as using "If... then... because" statements. To **appeal to emotions**, authors may ask readers how they would feel about something or to put themselves in another's place, present their argument as one that will make the audience feel good, or tell readers how they should feel. To **appeal to character**, **morality**, or **ethics**, authors present their points to readers as the right or most moral choices. Authors cite expert opinions to show readers that someone very knowledgeable about the subject or viewpoint agrees with the author's claims. **Testimonials**, usually via anecdotes or quotations regarding the author's subject, help build the audience's trust in an author's message through positive support from ordinary people. **Bandwagon appeals** claim that everybody else agrees with the author's argument and persuade readers to conform and agree, also. Authors **appeal to greed** by presenting their choice as cheaper, free, or more valuable for less cost. They **appeal to laziness** by presenting their views as more convenient, easy, or relaxing. Authors also anticipate potential objections and argue against them before audiences think of them, thereby depicting those objections as weak.

Authors can use **comparisons** like analogies, similes, and metaphors to persuade audiences. For example, a writer might represent excessive expenses as "hemorrhaging" money, which the author's recommended solution will stop. Authors can use negative word connotations to make some choices unappealing to readers, and positive word connotations to make others more appealing. Using **humor** can relax readers and garner their agreement. However, writers must take care: ridiculing opponents can be a successful strategy for appealing to readers who already agree with the author, but can backfire by angering other readers. **Rhetorical questions** need no answer, but create effect that can force agreement, such as asking the question, "Wouldn't you rather be paid more than less?" **Generalizations** persuade readers by being impossible to disagree with. Writers can easily make generalizations that appear to support their viewpoints, like saying, "We all want peace, not war" regarding more specific political arguments. **Transfer** and **association** persuade by example: if advertisements show attractive actors enjoying their products, audiences imagine they will experience the same. **Repetition** can also sometimes effectively persuade audiences.

Review Video: Using Rhetorical Strategies for Persuasion
Visit mometrix.com/academy and enter code: 302658

Classical Author Appeals

In his *On Rhetoric,* ancient Greek philosopher Aristotle defined three basic types of appeal used in writing, which he called *pathos*, *ethos*, and *logos*. ***Pathos*** means suffering or experience and refers to appeals to the emotions (the English word *pathetic* comes from this root). Writing that is meant to entertain audiences, by making them either happy, as with comedy, or sad, as with tragedy, uses *pathos*. Aristotle's *Poetics* states that evoking the emotions of terror and pity is one of the criteria for writing tragedy. ***Ethos*** means character and connotes ideology (the English word *ethics* comes from this root). Writing that appeals to credibility, based on academic, professional, or personal merit, uses *ethos*. ***Logos*** means "I say" and refers to a plea, opinion, expectation, word or speech, account, opinion, or reason (the English word *logic* comes from this root.) Aristotle used it to mean persuasion that appeals to the audience through reasoning and logic to influence their opinions.

Rhetorical Devices

- An **anecdote** is a brief story authors may relate to their argument, which can illustrate their points in a more real and relatable way.
- **Aphorisms** concisely state common beliefs and may rhyme. For example, Benjamin Franklin's "Early to bed and early to rise / Makes a man healthy, wealthy, and wise" is an aphorism.
- **Allusions** refer to literary or historical figures to impart symbolism to a thing or person and to create reader resonance. In John Steinbeck's *Of Mice and Men,* protagonist George's last name is Milton. This alludes to John Milton, who wrote *Paradise Lost*, and symbolizes George's eventual loss of his dream.
- **Satire** exaggerates, ridicules, or pokes fun at human flaws or ideas, as in the works of Jonathan Swift and Mark Twain.
- A **parody** is a form of satire that imitates another work to ridicule its topic or style.
- A **paradox** is a statement that is true despite appearing contradictory.
- **Hyperbole** is overstatement using exaggerated language.
- An **oxymoron** combines seeming contradictions, such as "deafening silence."
- **Analogies** compare two things that share common elements.
- **Similes** (stated comparisons using the words *like* or *as*) and **metaphors** (stated comparisons that do not use *like* or *as*) are considered forms of analogy.
- When using logic to reason with audiences, **syllogism** refers either to deductive reasoning or a deceptive, very sophisticated, or subtle argument.
- **Deductive reasoning** moves from general to specific, **inductive reasoning** from specific to general.
- **Diction** is author word choice that establishes tone and effect.
- **Understatement** achieves effects like contrast or irony by downplaying or describing something more subtly than warranted.
- **Chiasmus** uses parallel clauses, the second reversing the order of the first. Examples include T. S. Eliot's "Has the Church failed mankind, or has mankind failed the Church?" and John F. Kennedy's "Ask not what your country can do for you; ask what you can do for your country."
- **Anaphora** regularly repeats a word or phrase at the beginnings of consecutive clauses or phrases to add emphasis to an idea. A classic example of anaphora was Winston Churchill's emphasis of determination: "[W]e shall fight on the beaches, we shall fight on the landing grounds, we shall fight in the fields and in the streets, we shall fight in the hills; we shall never surrender..."

Reading Argumentative Writing

Author's Argument in Argumentative Writing

In argumentative writing, the argument is a belief, position, or opinion that the author wants to convince readers to believe as well. For the first step, readers should identify the **issue**. Some issues are controversial, meaning people disagree about them. Gun control, foreign policy, and the death penalty are all controversial issues. The next step is to determine the **author's position** on the issue. That position or viewpoint constitutes the author's argument. Readers should then identify the **author's assumptions**: things he or she accepts, believes, or takes for granted without needing proof. Inaccurate or illogical assumptions produce flawed arguments and can mislead readers. Readers should identify what kinds of **supporting evidence** the author offers, such as research results, personal observations or experiences, case studies, facts, examples, expert testimony and opinions, and comparisons. Readers should decide how relevant this support is to the argument.

Review Video: Argumentative Writing
Visit mometrix.com/academy and enter code: 561544

Evaluating an Author's Argument

The first three reader steps to **evaluate an author's argument** are to identify the **author's assumptions**, identify the **supporting evidence**, and decide **whether the evidence is relevant**. For example, if an author is not an expert on a particular topic, then that author's personal experience or opinion might not be relevant. The fourth step is to assess the **author's objectivity**. For example, consider whether the author introduces clear, understandable supporting evidence and facts to support the argument. The fifth step is evaluating whether the author's **argument is complete**. When authors give sufficient support for their arguments and also anticipate and respond effectively to opposing arguments or objections to their points, their arguments are complete. However, some authors omit information that could detract from their arguments. If instead they stated this information and refuted it, it would strengthen their arguments. The sixth step in evaluating an author's argumentative writing is to assess whether the **argument is valid**. Providing clear, logical reasoning makes an author's argument valid. Readers should ask themselves whether the author's points follow a sequence that makes sense, and whether each point leads to the next. The seventh step is to determine whether the author's **argument is credible**, meaning that it is convincing and believable. Arguments that are not valid are not credible, so step seven depends on step six. Readers should be mindful of their own biases as they evaluate and should not expect authors to conclusively prove their arguments, but rather to provide effective support and reason.

Evaluating an Author's Method of Appeal

To evaluate the effectiveness of an appeal, it is important to consider the author's purpose for writing. Any appeals an author uses in their argument must be relevant to the argument's goal. For example, a writer that argues for the reclassification of Pluto, but primarily uses appeals to emotion, will not have an effective argument. This writer should focus on using appeals to logic and support their argument with provable facts. While most arguments should include appeals to logic, emotion, and credibility, some arguments only call for one or two of these types of appeal. Evidence can support an appeal, but the evidence must be relevant to truly strengthen the appeal's effectiveness. If the writer arguing for Pluto's reclassification uses the reasons for Jupiter's classification as evidence, their argument would be weak. This information may seem relevant because it is related to the classification of planets. However, this classification is highly dependent on the size of the celestial object, and Jupiter is significantly bigger than Pluto. This use of evidence is illogical and does not support the appeal. Even when appropriate evidence and appeals are used, appeals and arguments lose their effectiveness when they create logical fallacies.

Evidence

The term **text evidence** refers to information that supports a main point or minor points and can help lead the reader to a conclusion about the text's credibility. Information used as text evidence is precise, descriptive, and factual. A main point is often followed by supporting details that provide evidence to back up a claim. For example, a passage may include the claim that winter occurs during opposite months in the Northern and

Southern hemispheres. Text evidence for this claim may include examples of countries where winter occurs in opposite months. Stating that the tilt of the Earth as it rotates around the sun causes winter to occur at different times in separate hemispheres is another example of text evidence. Text evidence can come from common knowledge, but it is also valuable to include text evidence from credible, relevant outside sources.

Review Video: Textual Evidence
Visit mometrix.com/academy and enter code: 486236

Evidence that supports the thesis and additional arguments needs to be provided. Most arguments must be supported by facts or statistics. A fact is something that is known with certainty, has been verified by several independent individuals, and can be proven to be true. In addition to facts, examples and illustrations can support an argument by adding an emotional component. With this component, you persuade readers in ways that facts and statistics cannot. The emotional component is effective when used alongside objective information that can be confirmed.

Credibility

The text used to support an argument can be the argument's downfall if the text is not credible. A text is **credible**, or believable, when its author is knowledgeable and objective, or unbiased. The author's motivations for writing the text play a critical role in determining the credibility of the text and must be evaluated when assessing that credibility. Reports written about the ozone layer by an environmental scientist and a hairdresser will have a different level of credibility.

Review Video: Author Credibility
Visit mometrix.com/academy and enter code: 827257

Appeal to Emotion

Sometimes, authors will appeal to the reader's emotion in an attempt to persuade or to distract the reader from the weakness of the argument. For instance, the author may try to inspire the pity of the reader by delivering a heart-rending story. An author also might use the bandwagon approach, in which he suggests that his opinion is correct because it is held by the majority. Some authors resort to name-calling, in which insults and harsh words are delivered to the opponent in an attempt to distract. In advertising, a common appeal is the celebrity testimonial, in which a famous person endorses a product. Of course, the fact that a famous person likes something should not really mean anything to the reader. These and other emotional appeals are usually evidence of poor reasoning and a weak argument.

Review Video: Emotional Language in Literature
Visit mometrix.com/academy and enter code: 759390

Counter Arguments

When authors give both sides to the argument, they build trust with their readers. As a reader, you should start with an undecided or neutral position. If an author presents only his or her side to the argument, then they are not exhibiting credibility and are weakening their argument.

Building common ground with readers can be effective for persuading neutral, skeptical, or opposed readers. Sharing values with undecided readers can allow people to switch positions without giving up what they feel is important. People who may oppose a position need to feel that they can change their minds without betraying who they are as a person. This appeal to having an open mind can be a powerful tool in arguing a position without antagonizing other views. Objections can be countered on a point-by-point basis or in a summary paragraph. Be mindful of how an author points out flaws in counter arguments. If they are unfair to the other side of the argument, then you should lose trust with the author.

Genres in Fiction

Common Genres in Prose Fiction

- The **mystery** genre includes stories with plots that follow a protagonist as they work to solve an unexplained situation, such as a murder, disappearance, or robbery. Protagonists of mysteries may be hired professionals or amateurs who solve the mystery despite their lack of experience and resources. Mysteries allow the reader to solve the case along with the protagonist, and often grant the reader an advantageous perspective, creating dramatic irony. The *Sherlock Holmes* novels by Sir Arthur Conan Doyle are examples of mystery novels.
- **Science fiction** is a genre that is based on the manipulation and exaggeration of real scientific discoveries and processes. These works are speculative and frequently depict a world where scientific discoveries and society have progressed beyond the point reached at the time of the work's creation. Works of science fiction often take place in a distant location or time, allowing for the dramatic advancements and conveniences they often depict. *Dune*, written by Frank Herbert, is an example of a science-fiction novel.
- The **fantasy** genre includes stories that feature imaginary creatures and supernatural abilities, but often take place in settings that resemble real places and cultures in history. Fantasy novels usually follow a gifted protagonist from humble beginnings as they embark on a quest, journey, or adventure and encounter mystical beings and personally challenging obstacles. Common themes in the fantasy genre include personal growth, good versus evil, and the value of the journey. J.R.R. Tolkien's *The Lord of the Rings* trilogy belongs to the fantasy genre.
- **Realistic fiction** describes fictional narratives that include events and characters that do not exist, but could appear in reality. Within the narrative, these characters and events may be depicted in real places. For example, Pip, the protagonist of Charles Dickens's *Great Expectations*, was not a real person, but the novel shows him living in London, England for much of his young adulthood. Realistic fiction contains no far-fetched or impossible elements and presents situations that can or do occur in real life. A contemporary example of realistic fiction is *Wonder* by R.J. Palacio.
- **Historical fiction** includes works that take place in the past and model their setting after real historical cultures, societies, and time periods. These works may include real historical figures and events, but they also may not. Works of historical fiction must be fully informed by the period and location they are set in, meaning both the major and minor details of the work must be historically compatible with the work's setting. Examples of historical fiction include Kathryn Stockett's *The Help* and Markus Zusak's *The Book Thief*.
- The phrase **literary nonfiction** describes nonfiction narratives that present true facts and events in a way that entertains readers and displays creativity. Literary nonfiction, also called creative nonfiction, may resemble fiction in its style and flow, but the truth of the events it describes sets it apart from fictional literature. Different types of books may be considered literary nonfiction, such as biographies, if they appear to employ creativity in their writing. An example of literary nonfiction is *The Immortal Life of Henrietta Lacks* by Rebecca Skloot.

Realism and Satire

Realism

Realism is a literary form with the goal of representing reality as faithfully as possible. Its genesis in Western literature was a reaction against the sentimentality and extreme emotionalism of the works written during the Romantic literary movement, which championed feelings and emotional expression. Realists focused in great detail on immediacy of time and place, on specific actions of their characters, and the justifiable consequences of those actions. Some techniques of **realism** include writing in vernacular (conversational language), using specific dialects, and placing an emphasis on character rather than plot. Realistic literature also often addresses ethical issues. Historically, realistic works have often concentrated on the middle classes of the authors' societies. Realists eschew treatments that are too dramatic or sensationalistic as exaggerations of the reality that they strive to portray as closely as they are able. Influenced by his own bleak past, Fyodor Dostoevsky wrote several novels, such as *Crime and Punishment* (1866) that shunned romantic ideals and sought to portray a stark reality. Henry James was a prominent writer of realism in novels such as *Daisy Miller* (1879). Samuel Clemens (Mark Twain) skillfully represented the language and culture of lower-class Mississippi in his novel *The Adventures of Huckleberry Finn* (1885).

SATIRE

Satire uses sarcasm, irony, and humor as social criticism to lampoon human folly. Unlike realism, which intends to depict reality as it exists without exaggeration, **satire** often involves creating situations or ideas that deliberately exaggerate reality to appear ridiculous to illuminate flawed behaviors. Ancient Roman satirists included Horace and Juvenal. Alexander Pope's poem "The Rape of the Lock" satirized the values of fashionable members of the 18th-century upper-middle class, which Pope found shallow and trivial. The theft of a lock of hair from a young woman is blown out of proportion: the poem's characters regard it as seriously as they would a rape. Irishman Jonathan Swift satirized British society, politics, and religion in works like "A Modest Proposal" and *Gulliver's Travels*. In "A Modest Proposal," Swift used essay form and mock-serious tone, satirically "proposing" cannibalism of babies and children as a solution to poverty and overpopulation. He satirized petty political disputes in *Gulliver's Travels*.

TYPES OF STORIES

OTHER COMMON TYPES OF PROSE

- A **narrative** is any composition that tells a story. Narratives have characters, settings, and a structure. Narratives may be fiction or nonfiction stories and may follow a linear or nonlinear structure. The purpose of a narrative is generally to entertain, but nonfiction narratives can be informative, as well. Narratives also appear in a variety of structures and formats.
- **Biographies** are books written about another person's life. Biographies can be valuable historical resources. Though they provide a narrow view of the relevant time period and culture, their specificity can also provide a unique context for that period or culture. Biographies, especially those whose subject was a well-known and influential figure, can provide a more complete picture of the figure's life or contributions. Biographies can also serve as a source of inspiration or communicate a moral because of their focus on one person over an extended period of time.
- **Myths** that explain how the world works, its creation, and human behavior exist in most ancient cultures and continue to influence modern cultures. Myths are stories that are part of a certain **mythology**, such as Norse mythology. Myths are so influential that they have even inspired numerous pieces of modern literature and media in popular culture. While popular culture most clearly references myths from the Ancient Greek and Roman cultures, literature has been influenced by mythologies from around the entire world. Since myths are so prevalent in ancient literature, it makes sense that universal themes and morals often appear in mythologies from different cultures. The similarities and parallels in different mythologies (e.g., Greek myths about Zeus are very similar to Roman myths about Jupiter) suggest connections between cultures.
- **Folktales** are stories that have withstood time and are usually popular in a particular region or culture. Folktales often depict the clever success of a common person, though the story may, alternatively, end poorly for the protagonist. A collection of folktales relevant to a particular region or culture is referred to as that culture's **folklore**. There are three common types of folktales: fables, fairy tales, and legends.
    - **Fables** are short, didactic stories that typically feature imaginary creatures or talking animals. The famous story "The Tortoise and the Hare" is a fable. Fables are still told and used today because of their universally understandable morals and characters, which also make them suitable for children's literature and media.
    - **Fairy tales** are stories that involve fictional creatures or realistic characters with fantastical traits and abilities. Fairy tales often end happily and depict the victory of good over evil. The plots and characters in fairy tales are often far-fetched and whimsical.

- Legends are stories that typically focus on one character and highlight their victory over a particular enemy or obstacle. Legends often feature some facts or are inspired by true events, but are generally considered both unproven and unprovable. Heroes are often the protagonists of legends, and they generally save or protect others as they conquer enemies and obstacles.

- A **short story** is a fictional narrative that is shorter than a novel. However, there is not a definite page or word count that defines the short story category. Short stories tend to focus on one or few elements of a story in order to efficiently tell the story. Though they are often brief, short stories may still contain a moral or impact their readers.

Review Video: Myths, Fables, Legends, and Fairy Tales
Visit mometrix.com/academy and enter code: 347199

Historical Forms of Prose

Historical, Picaresque, Gothic, and Psychological Fiction

Historical fiction is set in particular historical periods, including prehistoric and mythological. Examples include Walter Scott's *Rob Roy* and *Ivanhoe*; Leo Tolstoy's *War and Peace;* Robert Graves' *I, Claudius;* Mary Renault's *The King Must Die* and *The Bull from the Sea* (an historical novel using Greek mythology); Virginia Woolf's *Orlando* and *Between the Acts;* and John Dos Passos's *U.S.A* trilogy. **Picaresque** novels recount episodic adventures of a rogue protagonist or *pícaro,* like Miguel de Cervantes' *Don Quixote* or Henry Fielding's *Tom Jones.* **Gothic** novels originated as a reaction against 18th-century Enlightenment rationalism, featuring horror, mystery, superstition, madness, supernatural elements, and revenge. Early examples include Horace Walpole's *Castle of Otranto,* Matthew Gregory Lewis' *Monk,* Mary Shelley's *Frankenstein,* and Bram Stoker's *Dracula.* In America, Edgar Allan Poe wrote many Gothic works. Contemporary novelist Anne Rice has penned many Gothic novels under the pseudonym A. N. Roquelaure. **Psychological** novels, originating in 17th-century France, explore characters' motivations. Examples include Abbé Prévost's *Manon Lescaut;* George Eliot's novels; Fyodor Dostoyevsky's *Crime and Punishment;* Tolstoy's *Anna Karenina;* Gustave Flaubert's *Madame Bovary;* and the novels of Henry James, James Joyce, and Vladimir Nabokov.

Novels of Manners

Novels of manners are fictional stories that observe, explore, and analyze the social behaviors of a specific time and place. While deep psychological themes are more universal across different historical periods and countries, the manners of a particular society are shorter-lived and more varied; the **novel of manners** captures these societal details. Novels of manners can also be regarded as symbolically representing, in artistic form, certain established and secure social orders. Characteristics of novels of manners include descriptions of a society with defined behavioral codes; language that uses standardized, impersonal formulas; and inhibition of emotional expression, as contrasted with the strong emotions expressed in romantic or sentimental novels. Jane Austen's detailed descriptions of English society and characters struggling with the definitions and restrictions placed on them by society are excellent models of the novel of manners. In the 20th century, Evelyn Waugh's *Handful of Dust* is a novel of social manners, and his *Sword of Honour* trilogy contains novels of military manners. Another 20th-century example is *The Unbearable Bassington* by Saki (the pen name of writer H. H. Munro), focusing on Edwardian society.

Western-World Sentimental Novels

Sentimental love novels originated in the movement of Romanticism. Eighteenth-century examples of novels that emphasize the emotional aspect of love include Samuel Richardson's *Pamela* (1740) and Jean-Jacques Rousseau's *Nouvelle Héloïse* (1761). Also in the 18th century, Laurence Sterne's novel *Tristram Shandy* (1760-1767) is an example of a novel with elements of sentimentality. The Victorian era's rejection of emotionalism caused the term "sentimental" to have undesirable connotations. However, even non-sentimental novelists such as William Makepeace Thackeray and Charles Dickens incorporated sentimental elements in their writing. A 19th-century author of genuinely sentimental novels was Mrs. Henry Wood (e.g., *East Lynne,* 1861). In the 20th century, Erich Segal's sentimental novel *Love Story* (1970) was a popular bestseller.

Epistolary Novels

Epistolary novels are told in the form of letters written by their characters rather than in typical narrative form. Samuel Richardson, the best-known author of epistolary novels like *Pamela* (1740) and *Clarissa* (1748), widely influenced early Romantic epistolary novels throughout Europe that freely expressed emotions. Richardson, a printer, published technical manuals on letter-writing for young gentlewomen; his epistolary novels were fictional extensions of those nonfictional instructional books. Nineteenth-century English author Wilkie Collins' *The Moonstone* (1868) was a mystery written in epistolary form. By the 20th century, the format of well-composed written letters came to be regarded as artificial and outmoded. A 20th-century evolution of letters was tape-recording transcripts, such as in Irish playwright Samuel Beckett's drama *Krapp's Last Tape.* Though evoking modern alienation, Beckett still created a sense of fictional characters' direct communication without author intervention as Richardson had.

Pastoral Novels

Pastoral novels lyrically idealize country life as idyllic and utopian, akin to the Garden of Eden. *Daphnis and Chloe*, written by Greek novelist Longus around the second or third century, influenced Elizabethan pastoral romances like Thomas Lodge's *Rosalynde* (1590), which inspired Shakespeare's *As You Like It*, and Philip Sidney's *Arcadia* (1590). Jacques-Henri Bernardin de St. Pierre's French work *Paul et Virginie* (1787) demonstrated the early Romantic view of the innocence and goodness of nature. Though the style lost popularity by the 20th century, pastoral elements can still be seen in novels like *The Rainbow* (1915) and *Lady Chatterley's Lover* (1928), both by D. H. Lawrence. Growing realism transformed pastoral writing into less ideal and more dystopian, distasteful and ironic depictions of country life in George Eliot's and Thomas Hardy's novels. Saul Bellow's novel *Herzog* (1964) may demonstrate how urban ills highlight an alternative pastoral ideal. The pastoral style is commonly thought to be overly idealized and outdated today, as seen in Stella Gibbons' pastoral satire, Cold Comfort Farm (1932).

Bildungsroman

Bildungsroman is German for "education novel." This term is also used in English to describe "apprenticeship" novels focusing on coming-of-age stories, including youth's struggles and searches for things such as identity, spiritual understanding, or the meaning in life. Johann Wolfgang von Goethe's *Wilhelm Meisters Lehrjahre* (1796) is credited as the origin of this genre. Two of Charles Dickens' novels, *David Copperfield* (1850) and *Great Expectations* (1861), also fit this form. H. G. Wells wrote *bildungsromans* about questing for apprenticeships to address the complications of modern life in *Joan and Peter* (1918) and from a Utopian perspective in *The Dream* (1924). School *bildungsromans* include Thomas Hughes' *Tom Brown's School Days* (1857) and Alain-Fournier's *Le Grand Meaulnes* (1913). Many Hermann Hesse novels, including *Demian, Steppenwolf, Siddhartha, Magister Ludi,* and *Beneath the Wheel* are *bildungsromans* about a struggling, searching youth. Samuel Butler's *The Way of All Flesh* (1903) and James Joyce's *A Portrait of the Artist as a Young Man* (1916) are two modern examples. Variations include J. D. Salinger's *The Catcher in the Rye* (1951), set both within and beyond school, and William Golding's *Lord of the Flies* (1955), a novel not set in a school but one that is a coming-of-age story nonetheless.

Roman à Clef

Roman à clef, French for "novel with a key," refers to books that require a real-life frame of reference, or key, for full comprehension. In Geoffrey Chaucer's *Canterbury Tales,* the Nun's Priest's Tale contains details that confuse readers unaware of history about the Earl of Bolingbroke's involvement in an assassination plot. Other literary works fitting this form include John Dryden's political satirical poem "Absalom and Achitophel" (1681), Jonathan Swift's satire "A Tale of a Tub" (1704), and George Orwell's political allegory *Animal Farm* (1945), all of which cannot be understood completely without knowing their camouflaged historical contents. *Roman à clefs* disguise truths too dangerous for authors to state directly. Readers must know about the enemies of D. H. Lawrence and Aldous Huxley to appreciate their respective novels: *Aaron's Rod* (1922) and *Point Counter Point* (1928). Marcel Proust's *Remembrance of Things Past (À la recherché du temps perdu,* 1871-1922) is informed by his social context. James Joyce's *Finnegans Wake* is an enormous *roman à clef* containing multitudinous personal references.

Review Video: Major Forms of Prose
Visit mometrix.com/academy and enter code: 565543

POETRY

POETRY TERMINOLOGY

Unlike prose, which traditionally (except in forms like stream of consciousness) consists of complete sentences connected into paragraphs, poetry is written in **verses**. These may form complete sentences, clauses, or phrases. Poetry may be written with or without rhyme. It can be metered, following a particular rhythmic pattern such as iambic, dactylic, spondaic, trochaic, or **anapestic**, or may be without regular meter. The terms **iamb** and **trochee**, among others, identify stressed and unstressed syllables in each verse. Meter is also described by the number of beats or stressed syllables per verse: **dimeter** (2), **trimeter** (3), **tetrameter** (4), **pentameter** (5), and so forth. Using the symbol ᴗ to denote unstressed and / to denote stressed syllables, **iambic** = ᴗ/; **trochaic** = /ᴗ; **spondaic** =//; **dactylic** =/ᴗᴗ; **anapestic** =ᴗᴗ/. **Rhyme schemes** identify which lines rhyme, such as ABAB, ABCA, AABA, and so on. Poetry with neither rhyme nor meter is called **free verse**. Poems may be in free verse, metered but unrhymed, rhymed but without meter, or using both rhyme and meter. In English, the most common meter is iambic pentameter. Unrhymed iambic pentameter is called **blank verse**.

Review Video: Different Types of Rhyme
Visit mometrix.com/academy and enter code: 999342

Review Video: Evocative Words and Rhythm
Visit mometrix.com/academy and enter code: 894610

MAJOR FORMS OF POETRY

From man's earliest days, he expressed himself with poetry. A large percentage of the surviving literature from ancient times is in **epic poetry**, utilized by Homer and other Greco-Roman poets. Epic poems typically recount heroic deeds and adventures, using stylized language and combining dramatic and lyrical conventions. **Epistolary poems**, poems that are written and read as letters, also developed in ancient times. In the fourteenth and fifteenth centuries, the **ballad** became a popular convention. Ballads often follow a rhyme scheme and meter and focus on subjects such as love, death, and religion. Many ballads tell stories, and several modern ballads are put to music. From these early conventions, numerous other poetic forms developed, such as **elegies**, **odes**, and **pastoral poems**. Elegies are mourning poems written in three parts: lament, praise of the deceased, and solace for loss. Odes evolved from songs to the typical poem of the Romantic time period, expressing strong feelings and contemplative thoughts. Pastoral poems idealize nature and country living. Poetry can also be used to make short, pithy statements. **Epigrams** (memorable rhymes with one or two lines) and **limericks** (two lines of iambic dimeter followed by two lines of iambic dimeter and another of iambic trimeter) are known for humor and wit.

HAIKU

Haiku was originally a Japanese poetry form. In the 13th century, haiku was the opening phrase of renga, a 100-stanza oral poem. By the 16th century, haiku diverged into a separate short poem. When Western writers discovered haiku, the form became popular in English, as well as other languages. A haiku has 17 syllables, traditionally distributed across three lines as 5/7/5, with a pause after the first or second line. Haiku are syllabic and unrhymed. Haiku philosophy and technique are that brevity's compression forces writers to express images concisely, depict a moment in time, and evoke illumination and enlightenment. An example is 17th-century haiku master Matsuo Basho's classic: "An old silent pond... / A frog jumps into the pond, / splash! Silence again." Modern American poet Ezra Pound revealed the influence of haiku in his two-line poem "In a Station of the Metro." In this poem, line 1 has 12 syllables (combining the syllable count of the first two lines of a haiku) and line 2 has 7, but it still preserves haiku's philosophy and imagistic technique: "The apparition of these faces in the crowd; / Petals on a wet, black bough."

Sonnets

The sonnet traditionally has 14 lines of iambic pentameter, tightly organized around a theme. The Petrarchan sonnet, named for 14th-century Italian poet Petrarch, has an eight-line stanza, the octave, and a six-line stanza, the sestet. There is a change or turn, known as the volta, between the eighth and ninth verses, setting up the sestet's answer or summary. The rhyme scheme is ABBA/ABBA/CDECDE or CDCDCD. The English or Shakespearean sonnet has three quatrains and one couplet, with the rhyme scheme ABAB/CDCD/EFEF/GG. This format better suits English, which has fewer rhymes than Italian. The final couplet often contrasts sharply with the preceding quatrains, as in Shakespeare's sonnets—for example, Sonnet 130, "My mistress' eyes are nothing like the sun…And yet, by heaven, I think my love as rare / As any she belied with false compare." Variations on the sonnet form include Edmund Spenser's Spenserian sonnet in the 16th century, John Milton's Miltonic sonnet in the 17th century, and sonnet sequences. Sonnet sequences are seen in works such as John Donne's *La Corona* and Elizabeth Barrett Browning's *Sonnets from the Portuguese.*

Review Video: Structural Elements of Poetry
Visit mometrix.com/academy and enter code: 265216

Structure and Meaning in Poetry

Carpe Diem Tradition in Poetry

Carpe diem is Latin for "seize the day." A long poetic tradition, it advocates making the most of time because it passes swiftly and life is short. It is found in multiple languages, including Latin, Torquato Tasso's Italian, Pierre de Ronsard's French, and Edmund Spenser's English, and is often used in seduction to argue for indulging in earthly pleasures. Roman poet Horace's Ode 1.11 tells a younger woman, Leuconoe, to enjoy the present, not worrying about inevitable aging. Two Renaissance Metaphysical Poets, Andrew Marvell and Robert Herrick, treated *carpe diem* more as a call to action. In "To His Coy Mistress," Marvell points out that time is fleeting, arguing for love, and concluding that because they cannot stop time, they may as well defy it, getting the most out of the short time they have. In "To the Virgins, to Make Much of Time," Herrick advises young women to take advantage of their good fortune in being young by getting married before they become too old to attract men and have babies.

"To His Coy Mistress" begins, "Had we but world enough, and time, / This coyness, lady, were no crime." Using imagery, Andrew Marvell describes leisure they could enjoy if time were unlimited. Arguing for seduction, he continues famously, "But at my back I always hear/Time's winged chariot hurrying near; / And yonder all before us lie / Deserts of vast eternity." He depicts time as turning beauty to death and decay. Contradictory images in "amorous birds of prey" and "tear our pleasures with rough strife / Through the iron gates of life" overshadow romance with impending death, linking present pleasure with mortality and spiritual values with moral considerations. Marvell's concluding couplet summarizes *carpe diem*: "Thus, though we cannot make our sun / Stand still, yet we will make him run." "To the Virgins, to Make Much of Time" begins with the famous "Gather ye rosebuds while ye may." Rather than seduction to live for the present, Robert Herrick's experienced persona advises young women's future planning: "Old time is still a-flying / And this same flower that smiles today, / Tomorrow will be dying."

Effect of Structure on Meaning in Poetry

The way a poem is structured can affect its meaning. Different structural choices can change the way a reader understands a poem, so poets are careful to ensure that the form they use reflects the message they want to convey. The main structural elements in poetry include **lines** and **stanzas**. The number of lines within a stanza and the number of stanzas vary between different poems, but some poetic forms require a poem to have a certain number of lines and stanzas. Some of these forms also require each line to conform to a certain meter, or number and pattern of syllables. Many forms are associated with a certain topic or tone because of their meter. Poetic forms include sonnets, concrete poems, haiku, and villanelles. Another popular form of poetry is free verse, which is poetry that does not conform to a particular meter or rhyme scheme.

The arrangement of lines and stanzas determines the speed at which a poem is read. Long lines are generally read more quickly since the reader is often eager to reach the end of the line and does not have to stop to find the next word. Short lines cause the reader to briefly pause and look to the next line, so their reading is slowed. These effects often contribute to the meaning a reader gleans from a poem, so poets aim to make the line length compatible with the tone of their message.

For example, Edgar Allan Poe's poem "The Raven" is written with mostly long lines. The poem's speaker experiences troubling events and becomes paranoid throughout the poem, and he narrates his racing thoughts. Poe's use of long lines leads the reader to read each line quickly, allowing their reading experience to resemble the thoughts of the narrator:

> Deep into that darkness peering, long I stood there wondering, fearing,
> Doubting, dreaming dreams no mortal ever dared to dream before;
> But the silence was unbroken, and the stillness gave no token,
> And the only word there spoken was the whispered word, "Lenore?"
> This I whispered, and an echo murmured back the word, "Lenore!"—
> Merely this and nothing more.

The poem's meter also contributes to its tone, but consider the same stanza written using shorter lines:

> Deep into that darkness peering,
> long I stood there wondering, fearing,
> Doubting, dreaming dreams no mortal
> ever dared to dream before;
> But the silence was unbroken,
> and the stillness gave no token,
> And the only word there spoken
> was the whispered word, "Lenore?"
> This I whispered, and an echo
> murmured back the word, "Lenore!"—
> Merely this and nothing more.

Breaking the lines apart creates longer pauses and a slower, more suspenseful experience for the reader. While the tone of the poem is dark and suspense is appropriate, the longer lines allow Poe to emphasize and show the narrator's emotions. The narrator's emotions are more important to the poem's meaning than the creation of suspense, making longer lines more suitable in this case.

Concrete Poetry

A less common form of poetry is concrete poetry, also called shape poetry. **Concrete poems** are arranged so the full poem takes a shape that is relevant to the poem's message. For example, a concrete poem about the beach may be arranged to look like a palm tree. This contributes to a poem's meaning by influencing which aspect of the poem or message that the reader focuses on. In the beach poem example, the image of the palm tree leads the reader to focus on the poem's setting and visual imagery. The reader may also look for or anticipate the mention of a palm tree in the poem. This technique allows the poet to direct the reader's attention and emphasize a certain element of their work.

Free Verse

Free verse is a very common form of poetry. Because **free verse** poetry does not always incorporate meter or rhyme, it relies more heavily on punctuation and structure to influence the reader's experience and create emphasis. Free verse poetry makes strategic use of the length and number of both lines and stanzas. While meter and rhyme direct the flow and tone of other types of poems, poets of free verse pieces use the characteristics of lines and stanzas to establish flow and tone, instead.

Free verse also uses punctuation in each line to create flow and tone. The punctuation in each line directs the reader to pause after certain words, allowing the poet to emphasize specific ideas or images to clearly communicate their message. Similar to the effects of line length, the presence of punctuation at the end of a line can create pauses that affect a reader's pace. **End-stopped** lines, or lines with a punctuation mark at the end, create a pause that can contribute to the poem's flow or create emphasis. **Enjambed** lines, or lines that do not end with a punctuation mark, carry a sentence to the next line and create an effect similar to long lines. The use of enjambment can speed up a poem's flow and reflect an idea within the poem or contribute to tone.

Poetic Structure to Enhance Meaning

The opening stanza of Romantic English poet, artist and printmaker William Blake's famous poem "The Tyger" demonstrates how a poet can create tension by using line length and punctuation independently of one another: "Tyger! Tyger! burning bright / In the forests of the night, / What immortal hand or eye / Could frame thy fearful symmetry?" The first three lines of this stanza are **trochaic** (/˘), with "masculine" endings—that is, strongly stressed syllables at the ends of each of the lines. But Blake's punctuation contradicts this rhythmic regularity by not providing any divisions between the words "bright" and "In" or between "eye" and "Could." This irregular punctuation foreshadows how Blake disrupts the meter at the end of this first stanza by using a contrasting **dactyl** (/˘˘), with a "feminine" (unstressed) ending syllable in the last word, "symmetry." Thus, Blake uses structural contrasts to heighten the intrigue of his work.

In enjambment, one sentence or clause in a poem does not end at the end of its line or verse, but runs over into the next line or verse. Clause endings coinciding with line endings give readers a feeling of completion, but enjambment influences readers to hurry to the next line to finish and understand the sentence. In his blank-verse epic religious poem "Paradise Lost," John Milton wrote: "Anon out of the earth a fabric huge / Rose like an exhalation, with the sound / Of dulcet symphonies and voices sweet, / Built like a temple, where pilasters round / Were set, and Doric pillars overlaid / With golden architrave." Only the third line is end-stopped. Milton, describing the palace of Pandemonium bursting from Hell up through the ground, reinforced this idea through phrases and clauses bursting through the boundaries of the lines. A **caesura** is a pause in mid-verse. Milton's commas in the third and fourth lines signal caesuras. They interrupt flow, making the narration jerky to imply that Satan's glorious-seeming palace has a shaky and unsound foundation.

Couplets and Meter to Enhance Meaning in Poetry

When a poet uses a couplet—a stanza of two lines, rhymed or unrhymed—it can function as the answer to a question asked earlier in the poem, or the solution to a problem or riddle. Couplets can also enhance the establishment of a poem's mood, or clarify the development of a poem's theme. Another device to enhance thematic development is irony, which also communicates the poet's tone and draws the reader's attention to a point the poet is making. The use of meter gives a poem a rhythmic context, contributes to the poem's flow, makes it more appealing to the reader, can represent natural speech rhythms, and produces specific effects. For example, in "The Song of Hiawatha," Henry Wadsworth Longfellow uses trochaic (/ ˘) tetrameter (four beats per line) to evoke for readers the rhythms of Native American chanting: "*By* the *shores* of *Gitch*e *Gum*ee, / *By* the *shin*ing *Big*-Sea-*Wat*er / *Stood* the *wig*wam *of* No*kom*is." (Italicized syllables are stressed; non-italicized syllables are unstressed.)

Reflection of Content Through Structure

Wallace Stevens' short yet profound poem "The Snow Man" is reductionist: the snow man is a figure without human biases or emotions. Stevens begins, "One must have a mind of winter," the criterion for realizing nature and life does not inherently possess subjective qualities; we only invest it with these. Things are not as we see them; they simply are. The entire poem is one long sentence of clauses connected by conjunctions and commas, and modified by relative clauses and phrases. The successive phrases lead readers continually to reconsider as they read. Stevens' construction of the poem mirrors the meaning he conveys. With a mind of winter, the snow man, Stevens concludes, "nothing himself, beholds nothing that is not there, and the nothing that is."

CONTRAST OF CONTENT AND STRUCTURE

Robert Frost's poem "Stopping by Woods on a Snowy Evening" (1923) is deceptively short and simple, with only four stanzas, each of only four lines, and short and simple words. Reinforcing this is Frost's use of regular rhyme and meter. The rhythm is iambic tetrameter throughout; the rhyme scheme is AABA in the first three stanzas and AAAA in the fourth. In an additional internal subtlety, B ending "here" in the first stanza is rhymed with A endings "queer," "near," and "year" of the second; B ending "lake" in the second is rhymed in A endings "shake," "mistake," and "flake" of the third. The final stanza's AAAA endings reinforce the ultimate darker theme. Though the first three stanzas seem to describe quietly watching snow fill the woods, the last stanza evokes the seductive pull of mysterious death: "The woods are lovely, dark and deep," countered by the obligations of living life: "But I have promises to keep, / And miles to go before I sleep, / And miles to go before I sleep." The last line's repetition strengthens Frost's message that despite death's temptation, life's course must precede it.

EFFECTS OF FIGURATIVE DEVICES ON MEANING IN POETRY

Through exaggeration, **hyperbole** communicates the strength of a poet's or persona's feelings and enhances the mood of the poem. **Imagery** appeals to the reader's senses, creating vivid mental pictures, evoking reader emotions and responses, and helping to develop themes. **Irony** also aids thematic development by drawing the reader's attention to the poet's point and communicating the poem's tone. Thematic development is additionally supported by the comparisons of **metaphors** and **similes**, which emphasize similarities, enhance imagery, and affect readers' perceptions. The use of **mood** communicates the atmosphere of a poem, builds a sense of tension, and evokes the reader's emotions. **Onomatopoeia** appeals to the reader's auditory sense and enhances sound imagery even when the poem is visual (read silently) rather than auditory (read aloud). **Rhyme** connects and unites verses, gives the rhyming words emphasis, and makes poems more fluent. **Symbolism** communicates themes, develops imagery, evokes readers' emotions, and elicits a response from the reader.

Review Video: Sensory Language
Visit mometrix.com/academy and enter code: 177314

REPETITION TO ENHANCE MEANING

A **villanelle** is a nineteen-line poem composed of five tercets and one quatrain. The defining characteristic is the repetition: two lines appear repeatedly throughout the poem. In Theodore Roethke's "The Waking," the two repeated lines are "I wake to sleep, and take my waking slow," and "I learn by going where I have to go." At first these sound paradoxical, but the meaning is gradually revealed through the poem. The repetition also fits with the theme of cycle: the paradoxes of waking to sleep, learning by going, and thinking by feeling represent a constant cycle through life. They also symbolize abandoning conscious rationalism to embrace spiritual vision. We wake from the vision to "Great Nature," and "take the lively air." "This shaking keeps me steady"—another paradox—juxtaposes and balances fear of mortality with ecstasy in embracing experience. The transcendent vision of all life's interrelationship demonstrates, "What falls away is always. And is near." Readers experience the poem holistically, like music, through Roethke's integration of theme, motion, and sound.

Sylvia Plath's villanelle "Mad Girl's Love Song" narrows the scope from universal to personal but keeps the theme of cycle. The two repeated lines, "I shut my eyes and all the world drops dead" and "(I think I made you up inside my head.)" reflect the existential viewpoint that nothing exists in any absolute reality outside of our own perceptions. In the first stanza, the middle line, "I lift my lids and all is born again," in its recreating the world, bridges between the repeated refrain statements—one of obliterating reality, the other of having constructed her lover's existence. Unlike other villanelles wherein key lines are subtly altered in their repetitions, Plath repeats these exactly each time. This reflects the young woman's love, constant throughout the poem as it neither fades nor progresses.

DRAMA

EARLY DEVELOPMENT

English **drama** originally developed from religious ritual. Early Christians established traditions of presenting pageants or mystery plays, traveling on wagons and carts through the streets to depict Biblical events. Medieval tradition assigned responsibility for performing specific plays to the different guilds. In Middle English, "mystery" referred to craft, or trade, and religious ritual and truth. Historically, mystery plays were to be reproduced exactly the same every time they were performed, like religious rituals. However, some performers introduced individual interpretations of roles and even improvised. Thus, drama was born. Narrative detail and nuanced acting were evident in mystery cycles by the Middle Ages. As individualized performance evolved, plays on other subjects also developed. Middle English mystery plays that still exist include the York Cycle, Coventry Cycle, Chester Mystery Plays, N-Town Plays, and Towneley/Wakefield Plays. In recent times, these plays began to draw interest again, and several modern actors, such as Dame Judi Dench, began their careers with mystery plays.

Review Video: Dramas
Visit mometrix.com/academy and enter code: 216060

DEFINING CHARACTERISTICS

In the Middle Ages, plays were commonly composed in **verse**. By the time of the Renaissance, Shakespeare and other dramatists wrote plays that mixed **prose**, **rhymed verse**, and **blank verse**. The traditions of costumes and masks were seen in ancient Greek drama, medieval mystery plays, and Renaissance drama. Conventions like **asides**, in which actors make comments directly to the audience unheard by other characters, and **soliloquies** were also common during Shakespeare's Elizabethan dramatic period. **Monologues** date back to ancient Greek drama. Elizabethan dialogue tended to use colloquial prose for lower-class characters' speech and stylized verse for upper-class characters. Another Elizabethan convention was the play-within-a-play, as in *Hamlet*. As drama moved toward realism, dialogue became less poetic and more conversational, as in most modern English-language plays. Contemporary drama, both onstage and onscreen, includes a convention of **breaking the fourth wall**, as actors directly face and address audiences.

COMEDY

Today, most people equate the idea of **comedy** with something funny, and of **tragedy** with something sad. However, the ancient Greeks defined these differently. Comedy needed not be humorous or amusing; it needed only a happy ending. The classical definition of comedy, as included in Aristotle's works, is any work that tells the story of a sympathetic main character's rise in fortune. According to Aristotle, protagonists need not be heroic or exemplary, nor evil or worthless, but ordinary people of unremarkable morality. Comic figures who were sympathetic were usually of humble origins, proving their "natural nobility" through their actions as they were tested. Characters born into nobility were often satirized as self-important or pompous.

SHAKESPEAREAN COMEDY

William Shakespeare lived in England from 1564-1616. He was a poet and playwright of the Renaissance period in Western culture. He is generally considered the foremost dramatist in world literature and the greatest author to write in the English language. He wrote many poems, particularly sonnets, of which 154 survive today, and approximately 38 plays. Though his sonnets are greater in number and are very famous, he is best known for his plays, including comedies, tragedies, tragicomedies and historical plays. His play titles include: *All's Well That Ends Well, As You Like It, The Comedy of Errors, Love's Labour's Lost, Measure for Measure, The Merchant of Venice, The Merry Wives of Windsor, A Midsummer Night's Dream, Much Ado About Nothing, The Taming of the Shrew, The Tempest, Twelfth Night, The Two Gentlemen of Verona, The Winter's Tale, King John, Richard II, Henry IV, Henry V, Richard III, Romeo and Juliet, Coriolanus, Titus Andronicus, Julius Caesar, Macbeth, Hamlet, Troilus and Cressida, King Lear, Othello, Antony and Cleopatra,* and *Cymbeline.* Some scholars have suggested that Christopher Marlowe wrote several of Shakespeare's works. While most scholars reject this theory, Shakespeare did pay homage to Marlowe, alluding to several of his characters, themes, or verbiage, as well as borrowing themes from several of his plays (e.g., Marlowe's *Jew of Malta* influenced Shakespeare's *Merchant of Venice*).

When Shakespeare was writing, during the Elizabethan period of the Renaissance, Aristotle's version of comedies was popular. While some of Shakespeare's comedies were humorous and others were not, all had happy endings. *A Comedy of Errors* is a farce. Based and expanding on a Classical Roman comedy, it is lighthearted and includes slapstick humor and mistaken identity. *Much Ado About Nothing* is a romantic comedy. It incorporates some more serious themes, including social mores, perceived infidelity, marriage's duality as both trap and ideal, honor and its loss, public shame, and deception, but also much witty dialogue and a happy ending.

Dramatic Comedy

Three types of dramas classified as comedy include the farce, the romantic comedy, and the satirical comedy.

Farce

The **farce** is a zany, goofy type of comedy that includes pratfalls and other forms of slapstick humor. The characters in a farce tend to be ridiculous or fantastical in nature. The plot also tends to contain highly improbable events, featuring complications and twists that continue throughout, and incredible coincidences that would likely never occur in reality. Mistaken identity, deceptions, and disguises are common devices used in farcical comedies. Shakespeare's play *The Comedy of Errors,* with its cases of accidental mistaken identity and slapstick, is an example of farce. Contemporary examples of farce include the Marx Brothers' movies, the Three Stooges movies and TV episodes, and the *Pink Panther* movie series.

Romantic Comedy

Romantic comedies are probably the most popular of the types of comedy, in both live theater performances and movies. They include not only humor and a happy ending, but also love. In the typical plot of a **romantic comedy**, two people well suited to one another are either brought together for the first time, or reconciled after being separated. They are usually both sympathetic characters and seem destined to be together, yet they are separated by some intervening complication, such as ex-lovers, interfering parents or friends, or differences in social class. The happy ending is achieved through the lovers overcoming all these obstacles. William Shakespeare's *Much Ado About Nothing,* Walt Disney's version of *Cinderella* (1950), and Broadway musical *Guys and Dolls* (1955) are example of romantic comedies. Many live-action movies are also examples of romantic comedies, such as *The Princess Bride* (1987), *Sleepless in Seattle* (1993), *You've Got Mail* (1998), and *Forget Paris* (1995).

Satirical Comedy and Black Comedy

Satires generally mock and lampoon human foolishness and vices. **Satirical comedies** fit the classical definition of comedy by depicting a main character's rise in fortune, but they also fit the definition of satire by making that main character either a fool, morally corrupt, or cynical in attitude. All or most of the other characters in the satirical comedy display similar foibles. These include gullible types, such as cuckolded spouses and dupes, and deceptive types, such as tricksters, con artists, criminals, hypocrites, and fortune seekers, who prey on the gullible. Some classical examples of satirical comedies include *The Birds* by ancient Greek comedic playwright Aristophanes, and *Volpone* by 17th-century poet and playwright Ben Jonson, who made the comedy of humors popular. When satirical comedy is extended to extremes, it becomes **black comedy**, wherein the comedic occurrences are grotesque or terrible.

Tragedy

The opposite of comedy is tragedy, portraying a hero's fall in fortune. While by classical definitions, tragedies could be sad, Aristotle went further, requiring that they depict suffering and pain to cause "terror and pity" in audiences. Additionally, he decreed that tragic heroes be basically good, admirable, or noble, and that their downfalls result from personal action, choice, or error, not by bad luck or accident.

Aristotle's Features of Tragedy

In his *Poetics,* Aristotle identified various elements that appear in Greek tragedies:

- ***Anagnorisis***: Meaning tragic insight or recognition, this is a moment of realization by a tragic hero or heroine that he or she has become enmeshed in a "web of fate."
- ***Catharsis***: Meaning an emotional release on the part of the audience.
- ***Hamartia***: This is often called a "tragic flaw," but is better described as a tragic error. *Hamartia* is an archery term meaning a shot missing the bull's eye, used here as a metaphor for a mistake—often a simple one—which results in catastrophe.
- ***Hubris***: While often called "pride," this is actually translated as "violent transgression," and signifies an arrogant overstepping of moral or cultural bounds—the sin of the tragic hero who over-presumes or over-aspires.
- ***Mimesis***: This refers to the idea that works of art reflect the real world, including individuals, nature, human behavior, and social order.
- ***Nemesis***: translated as "retribution," this represents the cosmic punishment or payback that the tragic hero ultimately receives for committing hubristic acts.
- ***Peripateia***: Literally "turning," this is a plot reversal consisting of a tragic hero's pivotal action, which changes his or her status from safe to endangered.
- ***Spectacle***: Visual elements of the story, in the context of dramatic plays.

Hegel's Theory of Tragedy

Georg Wilhelm Friedrich Hegel (1770-1831) proposed a different theory of tragedy than Aristotle (384-322 BC), which was also very influential. Whereas Aristotle's criteria involved character and plot, Hegel defined tragedy as a dynamic conflict of opposite forces or rights. For example, if an individual believes in the moral philosophy of the conscientious objector (i.e., that fighting in wars is morally wrong) but is confronted with being drafted into military service, this conflict would fit Hegel's definition of a tragic plot premise. Hegel theorized that a tragedy must involve some circumstance in which two values, or two rights, are fatally at odds with one another and conflict directly. Hegel did not view this as good triumphing over evil, or evil winning out over good, but rather as one good fighting against another good unto death. He saw this conflict of two goods as truly tragic. In ancient Greek playwright Sophocles' tragedy *Antigone,* the main character experiences this tragic conflict between her public duties and her family and religious responsibilities.

Revenge Tragedy

Along with Aristotelian definitions of comedy and tragedy, ancient Greece was the origin of the **revenge tragedy**. This genre became highly popular in Renaissance England, and is still popular today in contemporary movies. In a revenge tragedy, the protagonist has suffered a serious wrong, such as the murder of a family member. However, the wrongdoer has not been punished. In contemporary plots, this often occurs when some legal technicality has interfered with the miscreant's conviction and sentencing, or when authorities are unable to locate and apprehend the criminal. The protagonist then faces the conflict of suffering this injustice, or exacting his or her own justice by seeking revenge. Greek revenge tragedies include *Agamemnon* and *Medea.* Playwright Thomas Kyd's *The Spanish Tragedy* (1582-1592) is credited with beginning the Elizabethan genre of revenge tragedies. Shakespearean revenge tragedies include *Hamlet* (1599-1602) and *Titus Andronicus* (1588-1593). A Jacobean example is Thomas Middleton's *The Revenger's Tragedy* (1606, 1607).

Hamlet's "Tragic Flaw"

Despite virtually limitless interpretations, one way to view Hamlet's tragic error generally is as indecision. He suffers the classic revenge tragedy's conflict of whether to suffer with his knowledge of his mother's and uncle's assassination of his father, or to exact his own revenge and justice against Claudius, who has assumed the throne after his crime went unknown and unpunished. Hamlet's famous soliloquy, "To be or not to be" reflects this dilemma. Hamlet muses "Whether 'tis nobler in the mind to suffer the slings and arrows of outrageous fortune, / Or to take arms against a sea of troubles, / And by opposing end them?" Hamlet both longs for and fears death, as "the dread of something after death ... makes us rather bear those ills we have / Than fly to others that we know not ... Thus, conscience does make cowards of us all." For most of the play, Hamlet struggles with his responsibility to avenge his father, who was killed by Hamlet's uncle, Claudius. So, Hamlet's tragic error at first might be considered a lack of action. But he then makes several attempts at revenge, each of which end in worse tragedy, until his efforts are ended by the final tragedy—Hamlet's own death.

Chapter Quiz

Ready to see how well you retained what you just read? Scan the QR code to go directly to the chapter quiz interface for this study guide. If you're using a computer, simply visit the online resources page at **mometrix.com/resources719/hiset-27339** and click the Chapter Quizzes link.

Language Arts—Writing

Development of Central Position or Claim

The Writing Process

Prewriting

The **prewriting stage** is the part of the process in which the writer focuses on **generating ideas** and developing a broad plan for what he or she wants to accomplish. **Brainstorming** is the process of thinking about a topic and writing down every thought that comes to mind. Brainstorming may also take the form of asking questions that need to be answered by the composition. **Free writing** has a similar goal of writing about a topic in a continuous flow for a short span of time (e.g., 2 to 3 minutes). The goal of these exercises is not to produce high-quality, polished thoughts, but to generate leads to follow when the more structured writing happens later in the process. In research writing, the prewriting stage may also include doing a literature review and **collecting information** to use as evidence in arguments later on. When collecting information, it is important to take clear notes of where an idea was originally found so it can be cited later on. Another key aspect of the prewriting process is **planning phase**. This entails deciding on the overall topic, purpose, tone, and general organization for the rest of the composition. The planning process may involve using aids like outlines, Venn diagrams, flowcharts, and other visual models to help collect and organize information. The planning process does not set the whole composition in stone, but it does help structure the ideas to be written in the drafting phase.

Drafting

The **drafting stage** of the writing process involves taking the plan for the composition and filling out all of the main ideas for the composition. Some writers prefer to start by writing the introduction and write their whole composition from start to finish, while others may prefer writing the main body paragraphs first and then coming back to the introduction and conclusion. In any case, the drafting process is a first attempt at writing the whole composition from start to finish. A writer may succeed in communicating what he or she wants in the first draft, but it often takes writing **several drafts** before the ideas and arguments take their final form. By the end of the drafting stage, the composition should be close to its final organization with its arguments clearly identified, but it will still need organizational, grammatical, and formatting improvements to be called complete.

Revising

The **revision stage** is when the writer reads back through his or her work and looks for big-picture issues that affect **clarity** and **cohesion**. These can include organizational issues or flaws in logical flow. Writers should look back through their work to find any assertions or arguments that may be misplaced or lacking in support. They should look also through their work to find any information that does not contribute to the main idea or goal of the composition. Beginning writers may find it difficult to clearly communicate more than two or three main points in their arguments. If this is the case, these writers should eliminate information that detracts from those main points. In this stage, clarity is often more important than comprehensiveness.

Editing/Proofreading

The **editing or proofreading stage** is focused specifically on improving the grammar and punctuation of the composition. The writer should read each paragraph closely and slowly to identify and fix any grammatical, spelling, or punctuation errors. Some of the worst offenders include subject-verb agreement in complex sentences, changes in tense throughout the document, and changes in perspective (first, second, or third person) or tone (professional, casual, opinionated, etc.). When writing at home, it is often helpful to have a friend or family member look for errors as well. Finally, this phase involves looking for very small errors, so multiple passes should be taken to catch as many problems as possible. One good rule of thumb is to keep reading through the whole document until a full read-through can be accomplished without finding any more errors.

Publishing

The **publishing stage** refers to putting the document into its final format and delivering it to the audience. This involves formatting the document for presentation. In research writing, the final document may need to conform to a specific publishing standard, such as MLA or APA. In literal publishing, this would also take the form of presenting the document to the final audience, which may involve physical printing or digital publication. Note that once a composition has been published, it is often difficult to change or retract. Before reaching the publishing stage, the writer should have looped through the drafting, revision, and editing process a few times to ensure the writer says exactly what he or she wants before putting it before the final audience.

Recursive Writing Process

However you approach writing, you may find comfort in knowing that the revision process can occur in any order. The **recursive writing process** is not as difficult as the phrase may make it seem. Simply put, the recursive writing process means that you may need to revisit steps after completing other steps. It also implies that the steps are not required to take place in any certain order. Indeed, you may find that planning, drafting, and revising can all take place at about the same time. The writing process involves moving back and forth between planning, drafting, and revising, followed by more planning, more drafting, and more revising until the writing is satisfactory.

Review Video: Recursive Writing Process
Visit mometrix.com/academy and enter code: 951611

Common Types of Writing

Autobiographical Narratives

Autobiographical narratives are narratives written by an author about an event or period in their life. Autobiographical narratives are written from one person's perspective, in first person, and often include the author's thoughts and feelings alongside their description of the event or period. Structure, style, or theme varies between different autobiographical narratives, since each narrative is personal and specific to its author and his or her experience.

Reflective Essay

A less common type of essay is the reflective essay. **Reflective essays** allow the author to reflect, or think back, on an experience and analyze what they recall. They should consider what they learned from the experience, what they could have done differently, what would have helped them during the experience, or anything else that they have realized from looking back on the experience. Reflection essays incorporate both objective reflection on one's own actions and subjective explanation of thoughts and feelings. These essays can be written for a number of experiences in a formal or informal context.

Journals and Diaries

A **journal** is a personal account of events, experiences, feelings, and thoughts. Many people write journals to express their feelings and thoughts or to help them process experiences they have had. Since journals are **private documents** not meant to be shared with others, writers may not be concerned with grammar, spelling, or other mechanics. However, authors may write journals that they expect or hope to publish someday; in this case, they not only express their thoughts and feelings and process their experiences, but they also attend to their craft in writing them. Some authors compose journals to record a particular time period or a series of related events, such as a cancer diagnosis, treatment, surviving the disease, and how these experiences have changed or affected them. Other experiences someone might include in a journal are recovering from addiction, journeys of spiritual exploration and discovery, time spent in another country, or anything else someone wants to personally document. Journaling can also be therapeutic, as some people use journals to work through feelings of grief over loss or to wrestle with big decisions.

Examples of Diaries in Literature

The Diary of a Young Girl by Dutch Jew Anne Frank (1947) contains her life-affirming, nonfictional diary entries from 1942-1944 while her family hid in an attic from World War II's genocidal Nazis. *Go Ask Alice* (1971) by Beatrice Sparks is a cautionary, fictional novel in the form of diary entries by Alice, an unhappy, rebellious teen who takes LSD, runs away from home and lives with hippies, and eventually returns home. Frank's writing reveals an intelligent, sensitive, insightful girl, raised by intellectual European parents—a girl who believes in the goodness of human nature despite surrounding atrocities. Alice, influenced by early 1970s counterculture, becomes less optimistic. However, similarities can be found between them: Frank dies in a Nazi concentration camp while the fictitious Alice dies from a drug overdose. Both young women are also unable to escape their surroundings. Additionally, adolescent searches for personal identity are evident in both books.

Review Video: Journals, Diaries, Letters, and Blogs
Visit mometrix.com/academy and enter code: 432845

Letters

Letters are messages written to other people. In addition to letters written between individuals, some writers compose letters to the editors of newspapers, magazines, and other publications, while some write "Open Letters" to be published and read by the general public. Open letters, while intended for everyone to read, may also identify a group of people or a single person whom the letter directly addresses. In everyday use, the most-used forms are business letters and personal or friendly letters. Both kinds share common elements: business or personal letterhead stationery; the writer's return address at the top; the addressee's address next; a salutation, such as "Dear [name]" or some similar opening greeting, followed by a colon in business letters or a comma in personal letters; the body of the letter, with paragraphs as indicated; and a closing, like "Sincerely/Cordially/Best regards/etc." or "Love," in intimate personal letters.

Early Letters

The Greek word for "letter" is *epistolē*, which became the English word "epistle." The earliest letters were called epistles, including the New Testament's epistles from the apostles to the Christians. In ancient Egypt, the writing curriculum in scribal schools included the epistolary genre. Epistolary novels frame a story in the form of letters. Examples of noteworthy epistolary novels include:

- *Pamela* (1740), by 18th-century English novelist Samuel Richardson
- *Shamela* (1741), Henry Fielding's satire of *Pamela* that mocked epistolary writing.
- *Lettres persanes* (1721) by French author Montesquieu
- *The Sorrows of Young Werther* (1774) by German author Johann Wolfgang von Goethe
- *The History of Emily Montague* (1769), the first Canadian novel, by Frances Brooke
- *Dracula* (1897) by Bram Stoker
- *Frankenstein* (1818) by Mary Shelley
- *The Color Purple* (1982) by Alice Walker

Blogs

The word "blog" is derived from "weblog" and refers to writing done exclusively on the internet. Readers of reputable newspapers expect quality content and layouts that enable easy reading. These expectations also apply to blogs. For example, readers can easily move visually from line to line when columns are narrow, while overly wide columns cause readers to lose their places. Blogs must also be posted with layouts enabling online readers to follow them easily. However, because the way people read on computer, tablet, and smartphone screens differs from how they read print on paper, formatting and writing blog content is more complex than writing newspaper articles. Two major principles are the bases for blog-writing rules: The first is while readers of print articles skim to estimate their length, online they must scroll down to scan; therefore, blog layouts need more subheadings, graphics, and other indications of what information follows. The second is onscreen reading can be harder on the eyes than reading printed paper, so legibility is crucial in blogs.

Rules and Rationales for Writing Blogs

1. Format all posts for smooth page layout and easy scanning.
2. Column width should not be too wide, as larger lines of text can be difficult to read
3. Headings and subheadings separate text visually, enable scanning or skimming, and encourage continued reading.
4. Bullet-pointed or numbered lists enable quick information location and scanning.
5. Punctuation is critical, so beginners should use shorter sentences until confident in their knowledge of punctuation rules.
6. Blog paragraphs should be far shorter—two to six sentences each—than paragraphs written on paper to enable "chunking" because reading onscreen is more difficult.
7. Sans-serif fonts are usually clearer than serif fonts, and larger font sizes are better.
8. Highlight important material and draw attention with **boldface**, but avoid overuse. Avoid hard-to-read *italics* and ALL CAPITALS.
9. Include enough blank spaces: overly busy blogs tire eyes and brains. Images not only break up text but also emphasize and enhance text and can attract initial reader attention.
10. Use background colors judiciously to avoid distracting the eye or making it difficult to read.
11. Be consistent throughout posts, since people read them in different orders.
12. Tell a story with a beginning, middle, and end.

Specialized Types of Writing

Editorials

Editorials are articles in newspapers, magazines, and other serial publications. Editorials express an opinion or belief belonging to the majority of the publication's leadership. This opinion or belief generally refers to a specific issue, topic, or event. These articles are authored by a member, or a small number of members, of the publication's leadership and are often written to affect their readers, such as persuading them to adopt a stance or take a particular action.

Resumes

Resumes are brief, but formal, documents that outline an individual's experience in a certain area. Resumes are most often used for job applications. Such resumes will list the applicant's work experience, certification, and achievements or qualifications related to the position. Resumes should only include the most pertinent information. They should also use strategic formatting to highlight the applicant's most impressive experiences and achievements, to ensure the document can be read quickly and easily, and to eliminate both visual clutter and excessive negative space.

Reports

Reports summarize the results of research, new methodology, or other developments in an academic or professional context. Reports often include details about methodology and outside influences and factors. However, a report should focus primarily on the results of the research or development. Reports are objective and deliver information efficiently, sacrificing style for clear and effective communication.

Memoranda

A memorandum, also called a memo, is a formal method of communication used in professional settings. Memoranda are printed documents that include a heading listing the sender and their job title, the recipient and their job title, the date, and a specific subject line. Memoranda often include an introductory section explaining the reason and context for the memorandum. Next, a memorandum includes a section with details relevant to the topic. Finally, the memorandum will conclude with a paragraph that politely and clearly defines the sender's expectations of the recipient.

Technology in the Writing Process

Modern technology has yielded several tools that can be used to make the writing process more convenient and organized. Word processors and online tools, such as databases and plagiarism detectors, allow much of the writing process to be completed in one place, using one device.

Technology for Planning and Drafting

For the planning and drafting stages of the writing process, word processors are a helpful tool. These programs also feature formatting tools, allowing users to create their own planning tools or create digital outlines that can be easily converted into sentences, paragraphs, or an entire essay draft. Online databases and references also complement the planning process by providing convenient access to information and sources for research. Word processors also allow users to keep up with their work and update it more easily than if they wrote their work by hand. Online word processors often allow users to collaborate, making group assignments more convenient. These programs also allow users to include illustrations or other supplemental media in their compositions.

Technology for Revising, Editing, and Proofreading

Word processors also benefit the revising, editing, and proofreading stages of the writing process. Most of these programs indicate errors in spelling and grammar, allowing users to catch minor errors and correct them quickly. There are also websites designed to help writers by analyzing text for deeper errors, such as poor sentence structure, inappropriate complexity, lack of sentence variety, and style issues. These websites can help users fix errors they may not know to look for or may have simply missed. As writers finish these steps, they may benefit from checking their work for any plagiarism. There are several websites and programs that compare text to other documents and publications across the internet and detect any similarities within the text. These websites show the source of the similar information, so users know whether or not they referenced the source and unintentionally plagiarized its contents.

Technology for Publishing

Technology also makes managing written work more convenient. Digitally storing documents keeps everything in one place and is easy to reference. Digital storage also makes sharing work easier, as documents can be attached to an email or stored online. This also allows writers to publish their work easily, as they can electronically submit it to other publications or freely post it to a personal blog, profile, or website.

Organization of Ideas

Outlining and Organizing Ideas

Essays

Essays usually focus on one topic, subject, or goal. There are several types of essays, including informative, persuasive, and narrative. An essay's structure and level of formality depend on the type of essay and its goal. While narrative essays typically do not include outside sources, other types of essays often require some research and the integration of primary and secondary sources.

The basic format of an essay typically has three major parts: the introduction, the body, and the conclusion. The body is further divided into the writer's main points. Short and simple essays may have three main points, while essays covering broader ranges and going into more depth can have almost any number of main points, depending on length.

An essay's introduction should answer three questions:

1. What is the **subject** of the essay?

If a student writes an essay about a book, the answer would include the title and author of the book and any additional information needed—such as the subject or argument of the book.

2. How does the essay **address** the subject?

   To answer this, the writer identifies the essay's organization by briefly summarizing main points and the evidence supporting them.

3. What will the essay **prove**?

   This is the thesis statement, usually the opening paragraph's last sentence, clearly stating the writer's message.

The body elaborates on all the main points related to the thesis, introducing one main point at a time, and includes supporting evidence with each main point. Each body paragraph should state the point in a topic sentence, which is usually the first sentence in the paragraph. The paragraph should then explain the point's meaning, support it with quotations or other evidence, and then explain how this point and the evidence are related to the thesis. The writer should then repeat this procedure in a new paragraph for each additional main point.

The conclusion reiterates the content of the introduction, including the thesis, to remind the reader of the essay's main argument or subject. The essay writer may also summarize the highlights of the argument or description contained in the body of the essay, following the same sequence originally used in the body. For example, a conclusion might look like: Point 1 + Point 2 + Point 3 = Thesis, or Point 1 → Point 2 → Point 3 → Thesis Proof. Good organization makes essays easier for writers to compose and provides a guide for readers to follow. Well-organized essays hold attention better and are more likely to get readers to accept their theses as valid.

Main Ideas, Supporting Details, and Outlining a Topic

A writer often begins the first paragraph of a paper by stating the **main idea** or point, also known as the **topic sentence**. The rest of the paragraph supplies particular details that develop and support the main point. One way to visualize the relationship between the main point and supporting information is by considering a table: the tabletop is the main point, and each of the table's legs is a supporting detail or group of details. Both professional authors and students can benefit from planning their writing by first making an outline of the topic. Outlines facilitate quick identification of the main point and supporting details without having to wade through the additional language that will exist in the fully developed essay, article, or paper. Outlining can also help readers to analyze a piece of existing writing for the same reason. The outline first summarizes the main idea in one sentence. Then, below that, it summarizes the supporting details in a numbered list. Writing the paper then consists of filling in the outline with detail, writing a paragraph for each supporting point, and adding an introduction and conclusion.

Introduction

The purpose of the introduction is to capture the reader's attention and announce the essay's main idea. Normally, the introduction contains 50-80 words, or 3-5 sentences. An introduction can begin with an interesting quote, a question, or a strong opinion—something that will **engage** the reader's interest and prompt them to keep reading. If you are writing your essay to a specific prompt, your introduction should include a **restatement or summarization** of the prompt so that the reader will have some context for your essay. Finally, your introduction should briefly state your **thesis or main idea**: the primary thing you hope to communicate to the reader through your essay. Don't try to include all of the details and nuances of your thesis, or all of your reasons for it, in the introduction. That's what the rest of the essay is for!

Review Video: Introduction
Visit mometrix.com/academy and enter code: 961328

THESIS STATEMENT

The thesis is the main idea of the essay. A temporary thesis, or working thesis, should be established early in the writing process because it will serve to keep the writer focused as ideas develop. This temporary thesis is subject to change as you continue to write.

The temporary thesis has two parts: a **topic** (i.e., the focus of your essay based on the prompt) and a **comment**. The comment makes an important point about the topic. A temporary thesis should be interesting and specific. Also, you need to limit the topic to a manageable scope. These three questions are useful tools to measure the effectiveness of any temporary thesis:

- Does the focus of my essay have enough interest to hold an audience?
- Is the focus of my essay specific enough to generate interest?
- Is the focus of my essay manageable for the time limit? Too broad? Too narrow?

The thesis should be a generalization rather than a fact because the thesis prepares readers for facts and details that support the thesis. The process of bringing the thesis into sharp focus may help in outlining major sections of the work. Once the thesis and introduction are complete, you can address the body of the work.

Review Video: Thesis Statements
Visit mometrix.com/academy and enter code: 691033

SUPPORTING THE THESIS

Throughout your essay, the thesis should be **explained clearly and supported** adequately by additional arguments. The thesis sentence needs to contain a clear statement of the purpose of your essay and a comment about the thesis. With the thesis statement, you have an opportunity to state what is noteworthy of this particular treatment of the prompt. Each sentence and paragraph should build on and support the thesis.

When you respond to the prompt, use parts of the passage to support your argument or defend your position. Using supporting evidence from the passage strengths your argument because readers can see your attention to the entire passage and your response to the details and facts within the passage. You can use facts, details, statistics, and direct quotations from the passage to uphold your position. Be sure to point out which information comes from the original passage and base your argument around that evidence.

BODY

In an essay's introduction, the writer establishes the thesis and may indicate how the rest of the piece will be structured. In the body of the piece, the writer **elaborates** upon, **illustrates**, and **explains** the **thesis statement**. How writers arrange supporting details and their choices of paragraph types are development techniques. Writers may give examples of the concept introduced in the thesis statement. If the subject includes a cause-and-effect relationship, the author may explain its causality. A writer will explain or analyze the main idea of the piece throughout the body, often by presenting arguments for the veracity or credibility of the thesis statement. Writers may use development to define or clarify ambiguous terms. Paragraphs within the body may be organized using natural sequences, like space and time. Writers may employ **inductive reasoning**, using multiple details to establish a generalization or causal relationship, or **deductive reasoning**, proving a generalized hypothesis or proposition through a specific example or case.

Review Video: Drafting Body Paragraphs
Visit mometrix.com/academy and enter code: 724590

PARAGRAPHS

After the introduction of a passage, a series of body paragraphs will carry a message through to the conclusion. Each paragraph should be **unified around a main point**. Normally, a good topic sentence summarizes the paragraph's main point. A topic sentence is a general sentence that gives an introduction to the paragraph.

The sentences that follow support the topic sentence. However, though it is usually the first sentence, the topic sentence can come as the final sentence to the paragraph if the earlier sentences give a clear explanation of the paragraph's topic. This allows the topic sentence to function as a concluding sentence. Overall, the paragraphs need to stay true to the main point. This means that any unnecessary sentences that do not advance the main point should be removed.

The main point of a paragraph requires adequate development (i.e., a substantial paragraph that covers the main point). A paragraph of two or three sentences does not cover a main point. This is especially true when the main point of the paragraph gives strong support to the argument of the thesis. An occasional short paragraph is fine as a transitional device. However, a well-developed argument will have paragraphs with more than a few sentences.

Methods of Developing Paragraphs

Common methods of adding substance to paragraphs include examples, illustrations, analogies, and cause and effect.

- **Examples** are supporting details to the main idea of a paragraph or a passage. When authors write about something that their audience may not understand, they can provide an example to show their point. When authors write about something that is not easily accepted, they can give examples to prove their point.
- **Illustrations** are extended examples that require several sentences. Well-selected illustrations can be a great way for authors to develop a point that may not be familiar to their audience.
- **Analogies** make comparisons between items that appear to have nothing in common. Analogies are employed by writers to provoke fresh thoughts about a subject. These comparisons may be used to explain the unfamiliar, to clarify an abstract point, or to argue a point. Although analogies are effective literary devices, they should be used carefully in arguments. Two things may be alike in some respects but completely different in others.
- **Cause and effect** is an excellent device to explain the connection between an action or situation and a particular result. One way that authors can use cause and effect is to state the effect in the topic sentence of a paragraph and add the causes in the body of the paragraph. This method can give an author's paragraphs structure, which always strengthens writing.

Types of Paragraphs

- A **paragraph of narration** tells a story or a part of a story. Normally, the sentences are arranged in chronological order (i.e., the order that the events happened). However, flashbacks (i.e., an anecdote from an earlier time) can be included.
- A **descriptive paragraph** makes a verbal portrait of a person, place, or thing. When specific details are used that appeal to one or more of the senses (i.e., sight, sound, smell, taste, and touch), authors give readers a sense of being present in the moment.
- A **process paragraph** is related to time order (i.e., First, you open the bottle. Second, you pour the liquid, etc.). Usually, this describes a process or teaches readers how to perform a process.
- **Comparing two things** draws attention to their similarities and indicates a number of differences. When authors contrast, they focus only on differences. Both comparing and contrasting may be done point-by-point, noting both the similarities and differences of each point, or in sequential paragraphs, where you discuss all the similarities and then all the differences, or vice versa.

Breaking Text into Paragraphs

For most forms of writing, you will need to use multiple paragraphs. As such, determining when to start a new paragraph is very important. Reasons for starting a new paragraph include:

- To mark off the introduction and concluding paragraphs
- To signal a shift to a new idea or topic
- To indicate an important shift in time or place
- To explain a point in additional detail
- To highlight a comparison, contrast, or cause and effect relationship

Paragraph Length

Most readers find that their comfort level for a paragraph is between 100 and 200 words. Shorter paragraphs cause too much starting and stopping and give a choppy effect. Paragraphs that are too long often test the attention span of readers. Two notable exceptions to this rule exist. In scientific or scholarly papers, longer paragraphs suggest seriousness and depth. In journalistic writing, constraints are placed on paragraph size by the narrow columns in a newspaper format.

The first and last paragraphs of a text will usually be the introduction and conclusion. These special-purpose paragraphs are likely to be shorter than paragraphs in the body of the work. Paragraphs in the body of the essay follow the subject's outline (e.g., one paragraph per point in short essays and a group of paragraphs per point in longer works). Some ideas require more development than others, so it is good for a writer to remain flexible. A paragraph of excessive length may be divided, and shorter ones may be combined.

Conclusion

Two important principles to consider when writing a conclusion are strength and closure. A strong conclusion gives the reader a sense that the author's main points are meaningful and important, and that the supporting facts and arguments are convincing, solid, and well developed. When a conclusion achieves closure, it gives the impression that the writer has stated all necessary information and points and completed the work, rather than simply stopping after a specified length. Some things to avoid when writing concluding paragraphs include:

- Introducing a completely new idea
- Beginning with obvious or unoriginal phrases like "In conclusion" or "To summarize"
- Apologizing for one's opinions or writing
- Repeating the thesis word for word rather than rephrasing it
- Believing that the conclusion must always summarize the piece

Coherence in Writing

Coherent Paragraphs

A smooth flow of sentences and paragraphs without gaps, shifts, or bumps will lead to paragraph **coherence**. Ties between old and new information can be smoothed using several methods:

- **Linking ideas clearly**, from the topic sentence to the body of the paragraph, is essential for a smooth transition. The topic sentence states the main point, and this should be followed by specific details, examples, and illustrations that support the topic sentence. The support may be direct or indirect. In **indirect support**, the illustrations and examples may support a sentence that in turn supports the topic directly.
- The **repetition of key words** adds coherence to a paragraph. To avoid dull language, variations of the key words may be used.
- **Parallel structures** are often used within sentences to emphasize the similarity of ideas and connect sentences giving similar information.

- Maintaining a **consistent verb tense** throughout the paragraph helps. Shifting tenses affects the smooth flow of words and can disrupt the coherence of the paragraph.

Review Video: How to Write a Good Paragraph
Visit mometrix.com/academy and enter code: 682127

Sequence Words and Phrases

When a paragraph opens with the topic sentence, the second sentence may begin with a phrase like *first of all*, introducing the first supporting detail or example. The writer may introduce the second supporting item with words or phrases like *also*, *in addition*, and *besides*. The writer might introduce succeeding pieces of support with wording like, *another thing*, *moreover*, *furthermore*, or *not only that, but*. The writer may introduce the last piece of support with *lastly*, *finally*, or *last but not least*. Writers get off the point by presenting off-target items not supporting the main point. For example, a main point *my dog is not smart* is supported by the statement, *he's six years old and still doesn't answer to his name*. But *he cries when I leave for school* is not supportive, as it does not indicate lack of intelligence. Writers stay on point by presenting only supportive statements that are directly relevant to and illustrative of their main point.

Review Video: Sequence
Visit mometrix.com/academy and enter code: 489027

Transitions

Transitions between sentences and paragraphs guide readers from idea to idea and indicate relationships between sentences and paragraphs. Writers should be judicious in their use of transitions, inserting them sparingly. They should also be selected to fit the author's purpose—transitions can indicate time, comparison, and conclusion, among other purposes. Tone is also important to consider when using transitional phrases, varying the tone for different audiences. For example, in a scholarly essay, *in summary* would be preferable to the more informal *in short*.

When working with transitional words and phrases, writers usually find a natural flow that indicates when a transition is needed. In reading a draft of the text, it should become apparent where the flow is disrupted. At this point, the writer can add transitional elements during the revision process. Revising can also afford an opportunity to delete transitional devices that seem heavy handed or unnecessary.

Review Video: Transitions in Writing
Visit mometrix.com/academy and enter code: 233246

Types of Transitional Words

Time	afterward, immediately, earlier, meanwhile, recently, lately, now, since, soon, when, then, until, before, etc.
Sequence	too, first, second, further, moreover, also, again, and, next, still, besides, finally
Comparison	similarly, in the same way, likewise, also, again, once more
Contrasting	but, although, despite, however, instead, nevertheless, on the one hand... on the other hand, regardless, yet, in contrast
Cause and Effect	because, consequently, thus, therefore, then, to this end, since, so, as a result, if... then, accordingly
Examples	for example, for instance, such as, to illustrate, indeed, in fact, specifically
Place	near, far, here, there, to the left/right, next to, above, below, beyond, opposite, beside
Concession	granted that, naturally, of course, it may appear, although it is true that
Repetition, Summary, or Conclusion	as mentioned earlier, as noted, in other words, in short, on the whole, to summarize, therefore, as a result, to conclude, in conclusion
Addition	and, also, furthermore, moreover
Generalization	in broad terms, broadly speaking, in general

Review Video: Transition Words
Visit mometrix.com/academy and enter code: 707563

Review Video: How to Effectively Connect Sentences
Visit mometrix.com/academy and enter code: 948325

Writing Style and Form

Writing Style and Linguistic Form

Linguistic form encodes the literal meanings of words and sentences. It comes from the phonological, morphological, syntactic, and semantic parts of a language. **Writing style** consists of different ways of encoding the meaning and indicating figurative and stylistic meanings. An author's writing style can also be referred to as his or her **voice**.

Writers' stylistic choices accomplish three basic effects on their audiences:

- They **communicate meanings** beyond linguistically dictated meanings,
- They communicate the **author's attitude**, such as persuasive or argumentative effects accomplished through style, and
- They communicate or **express feelings**.

Within style, component areas include:

- Narrative structure
- Viewpoint
- Focus
- Sound patterns
- Meter and rhythm
- Lexical and syntactic repetition and parallelism
- Writing genre
- Representational, realistic, and mimetic effects
- Representation of thought and speech

- Meta-representation (representing representation)
- Irony
- Metaphor and other indirect meanings
- Representation and use of historical and dialectal variations
- Gender-specific and other group-specific speech styles, both real and fictitious
- Analysis of the processes for inferring meaning from writing

Tone

Tone may be defined as the writer's **attitude** toward the topic, and to the audience. This attitude is reflected in the language used in the writing. The tone of a work should be **appropriate to the topic** and to the intended audience. While it may be fine to use slang or jargon in some pieces, other texts should not contain such terms. Tone can range from humorous to serious and any level in between. It may be more or less formal, depending on the purpose of the writing and its intended audience. All these nuances in tone can flavor the entire writing and should be kept in mind as the work evolves.

Review Video: Style, Tone, and Mood
Visit mometrix.com/academy and enter code: 416961

Word Selection

A writer's choice of words is a signature of their style. Careful thought about the use of words can improve a piece of writing. A passage can be an exciting piece to read when attention is given to the use of vivid or specific nouns rather than general ones.

Example:

> General: His kindness will never be forgotten.
>
> Specific: His thoughtful gifts and bear hugs will never be forgotten.

Active and Passive Language

Attention should also be given to the kind of verbs that are used in sentences. Active verbs (e.g., run, swim) are about an action. Whenever possible, an **active verb should replace a linking verb** to provide clear examples for arguments and to strengthen a passage overall. When using an active verb, one should be sure that the verb is used in the active voice instead of the passive voice. Verbs are in the active voice when the subject is the one doing the action. A verb is in the passive voice when the subject is the recipient of an action.

Example:

> Passive: The winners were called to the stage by the judges.
>
> Active: The judges called the winners to the stage.

Review Video: Word Usage In Sentences
Visit mometrix.com/academy and enter code: 197863

Conciseness

Conciseness is writing that communicates a message in the fewest words possible. Writing concisely is valuable because short, uncluttered messages allow the reader to understand the author's message more easily and efficiently. Planning is important in writing concise messages. If you have in mind what you need to write beforehand, it will be easier to make a message short and to the point. Do not state the obvious.

Revising is also important. After the message is written, make sure you have effective, pithy sentences that efficiently get your point across. When reviewing the information, imagine a conversation taking place, and concise writing will likely result.

Appropriate Kinds of Writing for Different Tasks, Purposes, and Audiences

When preparing to write a composition, consider the audience and purpose to choose the best type of writing. Four common types of writing are persuasive, expository, and narrative. **Persuasive**, or argumentative writing, is used to convince the audience to take action or agree with the author's claims. **Expository** writing is meant to inform the audience of the author's observations or research on a topic. **Narrative** writing is used to tell the audience a story and often allows more room for creativity. **Descriptive** writing is when a writer provides a substantial amount of detail to the reader so he or she can visualize the topic. While task, purpose, and audience inform a writer's mode of writing, these factors also impact elements such as tone, vocabulary, and formality.

For example, students who are writing to persuade their parents to grant them some additional privilege, such as permission for a more independent activity, should use more sophisticated vocabulary and diction that sounds more mature and serious to appeal to the parental audience. However, students who are writing for younger children should use simpler vocabulary and sentence structure, as well as choose words that are more vivid and entertaining. They should treat their topics more lightly, and include humor when appropriate. Students who are writing for their classmates may use language that is more informal, as well as age-appropriate.

Review Video: Writing Purpose and Audience
Visit mometrix.com/academy and enter code: 146627

Formality in Writing

Level of Formality

The relationship between writer and reader is important in choosing a **level of formality** as most writing requires some degree of formality. **Formal writing** is for addressing a superior in a school or work environment. Business letters, textbooks, and newspapers use a moderate to high level of formality. **Informal writing** is appropriate for private letters, personal emails, and business correspondence between close associates.

For your exam, you will want to be aware of informal and formal writing. One way that this can be accomplished is to watch for shifts in point of view in the essay. For example, unless writers are using a personal example, they will rarely refer to themselves (e.g., "*I* think that *my* point is very clear.") to avoid being informal when they need to be formal.

Also, be mindful of an author who addresses his or her audience **directly** in their writing (e.g., "Readers, *like you*, will understand this argument.") as this can be a sign of informal writing. Good writers understand the need to be consistent with their level of formality. Shifts in levels of formality or point of view can confuse readers and cause them to discount the message.

Clichés

Clichés are phrases that have been **overused** to the point that the phrase has no importance or has lost the original meaning. These phrases have no originality and add very little to a passage. Therefore, most writers will avoid the use of clichés. Another option is to make changes to a cliché so that it is not predictable and empty of meaning.

Examples:

When life gives you lemons, make lemonade.

Every cloud has a silver lining.

Jargon

Jargon is **specialized vocabulary** that is used among members of a certain trade or profession. Since jargon is understood by only a small audience, writers will use jargon in passages that will only be read by a specialized audience. For example, medical jargon should be used in a medical journal but not in a New York Times article. Jargon includes exaggerated language that tries to impress rather than inform. Sentences filled with jargon are not precise and are difficult to understand.

Examples:

"He is going to *toenail* these frames for us." (Toenail is construction jargon for nailing at an angle.)

"They brought in a *kip* of material today." (Kip refers to 1000 pounds in architecture and engineering.)

Slang

Slang is an **informal** and sometimes private language that is understood by some individuals. Slang terms have some usefulness, but they can have a small audience. So, most formal writing will not include this kind of language.

Examples:

"Yes, the event was a blast!" (In this sentence, *blast* means that the event was a great experience.)

"That attempt was an epic fail." (By *epic fail*, the speaker means that his or her attempt was not a success.)

Colloquialism

A colloquialism is a word or phrase that is found in informal writing. Unlike slang, **colloquial language** will be familiar to a greater range of people. However, colloquialisms are still considered inappropriate for formal writing. Colloquial language can include some slang, but these are limited to contractions for the most part.

Examples:

"Can *y'all* come back another time?" (Y'all is a contraction of "you all.")

"Will you stop him from building this *castle in the air*?" (A "castle in the air" is an improbable or unlikely event.)

Academic Language

In educational settings, students are often expected to use academic language in their schoolwork. Academic language is also commonly found in dissertations and theses, texts published by academic journals, and other forms of academic research. Academic language conventions may vary between fields, but general academic language is free of slang, regional terminology, and noticeable grammatical errors. Specific terms may also be used in academic language, and it is important to understand their proper usage. A writer's command of academic language impacts their ability to communicate in an academic or professional context. While it is acceptable to use colloquialisms, slang, improper grammar, or other forms of informal speech in social settings or at home, it is inappropriate to practice non-academic language in academic contexts.

Conventions and Language Facility

Parts of Speech

Nouns

A noun is a person, place, thing, or idea. The two main types of nouns are **common** and **proper** nouns. Nouns can also be categorized as abstract (i.e., general) or concrete (i.e., specific).

Common Nouns

Common nouns are generic names for people, places, and things. Common nouns are not usually capitalized.

Examples of common nouns:

People: boy, girl, worker, manager

Places: school, bank, library, home

Things: dog, cat, truck, car

Review Video: Nouns
Visit mometrix.com/academy and enter code: 344028

Proper Nouns

Proper nouns name specific people, places, or things. All proper nouns are capitalized.

Examples of proper nouns:

People: Abraham Lincoln, George Washington, Martin Luther King, Jr.

Places: Los Angeles, California; New York; Asia

Things: Statue of Liberty, Earth, Lincoln Memorial

Note: Some nouns can be either common or proper depending on their use. For example, when referring to the planet that we live on, *Earth* is a proper noun and is capitalized. When referring to the dirt, rocks, or land on our planet, *earth* is a common noun and is not capitalized.

General and Specific Nouns

General nouns are the names of conditions or ideas. **Specific nouns** name people, places, and things that are understood by using your senses.

General nouns:

Condition: beauty, strength

Idea: truth, peace

Specific nouns:

People: baby, friend, father

Places: town, park, city hall

Things: rainbow, cough, apple, silk, gasoline

Collective Nouns

Collective nouns are the names for a group of people, places, or things that may act as a whole. The following are examples of collective nouns: *class, company, dozen, group, herd, team,* and *public*. Collective nouns usually require an article, which denotes the noun as being a single unit. For instance, a choir is a group of singers. Even though there are many singers in a choir, the word choir is grammatically treated as a single unit. If we refer to the members of the group, and not the group itself, it is no longer a collective noun.

Incorrect: The *choir are* going to compete nationally this year.

Correct: The *choir is* going to compete nationally this year.

Incorrect: The *members* of the choir *is* competing nationally this year.

Correct: The *members* of the choir *are* competing nationally this year.

Pronouns

Pronouns are words that are used to stand in for nouns. A pronoun may be classified as personal, intensive, relative, interrogative, demonstrative, indefinite, and reciprocal.

Personal: *Nominative* is the case for nouns and pronouns that are the subject of a sentence. *Objective* is the case for nouns and pronouns that are an object in a sentence. *Possessive* is the case for nouns and pronouns that show possession or ownership.

Singular

	Nominative	Objective	Possessive
First Person	I	me	my, mine
Second Person	you	you	your, yours
Third Person	he, she, it	him, her, it	his, her, hers, its

Plural

	Nominative	Objective	Possessive
First Person	we	us	our, ours
Second Person	you	you	your, yours
Third Person	they	them	their, theirs

Intensive: I myself, you yourself, he himself, she herself, the (thing) itself, we ourselves, you yourselves, they themselves

Relative: which, who, whom, whose

Interrogative: what, which, who, whom, whose

Demonstrative: this, that, these, those

Indefinite: all, any, each, everyone, either/neither, one, some, several

Reciprocal: each other, one another

Review Video: Nouns and Pronouns
Visit mometrix.com/academy and enter code: 312073

VERBS

A verb is a word or group of words that indicates action or being. In other words, the verb shows something's action or state of being or the action that has been done to something. If you want to write a sentence, then you need a verb. Without a verb, you have no sentence.

TRANSITIVE AND INTRANSITIVE VERBS

A **transitive verb** is a verb whose action indicates a receiver. **Intransitive verbs** do not indicate a receiver of an action. In other words, the action of the verb does not point to an object.

> **Transitive**: He drives a car. | She feeds the dog.
>
> **Intransitive**: He runs every day. | She voted in the last election.

A dictionary will tell you whether a verb is transitive or intransitive. Some verbs can be transitive or intransitive.

ACTION VERBS AND LINKING VERBS

Action verbs show what the subject is doing. In other words, an action verb shows action. Unlike most types of words, a single action verb, in the right context, can be an entire sentence. **Linking verbs** link the subject of a sentence to a noun or pronoun, or they link a subject with an adjective. You always need a verb if you want a complete sentence. However, linking verbs on their own cannot be a complete sentence.

Common linking verbs include *appear, be, become, feel, grow, look, seem, smell, sound,* and *taste.* However, any verb that shows a condition and connects to a noun, pronoun, or adjective that describes the subject of a sentence is a linking verb.

Action: He sings. | Run! | Go! | I talk with him every day. | She reads.

Linking:

> Incorrect: I am.
>
> Correct: I am John. | The roses smell lovely. | I feel tired.

Note: Some verbs are followed by words that look like prepositions, but they are a part of the verb and a part of the verb's meaning. These are known as phrasal verbs, and examples include *call off, look up*, and *drop off.*

Review Video: Action Verbs and Linking Verbs
Visit mometrix.com/academy and enter code: 743142

VOICE

Transitive verbs may be in active voice or passive voice. The difference between active voice and passive voice is whether the subject is acting or being acted upon. When the subject of the sentence is doing the action, the verb is in **active voice**. When the subject is being acted upon, the verb is in **passive voice**.

> **Active**: Jon drew the picture. (The subject *Jon* is doing the action of *drawing a picture.*)
>
> **Passive**: The picture is drawn by Jon. (The subject *picture* is receiving the action from Jon.)

VERB TENSES

Verb **tense** is a property of a verb that indicates when the action being described takes place (past, present, or future) and whether or not the action is completed (simple or perfect). Describing an action taking place in the present (*I talk*) requires a different verb tense than describing an action that took place in the past (*I talked*).

Some verb tenses require an auxiliary (helping) verb. These helping verbs include *am, are, is | have, has, had | was, were, will* (or *shall*).

Present: I talk	Present perfect: I have talked
Past: I talked	Past perfect: I had talked
Future: I will talk	Future perfect: I will have talked

Present: The action is happening at the current time.

Example: He *walks* to the store every morning.

To show that something is happening right now, use the progressive present tense: I *am walking*.

Past: The action happened in the past.

Example: She *walked* to the store an hour ago.

Future: The action will happen later.

Example: I *will walk* to the store tomorrow.

Present perfect: The action started in the past and continues into the present or took place previously at an unspecified time.

Example: I *have walked* to the store three times today.

Past perfect: The action was completed at some point in the past. This tense is usually used to describe an action that was completed before some other reference time or event.

Example: I *had eaten* already before they arrived.

Future perfect: The action will be completed before some point in the future. This tense may be used to describe an action that has already begun or has yet to begin.

Example: The project *will have been completed* by the deadline.

Review Video: Present Perfect, Past Perfect, and Future Perfect Verb Tenses
Visit mometrix.com/academy and enter code: 269472

Conjugating Verbs

When you need to change the form of a verb, you are **conjugating** a verb. The key forms of a verb are present tense (sing/sings), past tense (sang), present participle (singing), and past participle (sung). By combining these forms with helping verbs, you can make almost any verb tense. The following table demonstrates some of the different ways to conjugate a verb:

Tense	First Person	Second Person	Third Person Singular	Third Person Plural
Simple Present	I sing	You sing	He, she, it sings	They sing
Simple Past	I sang	You sang	He, she, it sang	They sang
Simple Future	I will sing	You will sing	He, she, it will sing	They will sing
Present Progressive	I am singing	You are singing	He, she, it is singing	They are singing
Past Progressive	I was singing	You were singing	He, she, it was singing	They were singing
Present Perfect	I have sung	You have sung	He, she, it has sung	They have sung
Past Perfect	I had sung	You had sung	He, she, it had sung	They had sung

Mood

There are three **moods** in English: the indicative, the imperative, and the subjunctive.

The **indicative mood** is used for facts, opinions, and questions.

Fact: You can do this.

Opinion: I think that you can do this.

Question: Do you know that you can do this?

The **imperative** is used for orders or requests.

Order: You are going to do this!

Request: Will you do this for me?

The **subjunctive mood** is for wishes and statements that go against fact.

Wish: I wish that I were famous.

Statement against fact: If I were you, I would do this. (This goes against fact because I am not you. You have the chance to do this, and I do not have the chance.)

ADJECTIVES

An **adjective** is a word that is used to modify a noun or pronoun. An adjective answers a question: *Which one? What kind?* or *How many?* Usually, adjectives come before the words that they modify, but they may also come after a linking verb.

Which one? The *third* suit is my favorite.

What kind? This suit is *navy blue*.

How many? I am going to buy *four* pairs of socks to match the suit.

Review Video: Descriptive Text
Visit mometrix.com/academy and enter code: 174903

ARTICLES

Articles are adjectives that are used to distinguish nouns as definite or indefinite. *A*, *an*, and *the* are the only articles. **Definite** nouns are preceded by *the* and indicate a specific person, place, thing, or idea. **Indefinite** nouns are preceded by *a* or *an* and do not indicate a specific person, place, thing, or idea.

Note: *An* comes before words that start with a vowel sound. For example, "Are you going to get an **u**mbrella?"

Definite: I lost *the* bottle that belongs to me.

Indefinite: Does anyone have *a* bottle to share?

Review Video: Function of Articles in a Sentence
Visit mometrix.com/academy and enter code: 449383

COMPARISON WITH ADJECTIVES

Some adjectives are relative and other adjectives are absolute. Adjectives that are **relative** can show the comparison between things. **Absolute** adjectives can also show comparison, but they do so in a different way. Let's say that you are reading two books. You think that one book is perfect, and the other book is not exactly perfect. It is not possible for one book to be more perfect than the other. Either you think that the book is perfect, or you think that the book is imperfect. In this case, perfect and imperfect are absolute adjectives.

Relative adjectives will show the different **degrees** of something or someone to something else or someone else. The three degrees of adjectives include positive, comparative, and superlative.

The **positive** degree is the normal form of an adjective.

Example: This work is *difficult.* | She is *smart.*

The **comparative** degree compares one person or thing to another person or thing.

Example: This work is *more difficult* than your work. | She is *smarter* than me.

The **superlative** degree compares more than two people or things.

Example: This is the *most difficult* work of my life. | She is the *smartest* lady in school.

Review Video: Adjectives
Visit mometrix.com/academy and enter code: 470154

ADVERBS

An **adverb** is a word that is used to **modify** a verb, an adjective, or another adverb. Usually, adverbs answer one of these questions: *When? Where? How?* and *Why?* The negatives *not* and *never* are considered adverbs. Adverbs that modify adjectives or other adverbs **strengthen** or **weaken** the words that they modify.

Examples:

He walks *quickly* through the crowd.

The water flows *smoothly* on the rocks.

Note: Adverbs are usually indicated by the morpheme *-ly*, which has been added to the root word. For instance, *quick* can be made into an adverb by adding *-ly* to construct *quickly*. Some words that end in *-ly* do not follow this rule and can behave as other parts of speech. Examples of adjectives ending in *-ly* include: *early, friendly, holy, lonely, silly*, and *ugly*. To know if a word that ends in *-ly* is an adjective or adverb, check your dictionary. Also, while many adverbs end in *-ly*, you need to remember that not all adverbs end in *-ly*.

Examples:

He is *never* angry.

You are *too* irresponsible to travel alone.

Review Video: Adverbs
Visit mometrix.com/academy and enter code: 713951

Review Video: Adverbs that Modify Adjectives
Visit mometrix.com/academy and enter code: 122570

COMPARISON WITH ADVERBS

The rules for comparing adverbs are the same as the rules for adjectives.

The **positive** degree is the standard form of an adverb.

Example: He arrives *soon.* | She speaks *softly* to her friends.

The **comparative** degree compares one person or thing to another person or thing.

Example: He arrives *sooner* than Sarah. | She speaks *more softly* than him.

The **superlative** degree compares more than two people or things.

Example: He arrives *soonest* of the group. | She speaks the *most softly* of any of her friends.

PREPOSITIONS

A **preposition** is a word placed before a noun or pronoun that shows the relationship between that noun or pronoun and another word in the sentence.

Common prepositions:

about	before	during	on	under
after	beneath	for	over	until
against	between	from	past	up
among	beyond	in	through	with
around	by	of	to	within
at	down	off	toward	without

Examples:

The napkin is *in* the drawer.

The Earth rotates *around* the Sun.

The needle is *beneath* the haystack.

Can you find "me" *among* the words?

Review Video: Prepositions
Visit mometrix.com/academy and enter code: 946763

CONJUNCTIONS

Conjunctions join words, phrases, or clauses and they show the connection between the joined pieces. **Coordinating conjunctions** connect equal parts of sentences. **Correlative conjunctions** show the connection between pairs. **Subordinating conjunctions** join subordinate (i.e., dependent) clauses with independent clauses.

COORDINATING CONJUNCTIONS

The **coordinating conjunctions** include: *and, but, yet, or, nor, for,* and *so*

Examples:

The rock was small, *but* it was heavy.

She drove in the night, *and* he drove in the day.

Correlative Conjunctions

The **correlative conjunctions** are: *either...or* | *neither...nor* | *not only...but also*

Examples:

Either you are coming *or* you are staying.

He *not only* ran three miles *but also* swam 200 yards.

Review Video: Coordinating and Correlative Conjunctions
Visit mometrix.com/academy and enter code: 390329

Review Video: Adverb Equal Comparisons
Visit mometrix.com/academy and enter code: 231291

Subordinating Conjunctions

Common **subordinating conjunctions** include:

after	since	whenever
although	so that	where
because	unless	wherever
before	until	whether
in order that	when	while

Examples:

I am hungry *because* I did not eat breakfast.

He went home *when* everyone left.

Review Video: Subordinating Conjunctions
Visit mometrix.com/academy and enter code: 958913

Interjections

Interjections are words of exclamation (i.e., audible expressions of great feeling) that are used alone or as a part of a sentence. Often, they are used at the beginning of a sentence for an introduction. Sometimes, they can be used in the middle of a sentence to show a change in thought or attitude.

Common Interjections: Hey! | Oh, | Ouch! | Please! | Wow!

Agreement and Sentence Structure

Subjects and Predicates

Subjects

The **subject** of a sentence names who or what the sentence is about. The subject may be directly stated in a sentence, or the subject may be the implied *you*. The **complete subject** includes the simple subject and all of its modifiers. To find the complete subject, ask *Who* or *What* and insert the verb to complete the question. The answer, including any modifiers (adjectives, prepositional phrases, etc.), is the complete subject. To find the **simple subject**, remove all of the modifiers in the complete subject. Being able to locate the subject of a sentence helps with many problems, such as those involving sentence fragments and subject-verb agreement.

Examples:

The small, red **car** is the one that he wants for Christmas. (simple subject: car; complete subject: The small, red car)

The young **artist** is coming over for dinner. (simple subject: artist; complete subject: The young artist)

Review Video: Subjects in English
Visit mometrix.com/academy and enter code: 444771

In **imperative** sentences, the verb's subject is understood (e.g., [You] Run to the store), but is not actually present in the sentence. Normally, the subject comes before the verb. However, the subject comes after the verb in sentences that begin with *There are* or *There was.*

Direct:

John knows the way to the park.	Who knows the way to the park?	John
The cookies need ten more minutes.	What needs ten minutes?	The cookies
By five o'clock, Bill will need to leave.	Who needs to leave?	Bill
There are five letters on the table for him.	What is on the table?	Five letters
There were coffee and doughnuts in the house.	What was in the house?	Coffee and doughnuts

Implied:

Go to the post office for me.	Who is going to the post office?	You
Come and sit with me, please?	Who needs to come and sit?	You

Predicates

In a sentence, you always have a predicate and a subject. The subject tells who or what the sentence is about, and the **predicate** explains or describes the subject. The predicate includes the verb or verb phrase and any direct or indirect objects of the verb, as well as any words or phrases modifying these.

Think about the sentence *He sings*. In this sentence, we have a subject (He) and a predicate (sings). This is all that is needed for a sentence to be complete. Most sentences contain more information, but if this is all the information that you are given, then you have a complete sentence.

Now, let's look at another sentence: *John and Jane sing on Tuesday nights at the dance hall.*

subject: John and Jane | predicate: sing on Tuesday nights at the dance hall.

John and Jane sing on Tuesday nights at the dance hall.

Review Video: Complete Predicate
Visit mometrix.com/academy and enter code: 293942

Subject-Verb Agreement

Verbs must **agree** with their subjects in number and in person. To agree in number, singular subjects need singular verbs and plural subjects need plural verbs. A **singular** noun refers to **one** person, place, or thing. A **plural** noun refers to **more than one** person, place, or thing. To agree in person, the correct verb form must be chosen to match the first, second, or third person subject. The present tense ending *-s* or *-es* is used on a verb if its subject is third person singular; otherwise, the verb's ending is not modified.

Review Video: Subject-Verb Agreement
Visit mometrix.com/academy and enter code: 479190

Number Agreement Examples:

singular subject: Dan | singular verb: calls

Single Subject and Verb: Dan calls home.

Dan is one person. So, the singular verb *calls* is needed.

plural subject: Dan and Bob | plural verb: call

Plural Subject and Verb: Dan and Bob call home.

More than one person needs the plural verb *call.*

Person Agreement Examples:

First Person: I *am* walking.

Second Person: You *are* walking.

Third Person: He *is* walking.

Complications with Subject-Verb Agreement

Words Between Subject and Verb

Words that come between the simple subject and the verb have no bearing on subject-verb agreement.

Examples:

singular subject: joy | singular verb: returns

The joy of my life returns home tonight.

The phrase *of my life* does not influence the verb *returns.*

Language Arts—Writing

singular subject / singular verb

The question that still remains unanswered is "Who are you?"

Don't let the phrase *"that still remains..."* trouble you. The subject *question* goes with *is*.

Compound Subjects

A compound subject is formed when two or more nouns joined by *and*, *or*, or *nor* jointly act as the subject of the sentence.

Joined by And

When a compound subject is joined by *and*, it is treated as a plural subject and requires a plural verb.

Examples:

plural subject / plural verb

You and Jon are invited to come to my house.

plural subject / plural verb

The pencil and paper belong to me.

Joined by Or/Nor

For a compound subject joined by *or* or *nor*, the verb must agree in number with the part of the subject that is closest to the verb (italicized in the examples below).

Examples:

subject / verb

Today or tomorrow is the day.

subject / verb

Stan or Phil wants to read the book.

subject / verb

Neither the pen nor the book is on the desk.

subject / verb

Either the blanket or pillows arrive this afternoon.

Indefinite Pronouns as Subject

An indefinite pronoun is a pronoun that does not refer to a specific noun. Some indefinite pronouns function as only singular, some function as only plural, and some can function as either singular or plural depending on how they are used.

Always Singular

Pronouns such as *each*, *either*, *everybody*, *anybody*, *somebody*, and *nobody* are always singular.

Examples:

singular subject / singular verb

Each of the runners has a different bib number.

singular verb / singular subject

Is either of you ready for the game?

Note: The words *each* and *either* can also be used as adjectives (e.g., *each* person is unique). When one of these adjectives modifies the subject of a sentence, it is always a singular subject.

Everybody (singular subject) grows (singular verb) a day older every day.

Anybody (singular subject) is (singular verb) welcome to bring a tent.

Always Plural

Pronouns such as *both*, *several*, and *many* are always plural.

Examples:

Both (plural subject) of the siblings were (plural verb) too tired to argue.

Many (plural subject) have tried (plural verb), but none have succeeded.

Depend on Context

Pronouns such as *some*, *any*, *all*, *none*, *more*, and *most* can be either singular or plural depending on what they are representing in the context of the sentence.

Examples:

All (singular subject) of my dog's food was (singular verb) still there in his bowl.

By the end of the night, all (plural subject) of my guests were (plural verb) already excited about coming to my next party.

Other Cases Involving Plural or Irregular Form

Some nouns are **singular in meaning but plural in form**: news, mathematics, physics, and economics.

The *news is* coming on now.

Mathematics is my favorite class.

Some nouns are plural in form and meaning, and have **no singular equivalent**: scissors and pants.

Do these *pants come* with a shirt?

The *scissors are* for my project.

Mathematical operations are **irregular** in their construction, but are normally considered to be **singular in meaning**.

One plus one is two.

Three times three is nine.

Language Arts—Writing

Note: Look to your **dictionary** for help when you aren't sure whether a noun with a plural form has a singular or plural meaning.

COMPLEMENTS

A complement is a noun, pronoun, or adjective that is used to give more information about the subject or object in the sentence.

DIRECT OBJECTS

A direct object is a noun or pronoun that tells who or what **receives** the action of the verb. A sentence will only include a direct object if the verb is a transitive verb. If the verb is an intransitive verb or a linking verb, there will be no direct object. When you are looking for a direct object, find the verb and ask *who* or *what*.

Examples:

I took *the blanket.*

Jane read *books.*

INDIRECT OBJECTS

An indirect object is a noun or pronoun that indicates what or whom the action had an **influence** on. If there is an indirect object in a sentence, then there will also be a direct object. When you are looking for the indirect object, find the verb and ask *to/for whom or what.*

Examples:

We taught the old dog (indirect object) a new trick (direct object).

I gave them (indirect object) a math lesson (direct object).

Review Video: Direct and Indirect Objects
Visit mometrix.com/academy and enter code: 817385

PREDICATE NOMINATIVES AND PREDICATE ADJECTIVES

As we looked at previously, verbs may be classified as either action verbs or linking verbs. A linking verb is so named because it links the subject to words in the predicate that describe or define the subject. These words are called predicate nominatives (if nouns or pronouns) or predicate adjectives (if adjectives).

Examples:

My father (subject) is a lawyer (predicate nominative).

Your mother (subject) is patient (predicate adjective).

PRONOUN USAGE

The **antecedent** is the noun that has been replaced by a pronoun. A pronoun and its antecedent **agree** when they have the same number (singular or plural) and gender (male, female, or neutral).

Examples:

antecedent pronoun
Singular agreement: John came into town, and he played for us.

antecedent pronoun
Plural agreement: John and Rick came into town, and they played for us.

To determine which is the correct pronoun to use in a compound subject or object, try each pronoun **alone** in place of the compound in the sentence. Your knowledge of pronouns will tell you which one is correct.

Example:

Bob and (I, me) will be going.

Test: (1) *I will be going* or (2) *Me will be going*. The second choice cannot be correct because *me* cannot be used as the subject of a sentence. Instead, *me* is used as an object.

Answer: Bob and I will be going.

When a pronoun is used with a noun immediately following (as in "we boys"), try the sentence **without the added noun**.

Example:

(We/Us) boys played football last year.

Test: (1) *We played football last yea*r or (2) *Us played football last year*. Again, the second choice cannot be correct because *us* cannot be used as a subject of a sentence. Instead, *us* is used as an object.

Answer: We boys played football last year.

Review Video: Pronoun Usage
Visit mometrix.com/academy and enter code: 666500

Review Video: Pronoun-Antecedent Agreement
Visit mometrix.com/academy and enter code: 919704

A pronoun should point clearly to the **antecedent**. Here is how a pronoun reference can be unhelpful if it is puzzling or not directly stated.

antecedent pronoun
Unhelpful: Ron and Jim went to the store, and he bought soda.

Who bought soda? Ron or Jim?

antecedent pronoun
Helpful: Jim went to the store, and he bought soda.

The sentence is clear. Jim bought the soda.

Some pronouns change their form by their placement in a sentence. A pronoun that is a **subject** in a sentence comes in the **subjective case**. Pronouns that serve as **objects** appear in the **objective case**. Finally, the pronouns that are used as **possessives** appear in the **possessive case**.

Examples:

Subjective case: *He* is coming to the show.

The pronoun *He* is the subject of the sentence.

Objective case: Josh drove *him* to the airport.

The pronoun *him* is the object of the sentence.

Possessive case: The flowers are *mine*.

The pronoun *mine* shows ownership of the flowers.

The word *who* is a subjective-case pronoun that can be used as a **subject**. The word *whom* is an objective-case pronoun that can be used as an **object**. The words *who* and *whom* are common in subordinate clauses or in questions.

Examples:

He knows who (subject) wants (verb) to come.

He knows the man whom (object) we want (verb) at the party.

Clauses

A clause is a group of words that contains both a subject and a predicate (verb). There are two types of clauses: independent and dependent. An **independent clause** contains a complete thought, while a **dependent (or subordinate) clause** does not. A dependent clause includes a subject and a verb, and may also contain objects or complements, but it cannot stand as a complete thought without being joined to an independent clause. Dependent clauses function within sentences as adjectives, adverbs, or nouns.

Example:

I am running (independent clause) because I want to stay in shape. (dependent clause)

The clause *I am running* is an independent clause: it has a subject and a verb, and it gives a complete thought. The clause *because I want to stay in shape* is a dependent clause: it has a subject and a verb, but it does not express a complete thought. It adds detail to the independent clause to which it is attached.

Review Video: Clauses
Visit mometrix.com/academy and enter code: 940170

Review Video: Independent and Dependent Clauses
Visit mometrix.com/academy and enter code: 556903

Types of Dependent Clauses

Adjective Clauses

An **adjective clause** is a dependent clause that modifies a noun or a pronoun. Adjective clauses begin with a relative pronoun (*who, whose, whom, which,* and *that*) or a relative adverb (*where, when,* and *why*).

Also, adjective clauses usually come immediately after the noun that the clause needs to explain or rename. This is done to ensure that it is clear which noun or pronoun the clause is modifying.

Examples:

I learned the reason (independent clause) why I won the award. (adjective clause)

This is the place (independent clause) where I started my first job. (adjective clause)

An adjective clause can be an essential or nonessential clause. An essential clause is very important to the sentence. **Essential clauses** explain or define a person or thing. **Nonessential clauses** give more information about a person or thing but are not necessary to define them. Nonessential clauses are set off with commas while essential clauses are not.

Examples:

A person who works hard at first (essential clause) can often rest later in life.

Neil Armstrong, who walked on the moon, (nonessential clause) is my hero.

Review Video: Adjective Clauses and Phrases
Visit mometrix.com/academy and enter code: 520888

Adverb Clauses

An **adverb clause** is a dependent clause that modifies a verb, adjective, or adverb. In sentences with multiple dependent clauses, adverb clauses are usually placed immediately before or after the independent clause. An adverb clause is introduced with words such as *after, although, as, before, because, if, since, so, unless, when, where*, and *while*.

Examples:

When you walked outside, (adverb clause) I called the manager.

I will go with you unless you want to stay. (adverb clause)

Noun Clauses

A **noun clause** is a dependent clause that can be used as a subject, object, or complement. Noun clauses begin with words such as *how, that, what, whether, which, who,* and *why*. These words can also come with an adjective clause. Unless the noun clause is being used as the subject of the sentence, it should come after the verb of the independent clause.

Examples:

noun clause

The real mystery is how you avoided serious injury.

noun clause

What you learn from each other depends on your honesty with others.

Subordination

When two related ideas are not of equal importance, the ideal way to combine them is to make the more important idea an independent clause and the less important idea a dependent or subordinate clause. This is called **subordination**.

Example:

Separate ideas: The team had a perfect regular season. The team lost the championship.

Subordinated: Despite having a perfect regular season, *the team lost the championship.*

Phrases

A phrase is a group of words that functions as a single part of speech, usually a noun, adjective, or adverb. A **phrase** is not a complete thought and does not contain a subject and predicate, but it adds detail or explanation to a sentence, or renames something within the sentence.

Prepositional Phrases

One of the most common types of phrases is the prepositional phrase. A **prepositional phrase** begins with a preposition and ends with a noun or pronoun that is the object of the preposition. Normally, the prepositional phrase functions as an **adjective** or an **adverb** within the sentence.

Examples:

prepositional phrase

The picnic is on the blanket.

prepositional phrase

I am sick with a fever today.

prepositional phrase

Among the many flowers, John found a four-leaf clover.

Verbal Phrases

A **verbal** is a word or phrase that is formed from a verb but does not function as a verb. Depending on its particular form, it may be used as a noun, adjective, or adverb. A verbal does **not** replace a verb in a sentence.

Examples:

verb

Correct: Walk a mile daily.

This is a complete sentence with the implied subject *you*.

Incorrect: To walk (verbal) a mile.

This is not a sentence since there is no functional verb.

There are three types of verbal: **participles**, **gerunds**, and **infinitives**. Each type of verbal has a corresponding **phrase** that consists of the verbal itself along with any complements or modifiers.

Participles

A **participle** is a type of verbal that always functions as an adjective. The present participle always ends with -*ing*. Past participles end with *-d, -ed, -n,* or *-t*. Participles are combined with helping verbs to form certain verb tenses, but a participle by itself cannot function as a verb.

Examples: dance (verb) | dancing (present participle) | danced (past participle)

Participial phrases most often come right before or right after the noun or pronoun that they modify.

Examples:

Shipwrecked on an island (participial phrase), the boys started to fish for food.

Having been seated for five hours (participial phrase), we got out of the car to stretch our legs.

Praised for their work (participial phrase), the group accepted the first-place trophy.

Gerunds

A **gerund** is a type of verbal that always functions as a **noun**. Like present participles, gerunds always end with *-ing*, but they can be easily distinguished from participles by the part of speech they represent (participles always function as adjectives). Since a gerund or gerund phrase always functions as a noun, it can be used as the subject of a sentence, the predicate nominative, or the object of a verb or preposition.

Examples:

We want to be known for teaching (gerund) the poor (object of preposition: teaching the poor).

Coaching (gerund) this team (subject: Coaching this team) is the best job of my life.

We like practicing (gerund) our songs (object of verb: practicing our songs) in the basement.

Infinitives

An **infinitive** is a type of verbal that can function as a noun, an adjective, or an adverb. An infinitive is made of the word *to* and the basic form of the verb. As with all other types of verbal phrases, an infinitive phrase includes the verbal itself and all of its complements or modifiers.

Examples:

infinitive
To join the team is my goal in life.
noun

infinitive
The animals have enough food to eat for the night.
adjective

infinitive
People lift weights to exercise their muscles.
adverb

Review Video: Verbals
Visit mometrix.com/academy and enter code: 915480

Appositive Phrases

An **appositive** is a word or phrase that is used to explain or rename nouns or pronouns. Noun phrases, gerund phrases, and infinitive phrases can all be used as appositives.

Examples:

appositive
Terriers, hunters at heart, have been dressed up to look like lap dogs.

The noun phrase *hunters at heart* renames the noun *terriers*.

appositive
His plan, to save and invest his money, was proven as a safe approach.

The infinitive phrase explains what the plan is.

Appositive phrases can be **essential** or **nonessential**. An appositive phrase is essential if the person, place, or thing being described or renamed is too general for its meaning to be understood without the appositive.

Examples:

essential
Two of America's Founding Fathers, George Washington and Thomas Jefferson, served as presidents.

nonessential
George Washington and Thomas Jefferson, two Founding Fathers, served as presidents.

Absolute Phrases

An absolute phrase is a phrase that consists of **a noun followed by a participle**. An absolute phrase provides **context** to what is being described in the sentence, but it does not modify or explain any particular word; it is essentially independent.

Examples:

The alarm ringing, he pushed the snooze button. (noun: *The alarm*; participle: *ringing*; absolute phrase: *The alarm ringing*)

The music paused, she continued to dance through the crowd. (noun: *The music*; participle: *paused*; absolute phrase: *The music paused*)

PARALLELISM

When multiple items or ideas are presented in a sentence in series, such as in a list, the items or ideas must be stated in grammatically equivalent ways. For example, if two ideas are listed in parallel and the first is stated in gerund form, the second cannot be stated in infinitive form. (e.g., *I enjoy reading and to study.* [incorrect]) An infinitive and a gerund are not grammatically equivalent. Instead, you should write *I enjoy reading and studying* OR *I like to read and to study*. In lists of more than two, all items must be parallel.

Example:

> **Incorrect**: He stopped at the office, grocery store, and the pharmacy before heading home.
>
> The first and third items in the list of places include the article *the*, so the second item needs it as well.
>
> **Correct**: He stopped at the office, *the* grocery store, and the pharmacy before heading home.

Example:

> **Incorrect**: While vacationing in Europe, she went biking, skiing, and climbed mountains.
>
> The first and second items in the list are gerunds, so the third item must be as well.
>
> **Correct**: While vacationing in Europe, she went biking, skiing, and *mountain climbing*.

Review Video: Parallel Sentence Construction
Visit mometrix.com/academy and enter code: 831988

SENTENCE PURPOSE

There are four types of sentences: declarative, imperative, interrogative, and exclamatory.

A **declarative** sentence states a fact and ends with a period.

> *The football game starts at seven o'clock.*

An **imperative** sentence tells someone to do something and generally ends with a period. An urgent command might end with an exclamation point instead.

> *Don't forget to buy your ticket.*

An **interrogative** sentence asks a question and ends with a question mark.

> *Are you going to the game on Friday?*

An **exclamatory** sentence shows strong emotion and ends with an exclamation point.

> *I can't believe we won the game!*

Sentence Structure

Sentences are classified by structure based on the type and number of clauses present. The four classifications of sentence structure are the following:

Simple: A simple sentence has one independent clause with no dependent clauses. A simple sentence may have **compound elements** (i.e., compound subject or verb).

Examples:

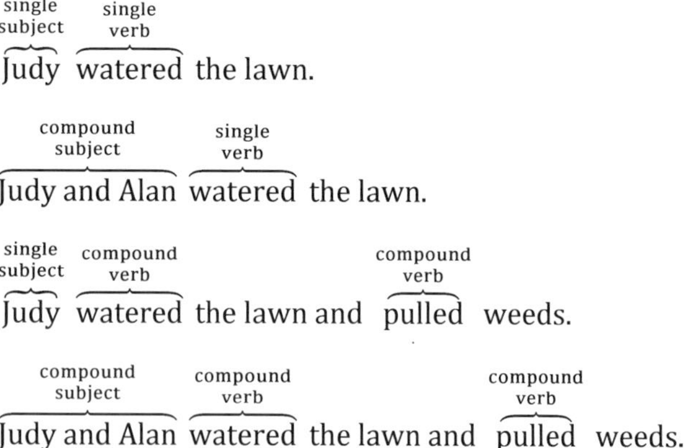

Compound: A compound sentence has two or more independent clauses with no dependent clauses. Usually, the independent clauses are joined with a comma and a coordinating conjunction or with a semicolon.

Examples:

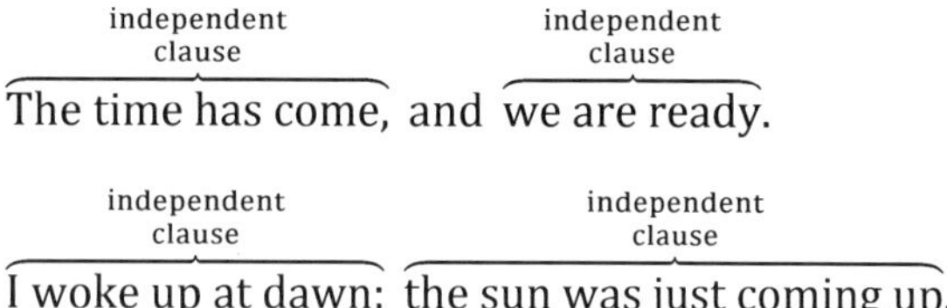

Complex: A complex sentence has one independent clause and at least one dependent clause. Punctuation depends on whether the dependent (subordinate) clause comes before or after the independent (or main) clause. If the subordinate clause comes first, it needs to be set apart with a comma.

Examples:

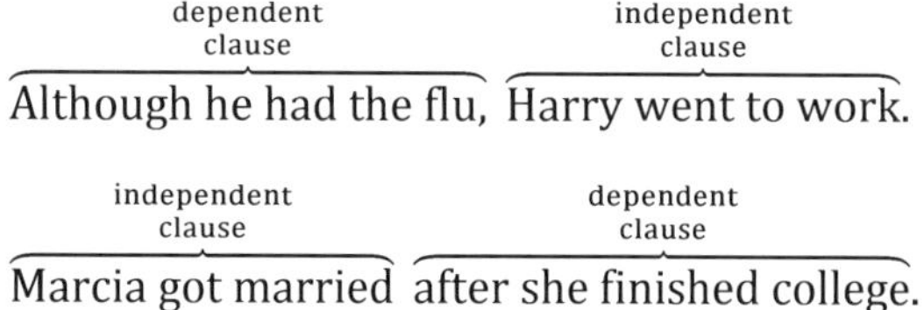

Compound-Complex: A compound-complex sentence has at least two independent clauses and at least one dependent clause.

Examples:

independent clause | dependent clause | independent clause
John is my friend who went to India, and he brought back souvenirs.

independent clause | independent clause | dependent clause
You may not realize this, but we heard the music that you played last night.

Review Video: Sentence Structure
Visit mometrix.com/academy and enter code: 700478

Sentence variety is important to consider when writing an essay or speech. A variety of sentence lengths and types creates rhythm, makes a passage more engaging, and gives writers an opportunity to demonstrate their writing style. Writing that uses the same length or type of sentence without variation can be boring or difficult to read. To evaluate a passage for effective sentence variety, it is helpful to note whether the passage contains diverse sentence structures and lengths. It is also important to pay attention to the way each sentence starts and avoid beginning with the same words or phrases.

Sentence Fragments

Recall that a group of words must contain at least one **independent clause** in order to be considered a sentence. If it doesn't contain even one independent clause, it is called a **sentence fragment**.

The appropriate process for **repairing** a sentence fragment depends on what type of fragment it is. If the fragment is a dependent clause, it can sometimes be as simple as removing a subordinating word (e.g., when, because, if) from the beginning of the fragment. Alternatively, a dependent clause can be incorporated into a closely related neighboring sentence. If the fragment is missing some required part, like a subject or a verb, the fix might be as simple as adding the missing part.

Examples:

Fragment: Because he wanted to sail the Mediterranean.

Removed subordinating word: He wanted to sail the Mediterranean.

Combined with another sentence: Because he wanted to sail the Mediterranean, he booked a Greek island cruise.

Run-on Sentences

Run-on sentences consist of multiple independent clauses that have not been joined together properly. Run-on sentences can be corrected in several different ways:

Join clauses properly: This can be done with a comma and coordinating conjunction, with a semicolon, or with a colon or dash if the second clause is explaining something in the first.

Example:

Incorrect: I went on the trip, we visited lots of castles.

Corrected: I went on the trip, and we visited lots of castles.

Split into separate sentences: This correction is most effective when the independent clauses are very long or when they are not closely related.

Example:

> **Incorrect**: The drive to New York takes ten hours, my uncle lives in Boston.
>
> **Corrected**: The drive to New York takes ten hours. My uncle lives in Boston.

Make one clause dependent: This is the easiest way to make the sentence correct and more interesting at the same time. It's often as simple as adding a subordinating word between the two clauses or before the first clause.

Example:

> **Incorrect**: I finally made it to the store and I bought some eggs.
>
> **Corrected**: When I finally made it to the store, I bought some eggs.

Reduce to one clause with a compound verb: If both clauses have the same subject, remove the subject from the second clause, and you now have just one clause with a compound verb.

Example:

> **Incorrect**: The drive to New York takes ten hours, it makes me very tired.
>
> **Corrected**: The drive to New York takes ten hours and makes me very tired.

Note: While these are the simplest ways to correct a run-on sentence, often the best way is to completely reorganize the thoughts in the sentence and rewrite it.

Review Video: Fragments and Run-on Sentences
Visit mometrix.com/academy and enter code: 541989

DANGLING AND MISPLACED MODIFIERS

DANGLING MODIFIERS

A dangling modifier is a dependent clause or verbal phrase that does not have a clear logical connection to a word in the sentence.

Example:

> dangling modifier
>
> **Incorrect**: Reading each magazine article, the stories caught my attention.
>
> The word *stories* cannot be modified by *Reading each magazine article*. People can read, but stories cannot read. Therefore, the subject of the sentence must be a person.
>
> gerund phrase
>
> **Corrected**: Reading each magazine article, I was entertained by the stories.

Example:

dangling modifier

Incorrect: Ever since childhood, my grandparents have visited me for Christmas.

The speaker in this sentence can't have been visited by her grandparents when *they* were children, since she wouldn't have been born yet. Either the modifier should be clarified or the sentence should be rearranged to specify whose childhood is being referenced.

dependent clause

Clarified: Ever since I was a child, my grandparents have visited for Christmas.

adverb phrase

Rearranged: Ever since childhood, I have enjoyed my grandparents visiting for Christmas.

Misplaced Modifiers

Because modifiers are grammatically versatile, they can be put in many different places within the structure of a sentence. The danger of this versatility is that a modifier can accidentally be placed where it is modifying the wrong word or where it is not clear which word it is modifying.

Example:

modifier

Incorrect: She read the book to a crowd that was filled with beautiful pictures.

The book was filled with beautiful pictures, not the crowd.

modifier

Corrected: She read the book that was filled with beautiful pictures to a crowd.

Example:

modifier

Ambiguous: Derek saw a bus nearly hit a man on his way to work.

Was Derek on his way to work or was the other man?

modifier

Derek: On his way to work, Derek saw a bus nearly hit a man.

modifier

The other man: Derek saw a bus nearly hit a man who was on his way to work.

Split Infinitives

A split infinitive occurs when a modifying word comes between the word *to* and the verb that pairs with *to.*

Example: To *clearly* explain vs. *To explain* clearly | To *softly* sing vs. *To sing* softly

Though considered improper by some, split infinitives may provide better clarity and simplicity in some cases than the alternatives. As such, avoiding them should not be considered a universal rule.

Double Negatives

Standard English allows **two negatives** only when a **positive** meaning is intended. (e.g., The team was *not displeased* with their performance.) Double negatives to emphasize negation are not used in standard English.

Negative modifiers (e.g., never, no, and not) should not be paired with other negative modifiers or negative words (e.g., none, nobody, nothing, or neither). The modifiers *hardly, barely,* and *scarcely* are also considered negatives in standard English, so they should not be used with other negatives.

Punctuation

End Punctuation

Periods

Use a period to end all sentences except direct questions and exclamations. Periods are also used for abbreviations.

Examples: 3 p.m. | 2 a.m. | Mr. Jones | Mrs. Stevens | Dr. Smith | Bill, Jr. | Pennsylvania Ave.

Note: An abbreviation is a shortened form of a word or phrase.

Question Marks

Question marks should be used following a **direct question**. A polite request can be followed by a period instead of a question mark.

Direct Question: What is for lunch today? | How are you? | Why is that the answer?

Polite Requests: Can you please send me the item tomorrow. | Will you please walk with me on the track.

Review Video: Question Marks
Visit mometrix.com/academy and enter code: 118471

Exclamation Marks

Exclamation marks are used after a word group or sentence that shows much feeling or has special importance. Exclamation marks should not be overused. They are saved for proper **exclamatory interjections**.

Example: We're going to the finals! | You have a beautiful car! | "That's crazy!" she yelled.

Review Video: Exclamation Points
Visit mometrix.com/academy and enter code: 199367

COMMAS

The comma is a punctuation mark that can help you understand connections in a sentence. Not every sentence needs a comma. However, if a sentence needs a comma, you need to put it in the right place. A comma in the wrong place (or an absent comma) will make a sentence's meaning unclear.

These are some of the rules for commas:

Use Case	Example
Before a **coordinating conjunction** joining independent clauses	Bob caught three fish, and I caught two fish.
After an **introductory phrase**	After the final out, we went to a restaurant to celebrate.
After an **adverbial clause**	Studying the stars, I was awed by the beauty of the sky.
Between **items in a series**	I will bring the turkey, the pie, and the coffee.
For **interjections**	Wow, you know how to play this game.
After ***yes*** **and** ***no*** **responses**	No, I cannot come tomorrow.
Separate **nonessential modifiers**	John Frank, who coaches the team, was promoted today.
Separate **nonessential appositives**	Thomas Edison, an American inventor, was born in Ohio.
Separate **nouns of direct address**	You, John, are my only hope in this moment.
Separate **interrogative tags**	This is the last time, correct?
Separate **contrasts**	You are my friend, not my enemy.
Writing **dates**	July 4, 1776, is an important date to remember.
Writing **addresses**	He is meeting me at 456 Delaware Avenue, Washington, D.C., tomorrow morning.
Writing **geographical names**	Paris, France, is my favorite city.
Writing **titles**	John Smith, PhD, will be visiting your class today.
Separate **expressions like** ***he said***	"You can start," she said, "with an apology."

A comma is also used **between coordinate adjectives** not joined with *and*. However, not all adjectives are coordinate (i.e., equal or parallel). To determine if your adjectives are coordinate, try connecting them with *and* or reversing their order. If it still sounds right, they are coordinate.

Incorrect: The kind, brown dog followed me home.

Correct: The kind, loyal dog followed me home.

Review Video: When to Use a Comma
Visit mometrix.com/academy and enter code: 786797

Language Arts—Writing

SEMICOLONS

The semicolon is used to join closely related independent clauses without the need for a coordinating conjunction. Semicolons are also used in place of commas to separate list elements that have internal commas. Some rules for semicolons include:

Use Case	Example
Between closely connected independent clauses **not connected with a coordinating conjunction**	You are right; we should go with your plan.
Between independent clauses **linked with a transitional word**	I think that we can agree on this; however, I am not sure about my friends.
Between items in a **series that has internal punctuation**	I have visited New York, New York; Augusta, Maine; and Baltimore, Maryland.

Review Video: How to Use Semicolons
Visit mometrix.com/academy and enter code: 370605

COLONS

The colon is used to call attention to the words that follow it. When used in a sentence, a colon should only come at the **end** of a **complete sentence**. The rules for colons are as follows:

Use Case	Example
After an independent clause to **make a list**	I want to learn many languages: Spanish, German, and Italian.
For **explanations**	There is one thing that stands out on your resume: responsibility.
To give a **quote**	He started with an idea: "We are able to do more than we imagine."
After the **greeting in a formal letter**	To Whom It May Concern:
Show **hours and minutes**	It is 3:14 p.m.
Separate a **title and subtitle**	The essay is titled "America: A Short Introduction to a Modern Country."

Review Video: Using Colons
Visit mometrix.com/academy and enter code: 868673

PARENTHESES

Parentheses are used for additional information. Also, they can be used to put labels for letters or numbers in a series. Parentheses should not be used very often. If they are overused, parentheses can be a distraction instead of a help.

Examples:

Extra Information: The rattlesnake (see Image 2) is a dangerous snake of North and South America.

Series: Include in the email (1) your name, (2) your address, and (3) your question for the author.

Review Video: Parentheses
Visit mometrix.com/academy and enter code: 947743

QUOTATION MARKS

Use quotation marks to close off **direct quotations** of a person's spoken or written words. Do not use quotation marks around indirect quotations. An indirect quotation gives someone's message without using the person's exact words. Use **single quotation marks** to close off a quotation inside a quotation.

Direct Quote: Nancy said, "I am waiting for Henry to arrive."

Indirect Quote: Henry said that he is going to be late to the meeting.

Quote inside a Quote: The teacher asked, "Has everyone read 'The Gift of the Magi'?"

Quotation marks should be used around the titles of **short works**: newspaper and magazine articles, poems, short stories, songs, television episodes, radio programs, and subdivisions of books or websites.

Examples:

"Rip Van Winkle" (short story by Washington Irving)

"O Captain! My Captain!" (poem by Walt Whitman)

Although it is not standard usage, quotation marks are sometimes used to highlight **irony** or the use of words to mean something other than their dictionary definition. This type of usage should be employed sparingly, if at all.

Examples:

The boss warned Frank that he was walking on "thin ice."	Frank is not walking on real ice. Instead, he is being warned to avoid mistakes.
The teacher thanked the young man for his "honesty."	The quotation marks around *honesty* show that the teacher does not believe the young man's explanation.

Review Video: Quotation Marks
Visit mometrix.com/academy and enter code: 884918

Periods and commas are put **inside** quotation marks. Colons and semicolons are put **outside** the quotation marks. Question marks and exclamation points are placed inside quotation marks when they are part of a quote. When the question or exclamation mark goes with the whole sentence, the mark is left outside of the quotation marks.

Examples:

Period and comma	We read "The Gift of the Magi," "The Skylight Room," and "The Cactus."
Semicolon	They watched "The Nutcracker"; then, they went home.
Exclamation mark that is a part of a quote	The crowd cheered, "Victory!"
Question mark that goes with the whole sentence	Is your favorite short story "The Tell-Tale Heart"?

Apostrophes

An apostrophe is used to show **possession** or the **deletion of letters in contractions**. An apostrophe is not needed with the possessive pronouns *his, hers, its, ours, theirs, whose*, and *yours*.

Singular Nouns: David's car | a book's theme | my brother's board game

Plural Nouns that end with -*s*: the scissors' handle | boys' basketball

Plural Nouns that end without -*s*: Men's department | the people's adventure

> **Review Video: When to Use an Apostrophe**
> Visit mometrix.com/academy and enter code: 213068
>
> **Review Video: Punctuation Errors in Possessive Pronouns**
> Visit mometrix.com/academy and enter code: 221438

Hyphens

Hyphens are used to **separate compound words**. Use hyphens in the following cases:

Use Case	Example
Compound numbers from 21 to 99 when written out in words	This team needs twenty-five points to win the game.
Written-out fractions that are used as adjectives	The recipe says that we need a three-fourths cup of butter.
Compound adjectives that come before a noun	The well-fed dog took a nap.
Unusual compound words that would be hard to read or easily confused with other words	This is the best anti-itch cream on the market.

Note: This is not a complete set of the rules for hyphens. A dictionary is the best tool for knowing if a compound word needs a hyphen.

> **Review Video: Hyphens**
> Visit mometrix.com/academy and enter code: 981632

Dashes

Dashes are used to show a **break** or a **change in thought** in a sentence or to act as parentheses in a sentence. When typing, use two hyphens to make a dash. Do not put a space before or after the dash. The following are the functions of dashes:

Use Case	Example
Set off parenthetical statements or an **appositive with internal punctuation**	The three trees—oak, pine, and magnolia—are coming on a truck tomorrow.
Show a **break or change in tone or thought**	The first question—how silly of me—does not have a correct answer.

Ellipsis Marks

The ellipsis mark has **three** periods (...) to show when **words have been removed** from a quotation. If a **full sentence or more** is removed from a quoted passage, you need to use **four** periods to show the removed text and the end punctuation mark. The ellipsis mark should not be used at the beginning of a quotation. The ellipsis mark should also not be used at the end of a quotation unless some words have been deleted from the end of the final quoted sentence.

Example:

> "Then he picked up the groceries...paid for them...later he went home."

Brackets

There are two main reasons to use brackets:

Use Case	Example
Placing **parentheses inside of parentheses**	The hero of this story, Paul Revere (a silversmith and industrialist [see Ch. 4]), rode through towns of Massachusetts to warn of advancing British troops.
Adding **clarification or detail to a quotation** that is not part of the quotation	The father explained, "My children are planning to attend my alma mater [State University]."

Review Video: Brackets
Visit mometrix.com/academy and enter code: 727546

Common Usage Mistakes

Commonly Confused Words

Which, That, and Who

The words *which, that,* and *who* can act as **relative pronouns** to help clarify or describe a noun.

Which is used for things only.

> Example: Andrew's car, *which is old and rusty,* broke down last week.

That is used for people or things. *That* is usually informal when used to describe people.

> Example: Is this the only book *that Louis L'Amour wrote?*

> Example: Is Louis L'Amour the author *that wrote Western novels?*

Who is used for people or for animals that have an identity or personality.

> Example: Mozart was the composer *who wrote those operas.*

> Example: John's dog, *who is called Max,* is large and fierce.

Then and Than

Then is an adverb that indicates sequence or order:

> Example: I'm going to run to the library and then come home.

Than is special-purpose word used only for comparisons:

> Example: Susie likes chips more than candy.

Language Arts—Writing

Saw and Seen

Saw is the past-tense form of *see*.

Example: I saw a turtle on my walk this morning.

Seen is the past participle of *see*.

Example: I have seen this movie before.

Affect and Effect

There are two main reasons that *affect* and *effect* are so often confused: 1) both words can be used as either a noun or a verb, and 2) unlike most homophones, their usage and meanings are closely related to each other. Here is a quick rundown of the four usage options:

Affect (n): feeling, emotion, or mood that is displayed

Example: The patient had a flat *affect.* (i.e., his face showed little or no emotion)

Affect (v): to alter, to change, to influence

Example: The sunshine *affects* the plant's growth.

Effect (n): a result, a consequence

Example: What *effect* will this weather have on our schedule?

Effect (v): to bring about, to cause to be

Example: These new rules will *effect* order in the office.

The noun form of *affect* is rarely used outside of technical medical descriptions, so if a noun form is needed on the test, you can safely select *effect*. The verb form of *effect* is not as rare as the noun form of *affect*, but it's still not all that likely to show up on your test. If you need a verb and you can't decide which to use based on the definitions, choosing *affect* is your best bet.

Homophones

Homophones are words that sound alike (or similar) but have different **spellings** and **definitions**. A homophone is a type of **homonym**, which is a pair or group of words that are pronounced or spelled the same, but do not mean the same thing.

To, Too, and Two

To can be an adverb or a preposition for showing direction, purpose, and relationship. See your dictionary for the many other ways to use *to* in a sentence.

Examples: I went to the store. | I want to go with you.

Too is an adverb that means *also, as well, very,* or *in excess.*

Examples: I can walk a mile too. | You have eaten too much.

Two is a number.

Example: You have two minutes left.

There, Their, and They're

There can be an adjective, adverb, or pronoun. Often, *there* is used to show a place or to start a sentence.

Examples: I went there yesterday. | There is something in his pocket.

Their is a pronoun that is used to show ownership.

Examples: He is their father. | This is their fourth apology this week.

They're is a contraction of *they are*.

Example: Did you know that they're in town?

Knew and New

Knew is the past tense of *know*.

Example: I knew the answer.

New is an adjective that means something is current, has not been used, or is modern.

Example: This is my new phone.

Its and It's

Its is a pronoun that shows ownership.

Example: The guitar is in its case.

It's is a contraction of *it is*.

Example: It's an honor and a privilege to meet you.

Note: The *h* in honor is silent, so *honor* starts with the vowel sound *o*, which must have the article *an*.

Your and You're

Your is a pronoun that shows ownership.

Example: This is your moment to shine.

You're is a contraction of *you are*.

Example: Yes, you're correct.

Homographs

Homographs are words that share the same spelling, but have different meanings and sometimes different pronunciations. To figure out which meaning is being used, you should be looking for context clues. The context clues give hints to the meaning of the word. For example, the word *spot* has many meanings. It can mean "a place" or "a stain or blot." In the sentence "After my lunch, I saw a spot on my shirt," the word *spot* means "a stain or blot." The context clues of "After my lunch" and "on my shirt" guide you to this decision. A homograph is another type of homonym.

Bank

(noun): an establishment where money is held for savings or lending

(verb): to collect or pile up

CONTENT

(noun): the topics that will be addressed within a book

(adjective): pleased or satisfied

(verb): to make someone pleased or satisfied

FINE

(noun): an amount of money that acts a penalty for an offense

(adjective): very small or thin

(adverb): in an acceptable way

(verb): to make someone pay money as a punishment

INCENSE

(noun): a material that is burned in religious settings and makes a pleasant aroma

(verb): to frustrate or anger

LEAD

(noun): the first or highest position

(noun): a heavy metallic element

(verb): to direct a person or group of followers

(adjective): containing lead

OBJECT

(noun): a lifeless item that can be held and observed

(verb): to disagree

PRODUCE

(noun): fruits and vegetables

(verb): to make or create something

REFUSE

(noun): garbage or debris that has been thrown away

(verb): to not allow

SUBJECT

(noun): an area of study

(verb): to force or subdue

TEAR

(noun): a fluid secreted by the eyes

(verb): to separate or pull apart

Commonly Misused Words and Phrases

A Lot

The phrase *a lot* should always be written as two words; never as *alot.*

Correct: That's a lot of chocolate!

Incorrect: He does that alot.

Can

The word *can* is used to describe things that are possible occurrences; the word *may* is used to described things that are allowed to happen.

Correct: May I have another piece of pie?

Correct: I can lift three of these bags of mulch at a time.

Incorrect: Mom said we can stay up thirty minutes later tonight.

Could Have

The phrase *could of* is often incorrectly substituted for the phrase *could have.* Similarly, *could of, may of,* and *might of* are sometimes used in place of the correct phrases *could have, may have,* and *might have.*

Correct: If I had known, I would have helped out.

Incorrect: Well, that could of gone much worse than it did.

Myself

The word *myself* is a reflexive pronoun, often incorrectly used in place of *I* or *me.*

Correct: He let me do it myself.

Incorrect: The job was given to Dave and myself.

Off

The phrase *off of* is a redundant expression that should be avoided. In most cases, it can be corrected simply by removing *of.*

Correct: My dog chased the squirrel off its perch on the fence.

Incorrect: He finally moved his plate off of the table.

Supposed To

The phrase *suppose to* is sometimes used incorrectly in place of the phrase *supposed to.*

Correct: I was supposed to go to the store this afternoon.

Incorrect: When are we suppose to get our grades?

Try To

The phrase *try and* is often used in informal writing and conversation to replace the correct phrase *try to.*

Correct: It's a good policy to try to satisfy every customer who walks in the door.

Incorrect: Don't try and do too much.

WORD ROOTS AND PREFIXES AND SUFFIXES

AFFIXES

Affixes in the English language are morphemes that are added to words to create related but different words. Derivational affixes form new words based on and related to the original words. For example, the affix *–ness* added to the end of the adjective *happy* forms the noun *happiness.* Inflectional affixes form different grammatical versions of words. For example, the plural affix *–s* changes the singular noun *book* to the plural noun *books*, and the past tense affix *–ed* changes the present tense verb *look* to the past tense *looked.* Prefixes are affixes placed in front of words. For example, *heat* means to make hot; *preheat* means to heat in advance. Suffixes are affixes placed at the ends of words. The *happiness* example above contains the suffix *–ness.* Circumfixes add parts both before and after words, such as how *light* becomes *enlighten* with the prefix *en-* and the suffix *–en.* Interfixes create compound words via central affixes: *speed* and *meter* become *speedometer* via the interfix *–o–*.

Review Video: Affixes
Visit mometrix.com/academy and enter code: 782422

WORD ROOTS, PREFIXES, AND SUFFIXES TO HELP DETERMINE MEANINGS OF WORDS

Many English words were formed from combining multiple sources. For example, the Latin *habēre* means "to have," and the prefixes *in-* and *im-* mean a lack or prevention of something, as in *insufficient* and *imperfect.* Latin combined *in-* with *habēre* to form *inhibēre,* whose past participle was *inhibitus.* This is the origin of the English word *inhibit,* meaning to prevent from having. Hence by knowing the meanings of both the prefix and the root, one can decipher the word meaning. In Greek, the root *enkephalo-* refers to the brain. Many medical terms are based on this root, such as encephalitis and hydrocephalus. Understanding the prefix and suffix meanings (*-itis* means inflammation; *hydro-* means water) allows a person to deduce that encephalitis refers to brain inflammation and hydrocephalus refers to water (or other fluid) in the brain.

Review Video: Root Words in English
Visit mometrix.com/academy and enter code: 896380

Review Video: Determining Word Meanings
Visit mometrix.com/academy and enter code: 894894

PREFIXES

Knowing common prefixes is helpful for all readers as they try to determining meanings or definitions of unfamiliar words. For example, a common word used when cooking is *preheat.* Knowing that *pre-* means in advance can also inform them that *presume* means to assume in advance, that *prejudice* means advance judgment, and that this understanding can be applied to many other words beginning with *pre-*. Knowing that the prefix *dis-* indicates opposition informs the meanings of words like *disbar, disagree, disestablish,* and many more. Knowing *dys-* means bad, impaired, abnormal, or difficult informs *dyslogistic, dysfunctional, dysphagia,* and *dysplasia.*

SUFFIXES

In English, certain suffixes generally indicate both that a word is a noun, and that the noun represents a state of being or quality. For example, *-ness* is commonly used to change an adjective into its noun form, as with *happy* and *happiness, nice* and *niceness,* and so on. The suffix *–tion* is commonly used to transform a verb into its noun form, as with *converse* and *conversation or move* and *motion*. Thus, if readers are unfamiliar with the second form of a word, knowing the meaning of the transforming suffix can help them determine meaning.

Prefixes for Numbers

Prefix	Definition	Examples
bi-	two	bisect, biennial
mono-	one, single	monogamy, monologue
poly-	many	polymorphous, polygamous
semi-	half, partly	semicircle, semicolon
uni-	one	uniform, unity

Prefixes for Time, Direction, and Space

Prefix	Definition	Examples
a-	in, on, of, up, to	abed, afoot
ab-	from, away, off	abdicate, abjure
ad-	to, toward	advance, adventure
ante-	before, previous	antecedent, antedate
anti-	against, opposing	antipathy, antidote
cata-	down, away, thoroughly	catastrophe, cataclysm
circum-	around	circumspect, circumference
com-	with, together, very	commotion, complicate
contra-	against, opposing	contradict, contravene
de-	from	depart
dia-	through, across, apart	diameter, diagnose
dis-	away, off, down, not	dissent, disappear
epi-	upon	epilogue
ex-	out	extract, excerpt
hypo-	under, beneath	hypodermic, hypothesis
inter-	among, between	intercede, interrupt
intra-	within	intramural, intrastate
ob-	against, opposing	objection
per-	through	perceive, permit
peri-	around	periscope, perimeter
post-	after, following	postpone, postscript
pre-	before, previous	prevent, preclude
pro-	forward, in place of	propel, pronoun
retro-	back, backward	retrospect, retrograde
sub-	under, beneath	subjugate, substitute
super-	above, extra	supersede, supernumerary
trans-	across, beyond, over	transact, transport
ultra-	beyond, excessively	ultramodern, ultrasonic

Negative Prefixes

Prefix	Definition	Examples
a-	without, lacking	atheist, agnostic
in-	not, opposing	incapable, ineligible
non-	not	nonentity, nonsense
un-	not, reverse of	unhappy, unlock

Extra Prefixes

Prefix	Definition	Examples
for-	away, off, from	forget, forswear

Prefix	Definition	Examples
fore-	previous	foretell, forefathers
homo-	same, equal	homogenized, homonym
hyper-	excessive, over	hypercritical, hypertension
in-	in, into	intrude, invade
mal-	bad, poorly, not	malfunction, malpractice
mis-	bad, poorly, not	misspell, misfire
neo-	new	Neolithic, neoconservative
omni-	all, everywhere	omniscient, omnivore
ortho-	right, straight	orthogonal, orthodox
over-	above	overbearing, oversight
pan-	all, entire	panorama, pandemonium
para-	beside, beyond	parallel, paradox
re-	backward, again	revoke, recur
sym-	with, together	sympathy, symphony

Below is a list of common suffixes and their meanings:

ADJECTIVE SUFFIXES

Suffix	Definition	Examples
-able (-ible)	capable of being	toler*able*, ed*ible*
-esque	in the style of, like	picturesque, grotesque
-ful	filled with, marked by	thankful, zestful
-ific	make, cause	terrific, beatific
-ish	suggesting, like	churlish, childish
-less	lacking, without	hopeless, countless
-ous	marked by, given to	religious, riotous

NOUN SUFFIXES

Suffix	Definition	Examples
-acy	state, condition	accuracy, privacy
-ance	act, condition, fact	acceptance, vigilance
-ard	one that does excessively	drunkard, sluggard
-ation	action, state, result	occupation, starvation
-dom	state, rank, condition	serfdom, wisdom
-er (-or)	office, action	teach*er*, elevat*or*, hon*or*
-ess	feminine	waitress, duchess
-hood	state, condition	manhood, statehood
-ion	action, result, state	union, fusion
-ism	act, manner, doctrine	barbarism, socialism
-ist	worker, follower	monopolist, socialist
-ity (-ty)	state, quality, condition	acid*ity*, civil*ity*, twen*ty*
-ment	result, action	Refreshment
-ness	quality, state	greatness, tallness
-ship	position	internship, statesmanship
-sion (-tion)	state, result	revi*sion*, expedi*tion*
-th	act, state, quality	warmth, width
-tude	quality, state, result	magnitude, fortitude

Verb Suffixes

Suffix	Definition	Examples
-ate	having, showing	separate, desolate
-en	cause to be, become	deepen, strengthen
-fy	make, cause to have	glorify, fortify
-ize	cause to be, treat with	sterilize, mechanize

Nuance and Word Meanings

Synonyms and Antonyms

When you understand how words relate to each other, you will discover more in a passage. This is explained by understanding **synonyms** (e.g., words that mean the same thing) and **antonyms** (e.g., words that mean the opposite of one another). As an example, *dry* and *arid* are synonyms, and *dry* and *wet* are antonyms.

There are many pairs of words in English that can be considered synonyms, despite having slightly different definitions. For instance, the words *friendly* and *collegial* can both be used to describe a warm interpersonal relationship, and one would be correct to call them synonyms. However, *collegial* (kin to *colleague*) is often used in reference to professional or academic relationships, and *friendly* has no such connotation.

If the difference between the two words is too great, then they should not be called synonyms. *Hot* and *warm* are not synonyms because their meanings are too distinct. A good way to determine whether two words are synonyms is to substitute one word for the other word and verify that the meaning of the sentence has not changed. Substituting *warm* for *hot* in a sentence would convey a different meaning. Although warm and hot may seem close in meaning, warm generally means that the temperature is moderate, and hot generally means that the temperature is excessively high.

Antonyms are words with opposite meanings. *Light* and *dark*, *up* and *down*, *right* and *left*, *good* and *bad*: these are all sets of antonyms. Be careful to distinguish between antonyms and pairs of words that are simply different. *Black* and *gray*, for instance, are not antonyms because gray is not the opposite of black. *Black* and *white*, on the other hand, are antonyms.

Not every word has an antonym. For instance, many nouns do not. What would be the antonym of *chair*? During your exam, the questions related to antonyms are more likely to concern adjectives. You will recall that adjectives are words that describe a noun. Some common adjectives include *purple*, *fast*, *skinny*, and *sweet*. From those four adjectives, *purple* is the item that lacks a group of obvious antonyms.

Review Video: Synonyms and Antonyms
Visit mometrix.com/academy and enter code: 105612

Denotative vs. Connotative Meaning

The **denotative** meaning of a word is the literal meaning. The **connotative** meaning goes beyond the denotative meaning to include the emotional reaction that a word may invoke. The connotative meaning often takes the denotative meaning a step further due to associations the reader makes with the denotative meaning. Readers can differentiate between the denotative and connotative meanings by first recognizing how authors use each meaning. Most non-fiction, for example, is fact-based and authors do not use flowery, figurative language. The reader can assume that the writer is using the denotative meaning of words. In fiction, the author may use the connotative meaning. Readers can determine whether the author is using the denotative or connotative meaning of a word by implementing context clues.

Review Video: Connotation and Denotation
Visit mometrix.com/academy and enter code: 310092

Nuances of Word Meaning

A word's denotation is simply its objective dictionary definition. However, its connotation refers to the subjective associations, often emotional, that specific words evoke in listeners and readers. Two or more words can have the same dictionary meaning, but very different connotations. Writers use diction (word choice) to convey various nuances of thought and emotion by selecting synonyms for other words that best communicate the associations they want to trigger for readers. For example, a car engine is naturally greasy; in this sense, "greasy" is a neutral term. But when a person's smile, appearance, or clothing is described as "greasy," it has a negative connotation. Some words have even gained additional or different meanings over time. For example, *awful* used to be used to describe things that evoked a sense of awe. When *awful* is separated into its root word, awe, and suffix, -ful, it can be understood to mean "full of awe." However, the word is now commonly used to describe things that evoke repulsion, terror, or another intense, negative reaction.

> **Review Video: Word Usage in Sentences**
> Visit mometrix.com/academy and enter code: 197863

Using Context to Determine Meaning

Context Clues

Readers of all levels will encounter words that they have either never seen or have encountered only on a limited basis. The best way to define a word in **context** is to look for nearby words that can assist in revealing the meaning of the word. For instance, unfamiliar nouns are often accompanied by examples that provide a definition. Consider the following sentence: *Dave arrived at the party in hilarious garb: a leopard-print shirt, buckskin trousers, and bright green sneakers.* If a reader was unfamiliar with the meaning of garb, he or she could read the examples (i.e., a leopard-print shirt, buckskin trousers, and bright green sneakers) and quickly determine that the word means *clothing*. Examples will not always be this obvious. Consider this sentence: *Parsley, lemon, and flowers were just a few of the items he used as garnishes.* Here, the word *garnishes* is exemplified by parsley, lemon, and flowers. Readers who have eaten in a variety of restaurants will probably be able to identify a garnish as something used to decorate a plate.

> **Review Video: Reading Comprehension: Using Context Clues**
> Visit mometrix.com/academy and enter code: 613660

Using Contrast in Context Clues

In addition to looking at the context of a passage, readers can use contrast to define an unfamiliar word in context. In many sentences, the author will not describe the unfamiliar word directly; instead, he or she will describe the opposite of the unfamiliar word. Thus, you are provided with some information that will bring you closer to defining the word. Consider the following example: *Despite his intelligence, Hector's low brow and bad posture made him look obtuse.* The author writes that Hector's appearance does not convey intelligence. Therefore, *obtuse* must mean unintelligent. Here is another example: *Despite the horrible weather, we were beatific about our trip to Alaska*. The word *despite* indicates that the speaker's feelings were at odds with the weather. Since the weather is described as *horrible*, then *beatific* must mean something positive.

Substitution to Find Meaning

In some cases, there will be very few contextual clues to help a reader define the meaning of an unfamiliar word. When this happens, one strategy that readers may employ is **substitution**. A good reader will brainstorm some possible synonyms for the given word, and he or she will substitute these words into the sentence. If the sentence and the surrounding passage continue to make sense, then the substitution has revealed at least some information about the unfamiliar word. Consider the sentence: *Frank's admonition rang in her ears as she climbed the mountain.* A reader unfamiliar with *admonition* might come up with some substitutions like *vow*, *promise*, *advice*, *complaint*, or *compliment*. All of these words make general sense of the sentence, though their meanings are diverse. However, this process has suggested that an admonition is some sort of message. The substitution strategy is rarely able to pinpoint a precise definition, but this process can be effective as a last resort.

Occasionally, you will be able to define an unfamiliar word by looking at the descriptive words in the context. Consider the following sentence: *Fred dragged the recalcitrant boy kicking and screaming up the stairs.* The words *dragged, kicking*, and *screaming* all suggest that the boy does not want to go up the stairs. The reader may assume that *recalcitrant* means something like unwilling or protesting. In this example, an unfamiliar adjective was identified.

Additionally, using description to define an unfamiliar noun is a common practice compared to unfamiliar adjectives, as in this sentence: *Don's wrinkled frown and constantly shaking fist identified him as a curmudgeon of the first order.* Don is described as having a *wrinkled frown and constantly shaking fist*, suggesting that a *curmudgeon* must be a grumpy person. Contrasts do not always provide detailed information about the unfamiliar word, but they at least give the reader some clues.

Words with Multiple Meanings

When a word has more than one meaning, readers can have difficulty determining how the word is being used in a given sentence. For instance, the verb *cleave*, can mean either *join* or *separate*. When readers come upon this word, they will have to select the definition that makes the most sense. Consider the following sentence: *Hermione's knife cleaved the bread cleanly.* Since a knife cannot join bread together, the word must indicate separation. A slightly more difficult example would be the sentence: *The birds cleaved to one another as they flew from the oak tree.* Immediately, the presence of the words *to one another* should suggest that in this sentence *cleave* is being used to mean *join*. Discovering the intent of a word with multiple meanings requires the same tricks as defining an unknown word: look for contextual clues and evaluate the substituted words.

Context Clues to Help Determine Meanings of Words

If readers simply bypass unknown words, they can reach unclear conclusions about what they read. However, looking for the definition of every unfamiliar word in the dictionary can slow their reading progress. Moreover, the dictionary may list multiple definitions for a word, so readers must search the word's context for meaning. Hence context is important to new vocabulary regardless of reader methods. Four types of context clues are examples, definitions, descriptive words, and opposites. Authors may use a certain word, and then follow it with several different examples of what it describes. Sometimes authors actually supply a definition of a word they use, which is especially true in informational and technical texts. Authors may use descriptive words that elaborate upon a vocabulary word they just used. Authors may also use opposites with negation that help define meaning.

Examples and Definitions

An author may use a word and then give examples that illustrate its meaning. Consider this text: "Teachers who do not know how to use sign language can help students who are deaf or hard of hearing understand certain instructions by using gestures instead, like pointing their fingers to indicate which direction to look or go; holding up a hand, palm outward, to indicate stopping; holding the hands flat, palms up, curling a finger toward oneself in a beckoning motion to indicate 'come here'; or curling all fingers toward oneself repeatedly to indicate 'come on', 'more', or 'continue.'" The author of this text has used the word "gestures" and then followed it with examples, so a reader unfamiliar with the word could deduce from the examples that "gestures" means "hand motions." Readers can find examples by looking for signal words "for example," "for instance," "like," "such as," and "e.g."

While readers sometimes have to look for definitions of unfamiliar words in a dictionary or do some work to determine a word's meaning from its surrounding context, at other times an author may make it easier for readers by defining certain words. For example, an author may write, "The company did not have sufficient capital, that is, available money, to continue operations." The author defined "capital" as "available money," and heralded the definition with the phrase "that is." Another way that authors supply word definitions is with appositives. Rather than being introduced by a signal phrase like "that is," "namely," or "meaning," an appositive comes after the vocabulary word it defines and is enclosed within two commas. For example, an author may write, "The Indians introduced the Pilgrims to pemmican, cakes they made of lean meat dried and mixed with fat, which proved greatly beneficial to keep settlers from starving while trapping." In this example, the appositive phrase following "pemmican" and preceding "which" defines the word "pemmican."

DESCRIPTIONS

When readers encounter a word they do not recognize in a text, the author may expand on that word to illustrate it better. While the author may do this to make the prose more picturesque and vivid, the reader can also take advantage of this description to provide context clues to the meaning of the unfamiliar word. For example, an author may write, "The man sitting next to me on the airplane was obese. His shirt stretched across his vast expanse of flesh, strained almost to bursting." The descriptive second sentence elaborates on and helps to define the previous sentence's word "obese" to mean extremely fat. A reader unfamiliar with the word "repugnant" can decipher its meaning through an author's accompanying description: "The way the child grimaced and shuddered as he swallowed the medicine showed that its taste was particularly repugnant."

OPPOSITES

Text authors sometimes introduce a contrasting or opposing idea before or after a concept they present. They may do this to emphasize or heighten the idea they present by contrasting it with something that is the reverse. However, readers can also use these context clues to understand familiar words. For example, an author may write, "Our conversation was not cheery. We sat and talked very solemnly about his experience and a number of similar events." The reader who is not familiar with the word "solemnly" can deduce by the author's preceding use of "not cheery" that "solemn" means the opposite of cheery or happy, so it must mean serious or sad. Or if someone writes, "Don't condemn his entire project because you couldn't find anything good to say about it," readers unfamiliar with "condemn" can understand from the sentence structure that it means the opposite of saying anything good, so it must mean reject, dismiss, or disapprove. "Entire" adds another context clue, meaning total or complete rejection.

SYNTAX TO DETERMINE PART OF SPEECH AND MEANINGS OF WORDS

Syntax refers to sentence structure and word order. Suppose that a reader encounters an unfamiliar word when reading a text. To illustrate, consider an invented word like "splunch." If this word is used in a sentence like "Please splunch that ball to me," the reader can assume from syntactic context that "splunch" is a verb. We would not use a noun, adjective, adverb, or preposition with the object "that ball," and the prepositional phrase "to me" further indicates "splunch" represents an action. However, in the sentence, "Please hand that splunch to me," the reader can assume that "splunch" is a noun. Demonstrative adjectives like "that" modify nouns. Also, we hand someone some*thing*—a thing being a noun; we do not hand someone a verb, adjective, or adverb. Some sentences contain further clues. For example, from the sentence, "The princess wore the glittering splunch on her head," the reader can deduce that it is a crown, tiara, or something similar from the syntactic context, without knowing the word.

SYNTAX TO INDICATE DIFFERENT MEANINGS OF SIMILAR SENTENCES

The syntax, or structure, of a sentence affords grammatical cues that aid readers in comprehending the meanings of words, phrases, and sentences in the texts that they read. Seemingly minor differences in how the words or phrases in a sentence are ordered can make major differences in meaning. For example, two sentences can use exactly the same words but have different meanings based on the word order:

- "The man with a broken arm sat in a chair."
- "The man sat in a chair with a broken arm."

While both sentences indicate that a man sat in a chair, differing syntax indicates whether the man's or chair's arm was broken.

> **Review Video: Syntax**
> Visit mometrix.com/academy and enter code: 242280

Determining Meaning of Phrases and Paragraphs

Like unknown words, the meanings of phrases, paragraphs, and entire works can also be difficult to discern. Each of these can be better understood with added context. However, for larger groups of words, more context is needed. Unclear phrases are similar to unclear words, and the same methods can be used to understand their meaning. However, it is also important to consider how the individual words in the phrase work together. Paragraphs are a bit more complicated. Just as words must be compared to other words in a sentence, paragraphs must be compared to other paragraphs in a composition or a section.

Determining Meaning in Various Types of Compositions

To understand the meaning of an entire composition, the type of composition must be considered. **Expository writing** is generally organized so that each paragraph focuses on explaining one idea, or part of an idea, and its relevance. **Persuasive writing** uses paragraphs for different purposes to organize the parts of the argument. **Unclear paragraphs** must be read in the context of the paragraphs around them for their meaning to be fully understood. The meaning of full texts can also be unclear at times. The purpose of composition is also important for understanding the meaning of a text. To quickly understand the broad meaning of a text, look to the introductory and concluding paragraphs. Fictional texts are different. Some fictional works have implicit meanings, but some do not. The target audience must be considered for understanding texts that do have an implicit meaning, as most children's fiction will clearly state any lessons or morals. For other fiction, the application of literary theories and criticism may be helpful for understanding the text.

Resources for Determining Word Meaning and Usage

While these strategies are useful for determining the meaning of unknown words and phrases, sometimes additional resources are needed to properly use the terms in different contexts. Some words have multiple definitions, and some words are inappropriate in particular contexts or modes of writing. The following tools are helpful for understanding all meanings and proper uses for words and phrases.

- **Dictionaries** provide the meaning of a multitude of words in a language. Many dictionaries include additional information about each word, such as its etymology, its synonyms, or variations of the word.
- **Glossaries** are similar to dictionaries, as they provide the meanings of a variety of terms. However, while dictionaries typically feature an extensive list of words and comprise an entire publication, glossaries are often included at the end of a text and only include terms and definitions that are relevant to the text they follow.
- **Spell Checkers** are used to detect spelling errors in typed text. Some spell checkers may also detect the misuse of plural or singular nouns, verb tenses, or capitalization. While spell checkers are a helpful tool, they are not always reliable or attuned to the author's intent, so it is important to review the spell checker's suggestions before accepting them.
- **Style Manuals** are guidelines on the preferred punctuation, format, and grammar usage according to different fields or organizations. For example, the Associated Press Stylebook is a style guide often used for media writing. The guidelines within a style guide are not always applicable across different contexts and usages, as the guidelines often cover grammatical or formatting situations that are not objectively correct or incorrect.

Plot and Story Structure

Plot and Story Structure

The **plot** includes the events that happen in a story and the order in which they are told to the reader. There are several types of plot structures, as stories can be told in many ways. The most common plot structure is the chronological plot, which presents the events to the reader in the same order they occur for the characters in the story. Chronological plots usually have five main parts, the **exposition**, **rising action**, the **climax**, **falling action**, and the **resolution**. This type of plot structure guides the reader through the story's events as the characters experience them and is the easiest structure to understand and identify. While this is the most common plot structure, many stories are nonlinear, which means the plot does not sequence events in the same order the characters experience them. Such stories might include elements like flashbacks that cause the story to be nonlinear.

Review Video: How to Make a Story Map
Visit mometrix.com/academy and enter code: 261719

Exposition

The **exposition** is at the beginning of the story and generally takes place before the rising action begins. The purpose of the exposition is to give the reader context for the story, which the author may do by introducing one or more characters, describing the setting or world, or explaining the events leading up to the point where the story begins. The exposition may still include events that contribute to the plot, but the **rising action** and main conflict of the story are not part of the exposition. Some narratives skip the exposition and begin the story with the beginning of the rising action, which causes the reader to learn the context as the story intensifies.

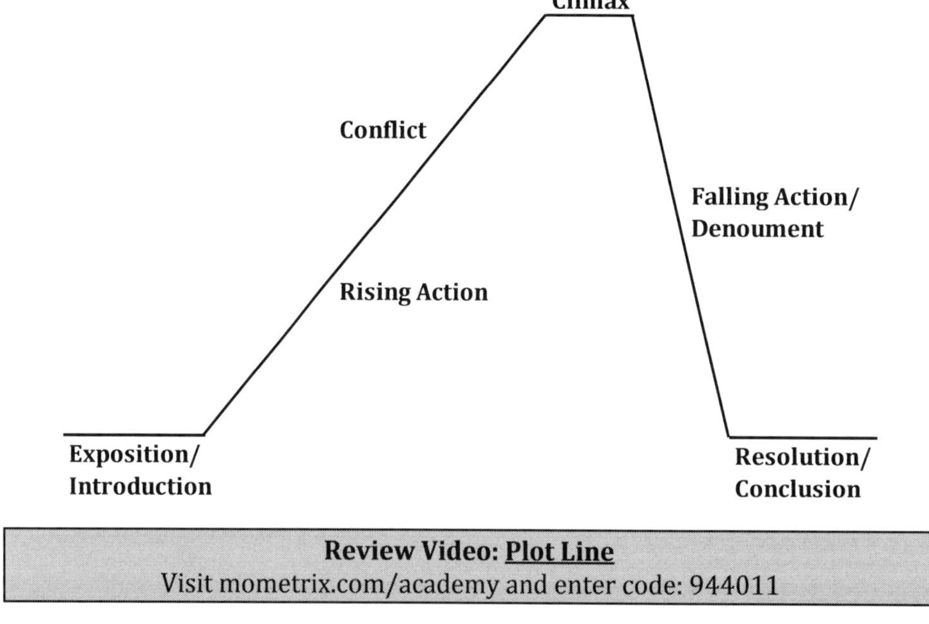

Review Video: Plot Line
Visit mometrix.com/academy and enter code: 944011

Conflict

A **conflict** is a problem to be solved. Literary plots typically include one conflict or more. Characters' attempts to resolve conflicts drive the narrative's forward movement. **Conflict resolution** is often the protagonist's primary occupation. Physical conflicts like exploring, wars, and escapes tend to make plots most suspenseful and exciting. Emotional, mental, or moral conflicts tend to make stories more personally gratifying or rewarding for many audiences. Conflicts can be external or internal. A major type of internal conflict is some inner personal battle, or **man versus self**. Major types of external conflicts include **man versus nature**, **man versus man**, and **man versus society**. Readers can identify conflicts in literary plots by identifying the protagonist and antagonist and asking why they conflict, what events develop the conflict, where the climax occurs, and how they identify with the characters.

Read the following paragraph and discuss the type of conflict present:

> Timothy was shocked out of sleep by the appearance of a bear just outside his tent. After panicking for a moment, he remembered some advice he had read in preparation for this trip: he should make noise so the bear would not be startled. As Timothy started to hum and sing, the bear wandered away.

There are three main types of conflict in literature: **man versus man**, **man versus nature**, and **man versus self**. This paragraph is an example of man versus nature. Timothy is in conflict with the bear. Even though no physical conflict like an attack exists, Timothy is pitted against the bear. Timothy uses his knowledge to "defeat" the bear and keep himself safe. The solution to the conflict is that Timothy makes noise, the bear wanders away, and Timothy is safe.

Review Video: Conflict
Visit mometrix.com/academy and enter code: 559550

Review Video: Determining Relationships in a Story
Visit mometrix.com/academy and enter code: 929925

Rising Action

The **rising action** is the part of the story where conflict **intensifies**. The rising action begins with an event that prompts the main conflict of the story. This may also be called the **inciting incident**. The main conflict generally occurs between the protagonist and an antagonist, but this is not the only type of conflict that may occur in a narrative. After this event, the protagonist works to resolve the main conflict by preparing for an altercation, pursuing a goal, fleeing an antagonist, or doing some other action that will end the conflict. The rising action is composed of several additional events that increase the story's tension. Most often, other developments will occur alongside the growth of the main conflict, such as character development or the development of minor conflicts. The rising action ends with the **climax**, which is the point of highest tension in the story.

Climax

The **climax** is the event in the narrative that marks the height of the story's conflict or tension. The event that takes place at the story's climax will end the rising action and bring about the results of the main conflict. If the conflict was between a good protagonist and an evil antagonist, the climax may be a final battle between the two characters. If the conflict is an adventurer looking for heavily guarded treasure, the climax may be the adventurer's encounter with the final obstacle that protects the treasure. The climax may be made of multiple scenes, but can usually be summarized as one event. Once the conflict and climax are complete, the **falling action** begins.

Falling Action

The **falling action** shows what happens in the story between the climax and the resolution. The falling action often composes a much smaller portion of the story than the rising action does. While the climax includes the end of the main conflict, the falling action may show the results of any minor conflicts in the story. For example, if the protagonist encountered a troll on the way to find some treasure, and the troll demanded the protagonist share the treasure after retrieving it, the falling action would include the protagonist returning to share the treasure with the troll. Similarly, any unexplained major events are usually made clear during the falling action. Once all significant elements of the story are resolved or addressed, the story's resolution will occur. The **resolution** is the end of the story, which shows the final result of the plot's events and shows what life is like for the main characters once they are no longer experiencing the story's conflicts.

RESOLUTION

The way the conflict is **resolved** depends on the type of conflict. The plot of any book starts with the lead up to the conflict, then the conflict itself, and finally the solution, or **resolution**, to the conflict. In **man versus man** conflicts, the conflict is often resolved by two parties coming to some sort of agreement or by one party triumphing over the other party. In **man versus nature** conflicts, the conflict is often resolved by man coming to some realization about some aspect of nature. In **man versus self** conflicts, the conflict is often resolved by the character growing or coming to an understanding about part of himself.

THEME

A **theme** is a central idea demonstrated by a passage. Often, a theme is a lesson or moral contained in the text, but it does not have to be. It also is a unifying idea that is used throughout the text; it can take the form of a common setting, idea, symbol, design, or recurring event. A passage can have two or more themes that convey its overall idea. The theme or themes of a passage are often based on **universal themes**. They can frequently be expressed using well-known sayings about life, society, or human nature, such as "Hard work pays off" or "Good triumphs over evil." Themes are not usually stated **explicitly**. The reader must figure them out by carefully reading the passage. Themes are created through descriptive language or events in the plot. The events of a story help shape the themes of a passage.

EXAMPLE

Explain why "if you care about something, you need to take care of it" accurately describes the theme of the following excerpt.

> Luca collected baseball cards, but he wasn't very careful with them. He left them around the house. His dog liked to chew. One day, Luca and his friend Bart were looking at his collection. Then they went outside. When Luca got home, he saw his dog chewing on his cards. They were ruined.

This excerpt tells the story of a boy who is careless with his baseball cards and leaves them lying around. His dog ends up chewing them and ruining them. The lesson is that if you care about something, you need to take care of it. This is the theme, or point, of the story. Some stories have more than one theme, but this is not really true of this excerpt. The reader needs to figure out the theme based on what happens in the story. Sometimes, as in the case of fables, the theme is stated directly in the text. However, this is not usually the case.

Review Video: Themes in Literature
Visit mometrix.com/academy and enter code: 732074

CHARACTER DEVELOPMENT AND DIALOGUE

CHARACTER DEVELOPMENT

When depicting characters or figures in a written text, authors generally use actions, dialogue, and descriptions as characterization techniques. Characterization can occur in both fiction and nonfiction and is used to show a character or figure's personality, demeanor, and thoughts. This helps create a more engaging experience for the reader by providing a more concrete picture of a character or figure's tendencies and features. Characterizations also gives authors the opportunity to integrate elements such as dialects, activities, attire, and attitudes into their writing.

To understand the meaning of a story, it is vital to understand the characters as the author describes them. We can look for contradictions in what a character thinks, says, and does. We can notice whether the author's observations about a character differ from what other characters in the story say about that character. A character may be dynamic, meaning they change significantly during the story, or static, meaning they remain the same from beginning to end. Characters may be two-dimensional, not fully developed, or may be well developed with characteristics that stand out vividly. Characters may also symbolize universal properties. Additionally, readers can compare and contrast characters to analyze how each one developed.

A well-known example of character development can be found in Charles Dickens's *Great Expectations*. The novel's main character, Pip, is introduced as a young boy, and he is depicted as innocent, kind, and humble. However, as Pip grows up and is confronted with the social hierarchy of Victorian England, he becomes arrogant and rejects his loved ones in pursuit of his own social advancement. Once he achieves his social goals, he realizes the merits of his former lifestyle, and lives with the wisdom he gained in both environments and life stages. Dickens shows Pip's ever-changing character through his interactions with others and his inner thoughts, which evolve as his personal values and personality shift.

DIALOGUE

Effectively written dialogue serves at least one, but usually several, purposes. It advances the story and moves the plot, develops the characters, sheds light on the work's theme or meaning, and can, often subtly, account for the passage of time not otherwise indicated. It can alter the direction that the plot is taking, typically by introducing some new conflict or changing existing ones. **Dialogue** can establish a work's narrative voice and the characters' voices and set the tone of the story or of particular characters. When fictional characters display enlightenment or realization, dialogue can give readers an understanding of what those characters have discovered and how. Dialogue can illuminate the motivations and wishes of the story's characters. By using consistent thoughts and syntax, dialogue can support character development. Skillfully created, it can also represent real-life speech rhythms in written form. Via conflicts and ensuing action, dialogue also provides drama.

DIALOGUE IN FICTION

In fictional works, effectively written dialogue does more than just break up or interrupt sections of narrative. While **dialogue** may supply exposition for readers, it must nonetheless be believable. Dialogue should be dynamic, not static, and it should not resemble regular prose. Authors should not use dialogue to write clever similes or metaphors, or to inject their own opinions. Nor should they use dialogue at all when narrative would be better. Most importantly, dialogue should not slow the plot movement. Dialogue must seem natural, which means careful construction of phrases rather than actually duplicating natural speech, which does not necessarily translate well to the written word. Finally, all dialogue must be pertinent to the story, rather than just added conversation.

Chapter Quiz

Ready to see how well you retained what you just read? Scan the QR code to go directly to the chapter quiz interface for this study guide. If you're using a computer, simply visit the online resources page at **mometrix.com/resources719/hiset-27339** and click the Chapter Quizzes link.

Mathematics

Numbers and Operations on Numbers

Number Basics

Classifications of Numbers

Numbers are the basic building blocks of mathematics. Specific features of numbers are identified by the following terms:

Integer – any positive or negative whole number, including zero. Integers do not include fractions $\left(\frac{1}{3}\right)$, decimals (0.56), or mixed numbers $\left(7\frac{3}{4}\right)$.

Prime number – any whole number greater than 1 that has only two factors, itself and 1; that is, a number that can be divided evenly only by 1 and itself.

Composite number – any whole number greater than 1 that has more than two different factors; in other words, any whole number that is not a prime number. For example: The composite number 8 has the factors of 1, 2, 4, and 8.

Even number – any integer that can be divided by 2 without leaving a remainder. For example: 2, 4, 6, 8, and so on.

Odd number – any integer that cannot be divided evenly by 2. For example: 3, 5, 7, 9, and so on.

Decimal number – any number that uses a decimal point to show the part of the number that is less than one. Example: 1.234.

Decimal point – a symbol used to separate the ones place from the tenths place in decimals or dollars from cents in currency.

Decimal place – the position of a number to the right of the decimal point. In the decimal 0.123, the 1 is in the first place to the right of the decimal point, indicating tenths; the 2 is in the second place, indicating hundredths; and the 3 is in the third place, indicating thousandths.

The **decimal**, or base 10, system is a number system that uses ten different digits (0, 1, 2, 3, 4, 5, 6, 7, 8, 9). An example of a number system that uses something other than ten digits is the **binary**, or base 2, number system, used by computers, which uses only the numbers 0 and 1. It is thought that the decimal system originated because people had only their 10 fingers for counting.

Rational numbers include all integers, decimals, and fractions. Any terminating or repeating decimal number is a rational number.

Irrational numbers cannot be written as fractions or decimals because the number of decimal places is infinite and there is no recurring pattern of digits within the number. For example, pi (π) begins with 3.141592 and continues without terminating or repeating, so pi is an irrational number.

Real numbers are the set of all rational and irrational numbers.

Review Video: Classification of Numbers
Visit mometrix.com/academy and enter code: 461071

Review Video: Prime and Composite Numbers
Visit mometrix.com/academy and enter code: 565581

Numbers in Word Form and Place Value

When writing numbers out in word form or translating word form to numbers, it is essential to understand how a place value system works. In the decimal or base-10 system, each digit of a number represents how many of the corresponding place value—a specific factor of 10—are contained in the number being represented. To make reading numbers easier, every three digits to the left of the decimal place is preceded by a comma. The following table demonstrates some of the place values:

Power of 10	10^3	10^2	10^1	10^0	10^{-1}	10^{-2}	10^{-3}
Value	1,000	100	10	1	0.1	0.01	0.001
Place	thousands	hundreds	tens	ones	tenths	hundredths	thousandths

For example, consider the number 4,546.09, which can be separated into each place value like this:

4: thousands
5: hundreds
4: tens
6: ones
0: tenths
9: hundredths

This number in word form would be *four thousand five hundred forty-six and nine hundredths.*

Review Video: Place Value
Visit mometrix.com/academy and enter code: 205433

Number Lines

A number line is a graph to see the distance between numbers. Basically, this graph shows the relationship between numbers. So a number line may have a point for zero and may show negative numbers on the left side of the line. Any positive numbers are placed on the right side of the line. For example, consider the points labeled on the following number line:

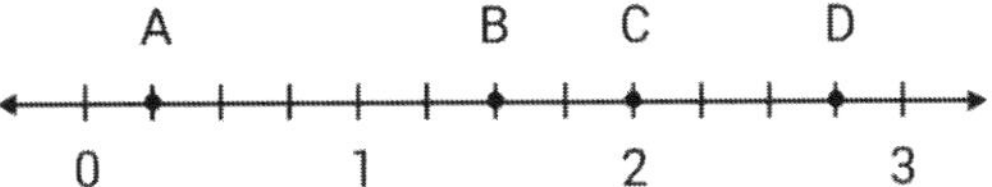

Mathematics

We can use the dashed lines on the number line to identify each point. Each dashed line between two whole numbers is $\frac{1}{4}$. The line halfway between two numbers is $\frac{1}{2}$.

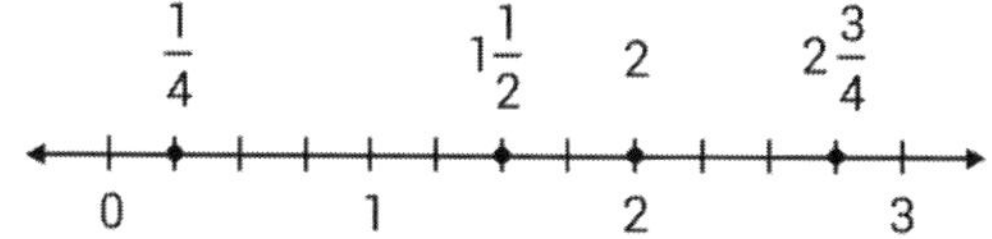

Review Video: The Number Line
Visit mometrix.com/academy and enter code: 816439

Comparing Numbers

Inequality Notation

The symbols < and > mean "is less than" and "is greater than," respectively. For instance, $3 < 5$ means "3 is less than 5," and $7 > 4$ means "7 is greater than 4." Statements like $3 < 5$ and $7 > 4$ are **inequalities**, and the symbols < and > are **inequality symbols**.

Whole Numbers and Decimal Numbers

To compare whole or decimal numbers, we look at the most significant place (the leftmost digit) at which they differ. The number with the larger digit in that place is larger. For instance, $0.3\underline{8}74$ and $0.3\underline{9}$ differ in the hundredths place (underlined). Since 8 is smaller than 9, we see $0.3874 < 0.39$. This is clearer if we make the decimals equal in length by writing extra zeroes: $0.3874 < 0.3900$. Similarly, $2\underline{3}.984 < 2\underline{5}.112$ because 3 is smaller than 5, or 23 is smaller than 25.

Fractions

If fractions have the same denominator, the fraction with the larger numerator is larger. For instance, $\frac{2}{7} < \frac{5}{7}$ since $2 < 5$. We compare fractions with different denominators by finding a common denominator. When comparing the fractions with a common denominator we only compare the numerator, so as a shortcut, we can multiply each numerator by the denominator of the other fraction. The numerator that produces the larger product belongs to the larger fraction. For example, to compare $\frac{7}{8}$ and $\frac{5}{6}$, we note that $7 \cdot 6 = 42$ is larger than $5 \cdot 8 = 40$. Since the numerator 7 produces the larger product, we see $\frac{7}{8} > \frac{5}{6}$. We can also compare fractions by converting them to decimals. For instance, since $\frac{3}{4} = 0.75$ and $\frac{4}{5} = 0.8$ and $0.75 < 0.8$, we conclude $\frac{3}{4} < \frac{4}{5}$.

Mixed Numbers

To compare mixed numbers we compare their whole number parts. If those are equal, then we compare their fractional parts. For instance, $5\frac{3}{8} > 4\frac{7}{8}$ because $5 > 4$, but $3\frac{5}{9} < 3\frac{8}{9}$ because $\frac{5}{9} < \frac{8}{9}$.

Square Roots

To compare square roots, we convert them to decimals, usually with a calculator. To compare two square roots, we compare their radicands. For instance, $\sqrt{11} < \sqrt{14}$ because $11 < 14$.

Negative Numbers

A negative number is always less than a positive number. Two negative numbers compare in the reverse order of their opposites. For instance, $-6 < -2$ (that is, -6 is smaller, more negative, than -2) because $6 > 2$.

Absolute Value

A precursor to working with negative numbers is understanding what **absolute values** are. A number's absolute value is simply the distance away from zero a number is on the number line. The absolute value of a number is always positive and is written $|x|$. For example, the absolute value of 3, written as $|3|$, is 3 because the distance between 0 and 3 on a number line is three units. Likewise, the absolute value of −3, written as $|-3|$, is 3 because the distance between 0 and −3 on a number line is three units. So $|3| = |-3|$.

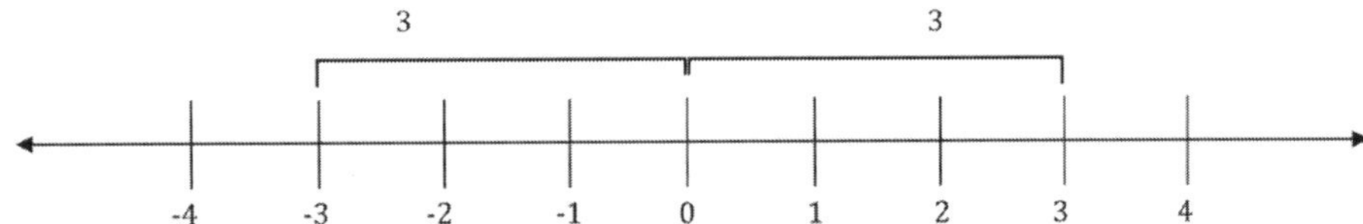

Review Video: Absolute Value
Visit mometrix.com/academy and enter code: 314669

Operations

An **operation** is simply a mathematical process that takes some value(s) as input(s) and produces an output. Elementary operations are often written in the following form: *value operation value*. For instance, in the expression $1 + 2$ the values are 1 and 2 and the operation is addition. Performing the operation gives the output of 3. In this way we can say that $1 + 2$ and 3 are equal, or $1 + 2 = 3$.

Addition

Addition increases the value of one quantity by the value of another quantity (both called **addends**). Example: $2 + 4 = 6$ or $8 + 9 = 17$. The result is called the **sum**. With addition, the order does not matter, $4 + 2 = 2 + 4$.

When adding signed numbers, if the signs are the same simply add the absolute values of the addends and apply the original sign to the sum. For example, $(+4) + (+8) = +12$ and $(-4) + (-8) = -12$. When the original signs are different, take the absolute values of the addends and subtract the smaller value from the larger value, then apply the original sign of the larger value to the difference. Example: $(+4) + (-8) = -4$ and $(-4) + (+8) = +4$.

Subtraction

Subtraction is the opposite operation to addition; it decreases the value of one quantity (the **minuend**) by the value of another quantity (the **subtrahend**). For example, $6 - 4 = 2$ or $17 - 8 = 9$. The result is called the **difference**. Note that with subtraction, the order does matter, $6 - 4 \neq 4 - 6$.

For subtracting signed numbers, change the sign of the subtrahend and then follow the same rules used for addition. Example: $(+4) - (+8) = (+4) + (-8) = -4$

Multiplication

Multiplication can be thought of as repeated addition. One number (the **multiplier**) indicates how many times to add the other number (the **multiplicand**) to itself. Example: $3 \times 2 = 2 + 2 + 2 = 6$. With multiplication, the order does not matter, $2 \times 3 = 3 \times 2$ or $3 + 3 = 2 + 2 + 2$, either way the result (the **product**) is the same.

If the signs are the same, the product is positive when multiplying signed numbers. Example: $(+4) \times (+8) = +32$ and $(-4) \times (-8) = +32$. If the signs are opposite, the product is negative. Example: $(+4) \times (-8) = -32$ and $(-4) \times (+8) = -32$. When more than two factors are multiplied together, the sign of the product is determined by how many negative factors are present. If there are an odd number of negative factors then the product is negative, whereas an even number of negative factors indicates a positive product. Example: $(+4) \times (-8) \times (-2) = +64$ and $(-4) \times (-8) \times (-2) = -64$.

Mathematics

Division

Division is the opposite operation to multiplication; one number (the **divisor**) tells us how many parts to divide the other number (the **dividend**) into. The result of division is called the **quotient**. Example: $20 \div 4 = 5$. If 20 is split into 4 equal parts, each part is 5. With division, the order of the numbers does matter, $20 \div 4 \neq 4 \div 20$.

The rules for dividing signed numbers are similar to multiplying signed numbers. If the dividend and divisor have the same sign, the quotient is positive. If the dividend and divisor have opposite signs, the quotient is negative. Example: $(-4) \div (+8) = -0.5$.

Review Video: Mathematical Operations
Visit mometrix.com/academy and enter code: 208095

Parentheses

Parentheses are used to designate which operations should be done first when there are multiple operations. Example: $4 - (2 + 1) = 1$; the parentheses tell us that we must add 2 and 1, and then subtract the sum from 4, rather than subtracting 2 from 4 and then adding 1 (this would give us an answer of 3).

Review Video: Mathematical Parentheses
Visit mometrix.com/academy and enter code: 978600

Exponents

An **exponent** is a superscript number placed next to another number at the top right. It indicates how many times the base number is to be multiplied by itself. Exponents provide a shorthand way to write what would be a longer mathematical expression. Example: $2^4 = 2 \times 2 \times 2 \times 2$. A number with an exponent of 2 is said to be "squared," while a number with an exponent of 3 is said to be "cubed." The value of a number raised to an exponent is called its power. So 8^4 is read as "8 to the 4th power," or "8 raised to the power of 4."

Review Video: Exponents
Visit mometrix.com/academy and enter code: 600998

Roots

A **root**, such as a square root, is another way of writing a fractional exponent. Instead of using a superscript, roots use the radical symbol ($\sqrt{\ }$) to indicate the operation. A radical will have a number underneath the bar, and may sometimes have a number in the upper left: $\sqrt[n]{a}$, read as "the nth root of a." The relationship between radical notation and exponent notation can be described by this equation:

$$\sqrt[n]{a} = a^{\frac{1}{n}}$$

The two special cases of $n = 2$ and $n = 3$ are called square roots and cube roots. If there is no number to the upper left, the radical is understood to be a square root ($n = 2$). Nearly all of the roots you encounter will be square roots. A square root is the same as a number raised to the one-half power. When we say that a is the square root of b ($a = \sqrt{b}$), we mean that a multiplied by itself equals b: ($a \times a = b$).

A **perfect square** is a number that has an integer for its square root. There are 10 perfect squares from 1 to 100: 1, 4, 9, 16, 25, 36, 49, 64, 81, 100 (the squares of integers 1 through 10).

Review Video: Roots
Visit mometrix.com/academy and enter code: 795655

Review Video: Perfect Squares and Square Roots
Visit mometrix.com/academy and enter code: 648063

Word Problems and Mathematical Symbols

When working on word problems, you must be able to translate verbal expressions or "math words" into math symbols. This chart contains several "math words" and their appropriate symbols:

Phrase	Symbol
equal, is, was, will be, has, costs, gets to, is the same as, becomes	$=$
times, of, multiplied by, product of, twice, doubles, halves, triples	$\times$
divided by, per, ratio of/to, out of	$\div$
plus, added to, sum, combined, and, more than, totals of	$+$
subtracted from, less than, decreased by, minus, difference between	$-$
what, how much, original value, how many, a number, a variable	x, n, etc.

Review Video: Understanding Word Problems
Visit mometrix.com/academy and enter code: 499199

Examples of Translated Mathematical Phrases

- The phrase four more than twice a number can be written algebraically as $2x + 4$.
- The phrase half a number decreased by six can be written algebraically as $\frac{1}{2}x - 6$.
- The phrase the sum of a number and the product of five and that number can be written algebraically as $x + 5x$.
- You may see a test question that says, "Olivia is constructing a bookcase from seven boards. Two of them are for vertical supports and five are for shelves. The height of the bookcase is twice the width of the bookcase. If the seven boards total 36 feet in length, what will be the height of Olivia's bookcase?" You would need to make a sketch and then create the equation to determine the width of the shelves. The height can be represented as double the width. (If x represents the width of the shelves in feet, then the height of the bookcase is $2x$. Since the seven boards total 36 feet, $2x + 2x + x + x + x + x + x = 36$ or $9x = 36$; $x = 4$. The height is twice the width, or 8 feet.)

Subtraction with Regrouping

A great way to make use of some of the features built into the decimal system would be regrouping when attempting longform subtraction operations. When subtracting within a place value, sometimes the minuend is smaller than the subtrahend; **regrouping** enables you to 'borrow' a unit from a place value to the left in order to get a positive difference. For example, consider subtracting 189 from 525 with regrouping.

First, set up the subtraction problem in vertical form:

$$\begin{array}{r} 525 \\ -\ 189 \\ \hline \end{array}$$

Notice that the numbers in the ones and tens columns of 525 are smaller than the numbers in the ones and tens columns of 189. This means you will need to use regrouping to perform subtraction:

$$\begin{array}{rrrr} & 5 & 2 & 5 \\ - & 1 & 8 & 9 \\ \hline \end{array}$$

To subtract 9 from 5 in the ones column you will need to borrow from the 2 in the tens column:

$$\begin{array}{rrrr} & 5 & 1 & 15 \\ - & 1 & 8 & 9 \\ \hline & & & 6 \end{array}$$

Next, to subtract 8 from 1 in the tens column you will need to borrow from the 5 in the hundreds column:

	4	11	15
–	1	8	9
		3	6

Last, subtract the 1 from the 4 in the hundreds column:

	4	11	15
–	1	8	9
	3	3	6

Review Video: Subtracting Large Numbers
Visit mometrix.com/academy and enter code: 603350

ORDER OF OPERATIONS

The **order of operations** is a set of rules that dictates the order in which we must perform each operation in an expression so that we will evaluate it accurately. If we have an expression that includes multiple different operations, the order of operations tells us which operations to do first. The most common mnemonic for the order of operations is **PEMDAS**, or "Please Excuse My Dear Aunt Sally." PEMDAS stands for parentheses, exponents, multiplication, division, addition, and subtraction. It is important to understand that multiplication and division have equal precedence, as do addition and subtraction, so those pairs of operations are simply worked from left to right in order.

For example, evaluating the expression $5 + 20 \div 4 \times (2 + 3)^2 - 6$ using the correct order of operations would be done like this:

- **P:** Perform the operations inside the parentheses: $(2 + 3) = 5$
- **E:** Simplify the exponents: $(5)^2 = 5 \times 5 = 25$
  - The expression now looks like this: $5 + 20 \div 4 \times 25 - 6$
- **MD:** Perform multiplication and division from left to right: $20 \div 4 = 5$; then $5 \times 25 = 125$
  - The expression now looks like this: $5 + 125 - 6$
- **AS:** Perform addition and subtraction from left to right: $5 + 125 = 130$; then $130 - 6 = 124$

Review Video: Order of Operations
Visit mometrix.com/academy and enter code: 259675

PROPERTIES OF OPERATIONS

THE COMMUTATIVE PROPERTY

The commutative property applies to addition and multiplication and states that these operations can be completed in any order. The **commutative property of addition** states that numbers and terms can be added together in any order to still get the same value. For example, $3 + 4 = 7$ and $4 + 3 = 7$. Also, we can use the commutative property of addition to show that $3x + 4 + 2^2$ is equivalent to $4 + 3x + 2^2$ and $2^2 + 4 + 3x$. When adding terms, you can add in any order and get the same value.

The **commutative property of multiplication** states that numbers and terms can be multiplied in any order to get the same value. For example, 12×3 is equivalent to 3×12. Additionally, we can use the commutative property of multiplication to assume that $(5 + 3) \times (36 - 6)$ is equivalent to $(36 - 6) \times (5 + 3)$. You can multiply terms in any order and still get the same value.

THE ASSOCIATIVE PROPERTY

The **associative property of addition** states that if three or more terms are being added together, the value is the same regardless of the groupings.

For example, given the expression $3 + 4 + 6$, these terms can be grouped and added in any form. $3 + 4 + 6$ is equivalent to $(3 + 4) + 6$ and is also equivalent to $3 + (4 + 6)$. This can be applied to write equivalent expressions in a variety of ways.

For example, suppose we are given the expression $5 + (y + 2) + 4$. We can generate equivalent expressions knowing the associative property. Knowing that when three or more terms are added, the grouping is irrelevant, we can say that this expression is equivalent to $5 + y + (2 + 4)$, and it is equivalent to $(5 + y) + (2 + 4)$. It is even equivalent to $5 + y + 2 + 4$.

The **associative property of multiplication** states that if three or more terms are being multiplied together, the value is the same regardless of the grouping. We can use this property to identify and generate equivalent expressions.

For example, given the expression $2 \times 7 \times 3$, these terms can be grouped in any way and still get the same value. $2 \times 7 \times 3$ is equivalent to $(2 \times 7) \times 3$ or $2 \times (7 \times 3)$.

THE IDENTITY PROPERTY

The **identity property of multiplication** states that when a number is multiplied by 1, you get the same number. That is, anything multiplied by 1 is itself. For example, $2 \times 1 = 2$, or $1 \times -36 = -36$. Using the identity property of multiplication, we can identify and generate equivalent expressions. Let's say that we are given the expression $15 - (3 \times 4)$. We can generate equivalent expressions using the identity property. One equivalent expression example would be $(15 \times 1) - (3 \times 4)$. Another example would be $15 - (1 \times 3 \times 4)$. We can say these expressions are equivalent because the identity property of multiplication states that we can multiply any portion of an expression by 1 to get the same value.

The **identity property of addition** states that when 0 is added to a number, you get the same number. For example, $2 + 0 = 2$, or $0 + -3 = -3$. We can also use this property to identify and generate equivalent expressions. For example, if we are given the expression $2 \times (1 + 2)$, we could write the equivalent expressions $2 \times (0 + 1 + 2)$ or $(2 + 0) \times (1 + 2)$.

THE INVERSE PROPERTY

The **inverse property of addition** states that the sum of a number and its opposite is always equal to 0. Remember, the opposite of a number is a number that is opposite on the number line from zero, or the same number with the opposite sign. For example, –4 is opposite to 4, and 1,726.9 is opposite to –1,726.9. So, the inverse property of addition states that if you add opposite numbers, their sum is zero. For example, $5 + (-5) = 0$ and $-5 + 5 = 0$.

The **inverse property of multiplication** states that a number multiplied by its reciprocal is always equal to 1. The **reciprocal** of a number is its "flipped" fraction. For example, the reciprocal of 5 is $\frac{1}{5}$, or the reciprocal of $\frac{2}{3}$ is $\frac{3}{2}$. The inverse property of multiplication can be applied for these values, $5 \times \frac{1}{5} = 1$ and $\frac{2}{3} \times \frac{3}{2} = 1$. This is because when you multiply across, you get a fraction that is equal to 1.

$$\frac{2}{3} \times \frac{3}{2} = \frac{6}{6} = 1$$

THE DISTRIBUTIVE PROPERTY

The **distributive property** explains how multiplication and addition interact. It says that when multiplying one number by the sum of two other numbers, the same result can also be obtained by multiplying the one

Mathematics

number by each of the numbers individually and then adding the products. For example, to multiply 2 by the sum of 7 and 3, the direct approach says, "the sum of 7 and 3 is 10, and 2 times 10 is 20." This would be expressed as $2 \times (7 + 3) = 2 \times 10 = 20$. On the other hand, the distributive property states that the same answer can be achieved by multiplying each number inside the parentheses and adding the products. That is, "the product of 2 and 7 is 14, the product of 2 and 3 is 6, and the sum of 14 and 6 is 20." This would be expressed as $2 \times (7 + 3) = 2 \times 7 + 2 \times 3 = 14 + 6 = 20$, and it is demonstrated below.

$$2 \times (7 + 3) = 2 \times 7 + 2 \times 3$$

This same concept can be used when multiplying a number by the difference of two numbers. For example, $5 \times (10 - 4) = 5 \times 10 - 5 \times 4$. Since $5 \times 10 = 50$ and $5 \times 4 = 20$, the result is $50 - 20 = 30$. This answer can be checked by subtracting inside the parentheses first and then multiplying: $5 \times (10 - 4) = 5 \times 6 = 30$.

Review Video: Commutative, Associative, and Distributive Properties
Visit mometrix.com/academy and enter code: 483176

PROPERTIES OF EXPONENTS

The properties of exponents are as follows:

Property	Description
$a^1 = a$	Any number to the power of 1 is equal to itself
$1^n = 1$	The number 1 raised to any power is equal to 1
$a^0 = 1$	Any number raised to the power of 0 is equal to 1
$a^n \times a^m = a^{n+m}$	Add exponents to multiply powers of the same base number
$a^n \div a^m = a^{n-m}$	Subtract exponents to divide powers of the same base number
$(a^n)^m = a^{n \times m}$	When a power is raised to a power, the exponents are multiplied
$(a \times b)^n = a^n \times b^n$ $(a \div b)^n = a^n \div b^n$	Multiplication and division operations inside parentheses can be raised to a power. This is the same as each term being raised to that power.
$a^{-n} = \frac{1}{a^n}$	A negative exponent is the same as the reciprocal of a positive exponent

Note that exponents do not have to be integers. Fractional or decimal exponents follow all the rules above as well. Example: $5^{\frac{1}{4}} \times 5^{\frac{3}{4}} = 5^{\frac{1}{4}+\frac{3}{4}} = 5^1 = 5$.

Review Video: Properties of Exponents
Visit mometrix.com/academy and enter code: 532558

FACTORS AND MULTIPLES

FACTORS AND GREATEST COMMON FACTOR

A whole number a is a **factor** (or **divisor**) of a whole number b if a divides b evenly. In other words, a is a factor of b if the quotient $b \div a$ is a whole number with a remainder of 0. For instance, 3 is a factor of 12 because $12 \div 3 = 4$ with no remainder. Another way to say this is that a is a factor of b if we can multiply a by another whole number to get b. So, we can also show that 3 is a factor of 12 by noting that $3 \times 4 = 12$.

Every positive whole number has 1 and itself as factors. If a whole number greater than one has *only* 1 and itself as factors, we call it a **prime number**. For instance, 5 is a prime number because its only factors are 1 and 5. The first several prime numbers are 2, 3, 5, 7, 11, and 13.

If a whole number greater than 1 is not prime—that is, if it has factors besides 1 and itself—then it is a **composite number.** For instance, 10 is a composite number because it has factors 2 and 5 in addition to 1 and 10. The first several composite numbers are 4, 6, 8, 9, 10, 12, 14, and 15.

A **prime factor** of a whole number is a factor that is also a prime number. For example, the prime factors of 12 are 2 and 3. The prime factors of 15 are 3 and 5.

A **common factor** of two (or more) whole numbers is a number that is a factor of both (or all) of them. For example, the factors of 12 are $\underline{1}$, 2, $\underline{3}$, 4, 6, and 12, while the factors of 15 are $\underline{1}$, $\underline{3}$, 5, and 15. The common factors (underlined) of 12 and 15 are 1 and 3.

The **greatest common factor** (**GCF**) of two (or more) whole numbers is the largest number that is a factor of both (or all) of them. For example, the factors of 15 are $\underline{1}$, 3, $\underline{5}$, and 15; the factors of 35 are $\underline{1}$, $\underline{5}$, 7, and 35. Therefore, the greatest common factor of 15 and 35 is 5.

Review Video: Factors
Visit mometrix.com/academy and enter code: 920086

Review Video: Prime Numbers and Factorization
Visit mometrix.com/academy and enter code: 760669

Multiples and Least Common Multiple

A whole number b is a **multiple** of a whole number a when a is a factor of b. This means that b is the product of a and another whole number. For example, the multiples of 7 are $0 \times 7 = 0, 1 \times 7 = 7, 2 \times 7 = 14, 3 \times 7 = 21, 4 \times 7 = 28, 5 \times 7 = 35, \ldots$. Dividing 0, 7, 14, 21, 28, and 35 by 7 results in the whole numbers 0, 1, 2, 3, 4, and 5, respectively, showing that 7 is a factor of these numbers.

The least common multiple (**LCM**) of two (or more) whole numbers is the smallest number that is a multiple of both (or all) of them. For example, the multiples of 3 are 3, 6, 9, 12, $\underline{15}$, ...; the multiples of 5 are 5, 10, $\underline{15}$, 20, ... The smallest number that appears in both lists is 15, so the least common multiple of 3 and 5 is 15.

Review Video: Multiples
Visit mometrix.com/academy and enter code: 626738

Review Video: Greatest Common Factor and Least Common Multiple
Visit mometrix.com/academy and enter code: 838699

Fractions

A **fraction** is a number that is expressed as one integer written above another integer, with a dividing line between them $\left(\frac{x}{y}\right)$. It represents the **quotient** of the two numbers "x divided by y." It can also be thought of as x out of y equal parts.

The top number of a fraction is called the **numerator**, and it represents the number of parts under consideration. The 1 in $\frac{1}{4}$ means that 1 part out of the whole is being considered in the calculation. The bottom number of a fraction is called the **denominator**, and it represents the total number of equal parts. The 4 in $\frac{1}{4}$

means that the whole consists of 4 equal parts. A fraction cannot have a denominator of zero; this is referred to as "*undefined.*"

Fractions can be manipulated, without changing the value of the fraction, by multiplying or dividing (but not adding or subtracting) both the numerator and denominator by the same number. If you divide both numbers by a common factor, you are **reducing** or simplifying the fraction. Two fractions that have the same value but are expressed differently are known as **equivalent fractions**. For example, $\frac{2}{10}, \frac{3}{15}, \frac{4}{20}$, and $\frac{5}{25}$ are all equivalent fractions. They can also all be reduced or simplified to $\frac{1}{5}$.

When two fractions are manipulated so that they have the same denominator, this is known as finding a **common denominator**. The number chosen to be that common denominator should be the least common multiple of the two original denominators. Example: $\frac{3}{4}$ and $\frac{5}{6}$; the least common multiple of 4 and 6 is 12. Manipulating to achieve the common denominator: $\frac{3}{4} = \frac{9}{12}; \frac{5}{6} = \frac{10}{12}$.

Review Video: Overview of Fractions
Visit mometrix.com/academy and enter code: 262335

Proper Fractions and Mixed Numbers

A fraction whose denominator is greater than its numerator is known as a **proper fraction**, while a fraction whose numerator is greater than its denominator is known as an **improper fraction**. Proper fractions have values *less than one* and improper fractions have values *greater than one.*

A **mixed number** is a number that contains both an integer and a fraction. Any improper fraction can be rewritten as a mixed number. Example: $\frac{8}{3} = \frac{6}{3} + \frac{2}{3} = 2 + \frac{2}{3} = 2\frac{2}{3}$. Similarly, any mixed number can be rewritten as an improper fraction. Example: $1\frac{3}{5} = 1 + \frac{3}{5} = \frac{5}{5} + \frac{3}{5} = \frac{8}{5}$.

Review Video: Proper and Improper Fractions and Mixed Numbers
Visit mometrix.com/academy and enter code: 211077

Adding and Subtracting Fractions

If two fractions have a common denominator, they can be added or subtracted simply by adding or subtracting the two numerators and retaining the same denominator. If the two fractions do not already have the same denominator, one or both of them must be manipulated to achieve a common denominator before they can be added or subtracted. Example: $\frac{1}{2} + \frac{1}{4} = \frac{2}{4} + \frac{1}{4} = \frac{3}{4}$.

Review Video: Adding and Subtracting Fractions
Visit mometrix.com/academy and enter code: 378080

Multiplying Fractions

Two fractions can be multiplied by multiplying the two numerators to find the new numerator and the two denominators to find the new denominator. Example: $\frac{1}{3} \times \frac{2}{3} = \frac{1\times2}{3\times3} = \frac{2}{9}$.

Dividing Fractions

Two fractions can be divided by flipping the numerator and denominator of the second fraction and then proceeding as though it were a multiplication problem. Example: $\frac{2}{3} \div \frac{3}{4} = \frac{2}{3} \times \frac{4}{3} = \frac{8}{9}$.

> **Review Video: Multiplying and Dividing Fractions**
> Visit mometrix.com/academy and enter code: 473632

Multiplying a Mixed Number by a Whole Number or a Decimal

When multiplying a mixed number by something, it is usually best to convert it to an improper fraction first. Additionally, if the multiplicand is a decimal, it is most often simplest to convert it to a fraction. For instance, to multiply $4\frac{3}{8}$ by 3.5, begin by rewriting each quantity as a whole number plus a proper fraction. Remember, a mixed number is a fraction added to a whole number and a decimal is a representation of the sum of fractions, specifically tenths, hundredths, thousandths, and so on:

$$4\frac{3}{8} \times 3.5 = \left(4 + \frac{3}{8}\right) \times \left(3 + \frac{1}{2}\right)$$

Next, the quantities being added need to be expressed with the same denominator. This is achieved by multiplying and dividing the whole number by the denominator of the fraction. Recall that a whole number is equivalent to that number divided by 1:

$$= \left(\frac{4}{1} \times \frac{8}{8} + \frac{3}{8}\right) \times \left(\frac{3}{1} \times \frac{2}{2} + \frac{1}{2}\right)$$

When multiplying fractions, remember to multiply the numerators and denominators separately:

$$= \left(\frac{4 \times 8}{1 \times 8} + \frac{3}{8}\right) \times \left(\frac{3 \times 2}{1 \times 2} + \frac{1}{2}\right)$$
$$= \left(\frac{32}{8} + \frac{3}{8}\right) \times \left(\frac{6}{2} + \frac{1}{2}\right)$$

Now that the fractions have the same denominators, they can be added:

$$= \frac{35}{8} \times \frac{7}{2}$$

Finally, perform the last multiplication and then simplify:

$$= \frac{35 \times 7}{8 \times 2} = \frac{245}{16} = \frac{240}{16} + \frac{5}{16} = 15\frac{5}{16}$$

Comparing Fractions

It is important to master the ability to compare and order fractions. This skill is relevant to many real-world scenarios. For example, carpenters often compare fractional construction nail lengths when preparing for a project, and bakers often compare fractional measurements to have the correct ratio of ingredients. There are three commonly used strategies when comparing fractions. These strategies are referred to as the common denominator approach, the decimal approach, and the cross-multiplication approach.

Mathematics

Using a Common Denominator to Compare Fractions

The fractions $\frac{2}{3}$ and $\frac{4}{7}$ have different denominators. $\frac{2}{3}$ has a denominator of 3, and $\frac{4}{7}$ has a denominator of 7. In order to precisely compare these two fractions, it is necessary to use a common denominator. A common denominator is a common multiple that is shared by both denominators. In this case, the denominators 3 and 7 share a multiple of 21. In general, it is most efficient to select the least common multiple for the two denominators.

Rewrite each fraction with the common denominator of 21. Then, calculate the new numerators as illustrated below.

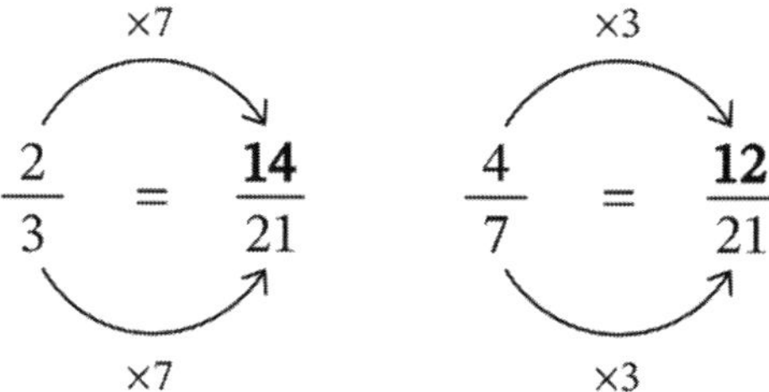

For $\frac{2}{3}$, multiply the numerator and denominator by 7. The result is $\frac{14}{21}$.

For $\frac{4}{7}$, multiply the numerator and denominator by 3. The result is $\frac{12}{21}$.

Now that both fractions have a denominator of 21, the fractions can accurately be compared by comparing the numerators. Since 14 is greater than 12, the fraction $\frac{14}{21}$ is greater than $\frac{12}{21}$. This means that $\frac{2}{3}$ is greater than $\frac{4}{7}$.

Using Decimals to Compare Fractions

Sometimes decimal values are easier to compare than fraction values. For example, $\frac{5}{8}$ is equivalent to 0.625 and $\frac{3}{5}$ is equivalent to 0.6. This means that the comparison of $\frac{5}{8}$ and $\frac{3}{5}$ can be determined by comparing the decimals 0.625 and 0.6. When both decimal values are extended to the thousandths place, they become 0.625 and 0.600, respectively. It becomes clear that 0.625 is greater than 0.600 because 625 thousandths is greater than 600 thousandths. In other words, $\frac{5}{8}$ is greater than $\frac{3}{5}$ because 0.625 is greater than 0.6.

Using Cross-Multiplication to Compare Fractions

Cross-multiplication is an efficient strategy for comparing fractions. This is a shortcut for the common denominator strategy. Start by writing each fraction next to one another. Multiply the numerator of the fraction on the left by the denominator of the fraction on the right. Write down the result next to the fraction on the left. Now multiply the numerator of the fraction on the right by the denominator of the fraction on the left. Write down the result next to the fraction on the right. Compare both products. The fraction with the larger result is the larger fraction.

Consider the fractions $\frac{4}{7}$ and $\frac{5}{9}$.

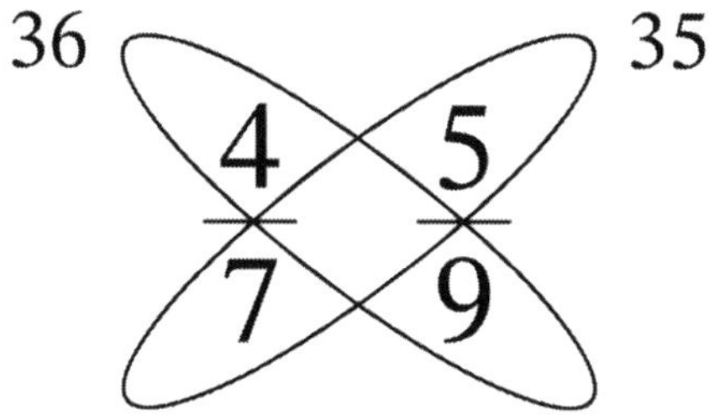

36 is greater than 35. Therefore, $\frac{4}{7}$ is greater than $\frac{5}{9}$.

DECIMALS

Decimals are one way to represent parts of a whole. Using the place value system, each digit to the right of a decimal point denotes the number of units of a corresponding *negative* power of ten. For example, consider the decimal 0.24. We can use a model to represent the decimal. Since a dime is worth one-tenth of a dollar and a penny is worth one-hundredth of a dollar, one possible model to represent this fraction is to have 2 dimes representing the 2 in the tenths place and 4 pennies representing the 4 in the hundredths place:

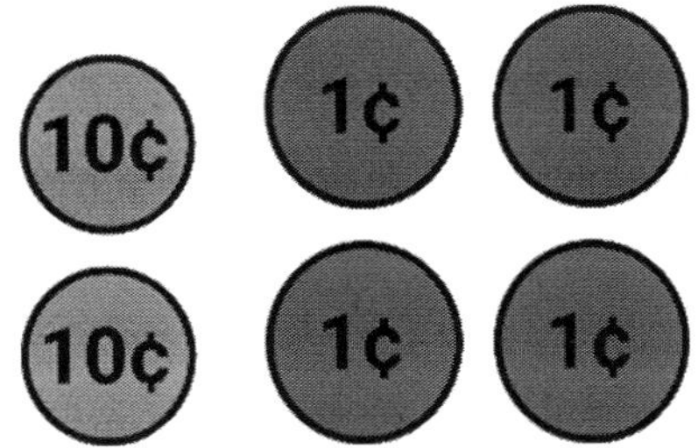

To write the decimal as a fraction, put the decimal in the numerator with 1 in the denominator. Multiply the numerator and denominator by tens until there are no more decimal places. Then simplify the fraction to lowest terms. For example, converting 0.24 to a fraction:

$$0.24 = \frac{0.24}{1} = \frac{0.24 \times 100}{1 \times 100} = \frac{24}{100} = \frac{6}{25}$$

Review Video: Decimals
Visit mometrix.com/academy and enter code: 837268

OPERATIONS WITH DECIMALS

ADDING AND SUBTRACTING DECIMALS

When adding and subtracting decimals, the decimal points must always be aligned. Adding decimals is just like adding regular whole numbers. Example: $4.5 + 2.0 = 6.5$.

If the problem-solver does not properly align the decimal points, an incorrect answer of 4.7 may result. An easy way to add decimals is to align all of the decimal points in a vertical column visually. This will allow you to see exactly where the decimal should be placed in the final answer. Begin adding from right to left. Add each column in turn, making sure to carry the number to the left if a column adds up to more than 9. The same rules apply to the subtraction of decimals.

Review Video: Adding and Subtracting Decimals
Visit mometrix.com/academy and enter code: 381101

MULTIPLYING DECIMALS

A simple multiplication problem has two components: a **multiplicand** and a **multiplier**. When multiplying decimals, work as though the numbers were whole rather than decimals. Once the final product is calculated, count the number of places to the right of the decimal in both the multiplicand and the multiplier. Then, count that number of places from the right of the product and place the decimal in that position.

For example, 12.3×2.56 has a total of three places to the right of the respective decimals. Multiply 123×256 to get 31,488. Now, beginning on the right, count three places to the left and insert the decimal. The final product will be 31.488.

Review Video: How to Multiply Decimals
Visit mometrix.com/academy and enter code: 731574

Dividing Decimals

Every division problem has a **divisor** and a **dividend**. The dividend is the number that is being divided. In the problem $14 \div 7$, 14 is the dividend and 7 is the divisor. In a division problem with decimals, the divisor must be converted into a whole number. Begin by moving the decimal in the divisor to the right until a whole number is created. Next, move the decimal in the dividend the same number of spaces to the right. For example, 4.9 into 24.5 would become 49 into 245. The decimal was moved one space to the right to create a whole number in the divisor, and then the same was done for the dividend. Once the whole numbers are created, the problem is carried out normally: $245 \div 49 = 5$.

Review Video: Dividing Decimals
Visit mometrix.com/academy and enter code: 560690

Review Video: Dividing Decimals by Whole Numbers
Visit mometrix.com/academy and enter code: 535669

Percentages

Percentages can be thought of as fractions that are based on a whole of 100; that is, one whole is equal to 100%. The word **percent** means "per hundred." Percentage problems are often presented in three main ways:

- Find what percentage of some number another number is.
  - Example: What percentage of 40 is 8?
- Find what number is some percentage of a given number.
  - Example: What number is 20% of 40?
- Find what number another number is a given percentage of.
  - Example: What number is 8 20% of?

There are three components in each of these cases: a **whole** (W), a **part** (P), and a **percentage** (%). These are related by the equation: $P = W \times \%$. This can easily be rearranged into other forms that may suit different questions better: $\% = \frac{P}{W}$ and $W = \frac{P}{\%}$. Percentage problems are often also word problems. As such, a large part of solving them is figuring out which quantities are what. For example, consider the following word problem:

In a school cafeteria, 7 students choose pizza, 9 choose hamburgers, and 4 choose tacos. What percentage of students choose tacos?

To find the whole, you must first add all of the parts: $7 + 9 + 4 = 20$. The percentage can then be found by dividing the part by the whole $\left(\% = \frac{P}{W}\right)$: $\frac{4}{20} = \frac{20}{100} = 20\%$.

Review Video: Computation with Percentages
Visit mometrix.com/academy and enter code: 693099

Calculating Percent Change

Suppose a quantity has a particular value (the *old value*) and then we add something (the *change*) to it to get another value (the *new value*). We can describe this process by the simple equation (old value) + change =

(new value). If we know the old and new values, we can rearrange this equation to find the change, getting change = (new value) − (old value). For instance, if a store's price for a box of computer paper goes from $20 last week to $25 this week, this is a change of (new value) − (old value) = $25 − $20 = $5. Or, if the size of the freshman class at a college goes from 500 students one year to 440 students the next year, this is a change of (new value) − (old value) = 440 − 500 = −60 students. So, we see that change can be positive or negative.

Instead of the word *change*, we sometimes use the words *increase* or *decrease* to specify whether the value goes up or down, respectively. In the examples above, the price of computer paper increases by $5 and the freshman class decreases by 60 students. Note that the decrease is 60 students and not −60 because the word *decrease* already means that the value goes down. So, *increase* is the same as positive change and *decrease* is the opposite or negative change.

If the changing quantity represents an amount (how much of something there is), we can also calculate the **percent change**. This is the change expressed as a percentage of the old amount. To calculate this, we divide the change by the old amount and express the quotient as a percent. That is, we use the formula $\text{percent change} = \frac{\text{change}}{\text{old value}}$, converting the resulting decimal answer to a percent. In the examples above, the price of a box of computer paper has a percent change of $\frac{\text{change in price}}{\text{old price}} = \frac{\$5}{\$20} = 0.25 = 25\%$, and the size of the freshman class at the college has a percent change of $\frac{\text{change in enrollment}}{\text{old enrollment}} = \frac{-60}{500} = -0.12 = -12\%$. We can also use the terms *percent increase* and *percent decrease*, saying that the price of computer paper increases by 25% and the size of the freshman class decreases by 12%. Note that the denominator is always the old amount, never the new amount.

Example: Your landlord raises your rent from $1,500 to $1,700 per month. To find the percent change in your rent (rounded to the nearest tenth of a percent), you calculate as follows.

$$\begin{aligned}\text{percent change in rent} &= \frac{\text{change in rent}}{\text{old rent}} = \frac{(\text{new rent}) - (\text{old rent})}{\text{old rent}} \\ &= \frac{\$1{,}700 - \$1{,}500}{\$1{,}500} = \frac{\$200}{\$1{,}500} = 0.1333\ldots \approx 13.3\%\end{aligned}$$

Therefore, the percent change in your rent is approximately 13.3%.

Review Video: Percent Change
Visit mometrix.com/academy and enter code: 907890

Converting Between Percentages, Fractions, and Decimals

Converting decimals to percentages and percentages to decimals is as simple as moving the decimal point. To *convert from a decimal to a percentage*, move the decimal point **two places to the right**. To *convert from a percentage to a decimal*, move it **two places to the left**. It may be helpful to remember that the percentage number will always be larger than the equivalent decimal number. Example:

$$\begin{array}{ccc} 0.23 = 23\% & 5.34 = 534\% & 0.007 = 0.7\% \\ 700\% = 7.00 & 86\% = 0.86 & 0.15\% = 0.0015 \end{array}$$

To convert a fraction to a decimal, simply divide the numerator by the denominator in the fraction. To convert a decimal to a fraction, put the decimal in the numerator with 1 in the denominator. Multiply the numerator

Mathematics

and denominator by tens until there are no more decimal places. Then simplify the fraction to lowest terms. For example, converting 0.24 to a fraction:

$$0.24 = \frac{0.24}{1} = \frac{0.24 \times 100}{1 \times 100} = \frac{24}{100} = \frac{6}{25}$$

Fractions can be converted to a percentage by finding equivalent fractions with a denominator of 100. Example:

$$\frac{7}{10} = \frac{70}{100} = 70\% \quad \frac{1}{4} = \frac{25}{100} = 25\%$$

To convert a percentage to a fraction, divide the percentage number by 100 and reduce the fraction to its simplest possible terms. Example:

$$60\% = \frac{60}{100} = \frac{3}{5} \quad 96\% = \frac{96}{100} = \frac{24}{25}$$

Review Video: Converting Fractions to Percentages and Decimals
Visit mometrix.com/academy and enter code: 306233

Review Video: Converting Percentages to Decimals and Fractions
Visit mometrix.com/academy and enter code: 287297

Review Video: Converting Decimals to Fractions and Percentages
Visit mometrix.com/academy and enter code: 986765

Review Video: Converting Decimals, Improper Fractions, and Mixed Numbers
Visit mometrix.com/academy and enter code: 696924

Rational and Irrational Numbers

The term **rational** means that the number can be expressed as a ratio or fraction. That is, a number, r, is rational if and only if it can be represented by a fraction $\frac{a}{b}$ where a and b are integers and b does not equal 0. The set of rational numbers includes integers and decimals. If there is no finite way to represent a value with a fraction of integers, then the number is **irrational**. Common irrational numbers are π and the square roots of whole numbers that are not perfect squares (e.g., $\sqrt{5}$ or $\sqrt{21}$). The sum or product of an integer and an irrational number is always irrational (e.g., 3π or $7 + \sqrt{6}$).

Review Video: Rational and Irrational Numbers
Visit mometrix.com/academy and enter code: 280645

Review Video: Ordering Rational Numbers
Visit mometrix.com/academy and enter code: 419578

Review Video: Irrational Numbers on a Number Line
Visit mometrix.com/academy and enter code: 433866

Measurement and Geometry

Metric and Customary Measurements

Metric Measurement Prefixes

Giga-	One billion	1 *giga*watt is one billion watts
Mega-	One million	1 *mega*hertz is one million hertz
Kilo-	One thousand	1 *kilo*gram is one thousand grams
Deci-	One-tenth	1 *deci*meter is one-tenth of a meter
Centi-	One-hundredth	1 *centi*meter is one-hundredth of a meter
Milli-	One-thousandth	1 *milli*liter is one-thousandth of a liter
Micro-	One-millionth	1 *micro*gram is one-millionth of a gram

Review Video: How the Metric System Works
Visit mometrix.com/academy and enter code: 163709

Measurement Conversion

When converting between units, the goal is to maintain the same meaning but change the way it is displayed. In order to go from a larger unit to a smaller unit, multiply the number of the known amount by the equivalent amount. When going from a smaller unit to a larger unit, divide the number of the known amount by the equivalent amount.

For complicated conversions, it may be helpful to set up conversion fractions. In these fractions, one fraction is the **conversion factor**. The other fraction has the unknown amount in the numerator. So, the known value is placed in the denominator. Sometimes, the second fraction has the known value from the problem in the numerator and the unknown in the denominator. Multiply the two fractions to get the converted measurement. Note that since the numerator and the denominator of the factor are equivalent, the value of the fraction is 1. That is why we can say that the result in the new units is equal to the result in the old units even though they have different numbers.

It can often be necessary to chain known conversion factors together. As an example, consider converting 512 square inches to square meters. We know that there are 2.54 centimeters in an inch and 100 centimeters in a meter, and we know we will need to square each of these factors to achieve the conversion we are looking for.

$$\frac{512\text{ in}^2}{1} \times \left(\frac{2.54\text{ cm}}{1\text{ in}}\right)^2 \times \left(\frac{1\text{ m}}{100\text{ cm}}\right)^2 = \frac{512\,\cancel{\text{in}^2}}{1} \times \left(\frac{6.4516\,\cancel{\text{cm}^2}}{1\,\cancel{\text{in}^2}}\right) \times \left(\frac{1\text{ m}^2}{10{,}000\,\cancel{\text{cm}^2}}\right) = 0.330\text{ m}^2$$

Review Video: Measurement Conversions
Visit mometrix.com/academy and enter code: 316703

Review Video: Converting Kilograms to Pounds
Visit mometrix.com/academy and enter code: 241463

COMMON UNITS AND EQUIVALENTS

METRIC EQUIVALENTS

1000 μg (microgram)	1 mg
1000 mg (milligram)	1 g
1000 g (gram)	1 kg
1000 kg (kilogram)	1 metric ton
1000 mL (milliliter)	1 L
1000 μm (micrometer)	1 mm
1000 mm (millimeter)	1 m
100 cm (centimeter)	1 m
1000 m (meter)	1 km

DISTANCE AND AREA MEASUREMENT

Unit	Abbreviation	US equivalent	Metric equivalent
Inch	in	1 inch	2.54 centimeters
Foot	ft	12 inches	0.305 meters
Yard	yd	3 feet	0.914 meters
Mile	mi	5280 feet	1.609 kilometers
Acre	ac	4840 square yards	0.405 hectares
Square Mile	sq. mi. or $mi.^2$	640 acres	2.590 square kilometers

CAPACITY MEASUREMENTS

Unit	Abbreviation	US equivalent	Metric equivalent
Fluid Ounce	fl oz	8 fluid drams	29.573 milliliters
Cup	c	8 fluid ounces	0.237 liter
Pint	pt.	16 fluid ounces	0.473 liter
Quart	qt.	2 pints	0.946 liter
Gallon	gal.	4 quarts	3.785 liters
Teaspoon	t or tsp.	1 fluid dram	5 milliliters
Tablespoon	T or tbsp.	4 fluid drams	15 or 16 milliliters
Cubic Centimeter	cc or cm^3	0.271 drams	1 milliliter

WEIGHT MEASUREMENTS

Unit	Abbreviation	US equivalent	Metric equivalent
Ounce	oz	16 drams	28.35 grams
Pound	lb	16 ounces	453.6 grams
Ton	tn.	2,000 pounds	907.2 kilograms

VOLUME AND WEIGHT MEASUREMENT CLARIFICATIONS

Always be careful when using ounces and fluid ounces. They are not equivalent.

1 pint = 16 fluid ounces	1 fluid ounce ≠ 1 ounce
1 pound = 16 ounces	1 pint ≠ 1 pound

Having one pint of something does not mean you have one pound of it. In the same way, just because something weighs one pound does not mean that its volume is one pint.

In the United States, the word "ton" by itself refers to a short ton or a net ton. Do not confuse this with a long ton (also called a gross ton) or a metric ton (also spelled *tonne*), which have different measurement equivalents.

$$1 \text{ US ton} = 2000 \text{ pounds} \quad \neq \quad 1 \text{ metric ton} = 1000 \text{ kilograms}$$

POINTS, LINES, AND PLANES

POINTS AND LINES

A **point** is a fixed location in space, has no size or dimensions, and is commonly represented by a dot. A **line** is a set of points that extends infinitely in two opposite directions. It has length, but no width or depth. A line can be defined by any two distinct points that it contains. A **line segment** is a portion of a line that has definite endpoints. A **ray** is a portion of a line that extends from a single point on that line in one direction along the line. It has a definite beginning, but no ending.

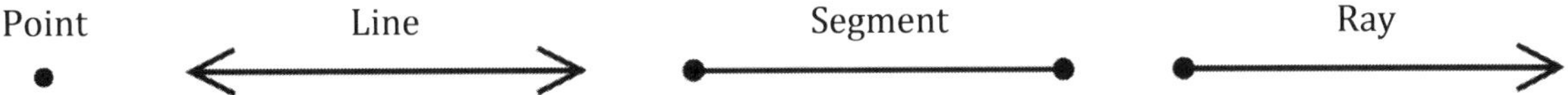

Points are **collinear** if there is a single line that passes through all of them. Otherwise, they are noncollinear. Two points are always collinear since two points define a line. Three points may be noncollinear. For example, the three vertices of a triangle are noncollinear since there is no line that goes through all three of them.

INTERACTIONS BETWEEN LINES

Intersecting lines are lines that have exactly one point in common. **Concurrent lines** are multiple lines that intersect at a single point. **Perpendicular lines** are lines that intersect at right angles. They are represented by the symbol ⊥. The shortest distance from a line to a point not on the line is a perpendicular segment from the point to the line. **Parallel lines** are lines in the same plane that have no points in common and never meet. Two distinct lines in a given plane are always either intersecting or parallel. **Skew lines** are two distinct lines in a three dimensional space that do not intersect and may also not be parallel because there is no single plane that contains them both.

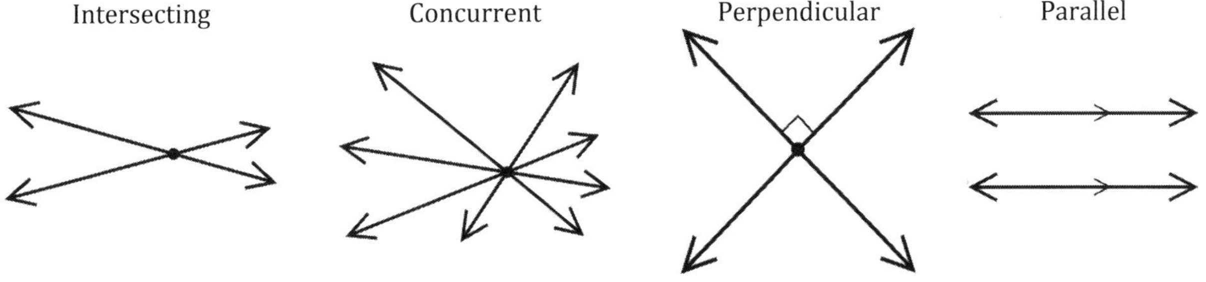

Review Video: Parallel and Perpendicular Lines
Visit mometrix.com/academy and enter code: 815923

A **transversal** is a line that intersects at least two other lines, which may or may not be parallel to one another. A transversal that intersects parallel lines is a common occurrence in geometry. A **bisector** is a line or line segment that divides another line segment into two equal lengths. A **perpendicular bisector** of a line segment is composed of points that are equidistant from the endpoints of the segment it is dividing.

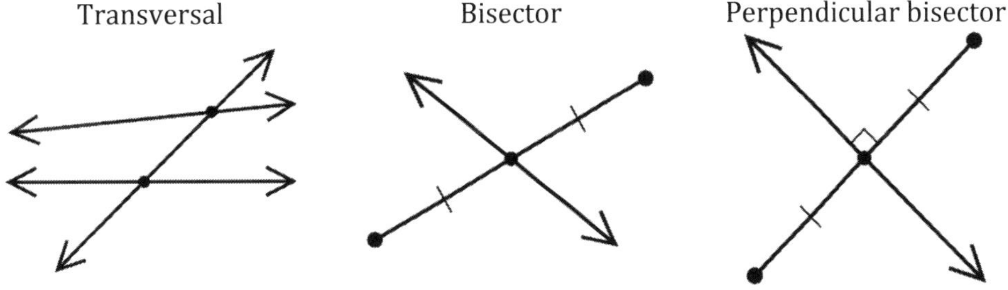

The **projection of a point on a line** is the point at which a perpendicular line drawn from the given point to the given line intersects the line. This is also the shortest distance from the given point to the line. The **projection of a segment on a line** is a segment whose endpoints are the points formed when perpendicular lines are drawn from the endpoints of the given segment to the given line. This is similar to the length a diagonal line appears to be when viewed from above.

Projection of a point on a line

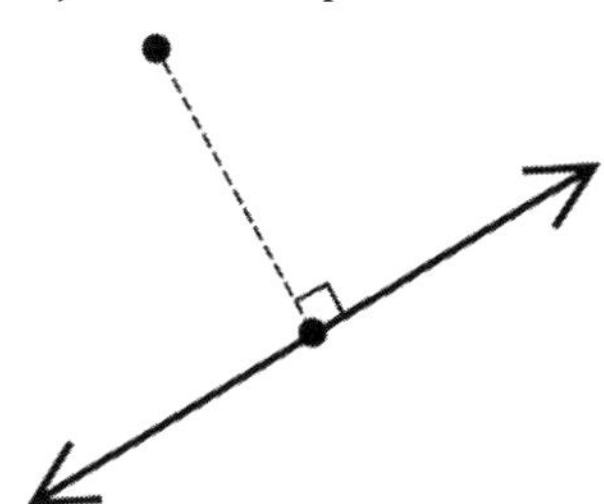

Projection of a segment on a line

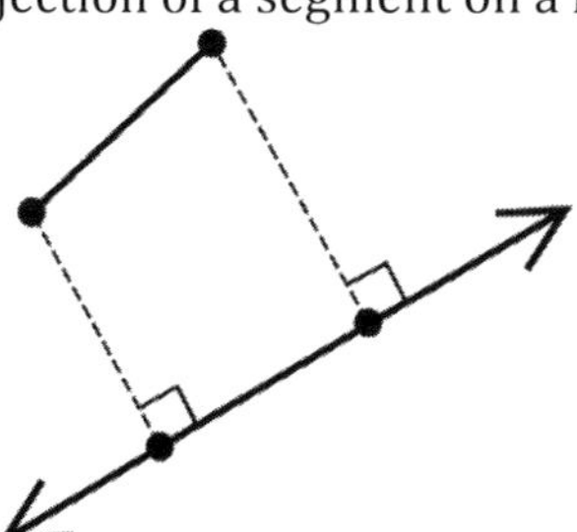

PLANES

A **plane** is a two-dimensional flat surface defined by three non-collinear points. A plane extends an infinite distance in all directions in those two dimensions. It contains an infinite number of points, parallel lines and segments, intersecting lines and segments, as well as parallel or intersecting rays. A plane will never contain a three-dimensional figure or skew lines. Two given planes are either parallel or they intersect at a line. A plane may intersect a circular conic surface to form **conic sections**, such as a parabola, hyperbola, circle or ellipse.

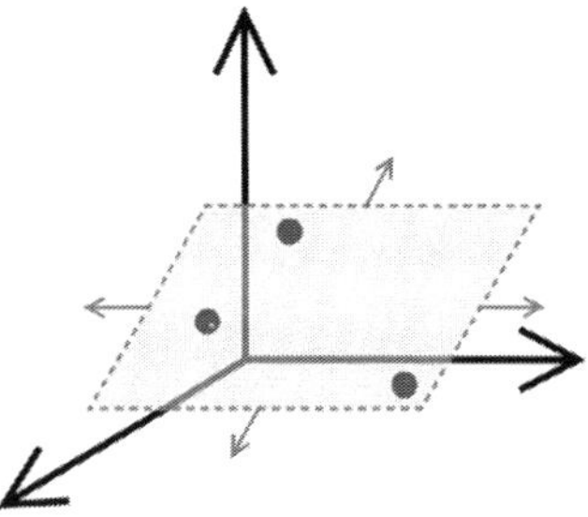

Review Video: Lines and Planes
Visit mometrix.com/academy and enter code: 554267

ANGLES

ANGLES AND VERTICES

An **angle** is formed when two lines or line segments meet at a common point. It may be a common starting point for a pair of segments or rays, or it may be the intersection of lines. Angles are represented by the symbol ∠.

The **vertex** is the point at which two segments or rays meet to form an angle. If the angle is formed by intersecting rays, lines, and/or line segments, the vertex is the point at which four angles are formed. The pairs of angles opposite one another are called vertical angles, and their measures are equal.

- An **acute** angle is an angle with a degree measure less than 90°.
- A **right** angle is an angle with a degree measure of exactly 90°.
- An **obtuse** angle is an angle with a degree measure greater than 90° but less than 180°.
- A **straight angle** is an angle with a degree measure of exactly 180°.
- A **reflex angle** is an angle with a degree measure greater than 180° but less than 360°.

- A **full angle** is an angle with a degree measure of exactly 360°.

Review Video: Angles
Visit mometrix.com/academy and enter code: 264624

Relationships Between Angles

Two angles whose sum is exactly 90° are said to be **complementary**. The two angles may or may not be adjacent. In a right triangle, the two acute angles are complementary.

Two angles whose sum is exactly 180° are said to be **supplementary**. The two angles may or may not be adjacent. Two intersecting lines always form two pairs of supplementary angles. Adjacent supplementary angles will always form a straight line.

Two angles that have the same vertex and share a side are said to be **adjacent**. Vertical angles are not adjacent because they share a vertex but no common side.

Review Video: Adjacent Angles
Visit mometrix.com/academy and enter code: 100375

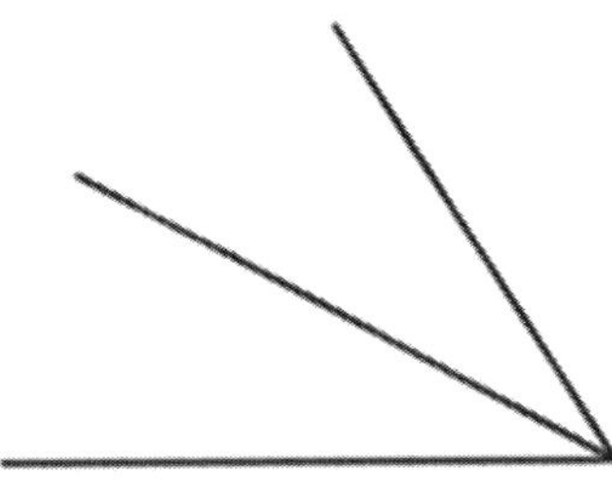

Adjacent
Share vertex and side

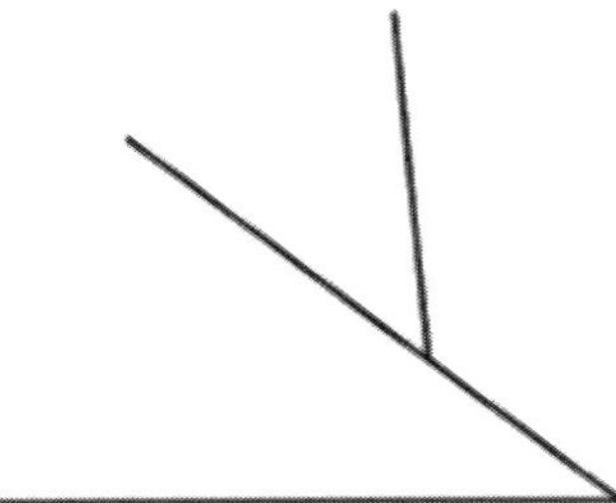

Not adjacent
Share part of a side, but not vertex

When two lines are cut by a transversal, the angles that are between the two lines are **interior angles**. In the diagram below, angles 3, 4, 5, and 6 are interior angles.

When two lines are cut by a transversal, the angles that are outside the lines are **exterior angles**. In the diagram below, angles 1, 2, 7, and 8 are exterior angles.

When two lines are cut by a transversal, the angles that are in the same position relative to the transversal and the cut lines are **corresponding angles**. The diagram below has four pairs of corresponding angles: angles 1 and 5, angles 2 and 6, angles 3 and 7, and angles 4 and 8. Corresponding angles formed by parallel lines are congruent.

When two lines are cut by a transversal, the two interior angles that are on opposite sides of the transversal are called **alternate interior angles**. In the diagram below, there are two pairs of alternate interior angles: angles 3 and 6, and angles 4 and 5. Alternate interior angles formed by parallel lines are congruent. Similarly, the two interior angles on the same side of the transversal (angles 3 and 5, and angles 4 and 6) are supplementary when the transversed lines are parallel. Some books call these angles **same side interior angles**.

When two lines are cut by a transversal, the two exterior angles that are on opposite sides of the transversal are called **alternate exterior angles**. In the diagram below, there are two pairs of alternate exterior angles: angles 1 and 8, and angles 2 and 7. Alternate exterior angles formed by parallel lines are congruent. Similarly, the two exterior angles on the same side of the transversal (angles 1 and 7, and angles 2 and 8) are supplementary when the transversed lines are parallel. Some books call these angles **same side exterior angles**.

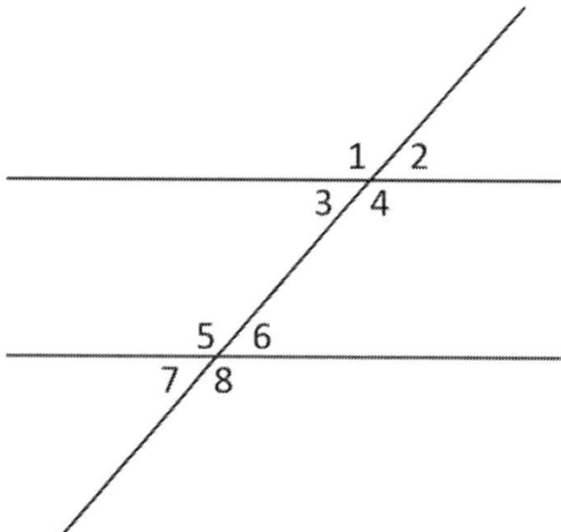

When two lines intersect, four angles are formed. The non-adjacent angles at this vertex are called vertical angles. Vertical angles are congruent. In the diagram, $\angle ABD \cong \angle CBE$ and $\angle ABC \cong \angle DBE$. The other pairs of angles, ($\angle ABC, \angle CBE$) and ($\angle ABD, \angle DBE$), are supplementary, meaning the pairs sum to 180°.

Review Video: Congruent Angles
Visit mometrix.com/academy and enter code: 642874

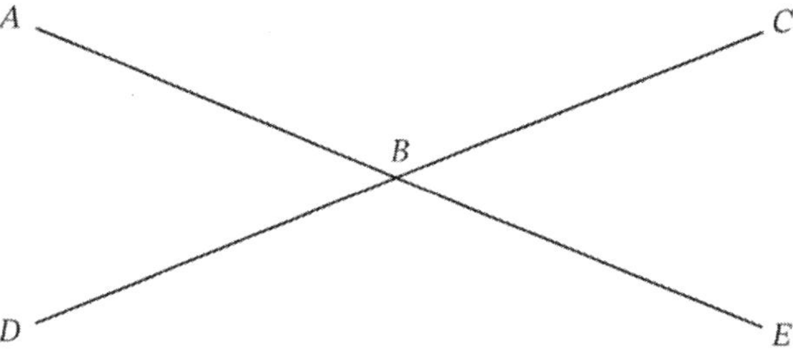

Polygons

A **polygon** is a closed, two-dimensional figure with three or more straight line segments called **sides**. The point at which two sides of a polygon intersect is called the **vertex**. In a polygon, the number of sides is always equal to the number of vertices. A polygon with all sides congruent and all angles equal is called a **regular polygon**. Common polygons are:

Triangle = 3 sides
Quadrilateral = 4 sides
Pentagon = 5 sides
Hexagon = 6 sides
Heptagon = 7 sides
Octagon = 8 sides
Nonagon = 9 sides
Decagon = 10 sides
Dodecagon = 12 sides

More generally, an n-gon is a polygon that has n angles and n sides.

Review Video: Intro to Polygons
Visit mometrix.com/academy and enter code: 271869

The sum of the interior angles of an n-sided polygon is $(n - 2) \times 180°$. For example, in a triangle $n = 3$. So the sum of the interior angles is $(3 - 2) \times 180° = 180°$. In a quadrilateral, $n = 4$, and the sum of the angles is $(4 - 2) \times 180° = 360°$.

Review Video: Sum of Interior Angles
Visit mometrix.com/academy and enter code: 984991

Convex and Concave Polygons

A **convex polygon** is a polygon whose diagonals all lie within the interior of the polygon. A **concave polygon** is a polygon with at least one diagonal that is outside the polygon. In the diagram below, quadrilateral $ABCD$ is concave because diagonal $\overline{AC}$ lies outside the polygon and quadrilateral $EFGH$ is convex because both diagonals lie inside the polygon.

Concave

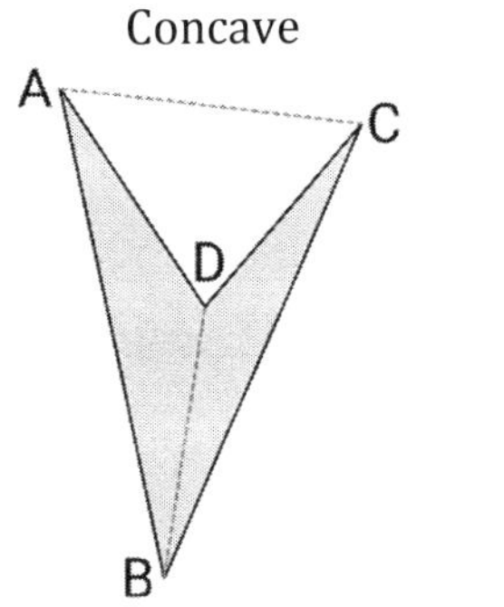

Convex

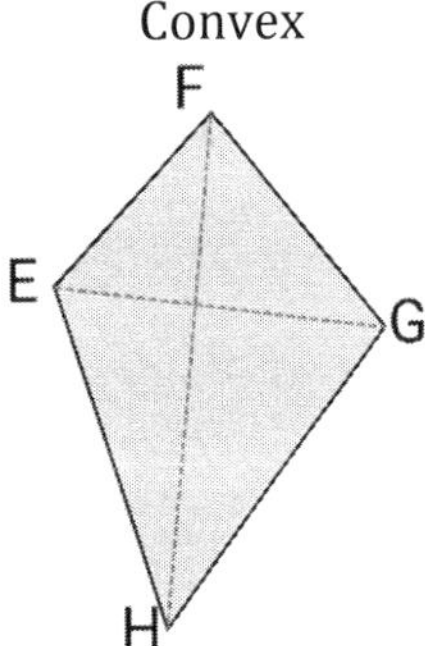

Apothem and Radius

A line segment from the center of a regular polygon that is perpendicular to a side of the polygon is called the **apothem**. A line segment from the center of a regular polygon to a vertex of the polygon is called a **radius**. In a regular polygon, the apothem can be used to find the area of the polygon using the formula $A = \frac{1}{2}ap$, where a is the apothem, and p is the perimeter.

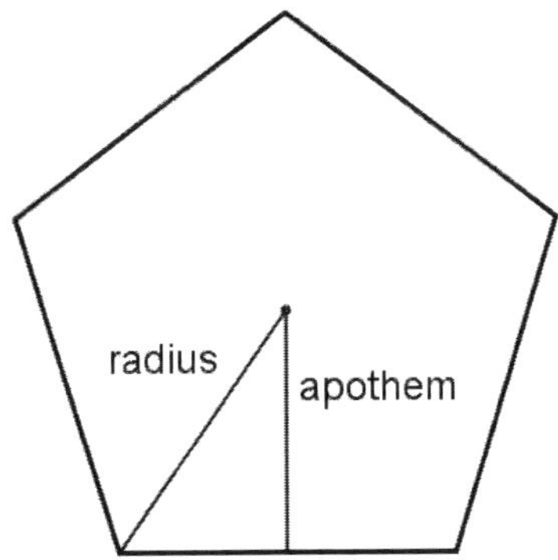

A **diagonal** is a line segment that joins two non-adjacent vertices of a polygon. The number of diagonals a polygon has can be found by using the formula:

$$\text{number of diagonals} = \frac{n(n-3)}{2}$$

Note that n is the number of sides in the polygon. This formula works for all polygons, not just regular polygons.

Mathematics

Congruence and Similarity

Congruent figures are geometric figures that have the same size and shape. For congruent polygons all corresponding angle measures are equal, and all corresponding side lengths are equal. Congruence is indicated by the symbol $\cong$. For instance, the expression $ABC \cong DEF$ indicates that the triangles below are congruent. The order of the letters is important, indicating which parts of the polygons correspond to each other. For example, since the letters A and D both come first, $\angle A$ and $\angle D$ have the same measure.

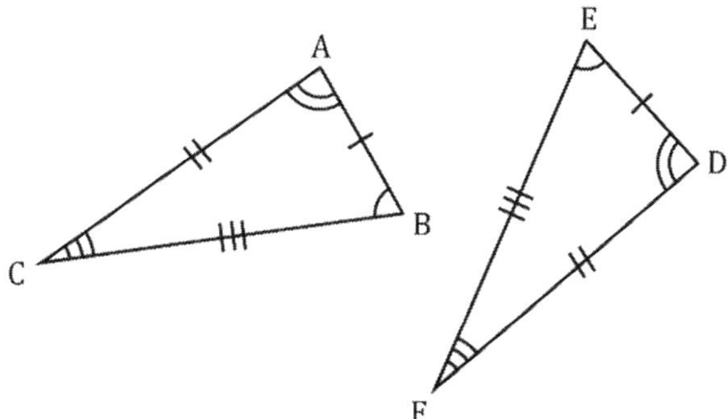

Similar figures are geometric figures that have the same shape, but do not necessarily have the same size. For similar polygons all corresponding angle measures are equal, and all corresponding side lengths are proportional, but they do not have to be equal. It is indicated by the symbol $\sim$. For instance, the expression $ABC \sim DEF$ indicates that the triangles below are similar. Again, the order of the letters indicates which parts of the polygons correspond to each other.

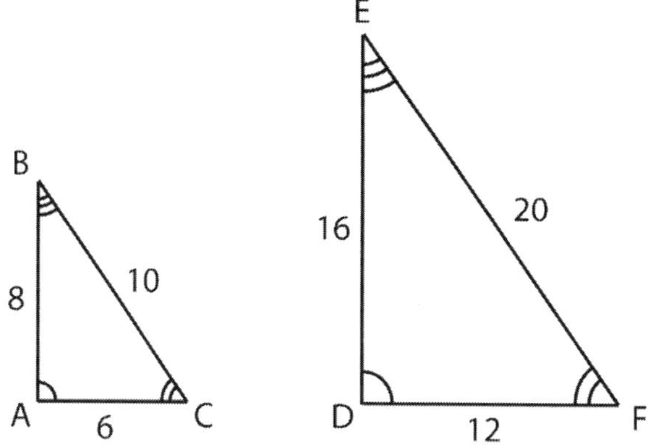

Note that all congruent figures are also similar, but not all similar figures are congruent.

Review Video: Congruent Shapes
Visit mometrix.com/academy and enter code: 492281

LINE OF SYMMETRY

A line that divides a figure or object into congruent parts that are mirror images of each other across the line is called a **line of symmetry**. An object may have no lines of symmetry, one line of symmetry, or multiple (i.e., more than one) lines of symmetry.

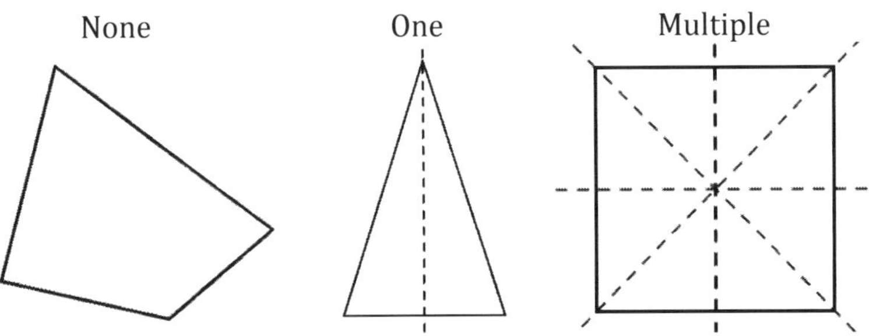

Review Video: Symmetry
Visit mometrix.com/academy and enter code: 528106

TRIANGLES

A triangle is a three-sided figure with the sum of its interior angles being 180°. The **perimeter of any triangle** is found by summing the three side lengths; $P = a + b + c$. For an equilateral triangle, this is the same as $P = 3a$, where a is any side length, since all three sides are the same length.

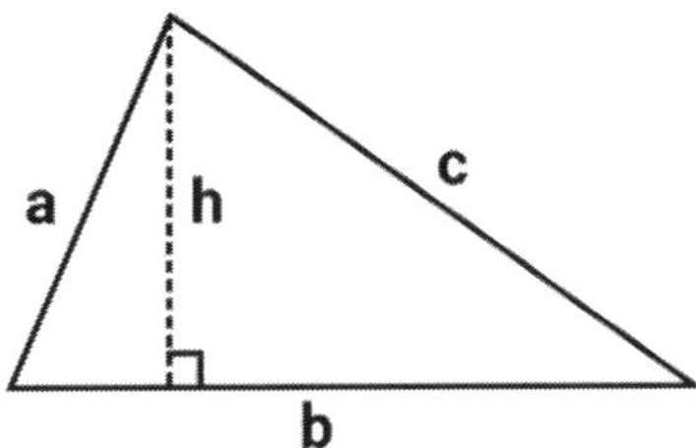

Review Video: Proof that a Triangle is 180 Degrees
Visit mometrix.com/academy and enter code: 687591

Review Video: Area and Perimeter of a Triangle
Visit mometrix.com/academy and enter code: 853779

The **area of any triangle** can be found by taking half the product of one side length referred to as the base, often given the variable b and the perpendicular distance from that side to the opposite vertex called the altitude or height and given the variable h. In equation form that is $A = \frac{1}{2}bh$. Another formula that works for any triangle is $A = \sqrt{s(s-a)(s-b)(s-c)}$, where s is the semiperimeter: $\frac{a+b+c}{2}$, and a, b, and c are the lengths of the three sides. Special cases include isosceles triangles, $A = \frac{1}{2}b\sqrt{a^2 - \frac{b^2}{4}}$, where b is the unique side and a is the length of one of the two congruent sides, and equilateral triangles, $A = \frac{\sqrt{3}}{4}a^2$, where a is the length of a side.

Review Video: Area of Any Triangle
Visit mometrix.com/academy and enter code: 138510

Mathematics

PARTS OF A TRIANGLE

An **altitude** of a triangle is a line segment drawn from one vertex perpendicular to the opposite side. In the diagram that follows, $\overline{BE}$, $\overline{AD}$, and $\overline{CF}$ are altitudes. The length of an altitude is also called the height of the triangle. The three altitudes in a triangle are always concurrent. The point of concurrency of the altitudes of a triangle, O, is called the **orthocenter**. Note that in an obtuse triangle, the orthocenter will be outside the triangle, and in a right triangle, the orthocenter is the vertex of the right angle.

A **median** of a triangle is a line segment drawn from one vertex to the midpoint of the opposite side. In the diagram that follows, $\overline{BH}$, $\overline{AG}$, and $\overline{CI}$ are medians. This is not the same as the altitude, except the altitude to the base of an isosceles triangle and all three altitudes of an equilateral triangle. The point of concurrency of the medians of a triangle, T, is called the **centroid**. This is the same point as the orthocenter only in an equilateral triangle. Unlike the orthocenter, the centroid is always inside the triangle. The centroid can also be considered the exact center of the triangle. Any shape triangle can be perfectly balanced on a tip placed at the centroid. The centroid is also the point that is two-thirds the distance from the vertex to the opposite side.

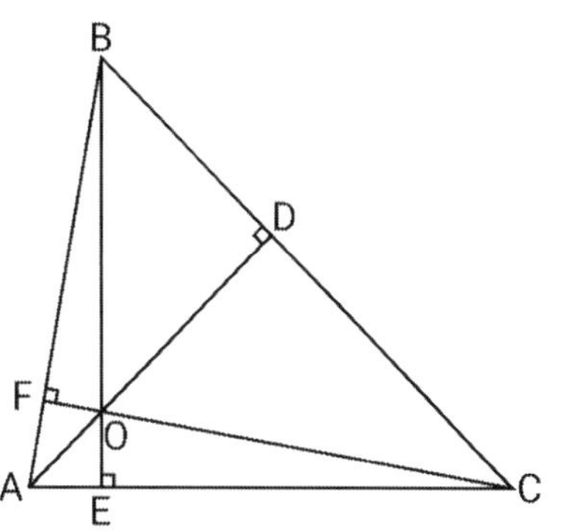

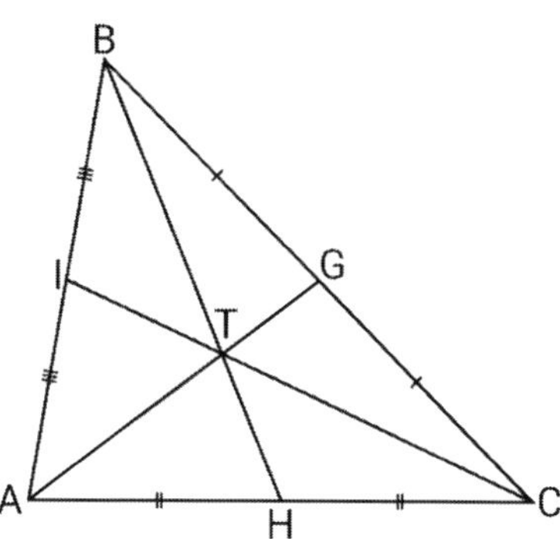

Review Video: Centroid, Incenter, Circumcenter, and Orthocenter
Visit mometrix.com/academy and enter code: 598260

TRIANGLE PROPERTIES

CLASSIFICATIONS OF TRIANGLES

A **scalene triangle** is a triangle with no congruent sides. A scalene triangle will also have three angles of different measures. The angle with the largest measure is opposite the longest side, and the angle with the smallest measure is opposite the shortest side. An **acute triangle** is a triangle whose three angles are all less than 90°. If two of the angles are equal, the acute triangle is also an **isosceles triangle**. An isosceles triangle will also have two congruent angles opposite the two congruent sides. If the three angles are all equal, the acute triangle is also an **equilateral triangle**. An equilateral triangle will also have three congruent angles, each 60°. All equilateral triangles are also acute triangles. An **obtuse triangle** is a triangle with exactly one angle greater than 90°. The other two angles may or may not be equal. If the two remaining angles are equal, the obtuse triangle is also an isosceles triangle. A **right triangle** is a triangle with exactly one angle equal to 90°. All right triangles follow the Pythagorean theorem. A right triangle can never be acute or obtuse.

The table below illustrates how each descriptor places a different restriction on the triangle:

Angles / Sides	Acute: All angles < 90°	Obtuse: One angle > 90°	Right: One angle = 90°
Scalene: No equal side lengths	$90° > \angle a > \angle b > \angle c$ $x > y > z$	$\angle a > 90° > \angle b > \angle c$ $x > y > z$	$90° = \angle a > \angle b > \angle c$ $x > y > z$
Isosceles: Two equal side lengths	$90° > \angle a, \angle b, or\ \angle c$ $\angle b = \angle c, \quad y = z$	$\angle a > 90° > \angle b = \angle c$ $x > y = z$	$\angle a = 90°$ $\angle b = \angle c = 45°$ $x > y = z$
Equilateral: Three equal side lengths	$60° = \angle a = \angle b = \angle c$ $x = y = z$		

Review Video: Introduction to Types of Triangles
Visit mometrix.com/academy and enter code: 511711

General Rules for Triangles

The **triangle inequality theorem** states that the sum of the measures of any two sides of a triangle is always greater than the measure of the third side. If the sum of the measures of two sides were equal to the third side, a triangle would be impossible because the two sides would lie flat across the third side and there would be no vertex. If the sum of the measures of two of the sides was less than the third side, a closed figure would be impossible because the two shortest sides would never meet. In other words, for a triangle with sides lengths A, B, and C: $A + B > C$, $B + C > A$, and $A + C > B$.

The sum of the measures of the interior angles of a triangle is always 180°. Therefore, a triangle can never have more than one angle greater than or equal to 90°.

In any triangle, the angles opposite congruent sides are congruent, and the sides opposite congruent angles are congruent. The largest angle is always opposite the longest side, and the smallest angle is always opposite the shortest side.

The line segment that joins the midpoints of any two sides of a triangle is always parallel to the third side and exactly half the length of the third side.

> **Review Video: General Rules (Triangle Inequality Theorem)**
> Visit mometrix.com/academy and enter code: 166488

Similarity and Congruence Rules

Similar triangles are triangles whose corresponding angles are equal and whose corresponding sides are proportional. Represented by AAA. Similar triangles whose corresponding sides are congruent are also congruent triangles.

Triangles can be shown to be **congruent** in 5 ways:

- **SSS**: Three sides of one triangle are congruent to the three corresponding sides of the second triangle.
- **SAS**: Two sides and the included angle (the angle formed by those two sides) of one triangle are congruent to the corresponding two sides and included angle of the second triangle.
- **ASA**: Two angles and the included side (the side that joins the two angles) of one triangle are congruent to the corresponding two angles and included side of the second triangle.
- **AAS**: Two angles and a non-included side of one triangle are congruent to the corresponding two angles and non-included side of the second triangle.
- **HL**: The hypotenuse and leg of one right triangle are congruent to the corresponding hypotenuse and leg of the second right triangle.

> **Review Video: Similar Triangles**
> Visit mometrix.com/academy and enter code: 398538

Quadrilaterals

A **quadrilateral** is a closed two-dimensional geometric figure that has four straight sides. The sum of the interior angles of any quadrilateral is 360°.

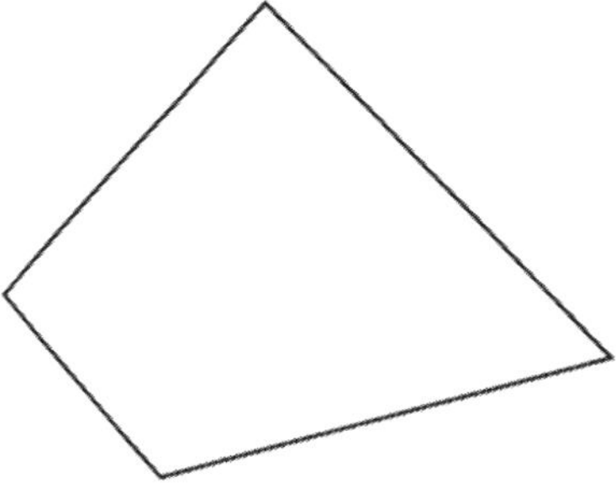

> **Review Video: Diagonals of Parallelograms, Rectangles, and Rhombi**
> Visit mometrix.com/academy and enter code: 320040

KITE

A **kite** is a quadrilateral with two pairs of adjacent sides that are congruent. A result of this is perpendicular diagonals. A kite can be concave or convex and has one line of symmetry.

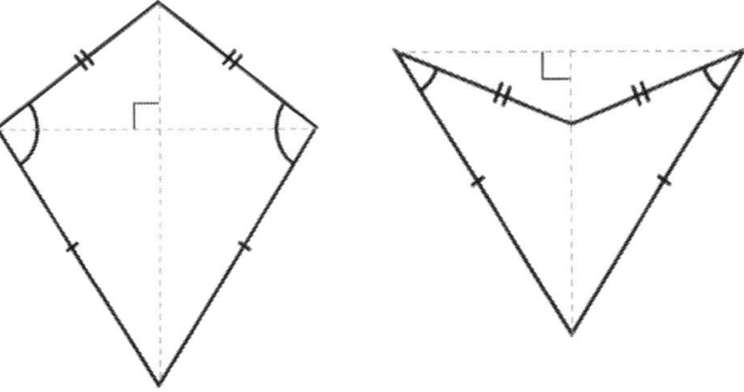

TRAPEZOID

Trapezoid: A trapezoid is defined as a quadrilateral that has at least one pair of parallel sides. There are no rules for the second pair of sides. So, there are no rules for the diagonals and no lines of symmetry for a trapezoid.

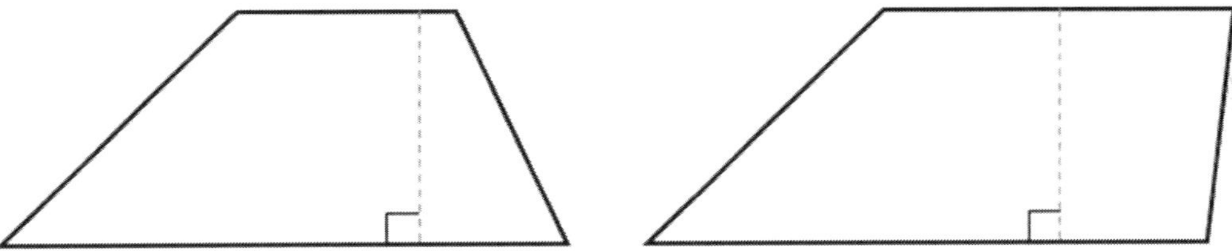

The **area of a trapezoid** is found by the formula $A = \frac{1}{2}h(b_1 + b_2)$, where h is the height (segment joining and perpendicular to the parallel bases), and b_1 and b_2 are the two parallel sides (bases). Do not use one of the other two sides as the height unless that side is also perpendicular to the parallel bases.

The **perimeter of a trapezoid** is found by the formula $P = a + b_1 + c + b_2$, where a, b_1, c, and b_2 are the four sides of the trapezoid.

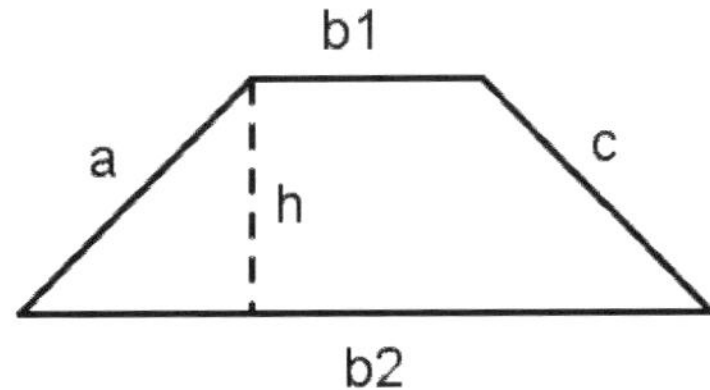

Review Video: Area and Perimeter of a Trapezoid
Visit mometrix.com/academy and enter code: 587523

Isosceles trapezoid: A trapezoid with equal base angles. This gives rise to other properties including: the two nonparallel sides have the same length, the two non-base angles are also equal, and there is one line of symmetry through the midpoints of the parallel sides.

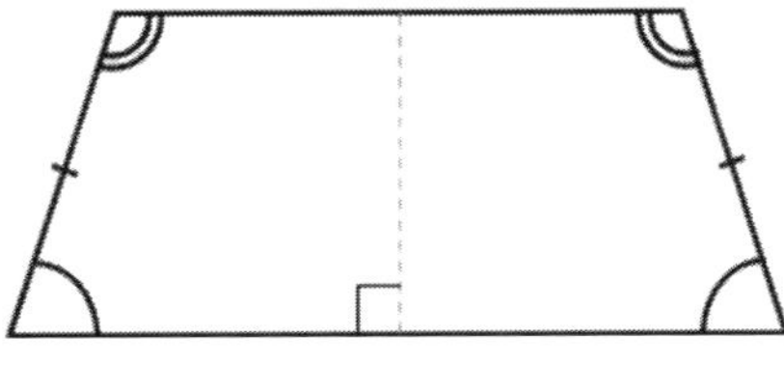

Parallelogram

A **parallelogram** is a quadrilateral that has two pairs of opposite parallel sides. As such it is a special type of trapezoid. The sides that are parallel are also congruent. The opposite interior angles are always congruent, and the consecutive interior angles are supplementary. The diagonals of a parallelogram divide each other. Each diagonal divides the parallelogram into two congruent triangles. A parallelogram has no line of symmetry, but does have 180-degree rotational symmetry about the midpoint.

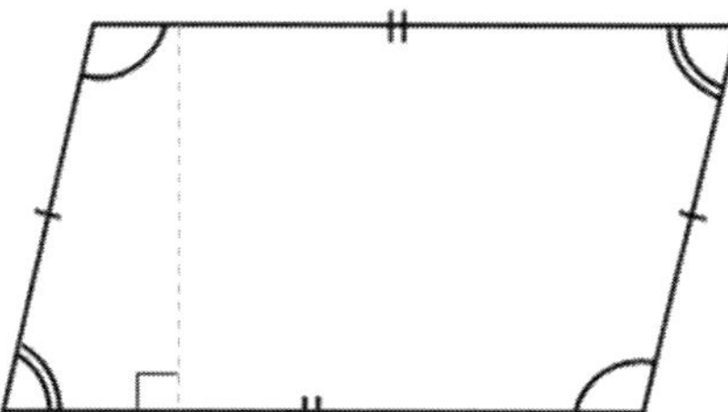

The **area of a parallelogram** is found by the formula $A = bh$, where b is the length of the base, and h is the height. Note that the base and height correspond to the length and width in a rectangle, so this formula would apply to rectangles as well. Do not confuse the height of a parallelogram with the length of the second side. The two are only the same measure in the case of a rectangle.

The **perimeter of a parallelogram** is found by the formula $P = 2a + 2b$ or $P = 2(a + b)$, where a and b are the lengths of the two sides.

Review Video: Area and Perimeter of a Parallelogram
Visit mometrix.com/academy and enter code: 718313

Rectangle

A **rectangle** is a quadrilateral with four right angles. All rectangles are parallelograms and trapezoids, but not all parallelograms or trapezoids are rectangles. The diagonals of a rectangle are congruent. Rectangles have two lines of symmetry (through each pair of opposing midpoints) and 180-degree rotational symmetry about the midpoint.

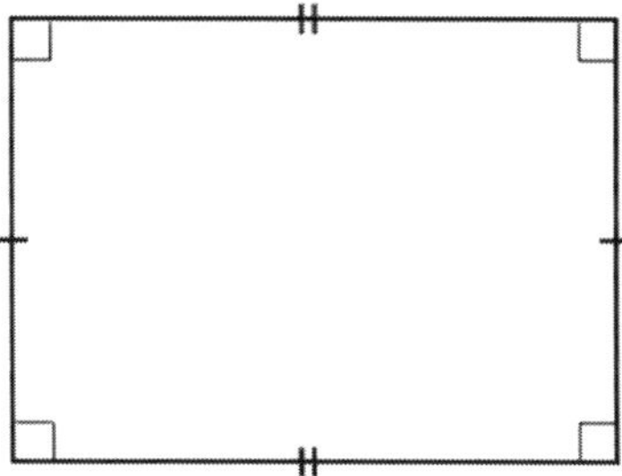

The **area of a rectangle** is found by the formula $A = lw$, where A is the area of the rectangle, l is the length (usually considered to be the longer side) and w is the width (usually considered to be the shorter side). The numbers for l and w are interchangeable.

The **perimeter of a rectangle** is found by the formula $P = 2l + 2w$ or $P = 2(l + w)$, where l is the length, and w is the width. It may be easier to add the length and width first and then double the result, as in the second formula.

Rhombus

A **rhombus** is a quadrilateral with four congruent sides. All rhombuses are parallelograms and kites; thus, they inherit all the properties of both types of quadrilaterals. The diagonals of a rhombus are perpendicular to each other. Rhombi have two lines of symmetry (along each of the diagonals) and 180° rotational symmetry. The

area of a rhombus is half the product of the diagonals: $A = \frac{d_1 d_2}{2}$ and the perimeter of a rhombus is: $P = 2\sqrt{(d_1)^2 + (d_2)^2}$.

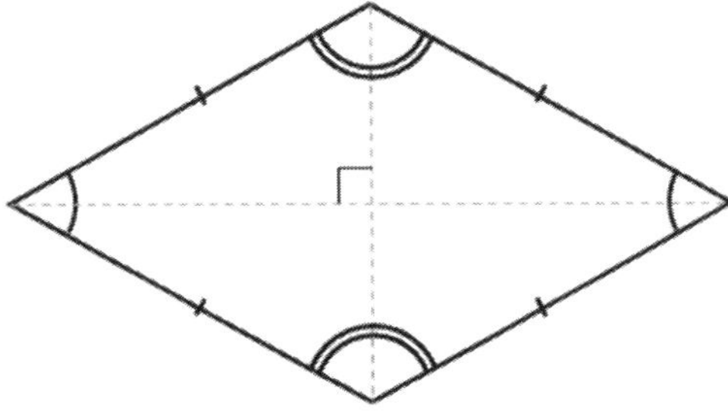

SQUARE

A **square** is a quadrilateral with four right angles and four congruent sides. Squares satisfy the criteria of all other types of quadrilaterals. The diagonals of a square are congruent and perpendicular to each other. Squares have four lines of symmetry (through each pair of opposing midpoints and along each of the diagonals) as well as 90° rotational symmetry about the midpoint.

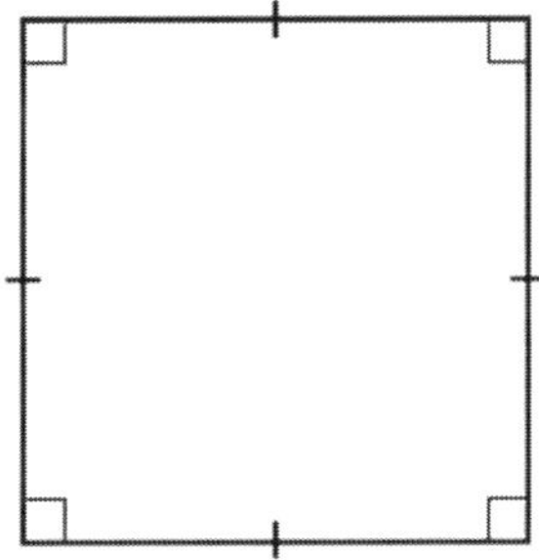

The **area of a square** is found by using the formula $A = s^2$, where s is the length of one side. The **perimeter of a square** is found by using the formula $P = 4s$, where s is the length of one side. Because all four sides are equal in a square, it is faster to multiply the length of one side by 4 than to add the same number four times. You could use the formulas for rectangles and get the same answer.

Review Video: Area and Perimeter of Rectangles and Squares
Visit mometrix.com/academy and enter code: 428109

Hierarchy of Quadrilaterals

The hierarchy of quadrilaterals is as follows:

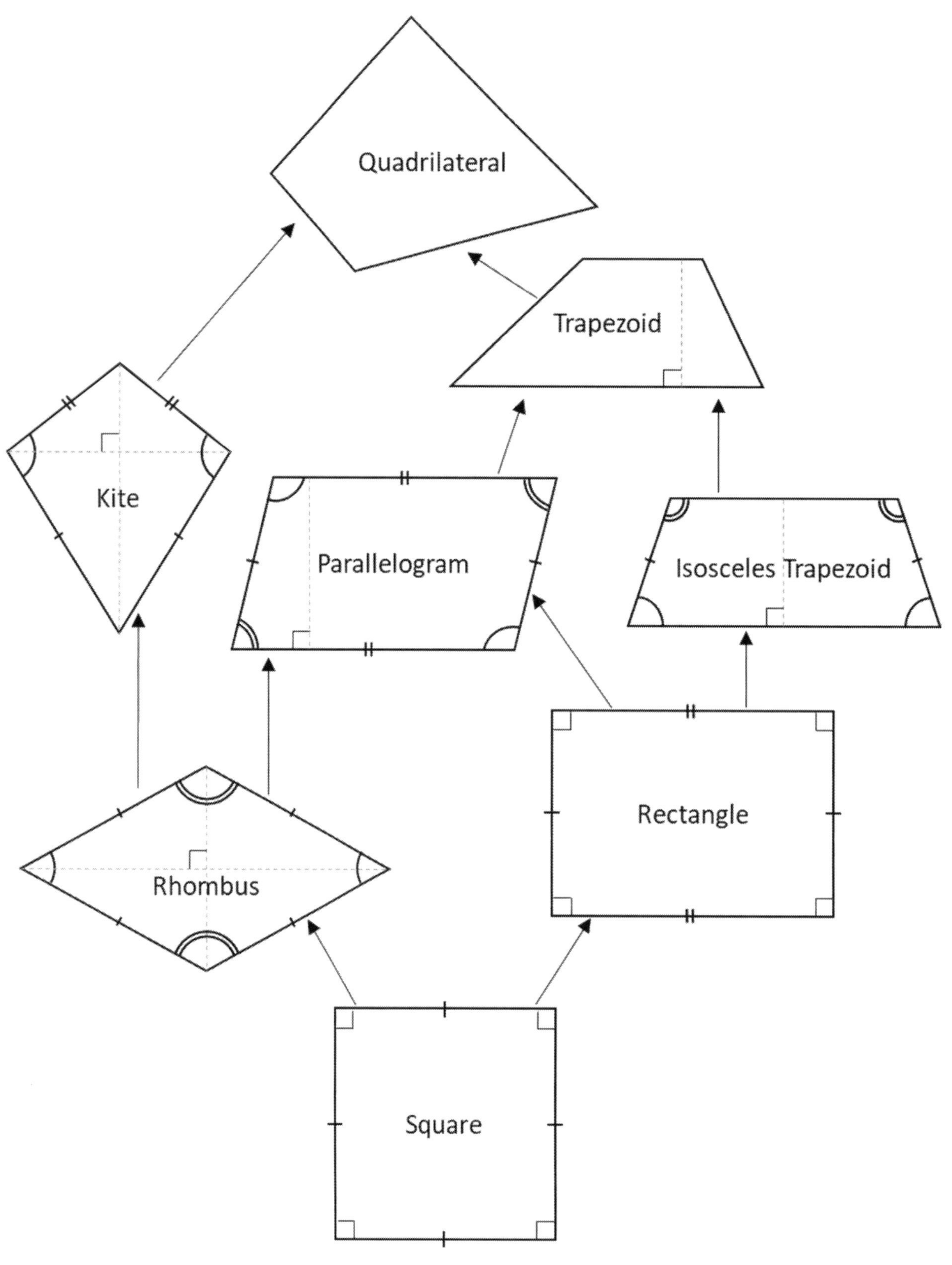

CIRCLES

The **center** of a circle is the single point from which every point on the circle is **equidistant**. The **radius** is a line segment that joins the center of the circle and any one point on the circle. All radii of a circle are equal. Circles that have the same center but not the same length of radii are **concentric**. The **diameter** is a line segment that passes through the center of the circle and has both endpoints on the circle. The length of the diameter is exactly twice the length of the radius. Point O in the diagram below is the center of the circle, segments $\overline{OX}$, $\overline{OY}$, and $\overline{OZ}$ are radii; and segment $\overline{XZ}$ is a diameter.

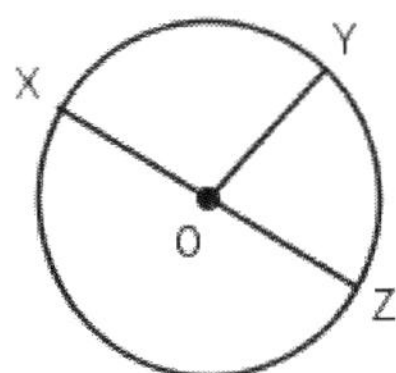

Review Video: Points of a Circle
Visit mometrix.com/academy and enter code: 420746

Review Video: Diameter, Radius, and Circumference
Visit mometrix.com/academy and enter code: 448988

The **area of a circle** is found by the formula $A = \pi r^2$, where r is the length of the radius. If the diameter of the circle is given, remember to divide it in half to get the length of the radius before proceeding.

The **circumference** of a circle is found by the formula $C = 2\pi r$, where r is the radius. Again, remember to convert the diameter if you are given that measure rather than the radius.

Review Video: Area and Circumference of a Circle
Visit mometrix.com/academy and enter code: 243015

INSCRIBED AND CIRCUMSCRIBED FIGURES

These terms can both be used to describe a given arrangement of figures, depending on perspective. If each of the vertices of figure A lie on figure B, then it can be said that figure A is **inscribed** in figure B, but it can also be said that figure B is **circumscribed** about figure A. The following table and examples help to illustrate the concept. Note that the figures cannot both be circles, as they would be completely overlapping and neither would be inscribed or circumscribed.

Given	Description	Equivalent Description	Figures
Each of the sides of a pentagon is tangent to a circle	The circle is inscribed in the pentagon	The pentagon is circumscribed about the circle	
Each of the vertices of a pentagon lie on a circle	The pentagon is inscribed in the circle	The circle is circumscribed about the pentagon	

TRANSFORMATIONS

ROTATION

A **rotation** is a transformation that turns a figure around a point called the **center of rotation**, which can lie anywhere in the plane. If a line is drawn from a point on a figure to the center of rotation, and another line is

Mathematics

drawn from the center to the rotated image of that point, the angle between the two lines is the **angle of rotation**. The vertex of the angle of rotation is the center of rotation.

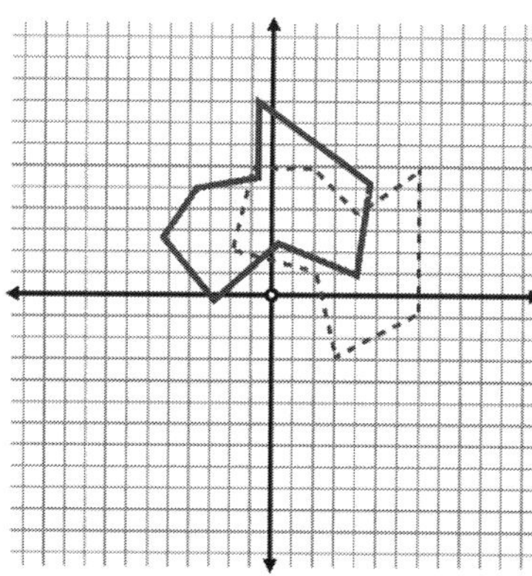

Review Video: Rotation
Visit mometrix.com/academy and enter code: 602600

Translation and Dilation

A **translation** is a transformation which slides a figure from one position in the plane to another position in the plane. The original figure and the translated figure have the same size, shape, and orientation. A **dilation** is a transformation which proportionally stretches or shrinks a figure by a **scale factor**. The dilated image is the same shape and orientation as the original image but a different size. A polygon and its dilated image are similar.

Translation

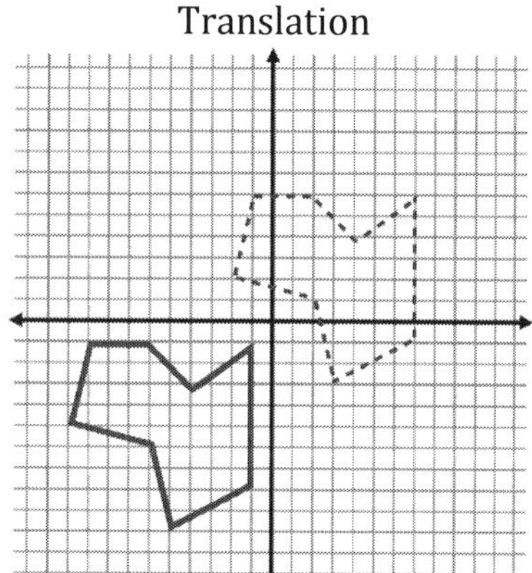

Dilation

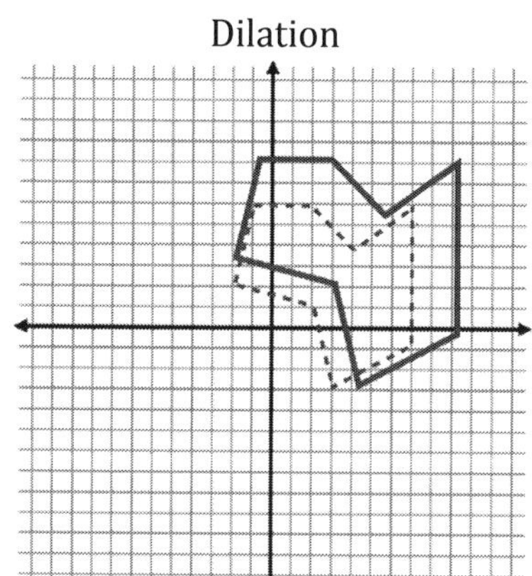

Review Video: Translation
Visit mometrix.com/academy and enter code: 718628

Review Video: Dilation
Visit mometrix.com/academy and enter code: 471630

A **reflection of a figure over a line** (a "flip") creates a congruent image that is the same distance from the line as the original figure but on the opposite side. The **line of reflection** is the perpendicular bisector of any line segment drawn from a point on the original figure to its reflected image (unless the point and its reflected image happen to be the same point, which happens when a figure is reflected over one of its own sides). A **reflection of a figure over a point** (an inversion) in two dimensions is the same as the rotation of the figure 180° about that point. The image of the figure is congruent to the original figure. The **point of reflection** is the midpoint of a line segment which connects a point in the figure to its image (unless the point and its reflected image happen to be the same point, which happens when a figure is reflected in one of its own points).

Reflection of a figure over a line

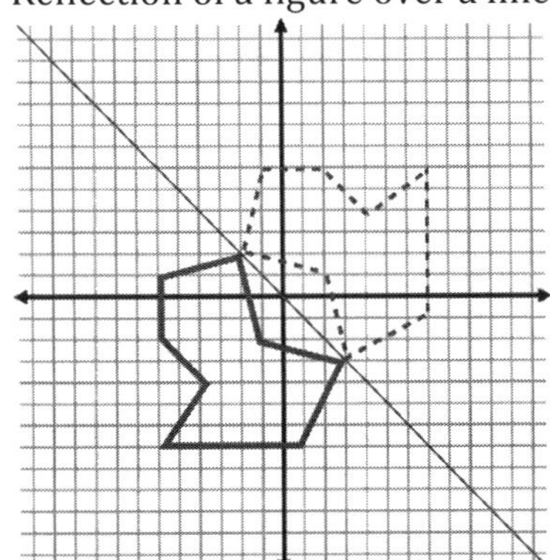

Reflection of a figure over a point

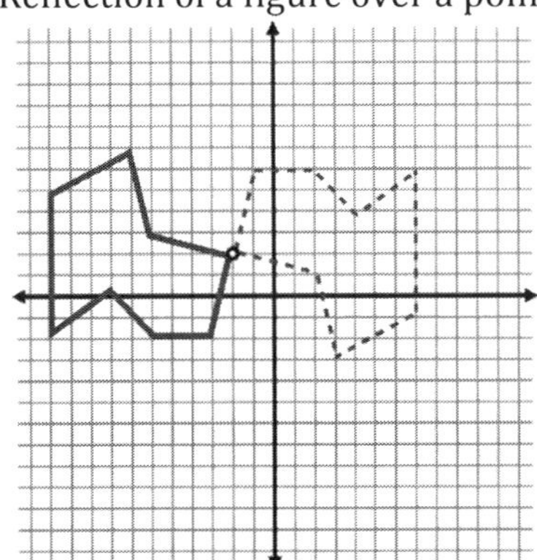

Review Video: Reflection
Visit mometrix.com/academy and enter code: 955068

3D Shapes

Solids

The **surface area of a solid object** is the area of all sides or exterior surfaces. For objects such as prisms and pyramids, a further distinction is made between base surface area (B) and lateral surface area (LA). For a prism, the total surface area (SA) is $SA = LA + 2B$. For a pyramid or cone, the total surface area is $SA = LA + B$.

The **surface area of a sphere** can be found by the formula $A = 4\pi r^2$, where r is the radius. The volume is given by the formula $V = \frac{4}{3}\pi r^3$, where r is the radius. Both quantities are generally given in terms of π.

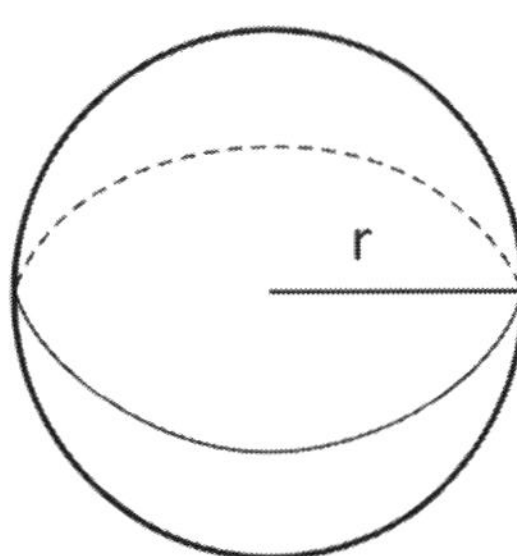

Review Video: Volume and Surface Area of a Sphere
Visit mometrix.com/academy and enter code: 786928

Review Video: How to Calculate the Volume of 3D Objects
Visit mometrix.com/academy and enter code: 163343

The **volume of any prism** is found by the formula $V = Bh$, where B is the area of the base, and h is the height (perpendicular distance between the bases). The surface area of any prism is the sum of the areas of both bases and all sides. It can be calculated as $SA = 2B + Ph$, where P is the perimeter of the base.

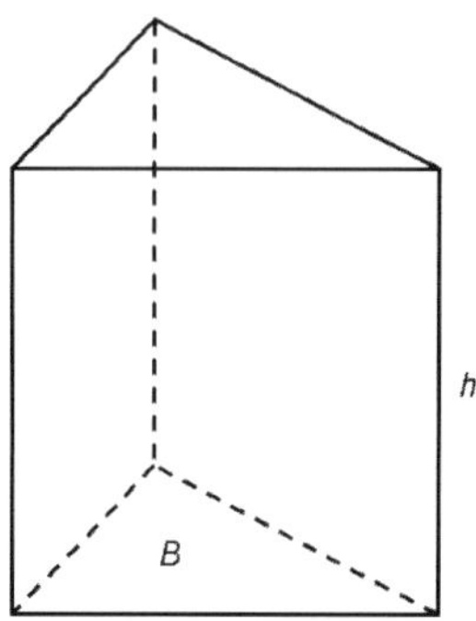

Review Video: Volume and Surface Area of a Prism
Visit mometrix.com/academy and enter code: 420158

For a **rectangular prism**, the volume can be found by the formula $V = lwh$, where V is the volume, l is the length, w is the width, and h is the height. The surface area can be calculated as $SA = 2lw + 2hl + 2wh$ or $SA = 2(lw + hl + wh)$.

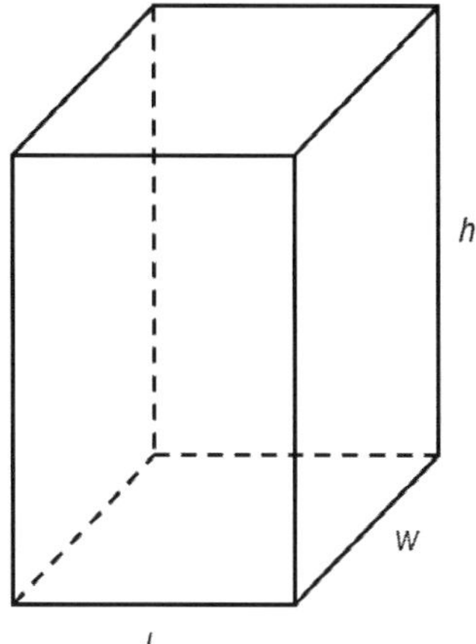

Review Video: Volume and Surface Area of a Rectangular Prism
Visit mometrix.com/academy and enter code: 282814

The **volume of a cube** can be found by the formula $V = s^3$, where s is the length of a side. The surface area of a cube is calculated as $SA = 6s^2$, where SA is the total surface area and s is the length of a side. These formulas are the same as the ones used for the volume and surface area of a rectangular prism, but simplified since all three quantities (length, width, and height) are the same.

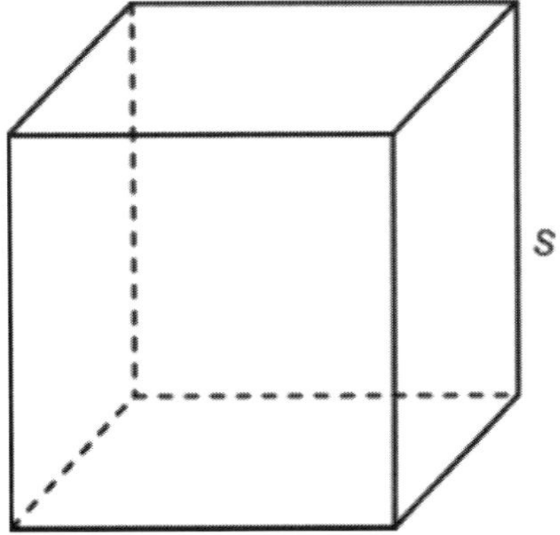

Review Video: Volume and Surface Area of a Cube
Visit mometrix.com/academy and enter code: 664455

The **volume of a cylinder** can be calculated by the formula $V = \pi r^2 h$, where r is the radius, and h is the height. The surface area of a cylinder can be found by the formula $SA = 2\pi r^2 + 2\pi rh$. The first term is the base area multiplied by two, and the second term is the perimeter of the base multiplied by the height.

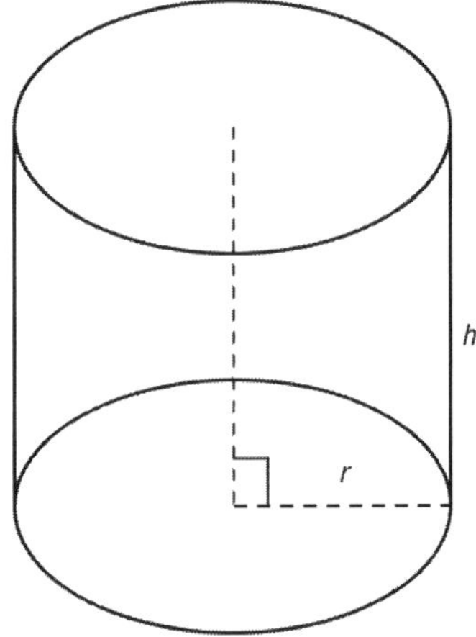

Review Video: Volume and Surface Area of a Right Circular Cylinder
Visit mometrix.com/academy and enter code: 226463

The **volume of a pyramid** is found by the formula $V = \frac{1}{3}Bh$, where B is the area of the base, and h is the height (perpendicular distance from the vertex to the base). Notice this formula is the same as $\frac{1}{3}$ times the volume of a prism. Like a prism, the base of a pyramid can be any shape.

Finding the **surface area of a pyramid** is not as simple as the other shapes we've looked at thus far. If the pyramid is a right pyramid, meaning the base is a regular polygon and the vertex is directly over the center of that polygon, the surface area can be calculated as $SA = B + \frac{1}{2}Ph_s$, where P is the perimeter of the base, and h_s

Mathematics

is the slant height (distance from the vertex to the midpoint of one side of the base). If the pyramid is irregular, the area of each triangle side must be calculated individually and then summed, along with the base.

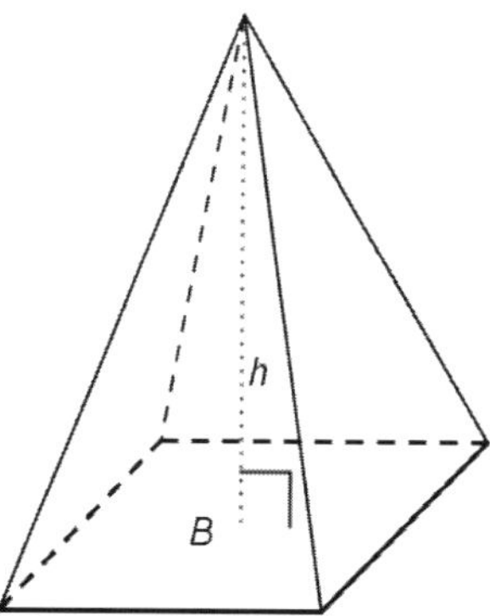

Review Video: Volume and Surface Area of a Pyramid
Visit mometrix.com/academy and enter code: 621932

The **volume of a cone** is found by the formula $V = \frac{1}{3}\pi r^2 h$, where r is the radius, and h is the height. Notice this is the same as $\frac{1}{3}$ times the volume of a cylinder. The surface area can be calculated as $SA = \pi r^2 + \pi r s$, where s is the slant height. The slant height can be calculated using the Pythagorean theorem to be $\sqrt{r^2 + h^2}$, so the surface area formula can also be written as $SA = \pi r^2 + \pi r\sqrt{r^2 + h^2}$.

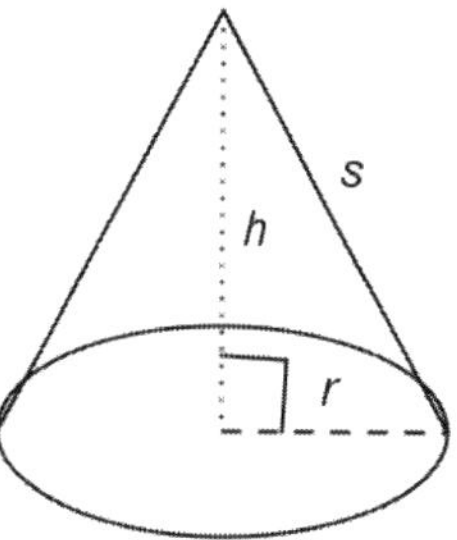

Review Video: Volume and Surface Area of a Right Circular Cone
Visit mometrix.com/academy and enter code: 573574

Data Analysis, Probability, and Statistics

Probability

Probability is the likelihood of a certain outcome occurring for a given event. An **event** is any situation that produces a result. It could be something as simple as flipping a coin or as complex as launching a rocket. Determining the probability of an outcome for an event can be equally simple or complex. As such, there are specific terms used in the study of probability that need to be understood:

- **Compound event**—an event that involves two or more independent events (rolling a pair of dice and taking the sum)
- **Desired outcome** (or success)—an outcome that meets a particular set of criteria (a roll of 1 or 2 if we are looking for numbers less than 3)
- **Independent events**—two or more events whose outcomes do not affect one another (two coins tossed at the same time)

- **Dependent events**—two or more events whose outcomes affect one another (two cards drawn consecutively from the same deck)
- **Certain outcome**—probability of outcome is 100% or 1
- **Impossible outcome**—probability of outcome is 0% or 0
- **Mutually exclusive outcomes**—two or more outcomes whose criteria cannot all be satisfied in a single event (a coin coming up heads and tails on the same toss)
- **Random variable**—refers to all possible outcomes of a single event which may be discrete or continuous.

Review Video: Intro to Probability
Visit mometrix.com/academy and enter code: 212374

Sample Space

The total set of all possible results of a test or experiment is called a **sample space**, or sometimes a universal sample space. The sample space, represented by one of the variables S, Ω, or U (for universal sample space) has individual elements called outcomes. Other terms for outcome that may be used interchangeably include elementary outcome, simple event, or sample point. The number of outcomes in a given sample space could be infinite or finite, and some tests may yield multiple unique sample sets. For example, tests conducted by drawing playing cards from a standard deck would have one sample space of the card values, another sample space of the card suits, and a third sample space of suit-denomination combinations. For most tests, the sample spaces considered will be finite.

An **event**, represented by the variable E, is a portion of a sample space. It may be one outcome or a group of outcomes from the same sample space. If an event occurs, then the test or experiment will generate an outcome that satisfies the requirement of that event. For example, given a standard deck of 52 playing cards as the sample space, and defining the event as the collection of face cards, then the event will occur if the card drawn is a J, Q, or K. If any other card is drawn, the event is said to have not occurred.

For every sample space, each possible outcome has a specific likelihood, or probability, that it will occur. The probability measure, also called the **distribution**, is a function that assigns a real number probability, from zero to one, to each outcome. For a probability measure to be accurate, every outcome must have a real number probability measure that is greater than or equal to zero and less than or equal to one. Also, the probability measure of the sample space must equal one, and the probability measure of the union of multiple outcomes must equal the sum of the individual probability measures.

Probabilities of events are expressed as real numbers from zero to one. They give a numerical value to the chance that a particular event will occur. The probability of an event occurring is the sum of the probabilities of the individual elements of that event. For example, in a standard deck of 52 playing cards as the sample space and the collection of face cards as the event, the probability of drawing a specific face card is $\frac{1}{52} = 0.019$, but the probability of drawing any one of the twelve face cards is $12(0.019) = 0.228$. Note that rounding of numbers can generate different results. If you multiplied 12 by the fraction $\frac{1}{52}$ before converting to a decimal, you would get the answer $\frac{12}{52} = 0.231$.

Theoretical and Experimental Probability

Theoretical probability can usually be determined without actually performing the event. The likelihood of an outcome occurring, or the probability of an outcome occurring, is given by the formula:

$$P(A) = \frac{\text{Number of acceptable outcomes}}{\text{Number of possible outcomes}}$$

Mathematics

Note that $P(A)$ is the probability of an outcome A occurring, and each outcome is just as likely to occur as any other outcome. If each outcome has the same probability of occurring as every other possible outcome, the outcomes are said to be equally likely to occur. The total number of acceptable outcomes must be less than or equal to the total number of possible outcomes. If the two are equal, then the outcome is certain to occur and the probability is 1. If the number of acceptable outcomes is zero, then the outcome is impossible and the probability is 0. For example, if there are 20 marbles in a bag and 5 are red, then the theoretical probability of randomly selecting a red marble is 5 out of 20, $\left(\frac{5}{20} = \frac{1}{4}, 0.25, \text{or } 25\%\right)$.

If the theoretical probability is unknown or too complicated to calculate, it can be estimated by an experimental probability. **Experimental probability**, also called empirical probability, is an estimate of the likelihood of a certain outcome based on repeated experiments or collected data. In other words, while theoretical probability is based on what *should* happen, experimental probability is based on what *has* happened. Experimental probability is calculated in the same way as theoretical probability, except that actual outcomes are used instead of possible outcomes. The more experiments performed or datapoints gathered, the better the estimate should be.

Theoretical and experimental probability do not always line up with one another. Theoretical probability says that out of 20 coin-tosses, 10 should be heads. However, if we were actually to toss 20 coins, we might record just 5 heads. This doesn't mean that our theoretical probability is incorrect; it just means that this particular experiment had results that were different from what was predicted. A practical application of empirical probability is the insurance industry. There are no set functions that define lifespan, health, or safety. Insurance companies look at factors from hundreds of thousands of individuals to find patterns that they then use to set the formulas for insurance premiums.

Review Video: Empirical Probability
Visit mometrix.com/academy and enter code: 513468

Objective and Subjective Probability

Objective probability is based on mathematical formulas and documented evidence. Examples of objective probability include raffles or lottery drawings where there is a pre-determined number of possible outcomes and a predetermined number of outcomes that correspond to an event. Other cases of objective probability include probabilities of rolling dice, flipping coins, or drawing cards. Most gambling games are based on objective probability.

In contrast, **subjective probability** is based on personal or professional feelings and judgments. Often, there is a lot of guesswork following extensive research. Areas where subjective probability is applicable include sales trends and business expenses. Attractions set admission prices based on subjective probabilities of attendance based on varying admission rates in an effort to maximize their profit.

Complement of an Event

Sometimes it may be easier to calculate the possibility of something not happening, or the **complement of an event**. Represented by the symbol $\bar{A}$, the complement of A is the probability that event A does not happen. When you know the probability of event A occurring, you can use the formula $P(\bar{A}) = 1 - P(A)$, where $P(\bar{A})$ is the probability of event A not occurring, and $P(A)$ is the probability of event A occurring.

Addition Rule

The **addition rule** for probability is used for finding the probability of a compound event. Use the formula $P(A \cup B) = P(A) + P(B) - P(A \cap B)$, where $P(A \cap B)$ is the probability of both events occurring to find the probability of a compound event. The probability of both events occurring at the same time must be subtracted to eliminate any overlap in the first two probabilities.

Conditional Probability

Given two events A and B, the **conditional probability** $P(A|B)$ is the probability that event A will occur, given that event B has occurred. The conditional probability cannot be calculated simply from $P(A)$ and $P(B)$; these probabilities alone do not give sufficient information to determine the conditional probability. It can, however, be determined if you are also given the probability of the intersection of events A and B, $P(A \cap B)$, the probability that events A and B both occur. Specifically, $P(A|B) = \frac{P(A \cap B)}{P(B)}$. For instance, suppose you have a jar containing two red marbles and two blue marbles, and you draw two marbles at random. Consider event A being the event that the first marble drawn is red, and event B being the event that the second marble drawn is blue. If we want to find the probability that B occurs given that A occurred, $P(B|A)$, then we can compute it using the fact that $P(A)$ is $\frac{1}{2}$, and $P(A \cap B)$ is $\frac{1}{3}$. (The latter may not be obvious, but may be determined by finding the product of $\frac{1}{2}$ and $\frac{2}{3}$). Therefore $P(B|A) = \frac{P(A \cap B)}{P(A)} = \frac{1/3}{1/2} = \frac{2}{3}$.

Conditional Probability in Everyday Situations

Conditional probability often arises in everyday situations in, for example, estimating the risk or benefit of certain activities. The conditional probability of having a heart attack given that you exercise daily may be smaller than the overall probability of having a heart attack. The conditional probability of having lung cancer given that you are a smoker is larger than the overall probability of having lung cancer. Note that changing the order of the conditional probability changes the meaning: the conditional probability of having lung cancer given that you are a smoker is a very different thing from the probability of being a smoker given that you have lung cancer. In an extreme case, suppose that a certain rare disease is caused only by eating a certain food, but even then, it is unlikely. Then the conditional probability of having that disease given that you eat the dangerous food is nonzero but low, but the conditional probability of having eaten that food given that you have the disease is 100%!

Review Video: Conditional Probability
Visit mometrix.com/academy and enter code: 397924

Independence

The conditional probability $P(A|B)$ is the probability that event A will occur given that event B occurs. If the two events are independent, we do not expect that whether or not event B occurs should have any effect on whether or not event A occurs. In other words, we expect $P(A|B) = P(A)$.

This can be proven using the usual equations for conditional probability and the joint probability of independent events. The conditional probability $P(A|B) = \frac{P(A \cap B)}{P(B)}$. If A and B are independent, then $P(A \cap B) = P(A)P(B)$. So $P(A|B) = \frac{P(A)P(B)}{P(B)} = P(A)$. By similar reasoning, if A and B are independent then $P(B|A) = P(B)$.

Multiplication Rule

The **multiplication rule** can be used to find the probability of two independent events occurring using the formula $P(A \cap B) = P(A) \times P(B)$, where $P(A \cap B)$ is the probability of two independent events occurring, $P(A)$ is the probability of the first event occurring, and $P(B)$ is the probability of the second event occurring.

The multiplication rule can also be used to find the probability of two dependent events occurring using the formula $P(A \cap B) = P(A) \times P(B|A)$, where $P(A \cap B)$ is the probability of two dependent events occurring and $P(B|A)$ is the probability of the second event occurring after the first event has already occurred.

Mathematics

Use a **combination of the multiplication** rule and the rule of complements to find the probability that at least one outcome of the element will occur. This is given by the general formula $P(\text{at least one event occurring}) = 1 - P(\text{no outcomes occurring})$. For example, to find the probability that at least one even number will show when a pair of dice is rolled, find the probability that two odd numbers will be rolled (no even numbers) and subtract from one. You can always use a tree diagram or make a chart to list the possible outcomes when the sample space is small, such as in the dice-rolling example, but in most cases it will be much faster to use the multiplication and complement formulas.

Review Video: Multiplication Rule
Visit mometrix.com/academy and enter code: 782598

Union and Intersection of Two Sets of Outcomes

If A and B are each a set of elements or outcomes from an experiment, then the **union** (symbol ∪) of the two sets is the set of elements found in set A or set B. For example, if $A = \{2, 3, 4\}$ and $B = \{3, 4, 5\}$, $A \cup B = \{2, 3, 4, 5\}$. Note that the outcomes 3 and 4 appear only once in the union. For statistical events, the union is equivalent to "or"; $P(A \cup B)$ is the same thing as $P(A \text{ or } B)$. The **intersection** (symbol ∩) of two sets is the set of outcomes common to both sets. For the above sets A and B, $A \cap B = \{3, 4\}$. For statistical events, the intersection is equivalent to "and"; $P(A \cap B)$ is the same thing as $P(A \text{ and } B)$. It is important to note that union and intersection operations commute. That is:

$$A \cup B = B \cup A \text{ and } A \cap B = B \cap A$$

Permutations and Combinations in Probability

When trying to calculate the probability of an event using the $\frac{\text{desired outcomes}}{\text{total outcomes}}$ formula, you may frequently find that there are too many outcomes to individually count them. **Permutation** and **combination formulas** offer a shortcut to counting outcomes. A permutation is an arrangement of a specific number of a set of objects in a specific order. The number of **permutations** of r items given a set of n items can be calculated as ${}_nP_r = \frac{n!}{(n-r)!}$. Combinations are similar to permutations, except there are no restrictions regarding the order of the elements. While ABC is considered a different permutation than BCA, ABC and BCA are considered the same combination. The number of **combinations** of r items given a set of n items can be calculated as ${}_nC_r = \frac{n!}{r!(n-r)!}$ or ${}_nC_r = \frac{{}_nP_r}{r!}$.

Suppose you want to calculate how many different 5-card hands can be drawn from a deck of 52 cards. This is a combination since the order of the cards in a hand does not matter. There are 52 cards available, and 5 to be selected. Thus, the number of different hands is ${}_{52}C_5 = \frac{52!}{5! \times 47!} = 2{,}598{,}960$.

Review Video: Probability - Permutation and Combination
Visit mometrix.com/academy and enter code: 907664

TREE DIAGRAMS

For a simple sample space, possible outcomes may be determined by using a **tree diagram** or an organized chart. In either case, you can easily draw or list out the possible outcomes. For example, to determine all the possible ways three objects can be ordered, you can draw a tree diagram:

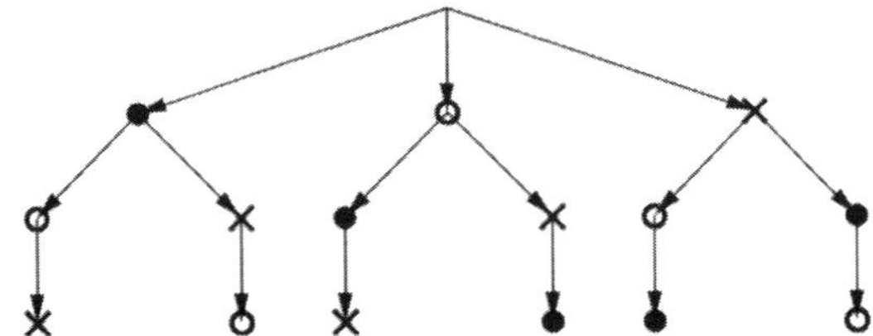

Review Video: Tree Diagrams
Visit mometrix.com/academy and enter code: 829158

You can also make a chart to list all the possibilities:

First object	Second object	Third object
●	x	o
●	o	x
o	●	x
o	x	●
x	●	o
x	o	●

Either way, you can easily see there are six possible ways the three objects can be ordered.

If two events have no outcomes in common, they are said to be **mutually exclusive**. For example, in a standard deck of 52 playing cards, the event of all card suits is mutually exclusive to the event of all card values. If two events have no bearing on each other so that one event occurring has no influence on the probability of another event occurring, the two events are said to be independent. For example, rolling a standard six-sided die multiple times does not change that probability that a particular number will be rolled from one roll to the next. If the outcome of one event does affect the probability of the second event, the two events are said to be dependent. For example, if cards are drawn from a deck, the probability of drawing an ace after an ace has been drawn is different than the probability of drawing an ace if no ace (or no other card, for that matter) has been drawn.

In probability, the **odds in favor of an event** are the number of times the event will occur compared to the number of times the event will not occur. To calculate the odds in favor of an event, use the formula $\frac{P(A)}{1-P(A)}$, where $P(A)$ is the probability that the event will occur. Many times, odds in favor is given as a ratio in the form $\frac{a}{b}$ or $a{:}\,b$, where a is the probability of the event occurring and b is the complement of the event, the probability of the event not occurring. If the odds in favor are given as 2:5, that means that you can expect the event to occur two times for every 5 times that it does not occur. In other words, the probability that the event will occur is $\frac{2}{2+5} = \frac{2}{7}$.

In probability, the **odds against an event** are the number of times the event will not occur compared to the number of times the event will occur. To calculate the odds against an event, use the formula $\frac{1-P(A)}{P(A)}$, where

Mathematics

$P(A)$ is the probability that the event will occur. Many times, odds against is given as a ratio in the form $\frac{b}{a}$ or $b\!:a$, where b is the probability the event will not occur (the complement of the event) and a is the probability the event will occur. If the odds against an event are given as 3:1, that means that you can expect the event to not occur 3 times for every one time it does occur. In other words, 3 out of every 4 trials will fail.

Two-Way Frequency Tables

If we have a two-way frequency table, it is generally a straightforward matter to read off the probabilities of any two events A and B, as well as the joint probability of both events occurring, $P(A \cap B)$. We can then find the conditional probability $P(A|B)$ by calculating $P(A|B) = \frac{P(A \cap B)}{P(B)}$. We could also check whether or not events are independent by verifying whether $P(A)P(B) = P(A \cap B)$.

For example, a certain store's recent T-shirt sales:

	Small	Medium	Large	Total
Blue	25	40	35	100
White	27	25	22	74
Black	8	23	15	46
Total	60	88	72	220

Suppose we want to find the conditional probability that a customer buys a black shirt (event A), given that the shirt he buys is size small (event B). From the table, the probability $P(B)$ that a customer buys a small shirt is $\frac{60}{220} = \frac{3}{11}$. The probability $P(A \cap B)$ that he buys a small, black shirt is $\frac{8}{220} = \frac{2}{55}$. The conditional probability $P(A|B)$ that he buys a black shirt, given that he buys a small shirt, is therefore $P(A|B) = \frac{2/55}{3/11} = \frac{2}{15}$.

Similarly, if we want to check whether the event a customer buys a blue shirt, A, is independent of the event that a customer buys a medium shirt, B. From the table, $P(A) = \frac{100}{220} = \frac{5}{11}$ and $P(B) = \frac{88}{220} = \frac{4}{10}$. Also, $P(A \cap B) = \frac{40}{220} = \frac{2}{11}$. Since $\left(\frac{5}{11}\right)\left(\frac{4}{10}\right) = \frac{20}{110} = \frac{2}{11}$, $P(A)P(B) = P(A \cap B)$ and these two events are indeed independent.

Expected Value

Expected value is a method of determining the expected outcome in a random situation. It is a sum of the weighted probabilities of the possible outcomes. Multiply the probability of an event occurring by the weight assigned to that probability (such as the amount of money won or lost). A practical application of the expected value is to determine whether a game of chance is really fair. If the sum of the weighted probabilities is equal to zero, the game is generally considered fair because the player has a fair chance to at least break even. If the expected value is less than zero, then players are expected to lose more than they win. For example, a lottery drawing might allow the player to choose any three-digit number, 000–999. The probability of choosing the winning number is 1:1000. If it costs \$1 to play, and a winning number receives \$500, the expected value is $\left(-\$1 \times \frac{999}{1{,}000}\right) + \left(\$499 \times \frac{1}{1{,}000}\right) = -\$0.50$. You can expect to lose on average 50 cents for every dollar you spend.

> **Review Video: Expected Value**
> Visit mometrix.com/academy and enter code: 643554

Expected Value and Simulators

A die roll simulator will show the results of n rolls of a die. The result of each die roll may be recorded. For example, suppose a die is rolled 100 times. All results may be recorded. The numbers of 1s, 2s, 3s, 4s, 5s, and 6s, may be counted. The experimental probability of rolling each number will equal the ratio of the frequency of the rolled number to the total number of rolls. As the number of rolls increases, or approaches infinity, the experimental probability will approach the theoretical probability of $\frac{1}{6}$. Thus, the expected value for the roll of a die is shown to be $\left(1 \times \frac{1}{6}\right) + \left(2 \times \frac{1}{6}\right) + \left(3 \times \frac{1}{6}\right) + \left(4 \times \frac{1}{6}\right) + \left(5 \times \frac{1}{6}\right) + \left(6 \times \frac{1}{6}\right)$, or 3.5.

Introduction to Statistics

Statistics is the branch of mathematics that deals with collecting, recording, interpreting, illustrating, and analyzing large amounts of **data**. The following terms are often used in the discussion of data and **statistics**:

- **Data** – the collective name for pieces of information (singular is datum)
- **Quantitative data** – measurements (such as length, mass, and speed) that provide information about quantities in numbers
- **Qualitative data** – information (such as colors, scents, tastes, and shapes) that cannot be measured using numbers
- **Discrete data** – information that can be expressed only by a specific value, such as whole or half numbers. (e.g., since people can be counted only in whole numbers, a population count would be discrete data.)
- **Continuous data** – information (such as time and temperature) that can be expressed by any value within a given range
- **Primary data** – information that has been collected directly from a survey, investigation, or experiment, such as a questionnaire or the recording of daily temperatures. (Primary data that has not yet been organized or analyzed is called **raw data**.)
- **Secondary data** – information that has been collected, sorted, and processed by the researcher
- **Ordinal data** – information that can be placed in numerical order, such as age or weight
- **Nominal data** – information that *cannot* be placed in numerical order, such as names or places

Data Collection

Population

In statistics, the **population** is the entire collection of people, plants, etc., that data can be collected from. For example, a study to determine how well students in local schools perform on a standardized test would have a population of all the students enrolled in those schools, although a study may include just a small sample of students from each school. A **parameter** is a numerical value that gives information about the population, such as the mean, median, mode, or standard deviation. Remember that the symbol for the mean of a population is μ and the symbol for the standard deviation of a population is σ.

Sample

A **sample** is a portion of the entire population. Whereas a parameter helped describe the population, a **statistic** is a numerical value that gives information about the sample, such as mean, median, mode, or standard deviation. Keep in mind that the symbols for mean and standard deviation are different when they are referring to a sample rather than the entire population. For a sample, the symbol for mean is $\bar{x}$ and the symbol for standard deviation is s. The mean and standard deviation of a sample may or may not be identical to that of the entire population due to a sample only being a subset of the population. However, if the sample is random and large enough, statistically significant values can be attained. Samples are generally used when the population is too large to justify including every element or when acquiring data for the entire population is impossible.

INFERENTIAL STATISTICS

Inferential statistics is the branch of statistics that uses samples to make predictions about an entire population. This type of statistic is often seen in political polls, where a sample of the population is questioned about a particular topic or politician to gain an understanding of the attitudes of the entire population of the country. Often, exit polls are conducted on election days using this method. Inferential statistics can have a large margin of error if you do not have a valid sample.

SAMPLING DISTRIBUTION

Statistical values calculated from various samples of the same size make up the **sampling distribution**. For example, if several samples of identical size are randomly selected from a large population and then the mean of each sample is calculated, the distribution of values of the means would be a sampling distribution.

The **sampling distribution of the mean** is the distribution of the sample mean, $\bar{x}$, derived from random samples of a given size. It has three important characteristics. First, the mean of the sampling distribution of the mean is equal to the mean of the population that was sampled. Second, assuming the standard deviation is non-zero, the standard deviation of the sampling distribution of the mean equals the standard deviation of the sampled population divided by the square root of the sample size. This is sometimes called the standard error. Finally, as the sample size gets larger, the sampling distribution of the mean gets closer to a normal distribution via the central limit theorem.

SURVEY STUDY

A **survey study** is a method of gathering information from a small group in an attempt to gain enough information to make accurate general assumptions about the population. Once a survey study is completed, the results are then put into a summary report.

Survey studies are generally in the format of surveys, interviews, or questionnaires as part of an effort to find opinions of a particular group or to find facts about a group.

It is important to note that the findings from a survey study are only as accurate as the sample chosen from the population.

CORRELATIONAL STUDIES

Correlational studies seek to determine how much one variable is affected by changes in a second variable. For example, correlational studies may look for a relationship between the amount of time a student spends studying for a test and the grade that student earned on the test or between student scores on college admissions tests and student grades in college.

It is important to note that correlational studies cannot show a cause and effect, but rather can show only that two variables are or are not potentially correlated.

EXPERIMENTAL STUDIES

Experimental studies take correlational studies one step farther, in that they attempt to prove or disprove a cause-and-effect relationship. These studies are performed by conducting a series of experiments to test the hypothesis. For a study to be scientifically accurate, it must have both an experimental group that receives the specified treatment and a control group that does not get the treatment. This is the type of study pharmaceutical companies do as part of drug trials for new medications. Experimental studies are only valid when the proper scientific method has been followed. In other words, the experiment must be well-planned and executed without bias in the testing process, all subjects must be selected at random, and the process of determining which subject is in which of the two groups must also be completely random.

OBSERVATIONAL STUDIES

Observational studies are the opposite of experimental studies. In observational studies, the tester cannot change or in any way control all of the variables in the test. For example, a study to determine which gender does better in math classes in school is strictly observational. You cannot change a person's gender, and you cannot change the subject being studied. The big downfall of observational studies is that you have no way of proving a cause-and-effect relationship because you cannot control outside influences. Events outside of school can influence a student's performance in school, and observational studies cannot take that into consideration.

RANDOM SAMPLES

For most studies, a **random sample** is necessary to produce valid results. Random samples should not have any particular influence to cause sampled subjects to behave one way or another. The goal is for the random sample to be a **representative sample**, or a sample whose characteristics give an accurate picture of the characteristics of the entire population. To accomplish this, you must make sure you have a proper **sample size**, or an appropriate number of elements in the sample.

BIASES

In statistical studies, biases must be avoided. **Bias** is an error that causes the study to favor one set of results over another. For example, if a survey to determine how the country views the president's job performance only speaks to registered voters in the president's party, the results will be skewed because a disproportionately large number of responders would tend to show approval, while a disproportionately large number of people in the opposite party would tend to express disapproval. **Extraneous variables** are, as the name implies, outside influences that can affect the outcome of a study. They are not always avoidable but could trigger bias in the result.

DATA ANALYSIS

DISPERSION

A **measure of dispersion** is a single value that helps to "interpret" the measure of central tendency by providing more information about how the data values in the set are distributed about the measure of central tendency. The measure of dispersion helps to eliminate or reduce the disadvantages of using the mean, median, or mode as a single measure of central tendency, and give a more accurate picture of the dataset as a whole. To have a measure of dispersion, you must know or calculate the range, standard deviation, or variance of the data set.

RANGE

The **range** of a set of data is the difference between the greatest and lowest values of the data in the set. To calculate the range, you must first make sure the units for all data values are the same, and then identify the greatest and lowest values. If there are multiple data values that are equal for the highest or lowest, just use one of the values in the formula. Write the answer with the same units as the data values you used to do the calculations.

Review Video: Statistical Range
Visit mometrix.com/academy and enter code: 778541

SAMPLE STANDARD DEVIATION

Standard deviation is a measure of dispersion that compares all the data values in the set to the mean of the set to give a more accurate picture. To find the **standard deviation of a sample**, use the formula

$$s = \sqrt{\frac{\sum_{i=1}^{n}(x_i - \bar{x})^2}{n-1}}$$

Note that s is the standard deviation of a sample, x_i represents the individual values in the data set, $\bar{x}$ is the mean of the data values in the set, and n is the number of data values in the set. The higher the value of the

Mathematics

standard deviation is, the greater the variance of the data values from the mean. The units associated with the standard deviation are the same as the units of the data values.

Review Video: Standard Deviation
Visit mometrix.com/academy and enter code: 419469

Sample Variance

The **variance of a sample** is the square of the sample standard deviation (denoted s^2). While the mean of a set of data gives the average of the set and gives information about where a specific data value lies in relation to the average, the variance of the sample gives information about the degree to which the data values are spread out and tells you how close an individual value is to the average compared to the other values. The units associated with variance are the same as the units of the data values squared.

Percentile

Percentiles and quartiles are other methods of describing data within a set. **Percentiles** tell what percentage of the data in the set fall below a specific point. For example, achievement test scores are often given in percentiles. A score at the 80th percentile is one which is equal to or higher than 80 percent of the scores in the set. In other words, 80 percent of the scores were lower than that score.

Quartiles are percentile groups that make up quarter sections of the data set. The first quartile is the 25th percentile. The second quartile is the 50th percentile; this is also the median of the dataset. The third quartile is the 75th percentile.

Skewness

Skewness is a way to describe the symmetry or asymmetry of the distribution of values in a dataset. If the distribution of values is symmetrical, there is no skew. In general the closer the mean of a data set is to the median of the data set, the less skew there is. Generally, if the mean is to the right of the median, the data set is *positively skewed*, or right-skewed, and if the mean is to the left of the median, the data set is *negatively skewed*, or left-skewed. However, this rule of thumb is not infallible. When the data values are graphed on a curve, a set with no skew will be a perfect bell curve.

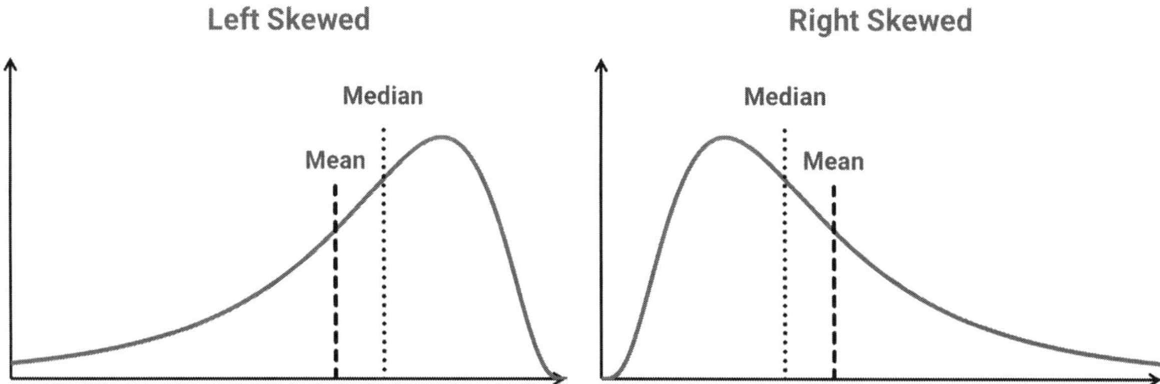

To estimate skew, use the formula:

$$\text{skew} = \frac{\sqrt{n(n-1)}}{n-2}\left(\frac{\frac{1}{n}\sum_{i=1}^{n}(x_i-\bar{x})^3}{\left(\frac{1}{n}\sum_{i=1}^{n}(x_i-\bar{x})^2\right)^{\frac{3}{2}}}\right)$$

Note that n is the datapoints in the set, x_i is the ith value in the set, and $\bar{x}$ is the mean of the set.

Review Video: Skew
Visit mometrix.com/academy and enter code: 661486

Unimodal vs. Bimodal

If a distribution has a single peak, it would be considered **unimodal**. If it has two discernible peaks it would be considered **bimodal**. Bimodal distributions may be an indication that the set of data being considered is actually the combination of two sets of data with significant differences. A **uniform distribution** is a distribution in which there is *no distinct peak or variation* in the data. No values or ranges are particularly more common than any other values or ranges.

Outlier

An outlier is an extremely high or extremely low value in the data set. It may be the result of measurement error, in which case, the outlier is not a valid member of the data set. However, it may also be a valid member of the distribution. Unless a measurement error is identified, the experimenter cannot know for certain if an outlier is or is not a member of the distribution. There are arbitrary methods that can be employed to designate an extreme value as an outlier. One method designates an outlier (or possible outlier) to be any value less than $Q_1 - 1.5(IQR)$ or any value greater than $Q_3 + 1.5(IQR)$.

Data Analysis

Simple Regression

In statistics, **simple regression** is using an equation to represent a relation between independent and dependent variables. The independent variable is also referred to as the explanatory variable or the predictor and is generally represented by the variable x in the equation. The dependent variable, usually represented by the variable y, is also referred to as the response variable. The equation may be any type of function – linear, quadratic, exponential, etc. The best way to handle this task is to use the regression feature of your graphing calculator. This will easily give you the curve of best fit and provide you with the coefficients and other information you need to derive an equation.

Line of Best Fit

In a scatter plot, the **line of best fit** is the line that best shows the trends of the data. The line of best fit is given by the equation $\hat{y} = ax + b$, where a and b are the regression coefficients. The regression coefficient a is also the slope of the line of best fit, and b is also the y-coordinate of the point at which the line of best fit crosses the y-axis. Not every point on the scatter plot will be on the line of best fit. The differences between the y-values of the points in the scatter plot and the corresponding y-values according to the equation of the line of best fit are the residuals. The line of best fit is also called the least-squares regression line because it is also the line that has the lowest sum of the squares of the residuals.

Correlation Coefficient

The **correlation coefficient** is the numerical value that indicates how strong the relationship is between the two variables of a linear regression equation. A correlation coefficient of –1 is a perfect negative correlation. A correlation coefficient of +1 is a perfect positive correlation. Correlation coefficients close to –1 or +1 are very strong correlations. A correlation coefficient equal to zero indicates there is no correlation between the two variables. This test is a good indicator of whether or not the equation for the line of best fit is accurate. The formula for the correlation coefficient is

$$r = \frac{\sum_{i=1}^{n}(x_i - \bar{x})(y_i - \bar{y})}{\sqrt{\sum_{i=1}^{n}(x_i - \bar{x})^2}\sqrt{\sum_{i=1}^{n}(y_i - \bar{y})^2}}$$

where r is the correlation coefficient, n is the number of data values in the set, (x_i, y_i) is a point in the set, and $\bar{x}$ and $\bar{y}$ are the means.

Mathematics

Z-Score

A **z-score** is an indication of how many standard deviations a given value falls from the sample mean. To calculate a z-score, use the formula:

$$\frac{x - \bar{x}}{\sigma}$$

In this formula x is the data value, $\bar{x}$ is the mean of the sample data, and σ is the standard deviation of the population. If the z-score is positive, the data value lies above the mean. If the z-score is negative, the data value falls below the mean. These scores are useful in interpreting data such as standardized test scores, where every piece of data in the set has been counted, rather than just a small random sample. In cases where standard deviations are calculated from a random sample of the set, the z-scores will not be as accurate.

Central Limit Theorem

According to the **central limit theorem**, regardless of what the original distribution of a sample is, the distribution of the means tends to get closer and closer to a normal distribution as the sample size gets larger and larger (this is necessary because the sample is becoming more all-encompassing of the elements of the population). As the sample size gets larger, the distribution of the sample mean will approach a normal distribution with a mean of the population mean and a variance of the population variance divided by the sample size.

Measures of Central Tendency

A **measure of central tendency** is a statistical value that gives a reasonable estimate for the center of a group of data. There are several different ways of describing the measure of central tendency. Each one has a unique way it is calculated, and each one gives a slightly different perspective on the data set. Whenever you give a measure of central tendency, always make sure the units are the same. If the data has different units, such as hours, minutes, and seconds, convert all the data to the same unit, and use the same unit in the measure of central tendency. If no units are given in the data, do not give units for the measure of central tendency.

Mean

The **statistical mean** of a group of data is the same as the arithmetic average of that group. To find the mean of a set of data, first convert each value to the same units, if necessary. Then find the sum of all the values, and count the total number of data values, making sure you take into consideration each individual value. If a value appears more than once, count it more than once. Divide the sum of the values by the total number of values and apply the units, if any. Note that the mean does not have to be one of the data values in the set, and may not divide evenly.

$$\text{mean} = \frac{\text{sum of the data values}}{\text{quantity of data values}}$$

For instance, the mean of the data set {88, 72, 61, 90, 97, 68, 88, 79, 86, 93, 97, 71, 80, 84, 89} would be the sum of the fifteen numbers divided by 15:

$$\frac{88 + 72 + 61 + 90 + 97 + 68 + 88 + 79 + 86 + 93 + 97 + 71 + 80 + 84 + 89}{15} = \frac{1242}{15}$$
$$= 82.8$$

While the mean is relatively easy to calculate and averages are understood by most people, the mean can be very misleading if it is used as the sole measure of central tendency. If the data set has outliers (data values that are unusually high or unusually low compared to the rest of the data values), the mean can be very distorted, especially if the data set has a small number of values. If unusually high values are countered with unusually low values, the mean is not affected as much. For example, if five of twenty students in a class get a 100 on a test, but the other 15 students have an average of 60 on the same test, the class average would appear as 70. Whenever the mean is skewed by outliers, it is always a good idea to include the median as an alternate measure of central tendency.

A **weighted mean**, or weighted average, is a mean that uses "weighted" values. The formula is weighted mean $= \frac{w_1x_1+w_2x_2+w_3x_3...+w_nx_n}{w_1+w_2+w_3+\cdots+w_n}$. Weighted values, such as $w_1, w_2, w_3, \ldots w_n$ are assigned to each member of the set $x_1, x_2, x_3, \ldots x_n$. When calculating the weighted mean, make sure a weight value for each member of the set is used.

Review Video: All About Averages
Visit mometrix.com/academy and enter code: 176521

Median

The **statistical median** is the value in the middle of the set of data. To find the median, list all data values in order from smallest to largest or from largest to smallest. Any value that is repeated in the set must be listed the number of times it appears. If there are an odd number of data values, the median is the value in the middle of the list. If there is an even number of data values, the median is the arithmetic mean of the two middle values.

For example, the median of the data set {88, 72, 61, 90, 97, 68, 88, 79, 86, 93, 97, 71, 80, 84, 88} is 86 since the ordered set is {61, 68, 71, 72, 79, 80, 84, **86**, 88, 88, 88, 90, 93, 97, 97}.

The big disadvantage of using the median as a measure of central tendency is that is relies solely on a value's relative size as compared to the other values in the set. When the individual values in a set of data are evenly dispersed, the median can be an accurate tool. However, if there is a group of rather large values or a group of rather small values that are not offset by a different group of values, the information that can be inferred from the median may not be accurate because the distribution of values is skewed.

Mode

The **statistical mode** is the data value that occurs the greatest number of times in the data set. It is possible to have exactly one mode, more than one mode, or no mode. To find the mode of a set of data, arrange the data like you do to find the median (all values in order, listing all multiples of data values). Count the number of times each value appears in the data set. If all values appear an equal number of times, there is no mode. If one value appears more than any other value, that value is the mode. If two or more values appear the same number of times, but there are other values that appear fewer times and no values that appear more times, all of those values are the modes.

For example, the mode of the data set {**88**, 72, 61, 90, 97, 68, **88**, 79, 86, 93, 97, 71, 80, 84, **88**} is 88.

The main disadvantage of the mode is that the values of the other data in the set have no bearing on the mode. The mode may be the largest value, the smallest value, or a value anywhere in between in the set. The mode only tells which value or values, if any, occurred the greatest number of times. It does not give any suggestions about the remaining values in the set.

Review Video: Mean, Median, and Mode
Visit mometrix.com/academy and enter code: 286207

Displaying Information

Frequency Tables

Frequency tables show how frequently each unique value appears in a set. A **relative frequency table** is one that shows the proportions of each unique value compared to the entire set. Relative frequencies are given as percentages; however, the total percent for a relative frequency table will not necessarily equal 100 percent due to rounding. An example of a frequency table with relative frequencies is below.

Favorite Color	Frequency	Relative Frequency
Blue	4	13%
Red	7	22%
Green	3	9%
Purple	6	19%
Cyan	12	38%

Review Video: Data Interpretation of Graphs
Visit mometrix.com/academy and enter code: 200439

Circle Graphs

Circle graphs, also known as *pie charts*, provide a visual depiction of the relationship of each type of data compared to the whole set of data. The circle graph is divided into sections by drawing radii to create central angles whose percentage of the circle is equal to the individual data's percentage of the whole set. Each 1% of data is equal to 3.6° in the circle graph. Therefore, data represented by a 90° section of the circle graph makes up 25% of the whole. When complete, a circle graph often looks like a pie cut into uneven wedges. The pie chart below shows the data from the frequency table referenced earlier where people were asked their favorite color.

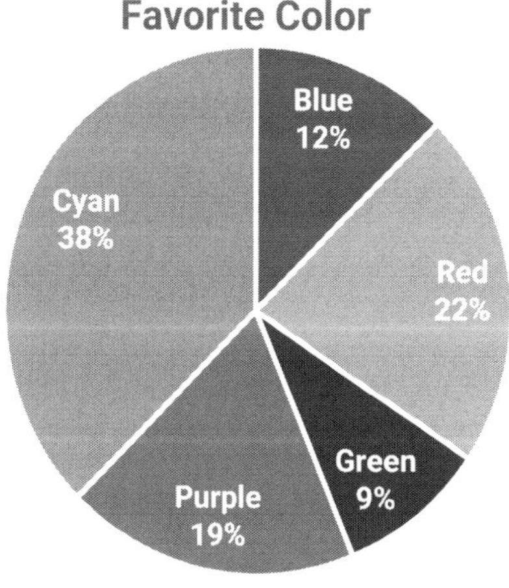

PICTOGRAPHS

A **pictograph** is a graph, generally in the horizontal orientation, that uses pictures or symbols to represent the data. Each pictograph must have a key that defines the picture or symbol and gives the quantity each picture or symbol represents. Pictures or symbols on a pictograph are not always shown as whole elements. In this case, the fraction of the picture or symbol shown represents the same fraction of the quantity a whole picture or symbol stands for. For example, a row with $3\frac{1}{2}$ ears of corn, where each ear of corn represents 100 stalks of corn in a field, would equal $3\frac{1}{2} \times 100 = 350$ stalks of corn in the field.

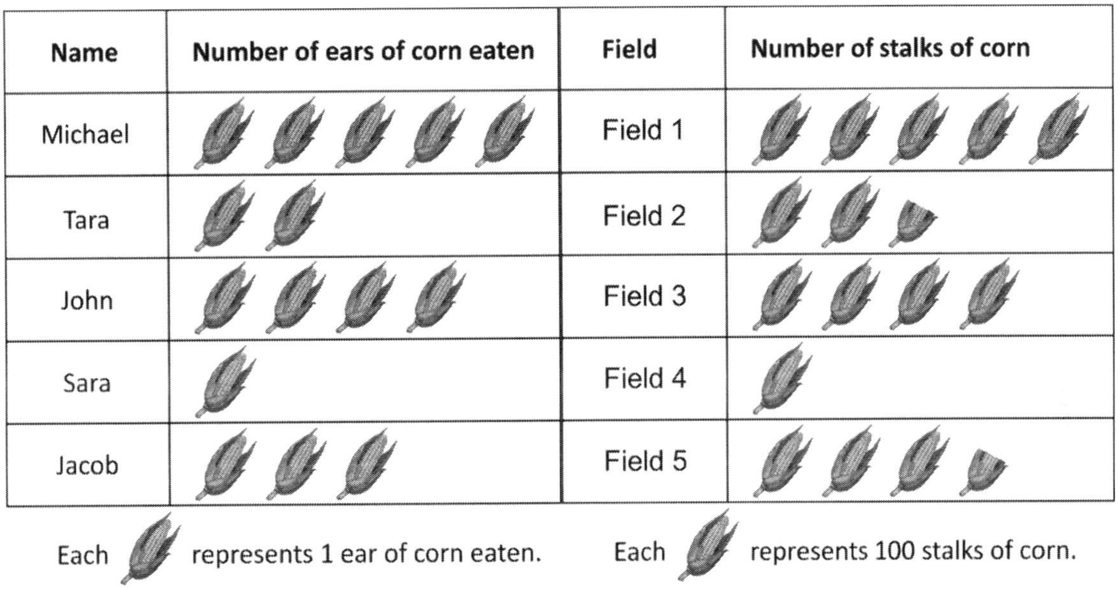

Name	Number of ears of corn eaten	Field	Number of stalks of corn
Michael		Field 1	
Tara		Field 2	
John		Field 3	
Sara		Field 4	
Jacob		Field 5	

Each represents 1 ear of corn eaten. Each represents 100 stalks of corn.

Review Video: Pictographs
Visit mometrix.com/academy and enter code: 147860

LINE GRAPHS

Line graphs have one or more lines of varying styles (solid or broken) to show the different values for a set of data. The individual data are represented as ordered pairs, much like on a Cartesian plane. In this case, the x- and y-axes are defined in terms of their units, such as dollars or time. The individual plotted points are joined by line segments to show whether the value of the data is increasing (line sloping upward), decreasing (line sloping downward), or staying the same (horizontal line). Multiple sets of data can be graphed on the same line graph to give an easy visual comparison. An example of this would be graphing achievement test scores for different groups of students over the same time period to see which group had the greatest increase or decrease in performance from year to year (as shown below).

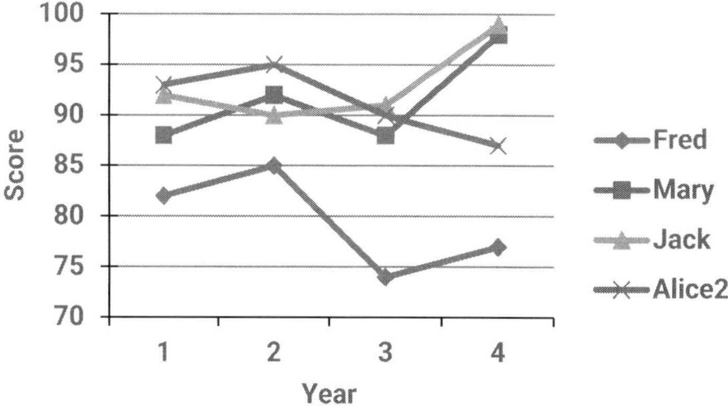

Review Video: How to Create a Line Graph
Visit mometrix.com/academy and enter code: 480147

Line Plots

A **line plot**, also known as a *dot plot*, has plotted points that are not connected by line segments. In this graph, the horizontal axis lists the different possible values for the data, and the vertical axis lists the number of times the individual value occurs. A single dot is graphed for each value to show the number of times it occurs. This graph is more closely related to a bar graph than a line graph. Do not connect the dots in a line plot or it will misrepresent the data.

Review Video: Line Plot
Visit mometrix.com/academy and enter code: 754610

Stem and Leaf Plots

A **stem and leaf plot** is useful for depicting groups of data that fall into a range of values. Each piece of data is separated into two parts: the first, or left, part is called the stem; the second, or right, part is called the leaf. Each stem is listed in a column from smallest to largest. Each leaf that has the common stem is listed in that stem's row from smallest to largest. For example, in a set of two-digit numbers, the digit in the tens place is the stem, and the digit in the ones place is the leaf. With a stem and leaf plot, you can easily see which subset of numbers (10s, 20s, 30s, etc.) is the largest. This information is also readily available by looking at a histogram, but a stem and leaf plot also allows you to look closer and see exactly which values fall in that range. Using a sample set of test scores (82, 88, 92, 93, 85, 90, 92, 95, 74, 88, 90, 91, 78, 87, 98, 99), we can assemble a stem and leaf plot like the one below.

Test Scores

7	4	8							
8	2	5	7	8	8				
9	0	0	1	2	2	3	5	8	9

Review Video: Stem and Leaf Plots
Visit mometrix.com/academy and enter code: 302339

Bar Graphs

A **bar graph** is one of the few graphs that can be drawn correctly in two different configurations – both horizontally and vertically. A bar graph is similar to a line plot in the way the data is organized on the graph. Both axes must have their categories defined for the graph to be useful. Rather than placing a single dot to mark the point of the data's value, a bar, or thick line, is drawn from zero to the exact value of the data, whether it is a number, percentage, or other numerical value. Longer bar lengths correspond to greater data values. To read a bar graph, read the labels for the axes to find the units being reported. Then, look where the bars end in relation to the scale given on the corresponding axis and determine the associated value.

The bar chart below represents the responses from our favorite-color survey.

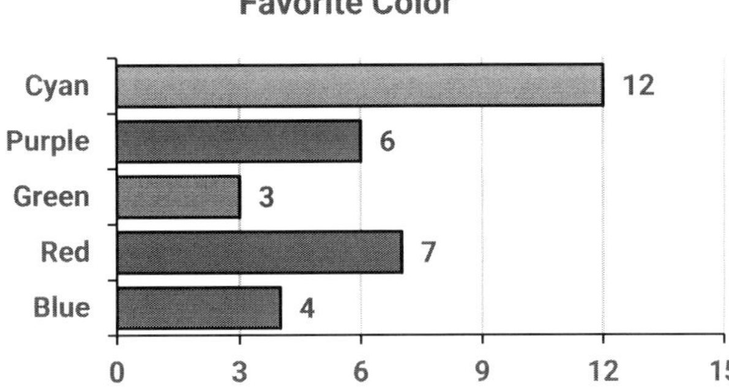

Histograms

At first glance, a **histogram** looks like a vertical bar graph. The difference is that a bar graph has a separate bar for each piece of data and a histogram has one continuous bar for each *range* of data. For example, a histogram may have one bar for the range 0–9, one bar for 10–19, etc. While a bar graph has numerical values on one axis, a histogram has numerical values on both axes. Each range is of equal size, and they are ordered left to right from lowest to highest. The height of each column on a histogram represents the number of data values within that range. Like a stem and leaf plot, a histogram makes it easy to glance at the graph and quickly determine which range has the greatest quantity of values. A simple example of a histogram is below.

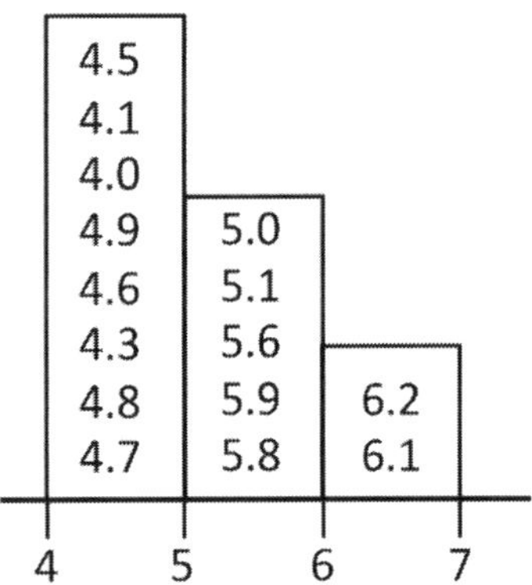

5-Number Summary

The **5-number summary** of a set of data gives a very informative picture of the set. The five numbers in the summary include the minimum value, maximum value, and the three quartiles. This information gives the reader the range and median of the set, as well as an indication of how the data is spread about the median.

Box and Whisker Plots

A **box-and-whiskers plot** is a graphical representation of the 5-number summary. To draw a box-and-whiskers plot, plot the points of the 5-number summary on a number line. Draw a box whose ends are through the points for the first and third quartiles. Draw a vertical line in the box through the median to divide the box in half. Draw a line segment from the first quartile point to the minimum value, and from the third quartile point to the maximum value.

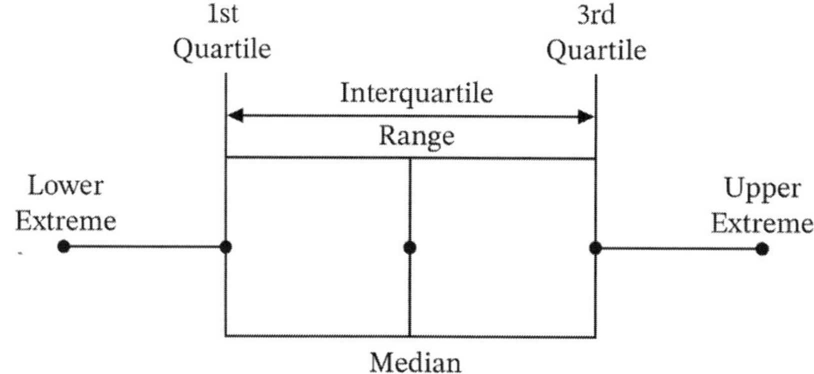

Review Video: Box and Whisker Plots
Visit mometrix.com/academy and enter code: 810817

Example

Given the following data (32, 28, 29, 26, 35, 27, 30, 31, 27, 32), we first sort it into numerical order: 26, 27, 27, 28, 29, 30, 31, 32, 32, 35. We can then find the median. Since there are ten values, we take the average of the 5th and 6th values to get 29.5. We find the lower quartile by taking the median of the data smaller than the median. Since there are five values, we take the 3rd value, which is 27. We find the upper quartile by taking the median of the data larger than the overall median, which is 32. Finally, we note our minimum and maximum, which are simply the smallest and largest values in the set: 26 and 35, respectively. Now we can create our box plot:

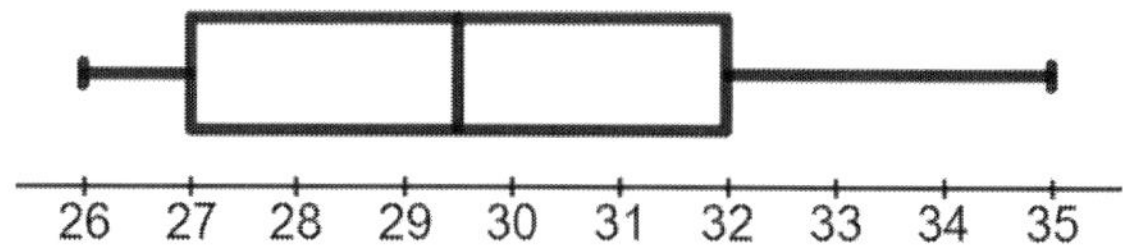

This plot is fairly "long" on the right whisker, showing one or more unusually high values (but not quite outliers). The other quartiles are similar in length, showing a fairly even distribution of data.

Interquartile Range

The **interquartile range, or IQR**, is the difference between the upper and lower quartiles. It measures how the data is dispersed: a high IQR means that the data is more spread out, while a low IQR means that the data is clustered more tightly around the median. To find the IQR, subtract the lower quartile value (Q_1) from the upper quartile value (Q_3).

Example

To find the upper and lower quartiles, we first find the median and then take the median of all values above it and all values below it. In the following data set (16, 18, 13, 24, 16, 51, 32, 21, 27, 39), we first rearrange the values in numerical order: 13, 16, 16, 18, 21, 24, 27, 32, 39, 51. There are 10 values, so the median is the average of the 5th and 6th: $\frac{21+24}{2} = \frac{45}{2} = 22.5$. We do not actually need this value to find the upper and lower quartiles. We look at the set of numbers below the median: 13, 16, 16, 18, 21. There are five values, so the 3rd is the median (16), or the value of the lower quartile (Q_1). Then we look at the numbers above the median: 24, 27, 32, 39, 51. Again there are five values, so the 3rd is the median (32), or the value of the upper quartile (Q_3). We find the IQR by subtracting Q_1 from Q_3: $32 - 16 = 16$.

68-95-99.7 RULE

The **68–95–99.7 rule** describes how a normal distribution of data should appear when compared to the mean. This is also a description of a normal bell curve. According to this rule, 68 percent of the data values in a normally distributed set should fall within one standard deviation of the mean (34 percent above and 34 percent below the mean), 95 percent of the data values should fall within two standard deviations of the mean (47.5 percent above and 47.5 percent below the mean), and 99.7 percent of the data values should fall within three standard deviations of the mean, again, equally distributed on either side of the mean. This means that only 0.3 percent of all data values should fall more than three standard deviations from the mean. On the graph below, the normal curve is centered on the y-axis. The x-axis labels are how many standard deviations away from the center you are. Therefore, it is easy to see how the 68-95-99.7 rule can apply.

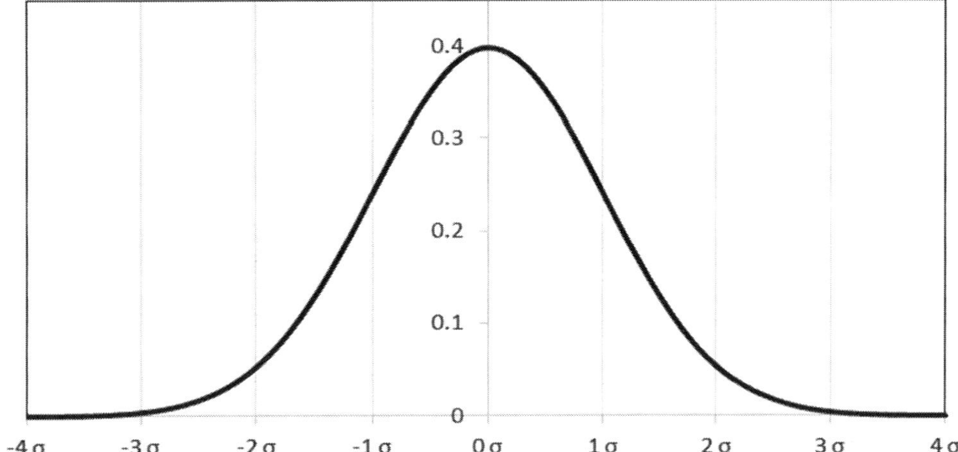

Mathematics

SCATTER PLOTS

BIVARIATE DATA

Bivariate data is simply data from two different variables. (The prefix *bi-* means *two.*) In a *scatter plot*, each value in the set of data is plotted on a grid similar to a Cartesian plane, where each axis represents one of the two variables. By looking at the pattern formed by the points on the grid, you can often determine whether or not there is a relationship between the two variables, and what that relationship is, if it exists. The variables may be directly proportionate, inversely proportionate, or show no proportion at all. It may also be possible to determine if the data is linear, and if so, to find an equation to relate the two variables. The following scatter plot shows the relationship between preference for brand "A" and the age of the consumers surveyed.

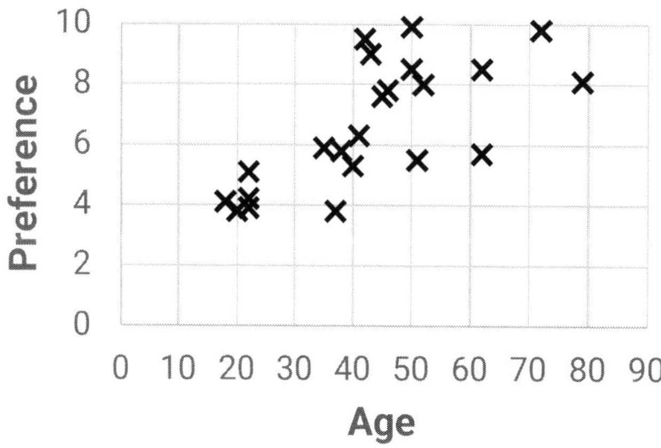

SCATTER PLOTS

Scatter plots are also useful in determining the type of function represented by the data and finding the simple regression. Linear scatter plots may be positive or negative. Nonlinear scatter plots are generally exponential or quadratic. Below are some common types of scatter plots:

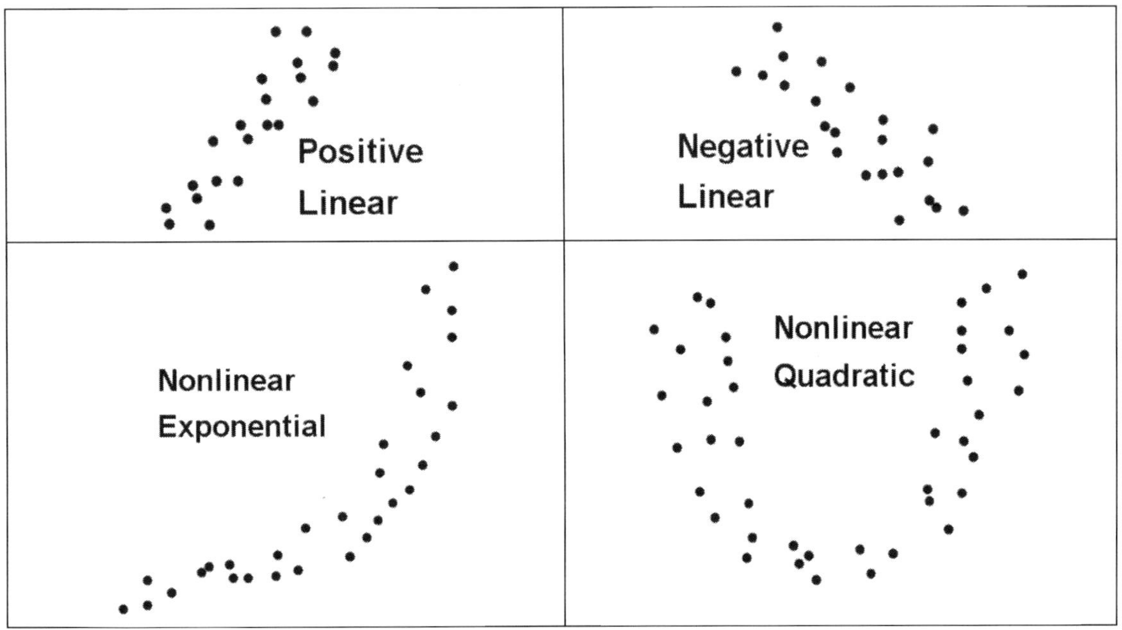

Review Video: Scatter Plot
Visit mometrix.com/academy and enter code: 596526

Algebraic Concepts

ROUNDING AND ESTIMATION

Rounding is reducing the digits in a number while still trying to keep the value similar. The result will be less accurate but in a simpler form and easier to use. Whole numbers can be rounded to the nearest ten, hundred, or thousand, for instance.

To round a number, we make it a little smaller (rounding down) or a little larger (rounding up) to get a number that ends in zeros. We specify the number of zeros by naming the last place that we will not "zero out." For example, to round 8,327 to the nearest hundred, we round down to 8,300, zeroing out every digit to the right of the hundreds place. To round 4,728 to the nearest thousand, we round up to 5,000, increasing the thousands digit by one (to make the number larger) and zeroing out every digit to the right of the thousands place.

We decide whether to round down or up by looking at the first digit we are going to zero out. If it is less than 5 (namely, 0, 1, 2, 3, or 4) we round down. If it is greater than or equal to 5 (namely, 5, 6, 7, 8, or 9) we round up by adding 1 to the place we are rounding to. So, rounding 8,327 to the nearest hundred, we round down to 8,300 because the tens digit, 2, is less than 5. And rounding 4,728 to the nearest thousand, we round up to 5,000, increasing the thousands digit by 1, because the hundreds digit, 7, is greater than or equal to 5.

This even works with decimals. For example, rounding 39.7426 to the nearest tenth, we round down to 39.7000 (or simply 39.7) because the hundredths digit, 4, is less than 5. And rounding 0.019823 to the nearest thousandth, we round up to 0.020000 (or simply 0.02) by increasing the thousandths digit by 1, because the ten-thousandths digit, 8, is greater than or equal to 5.

When you are asked to estimate the solution to a problem, you will need to provide only an approximate figure or **estimation** for your answer. In this situation, you will need to round each number in the calculation to the level indicated (nearest hundred, nearest thousand, etc.) or to a level that makes sense for the numbers involved. When estimating a sum **all numbers must be rounded to the same level**. You cannot round one number to the nearest thousand while rounding another to the nearest hundred.

For instance, suppose you are considering buying four pieces of equipment for your home office. Their prices are \$485, \$1,217, \$750, and \$643. To estimate their total cost, you might round each price to the nearest hundred and add the rounded figures, getting an estimate of $\$500 + \$1{,}200 + \$800 + \$600 = \$3{,}100$. By estimating instead of making an exact calculation, you give up a little accuracy to get a simpler calculation.

Review Video: Rounding and Estimation
Visit mometrix.com/academy and enter code: 126243

Scientific Notation

Scientific notation is a way of writing large numbers in a shorter form. The form $a \times 10^n$ is used in scientific notation, where a is greater than or equal to 1 but less than 10, and n is the number of places the decimal must move to get from the original number to a. Example: The number 230,400,000 is cumbersome to write. To write the value in scientific notation, place a decimal point between the first and second numbers, and include all digits through the last non-zero digit ($a = 2.304$). To find the appropriate power of 10, count the number of places the decimal point had to move ($n = 8$). The number is positive if the decimal moved to the left, and negative if it moved to the right. We can then write 230,400,000 as 2.304×10^8. If we look instead at the number 0.00002304, we have the same value for a, but this time the decimal moved 5 places to the right ($n = -5$). Thus, 0.00002304 can be written as 2.304×10^{-5}. Using this notation makes it simple to compare very large or very small numbers. By comparing exponents, it is easy to see that 3.28×10^4 is smaller than 1.51×10^5, because 4 is less than 5.

Review Video: Scientific Notation
Visit mometrix.com/academy and enter code: 976454

Proportions and Ratios

Proportions

There is a **proportion** between two variable quantities if there is a constant relationship between their products or quotients, a relationship that does not change as the quantities themselves change.

Given variable quantities x and y, we say that they are **directly proportional** (or that y **varies directly with** x) if their quotient or *ratio* is constant—that is, if there is a constant k such that $\frac{y}{x} = k$ is always true. Another way of saying this is that y is a constant multiple of x, so that $y = kx$ is always true. We call the number k the **constant of proportionality**. For example, if you drive at a constant 50 miles per hour, then the distance, y, that you travel in miles is 50 times the number of hours, x, that you drive. In symbols, $y = 50x$ miles (or $\frac{y}{x} = 50$ mph). So, the distance you travel, y, is directly proportional to (or varies directly with) the time you travel, x, with constant of proportionality $k = 50$ mph.

The quantities x and y are **inversely proportional** (or y varies inversely with x) if their product is constant—that is, if there is a constant k such that $xy = k$ is always true. Another way of saying this is to say that y is a constant multiple of the reciprocal of x so that $y = \frac{k}{x}$ is always true. For instance, suppose you drive at speed (rate) y mph for x hours, going a total of 120 miles. Since rate $\times$ time $=$ distance, we get $xy = 120$ miles (or

$y = \frac{120}{x}$ miles per hour). Thus, your driving speed, y, is inversely proportional to (or varies inversely with) your drive time, x, with constant of proportionality $k = 120$ miles.

Review Video: Proportions
Visit mometrix.com/academy and enter code: 505355

RATIOS

A **ratio** expresses the sizes of two quantities relative to each other. For instance, suppose we have 3 copies of sheet music to share among 6 singers. We can divide the singers into groups of 2 and give each group 1 copy of the music. Thus, there is 1 copy of the music for every 2 singers, and we say that the **ratio** of sheet music to singers is 1 to 2, which we write either as a fraction $\frac{1}{2}$ or using a colon $1 : 2$. Of course, it is also true there are 3 copies for every 6 singers so that the ratio of sheet music to singers is also 3 to 6, which we write as $\frac{3}{6}$ or $3 : 6$. So, the ratios $\frac{1}{2}$ and $\frac{3}{6}$ express the same relative quantities of music and singers. We say that these ratios are equal or **equivalent**, and we note that ratios are equal precisely when their fractions are equal (so, in this case, $\frac{1}{2} = \frac{3}{6}$ as fractions). We can also express the quantities in the other order and say that the ratio of singers to music is $\frac{2}{1}$ or $2 : 1$ (or $\frac{6}{3}$ or $6 : 3$).

Review Video: Ratios
Visit mometrix.com/academy and enter code: 996914

CONSTANT OF PROPORTIONALITY

If variable quantities x and y are proportional and we know a pair of corresponding values for them, then we can find their constant of proportionality. If they are directly proportional, we use the formula $\frac{y}{x} = k$. If they are inversely proportional, we use the formula $xy = k$.

Example: The cost in dollars, y, of buying fence posts is directly proportional to the number, x, that you buy. If it costs \$51 to buy 17 fence posts, what is the constant of proportionality? Because of direct proportionality, we know that $\frac{y}{x} = k$. Since this works for every pair of corresponding x- and y-values, it also works for $x = 17$ and $y = 51$. This gives us $\frac{51}{17} = k$, which simplifies to $k = 3$. Note also that this is the unit price, namely \$3 per fence post.

WORK/UNIT RATE

Unit rate expresses a quantity of one thing in terms of one unit of another. For example, if you travel 30 miles every two hours, a unit rate expresses this comparison in terms of one hour: in one hour you travel 15 miles, so your unit rate is 15 miles per hour. Other examples are how much one ounce of food costs (price per ounce) or figuring out how much one egg costs out of the dozen (price per 1 egg, instead of price per 12 eggs). The denominator of a unit rate is always 1. Unit rates are used to compare different situations to solve problems. For example, to make sure you get the best deal when deciding which kind of soda to buy, you can find the unit rate of each. If soda #1 costs \$1.50 for a 1-liter bottle, and soda #2 costs \$2.75 for a 2-liter bottle, it would be a better deal to buy soda #2, because its unit rate is only \$1.375 per liter, which is cheaper than soda #1. Unit rates can also help determine the length of time a given event will take. For example, if you can paint 2 rooms in 4.5 hours, you can determine how long it will take you to paint 5 rooms by solving for the unit rate per room and then multiplying that by 5.

Review Video: Rates and Unit Rates
Visit mometrix.com/academy and enter code: 185363

Cross Multiplication

Finding an Unknown in Equivalent Expressions

It is often necessary to apply information given about a rate or proportion to a new scenario. For example, if you know that Jedha can run a marathon (26.2 miles) in 3 hours, how long would it take her to run 10 miles at the same pace? Start by setting up equivalent expressions:

$$\frac{26.2\text{ mi}}{3\text{ hr}} = \frac{10\text{ mi}}{x\text{ hr}}$$

Now, cross multiply and solve for x:

$$\begin{aligned} 26.2x &= 30 \\ x &= \frac{30}{26.2} = \frac{15}{13.1} \\ x &\approx 1.15\text{ hrs } or \text{ } 1\text{ hr } 9\text{ min} \end{aligned}$$

So, at this pace, Jedha could run 10 miles in about 1.15 hours or about 1 hour and 9 minutes.

Review Video: Cross Multiplying Fractions
Visit mometrix.com/academy and enter code: 893904

Linear Expressions

Terms and Coefficients

Mathematical expressions consist of a combination of one or more values arranged in terms that are added together. As such, an expression could be just a single number, including zero. A **variable term** is the product of a real number, also called a **coefficient**, and one or more variables, each of which may be raised to an exponent. Expressions may also include numbers without a variable, called **constants** or **constant terms**. The expression $6s^2$, for example, is a single term where the coefficient is the real number 6 and the variable term is s^2. Note that if a term is written as simply a variable to some exponent, like t^2, then the coefficient is 1, because $t^2 = 1t^2$.

Linear Expressions

A **single variable linear expression** is the sum of a single variable term, where the variable has no exponent, and a constant, which may be zero. For instance, the expression $2w + 7$ has $2w$ as the variable term and 7 as the constant term. It is important to realize that terms are separated by addition or subtraction. Since an expression is a sum of terms, expressions such as $5x - 3$ can be written as $5x + (-3)$ to emphasize that the constant term is negative. A real-world example of a single variable linear expression is the perimeter of a square, four times the side length, often expressed: $4s$.

In general, a **linear expression** is the sum of any number of variable terms so long as none of the variables have an exponent and none of the terms have two variables multiplied together. For example, $3m + 8n - \frac{1}{4}p + 5.5q - 1$ is a linear expression, but $3y^3$ and $5xy$ are not. In the same way, the expression for the perimeter of a general triangle $(a + b + c)$ is linear, but the expression for the area of a square (s^2) is not.

Slope

Finding Slope Given Graph or Table

On a graph with two points, (x_1, y_1) and (x_2, y_2), the **slope** is found with the formula $m = \frac{y_2 - y_1}{x_2 - x_1}$; where $x_1 \neq x_2$ and m stands for slope. If the value of the slope is **positive**, the line has an *upward direction* from left to right. If the value of the slope is **negative**, the line has a *downward direction* from left to right. Consider the following example:

A new book goes on sale in bookstores and online stores. In the first month, 5,000 copies of the book are sold. Over time, the book continues to grow in popularity. The data for the number of copies sold is in the table below.

# of Months on Sale	1	2	3	4	5
# of Copies Sold (In Thousands)	5	10	15	20	25

So, the number of copies that are sold and the time that the book is on sale is a proportional relationship. In this example, an equation can be used to show the data: $y = 5x$, where x is the number of months that the book is on sale. Also, y is the number of copies sold. So, the slope of the corresponding line is $\frac{\text{rise}}{\text{run}} = \frac{5}{1} = 5$.

Finding Slope Given an Equation

When given an equation of a line, it is necessary to solve for y to determine the slope of the line. Given the equation $6x + 2y = 8$, find the slope. First, subtract $6x$ from both sides of the equation, resulting in $2y = -6x + 8$. Then divide both sides of the equation by 2, resulting in $y = -3x + 4$. This then allows us to conclude that the slope of the line is $m = -3$, the coefficient of x. Once an equation is in the form $y = mx + b$, the slope and y-intercept can easily be determined. For this reason, we refer to the equation $y = mx + b$ as "slope-intercept form" of the equation of a line.

> **Review Video: Finding the Slope of a Line**
> Visit mometrix.com/academy and enter code: 766664

Linear Equations

Equations like $5x = 100$ and $8x - 120 = 200$ and $6x + 4y = 240$ are **linear equations**. Linear equations are named based off the number of distinct variables they include. For example, the equation $3x + 30 = 8x$ is a **one-variable linear equation** because it involves only the single variable x. It does not matter that x appears more than once. Any equations that can be written as $ax + b = 0$, where $a \neq 0$, falls into this category. Furthermore, the equation $3x - 5y = 14 + 9y$ is a **two-variable linear equation** because it involves the two variables x and y. The equation $7x + 8y - 12z + 14w = 56$ is a linear equation in four variables.

Satisfying the Equation

When given a one-variable linear equation, the goal is typically to solve it. This means that we want to find the number that makes the equation true if we substitute it for the variable. That number is the **solution,** or root, of the equation. For instance, the equation $5x = 10$ has the solution $x = 2$. This is true because when 2 is substituted for x, the result is $5 \cdot 2 = 10$, which is true. On the other hand, $x = 6$ can not be a solution because $5 \cdot 6 \neq 10$, so it is false. Two equations with the same solution are **equivalent equations**. For example, the equations $5x = 10$ and $5x + 3 = 13$ are equivalent because both have the same solution of $x = 2$.

Determining a Solution Set

The **solution set** is the set of all solutions of an equation. In the previous example, the solution set would be 2. Solutions to a linear equation in two variables consist of pairs of numbers. For instance, the equation $6x + 4y = 240$ has the solution $x = 20$ and $y = 30$ since $6 \cdot 20 + 4 \cdot 30 = 240$ is true. We can write this solution as the ordered pair (20,30) and plot it as a point on the coordinate plane. Such equations usually have infinitely many solutions; and if we plot the points for all these solutions we get a line, which is a picture of all the solutions. We call this **graphing the equation**. When an equation has no true solutions, it is referred to as an **empty set**.

Linear Equation Forms

Linear equations can be written many ways. Below is a list of some forms linear equations can take:

- **Standard Form**: $Ax + By = C$; the slope is $\frac{-A}{B}$ and the y-intercept is $\frac{C}{B}$

- **Slope Intercept Form**: $y = mx + b$, where m is the slope and b is the y-intercept
- **Point-Slope Form**: $y - y_1 = m(x - x_1)$, where m is the slope and (x_1, y_1) is a point on the line
- **Two-Point Form**: $\frac{y-y_1}{x-x_1} = \frac{y_2-y_1}{x_2-x_1}$, where (x_1, y_1) and (x_2, y_2) are two points on the given line
- **Intercept Form**: $\frac{x}{x_1} + \frac{y}{y_1} = 1$, where $(x_1, 0)$ is the point at which a line intersects the x-axis, and $(0, y_1)$ is the point at which the same line intersects the y-axis

Review Video: Slope-Intercept and Point-Slope Forms
Visit mometrix.com/academy and enter code: 113216

Review Video: Converting Between Standard and Slope-Intercept Forms
Visit mometrix.com/academy and enter code: 982828

Review Video: Linear Equations Basics
Visit mometrix.com/academy and enter code: 793005

SOLVING EQUATIONS

MANIPULATING EQUATIONS

LIKE TERMS

Like terms are terms in an equation that have the same variable, regardless of whether they also have the same coefficient. This includes terms that *lack* a variable; all constants (i.e., numbers without variables) are considered like terms. If the equation involves terms with a variable raised to different powers, the like terms are those that have the variable raised to the same power.

For example, consider the equation $x^2 + 3x + 2 = 2x^2 + x - 7 + 2x$. In this equation, 2 and -7 are like terms; they are both constants. The terms $3x$, x, and $2x$ are like terms, they all include the variable x raised to the first power. The terms x^2 and $2x^2$ are like terms, they both include the variable x, raised to the second power. The terms $2x$ and $2x^2$ are not like terms; although they both involve the variable x, the variable is not raised to the same power in both terms. The fact that they have the same coefficient, 2, is not relevant.

Review Video: Rules for Manipulating Equations
Visit mometrix.com/academy and enter code: 838871

CARRYING OUT THE SAME OPERATION ON BOTH SIDES OF AN EQUATION

When solving an equation, the general procedure is to carry out a series of operations on both sides of an equation, choosing operations that simplify the equation when doing so. The reason why the same operation must be carried out on both sides of the equation is because that leaves the meaning of the equation unchanged, and yields a result that is equivalent to the original equation. This would not be the case if we carried out an operation on one side of an equation and not the other. Consider what an equation means: it is a statement that two values or expressions are equal. If we carry out the same operation on both sides of the equation—add 3 to both sides, for example—then the two sides of the equation are changed in the same way, and so remain equal. If we do that to only one side of the equation—add 3 to one side but not the other—then that wouldn't be true; if we change one side of the equation but not the other then the two sides are no longer equal.

COMBINING LIKE TERMS

Combining like terms refers to adding or subtracting like terms—terms with the same variable—and therefore reducing sets of like terms to a single term. The main advantage of doing this is that it simplifies the equation. Often, combining like terms can be done as the first step in solving an equation, though it can also be done later, such as after distributing terms in a product.

For example, consider the equation $2(x + 3) + 3(2 + x + 3) = -4$. The 2 and the 3 in the second set of parentheses are like terms, and we can combine them, yielding $2(x + 3) + 3(x + 5) = -4$. Now we can carry out the multiplications implied by the parentheses, distributing the outer 2 and 3 accordingly: $2x + 6 + 3x + 15 = -4$. The $2x$ and the $3x$ are like terms, and we can add them together: $5x + 6 + 15 = -4$. Now, the constants 6, 15, and –4 are also like terms, and we can combine them as well: subtracting 6 and 15 from both sides of the equation, we get $5x = -4 - 6 - 15$, or $5x = -25$, which simplifies further to $x = -5$.

Review Video: Solving Equations by Combining Like Terms
Visit mometrix.com/academy and enter code: 668506

Canceling Terms on Opposite Sides of an Equation

Two terms on opposite sides of an equation can be canceled if and only if they *exactly* match each other. They must have the same variable raised to the same power and the same coefficient. For example, in the equation $3x + 2x^2 + 6 = 2x^2 - 6$, $2x^2$ appears on both sides of the equation and can be canceled, leaving $3x + 6 = -6$. The 6 on each side of the equation *cannot* be canceled, because it is added on one side of the equation and subtracted on the other. While they cannot be canceled, however, the 6 and –6 are like terms and can be combined, yielding $3x = -12$, which simplifies further to $x = -4$.

It's also important to note that the terms to be canceled must be independent terms and cannot be part of a larger term. For example, consider the equation $2(x + 6) = 3(x + 4) + 1$. We cannot cancel the x's, because even though they match each other they are part of the larger terms $2(x + 6)$ and $3(x + 4)$. We must first distribute the 2 and 3, yielding $2x + 12 = 3x + 12 + 1$. Now we see that the terms with the x's do not match, but the 12s do, and can be canceled, leaving $2x = 3x + 1$, which simplifies to $x = -1$.

Isolating Variables

To isolate a variable means to manipulate the equation so that the variable appears by itself on one side of the equation, and does not appear at all on the other side. Generally, an equation or inequality is considered to be solved once the variable is isolated and the other side of the equation or inequality is simplified as much as possible. In the case of a two-variable equation or inequality, only one variable needs to be isolated; it will not usually be possible to simultaneously isolate both variables.

For a linear equation—an equation in which the variable only appears raised to the first power—isolating a variable can be done by first moving all the terms with the variable to one side of the equation and all other terms to the other side. (*Moving* a term really means adding the inverse of the term to both sides; when a term is *moved* to the other side of the equation its sign is flipped.) Then combine like terms on each side. Finally, divide both sides by the coefficient of the variable, if applicable. The steps need not necessarily be done in this order, but this order will always work.

Review Video: Solving Equations for Specific Variables
Visit mometrix.com/academy and enter code: 130695

Review Video: Solving Equations Involving Algebraic Fractions
Visit mometrix.com/academy and enter code: 237770

Review Video: Solving One-Step Equations
Visit mometrix.com/academy and enter code: 777004

Solving One-Variable Linear Equations

Equations with One Solution (the Usual Case)

To solve a one-variable linear equation, we use the techniques above to isolate the variable.

1. If any coefficients or constants are fractions, it is often helpful first to multiply both sides of the equation by the least common denominator (of all fractions) to clear the fractions.

2. Simplify both sides of the equation by combining any like terms.
3. Put all terms with the variable on one side of the equation and all constant terms on the other side, by adding or subtracting the same terms on both sides of the equation.
4. Divide both sides by the coefficient of the variable (or multiply both sides by its reciprocal).
5. When we have a value for the variable, we can check it by substituting the value into the original equation to make sure it produces a true result.

Consider the following example for solving the equation $\frac{2}{3}x + 8 = 14$:

$3 \cdot \left(\frac{2}{3}x + 8\right) = 3 \cdot 14$	Clear fractions by multiplying both sides by 3.
$2x + 24 = 42$	Simplify, remembering to apply the distributive property.
$2x + 24 - 24 = 42 - 24$	Subtract 24 from both sides to isolate $2x$.
$2x = 18$	Simplify by combining like terms.
$\frac{2x}{2} = \frac{18}{2}$	Divide both sides by 2 to isolate x.
$x = 9$	Simplify

Finally, we check this answer by substituting $x = 9$ into the original equation to make sure we get a true result.

$$\frac{2}{3}x + 8 = \frac{2}{3}(9) + 8 = 6 + 8 = 14$$

This is correct, so the value of x is 9.

Review Video: Solving Equations Using the Distributive Property
Visit mometrix.com/academy and enter code: 765499

Equations with More Than One Solution

Some types of non-linear equations, such as equations involving squares of variables, may have more than one solution. For example, the equation $x^2 = 4$ has two solutions: 2 and –2. Equations with absolute values can also have multiple solutions: $|x| = 1$ has the solutions $x = 1$ and $x = -1$.

It is possible for a linear equation to have more than one solution but only if the equation is true regardless of the value of the variable. We call such an equation an **identity**. In this case, the equation has infinitely many solutions, because every possible value of the variable is a solution. We discover that a linear equation is an identity when our attempts to isolate the variable cause the variable to disappear, leaving a *true* equation involving only constants. For example, consider the equation $2(3x + 5) = x + 5(x + 2)$. Distributing, we get $6x + 10 = x + 5x + 10$; combining like terms gives $6x + 10 = 6x + 10$, and the $6x$-terms cancel to leave $10 = 10$. This is clearly true, so the original equation is an identity. We could also cancel the 10's leaving $0 = 0$, which is also is clearly true—in general if both sides of the equation can be reduced to match one another exactly, the original equation is an identity.

Equations with No Solution

Some types of non-linear equations, such as equations involving squares of variables, may have no solution. For example, the equation $x^2 = -2$ has no solutions in the real numbers because the square of a real number must be positive. Similarly, $|x| = -1$ has no solution because the absolute value of a number is always positive.

It is also possible for a linear equation to have no solution. We call such an equation a **contradiction**. We discover that a linear equation is a contradiction when our attempts to isolate the variable cause the variable to disappear, leaving a *false* equation involving only constants. For example, the equation $2(x + 3) + x = 3x$

has no solution. We can see this by trying to solve it: first we distribute, leaving $2x + 6 + x = 3x$. Combining like terms gives us $3x + 6 = 3x$, and cancelling the term $3x$ on both sides leaves us with $6 = 0$. This is clearly false, so the original equation is a contradiction, having no solutions.

Features of Equations That Require Special Treatment

A linear equation is an equation in which variables only appear by themselves: not multiplied together, not with exponents other than one, and not inside absolute value signs or any other functions. For example, the equation $x + 1 - 3x = 5 - x$ is a linear equation; while x appears multiple times, it never appears with an exponent other than one, or inside any function. The two-variable equation $2x - 3y = 5 + 2x$ is also a linear equation. In contrast, the equation $x^2 - 5 = 3x$ is *not* a linear equation, because it involves the term x^2. The equation $\sqrt{x} = 5$ is not linear, because it involves a square root. The equation $(x - 1)^2 = 4$ is not linear because even though there's no exponent on the x directly, it appears as part of an expression that is squared. The two-variable equation $x + xy - y = 5$ is not linear because it includes the term xy, where two variables are multiplied together.

As we see above, linear equations can always be solved (or shown to have no solution) by combining like terms and performing simple operations on both sides of the equation. Some non-linear equations can be solved by similar methods, but others may require more advanced methods of solution, if they can be solved analytically at all.

Solving Equations Involving Roots

In an equation involving roots, the first step is to isolate the term with the root, if possible, and then raise both sides of the equation to the appropriate power to eliminate it. Consider an example equation, $2\sqrt{x + 1} - 1 = 3$. In this case, begin by adding 1 to both sides, yielding $2\sqrt{x + 1} = 4$, and then dividing both sides by 2, yielding $\sqrt{x + 1} = 2$. Now square both sides, yielding $x + 1 = 4$. Finally, subtracting 1 from both sides yields $x = 3$.

Squaring both sides of an equation (or raising both sides to any *even* power) may, however, yield a spurious solution—a solution to the squared equation that is *not* a solution of the original equation. It's therefore necessary to plug the solution back into the original equation to make sure it works. In this case, it does: $2\sqrt{3 + 1} - 1 = 2\sqrt{4} - 1 = 2(2) - 1 = 4 - 1 = 3$.

The same procedure applies for other roots as well. For example, given the equation $3 + \sqrt[3]{2x} = 5$, we can first subtract 3 from both sides, yielding $\sqrt[3]{2x} = 2$ and isolating the root. Raising both sides to the third power yields $2x = 2^3$; i.e., $2x = 8$. We can now divide both sides by 2 to get $x = 4$.

Review Video: Solving Equations Involving Roots
Visit mometrix.com/academy and enter code: 297670

Solving Equations with Exponents

In solving an equation with powers of a variable, sometimes it is possible to eliminate all but one term involving the variable. In that case, we can isolate the power of the variable and then take the appropriate root of both sides to eliminate the exponent. For instance, for the equation $2x^3 + 17 = 5x^3 - 7$, we can subtract $5x^3$ from both sides to get $-3x^3 + 17 = -7$, and then subtract 17 from both sides to get $-3x^3 = -24$. Finally, we can divide both sides by –3 to get $x^3 = 8$. Since this isolates the cube of the variable, we can take the cube root of both sides to get $x = \sqrt[3]{8} = 2$.

One important but often overlooked point is that equations with an exponent greater than 1 may have more than one answer. The solution to $x^2 = 9$ isn't simply $x = 3$; it's $x = \pm 3$ (that is, $x = 3$ or $x = -3$). For a slightly more complicated example, consider the equation $(x - 1)^2 - 1 = 3$. Adding 1 to both sides yields $(x - 1)^2 = 4$; taking the square root of both sides yields $x - 1 = 2$. We can then add 1 to both sides to get $x = 3$. However,

Mathematics

there's a second solution. We also have the possibility that $x - 1 = -2$, in which case $x = -1$. Both $x = 3$ and $x = -1$ are valid solutions, as can be verified by substituting them both into the original equation.

Review Video: Solving Equations with Exponents
Visit mometrix.com/academy and enter code: 514557

Review Video: Adding and Subtracting with Exponents
Visit mometrix.com/academy and enter code: 875756

SOLVING EQUATIONS WITH ABSOLUTE VALUES

When solving an equation with an absolute value, the first step is to isolate the absolute value term. We then consider two possibilities: when the expression inside the absolute value is positive or when it is negative. In the former case, the expression in the absolute value equals the expression on the other side of the equation; in the latter, it equals the additive inverse of that expression—the expression times negative one. We consider each case separately and finally check for spurious solutions.

For instance, consider solving $|2x - 1| + x = 5$ for x. We can first isolate the absolute value by moving the x to the other side: $|2x - 1| = -x + 5$. Now, we have two possibilities. First, that $2x - 1$ is positive, and hence $2x - 1 = -x + 5$. Rearranging and combining like terms yields $3x = 6$, and hence $x = 2$. The other possibility is that $2x - 1$ is negative, and hence $2x - 1 = -(-x + 5) = x - 5$. In this case, rearranging and combining like terms yields $x = -4$. Substituting $x = 2$ and $x = -4$ back into the original equation, we see that they are both valid solutions.

Note that the absolute value of a sum or difference applies to the sum or difference as a whole, not to the individual terms; in general, $|2x - 1|$ is not equal to $|2x + 1|$ or to $|2x| - 1$.

Review Video: Solving Absolute Value Equations
Visit mometrix.com/academy and enter code: 501208

EXTRANEOUS SOLUTIONS

An **extraneous solution** may arise when we square both sides of an equation (or raise both sides to an even power) as a step in solving it or under certain other operations on the equation. It is a solution to the squared or otherwise modified equation that is *not* a solution of the original equation. To identify an extraneous solution, it's useful when you solve an equation involving roots or absolute values to plug the solution back into the original equation to make sure it's valid.

TWO-VARIABLE EQUATIONS

Similar to methods for a one-variable equation, solving a two-variable equation involves isolating a variable: manipulating the equation so that a variable appears by itself on one side of the equation, and not at all on the other side. However, in a two-variable equation, you will usually only be able to isolate one of the variables; the other variable may appear on the other side along with constant terms, or with exponents or other functions. If an equation has multiple variables, the problem should tell you which variable to isolate.

Review Video: Solving Equations with Variables on Both Sides
Visit mometrix.com/academy and enter code: 402497

GRAPHING EQUATIONS

GRAPHICAL SOLUTIONS TO EQUATIONS

When equations are shown graphically, they are usually shown on a **Cartesian coordinate plane**. The Cartesian coordinate plane consists of two number lines placed perpendicular to each other and intersecting at the zero point, also known as the origin. The horizontal number line is known as the x-axis, with positive values to the right of the origin, and negative values to the left of the origin. The vertical number line is known as the y-axis, with positive values above the origin, and negative values below the origin. Any point on the plane can be identified by an ordered pair in the form (x, y), called coordinates. The x-value of the coordinate is called the abscissa, and the y-value of the coordinate is called the ordinate. The two number lines divide the plane into **four quadrants**: I, II, III, and IV.

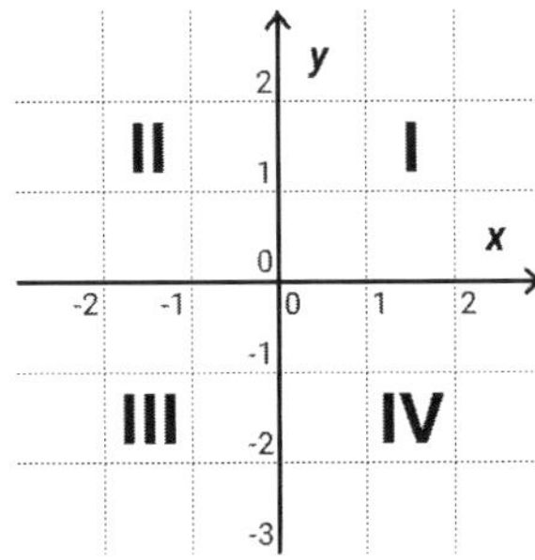

Note that in quadrant I $x > 0$ and $y > 0$, in quadrant II $x < 0$ and $y > 0$, in quadrant III $x < 0$ and $y < 0$, and in quadrant IV $x > 0$ and $y < 0$.

Recall that if the value of the slope of a line is positive, the line slopes upward from left to right. If the value of the slope is negative, the line slopes downward from left to right. If the y-coordinates are the same for two points on a line, the slope is 0 and the line is a **horizontal line**. If the x-coordinates are the same for two points on a line, there is no slope and the line is a **vertical line**. Two or more lines that have equivalent slopes are **parallel lines**. **Perpendicular lines** have slopes that are negative reciprocals of each other, such as $\frac{a}{b}$ and $\frac{-b}{a}$.

Review Video: Cartesian Coordinate Plane and Graphing
Visit mometrix.com/academy and enter code: 115173

Graphing Equations in Two Variables

One way of graphing an equation in two variables is to plot enough points to get an idea for its shape and then draw the appropriate curve through those points. A point can be plotted by substituting in a value for one variable and solving for the other. If the equation is linear, we only need two points and can then draw a straight line between them.

For example, consider the equation $y = 2x - 1$. This is a linear equation—both variables only appear raised to the first power—so we only need two points. When $x = 0, y = 2(0) - 1 = -1$. When $x = 2, y = 2(2) - 1 = 3$. We can therefore choose the points $(0, -1)$ and $(2, 3)$, and draw a line between them:

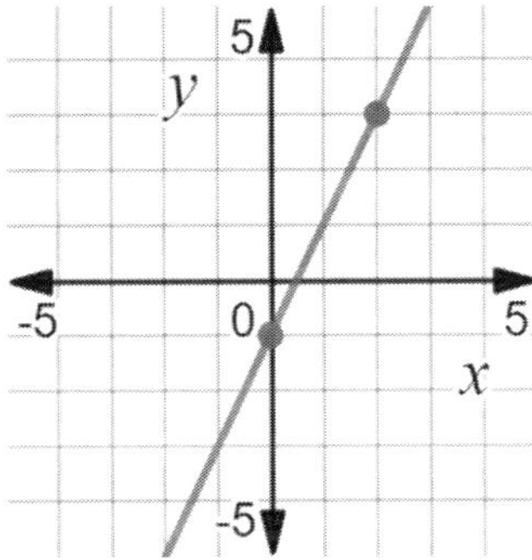

Inequalities

Commonly in algebra and other upper-level fields of math you find yourself working with mathematical expressions that do not equal each other. The statement comparing such expressions with symbols such as < (less than) or > (greater than) is called an *inequality*. An example of an inequality is $7x > 5$. To solve for x,

Mathematics

simply divide both sides by 7 and the solution is shown to be $x > \frac{5}{7}$. Graphs of the solution set of inequalities are represented on a number line. Open circles are used to show that an expression approaches a number but is never quite equal to that number.

Review Video: Solving One-Step Inequalities
Visit mometrix.com/academy and enter code: 229684

Review Video: Solving Multi-Step Inequalities
Visit mometrix.com/academy and enter code: 347842

Review Video: Solving Inequalities Using All 4 Basic Operations
Visit mometrix.com/academy and enter code: 401111

Types of Inequalities

Conditional inequalities are those with certain values for the variable that will make the condition true and other values for the variable where the condition will be false. **Absolute inequalities** can have any real number as the value for the variable to make the condition true, while there is no real number value for the variable that will make the condition false. Solving inequalities is done by following the same rules for solving equations with the exception that when multiplying or dividing by a negative number the direction of the inequality sign must be flipped or reversed. **Double inequalities** are situations where two inequality statements apply to the same variable expression. Example: $-c < ax + b < c$.

Review Video: Conditional and Absolute Inequalities
Visit mometrix.com/academy and enter code: 980164

Solving Inequalities

Determining Solutions to Inequalities

To determine whether a coordinate is a solution of an inequality, you can substitute the values of the coordinate into the inequality, simplify, and check whether the resulting statement holds true. For instance, to determine whether $(-2,4)$ is a solution of the inequality $y \geq -2x + 3$, substitute the values into the inequality, $4 \geq -2(-2) + 3$. Simplify the right side of the inequality and the result is $4 \geq 7$, which is a false statement. Therefore, the coordinate is not a solution of the inequality. You can also use this method to determine which part of the graph of an inequality is shaded. The graph of $y \geq -2x + 3$ includes the solid line $y = -2x + 3$ and, since it excludes the point $(-2,4)$ to the left of the line, it is shaded to the right of the line.

Review Video: Graphing Linear Inequalities
Visit mometrix.com/academy and enter code: 439421

Review Video: Graphing Solutions to Inequalities
Visit mometrix.com/academy and enter code: 391281

Flipping Inequality Signs

When given an inequality, we can always turn the entire inequality around, swapping the two sides of the inequality and changing the inequality sign. For instance, $x + 2 > 2x - 3$ is equivalent to $2x - 3 < x + 2$. Aside from that, normally the inequality does not change if we carry out the same operation on both sides of the inequality. There is, however, one principal exception: if we *multiply* or *divide* both sides of the inequality by a *negative number*, the inequality is flipped. For example, if we take the inequality $-2x < 6$ and divide both sides by –2, the inequality flips and we are left with $x > -3$. This *only* applies to multiplication and division, and only with negative numbers. Multiplying or dividing both sides by a positive number, or adding or subtracting any number regardless of sign, does not flip the inequality. Another special case that flips the inequality sign is when reciprocals are used. For instance, $3 > 2$ but the relation of the reciprocals is $\frac{1}{3} < \frac{1}{2}$.

Compound Inequalities

A **compound inequality** is an equality that consists of two inequalities combined with *and* or *or*. The two components of a proper compound inequality must be of opposite type: that is, one must be greater than (or greater than or equal to), the other less than (or less than or equal to). For instance, "$x + 1 < 2$ or $x + 1 > 3$" is a compound inequality, as is "$2x \geq 4$ and $2x \leq 6$." An *and* inequality can be written more compactly by having one inequality on each side of the common part: "$2x \geq 1$ and $2x \leq 6$," can also be written as $1 \leq 2x \leq 6$.

In order for the compound inequality to be meaningful, the two parts of an *and* inequality must overlap; otherwise, no numbers satisfy the inequality. On the other hand, if the two parts of an *or* inequality overlap, then *all* numbers satisfy the inequality and as such the inequality is usually not meaningful.

Solving a compound inequality requires solving each part separately. For example, given the compound inequality "$x + 1 < 2$ or $x + 1 > 3$," the first inequality, $x + 1 < 2$, reduces to $x < 1$, and the second part, $x + 1 > 3$, reduces to $x > 2$, so the whole compound inequality can be written as "$x < 1$ or $x > 2$." Similarly, $1 \leq 2x \leq 6$ can be solved by dividing each term by 2, yielding $\frac{1}{2} \leq x \leq 3$.

Review Video: Compound Inequalities
Visit mometrix.com/academy and enter code: 786318

Solving Inequalities Involving Absolute Values

To solve an inequality involving an absolute value, first isolate the term with the absolute value. Then proceed to treat the two cases separately as with an absolute value equation, but flipping the inequality in the case where the expression in the absolute value is negative (since that essentially involves multiplying both sides by –1.) The two cases are then combined into a compound inequality; if the absolute value is on the greater side of the inequality, then it is an *or* compound inequality, if on the lesser side, then it's an *and*.

Consider the inequality $2 + |x - 1| \geq 3$. We can isolate the absolute value term by subtracting 2 from both sides: $|x - 1| \geq 1$. Now, we're left with the two cases $x - 1 \geq 1$ or $x - 1 \leq -1$: note that in the latter, negative case, the inequality is flipped. $x - 1 \geq 1$ reduces to $x \geq 2$, and $x - 1 \leq -1$ reduces to $x \leq 0$. Since in the inequality $|x - 1| \geq 1$ the absolute value is on the greater side, the two cases combine into an *or* compound inequality, so the final, solved inequality is "$x \leq 0$ or $x \geq 2$."

Review Video: Solving Absolute Value Inequalities
Visit mometrix.com/academy and enter code: 997008

Solving Inequalities Involving Square Roots

Solving an inequality with a square root involves two parts. First, we solve the inequality as if it were an equation, isolating the square root and then squaring both sides of the equation. Second, we restrict the solution to the set of values of x for which the value inside the square root sign is non-negative.

For example, in the inequality, $\sqrt{x - 2} + 1 < 5$, we can isolate the square root by subtracting 1 from both sides, yielding $\sqrt{x - 2} < 4$. Squaring both sides of the inequality yields $x - 2 < 16$, so $x < 18$. Since we can't take the square root of a negative number, we also require the part inside the square root to be non-negative. In this case, that means $x - 2 \geq 0$. Adding 2 to both sides of the inequality yields $x \geq 2$. Our final answer is a compound inequality combining the two simple inequalities: $x \geq 2$ and $x < 18$, or $2 \leq x < 18$.

Note that we only get a compound inequality if the two simple inequalities are in opposite directions; otherwise, we take the one that is more restrictive.

The same technique can be used for other even roots, such as fourth roots. It is *not*, however, used for cube roots or other odd roots—negative numbers *do* have cube roots, so the condition that the quantity inside the root sign cannot be negative does not apply.

Review Video: Solving Inequalities Involving Square Roots
Visit mometrix.com/academy and enter code: 800288

SPECIAL CIRCUMSTANCES

Sometimes an inequality involving an absolute value or an even exponent is true for all values of x, and we don't need to do any further work to solve it. This is true if the inequality, once the absolute value or exponent term is isolated, says that term is greater than a negative number (or greater than or equal to zero). Since an absolute value or a number raised to an even exponent is *always* non-negative, this inequality is always true.

GRAPHING INEQUALITIES

GRAPHING SIMPLE INEQUALITIES

To graph a simple inequality, we first mark on the number line the value that signifies the end point of the inequality. If the inequality is strict (involves a less than or greater than), we use a hollow circle; if it is not strict (less than or equal to or greater than or equal to), we use a solid circle. We then fill in the part of the number line that satisfies the inequality: to the left of the marked point for less than (or less than or equal to), to the right for greater than (or greater than or equal to).

For example, we would graph the inequality $x < 5$ by putting a hollow circle at 5 and filling in the part of the line to the left:

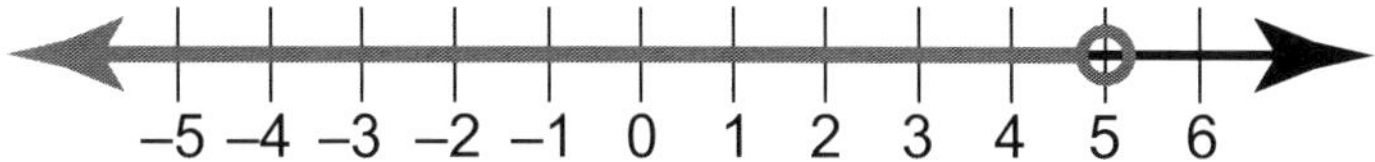

GRAPHING COMPOUND INEQUALITIES

To graph a compound inequality, we fill in both parts of the inequality for an *or* inequality, or the overlap between them for an *and* inequality. More specifically, we start by plotting the endpoints of each inequality on the number line. For an *or* inequality, we then fill in the appropriate side of the line for each inequality. Typically, the two component inequalities do not overlap, which means the shaded part is *outside* the two points. For an *and* inequality, we instead fill in the part of the line that meets both inequalities.

For the inequality "$x \leq -3$ or $x > 4$," we first put a solid circle at –3 and a hollow circle at 4. We then fill the parts of the line *outside* these circles:

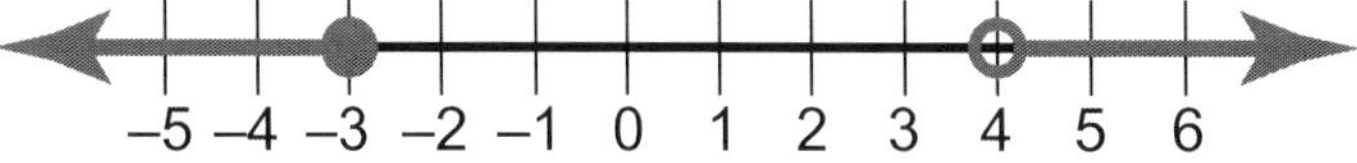

GRAPHING INEQUALITIES INCLUDING ABSOLUTE VALUES

An inequality with an absolute value can be converted to a compound inequality. To graph the inequality, first convert it to a compound inequality, and then graph that normally. If the absolute value is on the greater side of the inequality, we end up with an *or* inequality; we plot the endpoints of the inequality on the number line and fill in the part of the line *outside* those points. If the absolute value is on the smaller side of the inequality, we end up with an *and* inequality; we plot the endpoints of the inequality on the number line and fill in the part of the line *between* those points.

For example, the inequality $|x + 1| \geq 4$ can be rewritten as $x \geq 3$ or $x \leq -5$. We place solid circles at the points 3 and -5 and fill in the part of the line *outside* them:

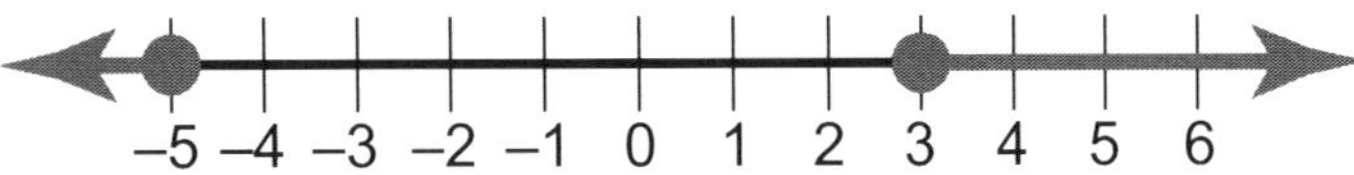

GRAPHING INEQUALITIES IN TWO VARIABLES

To graph an inequality in two variables, we first graph the border of the inequality. This means graphing the equation that we get if we replace the inequality sign with an equals sign. If the inequality is strict (> or <), we graph the border with a dashed or dotted line; if it is not strict (≥ or ≤), we use a solid line. We can then test any point not on the border to see if it satisfies the inequality. If it does, we shade in that side of the border; if not, we shade in the other side. As an example, consider $y > 2x + 2$. To graph this inequality, we first graph the border, $y = 2x + 2$. Since it is a strict inequality, we use a dashed line. Then, we choose a test point. This can be any point not on the border; in this case, we will choose the origin, (0,0). (This makes the calculation easy and is generally a good choice unless the border passes through the origin.) Putting this into the original inequality, we get $0 > 2(0) + 2$, i.e., $0 > 2$. This is *not* true, so we shade in the side of the border that does *not* include the point (0,0):

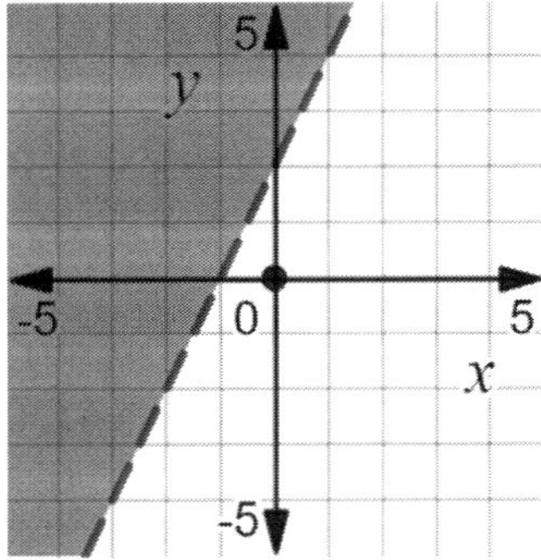

GRAPHING COMPOUND INEQUALITIES IN TWO VARIABLES

One way to graph a compound inequality in two variables is to first graph each of the component inequalities. For an *and* inequality, we then shade in only the parts where the two graphs overlap; for an *or* inequality, we shade in any region that pertains to either of the individual inequalities.

Consider the graph of "$y \geq x - 1$ and $y \leq -x$":

We first shade in the individual inequalities:

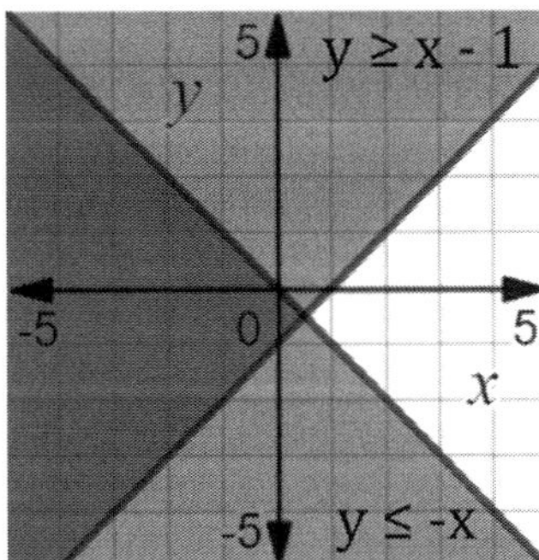

Now, since the compound inequality has an *and*, we only leave shaded the overlap—the part that pertains to *both* inequalities:

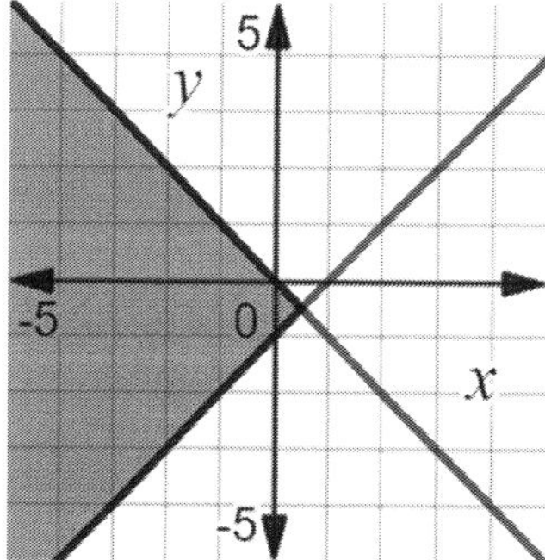

If instead the inequality had been "$y \geq x - 1$ or $y \leq -x$," our final graph would involve the *total* shaded area:

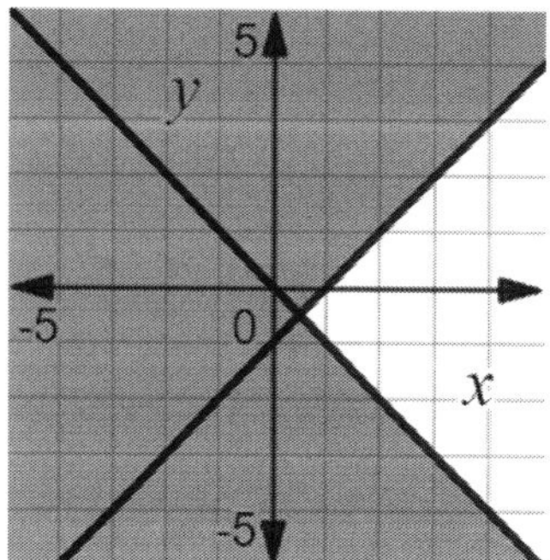

Review Video: Graphing Solutions to Inequalities
Visit mometrix.com/academy and enter code: 391281

Systems of Equations

Solving Systems of Equations

A **system of equations** is a set of simultaneous equations that all use the same variables. A solution to a system of equations must be true for each equation in the system. **Consistent systems** are those with at least one solution. **Inconsistent systems** are systems of equations that have no solution.

Review Video: Solving Systems of Linear Equations
Visit mometrix.com/academy and enter code: 746745

Substitution

To solve a system of linear equations by **substitution**, start with the easier equation and solve for one of the variables. Express this variable in terms of the other variable. Substitute this expression in the other equation and solve for the other variable. The solution should be expressed in the form (x, y). Substitute the values into both of the original equations to check your answer. Consider the following system of equations:

$$x + 6y = 15$$
$$3x - 12y = 18$$

Solving the first equation for x: $x = 15 - 6y$

Substitute this value in place of x in the second equation, and solve for y:

$$3(15 - 6y) - 12y = 18$$
$$45 - 18y - 12y = 18$$
$$30y = 27$$
$$y = \frac{27}{30} = \frac{9}{10} = 0.9$$

Plug this value for y back into the first equation to solve for x:

$$x = 15 - 6(0.9) = 15 - 5.4 = 9.6$$

Check both equations if you have time:

$$9.6 + 6(0.9) = 15$$
$$9.6 + 5.4 = 15$$
$$15 = 15$$

$$3(9.6) - 12(0.9) = 18$$
$$28.8 - 10.8 = 18$$
$$18 = 18$$

Therefore, the solution is (9.6,0.9).

Review Video: The Substitution Method
Visit mometrix.com/academy and enter code: 565151

Review Video: Substitution and Elimination
Visit mometrix.com/academy and enter code: 958611

ELIMINATION

To solve a system of equations using **elimination**, begin by rewriting both equations in standard form $Ax + By = C$. Check to see if the coefficients of one pair of like variables add to zero. If not, multiply one or both of the equations by a non-zero number to make one set of like variables add to zero. Add the two equations to solve for one of the variables. Substitute this value into one of the original equations to solve for the other variable. Check your work by substituting into the other equation. Now, let's look at solving the following system using the elimination method:

$$5x + 6y = 4$$
$$x + 2y = 4$$

If we multiply the second equation by -3, we can eliminate the y-terms:

$$5x + 6y = 4$$
$$-3x - 6y = -12$$

Add the equations together and solve for x:

$$2x = -8$$
$$x = \frac{-8}{2} = -4$$

Mathematics

Plug the value for x back in to either of the original equations and solve for y:

$$-4 + 2y = 4$$
$$y = \frac{4+4}{2} = 4$$

Check both equations if you have time:

$$\begin{aligned} 5(-4) + 6(4) &= 4 \\ -20 + 24 &= 4 \\ 4 &= 4 \end{aligned} \qquad \begin{aligned} -4 + 2(4) &= 4 \\ -4 + 8 &= 4 \\ 4 &= 4 \end{aligned}$$

Therefore, the solution is $(-4,4)$.

Review Video: The Elimination Method
Visit mometrix.com/academy and enter code: 449121

GRAPHICALLY

To solve a system of linear equations **graphically**, plot both equations on the same graph. The solution of the equations is the point where both lines cross. If the lines do not cross (are parallel), then there is **no solution**.

For example, consider the following system of equations:

$$y = 2x + 7$$
$$y = -x + 1$$

Since these equations are given in slope-intercept form, they are easy to graph; the y-intercepts of the lines are (0,7) and (0,1). The respective slopes are 2 and –1, thus the graphs look like this:

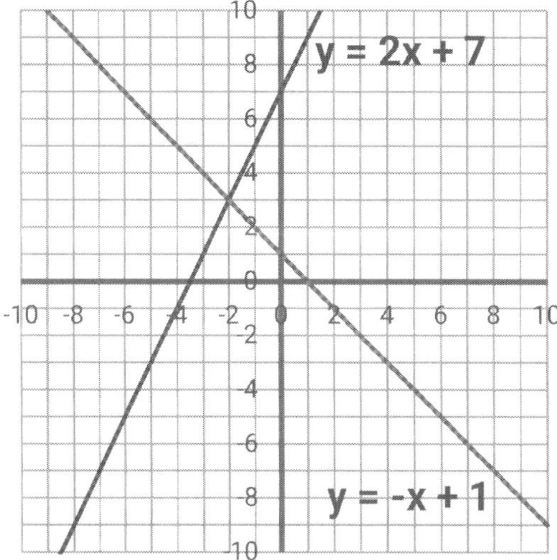

The two lines intersect at the point $(-2,3)$, thus this is the solution to the system of equations.

Solving a system graphically is generally only practical if both coordinates of the solution are integers; otherwise the intersection will lie between gridlines on the graph and the coordinates will be difficult or impossible to determine exactly. It also helps if, as in this example, the equations are in slope-intercept form or some other form that makes them easy to graph. Otherwise, another method of solution (by substitution or elimination) is likely to be more useful.

Review Video: Solving Systems by Graphing
Visit mometrix.com/academy and enter code: 634812

Solving Systems of Equations Using the Trace Feature

Using the trace feature on a calculator requires that you rewrite each equation, isolating the y-variable on one side of the equal sign. Enter both equations in the graphing calculator and plot the graphs simultaneously. Use the trace cursor to find where the two lines cross. Use the zoom feature if necessary to obtain more accurate results. Always check your answer by substituting into the original equations. The trace method is likely to be less accurate than other methods due to the resolution of graphing calculators but is a useful tool to provide an approximate answer.

Advanced Systems of Equations

Solving a System of Equations with a Linear Equation and a Quadratic Equation

Algebraically

Generally, the simplest way to solve a system of equations consisting of a linear equation and a quadratic equation algebraically is through the method of substitution. One possible strategy is to solve the linear equation for y and then substitute that expression into the quadratic equation. After expansion and combining like terms, this will result in a new quadratic equation for x, which, like all quadratic equations, may have zero, one, or two solutions. Plugging each solution for x back into one of the original equations will then produce the corresponding value of y.

For example, consider the following system of equations:

$$x + y = 1$$
$$y = (x + 3)^2 - 2$$

We can solve the linear equation for y to yield $y = -x + 1$. Substituting this expression into the quadratic equation produces $-x + 1 = (x + 3)^2 - 2$. We can simplify this equation:

$$\begin{aligned} -x + 1 &= (x + 3)^2 - 2 \\ -x + 1 &= x^2 + 6x + 9 - 2 \\ -x + 1 &= x^2 + 6x + 7 \\ 0 &= x^2 + 7x + 6 \end{aligned}$$

This quadratic equation can be factored as $(x + 1)(x + 6) = 0$. It therefore has two solutions: $x_1 = -1$ and $x_2 = -6$. Plugging each of these back into the original linear equation yields $y_1 = -x_1 + 1 = -(-1) + 1 = 2$ and $y_2 = -x_2 + 1 = -(-6) + 1 = 7$. Thus, this system of equations has two solutions, $(-1,2)$ and $(-6,7)$.

It may help to check your work by putting each x- and y-value back into the original equations and verifying that they do provide a solution.

Graphically

To solve a system of equations consisting of a linear equation and a quadratic equation graphically, plot both equations on the same graph. The linear equation will, of course, produce a straight line, while the quadratic equation will produce a parabola. These two graphs will intersect at zero, one, or two points; each point of intersection is a solution of the system.

Mathematics

For example, consider the following system of equations:

$$y = -2x + 2$$
$$y = -2x^2 + 4x + 2$$

The linear equation describes a line with a y-intercept of $(0,2)$ and a slope of -2.

To graph the quadratic equation, we can first find the vertex of the parabola: the x-coordinate of the vertex is $h = -\frac{b}{2a} = -\frac{4}{2(-2)} = 1$, and the y-coordinate is $k = -2(1)^2 + 4(1) + 2 = 4$. Thus, the vertex lies at $(1,4)$. To get a feel for the rest of the parabola, we can plug in a few more values of x to find more points; by putting in $x = 2$ and $x = 3$ in the quadratic equation, we find that the points $(2,2)$ and $(3,-4)$ lie on the parabola; by symmetry, so must $(0,2)$ and $(-1,-4)$. We can now plot both equations:

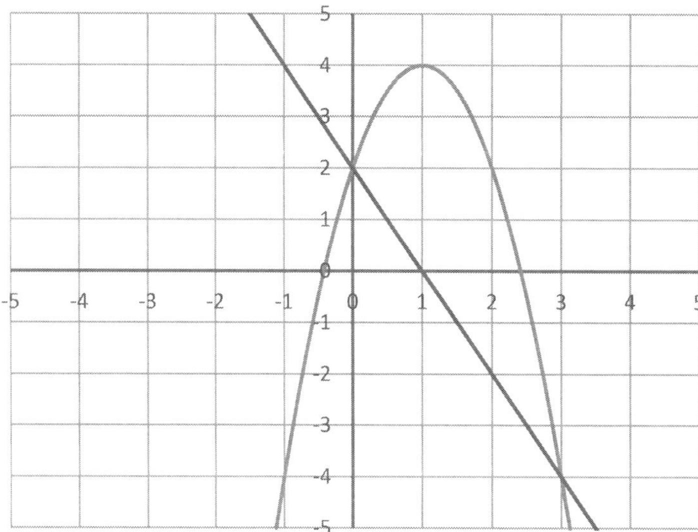

These two curves intersect at the points $(0,2)$ and $(3,-4)$, thus these are the solutions of the equation.

Review Video: Parabolas
Visit mometrix.com/academy and enter code: 129187

Review Video: Vertex of a Parabola
Visit mometrix.com/academy and enter code: 272300

Review Video: Solving a System of Linear and Quadratic Equations
Visit mometrix.com/academy and enter code: 194870

Midpoint and Distance Formulas

If you know the coordinates of the endpoints of a line segment, you can calculate the midpoint and length of the line segment. Conveniently, the length of the line segment is also the distance between the two endpoints.

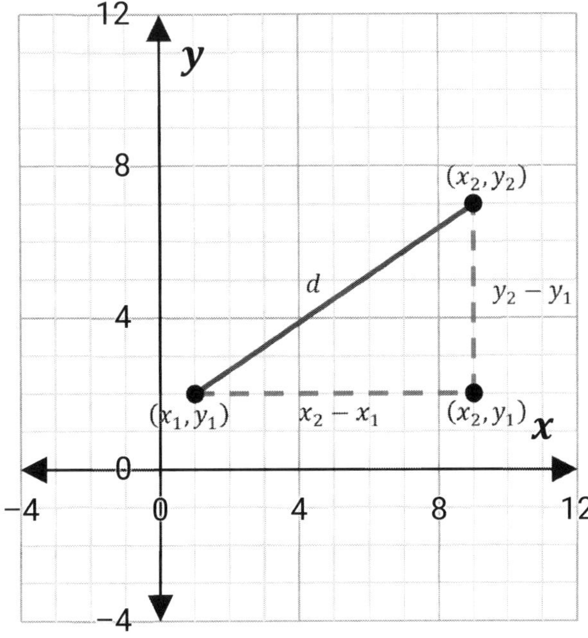

To find the **midpoint** of the line segment with endpoints (x_1, y_1) and (x_2, y_2), average the x-coordinates to get the x-coordinate of the midpoint, and average the y-coordinates to get the y-coordinate of the midpoint. Thus, the **midpoint formula** is:

$$\left(\frac{x_1 + x_2}{2}, \frac{y_1 + y_2}{2}\right)$$

The **distance** between points (x_1, y_1) and (x_2, y_2) is the same as the length of the hypotenuse of a right triangle with the two given points as endpoints, and the two sides of the right triangle parallel to the x-axis and y-axis, respectively. The length of the segment parallel to the x-axis is the difference between the x-coordinates of the two points. The length of the segment parallel to the y-axis is the difference between the y-coordinates of the two points. Use the Pythagorean theorem $a^2 + b^2 = c^2$ or $c = \sqrt{a^2 + b^2}$ to find the distance. Thus, the **distance formula** is:

$$d = \sqrt{(x_2 - x_1)^2 + (y_2 - y_1)^2}$$

Review Video: Calculations Using Points on a Graph
Visit mometrix.com/academy and enter code: 883228

Mathematics

Polynomials

Monomials and Polynomials

A **monomial** is a single constant, variable, or product of constants and variables, such as 7, x, $2x$, or x^3y. There will never be addition or subtraction symbols in a monomial. Like monomials have like variables, but they may have different coefficients. A **polynomial** is a monomial or the result of combining two or more monomials by sums or differences. In a polynomial we call each monomial a **term**. Two terms make a **binomial** (e.g., $2x + 3y$), three terms make a **trinomial** (e.g., $5x^2 - 4x + 9$). The **degree of a monomial** is the sum of the exponents of the variables. The **degree of a polynomial** is the highest degree of any individual term.

Review Video: Polynomials
Visit mometrix.com/academy and enter code: 305005

Simplifying Polynomials

Simplifying polynomials requires combining like terms. The like terms in a polynomial expression are those that have the same variables raised to the same powers. It is often helpful to connect the like terms with arrows or lines in order to separate them from the other monomials. Once you have determined the like terms, you can rearrange the polynomial by placing them together. Remember to include the sign that is in front of each term. Once the like terms are placed together, you can apply each operation and simplify. When adding and subtracting polynomials, only add and subtract the **coefficients**, or the number part; the variable and exponent stay the same.

Adding Polynomials

To add polynomials, you need to add like terms. These terms have the same variable part. For example, the terms $4x^2$ and $3x^2$ both include x^2 terms. To find the sum of like terms, find the sum of the coefficients. Then, keep the same variable part. You can use the distributive property to distribute the plus sign to each term of the polynomial. For example:

$(4x^2 - 5x + 7) + (3x^2 + 2x + 1) =$
$(4x^2 - 5x + 7) + 3x^2 + 2x + 1 =$
$(4x^2 + 3x^2) + (-5x + 2x) + (7 + 1) =$
$7x^2 - 3x + 8$

Subtracting Polynomials

To subtract polynomials, you need to subtract like terms. To find the difference of like terms, find the difference of the coefficients. Then, keep the same variable part. You can use the distributive property to distribute the minus sign to each term of the polynomial. For example:

$(-2x^2 - x + 5) - (3x^2 - 4x + 1) =$
$(-2x^2 - x + 5) - 3x^2 + 4x - 1 =$
$(-2x^2 - 3x^2) + (-x + 4x) + (5 - 1) =$
$-5x^2 + 3x + 4$

Review Video: Adding and Subtracting Polynomials
Visit mometrix.com/academy and enter code: 124088

Multiplying Polynomials

In general, multiplying polynomials is done by multiplying each term in one polynomial by each term in the other and adding the results. In the specific case for multiplying binomials, there is a useful acronym, FOIL, that can help you make sure to cover each combination of terms. The **FOIL method** for $(Ax + By)(Cx + Dy)$ would be:

F	Multiply the *first* terms of each binomial	$(\overbrace{Ax}^{first} + By)(\overbrace{Cx}^{first} + Dy)$	ACx^2
O	Multiply the *outer* terms	$(\overbrace{Ax}^{outer} + By)(Cx + \overbrace{Dy}^{outer})$	$ADxy$
I	Multiply the *inner* terms	$(Ax + \overbrace{By}^{inner})(\overbrace{Cx}^{inner} + Dy)$	$BCxy$
L	Multiply the *last* terms of each binomial	$(Ax + \overbrace{By}^{last})(Cx + \overbrace{Dy}^{last})$	BDy^2

Then, add up the result of each and combine like terms: $ACx^2 + (AD + BC)xy + BDy^2$.

For example, using the FOIL method on binomials $(x + 2)$ and $(x - 3)$:

$$\begin{aligned} \text{First:} \quad & (\boxed{x} + 2)(\boxed{x} + (-3)) \rightarrow (x)(x) = x^2 \\ \text{Outer:} \quad & (\boxed{x} + 2)(x + \boxed{(-3)}) \rightarrow (x)(-3) = -3x \\ \text{Inner:} \quad & (x + \boxed{2})(\boxed{x} + (-3)) \rightarrow (2)(x) = 2x \\ \text{Last:} \quad & (x + \boxed{2})(x + \boxed{(-3)}) \rightarrow (2)(-3) = -6 \end{aligned}$$

This results in: $(x^2) + (-3x) + (2x) + (-6)$

Combine like terms: $x^2 + (-3 + 2)x + (-6) = x^2 - x - 6$

Review Video: Multiplying Polynomials
Visit mometrix.com/academy and enter code: 598293

Review Video: Multiplying Terms Using the FOIL Method
Visit mometrix.com/academy and enter code: 854792

DIVIDING POLYNOMIALS

Use long division to divide a polynomial by either a monomial or another polynomial of equal or lesser degree.

When **dividing by a monomial**, divide each term of the polynomial by the monomial.

Review Video: Dividing Monomials
Visit mometrix.com/academy and enter code: 584409

When **dividing by a polynomial**, begin by arranging the terms of each polynomial in order of one variable. You may arrange in ascending or descending order, but be consistent with both polynomials. To get the first term of the quotient, divide the first term of the dividend by the first term of the divisor. Multiply the first term of the quotient by the entire divisor and subtract that product from the dividend. Repeat for the second and successive terms until you either get a remainder of zero or a remainder whose degree is less than the degree of the divisor. If the quotient has a remainder, write the answer as a mixed expression in the form:

$$\text{quotient} + \frac{\text{remainder}}{\text{divisor}}$$

For example, we can evaluate the following expression in the same way as long division:

$$\frac{x^3 - 3x^2 - 2x + 5}{x - 5}$$

$$\begin{array}{r} x^2 \quad +2x \quad +8 \\ x-5 \enclose{longdiv}{x^3 \quad -3x^2 \quad -2x \quad +5} \\ \underline{-(x^3 - 5x^2)} \qquad\qquad\quad \\ 2x^2 \quad -2x \qquad \\ \underline{-(2x^2 - 10x)} \qquad \\ 8x \quad +5 \\ \underline{-(8x - 40)} \\ 45 \end{array}$$

$$\frac{x^3 - 3x^2 - 2x + 5}{x - 5} = x^2 + 2x + 8 + \frac{45}{x - 5}$$

Review Video: Dividing Polynomials by Monomials
Visit mometrix.com/academy and enter code: 253551

Review Video: Dividing Trinomials by Binomials
Visit mometrix.com/academy and enter code: 651465

When **factoring** a polynomial, first see whether you can factor out a nontrivial greatest common factor (GCF). For example, the trinomial $3x^5 - 18x^4 + 15x^3$ has a GCF of $3x^3$ since the GCF of 3, 18, and 15 is 3 and the GCF of x^5, x^4, and x^3 is x^3. Factoring out the GCF simplifies the expression to $3x^3(x^2 - 6x + 5)$.

To factor a quadratic trinomial (this comes up frequently), first check whether it is a perfect square trinomial (see bulleted list below). If not, see if you can factor it by trial and error by making clever choices of values for a and b (or a, b, c, and d) in the formulas below (this amounts to trying to use the FOIL mnemonic backwards):

$$x^2 + (a + b)x + ab = (x + a)(x + b)$$
$$(ac)x^2 + (ad + bc)x + bd = (ax + b)(cx + d)$$

For instance, you would try to factor the trinomial $x^2 - 6x + 5$ using the equation $x^2 + (a + b)x + ab = (x + a)(x + b)$. This means that you need to find integers a and b such that $a + b = -6$ and $ab = 5$. Starting with $ab = 5$, you can see that the only ways to write 5 as a product of integers are $(1)(5) = 5$ and $(-1)(-5) = 5$. So, it is easy to see that you want $a = -1$ and $b = -5$ since $a + b = -1 + (-5) = -6$ and $ab = (-1)(-5) = 5$. This tells you that $x^2 - 6x + 5 = (x - 1)(x - 5)$.

For polynomials with four terms (usually a cubic polynomial), sometimes factoring by grouping works: You group the two higher-power terms and the two lower-power terms, factor the GCF out of each group, and then factor out the resulting common binomial factor, if there is one. For example, $x^3 + 5x^2 + 3x + 15 = (x^3 + 5x^2) + (3x + 15) = x^2(x + 5) + 3(x + 5) = (x^2 + 3)(x + 5)$.

Once you have found the factors, write the original polynomial as the product of all the factors. Make sure all of the factors are either monomials, or else linear or irreducible quadratic polynomials (*irreducible* means they have no real zeros, which is easy to check with the quadratic formula). Check your work by multiplying the factors to make sure you get the original polynomial.

Review Video: Factoring Out Common Monomial Factors
Visit mometrix.com/academy and enter code: 398578

Review Video: Factoring Trinomials of the Form x^2+bx+c
Visit mometrix.com/academy and enter code: 270556

Below are patterns of some special products to remember to help make factoring easier:

- Perfect square trinomials: $x^2 + 2xy + y^2 = (x + y)^2$ or $x^2 - 2xy + y^2 = (x - y)^2$. For example, $x^2 + 10x + 25 = (x + 5)^2$.
- Difference between two squares: $x^2 - y^2 = (x + y)(x - y)$. For example, $x^2 - 9 = (x + 3)(x - 3)$.
- Sum of two cubes: $x^3 + y^3 = (x + y)(x^2 - xy + y^2)$. For example, $x^3 + 27 = (x + 3)(x^2 - 3x + 9)$.
  - Note: the second factor is *not* the same as a perfect square trinomial, so do not try to factor it further.
- Difference between two cubes: $x^3 - y^3 = (x - y)(x^2 + xy + y^2)$. For example, $x^3 - 1000 = (x - 10)(x^2 + 10x + 100)$.
  - Again, the second factor is *not* the same as a perfect square trinomial.
- Perfect cubes: $x^3 + 3x^2y + 3xy^2 + y^3 = (x + y)^3$ and $x^3 - 3x^2y + 3xy^2 - y^3 = (x - y)^3$

Review Video: Factoring the Difference of Two Squares
Visit mometrix.com/academy and enter code: 128954

RATIONAL AND IRRATIONAL EXPRESSIONS

RATIONAL EXPRESSIONS

Rational expressions are fractions with polynomials in both the numerator and the denominator; the value of the polynomial in the denominator cannot be equal to zero. Be sure to keep track of values that make the denominator of the original expression zero as the final result inherits the same restrictions. For example, a denominator of $x - 3$ indicates that the expression is not defined when $x = 3$ and, as such, regardless of any operations done to the expression, it remains undefined there.

To **add or subtract** rational expressions, first find the common denominator, then rewrite each fraction as an equivalent fraction with the common denominator. Finally, add or subtract the numerators to get the numerator of the answer, and keep the common denominator as the denominator of the answer.

When **multiplying** rational expressions, factor each polynomial and cancel like factors (a factor which appears in both the numerator and the denominator). Then, multiply all remaining factors in the numerator to get the numerator of the product, and multiply the remaining factors in the denominator to get the denominator of the product. Remember: cancel entire factors, not individual terms.

To **divide** rational expressions, take the reciprocal of the divisor (the rational expression you are dividing by) and multiply by the dividend.

Review Video: Rational Expressions
Visit mometrix.com/academy and enter code: 415183

SIMPLIFYING RATIONAL EXPRESSIONS

To simplify a rational expression, factor the numerator and denominator completely. Factors that are the same and appear in the numerator and denominator have a ratio of 1. For example, look at the following expression:

$$\frac{x-1}{1-x^2}$$

The denominator, $(1-x^2)$, is a difference of squares. It can be factored as $(1-x)(1+x)$. The factor $1-x$ and the numerator $x-1$ are opposites and have a ratio of –1. Rewrite the numerator as $-1(1-x)$. So, the rational expression can be simplified as follows:

$$\frac{x-1}{1-x^2} = \frac{-1(1-x)}{(1-x)(1+x)} = \frac{-1}{1+x}$$

Note that since the original expression is only defined for $x \neq \{-1, 1\}$, the simplified expression has the same restrictions.

Review Video: Reducing Rational Expressions
Visit mometrix.com/academy and enter code: 788868

Review Video: Simplifying Algebraic Expressions with Parentheses
Visit mometrix.com/academy and enter code: 850843

IRRATIONAL EXPRESSIONS

Irrational expressions are mathematical expressions that contain an irrational number and cannot be simplified into a rational form. Usually, this includes expressions that contain radicals or constants such as π. Most commonly, you will encounter these in the forms of expressions containing roots of non-perfect squares.

BASIC OPERATIONS ON RADICAL EXPRESSIONS

To add or subtract radical numbers, the numbers within the radicals must match, similar to finding a common denominator in fractions:

$$a\sqrt{x} + b\sqrt{x} = (a+b)\sqrt{x}$$

$$a\sqrt{x} - b\sqrt{x} = (a-b)\sqrt{x}$$

To multiply radicals, the numbers outside the radical are multiplied together and the numbers inside the radical are multiplied together:

$$a\sqrt{x} \times b\sqrt{y} = ab\sqrt{xy}$$

To divide radicals, the radical must be eliminated from the denominator by multiplying both numerator and denominator by a value that will make the denominator a rational number:

$$\frac{a\sqrt{x}}{b\sqrt{y}} = \frac{a\sqrt{x}\sqrt{y}}{b\sqrt{y}\sqrt{y}} = \frac{a\sqrt{xy}}{by}$$

Review Video: Adding and Subtracting Radical Expressions
Visit mometrix.com/academy and enter code: 752176

EXAMPLE

To solve $\frac{(3\sqrt{6})(2\sqrt{3})}{4\sqrt{5}}$, we first multiply the numerator, inside the radical and out: $3 \times 2\sqrt{6 \times 3} = 6\sqrt{18} = 18\sqrt{2}$. To divide, we multiply both numerator and denominator by a value that will eliminate the radical:

$$\frac{18\sqrt{2} \times \sqrt{5}}{4\sqrt{5} \times \sqrt{5}} = \frac{18\sqrt{10}}{4 \times 5} = \frac{18\sqrt{10}}{20} = \frac{9\sqrt{10}}{10}$$

ALGEBRAIC THEOREMS

According to the **fundamental theorem of algebra**, every non-constant, single-variable polynomial has exactly as many roots as the polynomial's highest exponent. For example, if x^4 is the largest exponent of a term, the polynomial will have exactly 4 roots. However, some of these roots may have multiplicity or be complex numbers. For instance, in the polynomial function $f(x) = x^4 - 4x + 3$, the only real root is 1, though it has multiplicity of 2 – that is, it occurs twice. The other two roots, $(-1 - i\sqrt{2})$ and $(-1 + i\sqrt{2})$, are complex, consisting of both real and non-real components.

The **remainder theorem** is useful for determining the remainder when a polynomial is divided by a binomial. The remainder theorem states that if a polynomial function $f(x)$ is divided by a binomial $x - a$, where a is a real number, the remainder of the division will be the value of $f(a)$. If $f(a) = 0$, then a is a root of the polynomial.

The **factor theorem** is related to the remainder theorem and states that if $f(a) = 0$ then $(x - a)$ is a factor of the function.

According to the **rational root theorem,** any rational root of a polynomial function $f(x) = a_nx^n + a_{n-1}x^{n-1} + \cdots + a_1x + a_0$ with integer coefficients will, when reduced to its lowest terms, be a positive or negative fraction such that the numerator is a factor of a_0 and the denominator is a factor of a_n. For instance, if the polynomial function $f(x) = x^3 + 3x^2 - 4$ has any rational roots, the numerators of those roots can only be factors of 4 (1, 2, 4), and the denominators can only be factors of 1 (1). The function in this example has roots of 1 (or $\frac{1}{1}$) and –2 (or $\frac{-2}{1}$).

QUADRATICS

SOLVING QUADRATIC EQUATIONS

A quadratic equation is an equation that can be written (possibly after simplification) in the form $ax^2 + bx + c = 0$. Thus, the **solutions** of this equation are precisely the **zeros** of the quadratic polynomial $P(x) = ax^2 + bx + c$. On the graph of this polynomial the zeros, if any, appear as x-intercepts. There are several ways to find these solutions including the quadratic formula, factoring, completing the square, and graphing the function.

Review Video: Quadratic Equations Overview
Visit mometrix.com/academy and enter code: 476276

Review Video: Solutions of a Quadratic Equation on a Graph
Visit mometrix.com/academy and enter code: 328231

QUADRATIC FORMULA

The **quadratic formula** gives the zeros of a quadratic polynomial. It always works, but it is sometimes a little harder to use than other methods. To use it to solve a quadratic equation, rewrite the equation in the form $ax^2 + bx + c = 0$, where a, b, and c are coefficients. Now, as explained above, the solutions of the equation are the zeros of the quadratic polynomial $P(x) = ax^2 + bx + c$. To find them, substitute the values of a, b, and c into the Quadratic Formula:

$$x = \frac{-b \pm \sqrt{b^2 - 4ac}}{2a}$$

After simplification this formula produces two, one, or zero real solutions, depending on whether the **discriminant** (the number $b^2 - 4ac$ under the radical) is positive, zero, or negative. It is a good practice to check each solution by substituting it into the original equation. Incidentally, if the discriminant is negative, then the equation does have two complex solutions, but you often ignore these as meaningless in real-world settings.

Review Video: Using the Quadratic Formula
Visit mometrix.com/academy and enter code: 163102

Factoring

To solve a quadratic equation by factoring, begin by rewriting the equation in the standard form, $ax^2 + bx + c = 0$. In the important special case that $a = 1$, the goal of factoring is to find numbers f and g such that $x^2 + bx + c = (x + f)(x + g) = x^2 + (f + g)x + fg$. In other words, you want to choose f and g to make $fg = c$ and $f + g = b$. To do this, find pairs of numbers (factors) whose product is c and look for a pair whose sum is b.

For example, suppose you want to find the solutions of the equation $x^2 + 6x - 16 = 0$ by factoring. Here $b = 6$ and $c = -16$. First, you find the pairs of numbers whose product is -16. These are -4 and 4, -8 and 2, -2 and 8, -1 and 16, and 1 and -16. The pair -2 and 8 has a sum of 6. This means $f = -2$ and $g = 8$. So, the factorization is $x^2 + 6x - 16 = (x + f)(x + g) = (x - 2)(x + 8)$, allowing you to rewrite the original equation as $(x - 2)(x + 8) = 0$. The only way for a product to equal zero is for one of the factors to equal zero; so, either $x - 2 = 0$ (in which case $x = 2$) or $x + 8 = 0$ (in which case $x = -8$). Thus, the equation has the solution $x = 2$ or $x = -8$.

In the case that $a \neq 1$, you can attempt to factor the quadratic polynomial $ax^2 + bx + c$ in the form $(mx + f)(nx + g)$ by a similar trial-and-error procedure, but the work tends to be much harder.

Review Video: Factoring Quadratic Equations
Visit mometrix.com/academy and enter code: 336566

Completing the Square

The technique of completing the square comes from a simple observation: Suppose you have the expression $x^2 + bx$. If you take half the linear coefficient, b, square it, and add the result to the expression, the result is always a perfect square trinomial:

$$x^2 + bx + \left(\frac{b}{2}\right)^2 = \left(x + \frac{b}{2}\right)^2$$

For example, if you begin with $x^2 + 6x$ and add the square of half of 6 (half of 6 is 3, and $3^2 = 9$), then you get a perfect square trinomial:

$$x^2 + 6x + 9 = (x + 3)^2$$

This also works if b is negative. For instance, if you begin with the expression $x^2 - 10x$ and complete the square by adding 25 (half of -10 is -5, and $(-5)^2 = 25$), then you get another perfect square trinomial:

$$x^2 - 10x + 25 = (x - 5)^2$$

Now, suppose you want to solve the equation $x^2 + bx + c = 0$. Subtract c from both sides, to get the equation $x^2 + bx = -c$. Complete the square on the left side by adding $(b/2)^2$, but also add this same term to the right side so that the new equation is equivalent to the old one:

$$x^2 + bx + \left(\frac{b}{2}\right)^2 = -c + \left(\frac{b}{2}\right)^2$$
$$\left(x + \frac{b}{2}\right)^2 = -c + \left(\frac{b}{2}\right)^2$$

Take square roots of both sides:

$$x + \frac{b}{2} = \pm\sqrt{-c + \left(\frac{b}{2}\right)^2}$$

Remember to include $\pm$ since every positive number has both a positive and a negative square root. Subtract $b/2$ from both sides to isolate the variable x to finish the problem:

$$x = -\frac{b}{2} \pm \sqrt{-c + \left(\frac{b}{2}\right)^2}$$

This may sound complicated, but in practice it is not hard. For example, suppose you want to solve the equation $x^2 + 6x - 16 = 0$ by completing the square. First, add 16 to both sides:

$$x^2 + 6x = 16$$

Half of 6 is 3 and $3^2 = 9$, so complete the square by adding 9 to both sides of the equation:

$$x^2 + 6x + 9 = 16 + 9$$
$$(x + 3)^2 = 25$$

Now take square root of both sides, remembering to include the $\pm$:

$$\sqrt{(x + 3)^2} = \pm\sqrt{25}$$
$$x + 3 = \pm 5$$
$$x = -3 \pm 5$$

So we see that the two solutions to the equation are $x = 2$ and $x = -8$.

Review Video: Completing the Square
Visit mometrix.com/academy and enter code: 982479

Using Given Solutions to Find a Quadratic Equation

To find a quadratic equation with given numbers as solutions, simply find a quadratic polynomial that has those numbers as zeros and set that polynomial equal to zero. This is easy because a polynomial has the number p as a zero precisely when it has the binomial $x - p$ as a factor. Thus, for instance, to find a quadratic polynomial with zeros at $x = 3$ and $x = -5$, construct the polynomial $P(x) = (x - 3)(x - (-5)) = (x - 3)(x + 5) = x^2 + 2x - 15$. Setting this equal to zero produces an equation, $x^2 + 2x - 15 = 0$, whose solutions are $x = 3$ and $x = -5$.

Of course, any constant multiple $P(x) = a(x - 3)(x + 5)$ will also have the same zeros. For instance, if you choose $a = 4$, then you get the polynomial $P(x) = 4(x - 3)(x + 5) = 4x^2 + 8x - 60$, which also has zeros at

$x = 3$ and $x = -5$. From this you can get another equation, $4x^2 + 8x - 60 = 0$, with solutions $x = 3$ and $x = -5$.

Basics of Functions

Definition of a Function

A function is a rule that assigns to every number in a given set (called the **domain**) exactly one corresponding value. For example, if our domain is the set $\{-2,1,2,3\}$, we can define a function by assigning to each number its square. This function assigns to -2 the value 4, to 1 the value 1, to 2 the value 4, and to 3 the value 9 (since $(-2)^2 = 4$, $1^2 = 1$, $2^2 = 4$, and $3^2 = 9$). The set of all the values assigned by a function is the **range** of the function. The range of the function in our example is the set $\{1, 4, 9\}$. We may think of a function as a kind of machine: we give it a number as an input, and it uses its rule to produce a number as an output. In the squaring function above, the input 3 produces the output 9.

Review Video: What is a Function?
Visit mometrix.com/academy and enter code: 784611

Function Notation

We usually name a function by a letter, often the letter f (for *function*—if we need to talk about more than one function, we name the second one g, the third one h, etc.). To specify the value (the output) corresponding to a particular number in the domain (the input), we write the function letter followed by the input number in parentheses. For instance, in the example above the notation $f(3)$ means the value that the function assigns to the number 3, namely 9—that is, $f(3) = 9$. We read the symbols $f(3)$ as, "f of 3," and we call 3 the **argument** of the function and 9 the **value** of the function (so *argument* means *input* and *value* means *output*).

Using function notation we can define the squaring function above by listing the values the function assigns to each argument in the domain: $f(-2) = 4$. $f(1) = 1$, $f(2) = 4$, and $f(3) = 9$. More efficiently, we can define the function by the single equation $f(x) = x^2$, which says that if x is a number from the domain, then we calculate the value assigned to it by substituting the number x in the formula x^2. For instance, we calculate $f(5) = 5^2 = 25$. Similarly, if we define a function g by the equation $g(x) = x^2 - 4x + 7$, then we calculate the value $g(3)$ by substituting 3 for each x in the formula: $g(3) = 3^2 - 4 \cdot 3 + 7 = 9 - 12 + 7 = 4$.

Other Ways to Define Functions

Instead of denoting the value of the function by $f(x)$, sometimes we simply use another letter, usually y. For instance, instead of defining the squaring function by the equation $f(x) = x^2$, we might use the equation $y = x^2$. In this case, we refer to x (the input) as the **independent variable** and y (the output) as the **dependent variable** because the value, y, depends on the number we choose for x.

A formula (with y or $f(x)$) is the most common way to define a function; but sometimes, if the domain is small enough, we prefer to list explicitly the possible inputs and their corresponding outputs. Some ways of doing this appear above, but a more common approach is to put the input-output pairs in a table. For instance, we can define the squaring function above by the table

x	-2	1	2	3
y	4	1	4	9

We see that the domain of this function is the set of all numbers in the x-row and the range is the set of all numbers in the y-row. We note that numbers cannot repeat in the x-row (because a function assigns exactly one value to each argument in the domain) but they can repeat in the y-row (because the function can assign the same value to multiple arguments—for instance, the number 4 appears twice in the y-row).

We can also define a function by writing the inputs and corresponding outputs as ordered pairs of x- and y-values. For instance, we can write the squaring function above as the set of ordered pairs

$\{(-2,4), (1,1), (2,4), (3,9)\}$. Further, by treating these ordered pairs as coordinates and plotting the corresponding points on the coordinate plane, we get the **graph** of the function:

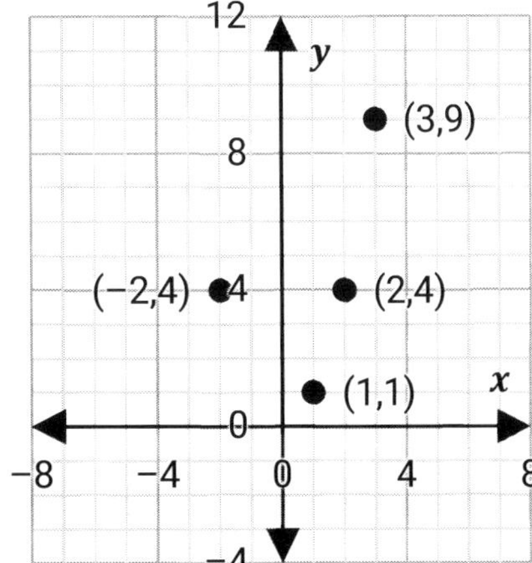

Turning this around, we can potentially use a graph to define a function, namely the function consisting of the coordinate pairs of all the points in the graph. This always works unless the graph has two points with the same x-coordinate (because then the function would assign two different y-values to the same x). It is easy to detect such points: because they have the same x-coordinate, a vertical line passes through both of them. Thus, a graph always defines a function unless it is possible to draw a vertical line that intersects the graph in two or more points. We call this condition the **vertical line test**. For example, if our graph is a circle, then by the Vertical Line Test the graph does not define a function because there are vertical lines that will intersect the circle in two different points.

More on Domains and Ranges

When we define a function by a formula and do not specify the domain, then by default the domain consists of all real numbers for which the formula produces an answer. For instance, suppose we define a function f by the formula $f(x) = 1/x$. If $x = 0$, then $1/x = 1/0$, which is undefined. But if x is any other real number, then we can calculate the value of $1/x$. So, the default domain of this function is all real numbers except zero. Because of this domain convention, the graph of a function defined by a formula usually consists of infinitely many points that "connect to" each other in a way that produces a line or curve (see examples below) rather than the isolated points we see in the squaring function above.

If we have the graph of a function, its domain consists of all numbers on the x-axis with corresponding points on the graph and its range consists of all numbers on the y-axis with corresponding points on the graph. For example, consider the function $f(x) = x^2 + 3$:

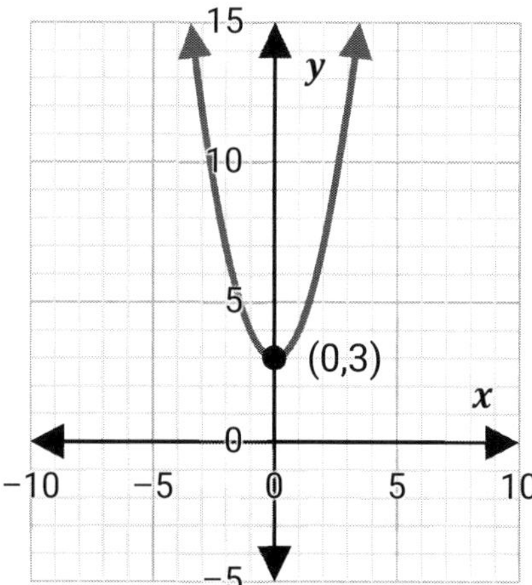

Since the graph continues infinitely to the left and right beyond what we can see, every point on the x-axis has a corresponding point on the graph; so, the domain of this function is all real numbers. On the other hand, the lowest point on this graph has a y-value of 3, and the graph passes through all higher y-values. So, the range of this function is all real numbers greater than or equal to 3, which we can denote algebraically by $y \geq 3$ or, using interval notation, by $[3, \infty)$.

Review Video: How to Find Domain and Range
Visit mometrix.com/academy and enter code: 778133

Review Video: Domain and Range of Quadratic Functions
Visit mometrix.com/academy and enter code: 331768

Monotonic and Even/Odd Functions

A function, f, is **increasing** if it always assigns larger values to larger arguments. It is **decreasing** if it always assigns smaller values to larger arguments. That is, f is increasing if $a < b$ always guarantees $f(a) < f(b)$, and it is decreasing if $a < b$ always guarantees $f(a) > f(b)$. The graph of an increasing function consistently rises from left to right, and the graph of a decreasing function consistently falls from left to right. For example, the function $f(x) = 2x$ is an increasing function because doubling a larger number always gives us a larger result than doubling a smaller number. The graph of $f(x) = 2x$ is a line with slope $m = 2$, which, as we expect, rises from left to right. We call a function **monotonic** if it is either increasing or decreasing.

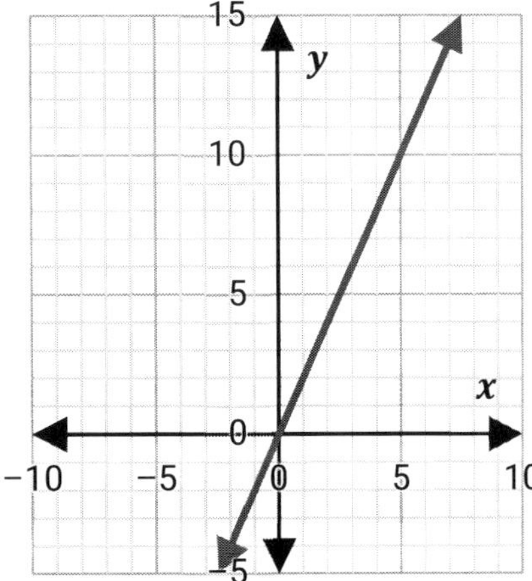

A function, f, is **even** if changing the sign of its argument produces the same value. It is **odd** if changing the sign of its argument produces the same value except with the opposite sign. That is, f is even if $f(-x) = f(x)$ and odd if $f(-x) = -f(x)$ for every argument x. The function $f(x) = x^2 + 3$ is even because substituting opposite arguments always produces the same value. For instance, $f(5) = 28$ and $f(-5) = 28$ because $5^2 + 3 = 25 + 3 = 28$ and $(-5)^2 + 3 = 25 + 3 = 28$. The function $f(x) = 2x$ is odd because substituting opposite arguments always produces opposite values. For instance, $f(10) = 20$ and $f(-10) = -20$ because $2(10) = 20$ and $2(-10) = -20$. The graph of an even function is always symmetric with respect to the y-axis, making the left and right halves of the graph mirror images of each other, as in the graph of the even function $f(x) = x^2 + 3$ above. The graph of an odd function is always symmetric with respect to the origin. This means that if we rotate the graph 180° around the origin (think of sticking a pin through the origin on a sheet of graph paper and rotating the paper halfway around) the graph looks the same, as in the graph of the odd function $f(x) = 2x$ above.

It is worth noting that most functions are neither increasing nor decreasing (that is, they are not monotonic) and most functions are neither even nor odd. For example, the function $f(x) = x^2 - x$ is neither increasing nor decreasing and neither even nor odd: its graph neither rises nor falls consistently, and it is symmetric with respect to neither the y-axis nor the origin.

Review Video: Even and Odd Functions
Visit mometrix.com/academy and enter code: 278985

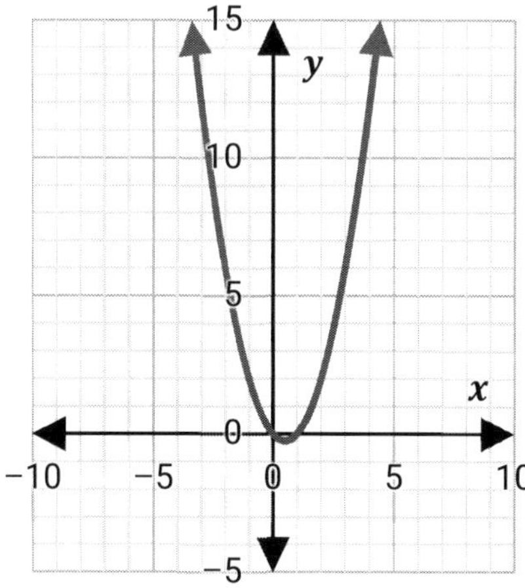

Invertible (One-to-One) Functions

A function, f, is one-to-one if it never assigns the same value to different arguments—that is, if $f(a)$ and $f(b)$ are different whenever a and b are different. The graph of a one-to-one function never has two points that lie on the same horizontal line because such points would have different x-values but the same y-value. Thus, a function is one-to-one if it is impossible to draw a horizontal line that intersects its graph in more than one point. We call this condition the **horizonal line test**. For example, the graph of the function $f(x) = 2x$ above is a line that rises from left to right. Every horizontal line intersects this line in exactly one point, so the function $f(x) = 2x$ is one-to-one. This is also clear without the graph because it is impossible to double two different numbers and get the same answer.

When a function, f, is one-to-one, it is possible to define its inverse function, f^{-1}, that "undoes" what f does, assigning to each output from f the input that produced it. That is, for each x in the domain of f, if $y = f(x)$, then $f^{-1}(y) = x$. For example, the inverse of the function $f(x) = 2x$ above is $f^{-1}(y) = y/2$. So, for instance, $f(5) = 2 \cdot 5 = 10$, and $f^{-1}(10) = 10/2 = 5$ (and similarly for every other value of x). Thus, the domain of f^{-1} is the range of f and vice versa. If a function, f, has an inverse, we say that f is **invertible**. Since a function has an inverse precisely when it is one-to-one, the terms *invertible* and *one-to-one* are synonyms.

If f is an invertible function defined by a formula, then to find its inverse we simply write the equation $y = f(x)$ and solve it for x (that is, we isolate the x). The result will be the equation $f^{-1}(y) = x$. For instance, starting with the function $f(x) = 2x$, we write $y = 2x$ and isolate the x by dividing both sides of the equation by 2. This gives us $y/2 = x$, so we know that $f^{-1}(y) = y/2$. Although this procedure is theoretically simple, in practice the algebra can be difficult.

Common Functions

Certain functions and certain kinds of functions are particularly useful, coming up frequently in mathematics and its applications. Once we know some basic function terminology and concepts, it is useful to begin developing a mental library of the most common and useful functions.

Review Video: Common Functions
Visit mometrix.com/academy and enter code: 629798

Constant Functions

A function of the form $f(x) = a$, where a is a real number, is a **constant function**. This function assigns the same value, a, to every real argument x. For instance, given the constant function $f(x) = 5$, we have $f(2) = 5$, $f(100) = 5$, and $f(-7.1) = 5$.

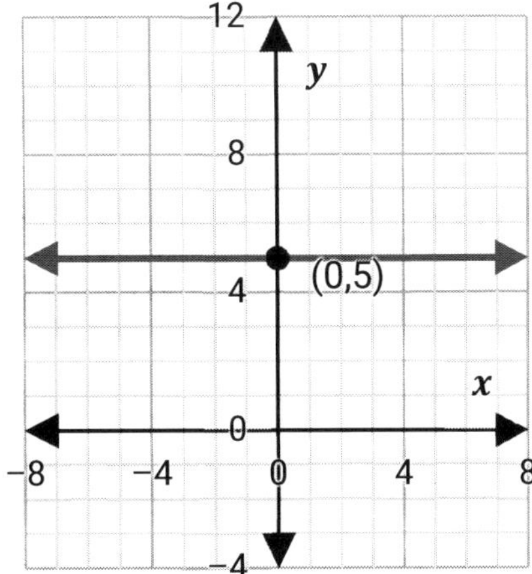

The domain of a constant function is the set of all real numbers, and the range is the set containing the single number a. Its graph is a horizontal line passing through the number $y = a$ on the y-axis (we call the number at which a function's graph intersects the y-axis the **y-intercept** of the function).

The Identity Function

The function $f(x) = x$ is the **identity function**. Its value always equals its argument. Thus, for instance, $f(2) = 2$, $f(100) = 100$, and $f(-7.1) = -7.1$.

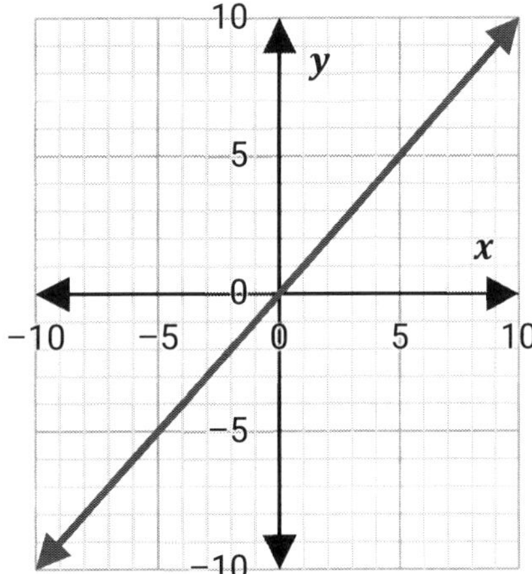

Its domain and range are the set of all real numbers. It is both an increasing function and an odd function. Its graph is a line that passes through the origin and rises from left to right at a 45° angle to the horizontal. Since it passes through the origin, its y intercept is $y = 0$ and it also has an **x-intercept** (a number at which the function's graph intersects the x-axis) of $x = 0$.

Linear Functions

A function of the form $f(x) = ax + b$, where a and b are real numbers (with $a \neq 0$), is a **linear function** (the identity function is a linear function with $a = 1$ and $b = 0$). Its domain and range are the set of all real numbers. Its graph is a line (the word *linear* contains the root word *line*) with one x-intercept (at $x = -b/a$), with a y-intercept at $y = b$, and with a direction and steepness that depend on the coefficient a, which we call the **slope**. Specifically, the slope a is the amount the y-value increases for each increase of 1 in the x-value. Thus, for $a > 0$, the line rises from left to right (making f an increasing function), and larger values of a produce steeper ascents. Similarly, for $a < 0$, the line falls from left to right (making f a decreasing function), and smaller (more negative) values of a produce steeper descents. For instance, the graph of the linear function $f(x) = (1/2)x + 3$ is a line that passes through the point $y = 3$ on the y-axis and that rises by $1/2$ unit for every unit that x increases.

Review Video: Linear Functions
Visit mometrix.com/academy and enter code: 200735

Review Video: Graphing Linear Functions
Visit mometrix.com/academy and enter code: 699478

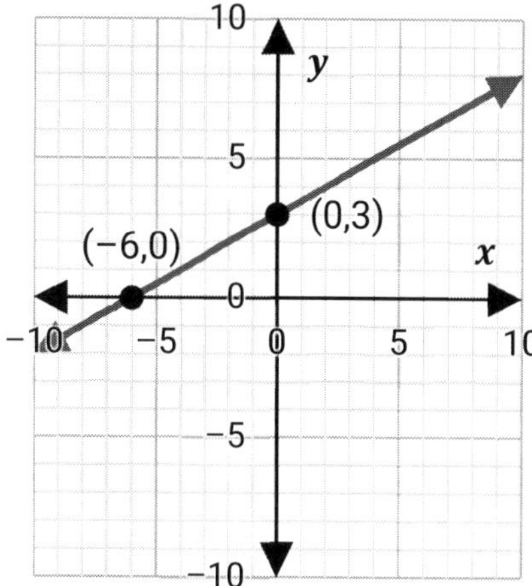

In many contexts it is standard to use the letter m for slope and thus to write the general form of a linear function as $f(x) = mx + b$, known as **slope-intercept form**.

The Squaring Function

The function $f(x) = x^2$ is the **squaring function**.

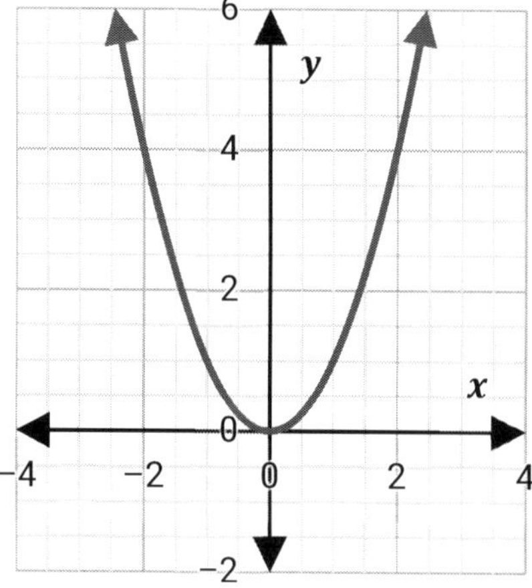

Its graph is U-shaped, opening upward as shown, a shape known as a **parabola**. It has a lowest point, its **vertex**, at the origin, which is also the location of its single x-intercept and single y-intercept. Thus, its **minimum** is $y = 0$, its domain is the set of all real numbers, and its range is the set of nonnegative real numbers (that is, $y \geq 0$). It is an even function and thus symmetric with respect to the y-axis (which we call the **axis of symmetry**), meaning that the left half of the graph is the mirror image of the right half, with the mirror standing on the y-axis.

QUADRATIC FUNCTIONS

A function of the form $f(x) = ax^2 + bx + c$, where a, b, and c are real numbers (with $a \neq 0$), is a **quadratic function** (the squaring function is a quadratic function with $a = 1, b = 0,$ and $c = 0$). Its domain is the set of all real numbers, and its graph is a parabola. It is symmetric with respect to its axis of symmetry, the vertical line $x = -b/(2a)$. If $a > 0$, the parabola opens upward, so that its vertex is at its lowest point (its minimum) and its range consists of all real numbers greater than or equal to this minimum y-value. If $a < 0$, the parabola opens downward, so that its vertex is at its highest point (its maximum) and its range consists of all real numbers less than or equal to this maximum y-value. Its y-intercept is $y = c$ since $f(0) = c$, and it may have zero, one, or two x-intercepts. For example, the function $f(x) = x^2 - 6x + 5$ has $a = 1, b = -6,$ and $c = 5$.

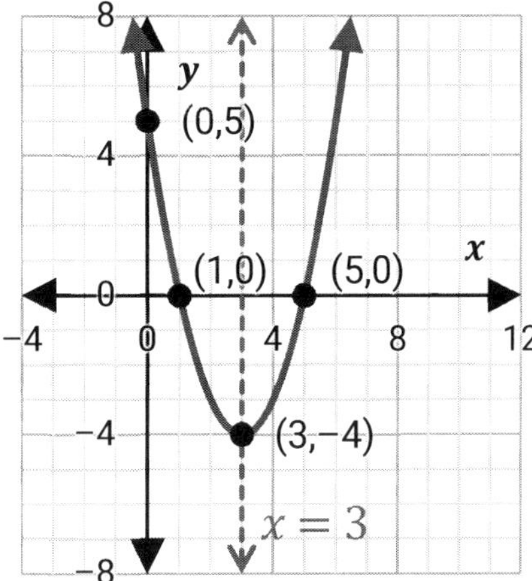

Its graph opens upward (because $a > 0$) and its axis of symmetry is the vertical line $x = 3$ (since $-b/(2a) = -(-6)/(2 \cdot 1) = 3$). Its y-intercept is at $y = 5$. It turns out to have its vertex at the point $(3, -4)$, making its minimum value $y = -4$. So, its domain is the set of all real numbers, and its range is $y \geq -4$. It also turns out to have two x-intercepts, at $x = 1$ and at $x = 5$ (since $f(1) = 0$ and $f(5) = 0$).

POLYNOMIAL FUNCTIONS

A function of the form $f(x) = a^n x^n + a^{n-1} x^{n-1} + \cdots + a_2 x^2 + a_1 x + a_0$, where n is a whole number and $a_0, a_1, a_2, \ldots a_{n-1}, a_n$ are real numbers, is a **polynomial function of degree n**. Its domain is the set of all real numbers (it is complicated to describe its range in general), and its y-intercept is $y = a_0$ (since $f(0) = a_0$). Constant functions, linear functions, and quadratic functions are polynomial functions of degrees 0, 1, and 2, respectively. In general, a polynomial function of degree n has up to n zeros (x-intercepts) and up to $n - 1$ "bends." For example, the fourth degree polynomial function $f(x) = x^4 - 11x^3 + 41x^2 - 61x + 30$, whose graph appears here, has four x-intercepts (at $x = 1, x = 2, x = 3$, and $x = 5$) and three "bends," and its y-intercept (not visible on the graph) is at $y = 30$.

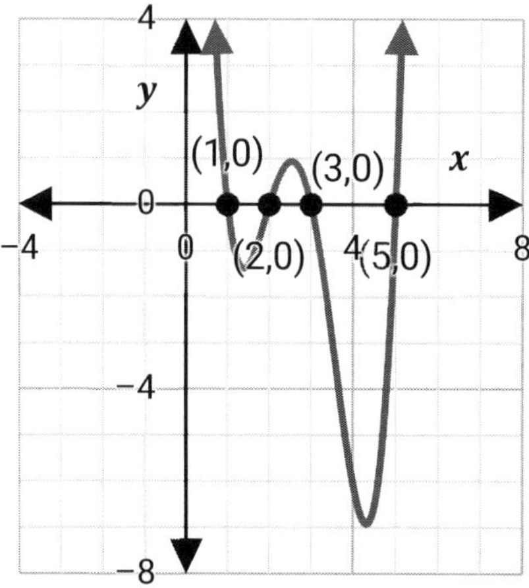

Rational Functions

A function of the form $f(x) = P(x)/Q(x)$, where P and Q are polynomials, is a rational function (we note that the word *rational* includes the root word *ratio*, indicating that a rational function is a ratio of polynomial functions). The domain of a rational function is all real numbers except the zeros of $Q(x)$ since division by zero is undefined (the range can be difficult to describe in general). Its y-intercept is $f(0)$, if this is defined; and its x-intercepts are the zeros of $P(x)$ that are in the domain of f, if there are any. A rational function may also have vertical asymptotes (vertical lines that the graph approaches without crossing) and a horizontal asymptote (a horizontal line that the curve approaches as x becomes very small or very large (toward the left and right edges of the graph). For example, the rational function $f(x) = (2x^2 + x - 1)/(x^2 + x - 2)$ has as its domain the set of all real numbers except $x = -2$ and $x = 1$ (since those numbers make the denominator zero).

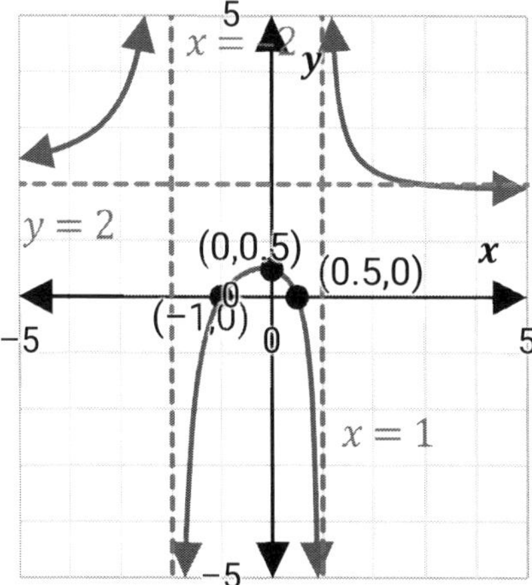

It has a y-intercept of $y = 1/2$ since $f(0) = (-1)/(-2) = 1/2$, and it has x-intercepts at $x = -1$ and at $x = 1/2$ since those numbers make the numerator zero. It has vertical asymptotes at $x = -2$ and $x = 1$ (not coincidentally, these are the numbers omitted from the domain) and a horizontal asymptote at $y = 2$. It is important to note that vertical asymptotes cannot be crossed in rational functions, but horizontal asymptotes can be crossed if the function tends near the asymptote at infinity and does not go past all possible turning points.

Review Video: Simplifying Rational Polynomial Functions
Visit mometrix.com/academy and enter code: 351038

Review Video: Horizontal Asymptotes
Visit mometrix.com/academy and enter code: 747796

The Square Root Function

The function $f(x) = \sqrt{x}$ is the square root function.

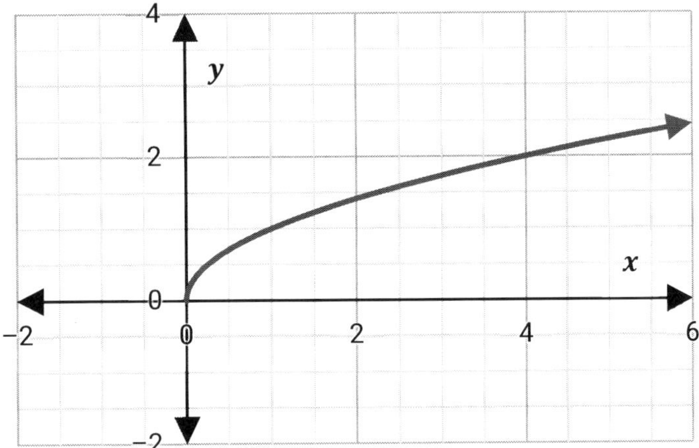

It is an increasing function, and its domain and range are both the set of all nonnegative real numbers. It has one x-intercept and one y-intercept, both appearing at the origin. Its graph is the upper half of a parabola opening to the right. The square root function is the inverse of the squaring function with domain restricted to the nonnegative real numbers (that is, $f(x) = x^2$ for $x \geq 0$).

Piecewise-Defined Functions

As the name suggests, a **piecewise-defined function** (or, simply, a **piecewise function**) is a function defined by different rules on different pieces of the domain. We define such a function using the following form:

Function Name	**Rule to Apply**	**Piece of the Domain on Which the Rule Applies**
$f(x) =$	Rule 1,	First Piece of the Domain
	Rule 2,	Second Piece of the Domain
	Rule 3,	Third Piece of the Domain
	etc.,	etc.

The pieces of the domain should not overlap, and together they should cover the whole domain. For example, we might craft a piecewise-defined function by

$$f(x) = \begin{cases} x^2, & \text{if } x < 2 \\ 3x - 5, & \text{if } x \geq 2 \end{cases}$$

The two pieces of the domain—namely, $x < 2$ and $x \geq 2$—do not overlap, and together they include all real numbers. To evaluate the function for a particular argument x, we determine which piece of the domain includes x and then apply the corresponding rule. For instance, to find $f(4)$, we note that $4 \geq 2$; so, we apply the rule $3x - 5$ to get the value $f(4) = 3 \cdot 4 - 5 = 7$. Similarly, to find $f(-6)$, we note that $-6 < 2$; so, we apply the rule x^2 to get the value $f(-6) = (-6)^2 = 36$.

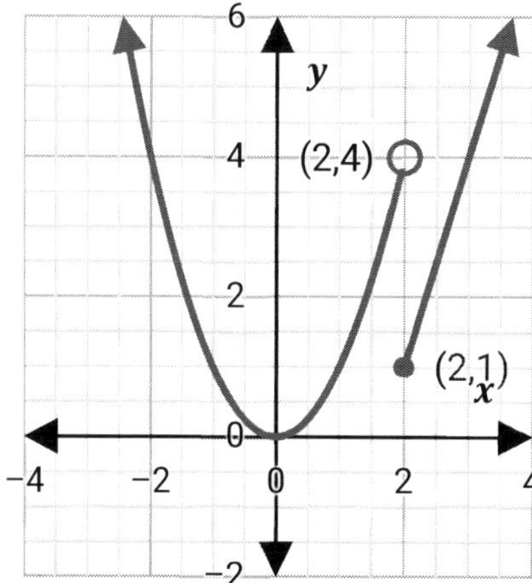

To graph this function, we sketch the graph of the parabola $y = x^2$ on the part of the plane where $x < 2$ and we sketch the line $y = 3x - 5$ on the part of the plane where $x \geq 2$. This produces a graph with a jump at $x = 2$ (a discontinuity—piecewise-defined functions are useful for producing graphs with discontinuities). We plot an open circle at the point (2,4), the end of the left part of the graph, to show that this point is not part of the graph. And we plot a solid dot at the point (2,1), the start of the right part of the graph, to show that this point *is* part of the graph.

Review Video: Piecewise Functions
Visit mometrix.com/academy and enter code: 707921

THE ABSOLUTE VALUE FUNCTION

A particularly useful piecewise-defined function is the absolute value function. It is so important that instead of naming it $f(x)$ or $g(x)$, we denote it using the special notation $|x|$. Its definition is

$$|x| = \begin{cases} -x, & \text{if } x < 0 \\ x, & \text{if } x \geq 0 \end{cases}$$

For instance, $|8| = 8$ (since $8 \geq 0$) and $|-5| = -(-5) = 5$, since $-5 < 0$. So, the absolute value function acts like the identity function for nonnegative numbers (it leaves them unchanged), and it gives the opposite of negative numbers (it effectively strips off the minus sign). Thus, we can think of the absolute value of a real number as its distance from zero on the number line, without taking into consideration whether the number is larger than or smaller than zero. For instance, $|-3| = 3$ and $|3| = 3$, showing that both -3 and 3 are three units away from zero. The absolute value function is an even function with a V-shaped graph that looks like the line $y = x$ (the identity function) on the right "half" of the plane (for $x \geq 0$) and the line $y = -x$ on the left "half" of the plane (for $x < 0$).

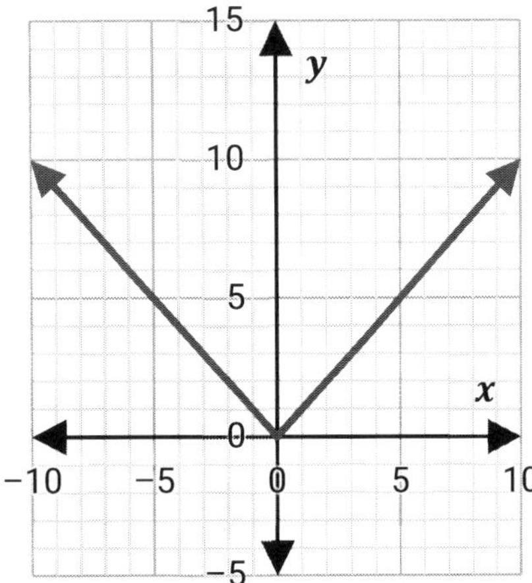

WORKING WITH FUNCTIONS

MANIPULATION OF FUNCTIONS

Translation occurs when values are added to or subtracted from the x- or y-values. If a constant is added to the y-portion of each point, the graph shifts up. If a constant is subtracted from the y-portion of each point, the graph shifts down. This is represented by the expression $f(x) \pm k$, where k is a constant. If a constant is added to the x-portion of each point, the graph shifts left. If a constant is subtracted from the x-portion of each point, the graph shifts right. This is represented by the expression $f(x \pm k)$, where k is a constant.

Stretching, compression, and reflection occur when different parts of a function are multiplied by different groups of constants. If the function as a whole is multiplied by a real number constant greater than 1, $(k \times f(x))$, the graph is stretched vertically. If k in the previous equation is greater than zero but less than 1, the graph is compressed vertically. If k is less than zero, the graph is reflected about the x-axis, in addition to being either stretched or compressed vertically if k is less than or greater than –1, respectively. If instead, just the x-term is multiplied by a constant greater than 1 $(f(k \times x))$, the graph is compressed horizontally. If k in the previous equation is greater than zero but less than 1, the graph is stretched horizontally. If k is less than zero, the graph is reflected about the y-axis, in addition to being either stretched or compressed horizontally if k is greater than or less than –1, respectively.

Review Video: Manipulation of Functions
Visit mometrix.com/academy and enter code: 669117

APPLYING THE BASIC OPERATIONS TO FUNCTIONS

For each of the basic operations, we will use these functions as examples: $f(x) = x^2$ and $g(x) = x$.

To find the sum of two functions f and g, assuming the domains are compatible, simply add the two functions together: $(f + g)(x) = f(x) + g(x) = x^2 + x$.

To find the difference of two functions f and g, assuming the domains are compatible, simply subtract the second function from the first: $(f - g)(x) = f(x) - g(x) = x^2 - x$.

To find the product of two functions f and g, assuming the domains are compatible, multiply the two functions together: $(f \times g)(x) = f(x) \times g(x) = x^2 \times x = x^3$.

To find the quotient of two functions f and g, assuming the domains are compatible, divide the first function by the second: $\left(\frac{f}{g}\right)(x) = \frac{f(x)}{g(x)} = \frac{x^2}{x} = x\,; x \neq 0$.

The example given in each case is fairly simple, but on a given problem, if you are looking only for the value of the sum, difference, product, or quotient of two functions at a particular x-value, it may be simpler to solve the functions individually and then perform the given operation using those values.

The composite of two functions f and g, written as $(f \circ g)(x)$ simply means that the output of the second function is used as the input of the first. This can also be written as $f\big(g(x)\big)$. In general, this can be solved by substituting $g(x)$ for all instances of x in $f(x)$ and simplifying. Using the example functions $f(x) = x^2 - x + 2$ and $g(x) = x + 1$, we can find that $(f \circ g)(x)$ or $f\big(g(x)\big)$ is equal to $f(x+1) = (x+1)^2 - (x+1) + 2$, which simplifies to $x^2 + x + 2$.

It is important to note that $(f \circ g)(x)$ is not necessarily the same as $(g \circ f)(x)$. The process is not always commutative like addition or multiplication expressions. It *can* be commutative, but most often this is not the case.

Evaluating Linear Functions

A **function** can be expressed as an equation that relates an input to an output where each input corresponds to exactly one output. The input of a function is defined by the x-variable, and the output is defined by the y-variable. For example, consider the function $y = 2x + 6$. The value of y, the output, is determined by the value of the x, the input. If the value of x is 3, the value of y is $y = 2(3) + 6 = 6 + 6 = 12$. This means that when $x = 3$, $y = 12$. This can be expressed as the ordered pair $(3,12)$.

It is common for function equations to use the form $f(x) =$ instead of $y =$. However, $f(x)$ and y represent the same thing. We read $f(x)$ as "f of x." The expression "f of x" implies that the value of f depends on the value of x. The function used in the example above could be expressed as $y = 2x + 6$ or $f(x) = 2x + 6$. Both functions represent the same line when graphed.

Functions that are expressed in the form $f(x) =$ are evaluated in the same way the equations are evaluated in the form $y =$. For example, when evaluating the function $f(x) = 3x - 2$ for $f(6)$, substitute 6 in for x, and simplify. In this case, $f(x) = 3x - 2$ becomes $f(6) = 3(6) - 2 = 18 - 2 = 16$. When x is 6, $f(x)$ is 16.

Example: To find the value of $f(8)$, calculate as follows:

$$f(x) = 3x - 2$$
$$f(8) = 3(8) - 2$$
$$f(8) = 22$$

Review Video: Evaluating Functions
Visit mometrix.com/academy and enter code: 588515

Advanced Functions

Step Functions

The double brackets indicate a step function. For a step function, the value inside the double brackets is rounded down to the nearest integer. The graph of the function $f_0(x) = [\![x]\!]$ appears on the left graph. In comparison $f(x) = 2\left[\!\!\left[\frac{1}{3}(x-1)\right]\!\!\right]$ is on the right graph. The coefficient of 2 shows that it's stretched vertically by a factor of 2 (so there's a vertical distance of 2 units between successive "steps"). The coefficient of $\frac{1}{3}$ in front of the x shows that it's stretched horizontally by a factor of 3 (so each "step" is three units long), and the $x - 1$ shows that it's displaced one unit to the right.

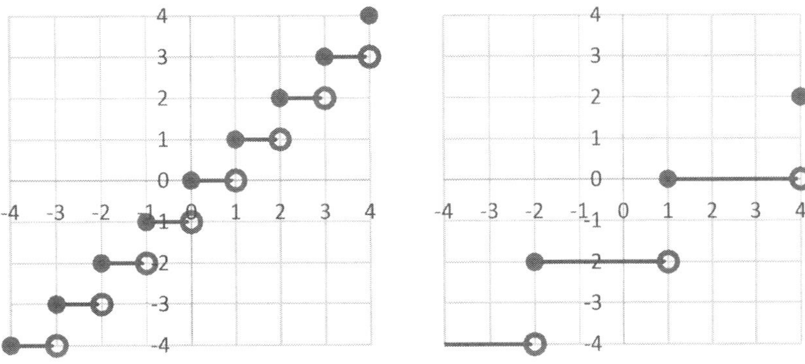

TRANSCENDENTAL FUNCTIONS

Roughly speaking, algebraic functions are functions defined by formulas involving numbers and variables combined by addition, subtraction, multiplication, division, powers (but not variable powers), and roots. **Transcendental functions** are functions that are not algebraic. A function that includes logarithms, trigonometric functions, or variables as exponents, is transcendental, not algebraic, even if the function also includes polynomials or roots.

EXPONENTIAL FUNCTIONS

Exponential functions are functions that have the form $y = b^x$, where base $b > 0$ and $b \neq 1$. The exponential function can also be written $f(x) = b^x$. The following properties apply to exponential expressions:

Property	Description
$a^x a^y = a^{x+y}$	The product of exponentials with the same base equals the base raised to the sum of the powers
$a^x / a^y = a^{x-y}$	The quotient of exponentials with the same base equals the base raised to the difference of the powers
$(a^x)^y = a^{xy}$	An exponential raised to a power equals the base raised to the product of the powers
$(ab)^x = a^x b^x$	Exponentiation distributes over multiplication
$(a/b)^x = a^x / b^x$	Exponentiation distributes over division

The graph of an example exponential function, $f(x) = 2^x$, is below:

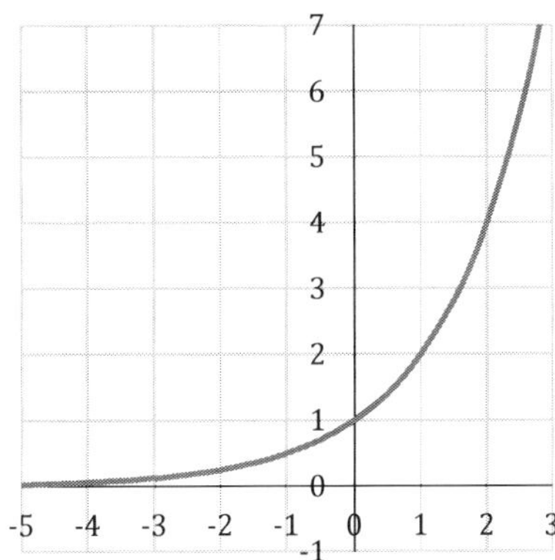

Mathematics

Note in the graph that the y-value approaches zero to the left and infinity to the right. One of the key features of an exponential function is that there will be one end that goes off to infinity and another that asymptotically approaches a lower bound. Common forms of exponential functions include the following:

Geometric sequences: The terms of a geometric sequence have the form $a_n = a_1 \times r^{n-1}$, where a_n is the value of the nth term, a_1 is the initial term, and r is the common ratio between succesive terms. Note that $a_1 \times r^{1-1} = a_1 \times r^0 = a_1 \times 1 = a_1$

Review Video: Geometric Sequences
Visit mometrix.com/academy and enter code: 140779

General exponential growth or decay: The general exponential growth or decay function is $f(t) = a(1+r)^t$, where the value of $f(t)$ is the amount (of whatever quantity we are measuring) at time t, the constant a is the initial amount (the amount at time $t = 0$), and the constant r is the fixed rate of increase (if $r > 0$) or decrease (if $r < 0$) per unit time. For example, if we invest \$1000 at an interest rate of 6% interest compounded annually and we measure time in years, then our investment will grow according to an exponential model with $a = \$1000$ and $r = 6\% = 0.06$. Thus, after t years the value of our investment will be $f(t) = \$1000(1+0.06)^t$. After 5 years, for instance, the investment will grow to $f(5) = \$1000(1+0.06)^5 \approx \$1338.23$.

Compound interest: We can modify the general exponential growth function above slightly to get a formula for interest compounded n times per year. Replacing the constant a with P (for principal, the initial amount we invest), the total value of our investment after t years is $f(t) = P\left(1+\frac{r}{n}\right)^{nt}$, where r is the nominal annual interest rate. Thus, if we change our \$1000 investment above by having the interest rate be 6% compounded *semiannually* (two times per year—so $n = 2$), the value of our investment after t years is $f(t) = \$1000\left(1+\frac{0.06}{2}\right)^{2t} = \$1000(1+0.03)^{2t}$. After 5 years, for instance, the investment will grow to $f(5) = \$1000(1+0.03)^{10} \approx \$1343.92$. This is slightly higher than the previous investment because the interest compounds twice as often.

Review Video: Compound Interest Formula
Visit mometrix.com/academy and enter code: 100366

Review Video: Interest Functions
Visit mometrix.com/academy and enter code: 559176

Population growth and continuously compounded interest: When a quantity grows (or decays) continuously at a rate that stays constant relative to the size the quantity has already attained, then we can model its size at time t with the function $f(t) = ae^{rt}$, where a is the initial amount, r is the relative growth rate (which we often call simply the **growth rate**), and e is the irrational constant known as Euler's number (approximately 2.718; scientific calculators have a button for finding e^x, which is known as the **natural exponential function**). For instance, under some circumstances, if an initial population (of people, plants, or animals, for example) of size a grows at constant relative rate r, then the size of the population at time t is $f(t) = ae^{rt}$. Similarly, if we invest principal P (instead of a) for t years at nominal annual interest rate r compounded *continuously*, then after t years the value of the investment is $f(t) = Pe^{rt}$.

For example, suppose the initial population of a town is $a = 1{,}200$ people and the relative annual growth rate is $r = 5\% = 0.05$. Then the population of the town after t years is $f(t) = ae^{rt} = 1200e^{0.05t}$. After 10 years, for instance, the town population is $f(10) = 1200e^{0.05\cdot 10} = 1200e^{0.5} \approx 1978$ people.

Review Video: Population Growth
Visit mometrix.com/academy and enter code: 109278

Logarithmic Functions

The **logarithmic function base b** is the function $y = \log_b x$ or $f(x) = \log_b x$, where the base b may be any positive number except one. The most common bases for logarithms are base 10 (the **common logarithm**) and base e (the **natural logarithm**). We usually write the common logarithm as $y = \log x$ (that is, $\log x$, with no base listed, means $\log_{10} x$) and the natural logarithm as $y = \ln x$ (that is, $\ln x$ means $\log_e x$).

Exponential functions and logarithmic functions with the same base are inverse functions. That is, if $f(x) = b^x$, then $f^{-1}(x) = \log_b x$. This means that the two equations $y = b^x$ (exponential form) and $x = \log_b y$ (logarithmic form) express the same relationship between the quantities x and y. We often solve problems involving logarithms by rewriting them in exponential form, and vice versa. Also, because of this inverse relationship, logarithms and exponentials cancel each other. That is, $\log_b b^x = x$ and $b^{\log_b x} = x$.

The following properties apply to logarithmic expressions:

Property	Description
$\log_b 1 = 0$	The log of 1 is equal to 0 for any base
$\log_b b = 1$	The log of the base is equal to 1
$\log_b b^p = p$	The log of the base raised to a power is equal to that power
$\log_b MN = \log_b M + \log_b N$	The log of a product is the sum of the log of each factor
$\log_b \frac{M}{N} = \log_b M - \log_b N$	The log of a quotient is equal to the log of the dividend minus the log of the divisor
$\log_b M^p = p \log_b M$	The log of a value raised to a power is equal to the power times the log of the value

Logarithms are helpful in solving equations in which the variable appears in an exponent. For instance, consider the example above in which we model the population of a town by the function $f(t) = 1200e^{0.05t}$. Suppose we want to know how long it will take the population of the town to double to 2400 people from its original value of 1200. We find this by solving the equation $1200e^{0.05t} = 2400$. First, we divide both sides of the equation by 1200 to get $e^{0.05t} = 2$. Then we take natural logarithms of both sides to get $\ln e^{0.05t} = \ln 2$, which simplifies (because natural logarithms and natural exponentials are inverse functions) to $0.05t = \ln 2$. Finally, we divide both sides by 0.05 to get $t = (\ln 2)/0.05$, which we evaluate with a calculator to get $t \approx 13.9$ years.

The graph of an example logarithmic function, $f(x) = \log_2(x + 2)$, is below:

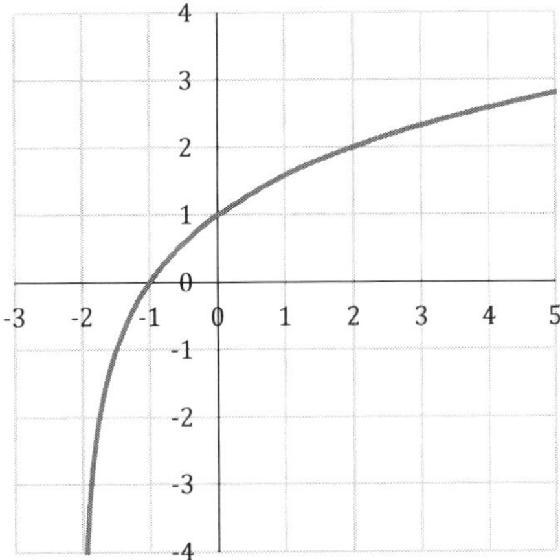

Review Video: Logarithmic Function
Visit mometrix.com/academy and enter code: 658985

Mathematics

Precision, Accuracy, and Error

Measurements of physical quantities (e.g., length, area, volume, weight, mass, and time) in the real world are never perfect. Measurements miss the true value, and repeated measurements produce different values. For this reason, fields that depend on good measurement have technical terms, precision and accuracy, that describe how particular ways of measuring a quantity produce good or bad results. Note that these terms apply not to single measurements but to repeated measurements of the same quantity using the same procedure.

Precision describes the consistency of measurements. Measurements that cluster closely together, with little variation from one measurement to the next, have high precision. Measurements that vary a great deal from one measurement to the next have low precision.

Accuracy describes the closeness of measurements to the true value of the quantity being measured or, more technically, the tendency of measurements to cluster around the true value (though we do not usually know the true value; otherwise, we would not bother to measure it).

An analogy from archery may help. An outstanding archer aiming at the center of the target (the true value) produces a tight cluster of arrows around the center (high accuracy, high precision). Under the same circumstances a modestly good archer produces a loose cluster around the center (high accuracy, low precision). If, however, there is a strong crosswind and the archers do nothing to compensate for it, the outstanding archer's shots will cluster tightly around a point away from the center (low accuracy, high precision); and the modestly good archer's shots will cluster loosely around a point away from the center (low accuracy, low precision).

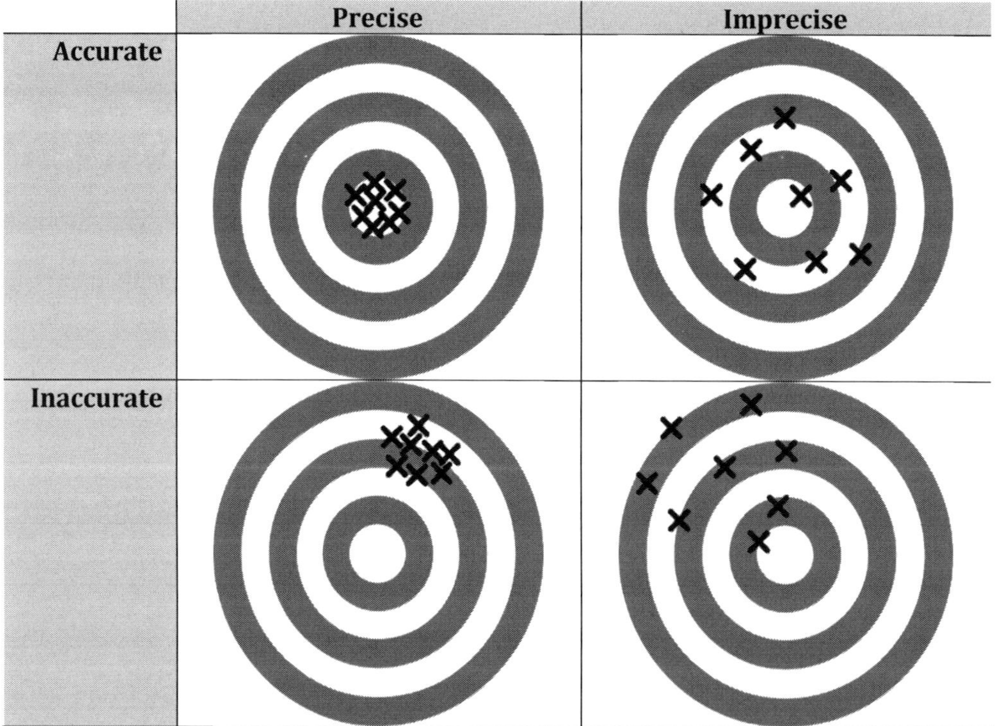

Error in measurement is not a mistake but simply the difference between the true value and the measured value. Since we seldom know the true value, we seldom know the exact error; but sometimes we know a limit on how big the error can be (an error bound), in which case we can use the plus-or-minus sign, $\pm$, to indicate how far the true value might lie from the measured value. For instance, if we measure the length of a metal bar as 25.6 cm and we know the error in our measurement is no more than 0.03 cm (some sources call this

approximate error), then we might report the length of the bar as 25.6 ± 0.03 cm, which means it lies between 25.57 cm and 25.63 cm.

A particularly important application of this comes from the necessity of rounding whenever we make a measurement. For instance, if we measure the length of a pencil using a ruler marked off in whole inches (no fractions), then we must round our measurement to the nearest inch. Thus, if we report the length as 8 inches, it means that the actual value lies somewhere between 7.5 inches and 8.5 inches, which is to say 8 ± 0.5 inches. This built-in error bound due to rounding is called the **maximum possible error**, and it is always half the magnitude of the smallest unit used in the measurement. Determining the smallest unit can be somewhat subtle, involving the rules for significant figures commonly used in physics, chemistry, and other fields.

Review Video: Precision, Accuracy, and Error
Visit mometrix.com/academy and enter code: 520377

Chapter Quiz

Ready to see how well you retained what you just read? Scan the QR code to go directly to the chapter quiz interface for this study guide. If you're using a computer, simply visit the online resources page at **mometrix.com/resources719/hiset-27339** and click the Chapter Quizzes link.

Science

Science as Inquiry

Safety and Equipment

Laboratory Accidents

Any spills or accidents should be **reported** to the teacher so that the teacher can determine the safest clean-up method. The student should start to wash off a **chemical** spilled on the skin while reporting the incident. Some spills may require removal of contaminated clothing and use of the **safety shower**. Broken glass should be disposed of in a designated container. If someone's clothing catches fire they should walk to the safety shower and use it to extinguish the flames. A fire blanket may be used to smother a **lab fire**. A fire extinguisher, phone, spill neutralizers, and a first aid box are other types of **safety equipment** found in the lab. Students should be familiar with **routes** out of the room and the building in case of fire. Students should use the **eye wash station** if a chemical gets in the eyes.

Safety Procedures

Students should wear a **lab apron** and **safety goggles**. Loose or dangling clothing and jewelry, necklaces, and earrings should not be worn. Those with long hair should tie it back. Care should always be taken not to splash chemicals. Open-toed shoes such as sandals and flip-flops should not be worn, nor should wrist watches. Glasses are preferable to contact lenses since the latter carry a risk of chemicals getting caught between the lens and the eye. Students should always be supervised. The area where the experiment is taking place and the surrounding floor should be free of clutter. Only the lab book and the items necessary for the experiment should be present. Smoking, eating, and chewing gum are not permitted in the lab. Cords should not be allowed to dangle from work stations. There should be no rough-housing in the lab. Hands should be washed after the lab is complete.

Fume Hoods

Because of the potential safety hazards associated with chemistry lab experiments, such as fire from vapors and the inhalation of toxic fumes, a **fume hood** should be used in many instances. A fume hood carries away vapors from reagents or reactions. Equipment or reactions are placed as far back in the hood as practical to help enhance the collection of the fumes. The **glass safety shield** automatically closes to the appropriate height, and it should be low enough to protect the face and body. The safety shield should only be raised to move equipment in and out of the hood. One should not climb inside a hood or stick one's head inside. All spills should be wiped up immediately, and the glass should be cleaned if a splash occurs.

Common Safety Hazards

Some specific safety hazards possible in a chemistry lab include:

- **Fire**: Fire can be caused by volatile solvents such as ether, acetone, or benzene being kept in an open beaker or Erlenmeyer flask. Vapors can creep along the table and ignite if they reach a flame or spark. Solvents should be heated in a hood with a steam bath, not on a hot plate.
- **Explosion**: Heating or creating a reaction in a closed system can cause an explosion, resulting in flying glass and chemical splashes. The system should be vented to prevent this.
- **Chemical and thermal burns**: Many chemicals are corrosive to the skin and eyes.
- **Inhalation of toxic fumes**: Some compounds severely irritate membranes in the eyes, nose, throat, and lungs.
- **Absorption** of toxic chemicals such as dimethyl sulfoxide (DMSO) and nitrobenzene through the skin.
- **Ingestion** of toxic chemicals.

Safety Gloves

There are many types of **gloves** available to help protect the skin from cuts, burns, and chemical splashes. There are many considerations when choosing a glove. For example, gloves that are highly protective may limit dexterity. Some gloves may not offer appropriate protection against a specific chemical. Other considerations include degradation rating, which indicates how effective a glove is when exposed to chemicals; breakthrough time, which indicates how quickly a chemical can break through the surface of the glove; and permeation rate, which indicates how quickly chemicals seep through after the initial breakthrough. Disposable latex, vinyl, or nitrile gloves are usually appropriate for most circumstances, and offer protection from incidental splashes and contact. Other types of gloves include butyl, neoprene, PVC, PVA, Viton, Silver Shield, and natural rubber. Each offers its own type of protection but may have drawbacks as well.

Proper Handling and Storage of Chemicals

Students should take care when **carrying chemicals** from one place to another. Chemicals should never be taken from the room, tasted, or touched with bare hands. **Safety gloves** should be worn when appropriate and glove/chemical interactions and glove deterioration should be considered. Hands should always be **washed** thoroughly after a lab. Potentially hazardous materials intended for use in chemistry, biology, or other science labs should be secured in a safe area where relevant **Safety Data Sheets (SDS)** can be accessed. Chemicals and solutions should be used as directed and labels should be read before handling solutions and chemicals. Extra chemicals should not be returned to their original containers, but should be disposed of as directed by the school district's rules or local ordinances. Local municipalities often have hazardous waste disposal programs. Acids should be stored separately from other chemicals. Flammable liquids should be stored away from acids, bases, and oxidizers.

Bunsen Burners

When using a **Bunsen burner**, loose clothing should be tucked in, long hair should be tied back, and safety goggles and aprons should be worn. Students should know what to do in case of a fire or accident. When lighting the burner, strikers should always be used instead of matches. Do not touch the hot barrel. Tongs (never fingers) should be used to hold the material in the flame. To heat liquid, a flask may be set upon wire gauze on a tripod and secured with an iron ring or clamp on a stand. The flame is extinguished by turning off the gas at the source.

Safety Procedures Related to Animals

Animals to be used for **dissections** should be obtained from a company that provides animals for this purpose. Road kill or decaying animals that a student brings in should not be used. It is possible that such an animal may have a pathogen or a virus, such as rabies, which can be transmitted via the saliva of even a dead animal. Students should use gloves and should not participate if they have open sores or moral objections to dissections. It is generally accepted that biological experiments may be performed on lower-order life forms and invertebrates, but not on mammalian vertebrates and birds. No animals should be harmed physiologically. Experimental animals should be kept, cared for, and handled in a safe manner and with compassion. Pathogenic (anything able to cause a disease) substances should not be used in lab experiments.

Lab Notebooks

A **lab notebook** is a record of all pre-lab work and lab work. It differs from a lab report, which is prepared after lab work is completed. A lab notebook is a formal record of lab preparations and what was done. **Observational recordings** should not be altered, erased, or whited-out to make corrections. Drawing a single line through an entry is sufficient to make changes. Pages should be numbered and should not be torn out. Entries should be made neatly, but don't necessarily have to be complete sentences. **Entries** should provide detailed information and be recorded in such a way that another person could use them to replicate the experiment. **Quantitative data** may be recorded in tabular form, and may include calculations made during an experiment. Lab book entries can also include references and research performed before the experiment. Entries may also consist of information about a lab experiment, including the objective or purpose, the procedures, data collected, and the results.

LAB REPORTS

A **lab report** is an item developed after an experiment that is intended to present the results of a lab experiment. Generally, it should be prepared using a word processor, not hand-written or recorded in a notebook. A lab report should be formally presented. It is intended to persuade others to accept or reject a hypothesis. It should include a brief but descriptive **title** and an **abstract**. The abstract is a summary of the report. It should include a purpose that states the problem that was explored or the question that was answered. It should also include a **hypothesis** that describes the anticipated results of the experiment. The experiment should include a **control** and one **variable** to ensure that the results can be interpreted correctly. Observations and results can be presented using written narratives, tables, graphs, and illustrations. The report should also include a **summation** or **conclusion** explaining whether the results supported the hypothesis.

TYPES OF LABORATORY GLASSWARE

Two types of flasks are Erlenmeyer flasks and volumetric flasks. **Volumetric flasks** are used to accurately prepare a specific volume and concentration of a solution. **Erlenmeyer flasks** can be used for mixing, transporting, and reacting, but are not appropriate for accurate measurements.

A **pipette** can be used to accurately measure small amounts of liquid. Liquid is drawn into the pipette through a bulb. The liquid measurement is read at the **meniscus**. There are also plastic disposable pipettes. A **repipette** is a hand-operated pump that dispenses solutions.

Beakers can be used to measure mass or dissolve a solvent into a solute. They do not measure volume as accurately as a volumetric flask, pipette, graduated cylinder, or burette.

Graduated cylinders are used for precise measurements and are considered more accurate than Erlenmeyer flasks or beakers. To read a graduated cylinder, it should be placed on a flat surface and read at eye level. The surface of a liquid in a graduated cylinder forms a lens-shaped curve. The measurement should be taken from the bottom of the curve. A ring may be placed at the top of tall, narrow cylinders to help avoid breakage if they are tipped over.

A **burette**, or buret, is a piece of lab glassware used to accurately dispense liquid. It looks similar to a narrow graduated cylinder, but it includes a stopcock and tip. It may be filled with a funnel or pipette.

MICROSCOPES

There are different kinds of microscopes, but **optical** or **light microscopes** are the most commonly used in lab settings. Light and lenses are used to magnify and view samples. A specimen or sample is placed on a slide, and the slide is placed on a stage with a hole in it. Light passes through the hole and illuminates the sample. The sample is magnified by lenses and viewed through the eyepiece. A simple microscope has one lens, while a typical compound microscope has three lenses. The light source can be room light redirected by a mirror, or the microscope can have its own independent light source that passes through a condenser. In this case, there are diaphragms and filters to allow light intensity to be controlled. Optical microscopes also have coarse and fine adjustment knobs.

Other types of microscopes include **digital microscopes**, which use a camera and a monitor to allow viewing of the sample. **Scanning electron microscopes (SEMs)** provide greater detail in terms of a sample's surface topography and can produce magnifications much greater than those possible with optical microscopes. The technology of an SEM is quite different from an optical microscope in that it does not rely on lenses to magnify objects, but uses samples placed in a chamber. In one type of SEM, a beam of electrons from an electron gun scans and actually interacts with the sample to produce an image.

Wet mount slides designed for use with a light microscope typically require a thin portion of the specimen to be placed on a standard glass slide. A drop of water is added, and a cover slip or cover glass is placed on top. Air bubbles and fingerprints can make viewing difficult. Placing the cover slip at a 45-degree angle and allowing it to drop into place can help avoid the problem of air bubbles. A **cover slip** should always be used when viewing wet mount slides. The viewer should start with the objective in its lowest position and then fine-focus. The microscope should be carried with two hands and stored with the low-power objective in the down position. **Lenses** should be cleaned with lens paper only. A **graticule slide** is marked with a grid line, and is useful for counting or estimating a quantity.

Balances

Balances such as triple-beam balances, spring balances, and electronic balances measure mass and force. An **electronic balance** is the most accurate, followed by a **triple-beam balance** and then a **spring balance**. One part of a **triple-beam balance** is the plate, which is where the item to be weighed is placed. There are also three beams, which have hash marks indicating amounts and which hold the weights that rest in the notches. The front beam measures weights between 0 and 10 grams, the middle beam measures weights in 100-gram increments, and the far beam measures weights in 10-gram increments. The sum of the weight of each beam is the total weight of the object. A triple beam balance also includes a set screw to calibrate the equipment, as well as a mark indicating that the object and counterweights are in balance.

Chromatography

Chromatography refers to a set of laboratory techniques used to separate or analyze **mixtures**. Mixtures are dissolved in their mobile phases. In the stationary or bonded phase, the desired component is separated from other molecules in the mixture. In chromatography, the analyte is the substance to be separated. **Preparative chromatography** refers to the type of chromatography that involves purifying a substance for further use rather than further analysis. **Analytical chromatography** involves analyzing the isolated substance. Other types of chromatography include column, planar, paper, thin layer, displacement, supercritical fluid, affinity, ion exchange, and size exclusion chromatography. Reversed phase, two-dimensional, simulated moving bed, pyrolysis, fast protein, counter current, and chiral are also types of chromatography. **Gas chromatography** refers to the separation technique in which the mobile phase of a substance is in gas form.

Review Video: Paper Chromatography
Visit mometrix.com/academy and enter code: 543963

Reagents and Reactants

A **reagent** or **reactant** is a chemical agent for use in chemical reactions. When preparing for a lab, it should be confirmed that glassware and other equipment have been cleaned and/or sterilized. There should be enough materials, reagents, or other solutions needed for the lab for every group of students completing the experiment. Distilled water should be used instead of tap water when performing lab experiments because distilled water has most of its impurities removed. Other needed apparatus such as funnels, filter paper, balances, Bunsen burners, ring stands, and/or microscopes should also be set up. After the lab, it should be confirmed that sinks, workstations, and any equipment used have been cleaned. If chemicals or specimens need to be kept at a certain temperature by refrigerating them or using another storage method, the temperature should be checked periodically to ensure the sample does not spoil.

Diluting Acids

When preparing a solution of **dilute acid**, always add the concentrated acid solution to water, not water to concentrated acid. Start by adding approximately $\frac{2}{3}$ of the total volume of water to the graduated cylinder or volumetric flask. Next, add the concentrated acid to the water. Add additional water to the diluted acid to bring the solution to the final desired volume.

Cleaning After Acid Spills

In the event of an **acid spill**, any clothes that have come into contact with the acid should be removed and any skin contacted with acid must be rinsed with clean water. To the extent a window can be opened or a fume hood can be turned on, do so. Do not try to force air circulation, such as by adding a fan, as acid fumes can be harmful if spread.

Next, pour one of the following over the spill area: sodium bicarbonate, baking soda, soda ash, or cat litter. Start from the outside of the spill and then move towards the center, in order to prevent splashing. When the clumps have thoroughly dried, sweep up the clumps and dispose of them as chemical waste.

Centrifuges

A centrifuge is used to separate the components of a heterogeneous mixture (consisting of two or more compounds) by spinning it. The solid precipitate settles in the bottom of the container, and the liquid component of the solution, called the **centrifugate**, is at the top. A well-known application of this process is using a centrifuge to separate blood cells and plasma. The heavier cells settle on the bottom of the test tube, and the lighter plasma stays on top. Another example is using a salad spinner to help dry lettuce.

Electrophoresis, Calorimetry, and Titration

- **Electrophoresis** is the separation of molecules based on electrical charge. This is possible because particles dispersed in a fluid usually carry electric charges on their surfaces. Molecules are pulled through the fluid toward the positive end if the molecules have a negative charge and are pulled through the fluid toward the negative end if the molecules have a positive charge.
- **Calorimetry** is used to determine the heat released or absorbed in a chemical reaction.
- **Titration** helps determine the precise endpoint of a reaction. With this information, the precise quantity of reactant in the titration flask can be determined. A burette is used to deliver the second reactant to the flask and an indicator or pH meter is used to detect the endpoint of the reaction.

Field Studies and Research Projects

Field studies may facilitate scientific inquiry in a manner similar to indoor lab experiments. Field studies can be interdisciplinary in nature and can help students learn and apply scientific concepts and processes. **Research projects** can be conducted in any number of locations, including school campuses, local parks, national parks, beaches, or mountains. Students can practice the general techniques of observation, data collection, collaborative planning, and analysis of experiments. Field studies give students the chance to learn through hands-on applications of scientific processes, such as map making in geography, observation of stratification in geology, observation of life cycles of plants and animals, and analysis of water quality.

Students should watch out for obvious outdoor **hazards**. These include poisonous flora and fauna such as poison ivy, poison oak, and sumac. Depending on the region of the United States in which the field study is being conducted, hazards may also include rattlesnakes and black widow or brown recluse spiders. Students should also be made aware of potentially hazardous situations specific to **geographic locales** and the possibility of coming into contact with **pathogens**.

Field studies allow for great flexibility in the use of traditional and technological methods for **making observations** and **collecting data**. For example, a nature study could consist of a simple survey of bird species within a given area. Information could be recorded using still photography or a video camera. This type of activity gives students the chance to use technologies other than computers. Computers could still be used to create a slide show of transferred images or a digital lab report. If a quantitative study of birds was being performed, the simple technique of using a pencil and paper to tabulate the number of birds counted in the field could also be used. Other techniques used during field studies could include collecting specimens for lab study, observing coastal ecosystems and tides, and collecting weather data such as temperature, precipitation amounts, and air pressure in a particular locale.

Scientific Inquiry and Reasoning

Scientific Inquiry

The concept of **scientific inquiry** refers to the idea of how one thinks and asks questions in a logical way to gain trustworthy information. The underlying motivation of science is to try to understand the natural world. Much of human thought is based on assumptions about how things work that may or may not be true. The goal of scientific inquiry is to test those assumptions to gain a greater understanding of the world with good questions and objective tests, and then re-use what was learned to ask better questions. The more we understand about the natural world, the better the questions we can ask, and that is the general idea behind scientific inquiry. The applied practice of scientific inquiry is to ask questions in a systematic method, called the scientific method.

Scientific Knowledge

Scientific knowledge refers to any topic that is studied **empirically**, meaning that it is based on observation of a **phenomenon** in an objective way. The body of **scientific knowledge** is often broken down into several domains including biology, ecology, Earth science, space science, physics, and chemistry. These each have further subdomains and are overlapping in many ways. For instance, ecology is the study of ecosystems, which are made up of biological factors and geological factors, so it contains elements of both biology and Earth science. Each of these domains is subject to the concepts of scientific inquiry, such as the scientific method, scientific facts, hypotheses, and scientific laws.

Important Terminology

- A **phenomenon** is an event or effect that is observed.
- A **scientific fact** is considered an objective and verifiable observation. Usually, a fact can be repeated or demonstrated to others.
- A **scientific theory** is a proposition explaining why or how something happens and is built on scientific facts and laws. Scientific theories can be tested, but are not fully proven. If new evidence is found that disproves the theory, it is no longer considered true.
- A **hypothesis** is an educated guess that is not yet proven. It is used to predict the outcome of an experiment in an attempt to solve a problem or answer a question.
- A **law** is an explanation of events that always leads to the same outcome. It is a fact that an object falls. The law of gravity explains why an object falls. The theory of relativity, although generally accepted, has been neither proven nor disproved.
- A **model** is used to explain something on a smaller scale or in simpler terms to provide an example. It is a representation of an idea that can be used to explain events or applied to new situations to predict outcomes or determine results.

History of Scientific Knowledge

When one examines the history of **scientific knowledge**, it is clear that it is constantly **evolving**. The body of facts, models, theories, and laws grows and changes over time. In other words, one scientific discovery leads to the next. Some advances in science and technology have important and long-lasting effects on science and society. Some discoveries were so alien to the accepted beliefs of the time that not only were they rejected as wrong, but were also considered outright blasphemy. Today, however, many beliefs once considered incorrect have become an ingrained part of scientific knowledge, and have also been the basis of new advances. Examples of advances include: Copernicus's heliocentric view of the universe, Newton's laws of motion and planetary orbits, relativity, geologic time scale, plate tectonics, atomic theory, nuclear physics, biological evolution, germ theory, industrial revolution, molecular biology, information and communication, quantum theory, galactic universe, and medical and health technology.

Scientific Inquiry and Scientific Method

Scientists use a number of generally accepted techniques collectively known as the **scientific method**. The scientific method generally involves carrying out the following steps:

- Identifying a problem or posing a question
- Formulating a hypothesis or an educated guess
- Conducting experiments or tests that will provide a basis to solve the problem or answer the question
- Observing the results of the test
- Drawing conclusions

An important part of the scientific method is using acceptable experimental techniques. Objectivity is also important if valid results are to be obtained. Another important part of the scientific method is peer review. It is essential that experiments be performed and data be recorded in such a way that experiments can be reproduced to verify results. Historically, the scientific method has been taught with a more linear approach, but it is important to recognize that the scientific method should be a cyclical or **recursive process**. This means that as hypotheses are tested and more is learned, the questions should continue to change to reflect the changing body of knowledge. One cycle of experimentation is not enough.

Review Video: The Scientific Method
Visit mometrix.com/academy and enter code: 191386

Metric and International System of Units

The **metric system** is the accepted standard of measurement in the scientific community. The **International System of Units (SI)** is a set of measurements (including the metric system) that is almost globally accepted. The United States, Liberia, and Myanmar have not accepted this system. **Standardization** is important because it allows the results of experiments to be compared and reproduced without the need to laboriously convert measurements. The SI is based partially on the **meter-kilogram-second (MKS) system** rather than the **centimeter-gram-second (CGS) system**. The MKS system considers meters, kilograms, and seconds to be the basic units of measurement, while the CGS system considers centimeters, grams, and seconds to be the basic units of measurement. Under the MKS system, the length of an object would be expressed as 1 meter instead of 100 centimeters, which is how it would be described under the CGS system.

Review Video: Metric System Conversions
Visit mometrix.com/academy and enter code: 163709

Basic Units of Measurement

Using the **metric system** is generally accepted as the preferred method for taking measurements. Having a **universal standard** allows individuals to interpret measurements more easily, regardless of where they are located. The basic units of measurement are: the **meter**, which measures length; the **liter**, which measures volume; and the **gram**, which measures mass. The metric system starts with a base unit and increases or decreases in units of 10. The prefix and the base unit combined are used to indicate an amount. For example, deka- is 10 times the base unit. A dekameter is 10 meters; a dekaliter is 10 liters; and a dekagram is 10 grams. The prefix hecto- refers to 100 times the base amount; kilo- is 1,000 times the base amount. The prefixes that indicate a fraction of the base unit are deci-, which is $\frac{1}{10}$ of the base unit; centi-, which is $\frac{1}{100}$ of the base unit; and milli-, which is $\frac{1}{1,000}$ of the base unit.

COMMON PREFIXES

The prefixes for multiples are as follows:

Deka	(da)	**10^1** (deka is the American spelling, but deca is also used)
Hecto	(h)	10^2
Kilo	(k)	10^3
Mega	(M)	10^6
Giga	(G)	10^9
Tera	(T)	10^{12}

The prefixes for subdivisions are as follows:

Deci	(d)	**10^{-1}**
Centi	(c)	10^{-2}
Milli	(m)	10^{-3}
Micro	(μ)	10^{-6}
Nano	(n)	10^{-9}
Pico	(p)	10^{-12}

The rule of thumb is that prefixes greater than 10^3 are capitalized when abbreviating. Abbreviations do not need a period after them. A decimeter (dm) is a tenth of a meter, a deciliter (dL) is a tenth of a liter, and a decigram (dg) is a tenth of a gram. Pluralization is understood. For example, when referring to 5 mL of water, no "s" needs to be added to the abbreviation.

BASIC SI UNITS OF MEASUREMENT

SI uses **second(s)** to measure time. Fractions of seconds are usually measured in metric terms using prefixes such as millisecond ($\frac{1}{1,000}$ of a second) or nanosecond ($\frac{1}{1,000,000,000}$ of a second). Increments of time larger than a second are measured in **minutes** and **hours**, which are multiples of 60 and 24. An example of this is a swimmer's time in the 800-meter freestyle being described as 7:32.67, meaning 7 minutes, 32 seconds, and 67 one-hundredths of a second. One second is equal to $\frac{1}{60}$ of a minute, $\frac{1}{3,600}$ of an hour, and $\frac{1}{86,400}$ of a day. Other SI base units are the **ampere** (A) (used to measure electric current), the **kelvin** (K) (used to measure thermodynamic temperature), the **candela** (cd) (used to measure luminous intensity), and the **mole** (mol) (used to measure the amount of a substance at a molecular level). **Meter** (m) is used to measure length and **kilogram** (kg) is used to measure mass.

SIGNIFICANT FIGURES

The mathematical concept of **significant figures** or **significant digits** is often used to determine the accuracy of measurements or the level of confidence one has in a specific measurement. The significant figures of a measurement include all the digits known with certainty plus one estimated or uncertain digit. There are a number of rules for determining which digits are considered "important" or "interesting." They are:

- All non-zero digits are *significant.*
- Zeros between digits are *significant.*
- Leading and trailing zeros are *not significant* unless they appear to the right of the non-zero digits in a decimal.

For example, in 0.01230, the significant digits are 1230, and this number would be said to be accurate to the hundred-thousandths place. The zero indicates that the amount has actually been measured as 0. Other zeros are considered placeholders and are not important. A decimal point may be placed after zeros to indicate their importance (in "100." for example).

Graphs and Charts

Graphs and charts are effective ways to present scientific data such as observations, statistical analyses, and comparisons between dependent variables and independent variables. On a line chart, the **independent variable** (the one that is being manipulated for the experiment) is represented on the horizontal axis (the x-axis). Any **dependent variables** (the ones that may change as the independent variable changes) are represented on the y-axis. An **XY** or **scatter plot** is often used to plot many points. A "best fit" line is drawn, which allows outliers to be identified more easily. Charts and their axes should have titles. The x and y interval units should be evenly spaced and labeled. Other types of charts are **bar charts** and **histograms**, which can be used to compare differences between the data collected for two variables. A **pie chart** can graphically show the relation of parts to a whole.

Review Video: Identifying Variables
Visit mometrix.com/academy and enter code: 627181

Review Video: Data Interpretation of Graphs
Visit mometrix.com/academy and enter code: 200439

Data Presentation

Data collected during a science lab can be organized and **presented** in any number of ways. While **straight narrative** is a suitable method for presenting some lab results, it is not a suitable way to present numbers and quantitative measurements. These types of observations can often be better presented with **tables** and **graphs**. Data that is presented in tables and organized in rows and columns may also be used to make graphs quite easily. Other methods of presenting data include illustrations, photographs, video, and even audio formats. In a **formal report**, tables and figures are labeled and referred to by their labels. For example, a picture of a bubbly solution might be labeled Figure 1, Bubbly Solution. It would be referred to in the text in the following way: "The reaction created bubbles 10 mm in size, as shown in Figure 1, Bubbly Solution." Graphs are also labeled as figures. Tables are labeled in a different way. Examples include: Table 1, Results of Statistical Analysis, or Table 2, Data from Lab 2.

Statistical Precision and Errors

Errors that occur during an experiment can be classified into two categories: random errors and systematic errors. **Random errors** can result in collected data that is wildly different from the rest of the data, or they may result in data that is indistinguishable from the rest. Random errors are not consistent across the data set. In large data sets, random errors may contribute to the variability of data, but they will not affect the average. Random errors are sometimes referred to as noise. They may be caused by a student's inability to take the same measurement in exactly the same way or by outside factors that are not considered variables, but influence the data. A **systematic error** will show up consistently across a sample or data set, and may be the result of a flaw in the experimental design. This type of error affects the average, and is also known as bias.

Scientific Notation

Scientific notation is used because values in science can be very large or very small, which makes them unwieldy. A number in **decimal notation** is 93,000,000. In **scientific notation**, it is 9.3×10^7. The first number, 9.3, is the **coefficient**. It is always greater than or equal to 1 and less than 10. This number is followed by a multiplication sign. The base is always 10 in scientific notation. If the number is greater than ten, the exponent is positive. If the number is between zero and one, the exponent is negative. The first digit of the number is followed by a decimal point and then the rest of the number. In this case, the number is 9.3, and the decimal point was moved seven places to the right from the end of the number to get 93,000,000. The number of places moved, seven, is the exponent.

Statistical Terminology

- **Mean**—The average, found by taking the sum of a set of numbers and dividing by the number of numbers in the set.
- **Median**—The middle number in a set of numbers sorted from least to greatest. If the set has an even number of entries, the median is the average of the two in the middle.
- **Mode**—The value that appears most frequently in a data set. There may be more than one mode. If no value appears more than once, there is no mode.
- **Range**—The difference between the highest and lowest numbers in a data set.
- **Standard deviation**—Measures the dispersion of a data set, or how far from the mean a single data point is likely to be.
- **Regression analysis**—A method of analyzing sets of data and sets of variables. It involves studying how the typical value of the dependent variable changes when any one of the independent variables is varied and the other independent variables remain fixed.

Review Video: Mean, Median, and Mode
Visit mometrix.com/academy and enter code: 286207

Review Video: Standard Deviation
Visit mometrix.com/academy and enter code: 419469

Physical Science

Work, Energy, and Power

Basic Equation for Work

The equation for **work** (W) is $W = \boldsymbol{Fd}$, where $\boldsymbol{F}$ is the force exerted and $\boldsymbol{d}$ is the displacement of the object on which the force is exerted. For the simplest case, when the vectors of force and displacement have the same direction, the work done is equal to the product of the magnitudes of the force and displacement. If this is not the case, then the work may be calculated as $W = \boldsymbol{Fd}\cos\theta$, where θ is the angle between the force and displacement vectors. If force and displacement have the same direction, then work is positive; if they are in opposite directions, however, work is negative; and if they are perpendicular, the work done by the force is zero.

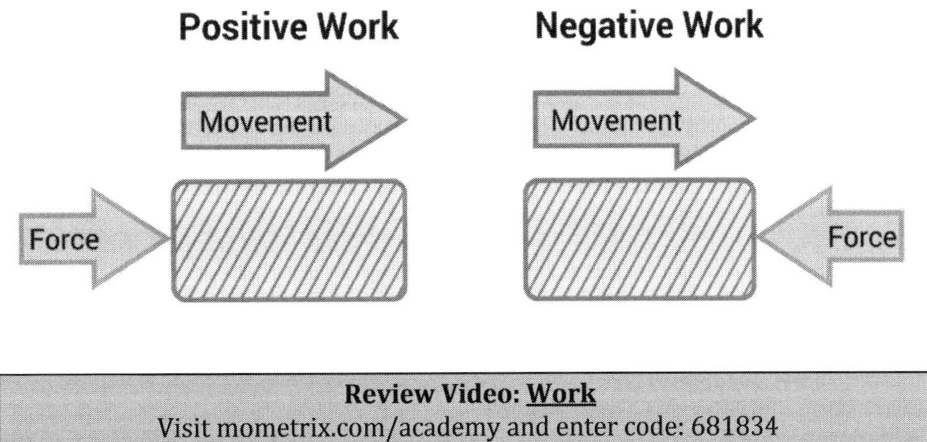

Review Video: Work
Visit mometrix.com/academy and enter code: 681834

For example, if a man pushes a block horizontally across a surface with a constant force of 10 N for a distance of 20 m, the work done by the man is 200 N-m or 200 J. If instead the block is sliding and the man tries to **slow its progress** by pushing against it, his work done is –200 J, since he is pushing in the direction opposite the

Science

motion. Also, if the man pushes vertically downward on the block while it slides, his work done is zero, since his force vector is perpendicular to the displacement vector of the block. It is important to note in each of these cases that neither the mass of the block nor the elapsed time is considered when calculating the amount of work done by the man.

Review Video: Push and Pull Forces
Visit mometrix.com/academy and enter code: 104731

Power

Put simply, **power** is the **rate at which work is done**. Power, like work, is a scalar quantity. If we know the amount of work, W, that has been performed in a given amount of time, Δt, then we may find average power, $P_{avg} = \frac{W}{\Delta t}$. If we are instead looking for the instantaneous power, there are two possibilities. If the force on an object is constant, and the object is moving at a constant velocity, then the instantaneous power is the same as the average power. If either the force or the velocity is varying, the instantaneous power should be computed by the equation $P = \boldsymbol{Fv}$, where $\boldsymbol{F}$ and $\boldsymbol{v}$ are the instantaneous force and velocity, respectively. This equation may also be used to compute average power if the force and velocity are constant. Power is typically expressed in joules per second, or watts.

Simple Machines

Simple machines include the pulley, lever, wheel and axle, wedge, inclined plane, and screw. These simple machines have no internal source of energy. More complex or compound machines can be formed from them. Simple machines provide a mechanical advantage and make it easier to accomplish a task. Single or double pulleys allow for easier direction of force. A lever enables a multiplication of force. The wheel and axle allows for movement with less resistance. The inclined plane enables a force less than an object's weight to be used to push it to a greater height. The wedge and screw are forms of the inclined plane. A wedge turns a smaller force working over a greater distance into a larger force. The screw is similar to an incline that is wrapped around a shaft.

Review Video: Simple Machines
Visit mometrix.com/academy and enter code: 950789

Mechanical Advantage

There is a certain amount of **work** required to move an object that cannot be reduced. However, using one or more simple machines can increase either the distance or force needed. Since work is defined as a force multiplied by a distance, force and distance are inversely proportional.

$$\textbf{Work}_{\textbf{input}} = \textbf{Work}_{\textbf{output}}$$

$$\textbf{force}_{\textbf{input}} \times \textbf{distance}_{\textbf{input}} = \textbf{force}_{\textbf{output}} \times \textbf{distance}_{\textbf{output}}$$

Simple machines can either reduce the amount of input force needed by increasing the input distance or they can reduce the input distance needed by increasing the required input force. The ratio of the output force over the input force is a measure of the **mechanical advantage** of a machine. Due to the inverse relationship between force and distance for these machines, mechanical advantage can also be expressed as the ratio of input distance over the output distance.

$$\textbf{Mechanical Advantage} = \frac{\textbf{force}_{\textbf{output}}}{\textbf{force}_{\textbf{input}}} = \frac{\textbf{distance}_{\textbf{input}}}{\textbf{distance}_{\textbf{output}}}$$

Levers

The **lever** is the most common kind of simple machine. See-saws, shovels, and baseball bats are all examples of levers. There are three classes of levers which are differentiated by the relative orientations of the fulcrum, resistance, and effort. The **fulcrum** is the point at which the lever rotates, the **effort** is the point on the lever where force is applied, and the **resistance** is the part of the lever that acts in response to the effort.

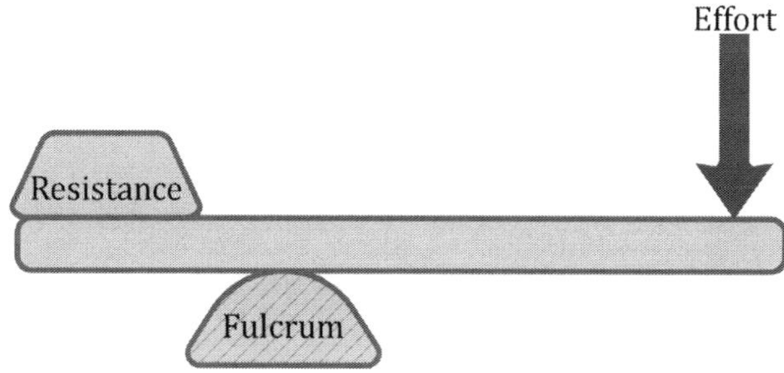

The mechanical advantage of a lever depends on the distances of the effort and resistance from the fulcrum.

$$\textbf{Mechanical Advantage} = \frac{\textbf{effort distance}}{\textbf{resistance distance}}$$

In a **first-class lever**, the fulcrum is between the effort and the resistance. A seesaw is a good example of a first-class lever when effort is applied to force one end up, the other end goes down, and vice versa. The shorter the distance between the fulcrum and the resistance, the easier it will be to move the resistance. As an example, consider whether it is easier to lift another person on a see-saw when they are sitting close to the middle or all the way at the end. A little practice will show you that it is much more difficult to lift a person the farther away he or she is on the see-saw.

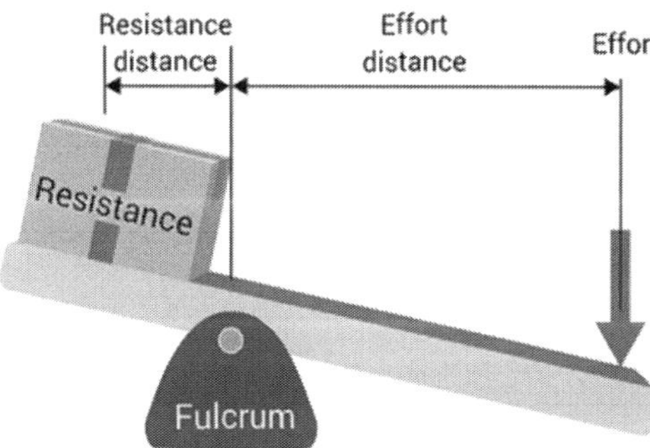

In a **second-class lever**, the resistance is in between the fulcrum and the effort. While a first-class lever is able to increase force and distance through mechanical advantage, a second-class lever is only able to increase force. A common example of a second-class lever is the wheelbarrow; the force exerted by your hand at one end of the wheelbarrow is magnified at the load. Basically, with a second-class lever, you are trading distance for force; by moving your end of the wheelbarrow a bit farther, you produce greater force at the load.

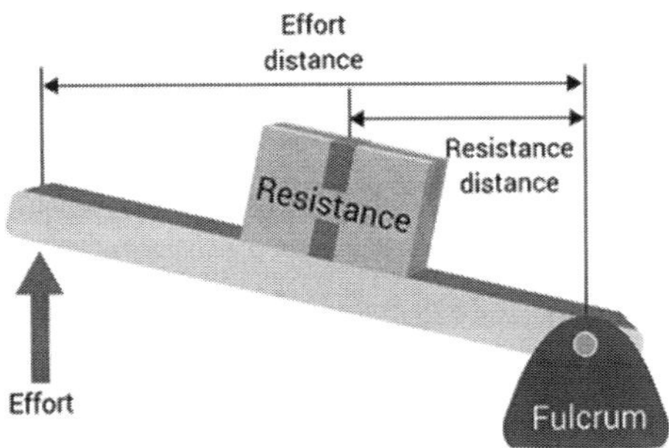

Third-class levers are used to produce greater distance. In a third-class lever, the force is applied in between the fulcrum and the resistance. A baseball bat is a classic example of a third-class lever; the bottom of the bat, below where you grip it, is considered the fulcrum. The end of the bat, where the ball is struck, is the resistance. By exerting effort at the base of the bat, close to the fulcrum, you are able to make the end of the bat fly quickly through the air. The closer your hands are to the base of the bat, the faster you will be able to make the other end of the bat travel.

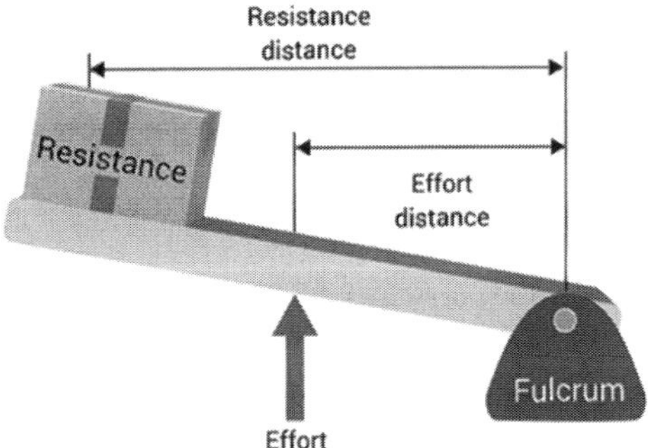

Review Video: Levers
Visit mometrix.com/academy and enter code: 103910

Wheel and Axle

Another basic arrangement that makes use of simple machines is called the wheel and axle. When most people think of a wheel and axle, they immediately envision an automobile tire. The steering wheel of the car, however, operates on the same mechanical principle, namely that the force required to move the center of a circle is much greater than the force required to move the outer rim of a circle. When you turn the steering wheel, you are essentially using a second-class lever by increasing the output force by increasing the input distance. The force required to turn the wheel from the outer rim is much less than would be required to turn the wheel from its center.

The equation for the mechanical advantage of a wheel and axle is:

$$\textbf{Mechanical Advantage} = \frac{\textbf{radius}_{\textbf{wheel}}}{\textbf{radius}_{\textbf{axle}}}$$

For instance, a steering wheel with a radius of 12 inches has a greater mechanical advantage than a steering wheel with a radius of 10 inches; the same amount of force exerted on the rim of each wheel will produce greater force on the axle of the larger wheel.

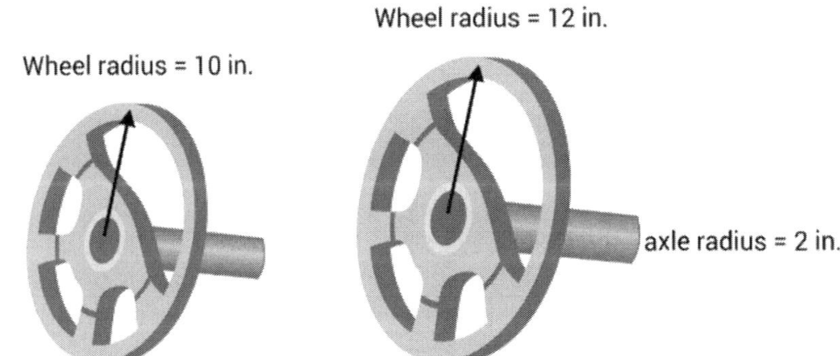

Thus, the mechanical advantage for each is:

$$\frac{10 \text{ inches}}{2 \text{ inches}} = 5 \qquad \frac{12 \text{ inches}}{2 \text{ inches}} = 6$$

Review Video: Wheel and Axle
Visit mometrix.com/academy and enter code: 574045

PULLEYS

The pulley is a simple machine in which a rope is carried by the rotation of a wheel. Another name for a pulley is a block. Pulleys are typically used to allow the force to be directed from a convenient location. For instance, imagine you are given the task of lifting a heavy and tall bookcase. Rather than tying a rope to the bookcase and trying to lift it, it would make sense to tie a pulley system to a rafter above the bookcase and run the rope through it, so that you could pull down on the rope and lift the bookcase. Pulling down allows you to incorporate your weight (normal force) into the act of lifting, thereby making it easier.

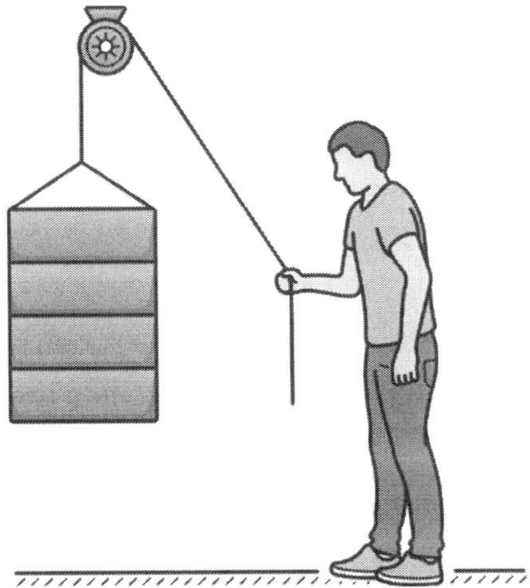

If there is just one pulley above the bookcase, you have created a first-class lever that will not diminish the amount of force that needs to be applied to lift the bookcase. There is another way to use a pulley, however, that can make the job of lifting a heavy object considerably easier. First, tie the rope directly to the rafter. Then, attach a pulley to the top of the bookcase and run the rope through it. If you can then stand so that you are above the bookcase, you will have a much easier time lifting this heavy object. This is because the weight of the bookcase is now being distributed: half of it is acting on the rafter, and half of it is acting on you. In other words, this arrangement allows you to lift an object with half the force. This simple pulley system, therefore, has a mechanical advantage of 2. Note that in this arrangement, the unfixed pulley is acting like a second-class lever. The price you pay for your mechanical advantage is that whatever distance you raise your end of the rope, the bookcase will only be lifted half as much.

Of course, it might be difficult for you to find a place high enough to enact this system. If this is the case, you can always tie another pulley to the rafter and run the rope through it and back down to the floor. Since this second pulley is fixed, the mechanical advantage will remain the same.

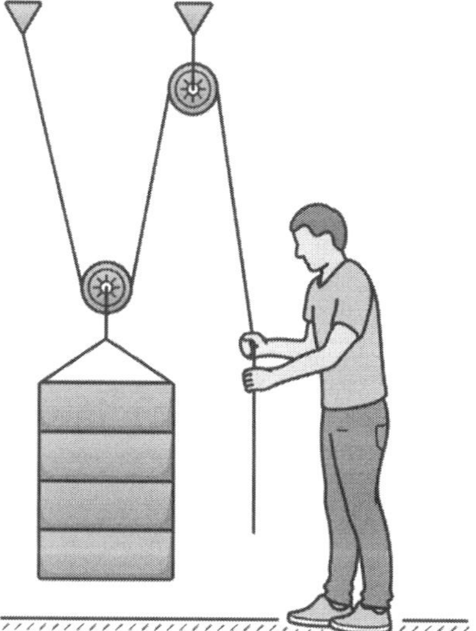

INCLINED PLANE

The inclined plane is perhaps the most common of the simple machines. It is simply a flat surface that elevates as you move from one end to the other. Consider how much easier it is for a person to walk up a long ramp than to climb a shorter but steeper flight of stairs; this is because the force required is diminished as the distance increases. Indeed, the longer the ramp, the easier it is to ascend.

Inclined planes often used to move heavy objects. For instance, moving a heavy box onto the back of a truck requires less force when pushing it up a ramp than when lifting it directly onto the truck bed. The longer the ramp, the greater the mechanical advantage, and the easier it will be to move the box. The mechanical advantage of an inclined plane is equal to the slant length divided by the rise of the plane.

$$\textbf{Mechanical Advantage} = \frac{\textbf{slant length}}{\textbf{rise}}$$

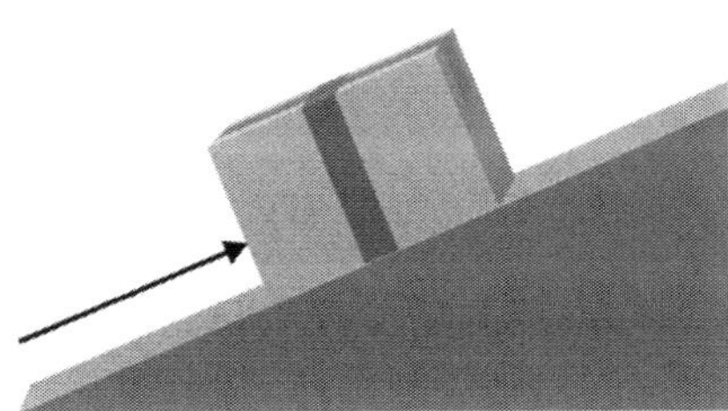

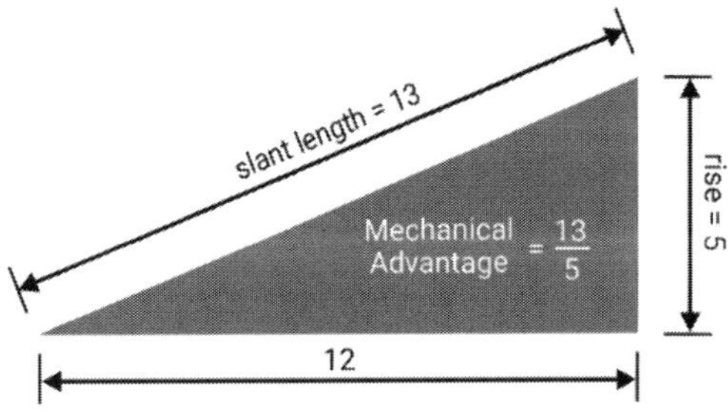

Screw

A screw is simply an inclined plane that has been wound around a cylinder so that it forms a sort of spiral.

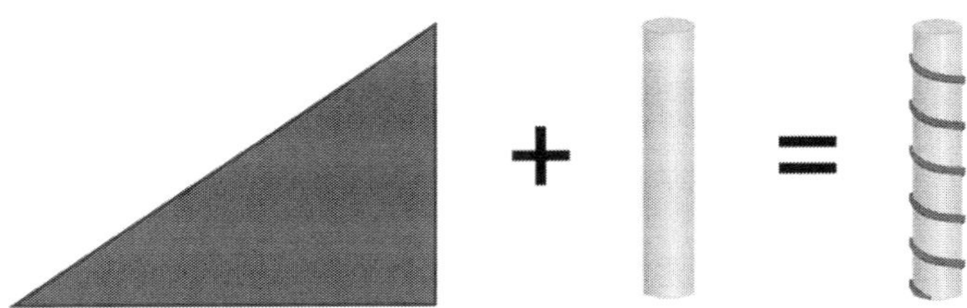

When it is placed into some medium, as for instance wood, the screw will move either forward or backward when it is rotated. The principle of the screw is used in a number of different objects, from jar lids to flashlights. The equation for the mechanical advantage is a modification of the inclined plane's equation.

Because the rise of the inclined plane is the length along a screw, length between rotations is the rise. The slant length is equal the circumference of one rotation ($2\pi r$).

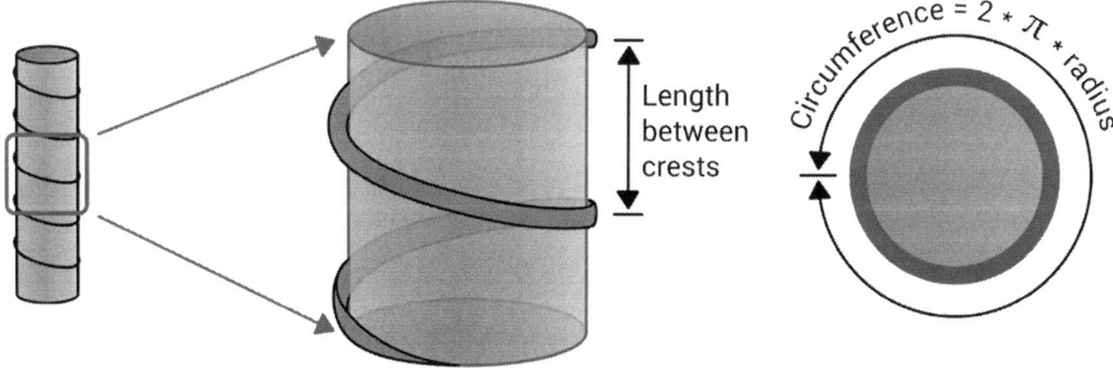

$$\textbf{Mechanical Advantage} = \frac{\mathbf{2 \times \pi \times radius}}{\textbf{length between crests}}$$

Wedge

A wedge is a variation on the inclined plane, in which the wedge moves between objects or parts and forces them apart. The unique characteristic of a wedge is that, unlike an inclined plane, it is designed to move. Perhaps the most familiar use of the wedge is in splitting wood. A wedge is driven into the wood by hitting the flat back end. The thin end of a wedge is easier to drive into the wood since it has less surface area and, therefore, transmits more force per area. As the wedge is driven in, the increased width helps to split the wood.

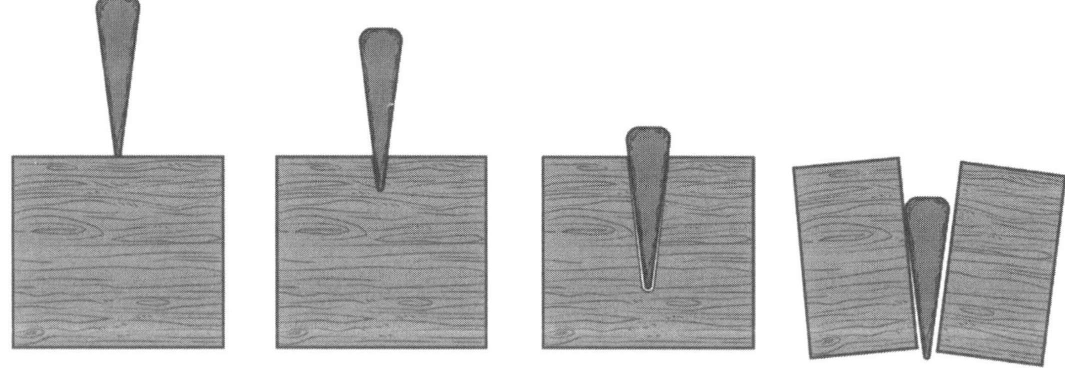

The longer and thinner the wedge, the greater the mechanical advantage. The equation for mechanical advantage of a wedge is:

$$\textbf{Mechanical Advantage} = \frac{\textbf{length}}{\textbf{width}}$$

Gears

Gears are a system of interlocking wheels that can create immense mechanical advantages. The amount of mechanical advantage, however, will depend on the gear ratio; that is, on the relation in size between the gears.

When a small gear is driving a big gear, the speed of the big gear is relatively slow; when a big gear is driving a small gear, the speed of the small gear is relatively fast.

The equation for the mechanical advantage is:

$$\textbf{Mechanical Advantage} = \frac{\textbf{torque}_{\textbf{output}}}{\textbf{torque}_{\textbf{input}}} = \frac{\textbf{r}_{\textbf{output}}}{\textbf{r}_{\textbf{input}}} = \frac{\textbf{\# of teeth}_{\textbf{output}}}{\textbf{\# of teeth}_{\textbf{input}}}$$

Note that mechanical advantage is greater than 1 when the output gear is larger. In these cases, the output velocity (ω) will be lower. The equation for the relative speed of a gear system is:

$$\frac{\omega_{\text{input}}}{\omega_{\text{output}}} = \frac{r_{\text{output}}}{r_{\text{input}}}$$

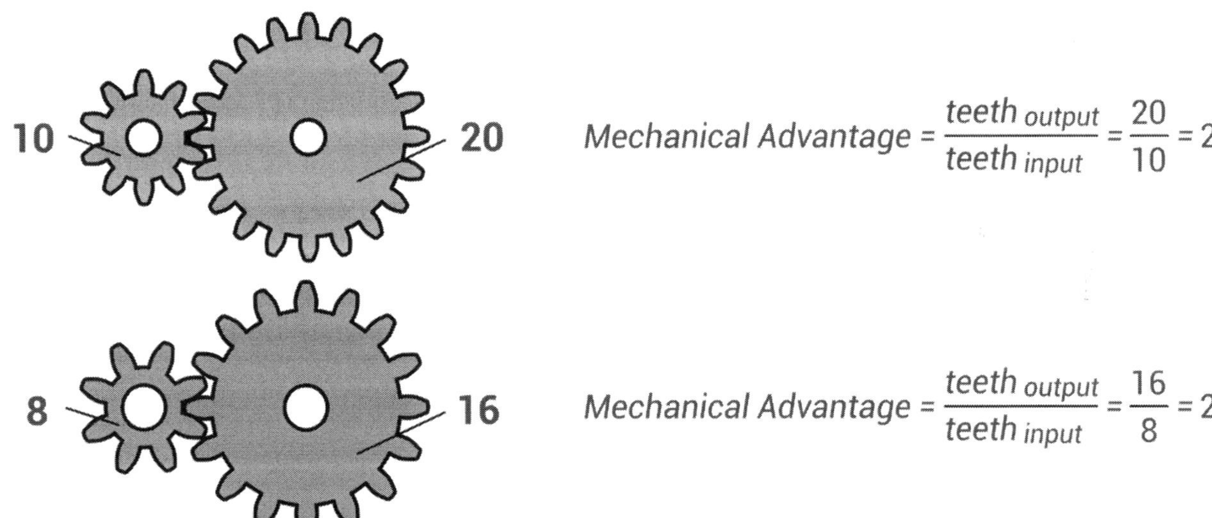

GEAR RATIOS

A gear ratio is a measure of how much the speed and torque are changing in a gear system. It is the ratio of output speed to input speed. Because the number of teeth is directly proportional to the speed in meshing gears, a gear ratio can also be calculated using the number of teeth on the gears. When the driving gear has 30 teeth and the driven gear has 10 teeth, the gear ratio is 3:1.

$$\text{Gear Ratio} = \frac{\text{\# of teeth}_{\text{driving}}}{\text{\# of teeth}_{\text{driven}}} = \frac{30}{10} = \frac{3}{1} = 3:1$$

This means that the smaller, driven gear rotates 3 times for every 1 rotation of the driving gear.

Science

Uses of Gears

Gears are used to change the direction, location, and amount of output torque, as well as change the angular velocity of output.

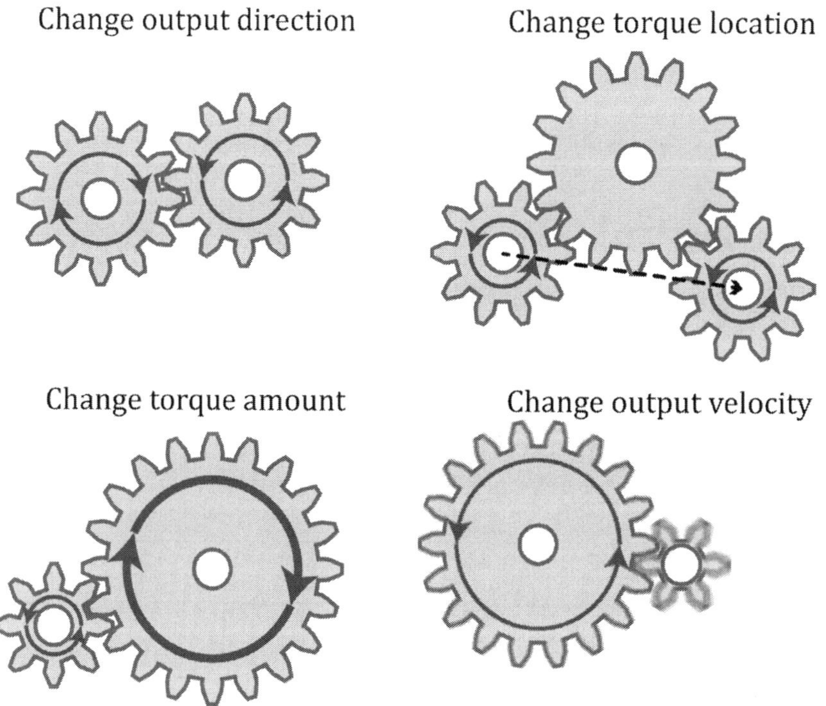

Cams

In the study of motion, a final application often tested is the cam. A cam and follower system allows mechanical systems to have timed, specified, and repeating motion. Although cams come in varied forms, tests focus on rotary cams. In engines, a cam shaft coordinates the valves for intake and exhaust. Cams are often used to convert rotational motion into repeating linear motion.

Cams rotate around one point. The follower sits on the edge of the cam and moves along with the edge. To understand simple cams, count the number of bumps on the cam. Each bump will cause the follower to move outwards.

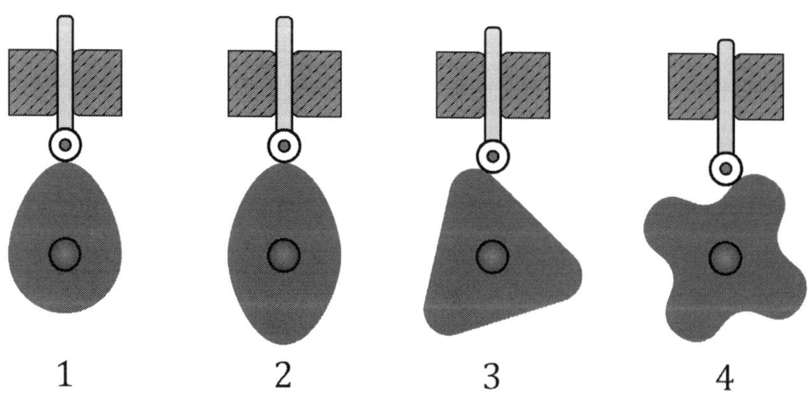

Another way to consider cams is to unravel the cam profile into a straight object. The follower will then follow the top of the profile.

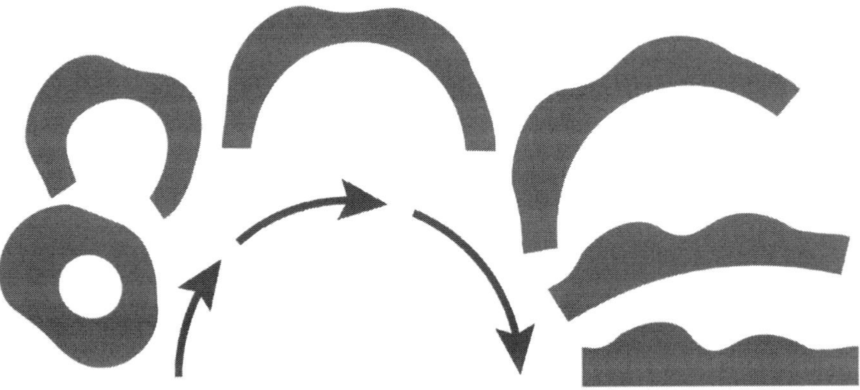

Energy

Energy is a word that has developed several different meanings in the English language, but in physics, it refers to the measure of a body's ability to do work. In physics, energy may not have a million meanings, but it does have many forms. Each of these forms, such as chemical, electric, and nuclear, is the capability of an object to perform work. However, the most commonly used concepts are mechanical energy and mechanical work. **Mechanical energy** is the sum of an object's kinetic and potential energies. While kinetic energy is linked to an object's motion, potential energy can be in a few different forms. The common forms of potential energy are gravitational and elastic.

Kinetic Energy

The **kinetic energy of an object** is that quality of its motion that can be related in a qualitative way to the amount of work performed on the object. Kinetic energy can be defined as $KE = \frac{mv^2}{2}$, in which m is the mass of an object and v is the magnitude of its velocity. Kinetic energy cannot be negative, since it depends on the square of velocity. Units for kinetic energy are the same as those for work: joules. Kinetic energy is a scalar quantity.

Changes in kinetic energy occur when a force does work on an object, such that the speed of the object is altered. This change in kinetic energy is equal to the amount of work that is done, and can be expressed as $W = KE_f - KE_i = \Delta KE$. This equation is commonly referred to as the work-kinetic energy theorem. If there are several different forces acting on the object, then W in this equation is the total work done by all the forces, or by the net force. This equation can be very helpful in solving some problems that would otherwise rely solely on Newton's laws of motion.

Potential Energy

Potential energy is the amount of energy that can be ascribed to a body or bodies based on configuration. There are a couple of different kinds of potential energy. **Gravitational potential energy** is the energy associated with the separation of bodies that are attracted to one another gravitationally. Any time you lift an object, you are increasing its gravitational potential energy. Gravitational potential energy can be found by the equation $PE = mgh$, where m is the mass of an object, $\boldsymbol{g}$ is the gravitational acceleration, and h is its height above a reference point, most often the ground.

Another kind of potential energy is **elastic potential energy**; elastic potential energy is associated with the compression or expansion of an elastic, or spring-like, object. Physicists will often refer to potential energy as being stored within a body, the implication being that it could emerge in the future.

Review Video: Potential and Kinetic Energy
Visit mometrix.com/academy and enter code: 491502

ELASTIC POTENTIAL ENERGY

Elastic potential energy is the potential for a certain amount of work to be done by one object on another using elastic compression or tension. The most common example is the spring. A spring will resist any compression or tension away from its equilibrium position (natural position). A small buggy is pressed into a large spring. The spring contains a large amount of elastic potential energy. If the buggy and spring are released, the spring will exert a force on the buggy, pushing it for a distance. This work will put kinetic energy into the buggy. The energy can be imagined as a liquid poured from one container into another. The spring pours its elastic energy into the buggy, which receives the energy as kinetic energy.

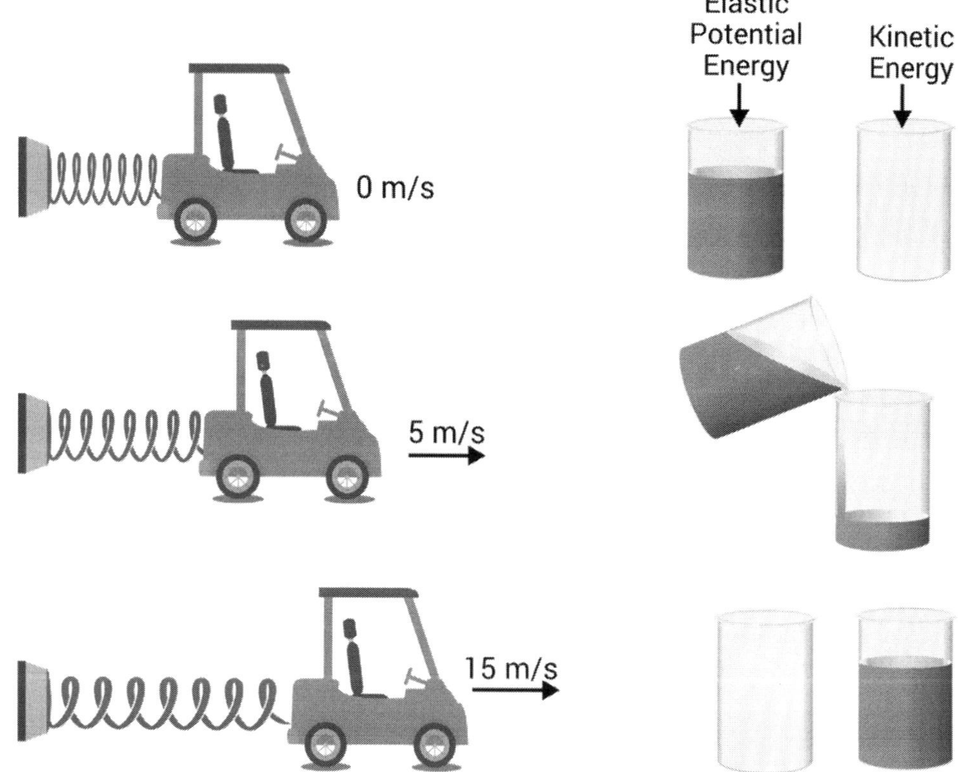

CONSERVATIVE AND NON-CONSERVATIVE FORCES

Forces that change the state of a system by changing kinetic energy into potential energy, or vice versa, are called **conservative forces**. This name arises because these forces conserve the total amount of kinetic and potential energy. Every other kind of force is considered non-conservative. One example of a conservative force is gravity. Consider the path of a ball thrown straight up into the air. Since the ball has the same amount of kinetic energy when it is thrown as it does when it returns to its original location (known as completing a closed path), gravity can be said to be a conservative force. More generally, a force can be said to be conservative if the work it does on an object through a closed path is zero. Frictional force would not meet this standard, of course, because it is only capable of performing negative work.

For example, imagine a ball moving perpendicular to the surface of the Earth, in other words straight up and down, with its weight being the only force acting on it. As the ball rises, the weight will be doing work on the ball, decreasing its speed and its kinetic energy and slowing it down until it momentarily stops. During this ascent, the potential energy of the ball will be rising. Once the ball begins to fall back down, it will lose potential energy as it gains kinetic energy. Mechanical energy is conserved throughout; the potential energy of the ball at its highest point is equal to the kinetic energy of the ball at its lowest point, just before to impact.

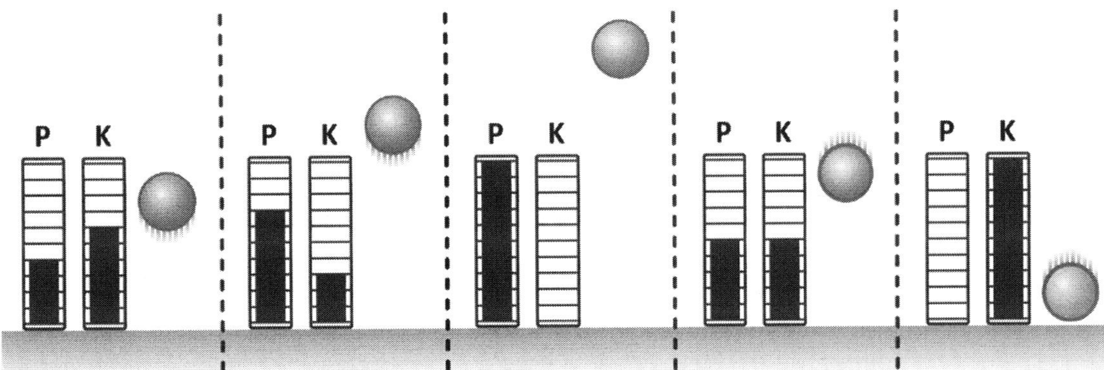

In systems where friction and air resistance are not negligible, we observe a different sort of result. For example, imagine a block sliding across the floor until it comes to a stop due to friction. Unlike a compressed spring or a ball flung into the air, there is no way for this block to regain its energy with a return trip. Therefore, we cannot say that the lost kinetic energy is being stored as potential energy. Instead, it has been dissipated and cannot be recovered. The total mechanical energy of the block-floor system has been not conserved in this case but rather reduced. The total energy of the system has not decreased, since the kinetic energy has been converted into thermal energy, but that energy is no longer useful for work.

One-Dimensional Analysis of Work Done By a Variable Force

If the force on an object varies across the distance the object is moved, then a simple product will not yield the work. If we consider the work performed by a variable force in one dimension, then we are assuming that the directions of the force and the displacement are the same. The magnitude of the force will depend on the position of the particle. In order to calculate the amount of work performed by a variable force over a given distance, we should first divide the total displacement into a number of intervals, each with a width of Δx. We may then say that the amount of work performed during any one interval is $\Delta W = \boldsymbol{F}_{avg}\Delta x$, where $\boldsymbol{F}_{avg}$ is the average force over the interval Δx. We can then say that the total amount of work performed is the sum of all work performed during the various intervals. By reducing the interval to an infinitesimal length, we obtain the integral:

$$W = \int_{x_1}^{x_2} \boldsymbol{F}_x dx$$

This integral requires that the force be a known function of x.

Work Performed by a Spring

If we move a block attached to a spring from point x_i to point x_f, we are doing work on the block, and the spring is also doing work on the block. To determine the work done by the spring on the block, we can substitute ***F*** from Hooke's law into our equation for work performed by a variable force, and arrive at this measure: $W = \frac{k(x_i^2 - x_f^2)}{2}$. This work will be positive if $x_i^2 > x_f^2$, and negative if the opposite is true. If $x_i = 0$ and we decide to call the final position x, then we may change our equation: $W = \frac{-kx^2}{2}$. It is important to keep in mind that this is the work done by the spring. The work done by the force that moves the block to its final position will be a positive quantity.

Like all simple harmonic oscillators, springs operate by **storing and releasing potential energy**. The amount of energy being stored or released by a spring is equal to the magnitude of the work done by the spring during that same operation. The total potential energy stored in a spring can be calculated as $PE = \frac{kx^2}{2}$. Neglecting the effects of friction and drag, an object oscillating on a spring will continue to do so indefinitely, since total mechanical energy (kinetic and potential) is conserved. In such a situation, the period of oscillation can be calculated as $T = 2\pi \times \sqrt{\frac{m}{k}}$.

Laws of Motion

Newton's Laws

Newton's First Law

Before Newton formulated his laws of mechanics, it was generally assumed that some force had to act on an object continuously in order to make the object move at a **constant velocity**. Newton, however, determined that unless some other force acted on the object (most notably friction or air resistance), it would continue in the direction it was pushed at the same velocity forever.

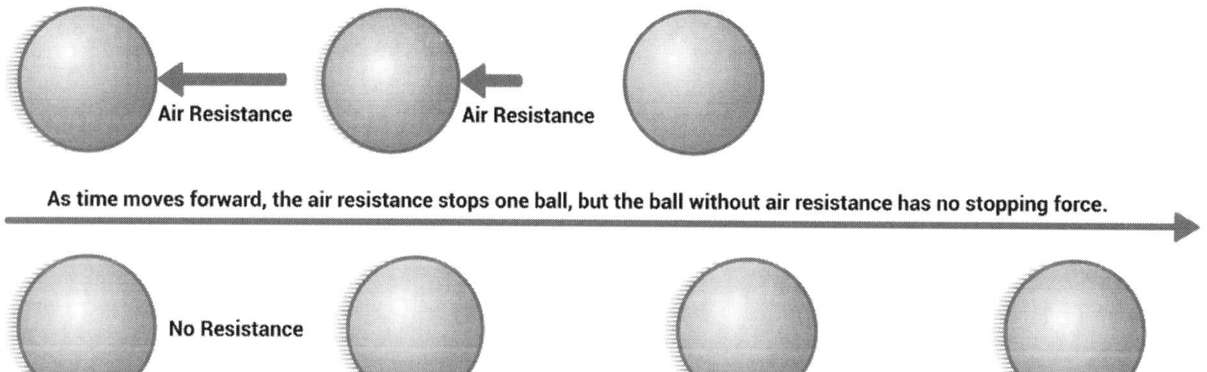

In this light, a body at rest and a body in motion are not all that different, and Newton's first law makes little distinction. It states that a body at rest will tend to remain at rest, while a body in motion will tend to remain in motion. This tendency of a body to remain in its present state of motion is referred to as **inertia**. In order for the body's state of motion to change, it must be acted on by a non-zero net force. **Net force** is the vector sum of all forces acting on a body. If this vector sum is zero, then there is no unbalanced force, and the body will remain in its present state of motion. It is important to remember that this law only holds in inertial reference frames.

Review Video: Newton's First Law of Motion
Visit mometrix.com/academy and enter code: 590367

NEWTON'S SECOND LAW

Newton's second law states that an **object's acceleration** is directly proportional to the net force acting on the object, and inversely proportional to the object's mass. It is generally written in equation form $\boldsymbol{F} = m\boldsymbol{a}$, where $\boldsymbol{F}$ is the net force acting on a body, m is the mass of the body, and $\boldsymbol{a}$ is its acceleration. It is important to note from this equation that since the mass is always a positive quantity, the acceleration vector is always pointed in the same direction as the net force vector. Of course, in order to apply this equation correctly, one must clearly identify the body to which it is being applied. Once this is done, we may say that $\boldsymbol{F}$ is the vector sum of all forces acting on that body, or the net force. This measure includes only those forces that are external to the body; any internal forces, in which one part of the body exerts force on another, are discounted.

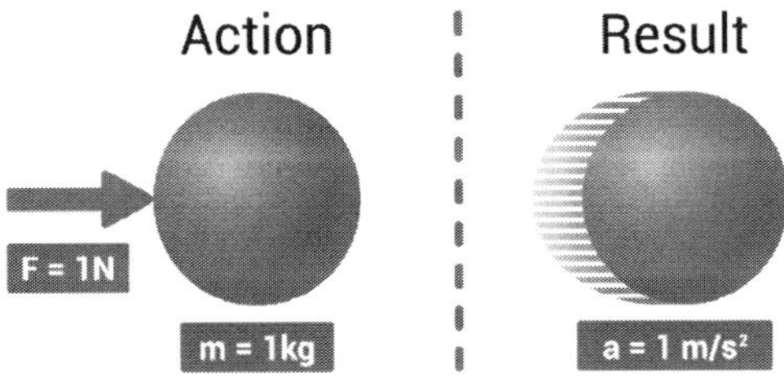

Newton's second law somewhat encapsulates his first, because it includes the principle that if no net force is acting on a body, the body will not accelerate. As was the case with his first law, Newton's second law may only be applied in inertial reference frames.

Review Video: Newton's Second Law of Motion
Visit mometrix.com/academy and enter code: 737975

NEWTON'S THIRD LAW

Newton's third law of motion can be stated as: **for every force, there is an equal and opposite force**. When a hammer strikes a nail, the nail hits the hammer just as hard. If we consider two objects, *A* and *B*, then we may express any contact between these two bodies with the equation $\boldsymbol{F}_{AB} = -\boldsymbol{F}_{BA}$. It is important to note in this kind of equation that the order of the subscripts denotes which body is exerting the force. Although the two forces are often referred to as the **action** and **reaction** forces, in physics there is really no such thing. There is no implication of cause and effect in the equation for Newton's third law. At first glance, this law might seem to forbid any movement at all. We must remember, however, that these equal, opposite forces are exerted on different bodies with different masses, so they will not cancel each other out.

As an example, consider two spring-based scales, both tipped on their sides, with the weighing surfaces facing each other. If scale #1 is pressing scale #2 into the wall, it exerts a force on scale #2, measurable by the reading

Science

on scale #2. However, because scale #1 is exerting a force on scale #2, scale #2 is exerting a force on scale #1 with an opposite direction, but the same magnitude.

Review Video: Newton's Third Law of Motion
Visit mometrix.com/academy and enter code: 838401

CONSERVATION OF ENERGY AND MOMENTUM

APPLYING CONSERVATION OF ROTATIONAL ENERGY AND ANGULAR MOMENTUM

A metal hoop of mass m and radius r is released from rest at the top of a hill of height h. Assuming that it rolls without sliding and does not lose energy to friction or drag, what will be the hoop's angular and linear velocities upon reaching the bottom of the hill?

The hoop's initial energy is all potential energy, $PE = mgh$. As the hoop rolls down, all of its energy is converted to **translational** and **rotational kinetic energy**. Thus, $mgh = \frac{1}{2}m\boldsymbol{v}^2 + \frac{1}{2}I\boldsymbol{\omega}^2$. Since the moment for a hoop is $I = mr^2$, and $\boldsymbol{\omega} = \frac{v}{r}$, the equation becomes $mgh = \frac{1}{2}m\boldsymbol{v}^2 + \frac{1}{2}mr^2\left(\frac{v^2}{r^2}\right)$, which further simplifies to $gh = \boldsymbol{v}^2$. Thus, the resulting velocity of the hoop is $\boldsymbol{v}_f = \sqrt{gh}$, with an angular velocity of $\boldsymbol{\omega}_f = \frac{v_f}{r}$. Note that if you were to forget about the energy converted to rotational motion, you would calculate a final velocity of $\boldsymbol{v}_f = \sqrt{2gh}$, which is the **impact velocity** of an object dropped from height h.

Angular momentum, $\boldsymbol{L}$, of an object is defined as its moment of inertia multiplied by its angular velocity, or $\boldsymbol{L} = I\boldsymbol{\omega}$. Consider a planet orbiting the sun with an elliptical orbit where the small radius is r_S and large radius is r_L. Find the angular velocity of the planet when it is at distance r_S from the sun if its velocity at r_L is $\boldsymbol{\omega}_L$.

Since the size of a planet is almost insignificant compared to the interplanetary distances, the planet may be treated as a single particle of mass m, giving it a moment about the sun of $I = mr^2$. Since the gravitational force is incapable of exerting a net torque on an object, we can assume that the planet's angular momentum about the sun is a constant, $\boldsymbol{L}_L = \boldsymbol{L}_S$. Thus, $m{r_L}^2\boldsymbol{\omega}_L = m{r_S}^2\boldsymbol{\omega}_S$. Solving this equation for $\boldsymbol{\omega}_S$ yields $\boldsymbol{\omega}_S = \boldsymbol{\omega}_L\left(\frac{r_L}{r_S}\right)^2$.

MASS-ENERGY RELATIONSHIP

Because mass consists of atoms, which are themselves formed of subatomic particles, there is an energy inherent in the composition of all mass. In other words, it would require a significant input of energy to form all the atoms in a given mass from their most basic particles. This rest energy is the energy that Einstein refers to in his famous mass-energy relation $E = mc^2$, where c is the speed of light in a vacuum. In theory, if all the particles in a given mass were converted directly to energy (e.g., by matter-antimatter annihilation), it would give off energy $E = mc^2$. For example, if this were to happen to a single gram of mass, the resulting outburst of energy would be $E = 9 \times 10^{13}$ J, enough energy to provide power for over 2,000 average households for a whole year.

In some nuclear reactions, small amounts of mass are converted to energy. The amount of energy released can be calculated through the same relation, $E = mc^2$. Most such reactions involve mass losses on the order of 10^{-30} kg.

WEIGHT AND MASS

WEIGHT

Not to be confused with mass (quantity of matter), weight the term for the force due to the gravitational attraction between the masses of the two bodies. This force is described by the expression $\frac{Gm_1m_2}{r^2}$, where G is the gravitational constant, m_1 and m_2 are the masses of the two objects, and r is the distance between the centers of mass. Since the majority of humans are concerned with events close to the surface of the Earth, one of the masses (M_E) and the distance (R_E) are essentially constant and are combined into $\boldsymbol{g}$, which is the acceleration due to gravity near the surface of the Earth $\left(\boldsymbol{g} = \frac{GM_E}{(R_E)^2}\right)$. Thus, we can express weight as $\boldsymbol{W} = m\boldsymbol{g}$. Since it is a force, the SI unit for weight is the Newton. As a vector, $\boldsymbol{W}$ can be expressed as either $-mg\mathbf{j}$ or $-W\mathbf{j}$, in which $\mathbf{j}$ is the direction on the axis pointing away from the Earth.

Review Video: Mass, Weight, Volume, Density, and Specific Gravity
Visit mometrix.com/academy and enter code: 920570

ELECTRICAL PROPERTIES OF MATERIALS

COMMON MEANS OF TRANSFERRING ELECTRICAL CHARGE

Charge is transferred in three common ways: conduction, induction, and friction. **Conduction**, as the name implies, takes place between conductive materials. There must be a point of contact between the two materials and a potential difference, such as when a battery is connected to a circuit. **Induction also requires conductive materials. It occurs when a conductive material encounters a changing magnetic field**. The change can be the result of a changing magnetic field or the material moving within a constant magnetic field. Charge transfer due to **friction** does not require conductive materials. When two materials are rubbed together, electrons may be transferred from one to the other, leaving the two materials with equal and opposite charges. This is observed when shoes are dragged across a carpeted floor.

Review Video: Charging by Conduction
Visit mometrix.com/academy and enter code: 502661

CONDUCTORS, INSULATORS, AND SEMICONDUCTORS

In many materials, electrons are able to move freely; these are known as **conductors**. Due to their atomic structure and delocalized electrons, **metals** tend to be the best conductors, particularly copper and silver. Highly conductive wires are instrumental in creating low-resistance pathways for electrons to travel along within a circuit.

Other materials naturally inhibit the movement of charge and are known as **insulators**. Their electrons are tightly held by the individual constituent atoms. Glass, pure water, wood, and plastic are all insulators. Insulators are necessary in circuits to prevent charge from escaping to undesirable places, such as an operator's hand. For this reason, most highly conductive materials are covered by insulators.

Semiconductors, as the name suggests, are materials that only partially conduct electrical charge. The elements silicon and germanium are both common semiconductors, and are frequently used in microelectronic devices because they allow for tight control of the rate of conduction. In many cases, the conduction ability of semiconductors can be controlled by adjusting the temperature of the material.

DOPING SEMICONDUCTORS

Resistivity is the physical property of resistance of different materials: metals, which easily conduct electricity, have low resistivity; insulators have high resistivity; and the resistivity of **semiconductors** falls in between (example: silicon). **Doping** is the process of mixing different semiconductor atoms in order to control conductivity of the material. **N-type semiconductors** have an excess of electrons as a result of the doping process; when an electric field is applied, a negative pole forms due to the buildup of negatively charged electrons (example: silicon doped with antimony). **P-type semiconductors** have a shortage of electrons; when an electric field is applied, a positive pole forms (example: silicon doped with boron).

PROPERTIES OF MAGNETS

MAGNETS AND MAGNETISM

A **magnet** is any object or material, such as iron, steel, or magnetite (lodestone), that can affect another substance within its **field of force** that has like characteristics. Magnets can either attract or repel other substances. Magnets have two **poles**: north and south. Like poles repel and opposite poles (pairs of north and south) attract. The magnetic field is a set of invisible lines representing the paths of attraction and repulsion.

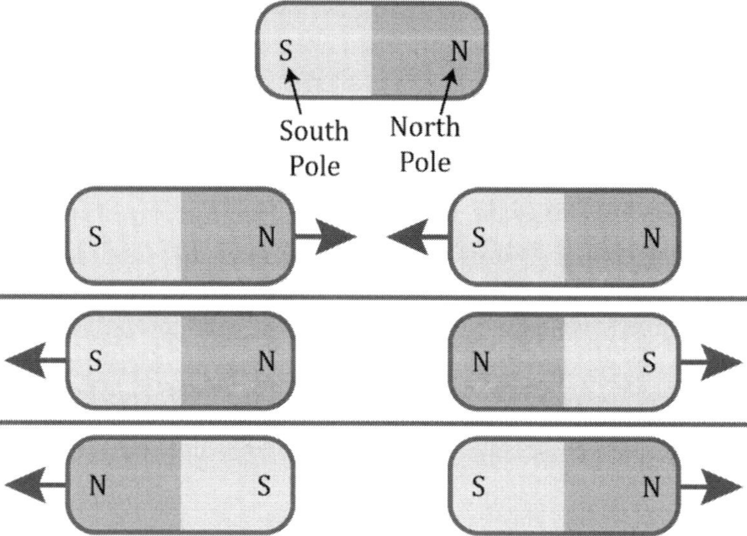

Magnetism can occur naturally, or ferromagnetic materials can be magnetized. Certain matter that is magnetized can retain its magnetic properties indefinitely and become a permanent magnet. Other matter can lose its magnetic properties. For example, an iron nail can be temporarily magnetized by stroking it repeatedly in the same direction using one pole of another magnet. Once magnetized, it can attract or repel other magnetically inclined materials, such as paper clips. Dropping the nail repeatedly will cause it to lose its magnetic properties.

Review Video: Magnets
Visit mometrix.com/academy and enter code: 570803

MAGNETIC FIELDS AND ATOMIC STRUCTURE

Motion of a charge produces a **magnetic field**. Within an atom, the negatively-charged electrons moving around the nucleus each generate a magnetic field. In most materials, these fields all perfectly oppose and cancel each other, but in certain elements (e.g., iron, cobalt, nickel) the fields are not completely canceled, which makes each atom a tiny magnet. The strength and direction of a magnetic field is known as the magnetic moment.

Pairs of electrons moving in opposite directions cancel each other out, creating a **net magnetic field** of zero. Materials that have an unpaired electron are magnetic. Those with a weak attractive force are referred to as **paramagnetic materials**, while **ferromagnetic materials** have a strong attractive force. A **diamagnetic material** has electrons that are paired, and therefore does not typically have a magnetic moment. There are, however, some diamagnetic materials that have a weak magnetic field.

A magnetic field can be formed not only by a magnetic material, but also by electric current flowing through a wire. When a coiled wire is attached to the two ends of a battery, for example, an **electromagnet** can be formed by inserting a ferromagnetic material such as an iron bar within the coil. When electric current flows through the wire, the bar becomes a magnet. If there is no current, the magnetism is lost. A **magnetic domain** occurs when the magnetic fields of atoms are grouped and aligned. These groups form what can be thought of as miniature magnets within a material. This is what happens when an object like an iron nail is temporarily magnetized. Prior to magnetization, the organization of atoms and their various polarities are somewhat random with respect to where the north and south poles are pointing. After magnetization, a significant percentage of the poles are lined up in one direction, which is what causes the magnetic force exerted by the material.

Sound Waves

The **pitch of a sound** as it reaches one's ear is based on the frequency of the sound waves. A high-pitched sound has a higher frequency than a low-pitched sound. Like all waves, sound waves transmit energy. The rate at which this energy is transmitted is the sonic power. Loudness, or intensity of sound, is the sonic power received per unit area.

When a pair of sound waves with slightly different frequencies interfere with one another causing a periodic variation in sound intensity or a **beat**. The frequency of the variation, called the **beat frequency**, is equal to the difference between frequencies of the two sound waves. The phenomenon is used when tuning two instruments to one another. As the two pitches get closer, the beat frequency will become smaller and smaller until it disappears entirely, indicating that the instruments are in tune.

Review Video: Sound
Visit mometrix.com/academy and enter code: 562378

Electromagnetic Waves and Electromagnetic Spectrum

Electromagnetic Spectrum

The **electromagnetic spectrum** is the range of all wavelengths and frequencies of known electromagnetic waves. Visible light occupies only a small portion of the electromagnetic spectrum. Some of the common classifications of electromagnetic waves are listed in the table below with their approximate frequency ranges.

Classification	Freq. (Hz)
Gamma Rays	$\sim 10^{19}$
X-Rays	$\sim 10^{17} - 10^{18}$
Ultraviolet	$\sim 10^{15} - 10^{16}$
Visible Light	$\sim 10^{14}$
Infra-red	$\sim 10^{11} - 10^{14}$
Microwaves	$\sim 10^{10} - 10^{11}$
Radio/TV	$\sim 10^{6} - 10^{9}$

Electromagnetic waves travel at the speed of light, $c = 3 \times 10^8$ m/s. To find the wavelength of any electromagnetic wave, simply divide c by the frequency. Visible light occupies a range of wavelengths from

Science

approximately 380 nm (violet) to 740 nm (red). The full spectrum of color can be found between these two wavelengths.

> **Review Video: Electromagnetic Spectrum**
> Visit mometrix.com/academy and enter code: 771761
>
> **Review Video: Light**
> Visit mometrix.com/academy and enter code: 900556

Geometric Optics

Thin Lenses

A **lens** is an optical device that **redirects light** to either converge or diverge in specific geometric patterns. Whether the lens converges or diverges is dependent on the lens being **convex** or **concave**, respectively. The particular angle of redirection is dictated by the lens's focal length. For a **converging lens**, this is the distance from the lens that parallel rays entering from the opposite side would intersect. For a **diverging lens**, it is the distance from the lens that parallel rays entering the lens would intersect if they were reverse extrapolated. However, the focal length of a diverging lens is always considered to be negative. A thin lens is a lens whose focal length is much greater than its thickness. By making this assumption, we can derive many helpful relations.

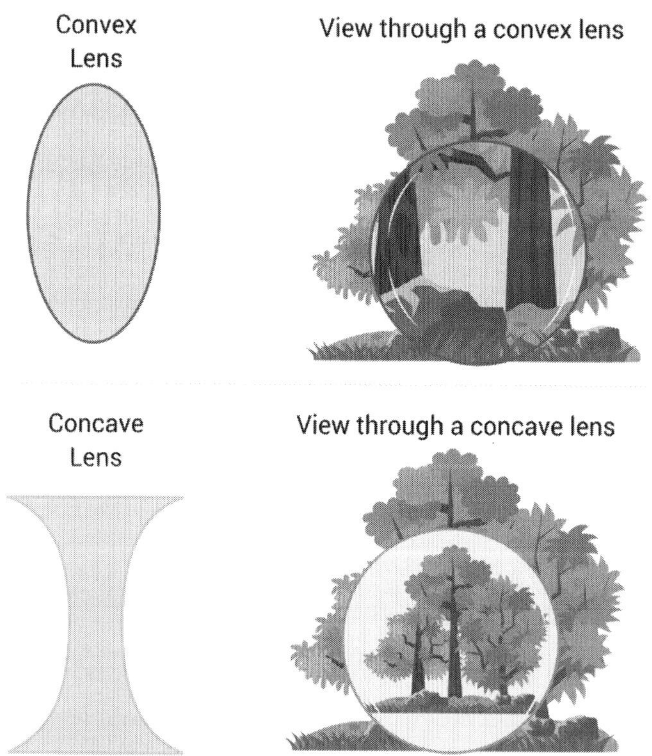

Real and Virtual Images

In optics, an **object's image** is what is seen when the object is viewed through a lens. The location of an object's image is related to the lens's **focal length** by the equation $\frac{1}{d_o} + \frac{1}{d_i} = \frac{1}{f}$, where f is the focal length, and d_o and d_i are the distance of the object and its image from the lens, respectively. A positive d_i indicates that the image is on the opposite side of the lens from the object. If the lens is a magnifying lens, the height of the object may be different from that of its image, and may even be inverted. The object's magnification, m, can be found as $m = \frac{-d_i}{d_o}$. The value for the magnification can then be used to relate the object's height to that of its image: $m = \frac{y_i}{y_o}$. Note that if the magnification is negative, then the image has been inverted.

Images may be either **real** or **virtual**. Real images are formed by light rays passing through the image location, while virtual images are only perceived by reverse extrapolating refracted light rays. Diverging lenses cannot create real images, only virtual ones. Real images are always on the opposite side of a converging lens from the object and are always inverted.

Concave Mirrors

Concave mirrors will create an image of an object in varying ways depending on the location of the object. The table below details the location, orientation, magnification, and nature of the image. The five object locations to be examined are between the mirror and the focal point (1), at the focal point (2), between the focal point and the center of curvature, or twice the focal point (3), at the center of curvature (4), and beyond the center of curvature (5).

Object	Image Location	Orientation	Magnification	Type
1	$d_i < 0$	upright	$m > 1$	virtual
2	none	none	none	none
3	$d_i > 2f$	inverted	$m < -1$	real
4	$d_i = 2f$	inverted	$m = -1$	real
5	$f < d_i < 2f$	inverted	$0 > m > -1$	real

Note in case 5 that the image may effectively be located at the focal point. This is the case for objects at extremely great, or near infinite, distances from the mirror. The magnification at these distances will be very small and a true infinite distance would result in a magnification of zero.

Plane Mirrors and Spherical Mirrors

Plane mirrors have very simple properties. They reflect only **virtual images**, they have no magnification, and the object's distance from the mirror is always equal to that of its image. Plane mirrors will also appear to reverse the directions left and right.

Spherical mirrors follow the same governing equations for finding image height, location, orientation, and magnification as do thin lenses; however, the sign convention for image location is reversed. A positive image location denotes that it is on the same side as the object. Spherical mirrors may be either **concave** or **convex**. Convex mirrors are by far the simpler of the two. They will always reflect virtual, upright images with magnification between zero and one. Concave mirrors have varying behavior based on the object location.

Simple Magnifier, the Microscope, and the Telescope

A simple magnifier, or commonly a **magnifying glass**, is a converging lens that creates an enlarged virtual image near the observer's eye. The object must be within a certain distance, about 25 cm or 10 inches, from the magnifier for it to operate properly. Otherwise, the image will be blurry.

A **microscope** is a magnifying device that is used to examine very small objects. It uses a series of lenses to capture light coming from the far side of the sample under examination. Often microscopes will have interchangeable magnification lenses mounted on a wheel, allowing the user to adjust the level of magnification by rotating in a different lens. Optical microscopes will generally be limited to a magnification of 1,500.

Telescopes are used to view very distant objects, most often celestial bodies. Telescopes use both lenses and mirrors to capture light from a distant source, focus it, and then magnify it. This creates a virtual image that is very much smaller than the object itself, and yet much larger than the object appears to the naked eye.

PRISMS

Prisms are optical devices that alter the path or nature of light waves. Glass and plastic are the two most prevalent materials used to make prisms. There are three different types of prisms in common use. The most familiar of these is the dispersive prism, which splits a beam of light into its constituent wavelengths. For sunlight, this results in the full spectrum of color being displayed. These prisms are generally in the familiar triangular prism shape.

Polarizing prisms, as their name suggests, polarize light, but without significantly reducing the intensity, as a simple filter would. Waves that are oscillating in planes other than the desired plane are caused to rotate, so that they are oscillating in the desired plane. This type of prism is commonly used in cameras.

Reflective prisms are much less common than either of the others. They reflect light, often through the use of the total internal reflection phenomenon. Their primary use is in binoculars.

HEAT TRANSFER

Heat transfer is the flow of thermal energy, which is measured by temperature. Heat will flow from warmer objects to cooler objects until an **equilibrium** is reached in which both objects are at the same temperature. Because the particles of warmer objects possess a higher kinetic energy than the particles of cooler objects, the particles of the warmer objects are vibrating more quickly and collide more often, transferring energy to the cooler objects in which the particles have less kinetic energy and are moving more slowly. Heat may be transferred by conduction, convection, or radiation. In **conduction**, heat is transferred by direct contact between two objects. In **convection**, heat is transferred by moving currents. In **radiation**, heat is transferred by electromagnetic waves.

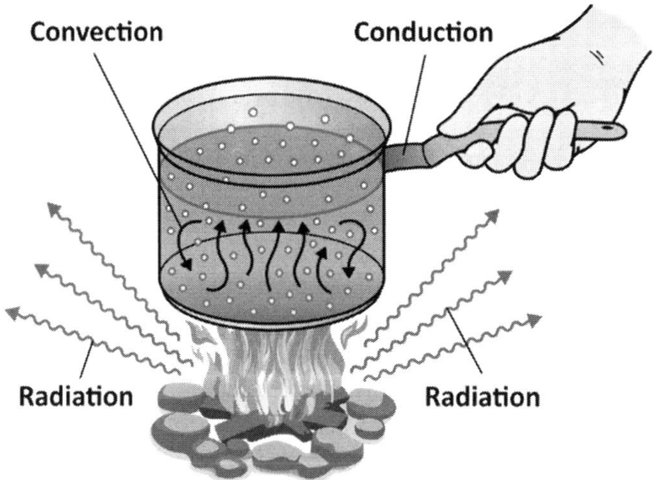

Review Video: Heat Transfer at the Molecular Level
Visit mometrix.com/academy and enter code: 451646

CONVECTION

Heat always flows from a region of higher temperature to a region of lower temperature. If two regions are at the same temperature, there is a thermal equilibrium between them and there will be no net heat transfer between them. Convection is a mode of heat transfer in which a surface in contact with a fluid experiences a heat flow. The heat rate for convection is given as $q = hA\Delta T$, where h is the convection coefficient, and q is the heat transferred per unit of time. The convection coefficient is dependent on a number of factors, including the configuration of the surface and the nature and velocity of the fluid. For complicated configurations, it often has to be determined experimentally.

Convection may be classified as either free or forced. In free convection, when a surface transfers heat to the surrounding air, the heated air becomes less dense and rises, allowing cooler air to descend and come into contact with the surface. Free convection may also be called natural convection. Forced convection in this example would involve forcibly cycling the air: for instance, with a fan. While this does generally require an additional input of work, the convection coefficient is always greater for forced convection.

Conduction

Conduction is a form of heat transfer that requires contact. Since heat is a measure of kinetic energy, most commonly vibration, at the atomic level, it may be transferred from one location to another or one object to another by contact. The rate at which heat is transferred is proportional to the material's thermal conductivity k, cross-sectional area A, and temperature gradient $\frac{\Delta T}{\Delta x}$:

$$q = kA\left(\frac{\Delta T}{\Delta x}\right)$$

If two ends of a rod are each held at a constant temperature, the heat transfer through the rod will be given as $q = k\text{A}\left(\frac{T_H - T_L}{d}\right)$, where d is the length of the rod. The heat will flow from the hot end to the cold end. The thermal conductivity is generally given in units of $\frac{\text{W}}{\text{m K}}$. Metals are some of the best conductors, many having a thermal conductivity around 400 $\frac{\text{W}}{\text{m K}}$. The thermal conductivity of wood is very small, generally less than 0.5 $\frac{\text{W}}{\text{m K}}$. Diamond is extremely thermally conductive and may have a conductivity of over 2,000 $\frac{\text{W}}{\text{m K}}$. Although fluids also have thermal conductivity, they will tend to transfer heat primarily through convection.

Radiation

Radiation heat transfer occurs via electromagnetic radiation between two bodies. Unlike conduction and convection, radiation requires no medium in which to take place. Indeed, the heat we receive from the sun is entirely radiation since it must pass through a vacuum to reach us. Every body at a temperature above absolute zero emits heat radiation at a rate of $q = e\sigma AT^4$, where e is the surface emissivity and σ is the Stefan-Boltzmann constant. The net radiation heat-transfer rate for a body is given by $q = e\sigma A(T^4 - T_0^4)$, where T_0 is the temperature of the surroundings. Emissivity, which has a value between 0 and 1, is a measure of how well a surface absorbs and emits radiation. Dark-colored surfaces tend to have high emissivity, while shiny or reflective surfaces have low emissivity. In the radiation heat-rate equation, it is important to remember to use absolute temperature units, since the temperature value is being raised to a power.

Types of Energy

Chemical, Electrical, Electromagnetic, Nuclear, and Thermal Energy

Different types of energy may be associated with systems:

- **Chemical energy** is the energy that is stored in chemical bonds and intermolecular forces.
- **Electrical energy** is the energy associated with the movement of electrons or ions through a material.
- **Electromagnetic energy** is the energy of electromagnetic waves of several frequencies including radio waves, microwaves, infrared light, visible light, ultraviolet light, x-rays, and gamma rays.
- **Nuclear energy** is the binding energy that is stored within an atom's nucleus.
- **Thermal energy** is the total internal kinetic energy of a system due to the random motions of the particles.

Phase Transitions

States of Matter

The four states of matter are solid, liquid, gas, and plasma. **Solids** have a definite shape and a definite volume. Because solid particles are held in fairly rigid positions, solids are the least compressible of the four states of matter. **Liquids** have definite volumes but no definite shapes. Because their particles are free to slip and slide over each other, liquids take the shape of their containers, but they still remain fairly incompressible by natural means. **Gases** have no definite shape or volume. Because gas particles are free to move, they move away from each other to fill their containers. Gases are compressible. **Plasmas** are high-temperature, ionized gases that exist only under very high temperatures at which electrons are stripped away from their atoms.

Review Video: States of Matter
Visit mometrix.com/academy and enter code: 742449

Review Video: Properties of Liquids
Visit mometrix.com/academy and enter code: 802024

Review Video: States of Matter [Advanced]
Visit mometrix.com/academy and enter code: 298130

The following table shows similarities and differences between solids, liquids, and gases:

	Solid	**Liquid**	**Gas**
Shape	Fixed shape	No fixed shape (assumes shape of container)	No fixed shape (assumes shape of container)
Volume	Fixed	Fixed	Changes to assume volume of container
Fluidity	Does not flow easily	Flows easily	Flows easily
Compressibility	Hard to compress	Hard to compress	Compresses

Six Different Types of Phase Change

A substance that is undergoing a change from a solid to a liquid is said to be melting. If this change occurs in the opposite direction, from liquid to solid, this change is called freezing. A liquid which is being converted to a gas is undergoing vaporization. The reverse of this process is known as condensation. Direct transitions from gas to solid and solid to gas are much less common in everyday life, but they can occur given the proper conditions. Solid to gas conversion is known as sublimation, while the reverse is called deposition.

Review Video: Chemical and Physical Properties of Matter
Visit mometrix.com/academy and enter code: 717349

Phase Diagram and Critical Point

A **phase diagram** is a graph or chart of pressure versus temperature that represents the solid, liquid, and gaseous phases of a substance and the transitions between these phases. Typically, **pressure** is located on the vertical axis, and temperature is located along the horizontal axis. The curves drawn on the graph represent points at which different phases are in an equilibrium state. These curves indicate at which pressure and temperature the phase changes of sublimation, melting, and boiling occur. Specifically, the curve between the liquid and gas phases indicates the pressures and temperatures at which the liquid and gas phases are in equilibrium. The curve between the solid and liquid phases indicates the temperatures and pressures at which the solid and liquid phases are in equilibrium. The open spaces on the graph represent the distinct phases solid, liquid, and gas. The point at which the solid–liquid, solid–gas, and liquid–gas phase boundaries intersect is called the triple point. At the triple point, the solid, liquid, and gas phases all exist in equilibrium. The critical point, by contrast, is the endpoint of the liquid–gas coexistence curve, where the liquid and gas phases become indistinguishable and form a supercritical fluid.

Lettered Regions of a Phase Diagram

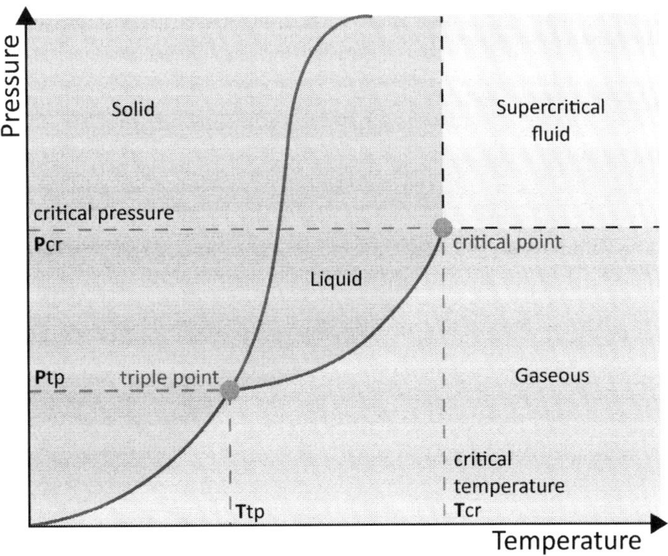

A—**Solid phase**: This is a region of high pressure and low temperature where the substance always exists as a solid.

B—**Liquid phase**: This is a region of pressure and temperature where the substance is in the liquid phase.

C—**Gas phase**: This is a region of pressure and temperature where the substance is in the gaseous phase.

D—**Sublimation point**: The portion of the curve that contains point D shows all the combinations of pressure and temperature at which the solid phase is in equilibrium with the gaseous phase.

E—**Triple point**: The point at which the solid, liquid, and gaseous phases are all in equilibrium.

F—**Boiling point**: The line that contains point F indicates all the combinations of pressure and temperature at which the liquid phase and gas phase are in equilibrium.

Laws of Thermodynamics

First Law

The **first law of thermodynamics** states that energy cannot be **created** or **destroyed**, but only **converted** from one form to another. It is generally applied as $Q = \Delta U + W$, where Q is the net heat energy added to a system, ΔU is the change in internal energy of the system, and W is the work done by the system. For any input of heat energy to a system, that energy must be either converted to internal energy through a temperature increase or expended in doing work. For a system that gives off heat, either the temperature of the system must decrease or work must be done on the system by its surroundings. By convention, work done by the system is positive while work done on the system is negative.

For instance, suppose a gas is compressed by a piston while the gas temperature remains constant. If we consider the gas to be the system, the work is negative, since the work is being performed on the gas. Since the temperature remains constant, $\Delta U = 0$. Thus, Q must be a negative quantity, indicating that heat is lost by the gas. Conversely, if the gas does positive work on the piston while remaining at a constant temperature, the gas must be receiving heat input from the surroundings.

SECOND LAW

The **second law of thermodynamics** is primarily a statement of the natural tendency of all things toward disorder rather than order. It deals with a quantity called **entropy**, which is an inverse measure of the remaining useful energy in a system. If we take a system of a pot of hot water and an ice cube, the system entropy initially has a value of s_1. After the ice cube melts in the water and the system reaches an equilibrium temperature, the system has larger entropy value s_2, which is the maximum entropy for the system. The system cannot return to its initial state without work put into the system to refreeze the ice cube and reheat the water. If this is done and the system returns to a state with entropy s_1, then the entropy of the surroundings must at the same time increase by more than $s_2 - s_1$, since the net entropy from any process is always greater than zero. Reversible processes are those that may be accomplished in reverse without requiring additional work input. These processes do not exist in the real world, but can be useful for approximating some situations. All real processes are irreversible, meaning they require additional work input to accomplish in reverse. Another important concept is that of spontaneity, the ability of a process to occur without instigation. An ice cube located in an environment at a temperature above the freezing point will spontaneously melt. Although some processes can decrease system entropy at a cost to the entropy of the surroundings, all spontaneous processes involve an increase in the total entropy of the universe.

THIRD AND ZEROTH LAWS

The **third law of thermodynamics** regards the behavior of systems as they **approach absolute zero temperature**. Actually reaching a state of absolute zero is impossible. According to this law, all activity disappears as molecules slow to a standstill near absolute zero, and the system achieves a perfect crystal structure while the system entropy approaches its minimum value. For most systems, this would in fact be a value of zero entropy. Note that this does not violate the second law since causing a system to approach absolute zero would require an immense increase in the entropy of the surroundings, resulting in a positive net entropy. This law is used to determine the value of a material's standard entropy, which is its entropy at the standard temperature of 25 °C.

The **zeroth law of thermodynamics** deals with thermal equilibrium between two systems. It states that if two systems are both in thermal equilibrium with a third system, then they are in thermal equilibrium with each other. This may seem intuitive, but it is an important basis for the other thermodynamic laws.

Review Video: Laws of Thermodynamics
Visit mometrix.com/academy and enter code: 253607

ENTROPY

Entropy (S) is the amount of **disorder** or **randomness of a system**. According to the second law of thermodynamics, systems tend toward a state of greater entropy. The second law of thermodynamics can also be stated as $\Delta S > 0$. Processes with positive changes in entropy tend to be spontaneous. For example, melting is a process with a positive ΔS. When a solid changes into a liquid state, the substance becomes more disordered; therefore, entropy increases. Entropy also will increase in a reaction in which the number of moles of gases increases due to the amount of disorder increasing. Entropy increases when a solute dissolves into a solvent due to the increase in the number of particles. Entropy increases when a system is heated due to the particles moving faster and the amount of disorder increasing.

SPONTANEOUS / REVERSIBLE PROCESSES

Some chemical processes are **spontaneous**. According to the second law of thermodynamics, systems or processes always **tend to a state of greater entropy** or lower potential energy. Some exothermic chemical systems are spontaneous because they can increase their stability by reaching a lower potential energy. If processes or reactions have products at a lower potential energy, these processes tend to be spontaneous.

Spontaneous reactions have only one direction as given by the second law of thermodynamics. Spontaneous processes go in the direction of greater entropy and lower potential energy. To be reversible, a reaction or process has to be able to go back and forth between two states. A spontaneous process is irreversible.

Concept of Change in Enthalpy

All chemical processes involve either the release or the absorption of heat. Enthalpy is this heat energy. **Enthalpy** is a state function that is equivalent to the amount of heat a system exchanges with its surroundings. For **exothermic processes**, which release heat, the change in enthalpy (ΔH) is negative because the final enthalpy is less than the initial enthalpy. For **endothermic processes**, which absorb heat, the change in enthalpy (ΔH) is positive because the final enthalpy is greater than the initial enthalpy.

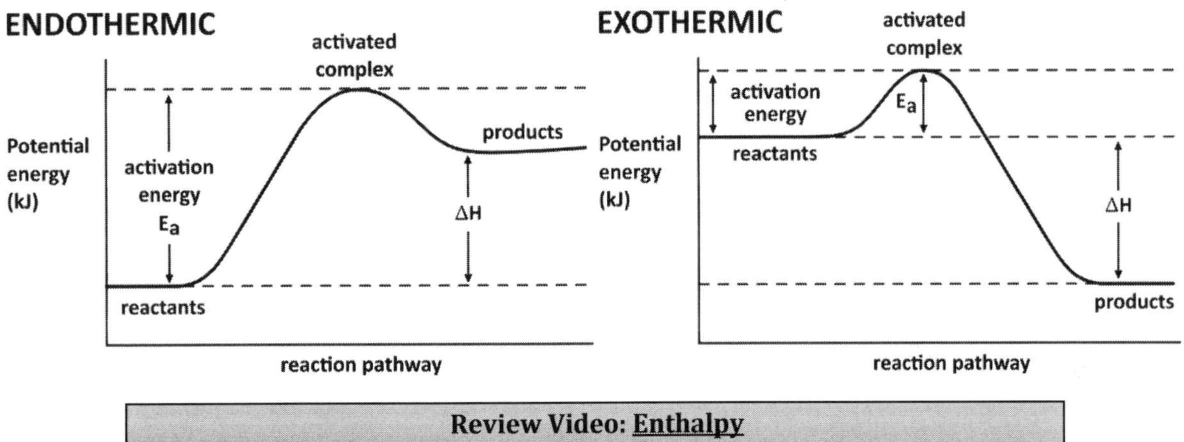

Review Video: Enthalpy
Visit mometrix.com/academy and enter code: 233315

Gibbs Energy

Gibbs energy (G), also known as Gibbs free energy, is the energy of the system that is available to do work. Gibbs energy determines the **spontaneity** of chemical and physical processes. Some processes are spontaneous because $\Delta H < 0$ or because $\Delta S > 0$. If one of the conditions is favorable but the other condition is not favorable, Gibbs energy can be used to determine if a process is spontaneous. Gibbs energy is given by $G = H - TS$. For processes that occur at constant temperature, $\Delta G = \Delta H - T\Delta S$. If ΔG is equal to zero, then the reaction is at equilibrium and neither the forward nor the reverse reaction is spontaneous. If ΔG is less than zero, then the forward reaction is spontaneous. If ΔG is greater than zero, then the reverse reaction is spontaneous.

Atomic and Subatomic Structure

Basic Organization of Matter

An **element** is the most basic type of matter. It has unique properties and cannot be broken down into other elements. The smallest unit of an element is the **atom**. Most elements are found somewhere in nature in single-atom form, but a few elements only exist naturally in pairs. These are called diatomic elements, and some of the most common of these are hydrogen, nitrogen, and oxygen. A chemical combination of two or more types of elements is called a compound. **Compounds** often have properties that are very different from those of their constituent elements. The smallest independent unit of an element or compound of two or more atoms is known as a **molecule**. Elements and compounds are represented by chemical symbols, one or two letters, most often the first in the element name. More than one atom of the same element in a compound is represented with a subscript number designating how many atoms of that element are present. Water, for instance, contains two hydrogens and one oxygen. Thus, the chemical formula is H_2O. Methane contains one carbon and four hydrogens, so its formula is CH_4.

Review Video: Molecules
Visit mometrix.com/academy and enter code: 349910

Protons, Neutrons, and Electrons

The three major subatomic particles are the proton, neutron, and electron. The **proton**, which is located in the nucleus, has a relative charge of +1. The **neutron**, which is located in the nucleus, has a relative charge of 0. The **electron**, which is located outside the nucleus, has a relative charge of –1. The proton and neutron, which are essentially the same mass, are much more massive than the electron and make up the mass of the atom. The electron's mass is insignificant compared to the mass of the proton and neutron.

Orbits and Orbitals

An orbit is a definite path, but an orbital is a region in space. The Bohr model described electrons as orbiting or following a definite path in space around the nucleus of an atom. But, according to **Heisenberg's uncertainty principle**, it is impossible to determine the location and the momentum of an electron simultaneously. Therefore, it is impossible to draw a definite path or orbit of an electron. An **orbital**, as described by the quantum-mechanical model or the electron-cloud model, is a region in space that is drawn in such a way as to indicate the probability of finding an electron at a specific location. The distance an orbital is located from the nucleus corresponds to the principal quantum number. The orbital shape corresponds to the subshell or azimuthal quantum number. The orbital orientation corresponds to the magnetic quantum number.

Quantum Numbers

The **principal quantum number** (n) describes an electron's shell or energy level and actually describes the size of the orbital. Electrons farther from the nucleus are at higher energy levels. The **subshell** or azimuthal quantum number (l) describes the electron's sublevel or subshell (s, p, d, or f) and specifies the shape of the orbital. Typical shapes include spherical, dumbbell, and clover leaf. The **magnetic quantum number** (m_l) describes the orientation of the orbital in space. The spin or magnetic moment quantum number (m_s) describes the direction of the spin of the electron in the orbital.

Atomic Number and Mass Number

The **atomic number** of an element is the number of protons in the nucleus of an atom of that element. This is the number that identifies the type of an atom. For example, all oxygen atoms have eight protons, and all carbon atoms have six protons. Each element is identified by its specific atomic number.

The **mass number** is the number of protons and neutrons in the nucleus of an atom. Although the atomic number is the same for all atoms of a specific element, the mass number can vary due to the varying numbers of neutrons in various isotopes of the atom.

Isotopes

Isotopes are atoms of the same element that vary in their number of neutrons. Isotopes of the same element have the same number of protons and thus the same atomic number. Because isotopes vary in the number of neutrons, they are identified by their mass numbers. For example, two naturally occurring carbon isotopes are carbon-12 and carbon-13, which have mass numbers 12 and 13, respectively. The symbols ${}^{12}_{6}C$ and ${}^{13}_{6}C$ also represent the carbon isotopes. The general form of the symbol is ${}^{M}_{A}X$, where X is the element symbol, M is the mass number, and A is the atomic number.

Average Atomic Mass

The **average atomic mass** is the weighted average of the masses of all the naturally occurring isotopes of an atom in comparison to the carbon-12 isotope. The unit for average atomic mass is the atomic mass unit (u). Atomic masses of isotopes are measured using a mass spectrometer by bombarding a gaseous sample of the isotope and measuring its relative deflections. Atomic masses can be calculated if the percent abundances and the atomic masses of the naturally occurring isotopes are known.

Cathode Ray Tube (CRT)

Electrons were discovered by Joseph John Thomson through scientific work with cathode ray tubes (CRTs). **Cathode rays** had been studied for many years, but it was Thomson who showed that cathode rays were

negatively charged particles. Although Thomson could not determine an electron's charge or mass, he was able to determine the ratio of the charge to the mass. Thomson discovered that this ratio was constant regardless of the gas in the CRT. He was able to show that the cathode rays were actually streams of negatively charged particles by deflecting them with a positively charged plate.

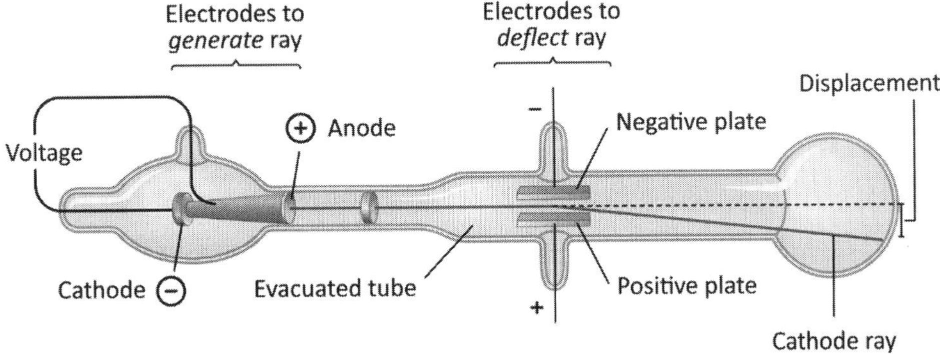

GOLD FOIL EXPERIMENT

After Thomson determined the ratio of the charge to the mass of an electron from studying cathode rays, he proposed the plum pudding model, in which he compared electrons to the raisins embedded in plum pudding. This model of the atom was disproved by the gold foil experiment. The gold foil experiment led to the discovery of the nucleus of an atom. Scientists at Rutherford's laboratory bombarded a thin gold foil with high-speed helium ions. Much to their surprise, some of the ions were reflected by the foil. The scientists concluded that the atom has a **hard central core**, which we now know to be the **nucleus**.

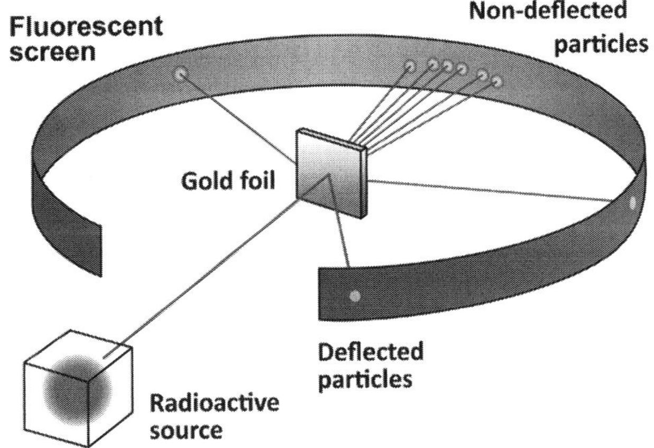

PROBLEMS THAT RUTHERFORD'S MODEL HAD WITH SPECTRAL LINES

Rutherford's model allowed for the electrons of an atom to be in an **infinite number of orbits** based on Newton's laws of motion. Rutherford believed that electrons could orbit the nucleus at any distance from the nucleus and that electrons could change velocity and direction at any moment. But, according to Rutherford's model, the electrons would lose energy and spiral into the nucleus. Unfortunately, if this was in fact true, then every atom would be **unstable**. Rutherford's model also does not correspond to the spectral lines emitted from gases at low pressure. The **spectral lines** are discrete bands of light at specific energy levels. These spectral lines indicate that electrons must be at specific distances from the nucleus. If electrons could be located at any distance from the nucleus, then these gases should emit continuous spectra instead of spectral lines.

Pure Substances and Mixtures

Pure Substances

Pure substances are substances that cannot be further broken down into simpler components or pieces and still retain their characteristics. Pure substances are categorized as either **elements** or **compounds**. Elements consist of only one type of atom may be monatomic, diatomic, or polyatomic. For example, helium (He) and copper (Cu) are monatomic elements, and hydrogen (H_2) and oxygen (O_2) are diatomic elements. Phosphorus (P_4) and sulfur (S_8) are polyatomic elements. Compounds consist of molecules of more than one type of atom. For example, pure water (H_2O) is made up of molecules consisting of two atoms of hydrogen bonded to one atom of oxygen, and glucose ($C_6H_{12}O_6$) is made up of molecules of six carbon atoms and twelve hydrogen atoms bonded together with six oxygen atoms.

Mixtures

Mixtures can be classified as either homogeneous or heterogeneous. The molecules of a **homogeneous mixture** are distributed uniformly throughout the mixture, whereas the molecules of a **heterogeneous mixture** are not. Air is an example of a homogeneous mixture, and a pile of sand and rock is an example of a heterogeneous mixture. Solutions are homogeneous mixtures consisting of a **solute** (the substance that is dissolved) and a **solvent** (the substance doing the dissolving).

Suspensions

Suspensions are heterogeneous mixtures in which the particle size of the substance **suspended** is too large to be kept in suspension by Brownian motion. Once left undisturbed, suspensions will settle out to form layers. An example of a suspension is sand stirred into water. Left undisturbed, the sand will fall out of suspension and the water will form a layer on top of the sand.

Mixtures with Compounds

Mixtures are similar to compounds in that they are produced when two or more substances are combined. However, there are some key differences as well. Compounds require a chemical combination of the constituent particles, while mixtures are simply the interspersion of particles. Unlike compounds, mixtures may be **separated** without a chemical change. A mixture retains the chemical properties of its constitutent particles, while a compound acquires a new set of properties. Given compounds can exist only in specific ratios, while mixtures may be any ratio of the involved substances.

Chemical and Physical Properties and Changes

Chemical and Physical Properties

Matter has both physical and chemical properties. **Physical properties** can be seen or observed without changing the identity or composition of matter. For example, the mass, volume, and density of a substance can be determined without permanently changing the sample. Other physical properties include color, boiling point, freezing point, solubility, odor, hardness, electrical conductivity, thermal conductivity, ductility, and malleability.

Chemical properties cannot be measured without changing the identity or composition of matter. Chemical properties describe how a substance reacts or changes to form a new substance. Examples of chemical properties include flammability, corrosivity, oxidation states, enthalpy of formation, and reactivity with other chemicals.

Intensive and Extensive Properties

Physical properties are categorized as either intensive or extensive. **Intensive properties** *do not* depend on the amount of matter or quantity of the sample. This means that intensive properties will not change if the sample size is increased or decreased. Intensive properties include color, hardness, melting point, boiling point, density, ductility, malleability, specific heat, temperature, concentration, and magnetization.

Extensive properties *do* depend on the amount of matter or quantity of the sample. Therefore, extensive properties do change if the sample size is increased or decreased. If the sample size is increased, the property increases. If the sample size is decreased, the property decreases. Extensive properties include volume, mass, weight, energy, entropy, number of moles, and electrical charge.

Atomic Properties of Neutral Atoms, Anions, and Cations

Neutral atoms have the same number of protons as electrons. **Cations** are positively-charged ions that are formed when atoms lose electrons. For example, the alkali metals sodium and potassium form the cations Na^+ and K^+, and the alkaline earth metals magnesium and calcium form the cations Mg^{2+} and Ca^{2+}. These elements easily lose electrons because the resulting ion is left with a full valence shell.

Anions are negatively-charged ions that are formed when atoms gain electrons. For example, the halogens fluorine and chlorine form the anions F^- and Cl^-. These elements easily gain electrons because the resulting ion has a full valence shell.

Chemical and Physical Changes

Physical changes do not produce new substances. The atoms or molecules may be rearranged, but no new substances are formed. **Phase changes**—changes of state such as melting, freezing, and sublimation—are physical changes. For example, physical changes include the melting of ice, the boiling of water, sugar dissolving into water, and the crushing of a piece of chalk into a fine powder.

Chemical changes involve a **chemical reaction** and do produce new substances. When iron rusts, iron oxide is formed, indicating a chemical change. Other examples of chemical changes include baking a cake, burning wood, digesting food, and mixing an acid and a base.

Conservation of Energy and Matter

Law of Conservation of Energy

The **law of conservation of energy** states that in a closed system, energy cannot be created or destroyed but only changed from one form to another. This is also known as the first law of thermodynamics. Another way to state this is that the **total energy in an isolated system is constant**. Energy comes in many forms that may be transformed from one kind to another, but in a closed system, the total amount of energy is conserved or remains constant. For example, potential energy can be converted to kinetic energy, thermal energy, radiant energy, or mechanical energy. In an isolated chemical reaction, there can be no energy created or destroyed. The energy simply changes forms.

Law of Conservation of Mass

The **law of conservation of mass** is also known as the **law of conservation of matter**. This law states that for a chemical reaction in a closed system, the total mass of the products must equal the total mass of the reactants. This could also be stated that in a closed system, mass never changes. A consequence of this law is that matter is never created or destroyed during a typical chemical reaction. The atoms of the reactants are only rearranged to form the products. The number and type of each specific atom involved in the reactants is identical to the number and type of atoms in the products. This is the key principle used when balancing chemical equations. In a balanced chemical equation, the number of moles of each element on the reactant side equals the number of moles of each element on the product side.

Review Video: Balancing Chemical Equations
Visit mometrix.com/academy and enter code: 341228

Conversion of Energy Within Chemical Systems

Chemical energy is the energy stored in molecules in the bonds between the atoms of those molecules and the energy associated with the intermolecular forces. This stored **potential energy** may be converted into **kinetic energy** and then into heat. During a chemical reaction, atoms may be rearranged and chemical bonds may be formed or broken accompanied by a corresponding absorption or release of energy, usually in the form of heat. According to the first law of thermodynamics, during these energy conversions, the **total amount of energy must be conserved**.

Reaction Types

Types of Reactions

One way to organize chemical reactions is to sort them into two categories: **oxidation/reduction reactions** (also called redox reactions) and **metathesis reactions** (which include acid/base reactions). Oxidation/reduction reactions can involve the transfer of one or more electrons, or they can occur as a result of the transfer of oxygen, hydrogen, or halogen atoms. The species that loses electrons (or increases its oxidation state) is oxidized and is referred to as the reducing agent. The species that gains electrons (or decreases its oxidation state) is reduced and is referred to as the oxidizing agent. **Single substitution reactions** are types of oxidation/reduction reactions. In a single substitution reaction, electrons are transferred from one chemical species to another. The transfer of electrons results in changes in the nature and charge of the species.

Review Video: Understanding Chemical Reactions
Visit mometrix.com/academy and enter code: 579876

Review Video: The Process of a Reaction
Visit mometrix.com/academy and enter code: 808039

Substitution Reactions

Single substitution, **displacement**, or **replacement reactions** are when one reactant is displaced by another to form the final product ($A + BC \rightarrow AB + C$). Single substitution reactions can be cationic or anionic. When a piece of copper (Cu) is placed into a solution of silver nitrate ($AgNO_3$), the solution turns blue. The copper appears to be replaced with a silvery white material. The equation is $2AgNO_3 + Cu \rightarrow Cu(NO_3)_2 + 2Ag$. When this reaction takes place, the copper dissolves and the silver in the silver nitrate solution precipitates (becomes a solid), resulting in copper nitrate and silver. Copper and silver have switched places in the nitrate.

Double substitution reactions, also called **double displacement**, **double replacement**, **metathesis**, or **ion exchange reactions**, are those where ions or bonds are exchanged by two compounds to form different compounds ($AC + BD \rightarrow AD + BC$). An example of this is that silver nitrate and sodium chloride form two different products (silver chloride and sodium nitrate) when they react. The formula for this reaction is $AgNO_3 + NaCl \rightarrow AgCl + NaNO_3$.

Review Video: Single-Replacement Reactions
Visit mometrix.com/academy and enter code: 442975

Combination and Decomposition Reactions

Combination, or **synthesis, reactions**: In a combination reaction, two or more reactants combine to form a single product ($A + B \rightarrow AB$). These reactions are also called synthesis or **addition reactions**. An example is burning hydrogen in air to produce water. The equation is $2H_2(g) + O_2(g) \rightarrow 2H_2O(l)$. Another example is when water and sulfur trioxide react to form sulfuric acid. The equation is $H_2O + SO_3 \rightarrow H_2SO_4$.

Decomposition (or desynthesis, decombination, or deconstruction) reactions: In a decomposition reaction, a reactant is broken down into two or more products ($AB \rightarrow A + B$). These reactions are also called analysis reactions. **Thermal decomposition** is caused by heat. **Electrolytic decomposition** is due to electricity. An example of this type of reaction is the decomposition of water into hydrogen and oxygen gas. The equation is $2H_2O \rightarrow 2H_2 + O_2$.

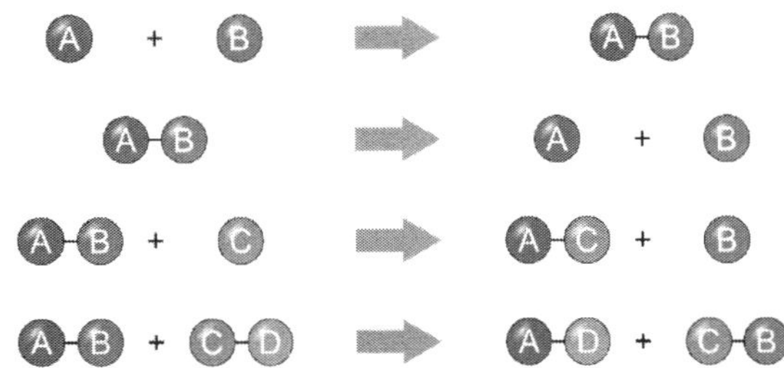

ACID/BASE REACTIONS

In **acid/base reactions**, an **acid** is a compound that can donate a proton, while a **base** is a compound that can accept a proton. In these types of reactions, the acid and base react to form a salt and water. When the proton is donated, the base becomes water and the remaining ions form a salt. One method of determining whether a reaction is an oxidation/reduction or a metathesis reaction is that the oxidation number of atoms does not change during a metathesis reaction.

ISOMERIZATION AND NEUTRALIZATION REACTIONS

Isomerization, or **rearrangement**, is the process changing a compound to an isomer. Within a compound, bonds are reformed. The reactant and product have the same molecular formula, but different structural formulas and different properties (A → A'). For example, butane (C_4H_{10}) is a hydrocarbon consisting of four carbon atoms in a straight chain. Heating it to 100 °C or higher in the presence of a catalyst forms isobutane (methylpropane), which has a branched-chain structure. Boiling and freezing points are greatly different for butane and isobutane.

A **neutralization**, **acid-base**, or **proton transfer reaction** occurs when one compound acquires H^+ from another. These types of reactions are also usually double displacement reactions. The acid has an H^+ that is transferred to the base and the acid and base are neutralized in the form of a salt that, depending on the salt's solubility, may precipitate from the solution.

TERMINOLOGY FOR SOLUTIONS AND SOLUBILITY

DILUTE AND CONCENTRATED

The terms *dilute* and *concentrated* have opposite meanings. In a **solution**, the **solute** is dissolved in the **solvent**. The more solute that is dissolved, the more **concentrated** is the solution. The less solute that is dissolved, the less concentrated and the more **dilute** is the solution. The terms are often associated with the preparation of a stock solution for a laboratory experiment. Stock solutions are typically acquired in a higly concentrated form. Typically, diluted forms of the solutions are used which must be prepared from the concentrated stock solutions. The desired dilutions are achieved by combining a specific amount of a solvent with a specific amount of stock solution.

SATURATED, UNSATURATED, AND SUPERSATURATED

Solutions can be categorized based on their saturation. In a **saturated** solution, the solute is added to the solvent until no more solute is able to dissolve. The undissolved solute will settle down to the bottom of the beaker. A solution is considered **unsaturated** as long as more solute is able to go into solution under ordinary conditions. The solubility of solids in liquids typically increases as temperature increases. If the temperature of a solution is increased as the solute is being added, more solute than is normally possible may go into solution, forming a **supersaturated** solution.

MIXTURE, SOLUTION, AND COLLOID

A **mixture** is made of two or more substances that are combined in various proportions. The exact proportion of the constituents is the defining characteristic of any mixture. There are two types of mixtures: homogeneous and heterogeneous. **Homogeneous** means that the mixture's composition and properties are uniform throughout. Conversely, **heterogeneous** means that the mixture's composition and properties are not uniform throughout.

A **solution** is a homogeneous mixture of substances that cannot be separated by filtration or centrifugation. Solutions are made by dissolving one or more solutes into a solvent. For example, in an aqueous glucose solution, glucose is the solute and water is the solvent. If there is more than one liquid present in the solution, then the most prevalent liquid is considered the solvent. The exact mechanism of dissolving varies depending on the mixture, but the result is always individual solute ions or molecules surrounded by solvent molecules. The proportion of solute to solvent for a particular solution is its **concentration**.

A **colloid** is a heterogeneous mixture in which small particles (<1 micrometer) are suspended, but not dissolved, in a liquid. As such, they can be separated by centrifugation. A commonplace example of a colloid is milk.

Review Video: Solutions
Visit mometrix.com/academy and enter code: 995937

Life Science

Differences Between Prokaryotic and Eukaryotic Cells

Prokaryotes and Eukaryotes

Sizes and Metabolism

Cells of the domains of Bacteria and Archaea are **prokaryotes**. Bacteria cells and Archaea cells are much smaller than cells of eukaryotes. Prokaryote cells are usually only 1 to 2 micrometers in diameter, but eukaryotic cells are usually at least 10 times and possibly 100 times larger than prokaryotic cells. Eukaryotic cells are usually 10 to 100 micrometers in diameter. Most prokaryotes are unicellular organisms, although some prokaryotes live in colonies. Because of their large surface-area-to-volume ratios, prokaryotes have a very high metabolic rate. **Eukaryotic cells** are much larger than prokaryotic cells. Due to their larger sizes, they have a much smaller surface-area-to-volume ratio and consequently have much lower metabolic rates.

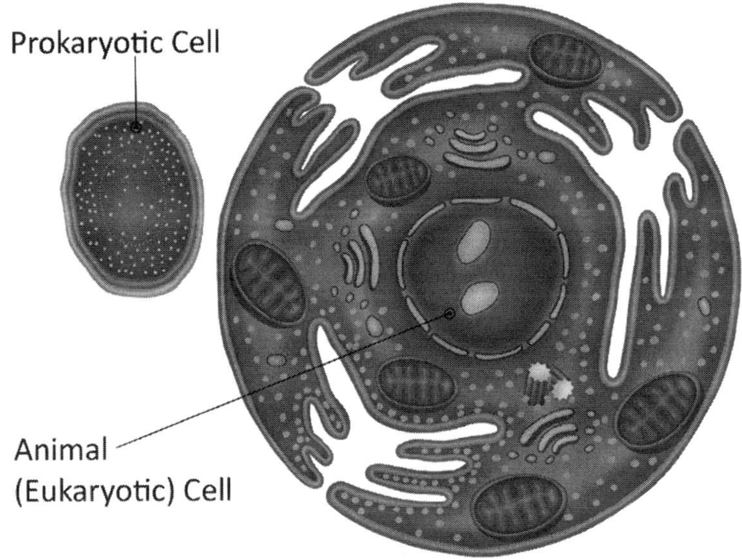

Review Video: Eukaryotic and Prokaryotic Cells
Visit mometrix.com/academy and enter code: 231438

Review Video: Cell Structure
Visit mometrix.com/academy and enter code: 591293

Membrane-Bound Organelles

Prokaryotic cells are much simpler than eukaryotic cells. Prokaryote cells do not have a nucleus due to their small size and their DNA is located in the center of the cell in a region referred to as a **nucleoid**. Eukaryote cells have a **nucleus** bound by a double membrane. Eukaryotic cells typically have hundreds or thousands of additional **membrane-bound organelles** that are independent of the cell membrane. Prokaryotic cells do not have any membrane-bound organelles that are independent of the cell membrane. Once again, this is probably due to the much larger size of the eukaryotic cells. The organelles of eukaryotes give them much higher levels of intracellular division than is possible in prokaryotic cells.

Cell Walls

Not all cells have cell walls, but most prokaryotes have cell walls. The cell walls of organisms from the domain Bacteria differ from the cell walls of the organisms from the domain Archaea. Some eukaryotes, such as some fungi, some algae, and plants, have cell walls that differ from the cell walls of the Bacteria and Archaea domains. The main difference between the cell walls of different domains or kingdoms is the composition of the cell walls. For example, most bacteria have cell walls outside of the plasma membrane that contains the molecule peptidoglycan. **Peptidoglycan** is a large polymer of amino acids and sugars. The peptidoglycan helps maintain the strength of the cell wall. Some of the Archaea cells have cell walls containing the molecule pseudopeptidoglycan, which differs in chemical structure from the peptidoglycan but basically provides the same strength to the cell wall. Some fungi cell walls contain **chitin**. The cell walls of diatoms, a type of yellow algae, contain silica. Plant cell walls contain cellulose, and woody plants are further strengthened by lignin. Some algae also contain lignin. Animal cells do not have cell walls.

CHROMOSOME STRUCTURE

Prokaryote cells have DNA arranged in a **circular structure** that should not be referred to as a chromosome. Due to the small size of a prokaryote cell, the DNA material is simply located near the center of the cell in a region called the nucleoid. A prokaryotic cell may also contain tiny rings of DNA called plasmids. Prokaryote cells lack histone proteins, and therefore the DNA is not actually packaged into chromosomes. Prokaryotes reproduce by binary fission, while eukaryotes reproduce by mitosis with the help of **linear chromosomes** and histone proteins. During mitosis, the chromatin is tightly wound on the histone proteins and packaged as a chromosome. The DNA in a eukaryotic cell is located in the membrane-bound nucleus.

Review Video: Chromosomes
Visit mometrix.com/academy and enter code: 132083

CELL CYCLE AND CELLULAR DIVISION

CELL CYCLE STAGES

The cell cycle consists of three stages: interphase, mitosis, and cytokinesis. **Interphase** is the longest stage of the cell cycle and involves the cell growing and making a copy of its DNA. Cells typically spend more than 90% of the cell cycle in interphase. Interphase includes two growth phases called G_1 and G_2. The order of interphase is the first growth cycle, **GAP 1** (G_1 phase), followed by the **synthesis phase** (S), and ending with the second growth phase, **GAP 2** (G_2 phase). During the G_1 phase of interphase, the cell increases the number of organelles by forming diploid cells. During the S phase of interphase, the DNA is replicated, and the chromosomes are doubled. During the G_2 phase of interphase, the cell synthesizes needed proteins and organelles, continues to increase in size, and prepares for mitosis. Once the G_2 phase ends, mitosis can begin.

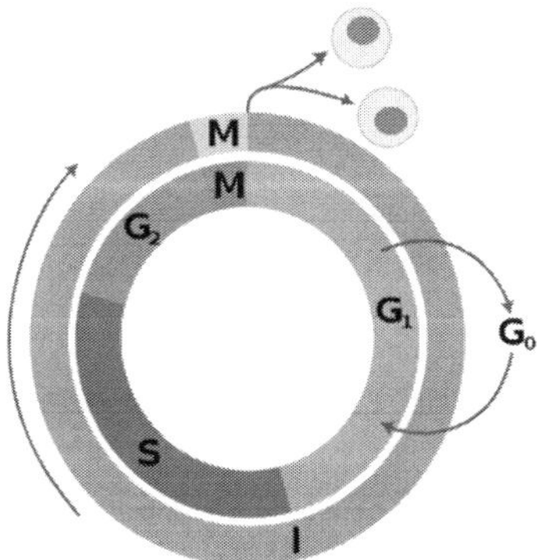

MITOSIS

Mitosis is the asexual process of cell division. During mitosis, one parent cell divides into two identical daughter cells. Mitosis is used for growth, repair, and replacement of cells. Some unicellular organisms reproduce asexually by mitosis. Some multicellular organisms can reproduce by fragmentation or budding, which involves mitosis. Mitosis consists of four phases: prophase, metaphase, anaphase, and telophase. During **prophase**, the spindle fibers appear and the DNA is condensed and packaged as chromosomes that become visible. The nuclear membrane also breaks down, and the nucleolus disappears. During **metaphase**, the spindle apparatus is formed and the centromeres of the chromosomes line up on the equatorial plane. During

anaphase, the centromeres divide and the two chromatids separate and are pulled toward the opposite poles of the cell. During **telophase**, the spindle fibers disappear, the nuclear membrane reforms, and the DNA in the chromatids is decondensed.

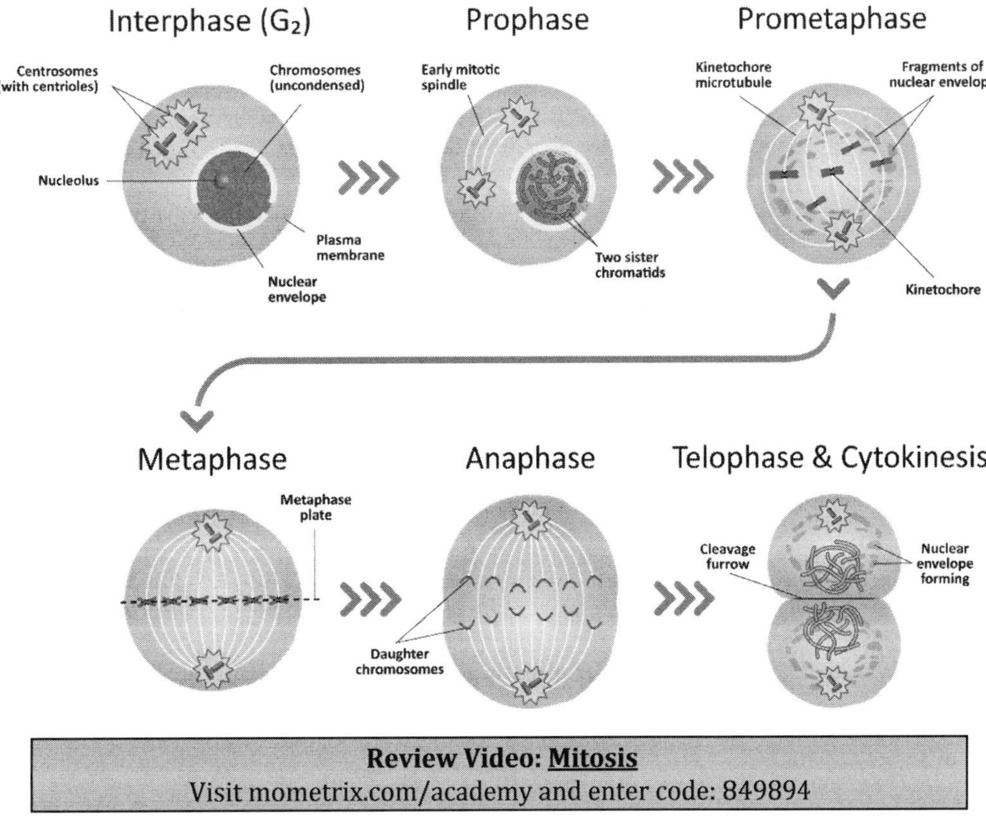

Review Video: Mitosis
Visit mometrix.com/academy and enter code: 849894

CYTOKINESIS

Cytokinesis is the dividing of the cytoplasm and cell membrane by the pinching of a cell into two new daughter cells at the end of mitosis. This occurs at the end of telophase when the actin filaments in the cytoskeleton form a contractile ring that narrows and divides the cell. In plant cells, a cell plate forms across the phragmoplast, which is the center of the spindle apparatus. In animal cells, as the contractile ring narrows, the cleavage furrow forms. Eventually, the contractile ring narrows down to the spindle apparatus joining the two cells and the cells eventually divide. Diagrams of the cleavage furrow of an animal cell and cell plate of a plant are shown below.

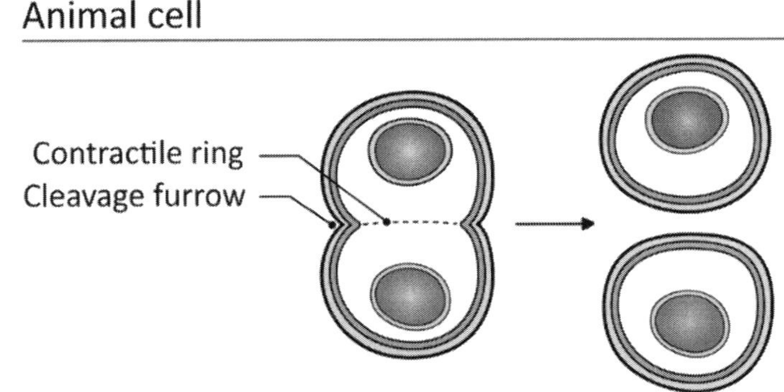

Science

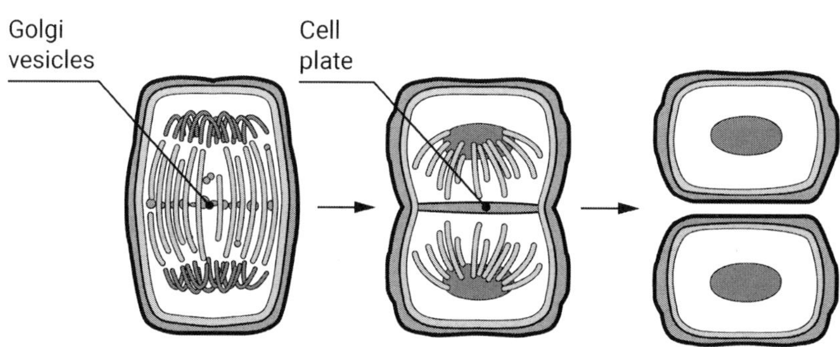

MEIOSIS

Meiosis is a type of cell division in which the number of chromosomes is reduced by half. Meiosis produces gametes, or egg and sperm cells. Meiosis occurs in two successive stages, which consist of a first mitotic division followed by a second mitotic division. During **meiosis I**, or the first meiotic division, the cell replicates its DNA in interphase and then continues through prophase I, metaphase I, anaphase I, and telophase I. At the end of meiosis I, there are two haploid daughter cells, each with half the number of chromosomes as the original diploid parent cell. Each chromosome consists of two sister chromatids, but these are considered a single chromosome. During **meiosis II**, the cell enters a brief interphase but does not replicate its DNA. Then, the cell continues through prophase II, metaphase II, anaphase II, and telophase II. During prophase II, the unduplicated chromosomes split. At the end of telophase II, there are four daughter cells that have half the number of chromosomes as the parent cell.

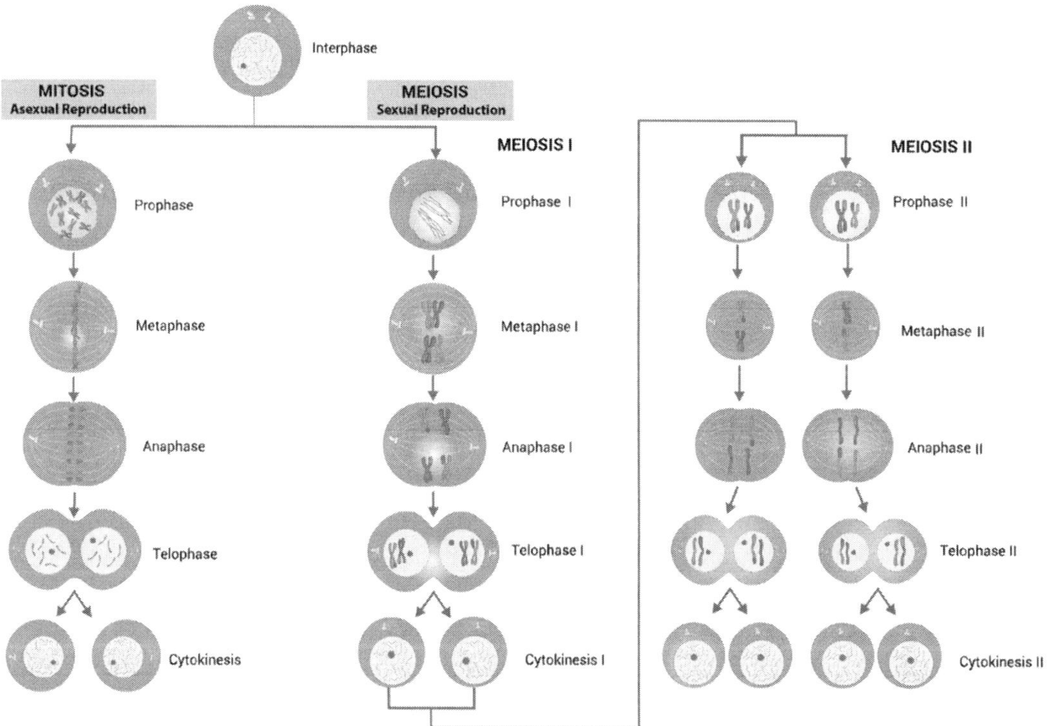

Cell Cycle Checkpoints

During the cell cycle, the cell goes through three checkpoints to ensure that the cell is dividing properly at each phase, that it is the appropriate time for division, and that the cell has not been damaged. The **first checkpoint** is at the end of the G_1 phase just before the cell undergoes the S phase, or synthesis. At this checkpoint, a cell may continue with cell division, delay the division, or rest. This **resting phase** is called G_0. In animal cells, the G_1 checkpoint is called **restriction**. Proteins called cyclin D and cyclin E, which are dependent on enzymes cyclin-dependent kinase 4 and cyclin-dependent kinase 2 (CDK4 and CDK2), respectively, largely control this first checkpoint. The **second checkpoint** is at the end of the G_2 phase just before the cell begins prophase during mitosis. The protein cyclin A, which is dependent on the enzyme CDK2, largely controls this checkpoint. During mitosis, the **third checkpoint** occurs at metaphase to check that the chromosomes are lined up along the equatorial plane. This checkpoint is largely controlled by cyclin B, which is dependent upon the enzyme CDK1.

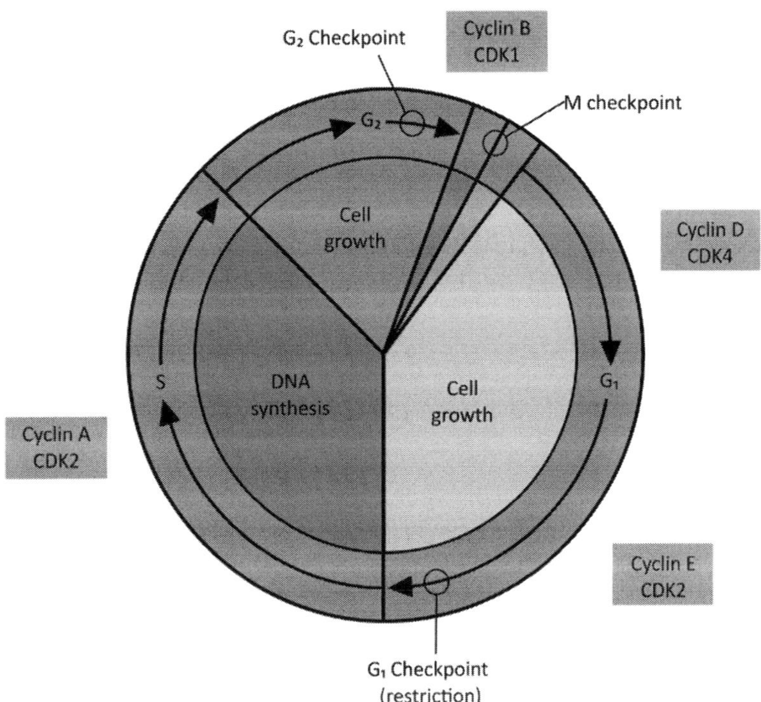

Mutations

Missense Mutations, Silent Mutations, and Nonsense Mutations

Mutations are changes in DNA sequences. **Point mutations** are changes in a single nucleotide in a DNA sequence. Three types of point mutations are missense, silent, and nonsense.

- **Missense mutations** result in a codon for a different amino acid. An example is mutating TGT (Cysteine codon) to TGG (Tryptophan codon).
- **Silent mutations** result in a codon for the same amino acid as the original sequence. An example is mutating TGT (Cysteine codon) to TGC (a different Cysteine codon).
- **Nonsense mutations** insert a premature stop codon, typically resulting in a non-functional protein. An example is mutating TGT (Cysteine codon) to TGA (STOP codon).

Review Video: Codons
Visit mometrix.com/academy and enter code: 978172

Science

FRAMESHIFT MUTATIONS AND INVERSION MUTATIONS

Deletions and insertions can result in the addition of amino acids, the removal of amino acids, or cause a frameshift mutation. A **frameshift mutation** changes the reading frame of the mRNA (a new group of codons will be read), resulting in the formation of a new protein product. Mutations can also occur on the chromosomal level. For example, an **inversion** is when a piece of the chromosome inverts or flips its orientation.

GERMLINE MUTATIONS AND SOMATIC MUTATIONS

Mutations can occur in somatic (body) cells and germ cells (egg and sperm). **Somatic mutations** develop after conception and occur in an organism's body cells such as bone cells, liver cells, or brain cells. Somatic mutations cannot be passed on from parent to offspring. The mutation is limited to the specific descendent of the cell in which the mutation occurred. The mutation is not in the other body cells unless they are descendants of the originally mutated cell. Somatic mutations may cause cancer or diseases. Some somatic mutations are silent. **Germline mutations** are present at conception and occur in an organism's germ cells, which are only egg and sperms cells. Germline mutations may be passed on from parent to offspring. Germline mutations will be present in every cell of an offspring that inherits a germline mutation. Germline mutations may cause diseases. Some germline mutations are silent.

MUTAGENS

Mutagens are physical and chemical agents that cause changes or errors in DNA replication. Mutagens are external factors to an organism. Examples include ionizing radiation such as ultraviolet radiation, x-rays, and gamma radiation. Viruses and microorganisms that integrate their DNA into host chromosomes are also mutagens. Mutagens include environmental poisons such as asbestos, coal tars, tobacco, and benzene. Alcohol and diets high in fat have been shown to be mutagenic. Not all mutations are caused by mutagens. **Spontaneous mutations** can occur in DNA due to molecular decay.

MENDEL'S LAWS

LAW OF SEGREGATION

The **law of segregation** states that the alleles for a trait separate when gametes are formed, which means that only one of the pair of alleles for a given trait is passed to the gamete. This can be shown in monohybrid crosses, which can be used to show which allele is **dominant** for a single trait. A **monohybrid cross** is a genetic cross between two organisms with a different variation for a single trait. The first monohybrid cross typically occurs between two **homozygous** parents. Each parent is homozygous for a separate allele (gg or GG) for a particular trait. For example, in pea plants, green seeds (G) are dominant over yellow seeds (g). Therefore, in a genetic cross of two pea plants that are homozygous for seed color, the F_1 generation will be 100% **heterozygous** green seeds.

	g	g
G	Gg	Gg
G	Gg	Gg

Review Video: Punnett Square
Visit mometrix.com/academy and enter code: 853855

MONOHYBRID CROSS FOR A CROSS BETWEEN TWO GG PARENTS

If the plants with the heterozygous green seeds are crossed, the F_1 generation should be 50% heterozygous green (Gg), 25% homozygous green (GG), and 25% homozygous yellow (gg).

	G	g
G	GG	Gg
g	Gg	gg

LAW OF INDEPENDENT ASSORTMENT

Mendel's law of independent assortment states that alleles of one characteristic or trait separate independently of the alleles of another characteristic. Therefore, the allele a gamete receives for one gene does not influence the allele received for another gene due to the allele pairs separating independently during gamete formation. This means that traits are transmitted independently of each other. This can be shown in dihybrid crosses.

GENE, GENOTYPE, PHENOTYPE, AND ALLELE

A **gene** is a portion of DNA that identifies how traits are expressed and passed on in an organism. A gene is part of the genetic code. Collectively, all genes form the **genotype** of an individual. The genotype includes genes that may not be expressed, such as recessive genes. The **phenotype** is the physical, visual manifestation of genes. It is determined by the basic genetic information and how genes have been affected by their environment.

An **allele** is a variation of a gene. Also known as a trait, it determines the manifestation of a gene. This manifestation results in a specific physical appearance of some facet of an organism, such as eye color or height. The genetic information for eye color is a gene. The gene variations responsible for blue, green, brown, or black eyes are called alleles. **Locus** (plural, *loci*) refers to the location of a gene or alleles.

> **Review Video: Genotype vs Phenotype**
> Visit mometrix.com/academy and enter code: 922853

DOMINANT AND RECESSIVE GENES

Gene traits are represented in pairs with an uppercase letter for the **dominant trait** (A) and a lowercase letter for the **recessive trait** (a). Genes occur in pairs (AA, Aa, or aa). There is one gene on each chromosome half supplied by each parent organism. Since half the genetic material is from each parent, the offspring's traits are represented as a combination of these. A dominant trait only requires one gene of a gene pair for it to be expressed in a phenotype, whereas a recessive requires both genes in order to be manifested. For example, if the mother's genotype is Dd and the father's is dd, the possible combinations are Dd and dd. The dominant trait will be manifested if the genotype is DD or Dd. The recessive trait will be manifested if the genotype is dd. Both DD and dd are **homozygous** pairs. Dd is **heterozygous**.

DIHYBRID CROSS FOR THE F_2 GENERATION OF A CROSS BETWEEN $GGRR$ AND $ggrr$ PARENTS

A **dihybrid cross** is a genetic cross for two traits that each have two alleles. For example, in pea plants, green seeds (G) are dominant over yellow seeds (g), and round seeds (R) are dominant over wrinkled seeds (r). In a genetic cross of two pea plants that are homozygous for seed color and seed shape (GGRR or ggRR), the F_1 generation will be 100% heterozygous green and round seeds (GgRr). If these F_1 plants (GgRr) are crossed, the resulting F_2 generation is shown below. Out of the 16 total genotypes for the cross of green, round seeds, there are only four possible phenotypes, or physical traits of the seed: green and round seed (GGRR, GGRr, GgRR, or GgRr), green and wrinkled seed (GGrr or Ggrr), yellow and round seed (ggRR or ggRr) , or yellow and wrinkled

Science

seed (ggrr). There are nine green and round seed plants, three green and wrinkled seed plants, three yellow and round seed plants, and only one yellow and wrinkled seed plant. This cross has a **9:3:3:1 ratio**.

	GR	**gR**	**Gr**	**gr**
GR	GGRR	GgRR	GGRr	GgRr
gR	GgRR	ggRR	GgRr	ggRr
Gr	GGRr	GgRr	GGrr	Ggrr
gr	GgRr	ggRr	Ggrr	ggrr

Pedigree

Pedigree analysis is a type of genetic analysis in which an inherited trait is studied and traced through several generations of a family to determine how that trait is inherited. A **pedigree** is a chart arranged as a type of family tree using symbols for people and lines to represent the relationships between those people. Squares usually represent males, and circles represent females. Horizontal lines represent a male and female mating, and the vertical lines beneath them represent their children. Usually, family members who possess the trait are fully shaded and those who only carry the trait are half-shaded. Genotypes and phenotypes are determined for each individual if possible. The pedigree below shows the family tree of a family in which the first male who was red-green color blind mated with the first female who was unaffected. They had five children. The three sons were unaffected, and the two daughters were carriers.

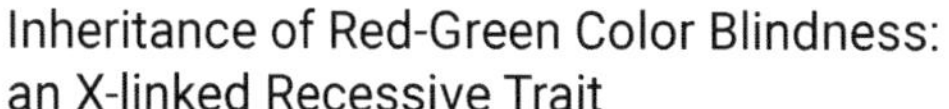

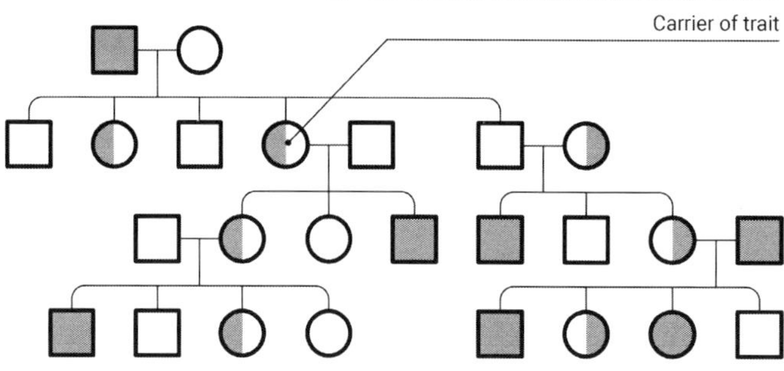

Processes Affecting the Gene Pool

Genetic Drift

Genetic drift is a microevolutionary process that causes random changes in allele frequencies that are not the result of natural selection. Genetic drift can result in a loss of genetic diversity. Genetic drift greatly impacts small populations. Two special forms of genetic drift are the genetic bottleneck and the founder effect. A **genetic bottleneck** occurs when there is a drastic reduction in population due to some change such as overhunting, disease, or habitat loss. When a population is greatly reduced in size, many alleles can be lost. Even if the population size greatly increases again, the lost alleles represent lost genetic diversity. The **founder effect** occurs when one individual or a few individuals populate a new area such as an island. This new population is limited to the alleles of the founder(s) unless mutations occur or new individuals immigrate to the region.

Gene Flow

Gene flow is a microevolutionary process in which alleles enter a population by immigration and leave a population by emigration. Gene flow helps counter genetic drift. When individuals from one genetically distinct population immigrate to a different genetically distinct population, alleles and their genetic information are added to the new population. The added alleles will change the gene frequencies within the population. This increases genetic diversity. If individuals with rare alleles emigrate from a population, the genetic diversity is decreased. Gene flow reduces the genetic differences between populations.

Mechanics of Evolution

Mechanisms of Evolution

Natural and Artificial Selection

Natural selection and artificial selection are both mechanisms of evolution. **Natural selection** is a process of nature in which a population can change over generations. Every population has variations in individual heritable traits and organisms best suited for survival typically reproduce and pass on those genetic traits to offspring to increase the likelihood of them surviving. Typically, the more advantageous a trait is, the more common that trait becomes in a population. Natural selection brings about evolutionary **adaptations** and is responsible for biological diversity. Artificial selection is another mechanism of evolution. **Artificial selection** is a process brought about by humans. Artificial selection is the selective breeding of domesticated animals and plants such as when farmers choose animals or plants with desirable traits to reproduce. Artificial selection has led to the evolution of farm stock and crops. For example, cauliflower, broccoli, and cabbage all evolved due to artificial selection of the wild mustard plant.

Sexual Selection

Sexual selection is a special case of natural selection in animal populations. **Sexual selection** occurs because some animals are more likely to find mates than other animals. The two main contributors to sexual selection are **competition** of males and **mate selection** by females. An example of male competition is in the mating practices of the redwing blackbird. Some males have huge territories and numerous mates that they defend. Other males have small territories, and some even have no mates. An example of mate selection by females is the mating practices of peacocks. Male peacocks display large, colorful tail feathers to attract females. Females are more likely to choose males with the larger, more colorful displays.

Coevolution

Coevolution describes a rare phenomenon in which two populations with a close ecological relationship undergo reciprocal adaptations simultaneously and evolve together, affecting each other's evolution. General examples of coevolution include predator and prey, or plant and pollinator, and parasites and their hosts. A specific example of coevolution is the yucca moths and the yucca plants. Yucca plants can only be pollinated by the yucca moths. The yucca moths lay their eggs in the yucca flowers, and their larvae grow inside the ovary.

Adaptive Radiation

Adaptive radiation is an evolutionary process in which a species branches out and adapts and fills numerous unoccupied ecological niches. The adaptations occur relatively quickly, driven by natural selection and resulting in new phenotypes and possibly new species eventually. An example of adaptive radiation is the finches that Darwin studied on the Galápagos Islands. Darwin recorded 13 different varieties of finches, which differed in the size and shape of their beaks. Through the process of natural selection, each type of finch adapted to the specific environment and specifically the food sources of the island to which it belonged. On newly formed islands with many unoccupied ecological niches, the adaptive radiation process occurred quickly due to the lack of competing species and predators.

Evidence Supporting Evolution

Molecular Evidence

Because all organisms are made up of cells, all organisms are alike on a fundamental level. Cells share similar components, which are made up of molecules. Specifically, all cells contain DNA and RNA. This should indicate that all species descended from a **common ancestor**. Humans and chimpanzees share approximately 98% of their genes in common, while humans and bacteria share approximately 7% of their genes in common suggesting that bacteria and humans are not closely related. Biologists have been able to use DNA sequence comparisons of modern organisms to reconstruct the "root" of the tree of life. The fact that RNA can store information, replicate itself, and code for proteins suggests that RNA could have could have evolved first, followed by DNA.

Homology

Homology is the similarity of structures of different species based on a similar anatomy in a common evolutionary ancestor. For instance, the forelimbs of humans, dogs, birds, and whales all have the same basic pattern of the bones. Specifically, all of these organisms have a humerus, radius, and ulna. They are all modifications of the same basic evolutionary structure from a common ancestor. Tetrapods resemble the fossils of extinct transitional animal called the *Eusthenopteron*. This would seem to indicate that evolution primarily modifies preexisting structures.

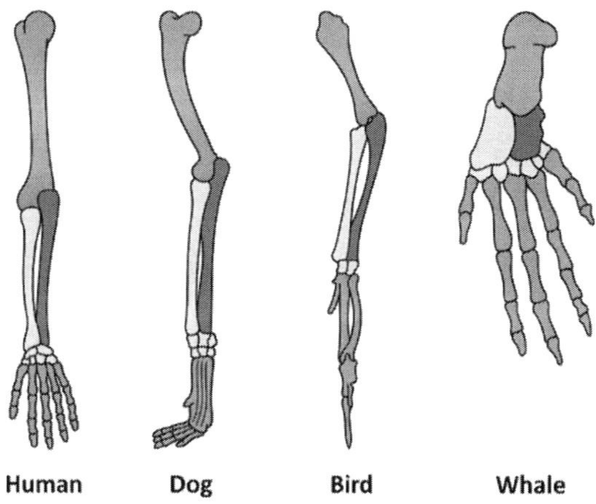

Review Video: Homologous vs Analogous Structures
Visit mometrix.com/academy and enter code: 355157

Embryology

The stages of **embryonic development** reveal homologies between species. These homologies are evidence of a **common ancestor**. For example, in chicken embryos and mammalian embryos, both include a stage in which slits and arches appear in the embryo's neck region that are strikingly similar to gill slits and gill arches in fish embryos. Adult chickens and adult mammals do not have gills, but this embryonic homology indicates that birds and mammals share a common ancestor with fish. As another example, some species of toothless whales have embryos that initially develop teeth that are later absorbed, which indicates that these whales have an ancestor with teeth in the adult form. Finally, most tetrapods have five-digit limbs, but birds have three-digit limbs in their wings. However, embryonic birds initially have five-digit limbs in their wings, which develop into a three-digit wing. Tetrapods such as reptiles, mammals, and birds all share a common ancestor with five-digit limbs.

Endosymbiosis Theory

The endosymbiosis theory is foundational to evolution. Endosymbiosis provides the path for prokaryotes to give rise to eukaryotes. Specifically, **endosymbiosis** explains the development of the organelles of mitochondria in animals and chloroplasts in plants. This theory states that some eukaryotic organelles such as mitochondria and chloroplasts originated as free living cells. According to this theory, primitive, heterotrophic eukaryotes engulfed smaller, autotrophic bacteria prokaryotes, but the bacteria were not digested. Instead, the eukaryotes and the bacteria formed a symbiotic relationship. Eventually, the bacteria transformed into mitochondrion or chloroplasts.

SUPPORTING EVIDENCE

Several facts support the endosymbiosis theory. Mitochondria and chloroplasts contain their own DNA and can both only arise from other preexisting mitochondria and chloroplasts. The genomes of mitochondria and chloroplasts consist of single, circular DNA molecules with no histones. This is similar to bacteria genomes, not eukaryote genomes. Also, the RNA, ribosomes, and protein synthesis of mitochondria and chloroplasts are remarkably similar to those of bacteria, and both use oxygen to produce ATP. These organelles have a double phospholipid layer that is typical of engulfed bacteria. This theory also involves a secondary endosymbiosis in which the original eukaryotic cells that have engulfed the bacteria are then engulfed themselves by another free-living eukaryote.

CONVERGENT EVOLUTION

Convergent evolution is the evolutionary process in which two or more unrelated species become increasingly similar in appearance. In convergent evolution, similar adaptations in these unrelated species occur due to these species inhabiting the same kind of environment. For example, the mammals shown below, although found in different parts of the world, developed similar appearances due to their similar environments.

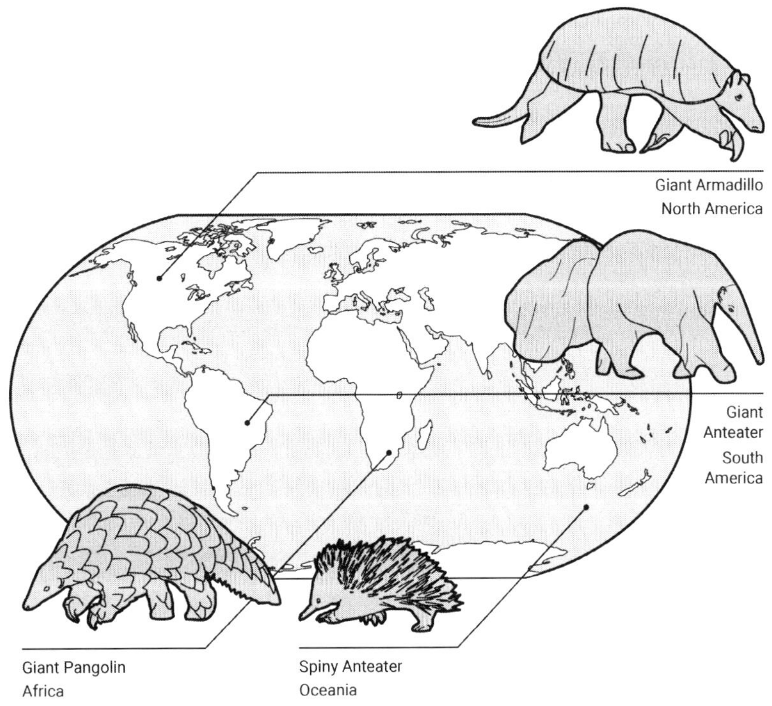

DIVERGENT EVOLUTION

Divergent evolution is the evolutionary process in which organisms of one species become increasingly dissimilar in appearance. As several small adaptations occur due to natural selection, the organisms will finally reach a point at which two new species are formed, also known as **speciation**. Then, these two species will further diverge from each other as they continue to evolve. Adaptive radiation is an example of divergent

Science

evolution. Another example is the divergent evolution of the wooly mammoth and the modern elephant from a common ancestor.

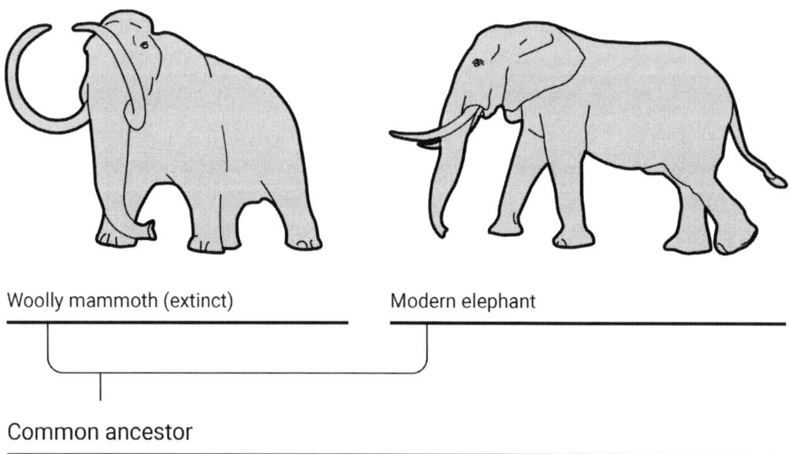

Fossil Record

The **fossil record** provides many types of support for evolution including comparisons from rock layers, transition fossils, and homologies with modern organisms. First, fossils from rock layers from all over the world have been compared, enabling scientists to develop a sequence of life from simple to complex. Based on the fossil record, the **geologic timeline** chronicles the history of all living things. For example, the fossil record clearly indicates that invertebrates developed before vertebrates and that fish developed before amphibians. Second, numerous transitional fossils have been found. **Transitional fossils** show an intermediate state between an ancestral form of an organism and the form of its descendants. These fossils show the path of evolutionary change. For example, many transition fossils documenting the evolutionary change from fish to amphibians have been discovered. In 2004, scientists discovered *Tiktaalik roseae*, or the "fishapod," which is a 375-million-year-old fossil that exhibits both fish and amphibian characteristics. Another example would be *Pakicetus*, an extinct land mammal, that scientists determined is an early ancestor of modern whales and dolphins based on the specialized structures of the inner ear. Most fossils exhibit homologies with modern organisms. For example, extinct horses are similar to modern horses, indicating a common ancestor.

Cephalization and Multicellularity

Cephalization is the evolutionary trend that can be summarized as "the evolution of the head." In most animals, nerve tissue has been concentrated into a brain at one end of an organism over many generations. Eventually, a head enclosing a brain and housing sensory organs was produced at one end of the organism. Many invertebrates, such as arthropods and annelids and all vertebrates, have undergone cephalization. However, some invertebrates, such as echinoderms and sponges, have not undergone cephalization, and these organisms literally do not have a head.

Another evolutionary trend is **multicellularity**. Life has evolved from simple, single-celled organisms to complex, multicellular organisms. Over millions of years, single-celled organisms gave rise to biofilms, which gave rise to multicellular organisms, which gave rise to all of the major phyla of multicellular organisms present today.

Scientific Explanations for the Origin of Life on Earth

Explanations for the Origin of Life on Earth

Panspermia

The word *panspermia* is a Greek work that means "seeds everywhere." **Panspermia** is one possible explanation for the origin of life on Earth that states that "seeds" of life exist throughout the universe and can be transferred from one location to another. Three types of panspermia based on the seed-dispersal method have been proposed. **Lithopanspermia** is described as rocks or dust transferring microorganisms between solar systems. **Ballistic panspermia** is described as rocks or dust transferring microorganisms between planets within the same solar system. **Directed panspermia** is described as intelligent extraterrestrials purposely spreading the seeds to other planets and solar systems. The panspermia hypothesis only proposes the origin of life on Earth. It does not offer an explanation for the origin of life in the universe or explain the origin of the seeds themselves.

Abiotic Synthesis of Organic Compounds

Scientists have performed sophisticated experiments to determine how the first organic compounds appeared on Earth. First, scientists performed controlled experiments that closely resembled the conditions similar to an early Earth. In the classic **Miller–Urey experiment** (1953), the Earth's early atmosphere was simulated with water, methane, ammonia, and hydrogen that were stimulated by an electric discharge. The Miller–Urey experiment produced complex organic compounds including several amino acids, sugars, and hydrocarbons. Later experiments by other scientists produced nucleic acids. Recently, Jeffrey Bada, a former student of Miller, was able to produce amino acids in a simulation using the Earth's current atmospheric conditions with the addition of iron and carbonate to the simulation. This is significant because in previous studies using Earth's current atmosphere, the amino acids were destroyed by the nitrites produced by the nitrogen.

Atmospheric Composition

The early atmosphere of Earth had little or possibly no oxygen. Early rocks had high levels of iron at their surfaces. Without oxygen, the iron just entered into the early oceans as ions. In the same time frame, early photosynthetic algae were beginning to grow abundantly in the early ocean. During photosynthesis, the algae would produce oxygen gas, which oxidized the iron at the rocks' surfaces, forming an iron oxide. This process basically kept the algae in an oxygen-free environment. As the algae population grew much larger, it eventually produced such a large amount of oxygen that it could not be removed by the iron in the rocks. Because the algae at this time were intolerant to oxygen, the algae became extinct. Over time, a new iron-rich layer of sediments formed, and algae populations reformed, and the cycle began again. This cycle repeated itself for millions of years. Iron-rich layers of sediment alternated with iron-poor layers. Gradually, algae and other life forms evolved that were tolerant to oxygen, stabilizing the oxygen concentration in the atmosphere at levels similar to those of today.

Development of Self-Replication

Several hypotheses for the origin of life involve the self-replication of molecules. In order for life to have originated on Earth, proteins and RNA must have been replicated. Hypotheses that combine the replication of proteins and RNA seem promising. One such hypothesis is called **RNA world**. RNA world explains how the pathway of DNA to RNA to protein may have originated by proposing the reverse process. RNA world proposes that self-replicating RNA was the precursor to DNA. Scientists have shown that RNA can actually function both as a gene and as an enzyme and could therefore have carried genetic information in earlier life stages. Also, RNA can be transcribed into DNA using reverse transcription. In RNA world, RNA molecules self-replicated and evolved through recombination and mutations. RNA molecules developed the ability to act as enzymes.

Eventually, RNA began to synthesize proteins. Finally, DNA molecules were copied from the RNA in a process of reverse transcription.

Historical and Current Biological Classifications of Organisms

Historical and Current Kingdom Systems

In 1735 Carolus Linnaeus devised a two-kingdom classification system. He placed all living things into either the *Animalia* kingdom or the *Plantae* kingdom. Fungi and algae were classified as plants. Also, Linnaeus developed the binomial nomenclature system that is still used today. In 1866, Ernst Haeckel introduced a three-kingdom classification system, adding the *Protista* kingdom to Linnaeus's animal and plant kingdoms. Bacteria were classified as protists and cyanobacteria were still classified as plants. In 1938, Herbert Copeland introduced a four-kingdom classification system in which bacteria and cyanobacteria were moved to the *Monera* kingdom. In 1969, Robert Whittaker introduced a five-kingdom system that moved fungi from the plant kingdom to the *Fungi* kingdom. Some algae were still classified as plants. In 1977, Carl Woese introduced a six-kingdom system in which in the *Monera* kingdom was replaced with the *Eubacteria* kingdom and the *Archaebacteria* kingdom.

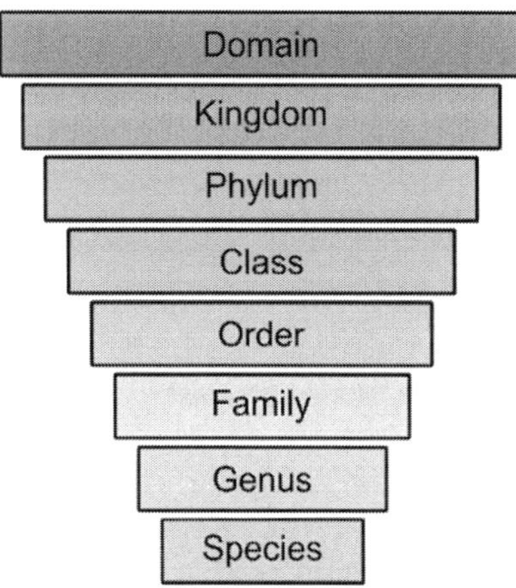

Domain Classification System

In 1990, Carl Woese introduced his domain classification system. **Domains** are broader groupings above the kingdom level. This system consists of three domains—*Archaea*, *Bacteria*, and *Eukarya*. All eukaryotes such as plants, animals, fungi, and protists are classified in the *Eukarya* domain. The *Bacteria* and *Archaea* domains consist of prokaryotes. Organisms previously classified in the *Monera* kingdom are now classified into either the *Bacteria* or *Archaea* domain based on their ribosomal RNA structure. Members of the *Archaea* domain often live in extremely harsh environments.

Review Video: Biological Classification Systems
Visit mometrix.com/academy and enter code: 736052

VIRUSES, BACTERIA, PROTISTS, FUNGI, PLANTS, AND ANIMALS

VIRUSES

Viruses are nonliving, infectious particles that act as parasites in living organisms. Viruses are acellular, which means that they lack cell structure. Viruses cannot reproduce outside of living cells. The structure of a virus is a nucleic acid genome, which may be either DNA or RNA, surrounded by a protective protein coat or **capsid**. In some viruses, the capsid may be surrounded by a lipid membrane or envelope. Viruses can contain up to 500 genes and have various shapes. They usually are too small to be seen without the aid of an electron microscope. Viruses can infect plants, animals, fungi, protists, and bacteria. Viruses can attack only specific types of cells that have specific receptors on their surfaces. Viruses do not divide or reproduce like living cells. Instead, they use the host cell they infect by "reprogramming" it, using the nucleic acid genome, to make more copies of the virus. The host cell usually bursts to release these copies.

Review Video: Viruses and Antiviral Drugs
Visit mometrix.com/academy and enter code: 984455

BACTERIA

Bacteria are small, prokaryotic, single-celled organisms. Bacteria have a circular loop of DNA (plasmid) that is not contained within a nuclear membrane. Bacterial ribosomes are not bound to the endoplasmic reticulum, as in eukaryotes. A cell wall containing peptidoglycan surrounds the bacterial plasma membrane. Some bacteria such as pathogens are further encased in a gel-like, sticky layer called the **capsule**, which enhances their ability to cause disease. Bacteria can be autotrophs or heterotrophs. Some bacterial heterotrophs are saprophytes that function as decomposers in ecosystems. Many types of bacteria share commensal or mutualistic relationships with other organisms. Most bacteria reproduce asexually by binary fission. Two identical daughter cells are produced from one parent cell. Some bacteria can transfer genetic material to other bacteria through a process called conjugation, while some bacteria can incorporate DNA from the environment in a process called transformation.

PROTISTS

Protists are small, eukaryotic, single-celled organisms. Although protists are small, they are much larger than prokaryotic bacteria. Protists have three general forms, which include plantlike protists, animal-like protists, and fungus-like protists. **Plantlike protists** are algae that contain chlorophyll and perform photosynthesis. Animal-like protists are **protozoa** with no cell walls that typically lack chlorophyll and are grouped by their method of locomotion, which may use flagella, cilia, or a different structure. **Fungus-like protists**, which do not have chitin in their cell walls, are generally grouped as either slime molds or water molds. Protists may be autotrophic or heterotrophic. Autotrophic protists include many species of algae, while heterotrophic protists include parasitic, commensal, and mutualistic protozoa. Slime molds are heterotrophic fungus-like protists, which consume microorganisms. Some protists reproduce sexually, but most reproduce asexually by binary fission. Some reproduce asexually by spores while others reproduce by alternation of generations and require two hosts in their life cycle.

FUNGI

Fungi are nonmotile organisms with eukaryotic cells and contain chitin in their cell walls. Most fungi are multicellular, but a few including yeast are unicellular. Fungi have multicellular filaments called **hyphae** that are grouped together into the mycelium. Fungi do not perform photosynthesis and are considered heterotrophs. Fungi can be parasitic, mutualistic or free living. Free-living fungi include mushrooms and toadstools. Parasitic fungi include fungi responsible for ringworm and athlete's foot. Mycorrhizae are mutualistic fungi that live in or near plant roots increasing the roots' surface area of absorption. Almost all fungi reproduce asexually by spores, but most fungi also have a sexual phase in the production of spores. Some fungi reproduce by budding or fragmentation.

> **Review Video: Feeding Among Heterotrophs**
> Visit mometrix.com/academy and enter code: 836017

Plants

Plants are multicellular organisms with eukaryotic cells containing cellulose in their cell walls. Plant cells have chlorophyll and perform photosynthesis. Plants can be vascular or nonvascular. **Vascular plants** have true leaves, stems, and roots that contain xylem and phloem. **Nonvascular plants** lack true leaves, stems and roots and do not have any true vascular tissue but instead rely on diffusion and osmosis to transport most of materials or resources needed to survive. Almost all plants are autotrophic, relying on photosynthesis for food. A small number do not have chlorophyll and are parasitic, but these are extremely rare. Plants can reproduce sexually or asexually. Many plants reproduce by seeds produced in the fruits of the plants, while some plants reproduce by seeds on cones. One type of plant, ferns, reproduce by a different system that utilizes spores. Some plants can even reproduce asexually by vegetative reproduction.

> **Review Video: Kingdom Plantae**
> Visit mometrix.com/academy and enter code: 710084

Structure, Organization, Modes of Nutrition, and Reproduction of Animals

Animals are multicellular organism with eukaryotic cells that do not have cell walls surrounding their plasma membranes. Animals have several possible structural body forms. Animals can be relatively simple in structure such as sponges, which do not have a nervous system. Other animals are more complex with cells organized into tissues, and tissues organized into organs, and organs even further organized into systems. Invertebrates such as arthropods, nematodes, and annelids have complex body systems. Vertebrates including fish, amphibians, reptiles, birds, and mammals are the most complex with detailed systems such as those with gills, air sacs, or lungs designed to exchange respiratory gases. All animals are heterotrophs and obtain their nutrition by consuming autotrophs or other heterotrophs. Most animals are motile, but some animals move their environment to bring food to them. All animals reproduce sexually at some point in their life cycle. Typically, this involves the union of a sperm and egg to produce a zygote.

Characteristics of the Major Animal Phyla

Characteristics of the Major Animal Phyla

Body Planes

Animals can exhibit bilateral symmetry, radial symmetry, or asymmetry. With **bilateral symmetry**, the organism can be cut in half along only one plane to produce two identical halves. Most animals, including all vertebrates such as mammals, birds, reptiles, amphibians, and fish, exhibit bilateral symmetry. Many invertebrates including arthropods and crustaceans also exhibit bilateral symmetry. With **radial symmetry**, the organism can be cut in half along several planes to produce two identical halves. Starfish, sea urchins, and jellyfish exhibit radial symmetry. With **asymmetry**, the organism exhibits no symmetry. Very few organisms in the animal phyla exhibit asymmetry, but a few species of sponges are asymmetrical.

Body Cavities

Animals can be grouped based on their types of body cavities. A **coelom** is a fluid-filled body cavity between the alimentary canal and the body wall. The three body plans based on the formation of the coelom are coelomates, pseudocoelomates, and acoelomates. **Coelomates** have a true coelom located within the mesoderm. Most animals including arthropods, mollusks, annelids, echinoderms, and chordates are coelomates. **Pseudocoelomates** have a body cavity called a pseudocoelom. **Pseudocoeloms** are not considered true coeloms. Pseudocoeloms are located between mesoderm and endoderm instead of actually in the mesoderm as in a true coelom. Pseudocoelomates include roundworms and rotifers. **Acoelomates** do not have body cavities. Simple or primitive animals such as sponges, jellyfish, sea anemones, hydras, flatworms, and ribbon worms are acoelomates.

MODES OF REPRODUCTION

Animals can reproduce sexually or asexually. Most animals reproduce sexually. In **sexual reproduction**, males and females have different reproductive organs that produce **gametes**. Males have testes that produce sperm, and females have ovaries that produce eggs. During fertilization, a sperm cell unites with an egg cell, forming a **zygote**. Fertilization can occur internally such as in most mammals and birds or externally such as aquatic animals such as fish and frogs. The zygote undergoes cell division, which develops into an embryo and eventually develops into an adult organism. Some embryos develop in eggs such as in fish, amphibians, reptiles, and birds. Some mammals are **oviparous** meaning that they lay eggs, but most are **viviparous** meaning they have a uterus in which the embryo develops. One particular type of mammal called **marsupials** give birth to an immature fetus that finishes development in a pouch. However, there are some animals reproduce **asexually**. For example, hydras reproduce by budding, and starfish and planarians can reproduce by fragmentation and regeneration. Some fish, frogs, and insects can even reproduce by parthenogenesis, which is a type of self-reproduction without fertilization.

MODES OF TEMPERATURE REGULATION

Animals can be classified as either homeotherms or poikilotherms. **Homeotherms**, also called warm-blooded animals or **endotherms**, maintain a constant body temperature regardless of the temperature of the environment. Homeotherms such as mammals and birds have a high metabolic rate because a lot of energy is needed to maintain the constant temperature. **Poikilotherms**, also called cold-blooded animals or **ectotherms**, do not maintain a constant body temperature. Their body temperature fluctuates with the temperature of the environment. Poikilotherms such as arthropods, fish, amphibians, and reptiles have metabolic rates that fluctuate with their body temperature.

HIERARCHY OF MULTICELLULAR ORGANISMS

ORGANIZATIONAL HIERARCHY WITHIN MULTICELLULAR ORGANISMS

Cells are the smallest living units of organisms. Tissues are groups of cells that work together to perform a specific function. Organs are groups of tissues that work together to perform a specific function. Organ systems are groups of organs that work together to perform a specific function. An organism is an individual that contains several body systems.

CELLS

Cells are the basic structural units of all living things. Cells are composed of various molecules including proteins, carbohydrates, lipids, and nucleic acids. All animal cells are eukaryotic and have a nucleus, cytoplasm, and a cell membrane. Organelles include mitochondria, ribosomes, endoplasmic reticulum, Golgi apparatuses, and vacuoles. Specialized cells are numerous, including but not limited to, muscle cells, nerve cells, epithelial cells, bone cells, blood cells, and cartilage cells. Cells can be grouped together in tissues to perform specific functions.

TISSUES

Tissues are groups of cells that work together to perform a specific function. Tissues can be grouped into four broad categories: muscle tissue, connective tissue, nerve tissue, and epithelial tissue. Muscle tissue is involved in body movement. **Muscle tissues** can be composed of skeletal muscle cells, cardiac muscle cells, or smooth muscle cells. Skeletal muscles include the muscles commonly called biceps, triceps, hamstrings, and quadriceps. Cardiac muscle tissue is found only in the heart. Smooth muscle tissue provides tension in the blood vessels, controls pupil dilation, and aids in peristalsis. **Connective tissues** include bone tissue, cartilage, tendons, ligaments, fat, blood, and lymph. **Nerve tissue** is located in the brain, spinal cord, and nerves. **Epithelial tissue** makes up the layers of the skin and various membranes. Tissues are grouped together as organs to perform specific functions.

Organs and Organ Systems

Organs are groups of tissues that work together to perform specific functions. **Organ systems** are groups of organs that work together to perform specific functions. Complex animals have several organs that are grouped together in multiple systems. In mammals, there are 11 major organ systems: integumentary system, respiratory system, cardiovascular system, endocrine system, nervous system, immune system, digestive system, excretory system, muscular system, skeletal system, and reproductive system.

Reproduction, Development, and Growth in Animals

Gamete Formation

Gametogenesis is the formation of gametes, or reproductive cells. Gametes are produced by meiosis. **Meiosis** is a special type of cell division that consists of two consecutive mitotic divisions referred to as meiosis I and meiosis II. **Meiosis I** is a reduction division in which a diploid cell is reduced to two haploid daughter cells that contain only one of each pair of homologous chromosomes. During **meiosis II**, those haploid cells are further divided to form four haploid cells. **Spermatogenesis** in males produces four viable sperm cells from each complete cycle of meiosis. **Oogenesis** produces four daughter cells, but only one is a viable egg and the other three are polar bodies.

Fertilization

Fertilization is the union of a sperm cell and an egg cell to produce a zygote. Many sperm may bind to an egg, but only one joins with the egg and injects its nuclei into the egg. Fertilization can be external or internal. **External fertilization** takes place outside of the female's body. For example, many fish, amphibians, crustaceans, mollusks, and corals reproduce externally by **spawning** or releasing gametes into the water simultaneously or right after each other. Reptiles and birds reproduce by **internal fertilization**. All mammals except monotremes (e.g. platypus) reproduce by internal fertilization.

Embryonic Development

Embryonic development in animals is typically divided into four stages: cleavage, patterning, differentiation, and growth. **Cleavage** occurs immediately after fertilization when the large single-celled zygote immediately begins to divide into smaller and smaller cells without an increase in mass. A hollow ball of cells forms a blastula. Next, during patterning, gastrulation occurs. During gastrulation, the cells are organized into three primary germ layers: ectoderm, mesoderm, and endoderm. Then, the cells in these layers differentiate into special tissues and organs. For example, the nervous system develops from the ectoderm. The muscular system develops from the mesoderm. Much of the digestive system develops from the endoderm. The final stage of embryonic development is growth and further tissue specialization. The embryo continues to grow until ready for hatching or birth.

Postnatal Growth

Postnatal growth occurs from hatching or birth until death. The length of the postnatal growth depends on the species. Elephants can live 70 years, but mice only about 4 years. Right after animals are hatched or born, they go through a period of rapid growth and development. In vertebrates, bones lengthen, muscles grow in bulk, and fat is deposited. At maturity, bones stop growing in length, but bones can grow in width and repair themselves throughout the animal's lifetime, and muscle deposition slows down. Fat cells continue to increase and decrease in size throughout the animal's life. Growth is controlled by genetics but is also influenced by nutrition and disease. Most animals are sexually mature in less than two years and can produce offspring.

Characteristics of Major Plant Divisions

Vascular and Nonvascular Plants

Vascular plants, also referred to as **tracheophytes**, have dermal tissue, meristematic tissue, ground tissues, and vascular tissues. Nonvascular plants, also referred to as **bryophytes**, do not have the vascular tissue xylem and phloem. Vascular plants can grow very tall, whereas nonvascular plants are short and close to the ground. Vascular plants can be found in dry regions, but nonvascular plants typically grow near or in moist areas. Vascular plants have leaves, roots, and stems, but nonvascular plants have leaf-like, root-like, and stem-like structures that do not have true vascular tissue. Nonvascular plants have hair-like **rhizoids**, that act like roots by anchoring them to the ground and absorbing water. Vascular plants include angiosperms, gymnosperms, and ferns. Nonvascular plants include mosses and liverworts.

Flowering Versus Nonflowering Plants

Angiosperms and gymnosperms are both vascular plants. **Angiosperms** are flowering plants, and **gymnosperms** are non-flowering plants. Angiosperms reproduce by seeds that are enclosed in an ovary, usually in a fruit, while gymnosperms reproduce by unenclosed or "naked" seeds on scales, leaves, or cones. Angiosperms can be further classified as either monocots or dicots, depending on if they have one or two cotyledons, respectively. Angiosperms include grasses, garden flowers, vegetables, and broadleaf trees such as maples, birches, elms, and oaks. Gymnosperms include conifers such as pines, spruces, cedars, and redwoods.

Review Video: Kingdom Plantae Characteristics
Visit mometrix.com/academy and enter code: 710084

Monocots and Dicots

Angiosperms can be classified as either monocots or dicots. The seeds of **monocots** have one cotyledon, and the seeds of **dicots** have two cotyledons. The flowers of monocots have petals in multiples of three, and the flowers of dicots have petals in multiples of four or five. The leaves of monocots are slender with parallel veins, while the leaves of dicots are broad and flat with branching veins. The vascular bundles in monocots are distributed throughout the stem, whereas the vascular bundles in dicots are arranged in rings. Monocots have a **fibrous root system**, and dicots have a **taproot system**.

Hierarchical Structure of the Biosphere

Biosphere

Components

The **biosphere** is the region of the earth inhabited by living things. The components of the biosphere from smallest to largest are organisms, populations, communities, ecosystems, and biomes. Organisms of the same species make up a **population**. All of the populations in an area make up the **community**. The community combined with the physical environment for a region forms an **ecosystem**. Several ecosystems are grouped together to form large geographic regions called **biomes**.

Population

A **population** is a group of all the individuals of one species in a specific area or region at a certain time. A **species** is a group of organisms that can breed and produce fertile offspring. There may be many populations of a specific species in a large geographic region. **Ecologists** study the size, density, and growth rate of populations to determine their stability. Population size continuously changes with births, deaths, and migrations. The population density is the number of individuals per unit of area. Growth rates for a population may be exponential or logistic. Ecologists also study how the individuals are dispersed within a population. Some species form clusters, while others are evenly or randomly spaced. However, every population has limiting factors. Changes in the environment or geography can reduce or limit population size. The individuals of a population interact with each other and with other organisms in the community in various ways, including competition and predation, which have direct impacts population size.

COMMUNITY INTERACTIONS

A **community** is all of the populations of different species that live in an area and interact with each other. Community interaction can be intraspecific or interspecific. **Intraspecific interactions** occur between members of the same species. **Interspecific interactions** occur between members of different species. Different types of interactions include competition, predation, and symbiosis. Communities with high diversity are more complex and more stable than communities with low diversity. The level of diversity can be seen in a food web of the community, which shows all the feeding relationships within the community.

ECOSYSTEMS

An **ecosystem** is the basic unit of ecology. An ecosystem is the sum of all the biotic and abiotic factors in an area. **Biotic factors** are all living things such as plants, animals, fungi, and microorganisms. **Abiotic factors** include the light, water, air, temperature, and soil in an area. Ecosystems obtain the energy they need from sunlight. Ecosystems also contain biogeochemical cycles such as the hydrologic cycle and the nitrogen cycle. Ecosystems are generally classified as either terrestrial or aquatic. All of the living things within an ecosystem are called its community. The number and variety of living things within a community describes the ecosystem's **biodiversity**. However, each ecosystem can only support a limited number of organisms known as the **carrying capacity**.

RELATIONSHIPS BETWEEN SPECIES

SYMBIOSIS

Many species share a special nutritional relationship with another species, called **symbiosis**. The term symbiosis means "living together." In symbiosis, two organisms share a close physical relationship that can be helpful, harmful, or neutral for each organism. Three forms of symbiotic relationships are parasitism, commensalism, and mutualism. **Parasitism** is a relationship between two organisms in which one organism is the parasite, and the other organism is the host. The parasite benefits from the relationship because the parasite obtains its nutrition from the host. The host is harmed from the relationship because the parasite is using the host's energy and giving nothing in return. For example, a tick and a dog share a parasitic relationship in which the tick is the parasite, and the dog is the host. **Commensalism** is a relationship between two organisms in which one benefits, and the other is not affected. For example, a small fish called a remora can attach to the belly of a shark and ride along. The remora is safe under the shark, and the shark is not affected. **Mutualism** is a relationship between two organisms in which both organisms benefit. For example, a rhinoceros usually can be seen with a few tick birds perched on its back. The tick birds are helped by the easy food source of ticks, and the rhino benefits from the tick removal.

PREDATION

Predation is a special nutritional relationship in which one organism is the predator, and the other organism is the prey. The predator benefits from the relationship, but the prey is harmed. The predator hunts and kills the prey for food. The predator is specially adapted to hunt its prey, and the prey is specially adapted to escape its predator. While predators harm (kill) their individual prey, predation usually helps the prey species. Predation keeps the population of the prey species under control and prevents them from overshooting the carrying capacity, which often leads to starvation. Also, predation usually helps to remove weak or slow members of the prey species leaving the healthier, stronger, and better adapted individuals to reproduce. Examples of predator-prey relationships include lions and zebras, snakes and rats, and hawks and rabbits.

COMPETITION AND TERRITORIALITY

Competition is a relationship between two organisms in which the organisms compete for the same vital resource that is in short supply. Typically, both organisms are harmed, but one is usually harmed more than the other, which provides an avenue for natural selection. Organisms compete for resources such as food, water, mates, and space. **Interspecific competition** is between members of different species, while **intraspecific competition** is between members of the same species. **Territoriality** can be considered to be a type of interspecific competition for space. Many animals including mammals, birds, reptiles, fish, spiders, and insects have exhibited territorial behavior. Once territories are established, there are fewer conflicts between organisms. For example, a male redwing blackbird can establish a large territory. By singing and flashing his red patches, he is able to warn other males to avoid his territory, and they can avoid fighting.

Altruistic Behaviors Between Animals

Altruism is a self-sacrificing behavior in which an individual animal may serve or protect another animal. For example, in a honey bee colony there is one queen with many workers (females). There are also drones (males), but only during the mating seasons. Adult workers do all the work of the hive and will die defending it. Another example of altruism is seen in a naked mole rat colony. Each colony has one queen that mates with a few males, and the rest of the colony is nonbreeding and lives to service the queen, her mates, and her offspring.

Review Video: Mutualism, Commensalism, and Parasitism
Visit mometrix.com/academy and enter code: 757249

Energy Flow in the Environment

Using Trophic Levels with an Energy Pyramid

Energy flow through an ecosystem can be tracked through an energy pyramid. An **energy pyramid** shows how energy is transferred from one trophic level to another. **Producers** always form the base of an energy pyramid, and the consumers form successive levels above the producers. Producers only store about 1% of the solar energy they receive. Then, each successive level only uses about 10% of the energy of the previous level. That means that **primary consumers** use about 10% of the energy used by primary producers, such as grasses and trees. Next, **secondary consumers** use 10% of primary consumers' 10%, or 1% overall. This continues up for as many trophic levels as exist in a particular ecosystem.

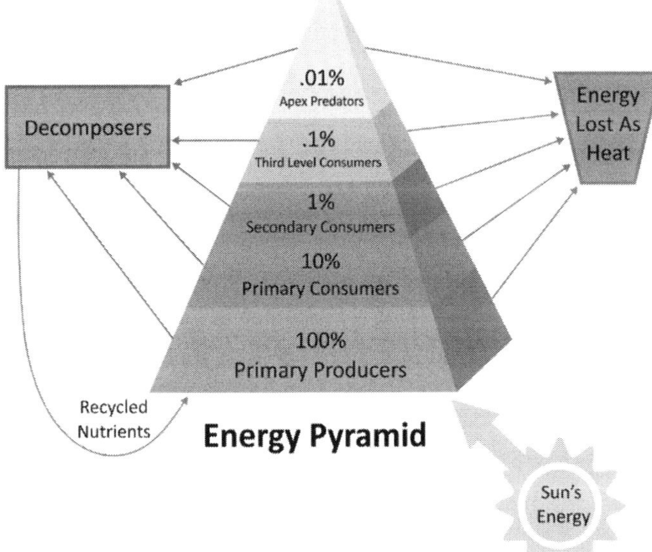

Food Web

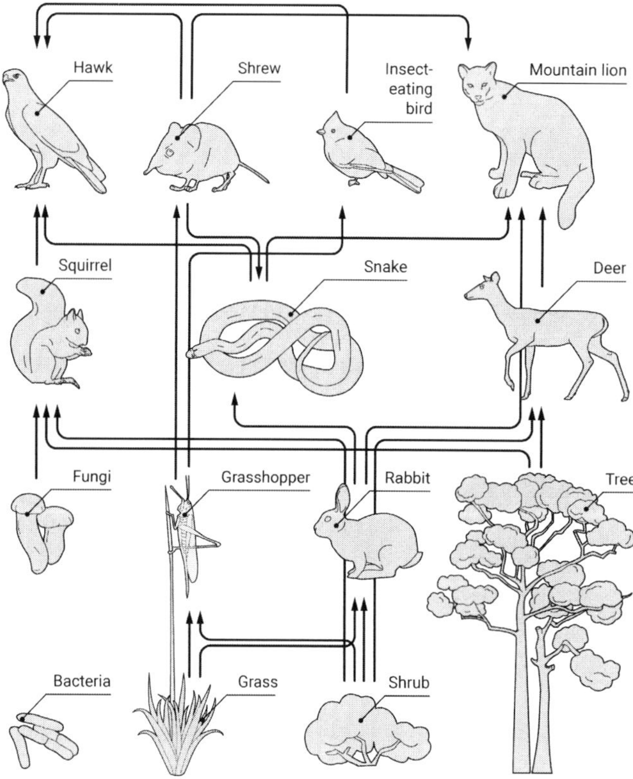

Energy flow through an ecosystem can be illustrated by a **food web**. Energy moves through the food web in the direction of the arrows. In the food web, producers such as grass, trees, and shrubs use energy from the sun to produce food through photosynthesis. Herbivores or primary consumers such as squirrels, grasshoppers, and rabbits obtain energy by eating the producers. Secondary consumers, which are carnivores such as snakes and shrews, obtain energy by eating the primary consumers. Tertiary consumers, which are carnivores such as hawks and mountain lions, obtain energy by eating the secondary consumers. Note that the hawk and the mountain lion can also be considered quaternary consumers in this food web if a different food chain within the web is followed.

Review Video: Food Webs
Visit mometrix.com/academy and enter code: 853254

Earth Science

Theory of Plate Tectonics

Plate Tectonics

Main Concepts

Plate tectonics is a geological theory that was developed to explain the process of continental drift. The theoretical separation of the Earth's lithosphere and asthenosphere is based upon the mechanical properties of the materials in the two respective layers and is distinct from the chemical separation of Earth's crust, mantle, and core. According to the theory of plate tectonics, the Earth's lithosphere is divided into **ten major plates**: African, Antarctic, Australian, Eurasian, North American, South American, Pacific, Cocos, Nazca, and Indian; it floats atop the asthenosphere. The plates of the lithosphere abut one another at plate boundaries (divergent, convergent, or transform fault), where the formation of topological features of Earth's surface begins.

THEORY

This theory of plate tectonics arose from the fusion of **continental drift** (first proposed in 1915 by Alfred Wegener) and **seafloor spreading** (first observed by Icelandic fishermen in the 1800s and later refined by Harry Hess and Robert Dietz in the early 1960s) in the late 1960s and early 1970s. Prior to this time, the generally accepted explanation for continental drift was that the continents were floating on the Earth's oceans. The discovery that mountains have "roots" (proved by George Airy in the early 1950s) did not categorically disprove the concept of floating continents; scientists were still uncertain as to where those mountainous roots were attached. It was not until the identification and study of the Mid-Atlantic Ridge and magnetic striping in the 1960s that plate tectonics became accepted as a scientific theory. Its conception was a landmark event in the field of Earth sciences—it provided an explanation for the empirical observations of continental drift and seafloor spreading.

TECTONIC PLATE MOTION

The two main sources of **tectonic plate motion** are **gravity** and **friction**. The energy driving tectonic plate motion comes from the dissipation of heat from the mantle in the relatively weak asthenosphere. This energy is converted into gravity or friction to incite the motion of plates. Gravity is subdivided by geologists into ridge-push and slab-pull. In the phenomenon of **ridge-push**, the motion of plates is instigated by the energy that causes low-density material from the mantle to rise at an oceanic ridge. This leads to the situation of certain plates at higher elevations; gravity causes material to slide downhill. In **slab-pull**, plate motion is thought to be caused by cold, heavy plates at oceanic trenches sinking back into the mantle, providing fuel for future convection. Friction is subdivided into mantle drag and trench suction. Mantle drag suggests that plates move due to the friction between the lithosphere and the asthenosphere. Trench suction involves a downward frictional pull on oceanic plates in subduction zones due to convection currents.

Review Video: Plate Tectonic Theory
Visit mometrix.com/academy and enter code: 535013

CONVERGENT PLATE BOUNDARIES

A **convergent** (destructive) **plate boundary** occurs when adjacent plats move toward one another. The Earth's diameter remains constant over time. Therefore, the formation of new plate material at diverging plate boundaries necessitates the destruction of plate material elsewhere. This process occurs at convergent (destructive) plate boundaries. One plate slips underneath the other at a subduction zone. The results of converging plates vary, depending on the nature of the lithosphere in said plates. When two oceanic plates converge, they form a deep underwater trench. If each of the converging plates at a destructive boundary carries a continent, the light materials of the continental lithosphere enables both plates to float above the subduction area. They crumple and compress, creating a mid-continent mountain range. When a continental plate converges with an oceanic plate, the denser oceanic lithosphere slides beneath the continental lithosphere. The result of such convergence is an oceanic trench on one side and a mountain range on the other.

DIVERGENT PLATE BOUNDARY

A **divergent**, or constructive, **plate boundary** exists when two adjacent plates move away from one another. Observation of activity at diverging boundaries provided unquestionable proof of the seafloor-spreading hypothesis. At this type of plate boundary, kinetic energy generated by asthenospheric convection cells cracks the lithosphere and pushes molten magma through the space left by separating tectonic plates. This magma cools and hardens, creating a new piece of the Earth's crust. In the oceanic lithosphere, diverging plate boundaries form a series of rifts known as the oceanic ridge system. The Mid-Atlantic Ridge is a consequence of undersea diverging boundaries. At divergent boundaries on the continental lithosphere, plate movement results in rift valleys, typified by the East African Rift Valley.

Transform Plate Boundary

A **transform** (conservative) **plate boundary** exists when two tectonic plates slide past each other laterally and in opposite directions. Due to the rocky composition of lithospheric plates, this motion causes the plates to grind against each other. Friction causes stress to build when the plates stick; this potential energy is finally released when the built-up pressure exceeds the slipping point of the rocks on the two plates. This sudden release of energy causes earthquakes. This type of plate boundary is also referred to as a **strike-slip fault**. The San Andreas Fault in California is the most famous example of such a boundary.

Geologic Faults

A **geologic fault** is a fracture in the Earth's surface created by movement of the crust. The majority of faults are found along **tectonic plate boundaries**; however, smaller faults have been identified at locations far from these boundaries. There are three types of geologic faults, which are named for the original direction of movement along the active fault line. The landforms on either side of a fault are called the footwall and the hanging wall, respectively. In a **normal fault**, the hanging wall moves downward relative to the footwall. A **reverse fault** is the opposite of a normal fault: The hanging wall moves upward relative to the footwall. The dip of a reverse fault is usually quite steep; when the dip is less than 45 degrees, the fault is called a thrust fault. In the third type of geologic fault, the **strike-slip fault**, the dip is virtually nonexistent, and the footwall moves vertically left (sinistral) or right (dextral). A transform plate boundary is a specific instance of a strike-slip fault.

Earth's Layers and Processes

Earth's Layers

Chemical Layers

The **crust** is the outermost layer of the Earth. It is located 0–35 kilometers below the surface. Earth's crust is composed mainly of basalt and granite. The crust is less dense, cooler, and more rigid than the planet's internal layers. This layer floats on top of the **mantle**. Located 35–2,890 kilometers below the Earth's surface, the mantle is separated from the crust by the **Mohorovicic discontinuity**, or Moho (which occurs at 30–70 kilometers below the continental crust and at 6–8 kilometers beneath the oceanic crust). The mantle is made up of rocks such as peridotite and eclogite; its temperature varies from 100 to 3,500 degrees Celsius. Material in the mantle cycles due to convection. The innermost layer of the Earth is the core, which consists of a liquid outer layer and a solid inner layer. It is located 2,890–6,378 kilometers below the surface. The core is thought to be composed of iron and nickel and is the densest layer of the Earth.

Sublayers

The **lithosphere** consists of the crust and the uppermost portion of the mantle of the Earth. It is located 0–60 kilometers below the surface. The lithosphere is the cooling layer of the planet's convection cycle and thickens over time. This solid shell is fragmented into pieces called tectonic plates. The oceanic lithosphere is made up of mafic basaltic rocks and is thinner and generally more dense than the continental lithosphere (composed of granite and sedimentary rock); the lithosphere floats atop Earth's mantle. The **asthenosphere** is the soft, topmost layer of the mantle. It is located 100–700 kilometers below the surface. A combination of heat and pressure keeps the asthenosphere's composite material plastic. The **mesosphere** is located 900–2,800 kilometers below the surface; it therefore spans from the lower part of the mantle to the mantle-core boundary. The liquid **outer core** exists at 2,890–5,100 kilometers below surface level, and the solid inner core exists at depths of 5,100–6,378 kilometers.

Review Video: Earth's Structure
Visit mometrix.com/academy and enter code: 713016

Cycling of Earth's Materials

Rock Cycle

The **rock cycle** is the process whereby the materials that make up the Earth transition through the three types of rock: igneous, sedimentary, and metamorphic. Rocks, like all matter, cannot be created or destroyed; rather, they undergo a series of changes and adopt different forms through the functions of the rock cycle. Plate tectonics and the water cycle are the driving forces behind the rock cycle; they force rocks and minerals out of equilibrium and force them to adjust to different external conditions. Viewed in a generalized, cyclical fashion, the rock cycle operates as follows: rocks beneath Earth's surface melt into magma. This **magma** either erupts through volcanoes or remains inside the Earth. Regardless, the magma cools, forming igneous rocks. On the surface, these rocks experience **weathering** and **erosion**, which break them down and distribute the fragments across the surface. These fragments form layers and eventually become **sedimentary rocks**. Sedimentary rocks are then either transformed to **metamorphic rocks** (which will become magma inside the Earth) or melted down into magma.

Rock Formation

Igneous Rocks: Igneous rocks can be formed from sedimentary rocks, metamorphic rocks, or other igneous rocks. Rocks that are pushed under the Earth's surface (usually due to plate subduction) are exposed to high mantle temperatures, which cause the rocks to melt into magma. The magma then rises to the surface through volcanic processes. The lower atmospheric temperature causes the magma to cool, forming grainy, extrusive igneous rocks. The creation of extrusive, or volcanic, rocks is quite rapid. The cooling process can occur so rapidly that crystals do not form; in this case, the result is a glass, such as obsidian. It is also possible for magma to cool down inside the Earth's interior; this type of igneous rock is called intrusive. Intrusive, or plutonic, rocks cool more slowly, resulting in a coarse-grained texture.

Sedimentary Rocks: Sedimentary rocks are formed when rocks at the Earth's surface experience weathering and erosion, which break them down and distribute the fragments across the surface. Fragmented material (small pieces of rock, organic debris, and the chemical products of mineral sublimation) is deposited and accumulates in layers, with top layers burying the materials beneath. The pressure exerted by the topmost layers causes the lower layers to compact, creating solid sedimentary rock in a process called lithification.

Metamorphic Rocks: Metamorphic rocks are igneous or sedimentary rocks that have "morphed" into another kind of rock. In metamorphism, high temperatures and levels of pressure change preexisting rocks physically and/or chemically, which produces different species of rocks. In the rock cycle, this process generally occurs in materials that have been thrust back into the Earth's mantle by plate subduction. Regional metamorphism refers to a large band of metamorphic activity; this often occurs near areas of high orogenic (mountain-building) activity. Contact metamorphism refers to metamorphism that occurs when "country rock" (that is, rock native to an area) comes into contact with high-heat igneous intrusions (magma).

Plate Tectonics Rock Cycle

The plate tectonics rock cycle expands the concept of the traditional rock cycle to include more specific information about the tectonic processes that propel the rock cycle, as well as an evolutionary component. Earth's materials do not cycle endlessly through the different rock forms; rather, these transitive processes cause, for example, increasing diversification of the rock types found in the crust. Also, the cycling of rock increases the masses of continents by increasing the volume of granite. Thus, the **tectonic rock cycle** is a model of an evolutionary rock cycle. In this model, new oceanic lithosphere is created at divergent plate boundaries. This new crust spreads outward until it reaches a **subduction zone**, where it is pushed back into the mantle, becomes magma, and is thrust out into the **atmosphere**. It experiences erosion and becomes **sedimentary rock**. At convergent continental plate boundaries, this crust is involved in mountain building and the associated metamorphic pressures. It is **eroded** again, and returns to the lithosphere.

Role of Water

Water plays an important role in the rock cycle through its roles in **erosion** and **weathering**: it wears down rocks; it contributes to the dissolution of rocks and minerals as acidic soil water; and it carries ions and rock fragments (sediments) to basins where they will be compressed into **sedimentary rock**. Water also plays a role in the **metamorphic processes** that occur underwater in newly-formed igneous rock at mid-ocean ridges. The presence of water (and other volatiles) is a vital component in the melting of rocky crust into magma above subduction zones.

Metamorphism

Metamorphism is the process whereby existing sedimentary, igneous, or metamorphic rocks (protoliths) are transformed due to a change in their original physiochemical environment, where they were mineralogically stable. This generally happens alongside sedimentation, orogenesis, or the movement of tectonic plates. Between the Earth's surface and a depth of 20 kilometers, there exists a wide range of temperatures, pressure levels, and chemical activity. Metamorphism is generally an **isochemical process**, which means that it does not alter the initial chemical composition of a rock. The changes a rock undergoes in metamorphism are usually physical. Neither a metamorphosing rock nor its component minerals are melted during this process—they remain almost exclusively in a solid state. Metamorphism, like the formation of plutonic rock bodies, can be studied only after metamorphic rocks have been exposed by weathering and erosion of the crustal rocks above.

Factors

Heat is a primary factor in metamorphism. When extreme heat is applied to existing rocks, their component minerals are able to recrystallize (which entails a reorganization of the grains or molecules of a mineral, resulting in increased density, as well as the possible expulsion of volatiles such as water and carbon dioxide). High levels of thermal energy may also cause rocks to contort and deform. **Pressure** is another factor affecting the metamorphism of rocks. Increased pressure can initiate recrystallization through compression. Pressure forces can also lead to spot-melting at individual grain boundaries. Lithostatic, or confining, pressure is created by the load of rocks above a metamorphosing rock. Pore-fluid pressure results from the release of volatiles due to thermal energy. Directed pressure is enforced in a certain direction due to orogenesis: This type of pressure is responsible for foliation, or layering, which entails parallel alignment of mineral particles in a rock, characteristic of metamorphism. **Chemical activity** affects metamorphism due to the presence of volatiles in pore fluids.

Biogeochemical Cycle

The term biogeochemical cycle refers to one of several chemical processes in which chemical elements are (re)cycled among **biotic** (living) and **abiotic** (nonliving) constituents of an ecosystem. The theory of relativity necessitates the presence of such cycles in nature by virtue of its supposition that energy and matter are not created or destroyed in a closed system such as Earth's ecosystem. Generally, a **biogeochemical cycle** operates as follows: inorganic compounds, such as carbon, are converted from water, air, and soil to organic molecules by organisms called **autotrophs. Heterotrophs** (organisms that cannot independently produce their own food) consume the autotrophs; some of the newly formed organic molecules are transferred. Finally, the organic molecules are broken down and processed once again into inorganic compounds by secondary and tertiary consumers and replaced within water, air, and soil. Carbon, nitrogen, and phosphorus provide examples of nutrients that are recycled in the Earth's ecosystem.

Water Cycle and Energy Transfers Involved

Hydrologic Cycle

The **hydrologic (water) cycle** refers to the circulation of water in the Earth's hydrosphere (below the surface, on the surface, and above the surface of the Earth). This continuous process involves five physical actions. Evaporation entails the change of water molecules from a liquid to gaseous state. Liquid water on the Earth's surface (often contained in a large body of water) becomes water vapor and enters the atmosphere when its component molecules gain enough kinetic (heat) energy to escape the liquid form. As the vapor rises, it cools and therefore loses its ability to maintain the gaseous form. It begins to the process of condensation (the return to a liquid or solid state) and forms clouds. When the clouds become sufficiently dense, the water falls back to Earth as precipitation. Water is then either trapped in vegetation (interception) or absorbed into the surface (infiltration). Runoff, caused by gravity, physically moves water downward into oceans or other water bodies.

Evaporation

Evaporation is the change of state in a substance from a liquid to a gaseous form at a temperature below its boiling point (the temperature at which all of the molecules in a liquid are changed to gas through vaporization). Some of the molecules at the surface of a liquid always maintain enough heat energy to escape the cohesive forces exerted on them by neighboring molecules. At higher temperatures, the molecules in a substance move more rapidly, increasing their number with enough energy to break out of the liquid form. The rate of evaporation is higher when more of the surface area of a liquid is exposed (as in a large water body, such as an ocean). The amount of moisture already in the air also affects the rate of evaporation—if there is a significant amount of water vapor in the air around a liquid, some evaporated molecules will return to the liquid. The speed of the evaporation process is also decreased by increased atmospheric pressure.

Condensation

Condensation is the phase change in a substance from a gaseous to liquid form; it is the opposite of evaporation or vaporization. When temperatures decrease in a gas, such as water vapor, the material's component molecules move more slowly. The decreased motion of the molecules enables intermolecular cohesive forces to pull the molecules closer together and, in water, establish hydrogen bonds. Condensation can also be caused by an increase in the pressure exerted on a gas, which results in a decrease in the substance's volume (it reduces the distance between particles). In the hydrologic cycle, this process is initiated when warm air containing water vapor rises and then cools. This occurs due to convection in the air, meteorological fronts, or lifting over high land formations.

Precipitation

Precipitation is water that falls back to Earth's surface from the atmosphere. This water may be in the form of rain, which is water in the liquid form. Raindrops are formed in clouds due to the process of condensation. When the drops become too heavy to remain in the cloud (due to a decrease in their kinetic energy), gravity causes them to fall down toward Earth's surface. Extremely small raindrops are called drizzle. If the temperature of a layer of air through which rain passes on its way down is below the freezing point, the rain may take the form of sleet (partially frozen water). Precipitation may also fall in the form of snow, or water molecules sublimated into ice crystals. When clumps of snowflakes melt and refreeze, hail is formed. Hail may also be formed when liquid water accumulates on the surface of a snowflake and subsequently freezes.

Transportation of Water in the Water Cycle

In the **hydrologic cycle**, the principal movement of water in the atmosphere is its transport from the area above an ocean to an area over land. If this transport did not occur, the hydrologic cycle would be less a cycle than the vertical motion of water from the oceans to the atmosphere and back again. Some evaporated water is transported in the form of clouds consisting of condensed water droplets and small ice crystals. The clouds are moved by the jet stream (strong winds in the upper levels of the atmosphere that are related to surface temperatures) or by surface winds (land or sea breezes). Most of the water that moves through the atmosphere is water vapor (water in the gaseous form).

> **Review Video: Hydrologic Cycle**
> Visit mometrix.com/academy and enter code: 426578

Structure of the Atmosphere

Layers of the Atmosphere

The **atmosphere** consists of 78% nitrogen, 21% oxygen, and 1% argon. It also includes traces of water vapor, carbon dioxide and other gases, dust particles, and chemicals from Earth. The atmosphere becomes thinner the farther it is from the Earth's surface. It becomes difficult to breathe at about 3 km above sea level. The atmosphere gradually fades into space.

The main layers of the Earth's atmosphere (from lowest to highest) are:

- **Troposphere** (lowest layer): where life exists and most weather occurs; elevation 0–15 km
- **Stratosphere**: has the ozone layer, which absorbs UV radiation; elevation 15–50 km
- **Mesosphere**: coldest layer; where meteors will burn up; elevation 50–80 km
- **Thermosphere**: where the international space station and most satellites orbit; hottest layer; elevation 80–600 km
- **Exosphere** (outermost layer): consists mainly of hydrogen and helium; extends to ~10,000 km

> **Review Video: Earth's Atmosphere**
> Visit mometrix.com/academy and enter code: 417614

Tropospheric Circulation

Most weather takes place in the **troposphere**. Air circulates in the atmosphere by convection and in various types of "cells." Air near the equator is warmed by the Sun and rises. Cool air rushes under it, and the higher, warmer air flows toward Earth's poles. At the poles, it cools and descends to the surface. It is now under the hot air, and flows back to the equator. Air currents coupled with ocean currents move heat around the planet, creating winds, weather, and climate. Winds can change direction with the seasons. For example, in Southeast Asia and India, summer monsoons are caused by air being heated by the Sun. This air rises, draws moisture from the ocean, and causes daily rains. In winter, the air cools, sinks, pushes the moist air away, and creates dry weather.

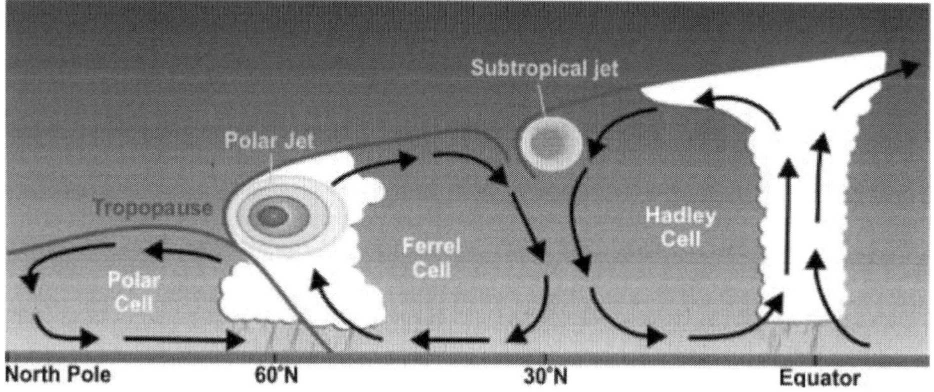

Weather Systems

Weather

Weather is the result of transfers of kinetic (heat) energy due to differences in temperature between objects as well as transfers of moisture in Earth's atmosphere. **Meteorology**, the study of weather, covers the same natural events as climatology, but observes them on a shorter time scale (usually no more than a few days). Rain, fog, snow, and wind are all examples of weather phenomena. The processes that occur at different stages in the hydrologic cycle form the basis of meteorological events. Most of the activity that produces the weather we experience on Earth takes place in the **troposphere**, the lowest level of the atmosphere. Atmospheric pressure, temperature, humidity, elevation, wind speed, and cloud cover are all factors in the study of weather.

Ozone Layer

The **Earth's ozone layer** is the region of the stratosphere with a high concentration of ozone (a form of oxygen) particles. These molecules are formed through the process of **photolysis**, which occurs when ultraviolet light from the sun collides with oxygen molecules (O_2) in the atmosphere. The ultraviolet radiation splits the oxygen atoms apart; when a free oxygen atom strikes an oxygen molecule, it combines with the molecule to create an **ozone particle** (O_3). Ozone molecules may be broken down by interaction with nitrogen-, chlorine-, and hydrogen-containing compounds, or by thermal energy from the sun. Under normal conditions, these creative and destructive processes balance the levels of ozone in the stratosphere. The concentration of ozone molecules in the atmosphere absorbs ultraviolet radiation, thus preventing this harmful energy from reaching the Earth's surface. Ozone particles form in the region of the atmosphere over the equator, which receives the most direct sunlight. Atmospheric winds then disperse the particles throughout the rest of the stratosphere.

Air Mass

An **air mass** is a body of air that exhibits consistent temperatures and levels of moisture throughout. These (usually large) pockets of air tend to come together under relatively still conditions, where air can remain in one place long enough to adopt the temperature and moisture characteristics of the land below it; this often occurs above wide areas of flat land. The region in which an air mass originates and the course of its motion are used to name it. For example, a maritime tropical air mass (denoted mT) is formed over the Gulf of Mexico (a tropical climate) and moves across the Atlantic Ocean (a maritime area). The conditions of an air mass will remain constant as long as the body is still, but when it moves across surfaces with different conditions, it may adopt those qualities. For example, polar air that moves over tropical land areas will be heated by the conditions below. Generally, maritime air masses contain high levels of moisture, and continental air masses are drier.

Meteorological Depression

A **meteorological depression** refers to a **low-pressure zone** (created by rising air) situated between 30- and 60-degrees latitude. These zones vary from approximately 321–3,218 kilometers in diameter. The rising air associated with a depression usually condenses at higher levels in the atmosphere and causes precipitation. Depressions are formed when warm air masses and cold air masses converge. At first, a single front (boundary between converging masses of air with different temperatures) separates the air masses.

A distortion similar to the crest of a water wave develops, creating a small center of low pressure. Then, differentiated warm and cold fronts develop from that center. A mass of warm air forms and rises over the body of cold air. The cold front and the cold air eventually catch up with the warm air, creating an occluded front and causing pressure to rise, effectually slowing the depression's movement. Depressions usually have life spans of four to seven days.

Prevailing Winds and Wind Belts

Wind (the horizontal movement of air with respect to Earth's surface) forms due to pressure gradients (differences) in the atmosphere. Air tends to move from areas of **high pressure** (such as the poles) to areas of

low pressure (such as the tropics). Prevailing winds, or trade winds, are the winds (named in meteorology for the direction they come from) that blow most frequently in a particular region. For instance, the prevailing winds most common in the region from 90 to 60 degrees north latitude blow from the northeast, and are generally called the Polar Easterlies. Wind belts are created in areas where prevailing winds converge with other prevailing winds or air masses. The Inter-Tropical Convergence Zone (ITCZ), where air coming from tropical areas north and south of the equator come together, is an example of a wind belt.

Review Video: Source of Wind
Visit mometrix.com/academy and enter code: 451712

Coriolis Force

The **Coriolis force**, which gives rise to the **Coriolis effect**, is not really a force at all. Rather, it appears to be there to us because the Earth is a rotating frame of reference and we are inside it. In the atmosphere, air tends to move from areas of high pressure to areas of lower pressure. This air would move in a straight line but for the Coriolis force, which appears to deflect the air and cause it to **swirl**. Really, however, the Earth moves underneath the wind, which creates the impression of swirling air to someone standing on the Earth's surface. The Coriolis force causes winds to swing to the right as they approach the Northern Hemisphere and to the left as they approach the Southern Hemisphere.

Air Stability in the Atmosphere

Air stability is the tendency for air to rise or fall through the atmosphere under its own power. Heated air rises because it is less dense than the surrounding air. As a pocket of air rises, however, it will expand and become cooler with changes in atmospheric pressure. If the ambient air into which rising air ascends does not cool as quickly with altitude as the rising air does, that air will rapidly become cooler (and heavier) than the surrounding air and descend back to its original position. The air in this situation is said to be stable. However, if the air into which the warm pocket rises becomes colder with increased altitude, the warm air will continue its ascent. In this case, the air is unstable. Unstable air conditions (such as those that exist in depressions) lead to the formation of large clouds of precipitation.

Clouds

The four main **types of clouds** are cirrus, cumulous, nimbus, and stratus. A **cirrus** cloud forms high in a stable atmosphere, generally at altitudes of 6,000 meters or higher. Temperatures at these altitudes (in the troposphere) decrease with increased altitude; therefore, the precipitation in a cirrus cloud adopts the form of ice crystals. These usually thin traces of clouds may indicate an approaching weather depression. A cumulous cloud is a stereotypical white, fluffy ball. **Cumulous** clouds are indicators of a stable atmosphere, and also of the vertical extent of convection in the atmosphere—condensation and cloud formation begin at the flat base of a cumulous cloud. The more humid the air, the lower a cumulous cloud will form. A **nimbus** cloud is, generally speaking, a rain cloud. Nimbus clouds are usually low, dark, and formless, sometimes spanning the entire visible sky. A **stratus** cloud is basically a cloud of fog which forms at a distance above the Earth's surface. This type of cloud forms when weak convective currents bring moisture just high enough to initiate condensation (if the temperature is below the dew point).

The four cloud subtypes are cumulonimbus, cirrostratus, altocumulus, and stratocumulus. A **cumulonimbus** cloud is produced by rapid convection in unstable air. This type of cloud (which is often dark) is formed as a large, tall "tower." Collections of these towers (squall lines) often signal a coming cold front. Thunderstorms often involve cumulonimbus clouds. A **cirrostratus** cloud is an ultra-thin formation with a white tint and a transparent quality. An **altocumulus** cloud forms at an altitude from 1,980 to 6,100 meters. Clouds of this type, which appear to be flattened spheres, often form in clumps, waves, or lines. A **stratocumulus** cloud forms as a globular mass or flake. Stratocumulus clouds usually come together in layers or clumps.

Review Video: Types of Clouds
Visit mometrix.com/academy and enter code: 803166

LIGHTNING

Lightning is a natural electrostatic discharge that produces light and releases electromagnetic radiation. It is believed that the separation of positive and negative charge carriers within a cloud is achieved by the polarization mechanism. The first step of this mechanism occurs when falling precipitation particles become **electrically polarized** after they move through the Earth's magnetic field. The second step of the polarization mechanism involves **electrostatic induction**, the process whereby electrically charged particles create charges in other particles without direct contact. Ice particles are charged though this method, and then energy-storing electric fields are formed between the charged particles. The positively-charged ice crystals tend to rise to the top of the cloud, effectively polarizing the cloud with positive charges on top and negative charges at the middle and bottom. When charged clouds conglomerate, an electric discharge (a lightning bolt) is produced, either between clouds or between a cloud and the Earth's surface.

THUNDERSTORMS

A **thunderstorm** is a weather phenomenon that includes lightning, thunder, and usually large amounts of precipitation and strong winds. Thunder is the noise made by the rapid expansion and contraction of air due to the heat energy produced by lightning bolts. A thunderstorm develops when heating on the Earth's surface causes large amounts of air to rise into an unstable atmosphere. This results in large clouds of rain and ice crystals. The associated condensation releases high levels of heat, which in turn power the growth cycle of the cloud. The clouds created during thunderstorms are immense, sometimes reaching widths of several miles and extending to heights of 10,000 meters or more. The precipitation in such clouds eventually becomes heavy enough to fall against the updraft of unstable air; the consequent downpour is often short but intense. The differential speeds at which light and sound travel through the atmosphere enable one to estimate the distance between oneself and the storm by observing the interval between a lightning bolt and a thunderclap.

HURRICANES

Hurricanes form when several conditions are met: Oceanic water must be at least 26 degrees Celsius, the general circulation pattern of wind must be disrupted (this disruption usually takes the form of an atmospheric wave in the easterly trade winds), and the Coriolis force must be in effect. During hurricane season (June to November), easterly waves appear in the trade winds every few days. When such a wave occurs over a body of particularly warm, deep water, it is strengthened by the evaporation of warm air from below. Surrounding winds converge at the low-pressure zone created by the wave; air brought by these winds rises because it has nowhere else to go. The large body of warm, moist air rises high into the atmosphere and consequently condenses into huge clouds. As more and more humid air is drawn upward, this air begins to rotate around the area of low pressure. The storm continues to gain strength and may move toward land.

TORNADO

A tornado is a violent rotating column of air that is in contact with both the ground and a cloud. The column is visible because the very low pressure causes water vapor to condense out as visible water droplets. Where the tornado touches the ground it usually stirs up a cloud of dirt and debris like the one in this photo. Tornadoes are the most violent storms on Earth, and the strongest spin at 300 miles per hour.

Review Video: Tornadoes
Visit mometrix.com/academy and enter code: 540439

El Nino

El Niño refers to the **unusual warming of surface waters** near the equatorial coast of South America. This phenomenon occurs during the winter approximately every two to seven years, lasting from a few weeks to a few months. El Nino can cause torrential rains, violent winds, drought, and dangerously high temperatures in surrounding areas. El Nino is caused by a reversal of the atmospheric pressures on the eastern and western sides of the Pacific (normally, pressure is high on the eastern side near South America and lower on the western side near the Indonesian coast). This reversal causes a wave of warm water to flow eastward and sea levels to fall on the western side. The changes in air pressure and ocean temperature cause moisture levels in the western Pacific to rise drastically while the region east of the Pacific experiences drought. The air pressure changes also weaken the region's trade winds, which normally serve to distribute heat and moisture.

Monsoons and Savannahs

The term **monsoon** refers to a unique pattern of moving air and currents that occurs when winds reverse direction with a change in season. India and Southeast Asia experience the most intense monsoons. This area lies between tropical and subtropical climate zones. During the winter season, northeasterly winds (which are generally dry) move from high-pressure subtropical areas to lower-pressure tropical areas. During the summer season, the continents of India and Asia heat up, creating a low-pressure zone. This causes winds to reverse and blow southwesterly across the Indian Ocean, accumulating high levels of moisture, thereby creating large amounts of precipitation during this season.

Savannahs also exist between wet equatorial and dry subtropical climate zones. These regions are characterized by vegetation consisting mainly of shrubs and grass. Savannahs experience dry weather throughout most of the year. A single, brief rainy season that occurs when the Sun is directly above the region interrupts prolonged dry spells.

Influence of Mountains on Climate

At the level of local climate, the presence of mountains forces air to rise to travel above them; this contributes to increased formation of clouds and consequently, increases in levels of precipitation. Mountain chains can affect regional and even global climates by deflecting airflow. The Coriolis force causes most of Earth's atmospheric airflow to move east and west. Therefore, the presence of north-south–oriented mountain chains can alter general circulation patterns. For example, the Rocky Mountains force air to move northward; the air cools near the North Pole before blowing back down. This causes winter temperatures in Canada and parts of the United States to be very cold.

Humidity and Cloud Cover

Humidity is a measure of the amount of water vapor in the air. **Specific humidity** is the expression of humidity as a ratio of aqueous vapor to dry air; it is expressed as a ratio of mass of water vapor per unit mass of natural (dry) air. **Absolute humidity** measures the mass of water vapor in a given volume of moist air or gas; it is expressed in grams per cubic foot or per cubic meter. The equilibrium (or saturated) vapor pressure of a gas is the vapor pressure (created by the movement of molecules) of water vapor when air is saturated with water vapor. **Relative humidity**, usually expressed as a percentage, is the ratio of the vapor pressure of water in air (or another gas) to the equilibrium vapor pressure. In other words, it is a ratio of the mass of water per volume of gas and the mass per volume of a saturated gas. Cloud cover refers to the amount of sky blocked by clouds at a given location.

Measuring Weather

Weather can be measured by a variety of methods. The simplest include measurement of rainfall, sunshine, pressure, humidity, temperature, and cloudiness with basic instruments such as thermometers, barometers, and rain gauges. However, the use of radar (which involves analysis of microwaves reflecting off of raindrops) and satellite imagery grants meteorologists a look at the big picture of weather across, for example, an entire continent. This helps them understand and make predictions about current and developing weather systems. Infrared (heat-sensing) imaging allows meteorologists to measure the temperature of clouds above ground. Using weather reports gathered from different weather stations spread over an area, meteorologists create synoptic charts. The locations and weather reports of several stations are plotted on a chart; analysis of the pressures reported from each location, as well as rainfall, cloud cover, and so on, can reveal basic weather patterns.

Global Warming

The **natural greenhouse effect** of the atmosphere is beneficial to life on Earth; it keeps temperatures on the planet 33 degrees higher than they would be without this phenomenon. Originally, this helped sustain life. However, it has been discovered in the last 20 years that this effect is being intensified by the actions of humans. In the twentieth century, certain activities of mankind, including the burning of fossils fuels like coal and oil, have resulted in an **increase in the levels of greenhouse gases** (such as methane and carbon dioxide) being released into the atmosphere. Also, increasing deforestation has affected the number of photosynthesis-practicing plants. The combined effect of these trends is a higher-than-normal concentration of greenhouse gases in the atmosphere. This, in turn, produces the effect of global warming. The average temperature at the Earth's surface has gone up 0.6 degrees Celsius in the last 100 years. Continuation of this trend is likely to have a detrimental effect on many of the planet's ecosystems, including that of human beings.

Earth-Moon-Sun System

Earth's Rotation

The **Earth rotates** west to east about its axis, an imaginary straight line that runs nearly vertically through the center of the planet. This rotation (which takes 23 hours, 56 minutes, and 5 seconds) places each section of the Earth's surface in a position facing the Sun for a period of time, thus creating the alternating periods of light and darkness we experience as **day and night**. This rotation constitutes a sidereal day; it is measured as the amount of time required for a reference star to cross the meridian (an imaginary north-south line above an observer). Each star crosses the meridian once every (sidereal) day. Since the speed at which Earth rotates is not exactly constant, we use the mean solar day (a 24-hour period) in timekeeping rather than the slightly variable sidereal day.

SUN

The **Sun** is the vital force of life on Earth; it is also the central component of our solar system. It is basically a sphere of extremely hot gases (close to 15 million degrees at the core) held together by gravity. Some of these gaseous molecules are ionized due to the high temperatures. The balance between its gravitational force and the pressure produced by the hot gases is called **hydrostatic equilibrium**. The source of the solar energy that keeps the Sun alive and plays a key role in the perpetuation of life on Earth is located in the Sun's core, where nucleosynthesis produces heat energy and photons. The Sun's atmosphere consists of the photosphere, the surface visible from Earth, the chromosphere, a layer outside of and hotter than the photosphere, the transition zone (the region where temperatures rise between the chromosphere and the corona), and the corona, which is best viewed at x-ray wavelengths. A solar flare is an explosive emission of ionized particles from the Sun's surface.

Review Video: The Sun
Visit mometrix.com/academy and enter code: 699233

EARTH'S REVOLUTION AROUND THE SUN

Like all celestial objects in our solar system, planet Earth revolves around the Sun. This process takes approximately 365 1/4 days, the period of time that constitutes a calendar year. The path of the orbit of Earth around the Sun is not circular but **elliptical**. Therefore, the distances between the Earth and the Sun at points on either extreme of this counterclockwise orbit are not equal. In other words, the distance between the two objects varies over the course of a year. At **perihelion**, the minimum heliocentric distance, Earth is 147 million kilometers from the Sun. At **aphelion**, the maximum heliocentric distance, Earth is 152 million kilometers from the Sun. This movement of the Earth is responsible for the apparent annual motions of the Sun (in a path referred to as the ecliptic) and other celestial objects visible from Earth's surface.

Review Video: Astronomy
Visit mometrix.com/academy and enter code: 640556

Review Video: The Solar System
Visit mometrix.com/academy and enter code: 273231

SEASONS

The combined effects of Earth's revolution around the Sun and the tilt of the planet's rotational axis create the **seasons**. Earth's axis is not perfectly perpendicular to its orbital plane; rather, it is **tilted** about 23.5 degrees. Thus, at different times of the year, certain areas of the surface receive different amounts of sunlight. For example, during the period of time in Earth's orbit when the Northern Hemisphere is tipped toward the Sun, it is exposed to higher amounts of nearly direct sunlight than at any other time of year (days are longer, and the direction of Sun's rays striking the surface is nearly perpendicular). This period of time is summer in the Northern Hemisphere and winter in the Southern Hemisphere; on the opposite side of the orbit, the seasons are reversed in each hemisphere.

Review Video: Earth's Tilt and Seasons
Visit mometrix.com/academy and enter code: 602892

SUMMER AND WINTER SOLSTICES

The **summer solstice** occurs when Earth's orbital position and axial tilt point the North Pole most directly toward the Sun. This happens on or near June 21 each year. On this day in the Northern Hemisphere, the Sun appears to be directly overhead (at its zenith) at 12:00 noon. The entire Arctic Circle (the north polar region above approximately 66.5 degrees north latitude) is bathed in sunlight for a complete solar day. The North Pole itself experiences constant daylight for six full months. Conversely, the **winter solstice** occurs when the South Pole is oriented most directly toward the Sun. This phenomenon, which falls on or near December 22 each year, orients the Sun as viewed from the Northern Hemisphere at its lowest point above the horizon.

Equinoxes

The **ecliptic** (the Sun's apparent path through the sky) crosses Earth's equatorial plane twice during the year; these intersections occur when the North Pole is at a right angle from the line connecting the Earth and the Sun. At these times, the two hemispheres experience equal periods of light and dark. These two points in time are respectively referred to as the vernal (spring) equinox (on or about March 21) and the autumnal (fall) equinox (on or about September 23). A calendar year is measured as the length of time between vernal equinoxes.

Moon

Earth's Moon is historically one of the most studied celestial bodies. Its mass is approximately 1.2% of the Earth's mass, and its radius is just over one-fourth of the size of the Earth's radius. Measurements of the Moon's density suggest that its characteristics are similar to those of the rocks that make up Earth's crust. The **landscape** of the Moon consists mostly of mountains and craters formed by collisions of this surface with meteors and other interplanetary materials. The Moon's crust (estimated to be 50 to 100 kilometers in thickness) is made up of a layer of regolith (lunar soil) supported by a layer of loose rocks and gravel. Beneath the crust is a mantle made up of a solid lithosphere and a semiliquid asthenosphere. The Moon's **core** (the innermost 500 kilometers of the body) is not as dense as that of the Earth. The Moon is made up mostly of refractory elements with high melting and boiling points with low levels of heavy elements such as iron.

Formation Theories

The **fission model** of Moon origin suggests that the Moon is actually a piece of the Earth that split off early during the planet's formation. In this model, a portion of the Earth's mantle fissioned off during a liquid stage in its formation, creating the Moon. According to the **capture model**, the Moon formed elsewhere in the solar system and was subsequently captured by the Earth's gravitational field. The **double-impact model** states that the Earth and the Moon formed during the same period of time from the same accretion material. Each of these theories has its strengths, but none of them can explain all of the properties of the Moon and its relationship to the Earth. Recently, a fourth (widely accepted) hypothesis has been suggested, which involves the **collision** between the Earth and a large asteroid. This hypothetical collision is said to have released a large amount of Earth's crustal material into its orbit; the Moon accreted from that material and the material displaced from the asteroid due to the collision.

Earth-Moon System

While the Moon is commonly referred to as a satellite of the Earth, this is not entirely accurate. The ratio of the masses of the two bodies is much larger than that of any other planet-satellite system. Also, the Moon does not truly **revolve** around the Earth. Rather, the two bodies revolve around a common center of mass beneath the surface of the Earth (approximately 4,800 kilometers from Earth's core). The **orbital planes** of the Moon and the Earth are nearly aligned; therefore, the Moon moves close to the ecliptic, as seen from Earth. Due to the Moon's synchronous rotation (its rotation period and orbital period are equal); the same side of the Moon is always facing Earth. This occurs because of the **mutual gravitational** pull between the two bodies.

Phases

The **sidereal period** of the Moon (the time it takes the Moon to orbit the Earth with the fixed stars as reference points) is about 27 days. The **lunar month** (or synodic period) is the period of time required for the Moon to return to a given alignment as observed from the Earth with the Sun as a reference point; this takes 29 days, 12 hours, 44 minutes, and 28 seconds. A discrepancy exists between the two periods of time because the Earth and the Moon move at the same time. Sunlight reflected off of the Moon's surface at different times during the lunar month causes its apparent shape to change. The sequence of the Moon's shapes is referred to as the **phases of the Moon**. The full Moon can be viewed when the body is directly opposite from the Sun. The opposite end of the cycle, the new Moon, occurs when the Moon is not visible from Earth because it is situated between the Earth and the Sun.

Configurations

The **configurations of the Moon** describe its position with respect to the Earth and the Sun. We can thus observe a correlation between the phases of the Moon and its configuration. The Moon is at **conjunction** at the time of the new Moon—it is situated in the same direction as the Sun. **Quadrature** (which signals the first quarter phase) is the position of the Moon at a right angle between the Earth-Sun line; we see exactly half of the Moon's sunlit hemisphere. This is the **waxing crescent phase**, in which we see more of the Moon each night. Then comes opposition (which occurs when the Moon lies in the direction opposite the Sun)—we see the full Moon. After this point, the Moon enters its **waning gibbons phase** as it travels back toward quadrature. When it reaches that point again, it has entered the third-quarter phase. Finally, as the Moon circles back toward conjunction, it is in its waning crescent phase.

Review Video: Moon
Visit mometrix.com/academy and enter code: 880415

The Solar System

Terrestrial Planets

The term **terrestrial planets** refers to the four planets closest to the Sun (Mercury, Venus, Earth, and Mars). They are classified together because they share many similarities that distinguish them from the giant planets. The terrestrial planets have **high densities and atmospheres** that constitute a small percentage of their total masses. These atmospheres consist mostly of heavy elements, such as carbon dioxide, nitrogen, and water, and are maintained by the gravitational field of the planets (which could not prevent hydrogen from escaping). These planets exhibit magnetic fields of varying intensity. An important characteristic that distinguishes the terrestrial planets from the giant planets is the evidence of various levels of internally generated activity, which caused these planets to evolve from their original states. These processes are thought to have been caused by constant meteoritic impacts during the first few hundred million years of the planets' existence. Radioactive decay of certain isotopes increased the internal temperatures of these planets, leading to volcanic activity on all of the terrestrial planets except Venus.

Review Video: Terrestrial Planets
Visit mometrix.com/academy and enter code: 100346

Mercury

Mercury, the smallest interior planet, is the least well known of the four. This is due to its close proximity to the Sun and high temperatures. Mercury's atmosphere is not very dense; this means that the planet's surface experiences wide temperature differentials from day to night. Mercury's density is close to that of Earth. As the smallest planet known to have experienced planetary evolution, Mercury's internal activity ceased (it became extinct) thousands of millions of years ago. The size of the planet is relevant because less massive bodies cool more quickly than larger ones after cessation of radioactivity. Mercury's surface is characterized by craters produced by meteoritic impact.

Venus

Venus is comparable to Earth in both size and mass. Venus is the brightest planet in the sky, partially due to the fact that it is proximate to the Sun. This proximity to the Sun makes exploration of its surface difficult. This planet's atmosphere consists mainly of carbon dioxide, with trace amounts of water and carbon oxide molecules, as well as high levels of sulfuric, nitric, and hydrofluoric acids in the clouds that characterize this atmosphere. The concentration of clouds, coupled with the chemical makeup of Venus's atmosphere, result in a strong greenhouse effect at the planet's surface. This surface consists of large plains (thought to be created by either volcanic activity or by meteoritic impacts) and large impact craters. The materials that compose Venus's surface are highly radioactive. Some astronomers have suggested past single-plate tectonic activity; again, however, the planet's dense atmosphere makes valid surface observation quite difficult. Recent evidence points to the likelihood of current volcanic activity.

MARS

Mars and Earth exhibit many similarities. For example, Mars has an internal structure that includes a central metallic core, a mantle rich in olivine and iron oxide, and a crust of hydrated silicates. Martian soil consists largely of basalts and clay silicate, with elements of sulfur, silicon oxide, and iron oxide. The planet's surface belies high levels of past volcanic activity (though, due to its relatively small mass, it is probably extinct). In fact, Mars is home to the largest known volcano in the solar system. The Martian landscape also includes two major basins, ridges and plateaus, and, most notably, apparent evidence of fluvial (water-based) erosion landforms, such as canyons and canals. It is possible that the past pressures and temperatures on Mars allowed water to exist on the red planet. Some have gone so far as to suggest that this planet was a site of biochemical evolution. So far, however, no evidence of life has been found.

MARS'S SATELLITES

Two Martian satellites have been observed: **Phobos** and **Deimos**. Each of these bodies is ellipsoidal; the circular orbits of the two satellites lie in Mars's equatorial plane. The gravitational forces between this planet and Phobos and Deimos have caused both satellites to settle into synchronous rotation (the same parts of their surfaces are always facing Mars). This feature exerts a braking force on Phobos's orbit. In other words, its orbit is decreasing in size. The relationship between Deimos and Mars is similar to the Earth-Moon system, in which the radius of the satellite's orbit is gradually growing. The differential compositions and densities of Mars and its satellites indicate that Phobos and Deimos probably did not break off from Mars.

GIANT PLANETS

The **large diameters** of Jupiter, Saturn, Uranus, and Neptune gave rise to the name of the category into which they fall. The **hypothetical icy cores** of these planets cause them to exhibit primary atmospheres, because the large levels of mass they accreted prevented even the lightest elements from escaping their gravitational pulls. The atmospheres of the giant planets thus consist mostly of hydrogen and helium. The giant planets do not have solid surfaces like those of the terrestrial planets. Jupiter probably consists of a core (made of ice and rock) surrounded by a layer of metallic hydrogen, which is covered by a convective atmosphere of hydrogen and helium. Saturn is believed to have the same type of core and hydrogen mantle, enriched by the helium missing from the atmosphere, surrounded by a differentiation zone and a hydrogenic atmosphere. Uranus and Neptune probably have the same type of core, surrounded by ionic materials, bounded by methane-rich molecular envelopes. Uranus is the only giant planet that exhibits no evidence of internal activity.

Review Video: Giant Planets
Visit mometrix.com/academy and enter code: 563115

RINGS

Each of the four giant planets exhibits **rings**. These are flat disks of fragmented material that orbit just next to their respective planets. Many of the giant planets' smaller satellites are embedded in these rings. There are two main hypotheses regarding the formation of such rings. One theory suggests that the tidal force exerted on a satellite by its planet may surpass the **Roche limit** (the point at which particle cohesion is no longer possible) and break the satellite into fragments, which then collide and become smaller. This material then spreads out and forms a ring. An alternate theory of the formation of the rings of the giant planets suggests that there was unaccreted material left over after the formation of these planets. Below the Roche limit (within a certain vicinity to the planet), these particles could not join together to form satellites and would consequently settle into orbital rings.

SATELLITES

Each of the giant planets possesses a number of **satellites**. **Jupiter** has over 50 known satellites—they are grouped according to size. Each of the four largest satellites of Jupiter exhibits evidence of internal activity at some point in their evolutions. In fact, Io, the densest satellite and the one closest to Jupiter, is the only celestial body besides Earth known to be currently volcanically active. **Saturn** has 21 satellites. Titan, the second-largest known satellite, has its own atmosphere. The other six largest of Saturn's satellites all have icy surfaces;

some of these show evidence of past internal activity. The smaller 14 are relatively unknown. **Uranus** has five satellites. Each of them displays evidence of geological activity, in the form of valleys, smoothed surfaces, cliffs, mountains, and depressions. **Neptune** has eight known satellites. The larger, Triton, is similar to Titan in that it has an atmosphere. The other seven satellites of Neptune are relatively unknown.

Pluto and Charon

Though Charon was originally considered a satellite of Pluto, it now appears that the two are more accurately described as a double dwarf planet system (largely because of the similarity in the sizes of the two and the recurring debate over how Pluto should be classified). It is believed that these bodies formed from the solar nebula like most other objects in the solar system. Pluto has a highly irregular orbit, which places it closer to the Sun than Neptune for periods of time. In sharp contrast to its giant neighbors, this planet's density is higher than that of water ice. The surface of Pluto consists of high levels of methane absorbed into ice, with trace amounts of carbon oxide and nitrogen. Charon resembles the major Uranian satellites more so than it does Pluto. It consists of water ice with a siliceous or hydrocarbonate contaminant.

Review Video: Pluto and Charon
Visit mometrix.com/academy and enter code: 426296

Kepler's Laws

Kepler's laws are a collection of observations about the motion of planets in the solar system. Formulated by Johannes Kepler in the 1600s, these laws are still vital to our understanding of the way the universe works. **Kepler's first law** states that each planet moves in its own elliptical path and that all of these orbits have the Sun as their singular focal point. Before Kepler's discovery, astronomers had assumed that planetary orbits were circular (because the heavens were assumed to be geometrically perfect). **Kepler's second law** says that a straight line between a planet and the Sun sweeps out equal areas in equal time. In other words, planets move quickest in the part of their orbit that is closest to the Sun, and vice versa. **Kepler's third law** states that the further a planet is from the Sun, the longer its orbital period will be. In mathematical terms, the square of a planet's period is directly proportional to the cube of the radius of its orbit.

Stars and Other Objects in Space

Stellar Observation

The observation of stars relates to one of three stellar properties: position, brightness, and spectra. **Positional stellar observation** is principally performed through study of the positions of stars on multiple photographic plates. Historically, this type of analysis was done through measurement of the angular positions of the stars in the sky. **Parallax** of a star is its apparent shift in position due to the revolution of the Earth about the Sun; this property can be used to establish the distance to a star. Observation of the **brightness** of a star involves the categorization of stars according to their magnitudes. There is a fixed intensity ratio between each of the six magnitudes. Since stars emit light over a range of wavelengths, viewing a star at different wavelengths can give an indication of its temperature. The analysis of stars' **spectra** provides information about the temperatures of stars—the higher a star's temperature, the more ionized the gas in its outer layer. A star's spectrum also relates to its chemical composition.

Binary Star

Binary star systems, of which about fifty percent of the stars in the sky are members, consist of two stars that orbit each other. The orbits of and distances between members of a binary system vary. A **visual binary** is a pair of stars that can be visually observed. Positional measurements of a visual binary reveal the orbital paths of the two stars. Astronomers can identify astrometric binaries through long-term observation of a visible star—if the star appears to wobble, it may be inferred that it is orbiting a companion star that is not visible. An **eclipsing binary** can be identified through observation of the brightness of a star. Variations in the visual brightness of a star can occur when one star in a binary system passes in front of the other. Sometimes, variations in the spectral lines of a star occur because it is in a binary system. This type of binary is a spectroscopic binary.

Review Video: Types of Stars
Visit mometrix.com/academy and enter code: 831934

HERTZSPRUNG-RUSSELL DIAGRAM

The **Hertzsprung-Russell (H-R) diagram** was developed to explore the relationships between the luminosities and spectral qualities of stars. This diagram involves plotting these qualities on a graph, with absolute magnitude (luminosity) on the vertical and spectral class on the horizontal. Plotting a number of stars on the H-R diagram demonstrates that stars fall into narrowly defined regions, which correspond to stages in stellar evolution. Most stars are situated in a diagonal strip that runs from the top-left (high temperature, high luminosity) to the lower-right (low temperature, low luminosity). This diagonal line shows stars in the main sequence of evolution (often called dwarfs). Stars that fall above this line on the diagram (low temperature, high luminosity) are believed to be much larger than the stars on the main sequence (because their high luminosities are not due to higher temperatures than main sequence stars); they are termed giants and supergiants. Stars below the main sequence (high temperature, low luminosity) are called white dwarfs. The H-R diagram is useful in calculating distances to stars.

STELLAR EVOLUTION

The life cycle of a star is closely related to its **mass**—low-mass stars become white dwarfs, while high-mass stars become **supernovae**. A star is born when a **protostar** is formed from a **collapsing interstellar cloud**. The temperature at the center of the protostar rises, allowing nucleosynthesis to begin. **Nucleosynthesis**, or hydrogen-burning through fusion, entails a release of energy. Eventually, the star runs out of fuel (hydrogen). If the star is relatively low mass, the disruption of hydrostatic equilibrium allows the star to contract due to gravity. This raises the temperature just outside the core to a point at which nucleosynthesis and a different kind of fusion (with helium as fuel) that produces a carbon nucleus can occur. The star swells with greater energy, becoming a red giant. Once this phase is over, gravity becomes active again, shrinking the star until the degeneracy pressure of electrons begins to operate, creating a white dwarf that will eventually burn out. If the star has a high mass, the depletion of hydrogen creates a supernova.

SUPERNOVA

When a star on the main sequence runs out of hydrogen fuel, it begins to burn helium (the by-product of nucleosynthesis). Once helium-burning is complete in a massive star, the mass causes the core temperature to rise, enabling the fusion of carbon, then silicon, and a succession of other atomic nuclei, each of which takes place in a new shell further out of the core. When the fusion cycle reaches iron (which cannot serve as fuel for a nuclear reaction), an iron core begins to form, which accumulates over time. Eventually, the temperature and pressure in the core become high enough for electrons to interact with protons in the iron nuclei to produce neutrons. In a matter of moments, this reaction is complete. The core falls and collides with the star's outer envelope, causing a massive explosion (a supernova). This continues until the neutrons exert degeneracy pressure; this creates a pulsar. In more massive stars, nothing can stop the collapse, which ends in the creation of a black hole.

METEOROID

A **meteoroid** is a small, solid fragment of material in the solar system. An enormous number of these objects are present in the system. The term meteor is used to refer to such a body when it enters the Earth's atmosphere. Interaction (friction) between meteors and the upper levels of the atmosphere cause them to break up; most disintegrate before they reach the surface. The heat associated with frictional forces causes meteors to glow, creating the phenomena of shooting stars. The meteors that are large enough to avoid complete disintegration, and can therefore travel all the way down through the atmosphere to Earth's surface, are termed meteorites. Analysis of these fragments indicates that these bodies originate from the Moon, Mars, comets, and small asteroids that cross Earth's orbital path. The forceful impacts of meteorites on Earth's surface compress, heat, and vaporize some of the materials of the meteorite as well as crustal materials, producing gases and water vapor.

Asteroid

An **asteroid** is a small, solid planet (planetoid) that orbits the Sun. The orbital paths of most asteroids are between the orbits of Jupiter and Mars. Many of these bodies have been studied extensively and given names; those in the main belt (which tend to be carbonaceous) are classified into subgroups based on their distance from a large, named asteroid (for example, Floras, Hildas, Cybeles). **Atens** are asteroids whose orbits lie between the Earth and the Sun, and Apollos are asteroids with orbits that mimic Earth's. Asteroids may also be classified based on their composition. **C-type asteroids are similar in composition to the non-volatile elements of the sun. The sun is composed of about 74% hydrogen, 24% helium, and about 2% heavier elements**. S-type asteroids are made up of nickel-iron and iron- and magnesium-silicates; these are relatively bright. **Bright asteroids** made up exclusively of nickel-iron are classified as M-type. Observation of the relative brightness of an asteroid allows astronomers to estimate its size.

Review Video: Comets, Asteroids, and Meteoroids
Visit mometrix.com/academy and enter code: 100347

Interstellar Medium

The **interstellar**, or interplanetary, **medium** (the space between planets and stars) is populated by comets, asteroids, and meteoroids. However, particles exist in this medium on an even smaller scale. Tiny solid bodies (close to a millionth of a meter in diameter) are called **interplanetary dust**. The accumulation of this material in arctic lakes, for example, allows scientists to study it. Such analysis has revealed that these grains are most likely miniscule fragments of the **nuclei of dead comets**. They possess low density, for they are really many microscopic particles stuck together. The interplanetary dust refracts sunlight, which produces a visible (but faint) glow in parts of the sky populated by clouds of this dust. The interstellar medium also contains particle remnants of **dead stars** and **gases** (such as hydrogen molecules ionized by ultraviolet photons). **Black holes** (objects that collapse under their own gravitational forces), which trap photons, are also believed to populate the interstellar medium. Black holes are a form of dark matter.

Dark Matter

Observations of the **gravitational force** in the solar system (based on Kepler's laws) have indicated for years that there are bodies in the system that we cannot see. **Dark matter** (sometimes called missing matter) is thought to account for the unseen masses, though its exact nature is unknown. Some dark matter may simply be **ordinary celestial bodies** too small to be observed from Earth, even with technology such as high-powered telescopes. The presence of MACHOs (massive compact halo objects) has been noted through observation of distant galaxies—at certain times astronomers can discern dips in the brightness of these galaxies, thought to be caused by a large object (a MACHO) passing between Earth and the galaxy under observation. Some have postulated that dark matter is made up of **WIMPs** (weakly interacting massive particles), which do not interact with photons or other forms of electromagnetic radiation; these particles are hypothetical, because astronomers cannot detect or study them.

Review Video: Dark Matter
Visit mometrix.com/academy and enter code: 251909

Eclipses

Eclipses occur when one celestial body obscures the view of another, either partially or completely. A **solar eclipse**, or eclipse of the Sun by the Moon, happens when the Moon passes directly in front of the Sun (as observed from Earth). Alternately, a **lunar eclipse** occurs when the Moon is situated in the Earth's shadow and is therefore completely invisible. These events do not happen every month because of the differential between the orbital planes of the Moon and the Earth—the Moon's orbit is about five degrees off from the ecliptic. The Moon's orbital path is subject to the same precession that occurs in the Earth's rotational axis; this causes the occasional intersection of the orbital planes of the two bodies. Therefore, eclipses are produced by a combination of the effects of the precession of the Moon's orbit, the orbit itself, and the Earth's orbit.

Review Video: Eclipses
Visit mometrix.com/academy and enter code: 691598

NEWTON'S LAW OF GRAVITATION

Newton's law of gravitation (sometimes referred to as the law of universal gravitation) states that the force of gravity operates as an attractive force between all bodies in the universe. Prior to Newton's formulation of this law, scientists believed that two gravitational forces were at work in the universe—that gravity operated differently on Earth than it did in space. Newton's discovery served to unify these two conceptions of gravity. This law is expressed as a mathematical formula: $F = \frac{GMm}{D^2}$, in which F is the gravitational force, M and m are the masses of two bodies, D is the distance between them, and G is the gravitational constant ($6.67 \times 10^{-11} \frac{\text{m}^3}{\text{kg s}^2}$). The gravitational attraction between two objects, therefore, depends on the distance between them and their relative masses. Newton's law of gravitation served to clarify the mechanisms by which Kepler's laws operated. In effect, Newton proved Kepler's laws to be true through the development of this law.

Review Video: Newton's Law of Gravitation
Visit mometrix.com/academy and enter code: 709086

CHARACTERISTICS OF THE MILKY WAY AND OTHER GALAXIES

MILKY WAY

The **Milky Way**, which houses the Earth's solar system, is a spiral galaxy. It consists of a central bulging disk, the center of which is referred to as a **nucleus**. Most of a galaxy's visible light comes from stars in this region. The disk is surrounded by a halo of stars and star clusters that spread above, next to, and beneath the nucleus. **Globular clusters** (dense, spherical clusters of ancient stars) are often found in the halo. Spiral arms of high-luminosity stars (from which this type of galaxy gets its name) fan out from the nucleus as well, with stars that are less bright in between. Interstellar dust populates the entire galaxy between celestial bodies. The entire galaxy rotates about the center. While Earth, the Sun, and its solar system are located on the disk, we are far from the center of the Milky Way. The galaxy's mass is about 1.5 trillion solar masses.

STRUCTURES OF GALAXIES

Elliptical galaxies are roughly spherical. Within this category, subgroups based on the degree of flattening exhibited in the galaxy's shape range from E0 (spherical) to E7 (flat). A dwarf elliptical galaxy has a spheroidal shape, with low mass and low luminosity. An S0 galaxy is similar in shape to a spiral galaxy, but lacks spiral arms. Spiral galaxies such as the Milky Way are characterized by disk-like nuclei with spiral arms. Subtypes of this category are determined by the tightness of the spiral arms and the size of the nucleus; a spiral galaxy of Sa type has a large nucleus and tightly wound arms, and an Sc-type galaxy consists of a small nucleus with open spiral arms. A barred spiral galaxy exhibits an elongated nucleus. The subtypes of barred spiral galaxies are determined like those of spiral galaxies. Some irregular galaxies (type I) display a loose spiral structure with high levels of disorganization. Other irregular galaxies (type II) can be of any shape.

Review Video: Galaxies
Visit mometrix.com/academy and enter code: 226539

Theories Relating to the Origin of the Universe

Model of the Inflationary Universe

Hubble's law states that the speed at which a galaxy appears to be moving away from the Earth is proportional to its distance from Earth. This relatively simple formula ($v = Hr$, where v is the **velocity of a receding galaxy**, r is its distance from Earth, and H is the Hubble constant) had an important implication at the time that it was developed—the universe is expanding. This fact, in turn, implies that the universe began at a **specific point** in the past. This model suggests that a random conglomeration of quarks and leptons, along with the strong force (all the forces in the universe unified as one), existed in the very dense, very hot, early universe. When the universe was a certain age (about 10–35 seconds old), the strong force separated out from the mass. This enabled the rapid expansion of the particles that formed the universe.

Big Bang Theory

The **theory of the big bang** expands upon the model of the **inflationary universe**. This theory hypothesizes that the early universe consisted of elementary particles, high energy density and high levels of pressure and heat. This single mass experienced a **phase change** (similar to that of freezing water) when it cooled and expanded. This transition caused the early universe to expand exponentially; this period of growth is called **cosmic inflation**. As it continued to grow, the temperature continued to fall. At some point, **baryogenesis** (an unknown process in which quarks and gluons become baryons, such as protons and neutrons) occurred, somehow creating the distinction between matter and antimatter. As the universe continued to cool, the **elementary forces** reached their present form, and **elementary particles** engaged in big bang **nucleosynthesis** (a process that produced helium and deuterium nuclei). **Gravity** became the predominant force governing interactions between particles; this enabled increasing accretion of particles of matter, which eventually formed the universal constituents as we recognize them today.

Chapter Quiz

Ready to see how well you retained what you just read? Scan the QR code to go directly to the chapter quiz interface for this study guide. If you're using a computer, simply visit the online resources page at **mometrix.com/resources719/hiset-27339** and click the Chapter Quizzes link.

Social Studies

American History

American History Pre-Columbian to 1789

Prior to European colonization, the land that would become the United States was populated by millions of Native Americans belonging to hundreds of distinct tribes. Native American societies were diverse and sophisticated, with political structures, religious beliefs, domesticated animals, agricultural practices, and trade networks. Native Americans adapted their societies and cultures to the environments in which they settled, which led to distinct cultures, beliefs, practices, and languages all across the continent.

Well-Known Native Americans

The following are five well-known Native Americans and their roles in early US history:

1. **Squanto**, an Algonquian, helped early English settlers survive the hard winter by teaching them the native methods of planting corn, squash, and pumpkins.
2. **Pocahontas**, also Algonquian, became famous as a liaison with John Smith's Jamestown colony in 1607.
3. **Sacagawea**, a Shoshone, served a vital role in the Lewis and Clark expedition when the two explorers hired her as their guide in 1805.
4. **Crazy Horse** and **Sitting Bull** led Sioux and Cheyenne troops in the Battle of the Little Bighorn in 1876, soundly defeating George Armstrong Custer.
5. **Chief Joseph**, a leader of the Nez Perce who supported peaceful interaction with white settlers, attempted to relocate his tribe to Canada rather than move them to a reservation.

Major Regional Native American Groups

The major regional Native American groups and the major traits of each are as follows:

- The **Algonquians** in the eastern part of the United States lived in wigwams. The northern tribes subsisted on hunting and gathering, while those who were farther south grew crops such as corn.
- The **Iroquois**, also an east coast tribe, spoke a different language from the Algonquians and lived in rectangular longhouses.
- The **Plains tribes** lived between the Mississippi River and the Rocky Mountains. These nomadic tribes lived in teepees and followed the buffalo herds. Plains tribes included the Sioux, Cheyenne, Comanche, and Blackfoot.
- **Pueblo tribes** included the Zuni, Hopi, and Acoma. They lived in the Southwest deserts in homes made of stone or adobe. They domesticated animals and cultivated corn and beans.
- On the Pacific coast, tribes such as the **Tlingit**, **Chinook**, and **Salish** lived on fish,deer, native berries, and roots. Their rectangular homes housed large family groups, and they used totem poles.
- In the far north, the **Aleuts** and **Inuit** lived in skin tents or igloos. Talented fishermen, they built kayaks and umiaks and also hunted caribou, seals, whales, and walrus.

Review Video: Major Regional Native American Groups
Visit mometrix.com/academy and enter code: 550136

Age of Exploration

The Age of Exploration is also called the **Age of Discovery**. It is generally considered to have begun in the early 15th century and continued into the 17th century. Major developments of the **Age of Exploration** included technological advances in navigation, mapmaking, and shipbuilding. These advances led to expanded European exploration of the rest of the world. Explorers set out from several European countries, including Portugal,

Spain, France, and England, seeking new routes to Asia. These efforts led to the discovery of new lands, as well as colonization in India, Asia, Africa, and North America.

Review Video: Age of Exploration
Visit mometrix.com/academy and enter code: 612972

Impact of Technological Advances in Navigation and Seafaring Exploration

For long ocean journeys, it was important for sailors to be able to find their way home even when their vessels sailed far out to sea. A variety of navigational tools enabled them to launch ambitious journeys over long distances. The **compass** and **astrolabe** were particularly important advancements. Chinese navigators used the magnetic compass in approximately 200 BC, and knowledge of the astrolabe came to Europe from Arab navigators and traders who had refined designs developed by the ancient Greeks. The Portuguese developed a ship called a **caravel** in the 1400s that incorporated navigational advancements with the ability to make long sea journeys. Equipped with this advanced vessel, the Portuguese achieved a major goal of the Age of Exploration by discovering a **sea route** from Europe to Asia in 1498.

Significance of Christopher Columbus's Voyage

In 1492, Columbus, a Genoan explorer, obtained financial backing from King Ferdinand and Queen Isabella of Spain to seek a sea route to Asia. He sought a trade route with the Asian Indies to the west. With three ships, the *Niña*, the *Pinta*, and the *Santa Maria*, he eventually landed in the **West Indies**. While Columbus failed in his effort to discover a western route to Asia, he is credited with the discovery of the **Americas**.

Review Video: Christopher Columbus
Visit mometrix.com/academy and enter code: 496598

French, Spanish, Dutch, and British Goals in Colonization of the Americas

France, Spain, the Netherlands, and England each had specific goals in the colonization of the Americas:

- Initial **French colonies** were focused on expanding the fur trade. Later, French colonization led to the growth of plantations in Louisiana, which brought numerous African slaves to the New World.
- **Spanish colonists** came to look for wealth and to convert the natives to Christianity. For some, the desire for gold led to mining in the New World, while others established large ranches.
- The **Dutch** were also involved in the fur trade and imported slaves as the need for laborers increased.
- **British colonists** arrived with various goals. Some were simply looking for additional income, while others were fleeing Britain to escape religious persecution.

Review Video: European Colonization of the Americas
Visit mometrix.com/academy and enter code: 438412

Interactions Between the Colonies and Native Americans

While there were examples of peaceful relations between Native Americans and European colonists, these two groups were often in conflict. The colonists constantly attempted to expand their territories and take Native American land. Native Americans often tried to stop the expansion of European colonies via war and diplomacy, both of which usually resulted in failure due to European advantages in technology and shifting alliances. Both the colonists and the Native Americans committed atrocities against the other in these conflicts. Many Native Americans captured in war were made slaves; however, the most fatal attack suffered by the Native Americans came in the form of disease. Foreign diseases like small pox ravaged through the Native American population. Some researchers estimate that up to 90% of the Native American population died as a result of foreign diseases brought to America by colonists.

NEW ENGLAND COLONIES

The New England colonies were New Hampshire, Connecticut, Rhode Island and Massachusetts. These colonies were founded largely to escape **religious persecution** in England. The beliefs of the **Puritans**, who migrated to America in the 1600s, significantly influenced the development of these colonies. Situated in the northeast coastal areas of America, the New England colonies featured numerous harbors as well as dense forests. The soil, however, was rocky and had a very short growing season, so was not well suited for agriculture. The economy of New England during the colonial period centered around fishing, shipbuilding and trade along with some small farms and lumber mills. Although some groups congregated in small farms, life centered mainly in towns and cities where **merchants** largely controlled the trade economy. Coastal cities such as Boston grew and thrived.

Review Video: The Massachusetts Bay Colony
Visit mometrix.com/academy and enter code: 407058

MIDDLE OR MIDDLE ATLANTIC COLONIES

The Middle or Middle Atlantic Colonies were New York, New Jersey, Pennsylvania, and Delaware. Unlike the New England colonies, where most colonists were from England and Scotland, the Middle Colonies founders were from various countries, including the Netherlands and Sweden. Various factors led these colonists to America. More fertile than New England, the Middle Colonies became major producers of **crops**, including rye, oats, potatoes, wheat, and barley. Some particularly wealthy inhabitants owned large farms and/or businesses. Farmers, in general, were able to produce enough to have a surplus to sell. Tenant farmers also rented land from larger landowners.

SOUTHERN COLONIES

The Southern Colonies were Maryland, Virginia, North Carolina, South Carolina, and Georgia. Of the Southern Colonies, Virginia was the first permanent English colony and Georgia the last. The warm climate and rich soil of the south encouraged **agriculture**, and the growing season was long. As a result, economy in the south was based largely on labor-intensive **plantations**. Crops included tobacco, rice, and indigo, all of which became valuable cash crops. Most land in the south was controlled by wealthy plantation owners and farmers. Labor on the farms came in the form of indentured servants and African slaves. The first of these **African slaves** arrived in Virginia in 1619.

Review Video: The Southern Colonies
Visit mometrix.com/academy and enter code: 703830

Review Video: The English Colony of Virginia
Visit mometrix.com/academy and enter code: 537399

SIGNIFICANCE OF THE FRENCH AND INDIAN WARS

The **British defeat of the Spanish Armada** in 1588 led to the decline of Spanish power in Europe. This, in turn, led the British and French into battle several times between 1689 and 1748. These wars were:

- King William's War, or the Nine Years War, 1689-1697. This war was fought largely in Flanders.
- The War of Spanish Succession, or Queen Anne's War, 1702-1713
- War of Austrian Succession, or King George's War, 1740-1748

The fourth and final war, the **French and Indian War** (1754-1763), was fought largely in the North American territory and resulted in the end of France's reign as a colonial power in North America. Although the French held many advantages, including more cooperative colonists and numerous Native American allies, the strong leadership of **William Pitt** eventually led the British to victory. Costs incurred during the wars eventually led to discontent in the colonies and helped spark the **American Revolution**.

Review Video: French and Indian Wars
Visit mometrix.com/academy and enter code: 502183

Navigation Acts

The Navigation Acts, enacted in 1651, were an attempt by Britain to dominate international trade. Aimed largely at the Dutch, the acts banned foreign ships from transporting goods to the British colonies and from transporting goods to Britain from elsewhere in Europe. While the restrictions on trade angered some colonists, these acts were helpful to other American colonists who, as members of the British Empire, were legally able to provide ships for Britain's growing trade interests and use the ships for their own trading ventures. By the time the French and Indian War had ended, one-third of British merchant ships were built in the American colonies. Many colonists amassed fortunes in the shipbuilding trade.

Acts of British Parliament that Occurred After the French and Indian Wars

After the French and Indian Wars, the British Parliament passed four major acts:

1. The **Sugar Act**, 1764—this act not only required taxes to be collected on molasses brought into the colonies but gave British officials the right to search the homes of anyone suspected of violating it.
2. The **Stamp Act**, 1765—this act taxed printed materials such as newspapers and legal documents. Protests led the Stamp Act to be repealed in 1766, but the repeal also included the Declaratory Act, which stated that Parliament had the right to govern the colonies.
3. The **Quartering Act**, 1765—this act required colonists to provide accommodations and supplies for British troops. In addition, colonists were prohibited from settling west of the Appalachians until given permission by Britain.
4. The **Townshend Acts**, 1767—these acts taxed paper, paint, lead, and tea that came into the colonies. Colonists led boycotts in protest, and in Massachusetts leaders like Samuel and John Adams began to organize resistance against British rule.

Britain's Taxation of the American Colonies After the French and Indian War

The French and Indian War created circumstances for which the British desperately needed more revenue. These needs included:

- Paying off the war debt
- Defending the expanding empire
- Governing Britain's 33 far-flung colonies, including the American colonies

To meet these needs, the British passed additional laws, increasing revenues from the colonies. Because they had spent so much money to defend the American colonies, the British felt it was appropriate to collect considerably higher **taxes** from them. The colonists felt this was unfair, and many were led to protest the increasing taxes. Eventually, protest led to violence.

Triangular Trade

Triangular trade began in the colonies with ships setting off for **Africa**, carrying rum. In Africa, the rum was traded for gold or slaves. Ships then went from Africa to the **West Indies**, trading slaves for sugar, molasses, or money. To complete the triangle, the ships returned to the **colonies** with sugar or molasses to make more rum, as well as stores of gold and silver. This trade triangle violated the Molasses Act of 1733, which required the colonists to pay high duties to Britain on molasses acquired from French, Dutch, and Spanish colonies. The colonists ignored these duties, and the British government adopted a policy of salutary neglect by not enforcing them.

Review Video: The Triangular Trade
Visit mometrix.com/academy and enter code: 415470

Effects of New Laws on British-Colonial Relations

While earlier revenue-generating acts such as the Navigation Acts brought money to the colonists, the new laws after 1763 required colonists to pay money back to **Britain**. The British felt this was fair since the colonists were British subjects and since they had incurred debt protecting the Colonies. The colonists felt it was not only unfair but illegal.

The development of **local government** in America had given the colonists a different view of the structure and role of government. This made it difficult for the British to understand the colonists' protests against what the British felt was a fair and reasonable solution to the mother country's financial problems.

Factors That Led to Increasing Discontent in the American Colonies

More and more colonists were born on American soil, decreasing any sense of kinship with the far-away British rulers. Their new environment had led to new ideas of government and a strong view of the colonies as a separate entity from Britain. Colonists were allowed to **self-govern** in domestic issues, but **Britain** controlled international issues. In fact, the American colonies were largely left to form their own local government bodies, giving them more freedom than any other colonial territory. This gave the colonists a sense of **independence**, which led them to resent control from Britain. Threats during the French and Indian War led the colonists to call for unification in order to protect themselves.

Colonial and British Government Differences That Caused Tension

As new towns and other legislative districts developed in America, the colonists began to practice **representative government**. Colonial legislative bodies were made up of elected representatives chosen by male property owners in the districts. These individuals represented the interests of the districts from which they had been elected.

By contrast, in Britain, the **Parliament** represented the entire country. Parliament was not elected to represent individual districts. Instead, they represented specific classes. Because of this drastically different approach to government, the British did not understand the colonists' statement that they had no representation in the British Parliament.

Factors That Led to the Boston Massacre

With the passage of the **Stamp Act**, nine colonies met in New York to demand its repeal. Elsewhere, protest arose in New York City, Philadelphia, Boston, and other cities. These protests sometimes escalated into violence, often targeting ruling British officials. The passage of the **Townshend Acts** in 1767 led to additional tension in the colonies. The British sent troops to New York City and Boston. On March 5, 1770, protesters began to taunt the British troops, throwing snowballs. The soldiers responded by firing into the crowd. This clash between protesters and soldiers led to five deaths and eight injuries, and was christened the **Boston Massacre**. Shortly thereafter, Britain repealed the majority of the Townshend Acts.

Tea Act That Led to the Boston Tea Party

The majority of the **Townshend Acts** were repealed after the Boston Massacre in 1770, but Britain kept the tax on tea. In 1773, the **Tea Act** was passed. This allowed the East India Company to sell tea for much lower prices and also allowed them to bypass American distributors, selling directly to shopkeepers instead. Colonial tea merchants saw this as a direct assault on their business. In December of 1773, the **Sons of Liberty** boarded ships in Boston Harbor and dumped 342 chests of tea into the sea in protest of the new laws. This act of protest came to be known as the **Boston Tea Party**.

COERCIVE ACTS PASSED AFTER THE BOSTON TEA PARTY

The Coercive Acts passed by Britain in 1774 were meant to punish Massachusetts for defying British authority. These became collectively known as the **Intolerable Acts** in the colonies and mandated the following:

- Shut down ports in Boston until the city paid back the value of the tea destroyed during the Boston Tea Party
- Required that local government officials in Massachusetts be appointed by the governor rather than being elected by the people
- Allowed trials of British soldiers to be transferred to Britain rather than being held in Massachusetts
- Required locals to provide lodging for British soldiers any time there was a disturbance, even if lodging required them to stay in private homes

These acts led to the assembly of the First Continental Congress in Philadelphia on September 5, 1774. Fifty-five delegates met, representing 12 of the American colonies. They sought compromise with England over England's increasingly harsh efforts to control the colonies.

FIRST CONTINENTAL CONGRESS

The goal of the First Continental Congress was to achieve a peaceful agreement with Britain. Made up of delegates from 12 of the 13 colonies, the Congress affirmed loyalty to Britain and the power of Parliament to dictate foreign affairs in the colonies. However, they demanded that the **Intolerable Acts** be repealed, and instituted a trade embargo with Britain until this came to pass.

In response, George III of England declared that the American colonies must submit or face military action. The British sought to end assemblies that opposed their policies. These assemblies gathered weapons and began to form militias. On April 19, 1775, the British military was ordered to disperse a meeting of the Massachusetts Assembly. A battle ensued on Lexington Common as the armed colonists resisted. The resulting battles became the **Battle of Lexington and Concord**—the first battles of the **American Revolution**.

SIGNIFICANCE OF THE SECOND CONTINENTAL CONGRESS

The Second Continental Congress met in Philadelphia on May 10, 1775, a month after Lexington and Concord. Their discussions centered on the defense of the American colonies and how to conduct the growing war, as well as local government. The delegates also discussed declaring independence from Britain, with many members in favor of this drastic move. They established an army, and on June 15, named **George Washington** as its commander in chief. By 1776, it was obvious that there was no turning back from full-scale war with Britain. The colonial delegates of the Continental Congress signed the **Declaration of Independence** on July 4, 1776.

Review Video: The First and Second Continental Congress
Visit mometrix.com/academy and enter code: 835211

ORIGINS AND BASIC IDEAS OF THE DECLARATION OF INDEPENDENCE

Penned by Thomas Jefferson and signed on July 4, 1776, the **Declaration of Independence** stated that King George III had violated the rights of the colonists and was establishing a tyrannical reign over them. Many of Jefferson's ideas of natural rights and property rights were shaped by 17th-century philosopher **John Locke**. Jefferson asserted all people's rights to "life, liberty and the pursuit of happiness." Locke's comparable idea asserted "life, liberty, and private property." Both felt that the purpose of government was to protect the rights of the people, and that individual rights were more important than individuals' obligations to the state.

Review Video: Declaration of Independence
Visit mometrix.com/academy and enter code: 256838

Battles of the Revolutionary War

The following are five major battles of the Revolutionary War and their significance:

- The **Battle of Lexington and Concord** (April 1775) is considered the first engagement of the Revolutionary War.
- The **Battle of Bunker Hill** (June 1775) was one of the bloodiest of the entire war. Although American troops withdrew, about half of the British army was lost. The colonists proved they could stand against professional British soldiers. In August, Britain declared that the American colonies were officially in a state of rebellion.
- The first colonial victory occurred in Trenton, New Jersey, when Washington and his troops **crossed the Delaware River** on Christmas Day, 1776, for a December 26 surprise attack on British and Hessian troops.
- The **Battle of Saratoga** effectively ended a plan to separate the New England colonies from their Southern counterparts. The surrender of British general John Burgoyne led to France joining the war as allies of the Americans and is generally considered a turning point of the war.
- On October 19, 1781, General Cornwallis surrendered after a defeat in the **Battle of Yorktown**, ending the Revolutionary War.

Review Video: The American Revolutionary War
Visit mometrix.com/academy and enter code: 935282

Significance of the Treaty of Paris

The Treaty of Paris was signed on September 3, 1783, bringing an official end to the Revolutionary War. In this document, Britain officially recognized the United States of America as an **independent nation**. The treaty established the Mississippi River as the country's western border. The treaty also restored Florida to Spain, while France reclaimed African and Caribbean colonies seized by the British in 1763. On November 25, 1783, the last British troops departed from the newly born United States of America.

Significance of the Articles of Confederation

A precursor to the Constitution, the **Articles of Confederation** represented the first attempt of the newly independent colonies to establish the basics of government. The Continental Congress approved the Articles on November 15, 1777. They went into effect on March 1, 1781, following ratification by the thirteen states. The articles prevented a central government from gaining too much power, instead giving power to a **congressional body** made up of **delegates** from all thirteen states. However, the individual states retained final authority.

Without a strong central **executive**, though, this weak alliance among the new states proved ineffective in settling disputes or enforcing laws. The idea of a weak central government needed to be revised. Recognition of these weaknesses eventually led to the drafting of a new document, the **Constitution**.

Review Video: Articles of Confederation
Visit mometrix.com/academy and enter code: 927401

Initial Proposition and Draft of the Constitution

Delegates from twelve of the thirteen states (Rhode Island was not represented) met in Philadelphia in May of 1787, initially intending to revise the Articles of Confederation. However, it quickly became apparent that a simple revision would not provide the workable governmental structure the newly formed country needed. After vowing to keep all the proceedings secret until the final document was completed, the delegates set out to draft what would eventually become the **Constitution of the United States of America**. By keeping the negotiations secret, the delegates were able to present a completed document to the country for ratification, rather than having every small detail hammered out by the general public.

General Structure of Government Proposed by the Delegates

The delegates agreed that the new nation required a **strong central government** but that its overall power should be **limited**. The various branches of the government should have **balanced power**, so that no one group could control the others. Final power belonged to the **citizens** who voted officials into office based on who would provide the best representation.

Objections Against the Constitution

Once the Constitution was drafted, it was presented for approval by the states. Nine states needed to approve the document for it to become official. However, debate and discussion continued. Major **concerns** included:

- There was no bill of rights to protect individual freedoms.
- States felt too much power was being handed over to the central government.
- Voters wanted more control over their elected representatives.

Discussion about necessary changes to the Constitution was divided into two camps: Federalists and Anti-Federalists. **Federalists** wanted a strong central government. **Anti-Federalists** wanted to prevent a tyrannical government from developing if a central government held too much power

Major Players in the Federalist and Anti-Federalist camps

Major Federalist leaders included Alexander Hamilton, John Jay, and James Madison. They wrote a series of letters, called the **Federalist Papers**, aimed at convincing the states to ratify the Constitution. These were published in New York papers. Anti-Federalists included Thomas Jefferson and Patrick Henry. They argued against the Constitution as it was originally drafted in a series of **Anti-Federalist Papers**.

The final compromise produced a strong central government controlled by checks and balances. A **Bill of Rights** was also added, becoming the first ten amendments to the Constitution. These amendments protected rights such as freedom of speech, freedom of religion, and other basic rights. Aside from various amendments added throughout the years, the United States Constitution has remained unchanged.

Individuals Who Formed the First Administration of the New Government

The individuals who formed the first administration of the new government were:

- **George Washington**—elected as the first President of the United States in 1789
- **John Adams**—finished second in the election and became the first Vice President
- **Thomas Jefferson**—appointed by Washington as Secretary of State
- **Alexander Hamilton**—appointed Secretary of the Treasury

The Virginia Plan, the New Jersey Plan, and the Great Compromise

Disagreement immediately occurred between delegates from large states and those from smaller states. James Madison and Edmund Randolph (the governor of Virginia) felt that representation in Congress should be based on state population. This was the **Virginia Plan**. The **New Jersey Plan**, presented by William Paterson from New Jersey, proposed that each state should have equal representation. Finally, Roger Sherman from Connecticut formulated the **Connecticut Compromise**, also called the Great Compromise. The result was the familiar structure we have today. Each state has the equal representation of two Senators in the Senate, with the number of representatives in the House of Representatives based on population. This is called a **bicameral congress**. Both houses may draft bills, but financial matters must originate in the House of Representatives.

The Three-fifths Compromise and Number of Representatives for Each State

During debate on the US Constitution, a disagreement arose between the Northern and Southern states involving how **slaves** should be counted when determining a state's quota of representatives. In the South, large numbers of slaves were commonly used to run plantations. Delegates wanted slaves to be counted to determine the number of representatives but not counted to determine the amount of taxes the states would pay. The Northern states wanted exactly the opposite arrangement. The final decision was to count three-fifths of the slave population both for tax purposes and to determine representation. This was called the **Three-fifths Compromise**.

Provisions of the Commerce Compromise

The Commerce Compromise also resulted from a North/South disagreement. In the North, the economy was centered on **industry and trade**. The Southern economy was largely **agricultural**. The Northern states wanted to give the new government the ability to regulate exports as well as trade between the states. The South opposed this plan. Another compromise was in order. In the end, Congress received regulatory power over all trade, including the ability to collect **tariffs** on exported goods. In the South, this raised another red flag regarding the slave trade, as they were concerned about the effect on their economy if tariffs were levied on slaves. The final agreement allowed importing slaves to continue for twenty years without government intervention. Import taxes on slaves were limited, and after the year 1808, Congress could decide whether to allow continued imports of slaves.

American History 1790 to 1898

Alien and Sedition Acts

When **John Adams** became president, a war was raging between Britain and France. While Adams and the Federalists backed the British, Thomas Jefferson and the Democratic-Republican Party supported the French. The United States nearly went to war with France during this time period, while France worked to spread its international standing and influence under the leadership of **Napoleon Bonaparte**. The **Alien and Sedition Acts** grew out of this conflict and made it illegal to speak in a hostile fashion against the existing government. They also allowed the president to deport anyone in the US who was not a citizen and who was suspected of treason or treasonous activity. When Jefferson became the third president in 1800, he repealed these four laws and pardoned anyone who had been convicted under them.

Development of Political Parties in Early US Government

Many in the US were against political parties after seeing the way parties, or factions, functioned in Britain. The factions in Britain were more interested in personal profit than the overall good of the country, and they did not want this to happen in the US.

However, the differences of opinion between Thomas Jefferson and Alexander Hamilton led to the formation of **political parties**. Hamilton favored a stronger central government, while Jefferson felt that more power should remain with the states. Jefferson was in favor of strict Constitutional interpretation, while Hamilton believed in a more flexible approach. As others joined the two camps, Hamilton backers began to call themselves **Federalists**, while those supporting Jefferson became identified as **Democratic-Republicans**.

Development of the Whig, the Democratic, and the Republican Parties

Thomas Jefferson was elected president in 1800 and again in 1804. The **Federalist Party** began to decline, and its major figure, Alexander Hamilton, died in a duel with Aaron Burr in 1804. By 1816, the Federalist Party had virtually disappeared.

New parties sprang up to take its place. After 1824, the **Democratic-Republican Party** suffered a split. The **Whigs** rose, backing John Quincy Adams and industrial growth. The new Democratic Party formed in opposition to the Whigs, and their candidate, Andrew Jackson, was elected as president in 1828.

By the 1850s, issues regarding slavery led to the formation of the **Republican Party**, which was anti-slavery, while the Democratic Party, with a larger interest in the South, favored slavery. This Republican/Democrat division formed the basis of today's **two-party system**.

SIGNIFICANCE OF MARBURY V. MADISON

The main duty of the Supreme Court today is **judicial review**. This power was largely established by **Marbury v. Madison**. When John Adams was voted out of office in 1800, he worked during his final days in office to appoint Federalist judges to Supreme Court positions, knowing Jefferson, his replacement, held opposing views. As late as March 3, the day before Jefferson was to take office, Adams made last-minute appointments referred to as "Midnight Judges." One of the late appointments was William Marbury. The next day, March 4, Jefferson ordered his Secretary of State, James Madison, not to deliver Marbury's commission. This decision was backed by Chief Justice Marshall, who determined that the **Judiciary Act of 1789**, which granted the power to deliver commissions, was illegal in that it gave the Judicial Branch powers not granted in the Constitution. This case set precedent for the Supreme Court to nullify laws it found to be **unconstitutional**.

Review Video: Marbury v Madison
Visit mometrix.com/academy and enter code: 573964

POLITICAL MOTIVATIONS BEHIND FRANCE SELLING THE LOUISIANA PURCHASE

With tension still high between France and Britain, Napoleon was in need of money to support his continuing war efforts. To secure necessary funds, he decided to sell the **Louisiana Territory** to the US. President **Thomas Jefferson** wanted to buy New Orleans, feeling US trade was made vulnerable to both Spain and France at that port. Instead, Napoleon sold him the entire territory for the bargain price of $15 million. The Louisiana Territory was larger than all the rest of the United States put together, and it eventually became 15 additional states.

Federalists in Congress were opposed to the purchase. They feared that the Louisiana Purchase would extend slavery, and that further western growth would weaken the power of the northern states.

LEWIS AND CLARK EXPEDITION

The purchase of the **Louisiana Territory** from France in 1803 more than doubled the size of the United States. President Thomas Jefferson wanted to have the area mapped and explored, since much of the territory was wilderness. He chose Meriwether Lewis and William Clark to head an expedition into the Louisiana Territory. After two years, Lewis and Clark returned, having traveled all the way to the Pacific Ocean. They brought maps, detailed journals, and a multitude of information about the wide expanse of land they had traversed. The **Lewis and Clark Expedition** opened up the west in the Louisiana Territory and beyond for further exploration and settlement.

Review Video: Purpose of the Lewis and Clark Expedition
Visit mometrix.com/academy and enter code: 570657

CAUSES AND RESULT OF THE WAR OF 1812

The War of 1812 grew out of the continuing tension between France and Great Britain. Napoleon continued striving to conquer Britain, while the US continued trade with both countries but favored France and the French colonies. Because of what Britain saw as an alliance between America and France, they determined to bring an end to trade between the two nations.

With the British preventing US trade with the French and the French preventing trade with the British, James Madison's presidency introduced acts to **regulate international trade**. If either Britain or France removed their restrictions, America would not trade with the other country. Napoleon acted first, and Madison prohibited trade with England. England saw this as the US formally siding with the French, and war ensued in 1812.

The **War of 1812** has been called the **Second American Revolution**. It established the superiority of the US naval forces and reestablished US independence from Britain and Europe.

The British had two major objections to America's continued trade with France. First, they saw the US as helping France's war effort by providing supplies and goods. Second, the United States had grown into a competitor, taking trade and money away from British ships and tradesmen. In its attempts to end American trade with France, the British put into effect the **Orders in Council**, which made any and all French-owned ports off-limits to American ships. They also began to seize American ships and conscript their crews.

Review Video: Overview of the War of 1812
Visit mometrix.com/academy and enter code: 507716

Review Video: Opinions About the War of 1812
Visit mometrix.com/academy and enter code: 274558

Major Military Events of the War of 1812

Two major naval battles, at **Lake Erie** and **Lake Champlain**, kept the British from invading the US via Canada. American attempts to conquer Canadian lands were not successful.

In another memorable British attack, the British invaded Washington, DC and burned the White House on August 24, 1814. Legend has it that **Dolley Madison**, the First Lady, salvaged the portrait of George Washington from the fire. On Christmas Eve, 1814, the **Treaty of Ghent** officially ended the war. However, Andrew Jackson, unaware that the war was over, managed another victory at New Orleans on January 8, 1815. This victory improved American morale and led to a new wave of national pride and support known as the "**Era of Good Feelings**."

Influence of the American System on American Economics

Spurred by the trade conflicts of the War of 1812 and supported by Henry Clay among others, the **American System** set up tariffs to help protect American interests from competition with overseas products. Reducing competition led to growth in employment and an overall increase in American industry. The higher tariffs also provided funds for the government to pay for various improvements. Congress passed high tariffs in 1816 and also chartered a federal bank. The **Second Bank of the United States** was given the job of regulating America's money supply.

McCulloch v. Maryland

Judicial review was further exercised by the Supreme Court in **McCulloch v. Maryland**. When Congress chartered a national bank, the **Second Bank of the United States**, Maryland voted to tax any bank business dealing with banks chartered outside the state, including the federally chartered bank. Andrew McCulloch, an employee of the Second Bank of the US in Baltimore, refused to pay this tax. The resulting lawsuit from the State of Maryland went to the Supreme Court for judgment.

John Marshall, Chief Justice of the Supreme Court, stated that Congress was within its rights to charter a national bank. In addition, the State of Maryland did not have the power to levy a tax on the federal bank or on the federal government in general. In cases where state and federal government collided, precedent was set for the **federal government** to prevail.

Effects of the Missouri Compromise on the Tensions Between the North and South

By 1819, the United States had developed a tenuous balance between slave and free states, with exactly 22 senators in Congress from each faction. However, Missouri was ready to join the union. As a slave state, it would tip the balance in Congress. To prevent this imbalance, the **Missouri Compromise** brought the northern part of Massachusetts into the union as Maine, establishing it as a free state to balance the admission of Missouri as a slave state. In addition, the remaining portion of the Louisiana Purchase was to remain free north of **latitude 36°30'**. Since cotton did not grow well this far north, this limitation was acceptable to congressmen representing the slave states.

However, the proposed Missouri constitution presented a problem, as it outlawed immigration of free blacks into the state. Another compromise was in order, this time proposed by **Henry Clay**. According to this new compromise, Missouri would never pass a law that prevented anyone from entering the state. Through this and other work, Clay earned his title of the "**Great Compromiser**."

Review Video: The Missouri Compromise
Visit mometrix.com/academy and enter code: 848091

MONROE DOCTRINE

On December 2, 1823, President Monroe delivered a message to Congress in which he introduced the **Monroe Doctrine**. In this address, he stated that any attempts by European powers to establish new colonies on the North American continent would be considered interference in American politics. The US would stay out of European matters, and expected Europe to offer America the same courtesy. This approach to foreign policy stated in no uncertain terms that America would not tolerate any new European colonies in the New World, and that events occurring in Europe would no longer influence the policies and doctrines of the US.

Review Video: What was the Monroe Doctrine?
Visit mometrix.com/academy and enter code: 953021

EFFECT OF THE TREATY OF PARIS ON NATIVE AMERICANS

After the Revolutionary War, the **Treaty of Paris**, which outlined the terms of surrender of the British to the Americans, granted large parcels of land to the US that were occupied by Native Americans. The new government attempted to claim the land, treating the natives as a conquered people. This approach proved unenforceable.

Next, the government tried purchasing the land from the Native Americans via a series of **treaties** as the country expanded westward. In practice, however, these treaties were not honored, and Native Americans were simply dislocated and forced to move farther and farther west, often with military action, as American expansion continued.

INDIAN REMOVAL ACT OF 1830 AND THE TREATY OF NEW ECHOTA

The Indian Removal Act of 1830 gave the new American government power to form treaties with Native Americans. In theory, America would claim land east of the Mississippi in exchange for land west of the Mississippi, to which the natives would relocate voluntarily. In practice, many tribal leaders were forced into signing the treaties, and relocation at times occurred by force.

The **Treaty of New Echota** in 1835 was supposedly a treaty between the US government and Cherokee tribes in Georgia. However, the treaty was not signed by tribal leaders but rather by a small portion of the represented people. The leaders protested and refused to leave, but President Martin Van Buren enforced the treaty by sending soldiers. During their forced relocation, more than 4,000 Cherokees died on what became known as the **Trail of Tears**.

Review Video: Indian Removal Act
Visit mometrix.com/academy and enter code: 666738

JACKSONIAN DEMOCRACY VS. PRECEDING POLITICAL CLIMATE

Jacksonian Democracy is largely seen as a shift from politics favoring the wealthy to politics favoring the common man. The right to vote was given to all free white males, not just property owners, as had been the case previously. Jackson's approach favored the patronage system, laissez-faire economics, and relocation of the Native American tribes from the Southeast portion of the country. Jackson opposed the formation of a federal bank and allowed the Second Bank of the United States to collapse by vetoing a bill to renew the charter. Jackson also faced the challenge of the **Nullification Crisis** when South Carolina claimed that it could ignore or nullify any federal law it considered unconstitutional. Jackson sent troops to the state to enforce the protested tariff laws, and a compromise engineered by Henry Clay in 1833 settled the matter for the time being.

Second Great Awakening

Led by Protestant evangelical leaders, the **Second Great Awakening** occurred between 1800 and 1830. Several missionary groups grew out of the movement, including the **American Home Missionary Society**, which formed in 1826. The ideas behind the Second Great Awakening focused on personal responsibility, both as an individual and in response to injustice and suffering. The **American Bible Society** and the **American Tract Society** provided literature, while various traveling preachers spread the word. New denominations arose, including the Latter-day Saints and Seventh-day Adventists.

Another movement associated with the Second Great Awakening was the **temperance movement**, focused on ending the production and use of alcohol. One major organization behind the temperance movement was the **Society for the Promotion of Temperance**, formed in 1826 in Boston.

Attitudes Toward Education in the Early 19th Century

Horace Mann, among others, felt that schools could help children become better citizens, keep them away from crime, prevent poverty, and help American society become more unified. His *Common School Journal* brought his ideas of the importance of education into the public consciousness and proposed his suggestions for an improved American education system. Increased literacy led to increased awareness of current events, Western expansion, and other major developments of the time period. Public interest and participation in the arts and literature also increased. By the end of the 19th century, all children had access to a **free public elementary education**.

Development of Economic Trends as the US Continued to Grow

In the Northeast, the economy mostly depended on **manufacturing, industry, and industrial development**. This led to a dichotomy between rich business owners and industrial leaders and the much poorer workers who supported their businesses. The South continued to depend on **agriculture**, especially on large-scale farms or plantations worked mostly by slaves and indentured servants. In the West, where new settlements had begun to develop, the land was largely wild. Growing communities were essentially **agricultural**, raising crops and livestock. The differences between regions led each to support different interests both politically and economically.

Industrial Activity Before and After 1800

During the 18th century, goods were often manufactured in houses or small shops. With increased technology allowing for the use of machines, **factories** began to develop. In factories, a large volume of salable goods could be produced in a much shorter amount of time. Many Americans, including increasing numbers of **immigrants**, found jobs in these factories, which were in constant need of labor. Another major invention was the **cotton gin**, which significantly decreased the processing time of cotton and was a major factor in the rapid expansion of cotton production in the South.

Development of Labor Movements in the 1800s

In 1751, a group of bakers held a protest in which they stopped baking bread. This was technically the first American **labor strike**. In the 1830s and 1840s, labor movements began in earnest. Boston's masons, carpenters, and stoneworkers protested the length of the workday, fighting to reduce it to ten hours. In 1844, a group of women in the textile industry also fought to reduce their workday to ten hours, forming the **Lowell Female Labor Reform Association**. Many other protests occurred and organizations developed through this time period with the same goal in mind.

MAJOR IDEAS DRIVING AMERICAN FOREIGN POLICY

The three major ideas driving American foreign policy during its early years were:

- **Isolationism**—the early US government did not intend to establish colonies, though they did plan to grow larger within the bounds of North America.
- **No entangling alliances**—both George Washington and Thomas Jefferson were opposed to forming any permanent alliances with other countries or becoming involved in other countries' internal issues.
- **Nationalism**—a positive patriotic feeling about the United States blossomed quickly among its citizens, particularly after the War of 1812, when the US once again defeated Britain. The Industrial Revolution also sparked increased nationalism by allowing even the most far-flung areas of the US to communicate with each other via telegraph and the expanding railroad.

EFFECTS OF MANIFEST DESTINY ON AMERICAN POLITICS

In the 1800s, many believed America was destined by God to expand west, bringing as much of the North American continent as possible under the umbrella of the US government. With the Northwest Ordinance and the Louisiana Purchase, over half of the continent became American. However, the rapid and relentless expansion brought conflict with the Native Americans, Great Britain, Mexico, and Spain. One result of "**Manifest Destiny**" was the **Mexican-American War** from 1846 to 1848. By the end of the war, Texas, California, and a large portion of what is now the American Southwest joined the growing nation. Conflict also arose over the **Oregon Territory**, shared by the US and Britain. In 1846, President James Polk resolved this problem by compromising with Britain, establishing a US boundary south of the 49th parallel.

Review Video: Manifest Destiny
Visit mometrix.com/academy and enter code: 957409

MEXICAN-AMERICAN WAR

Spain had held colonial interests in America since the 1540s—earlier even than Great Britain. In 1810, **Mexico** revolted against Spain, becoming a free nation in 1821. **Texas** followed suit, declaring its independence after an 1836 revolution. In 1844, the Democrats pressed President Tyler to annex Texas. Unlike his predecessor, Andrew Jackson, Tyler agreed to admit Texas into the Union, and in 1845, Texas became a state.

During Mexico's war for independence, the nation incurred $4.5 million in war debts to the US. Newly elected James K. Polk offered to forgive the debts in return for New Mexico and Upper California, but Mexico refused. In 1846, war was declared in response to a Mexican attack on American troops that President Polk had moved into a disputed zone between the Rio Grande and Nueces River. As US victory grew more certain, dispute arose over how to handle slavery in any newly acquired territory. The **Wilmot Proviso**, though it was never passed, was a large source of contention, as it aimed to prohibit slavery in any territory acquired from Mexico—sowing further seeds of tension between the North and the South. The Mexican-American War ended in 1848 with Mexico agreeing to sell California and its remaining territory north of the Rio Grande.

Review Video: The Mexican-American War
Visit mometrix.com/academy and enter code: 271216

Review Video: Sectional Crisis: The Wilmot Proviso
Visit mometrix.com/academy and enter code: 974842

POPULAR SOVEREIGNTY AND THE COMPROMISE OF 1850

In addition to the pro-slavery and anti-slavery factions, a third group rose, who felt that each individual state should decide whether to allow or permit slavery within its borders. The idea that a state could make its own choices was referred to as **popular sovereignty**.

When California applied to join the union in 1849, the balance of congressional power was again threatened. The **Compromise of 1850** introduced a group of laws meant to bring an end to the conflict:

- California's admittance as a free state
- The outlaw of the slave trade in Washington, DC
- An increase in efforts to capture escaped slaves
- The right of New Mexico and Utah territories to decide individually whether to allow slavery

In spite of these measures, debate raged each time a new state prepared to enter the union.

Gadsden Purchase and the 1853 Post-War Treaty with Mexico

After the Mexican-American war, a **second treaty** in 1853 determined hundreds of miles of America's southwest borders. In 1854, the **Gadsden Purchase** was finalized, providing even more territory to aid in the building of the transcontinental railroad. This purchase added what would eventually become the southernmost regions of Arizona and New Mexico to the growing nation. The modern outline of the United States was by this time nearly complete.

Kansas-Nebraska Act Trigger of Additional Conflict

With the creation of the Kansas and Nebraska territories in 1854, another debate began. Congress allowed popular sovereignty in these territories, but slavery opponents argued that the Missouri Compromise had already made slavery illegal in this region. In Kansas, two separate governments arose, one pro-slavery and one anti-slavery. Conflict between the two factions rose to violence, leading Kansas to gain the nickname of "**Bleeding Kansas.**"

Review Video: Sectional Crisis: The Kansas-Nebraska Act
Visit mometrix.com/academy and enter code: 982119

Early Leaders in the Women's Rights Movement

The women's rights movement began in the 1840s, with leaders including Elizabeth Cady Stanton, Sojourner Truth, Ernestine Rose, and Lucretia Mott. In 1869, Elizabeth Cady Stanton and Susan B. Anthony formed the **National Woman Suffrage Association**, fighting for women's right to vote.

In 1848, in Seneca Falls, the first women's rights convention was held, with about 300 attendees. The two-day **Seneca Falls Convention** discussed the rights of women to vote (suffrage) as well as equal treatment in careers, legal proceedings, etc. The convention produced a "Declaration of Sentiments," which outlined a plan for women to attain the rights they deserved. **Frederick Douglass** supported the women's rights movement, as well as the abolition movement. In fact, women's rights and abolition movements often went hand-in-hand during this time period.

Review Video: The Women's Rights Movement in America
Visit mometrix.com/academy and enter code: 987734

Events and Developments that Brought the North and South into Conflict

The conflict between the North and South coalesced around the issue of **slavery**, but other elements contributed to the growing disagreement. Though most farmers in the South worked small farms with little or no slave labor, the huge plantations run by the South's rich depended on slaves or indentured servants to remain profitable. They had also become more dependent on **cotton**, with slave populations growing in concert with the rapid increase in cotton production. In the North, a more diverse agricultural economy and the growth of **industry** made slaves rarer. The **abolitionist movement** grew steadily, with Harriet Beecher Stowe's *Uncle Tom's Cabin* giving many an idea to rally around. A collection of anti-slavery organizations formed, with many actively working to free slaves in the South, often bringing them to the northern states or Canada.

Dred Scott Decision

Abolitionist factions coalesced around the case of **Dred Scott**, using his case to test the country's laws regarding slavery. Scott, a slave, had been taken by his owner from Missouri, which was a slave state. He then traveled to Illinois, a free state, then on to the Minnesota Territory, also free based on the Missouri Compromise. After several years, he returned to Missouri, and his owner subsequently died. Abolitionists took Scott's case to court, stating that Scott was no longer a slave but free, since he had lived in free territory. The case went to the Supreme Court.

The Supreme Court stated that, because Scott, as a slave, was not a US citizen, his time in free states did not change his status. He also did not have the right to sue. In addition, the Court determined that the **Missouri Compromise** was unconstitutional, stating that Congress had overstepped its bounds by outlawing slavery in the territories.

Review Video: The Dred Scott Act
Visit mometrix.com/academy and enter code: 364838

Anti-Slavery Organizations

Five anti-slavery organizations and their significance are:

- **American Colonization Society**—Protestant churches formed this group, aimed at returning black slaves to Africa. Former slaves subsequently formed Liberia, but the colony did not do well, as the region was not well-suited for agriculture.
- **American Anti-Slavery Society**—William Lloyd Garrison, a Quaker, was the major force behind this group and its newspaper, *The Liberator*.
- **Philadelphia Female Anti-Slavery Society**—this women-only group was formed by Margaretta Forten because women were not allowed to join the Anti-Slavery Society formed by her father.
- **Anti-Slavery Convention of American Women**—this group continued meeting even after pro-slavery factions burned down their original meeting place.
- **Female Vigilant Society**—this organization raised funds to help the Underground Railroad, as well as slave refugees.

Incidents at Harper's Ferry and John Brown's Role

John Brown, an abolitionist, had participated in several anti-slavery activities, including killing five pro-slavery men in retaliation, after the sacking of Lawrence, Kansas, an anti-slavery town. He and other abolitionists also banded together to pool their funds and build a runaway slave colony.

In 1859, Brown seized a federal arsenal in **Harper's Ferry**, located in what is now West Virginia. Brown intended to seize guns and ammunition and lead a slave rebellion. **Robert E. Lee** captured Brown and 21 followers, who were subsequently tried and hanged. While Northerners took the executions as an indication that the government supported slavery, Southerners were of the opinion that most of the North supported Brown and were, in general, anti-slavery.

Presidential Candidates for the 1860 Election

The 1860 presidential candidates represented four different parties, each with a different opinion on slavery:

- **John Breckinridge**, representing the Southern Democrats, was pro-slavery but urged compromise to preserve the Union.
- **Abraham Lincoln**, of the Republican Party, was anti-slavery.
- **Stephen Douglas**, of the Northern Democrats, felt that the issue should be determined locally, on a state-by-state basis.
- **John Bell**, of the Constitutional Union Party, focused primarily on keeping the Union intact.

In the end, Abraham Lincoln won both the popular and electoral election. Southern states, who had sworn to secede from the Union if Lincoln was elected, did so, led by South Carolina and followed by the rest of the Deep South (Mississippi, Alabama, Georgia, Louisiana, Florida, and Texas). These states established the **Confederate States of America**, with its capital in Montgomery, Alabama. The president of the CSA was **Jefferson Davis**. Outgoing US President Buchanan claimed that he had no constitutional authority to stop the secession, but upon entering office, Lincoln attempted to maintain control of all Southern forts. This led to the firing on **Ft. Sumter** (SC) by the Confederates. As Lincoln called for aid, the Upper South (Virginia, Arkansas, North Carolina, and Tennessee) seceded as well, and the CSA made Richmond, Virginia its new capital.

Compromises to Save the Union

The US government made a number of compromises in an attempt to preserve the Union after Lincoln's election. The **Crittenden Compromise** extended the line of the Missouri Compromise and promised federal protection of slavery south of that line. The **House of Representatives Compromise** offered an extension of the Missouri Compromise and a Constitutional amendment to protect slavery. The **Virginia Peace Convention** produced an offer to extend the line of the Missouri Compromise and establish that slavery can never be outlawed except by the permission of the owner. Finally, Congress offered $300 for each slave. The South said that this was not enough money, and the North was appalled by the offer, regardless. It became clear that such compromises would not be enough to save the Union.

North vs. South in the Civil War

The Northern states had significant advantages, including:

- **Larger population**—the North consisted of 24 states, while the South had 11.
- **Better transportation and finances**—with railroads primarily in the North, supply chains were much more dependable, as was overseas trade.
- **Raw materials**—the North held the majority of America's gold, as well as iron, copper, and other minerals vital to wartime.

The South's advantages included the following:

- **Better-trained military officers**—many of the Southern officers were West Point trained and had commanded in the Mexican and Indian wars.
- **Familiarity with weapons**—the climate and lifestyle of the South meant most of the people were experienced with both guns and horses. The industrial North had less extensive experience.
- **Defensive position**—the South felt that victory was guaranteed, since they were protecting their own lands, while the North would be invading.
- **Well-defined goals**—the South fought an ideological war to be allowed to govern themselves and preserve their way of life. The North originally fought to preserve the Union and later to free the slaves.

Review Video: American Civil War: North vs. South Overview
Visit mometrix.com/academy and enter code: 370788

Benefit of the Emancipation Proclamation on the Union's Military Strategy

The Emancipation Proclamation, issued by President Lincoln on January 1, 1863, freed all slaves in **Confederate states** that were still in rebellion against the Union. While the original proclamation did not free any slaves in the states actually under Union control, it did set a precedent for the emancipation of slaves as the war progressed.

The **Emancipation Proclamation** worked in the Union's favor, as many freed slaves and other black troops joined the **Union Army**. Almost 200,000 blacks fought in the Union army, and over 10,000 served in the navy.

By the end of the war, over 4 million slaves had been freed, and in 1865 slavery was abolished in the **13th amendment** to the Constitution.

> **Review Video: The Civil War: The Emancipation Proclamation**
> Visit mometrix.com/academy and enter code: 181778

Major Events of the Civil War

Six major events of the Civil War and their outcomes or significance are:

- The **First Battle of Bull Run** (July 21, 1861)—this was the first major land battle of the war. Observers, expecting to enjoy an entertaining skirmish, set up picnics nearby. Instead, they found themselves witness to a bloodbath. Union forces were defeated, and the battle set the course of the Civil War as long, bloody, and costly.
- The **Capture of Fort Henry** by Ulysses S. Grant—this battle in February of 1862 marked the Union's first major victory.
- The **Battle of Gettysburg** (July 1-3, 1863)—often seen as the turning point of the war, Gettysburg also saw the largest number of casualties of the war, with over 50,000 dead, wounded, or missing. Robert E. Lee was defeated, and the Confederate army, significantly crippled, withdrew.
- The **Overland Campaign** (May and June of 1864)—Grant, now in command of all the Union armies, led this high casualty campaign that eventually positioned the Union for victory.
- **Sherman's March to the Sea**—William Tecumseh Sherman, in May of 1864, conquered Atlanta. He then continued to Savannah, destroying vast amounts of property as he went.
- Following Lee's defeat at the Appomattox Courthouse, General Grant accepted **Lee's surrender** in the home of Wilmer McLean in Appomattox, Virginia on April 9, 1865.

Impact of the Civil War across America

The Civil War impacted various people in America in remarkable ways. The people most affected were likely African Americans, who were at the center of the divide between the North and the South. Many African Americans directly fought in the war on both sides. Those in the Southern states were ultimately freed as a result of the Emancipation Proclamation of 1863. Soldiers in the war saw brutal warfare and faced physical and psychological repercussions of combat. It has long been said about the Civil War that soldiers often knew or were related to the very people they were fighting. This was especially so in states that hosted battles or lied on the borders between Southern and Northern states, such as Virginia and Tennessee. Others affected included women and children who were, in some cases, located fairly near the fights and played roles as suppliers, medics, and activists, leading to some precursors to the women's rights movement. In the reconstruction, economic, political, legal, and emotional fallout had to be dealt with, leading to many decades of repair following the war.

Circumstances of Lincoln's Assassination

The Civil War ended with the surrender of the South on April 9, 1865. Five days later, Lincoln and his wife, Mary, went to the play *Our American Cousin* at the Ford Theater. John Wilkes Booth, who did not know that the war was over, did his part in a plot to help the Confederacy by shooting Lincoln. He was carried from the theater to a nearby house, where he died the next morning. Booth was tracked down and killed by Union soldiers twelve days later.

> **Review Video: Overview of the American Civil War**
> Visit mometrix.com/academy and enter code: 239557

Goals of Reconstruction and the Freedmen's Bureau

In the aftermath of the Civil War, the South was left in chaos. From 1865 to 1877, government on all levels worked to help restore order to the South, ensure civil rights to the freed slaves, and bring the Confederate states back into the Union. This became known as the **Reconstruction period**. In 1866, Congress passed the

Reconstruction Acts, placing former Confederate states under military rule and stating the grounds for readmission into the Union.

The **Freedmen's Bureau** was formed to help freedmen both with basic necessities like food and clothing and also with employment and finding of family members who had been separated during the war. Many in the South felt the Freedmen's Bureau worked to set freed slaves against their former owners. The Bureau was intended to help former slaves become self-sufficient, and to keep them from falling prey to those who would take advantage of them. It eventually closed due to lack of funding and to violence from the **Ku Klux Klan**.

Policies of the Radical and Moderate Republicans

The **Radical Republicans** wished to treat the South quite harshly after the war. **Thaddeus Stevens**, the House Leader, suggested that the Confederate states be treated as if they were territories again, with ten years of military rule and territorial government before they would be readmitted. He also wanted to give all black men the right to vote. Former Confederate soldiers would be required to swear they had never supported the Confederacy (knows as the "Ironclad Oath") in order to be granted full rights as American citizens.

In contrast, the **moderate Republicans** wanted only black men who were literate or who had served as Union troops to be able to vote. All Confederate soldiers except troop leaders would also be able to vote. Before his death, **Lincoln** had favored a more moderate approach to Reconstruction, hoping this approach might bring some states back into the Union before the end of the war.

Phases of Reconstruction

The three phases of Reconstruction are:

- **Presidential Reconstruction**—largely driven by President Andrew Johnson's policies, the presidential phase of Reconstruction was lenient on the South and allowed continued discrimination against and control over blacks.
- **Congressional Reconstruction**—Congress, controlled largely by Radical Republicans, took a different stance, providing a wider range of civil rights for blacks and greater control over Southern government. Congressional Reconstruction is marked by military control of the former Confederate States.
- **Redemption**—gradually, the Confederate states were readmitted into the Union. During this time, white Democrats took over the government of most of the South. In 1877, President Rutherford Hayes withdrew the last federal troops from the South.

Carpetbaggers and Scalawags

The chaos in the South attracted a number of people seeking to fill the power vacuums and take advantage of the economic disruption. **Scalawags** were southern whites who aligned with freedmen to take over local governments. Many in the South who could have filled political offices refused to take the necessary oath required to grant them the right to vote, leaving many opportunities for Scalawags and others. **Carpetbaggers** were Northerners who traveled to the South for various reasons. Some provided assistance, while others sought to make money or to acquire political power during this chaotic period.

Black Codes and the Civil Rights Bill

The Black Codes were proposed to control freed slaves. They would not be allowed to bear arms, assemble, serve on juries, or testify against whites. Schools would be segregated, and unemployed blacks could be arrested and forced to work. The **Civil Rights Act** countered these codes, providing much wider rights for the freed slaves.

Andrew Johnson, who became president after Lincoln's death, supported the Black Codes and vetoed the Civil Rights Act in 1865 and again in 1866. The second time, Congress overrode his veto, and it became law.

Two years later, Congress voted to **impeach** Johnson, the culmination of tensions between Congress and the president. He was tried and came within a single vote of being convicted, but ultimately was acquitted and finished his term in office.

Purpose of the Thirteenth, Fourteenth, and Fifteenth Amendments

The Thirteenth, Fourteenth and Fifteenth Amendments were all passed shortly after the end of the Civil War:

- The **Thirteenth Amendment** was ratified by the states on December 6, 1865. This amendment prohibited slavery in the United States.
- The **Fourteenth Amendment** overturned the Dred Scott decision and was ratified July 9, 1868. American citizenship was redefined: a citizen was any person born or naturalized in the US, with all citizens guaranteed equal legal protection by all states. It also guaranteed citizens of any race the right to file a lawsuit or serve on a jury.
- The **Fifteenth Amendment** was ratified on February 3, 1870. It states that no citizen of the United States can be denied the right to vote based on race, color, or previous status as a slave.

Black Southerners and Segregation

Most Southern Democrats supported **segregation**, or the separation of the races. Although the **Civil Rights Act of 1875** had outlawed segregated restaurants and hotels, among other things, the Supreme Court ruled in 1883 that this act violated the 14th amendment because only states, and not individuals, could be forbidden from segregation. The **Jim Crow laws** were those rules that segregated black people and white people. Although de facto (by custom) segregation had existed in the North for years, the South began to implement segregation de jure (by law). In **Plessy v. Ferguson** (1896), the Supreme Court ruled that accommodations should be "separate but equal." In **Cummings v. Board of Education** (1898), the Supreme Court allowed public schools to be segregated.

Developments in Transportation

As America expanded its borders, it also developed new technology to travel the rapidly growing country. Roads and railroads traversed the nation, with the **Transcontinental Railroad** eventually allowing travel from one coast to the other. Canals and steamboats simplified water travel and made shipping easier and less expensive. The **Erie Canal** (1825) connected the Great Lakes to the Hudson River. Other canals connected other major waterways, further facilitating transportation and the shipment of goods.

Transcontinental Railroad

In 1869, the **Union Pacific Railroad** completed the first section of a planned **transcontinental railroad.** This section went from Omaha, Nebraska to Sacramento, California. Ninety percent of the workers were Chinese, working in very dangerous conditions for very low pay. With the rise of the railroad, products were much more easily transported across the country. While this was positive overall for industry throughout the country, it was often damaging to family farmers, who found themselves paying high shipping costs for smaller supply orders while larger companies received major discounts.

Measures to Limit Immigration in the 19th Century

In 1870, the **Naturalization Act** put limits on US citizenship, allowing full citizenship only to whites and those of African descent. The **Chinese Exclusion Act of 1882** put limits on Chinese immigration. The **Immigration Act of 1882** taxed immigrants, charging 50 cents per person. These funds helped pay administrative costs for regulating immigration. **Ellis Island** opened in 1892 as a processing center for those arriving in New York. The year 1921 saw the **Emergency Quota Act** passed, also known as the **Johnson Quota Act**, which severely limited the number of immigrants allowed into the country.

Agriculture in the 19th Century

Technological Advances in Agricultural Changes

During the mid-1800s, irrigation techniques improved significantly. Advances occurred in cultivation and breeding, as well as fertilizer use and crop rotation. In the Great Plains, also known as the Great American Desert, the dense soil was finally cultivated with steel plows. In 1892, gasoline-powered tractors arrived, and they were widely used by 1900. Other advancements in agriculture's toolset included barbed wire fences, combines, silos, deep-water wells, and the cream separator.

Major Actions that Helped Improve Agriculture

Four major government actions that helped improve US agriculture in the 19th century are:

- The **Department of Agriculture** came into being in 1862, working for the interests of farmers and ranchers across the country.
- The **Morrill Land-Grant Acts** were a series of acts passed between 1862 and 1890, allowing land-grant colleges.
- In conjunction with land-grant colleges, the **Hatch Act of 1887** brought agriculture experiment stations into the picture, helping discover new farming techniques.
- In 1914, the **Smith-Lever Act** provided cooperative programs to help educate people about food, home economics, community development, and agriculture. Related agriculture extension programs helped farmers increase crop production to feed the rapidly growing nation.

Inventors from the 1800s

Major inventors from the 1800s and their inventions include:

- Alexander Graham Bell—the telephone
- Orville and Wilbur Wright—the airplane
- Richard Gatling—the machine gun
- Walter Hunt, Elias Howe, and Isaac Singer—the sewing machine
- Nikola Tesla—alternating current motor
- George Eastman—the Kodak camera
- Thomas Edison—the first commercially practical light bulbs, motion pictures, and the phonograph
- Samuel Morse—the telegraph
- Charles Goodyear—vulcanized rubber
- Cyrus McCormick—the reaper
- George Westinghouse—the transformer, the air brake

This was an active period for invention, with about 700,000 patents registered between 1860 and 1900.

Gilded Age

The time period from the end of the Civil War to the beginning of the First World War is often referred to as the **Gilded Age**, or the **Second Industrial Revolution**. The US was changing from an agricultural-based economy to an **industrial economy**, with rapid growth accompanying the shift. In addition, the country itself was expanding, spreading into the seemingly unlimited west.

This time period saw the beginning of banks, department stores, chain stores, and trusts—all familiar features of the modern-day landscape. Cities also grew rapidly, and large numbers of immigrants arrived in the country, swelling the urban ranks.

Review Video: The Gilded Age: An Overview
Visit mometrix.com/academy and enter code: 684770

Factors Leading to the Development of the Populist Party

A major **recession** struck the United States during the 1890s, with crop prices falling dramatically. **Drought** compounded the problems, leaving many American farmers in crippling debt. The **Farmers' Alliance** formed in 1875, drawing the rural poor into a single political entity.

Recession also affected the more industrial parts of the country. The **Knights of Labor**, formed in 1869 by **Uriah Stephens**, was able to unite workers into a union to protect their rights. Dissatisfied by views espoused by industrialists, the Farmers Alliance and the Knights of Labor, joined to form the **Populist Party**, also known as the People's Party, in 1892. Some of the elements of the party's platform included:

- National currency
- Graduated income tax
- Government ownership of railroads as well as telegraph and telephone systems
- Secret ballots for voting
- Immigration restriction
- Single-term limits for president and vice-president

The Populist Party was in favor of decreasing elitism and making the voice of the common man more easily heard in the political process.

Growth of the Labor Movement Through the Late 19th Century

One of the first large, well-organized strikes occurred in 1892. Called the **Homestead Strike**, it occurred when the Amalgamated Association of Iron and Steel Workers struck against the Carnegie Steel Company. Gunfire ensued, and Carnegie was able to eliminate the plant's union. In 1894, workers in the American Railway Union, led by Eugene Debs, initiated the **Pullman Strike** after the Pullman Palace Car Co. cut their wages by 28 percent. President Grover Cleveland called in troops to break up the strike on the grounds that it interfered with mail delivery. Mary Harris "Mother" Jones organized the **Children's Crusade** to protest child labor. A protest march proceeded to the home of President Theodore Roosevelt in 1903. Jones also worked with the United Mine Workers of America and helped found the **Industrial Workers of the World**.

Panic of 1893

Far from a US-centric event, the **Panic of 1893** was an economic crisis that affected most of the globe. As a response, President Grover Cleveland repealed the **Sherman Silver Purchase Act**, afraid it had caused the downturn rather than boosting the economy as intended. The Panic led to bankruptcies, with banks and railroads going under and factory unemployment rising as high as 25 percent. In the end, the **Republican Party** regained power due to the economic crisis.

Progressive Era

From the 1890s to the end of the First World War, **Progressives** set forth an ideology that drove many levels of society and politics. The Progressives were in favor of workers' rights and safety and wanted measures taken against waste and corruption. They felt science could help improve society and that the government could—and should—provide answers to a variety of social problems. Progressives came from a wide variety of backgrounds but were united in their desire to improve society.

MUCKRAKERS AND THE PROGRESSIVE MOVEMENT

"Muckrakers" was a term used to identify aggressive investigative journalists who exposed scandals, corruption, and many other wrongs in late 19th-century society. Among these intrepid writers were:

- **Ida Tarbell**—she exposed John D. Rockefeller's Standard Oil Trust.
- **Jacob Riis**—a photographer, he brought the living conditions of the poor in New York to the public's attention.
- **Lincoln Steffens**—he worked to expose political corruption in municipal government.
- **Upton Sinclair**—his book *The Jungle* led to reforms in the meat-packing industry.

Through the work of these journalists, many new policies came into being, including workmen's compensation, child labor laws, and trust-busting.

DEALINGS WITH NATIVE AMERICANS THROUGH THE END OF THE 19TH CENTURY

America's westward expansion led to conflict and violent confrontations with Native Americans such as the **Battle of Little Bighorn**. In 1876, the American government ordered all Native Americans to relocate to reservations. Lack of compliance led to the **Dawes Act** in 1887, which ordered assimilation rather than separation: Native Americans were offered American citizenship and a piece of their tribal land if they would accept the lot chosen by the government and live on it separately from the tribe. This act remained in effect until 1934. Reformers also forced Native American children to attend **boarding schools**, where they were not allowed to speak their native language and were immersed into a Euro-American culture and religion. Children were often abused in these schools and were indoctrinated to abandon their identity as Native Americans.

In 1890, the massacre at **Wounded Knee**, accompanied by Geronimo's surrender, led the Native Americans to work to preserve their culture rather than fight for their lands.

Review Video: Government Dealings with Native Americans Through 1900
Visit mometrix.com/academy and enter code: 635645

NATIVE AMERICANS IN WARTIME THROUGH THE BEGINNING OF THE 20TH CENTURY

The **Spanish-American War** (1898) saw a number of Native Americans serving with Teddy Roosevelt in the Rough Riders. Apache scouts accompanied General John J. Pershing to Mexico, hoping to find **Pancho Villa**. More than 17,000 Native Americans were drafted into service for **World War I**, though at the time, they were not considered legal citizens. In 1924, Native Americans were finally granted official citizenship by the **Indian Citizenship Act**.

After decades of relocation, forced assimilation, and genocide, the number of Native Americans in the US has greatly declined. Though many Native Americans have chosen—or have been forced—to assimilate, about 300 reservations exist today, with most of their inhabitants living in abject poverty.

Review Video: Wartime Role of Native Americans
Visit mometrix.com/academy and enter code: 419128

EVENTS LEADING UP TO THE SPANISH-AMERICAN WAR

Spain had controlled **Cuba** since the 15th century. Over the centuries, the Spanish had quashed a variety of revolts. In 1886, slavery ended in Cuba, and another revolt was rising.

In the meantime, the US had expressed interest in Cuba, offering Spain $130 million for the island in 1853, during Franklin Pierce's presidency. In 1898, the Cuban revolt was underway. In spite of various factions supporting the Cubans, the US President, William McKinley, refused to recognize the rebellion, preferring negotiation over involvement in war. Then, the *Maine*, a US battleship in Havana Harbor, was blown up, killing

266 crew members. The US declared war two months later, and the war ended with a **Spanish surrender** in less than four months.

American History 1899 to Present

Influence of Big Stick Diplomacy on American Foreign Policy in Latin America

Theodore Roosevelt's famous quote, "Speak softly and carry a big stick," is supposedly of African origins, at least according to Roosevelt. He used this proverb to justify expanded involvement in foreign affairs during his tenure as President. The US military was deployed to protect American interests in **Latin America**. Roosevelt also worked to maintain an equal or greater influence in Latin America than those held by European interests. As a result, the US Navy grew larger, and the US generally became more involved in foreign affairs. Roosevelt felt that if any country was left vulnerable to control by Europe due to economic issues or political instability, the US had not only a right to intervene but was **obligated** to do so. This led to US involvement in Cuba, Nicaragua, Haiti, and the Dominican Republic over several decades leading into the First and Second World Wars.

Importance of the Panama Canal

Initial work began on the **Panama Canal** in 1881, though the idea had been discussed since the 1500s. The canal greatly reduces the length and time needed to sail from one ocean to the other by connecting the Atlantic to the Pacific through the Isthmus of Panama, which joins South America to North America. Before the canal was built, travelers had to sail around the entire perimeter of South America to reach the West Coast of the US. The French began the work after successfully completing the **Suez Canal**, which connected the Mediterranean Sea to the Red Sea. However, due to disease and high expense, the work moved slowly, and after eight years, the company went bankrupt, suspending work. The US purchased the holdings, and the first ship sailed through the canal in 1914. The Panama Canal was constructed as a lock-and-lake canal, with ships lifted on locks to travel from one lake to another over the rugged, mountainous terrain. In order to maintain control of the Canal Zone, the US assisted Panama in its battle for independence from **Colombia**.

Taft's Dollar Diplomacy vs. Roosevelt's Diplomatic Theories

During William Howard Taft's presidency, Taft instituted "**Dollar Diplomacy**." This approach was America's effort to influence Latin America and East Asia through economic rather than military means. Taft saw past efforts in these areas to be political and warlike, while his efforts focused on peaceful economic goals. His justification of the policy was to protect the **Panama Canal**, which was vital to US trade interests.

In spite of Taft's assurance that Dollar Diplomacy was a peaceful approach, many interventions proved violent. During Latin American revolts, such as those in **Nicaragua**, the US sent troops to settle the revolutions. Afterward, bankers moved in to help support the new leaders through loans. Dollar Diplomacy continued until 1913, when Woodrow Wilson was elected president.

Growth of Civil Rights for African Americans

Marcus Garvey founded the **Universal Negro Improvement Association and African Communities League (UNIA-ACL)**, which became a large and active organization focused on building black nationalism. In 1909, the **National Association for the Advancement of Colored People (NAACP)** came into being, working to defeat Jim Crow laws. The NAACP also helped prevent racial segregation from becoming federal law, fought against lynchings, helped black soldiers in WWI become officers, and helped defend the Scottsboro Boys, who were unjustly accused of rape.

Wilson's Approach to International Diplomacy

Turning away from Taft's "Dollar Diplomacy," Wilson instituted a foreign policy he referred to as "**moral diplomacy**." This approach still influences American foreign policy today.

Wilson felt that **representative government and democracy** in all countries would lead to worldwide stability. Democratic governments, he felt, would be less likely to threaten American interests. He also saw the

US and Great Britain as the great role models in this area, as well as champions of world peace and self-government. Free trade and international commerce would allow the US to speak out regarding world events.

Main elements of Wilson's policies included:

- Maintaining a strong military
- Promoting democracy throughout the world
- Expanding international trade to boost the American economy

The Sixteenth, Seventeenth, Eighteenth, and Nineteenth Amendments

The early 20th century saw several amendments made to the US Constitution:

- The **Sixteenth Amendment** (1913) established a federal income tax.
- The **Seventeenth Amendment** (1913) allowed popular election of senators.
- The **Eighteenth Amendment** (1919) prohibited the sale, production, and transportation of alcohol. This amendment was later repealed by the Twenty-first Amendment.
- The **Nineteenth Amendment** (1920) gave women the right to vote.

These amendments largely grew out of the Progressive Era, as many citizens worked to improve American society.

Goals of the Anti-Defamation League

In 1913, the Anti-Defamation League was formed to prevent anti-Semitic behavior and practices. Its actions also worked to prevent all forms of racism and to prevent individuals from being discriminated against for any reason involving their race. They spoke against the Ku Klux Klan, as well as other racist or anti-Semitic organizations. This organization still works to fight discrimination against all minorities.

Role of the Federal Trade Commission in Eliminating Trusts

Muckrakers such as Ida Tarbell and Lincoln Steffens brought to light the damaging trend of trusts—huge corporations working to monopolize areas of commerce so they could control prices and distribution. The **Sherman Antitrust Act** and the **Clayton Antitrust Act** set out guidelines for competition among corporations and set out to eliminate these trusts. The **Federal Trade Commission** was formed in 1914 in order to enforce antitrust measures and ensure that companies were operated fairly and did not create controlling monopolies.

Major Events of World War I

World War I occurred from 1914 to 1918 and was fought largely in Europe. The rise in **nationalism** at the beginning of the 20th century helped contribute to the possibility of war. There was also some conflict between the **imperialist** (France, Britain, and the US) and the **non-imperialist** (Germany, Italy) nations. Many large nations were seeking economic expansion outside of their own borders, and the competition for foreign markets was intense. There was also a complex system of entangling alliances; many countries were involved in several different alliances at the same time. The spark for World War I, though, was the assassination of **Archduke Franz Ferdinand**, heir to the throne of Austria-Hungary, in April of 1914 by a Serbian nationalist. When Emperor Franz Joseph declared war on Serbia, it set off a chain reaction that involved virtually every nation in Europe. At the beginning of the conflict, Woodrow Wilson declared the US neutral. Eventually, however, the US joined the war. Major events influencing US involvement included:

- **Sinking of the *Lusitania***—the British passenger liner RMS *Lusitania* was sunk by a German U-boat in 1915. Among the 1,000 civilian victims were over 100 American citizens. Outraged by this act, many Americans began to push for US involvement in the war, using the *Lusitania* as a rallying cry.

- **German U-boat aggression**—Wilson continued to keep the US out of the war, using as his 1916 reelection slogan, "He kept us out of war." While he continued to work toward an end of the war, German U-boats began to indiscriminately attack American and Canadian merchant ships carrying supplies to Germany's enemies in Europe.
- **Zimmerman Telegram** —the final event that brought the US into World War I was the interception of the Zimmerman Telegram (also known as the Zimmerman Note) on January 17th, 1917. In this telegram, Germany proposed forming an alliance with Mexico if the US entered the war.

Efforts in the US During World War I Supporting the War Effort

American **railroads** came under government control in December 1917. The widespread system was consolidated into a single system, with each region assigned a director. This greatly increased the efficiency of the railroad system, allowing the railroads to supply both domestic and military needs. Control returned to private ownership in 1920. In 1918, **telegraph, telephone, and cable services** also came under Federal control, to be returned to private management the next year. The **American Red Cross** supported the war effort by knitting clothes for Army and Navy troops. They also helped supply hospital and refugee clothing and surgical dressings. Over 8 million people participated in this effort. To generate wartime funds, the US government sold **Liberty Bonds**. In four issues, they sold nearly $25 billion—more than one-fifth of Americans purchased them. After the war, a fifth bond drive was held but sold "**Victory Liberty Bonds**."

Review Video: WWI Overview
Visit mometrix.com/academy and enter code: 659767

Influence of Wilson's Fourteen Points on Final Peace Treaties

President Woodrow Wilson proposed **Fourteen Points** as the basis for a peace settlement to end the war. Presented to the US Congress in January 1918, the Fourteen Points included:

- Five points outlining **general ideals**
- Eight points to resolve **immediate problems** of political and territorial nature
- One point proposing an **organization of nations** (the League of Nations) with the intent of maintaining world peace

In November of that same year, Germany agreed to an **armistice**, assuming the final treaty would be based on the Fourteen Points. However, during the peace conference in Paris 1919, there was much disagreement, leading to a final agreement that punished Germany and the other Central Powers much more than originally intended. Henry Cabot Lodge, who had become the Foreign Relations Committee chairman in 1918, wanted an unconditional surrender from Germany and was concerned about the article in the **Treaty of Versailles** that gave the League of Nations power to declare war without a vote from the US Congress. A **League of Nations** was included in the Treaty of Versailles at Wilson's insistence. The Senate rejected the Treaty of Versailles, and in the end, Wilson refused to concede to Lodge's demands. As a result, the US did not join the League of Nations.

Origins of the Red Scare

World War I created many jobs, but after the war ended, these jobs disappeared, leaving many unemployed. In the wake of these employment changes, the **International Workers of the World** and the **Socialist Party**, headed by Eugene Debs, became more and more visible. Workers initiated strikes in an attempt to regain the favorable working conditions that had been put into place before the war. Unfortunately, many of these strikes became violent, and the actions were blamed on "Reds," or Communists, for trying to spread their views into America. With the recent Bolshevik Revolution in Russia, many Americans feared a similar revolution might occur in the US. The **Red Scare** ensued, with many individuals jailed for supposedly holding communist, anarchist, or socialist beliefs.

Major Changes and Events that Took Place in America During the 1920s

The post-war 1920s saw many Americans moving from the farm to the city, with growing prosperity in the US. The **Roaring Twenties**, or the **Jazz Age**, was driven largely by growth in the automobile and entertainment industries. Individuals like Charles Lindbergh, the first aviator to make a solo flight across the Atlantic Ocean, added to the American admiration of individual accomplishment. Telephone lines, distribution of electricity, highways, the radio, and other inventions brought great changes to everyday life.

Review Video: 1920's
Visit mometrix.com/academy and enter code: 124996

Prohibition

The Eighteenth Amendment was ratified by most states in 1919, making the manufacture, sale, transportation, importation, and exportation of alcohol illegal; however, this change was not enforced with much success. Instead of curbing the production and consumption of alcohol, Prohibition led to the creation of a large, illegal alcohol market dominated by organized crime. Criminal organizations, like the Mafia crime syndicate, grew massively in power and influence during the 1920s and 1930s by cornering the market on the production, distribution, and sale of alcohol. Americans continued to drink alcohol in speakeasies—hidden, illegal drinking establishments. The huge illegal market for alcohol contributed to increased crime and unregulated, sometimes dangerous, alcohol.

Major Cultural Movements of the 1920s Influenced by African Americans

The **Harlem Renaissance** saw a number of African-American artists settling in Harlem in New York. This community produced a number of well-known artists and writers, including Langston Hughes, Nella Larsen, Zora Neale Hurston, Claude McKay, Countee Cullen, and Jean Toomer. The growth of jazz, also largely driven by African Americans, defined the **Jazz Age**. Its unconventional, improvisational style matched the growing sense of optimism and exploration of the decade. Originating as an offshoot of the blues, jazz began in New Orleans. Some significant jazz musicians were Duke Ellington, Louis Armstrong, and Jelly Roll Morton. **Big Band** and **Swing Jazz** also developed in the 1920s. Well-known musicians of this movement included Bing Crosby, Frank Sinatra, Count Basie, Benny Goodman, Billie Holiday, Ella Fitzgerald, and The Dorsey Brothers.

American Civil Liberties Union

The American Civil Liberties Union (**ACLU**), founded in 1920, grew from the American Union Against Militarism. The ACLU helped conscientious objectors avoid going to war during WWI, and also helped those being prosecuted under the **Espionage Act** (1917) and the **Sedition Act** (1918), many of whom were immigrants. Their major goals were to protect immigrants and other citizens who were threatened with prosecution for their political beliefs, and to support labor unions, which were also under threat by the government during the Red Scare.

Womens' Suffrage

The Nineteenth Amendment gave **women the right to vote**. This amendment was proposed on June 4, 1919, and was ratified on August 18, 1920. An amendment to give women the right to vote was first introduced in Congress in 1878, but it failed to pass. For the next four decades, the amendment was reintroduced in every session of Congress but was defeated each time. The involvement of women in the war effort during World War I spawned increased support for women's suffrage. Finally, in 1918, the House of Representatives approved the amendment to grant women suffrage, but the Senate defeated it. In 1919, the Senate also passed the amendment and sent it to the states for approval, where it was ratified in 1920.

Provisions and Importance of the National Origins Act of 1924

The National Origins Act (Johnson-Reed Act) placed limitations on **immigration**. The number of immigrants allowed into the US was based on the population of each nationality of immigrants who were living in the country in 1890. Only two percent of each nationality's 1890 population numbers were allowed to immigrate.

This led to great disparities between immigrants from various nations, and Asian immigration was not allowed at all. Some of the impetus behind the Johnson-Reed Act came as a result of paranoia following the **Russian Revolution**. Fear of communist influences in the US led to a general fear of immigrants.

Ku Klux Klan

In 1866, Confederate Army veterans came together to fight against Reconstruction in the South, forming a group called the **Ku Klux Klan (KKK)**. With white supremacist beliefs, including anti-Semitism, nativism, anti-Catholicism, and overt racism, this organization relied heavily on violence to get its message across. In 1915, they grew again in power, using a film called *The Birth of a Nation*, by D.W. Griffith, to spread their ideas. In the 1920s, the reach of the KKK spread far into the north and midwest, and members controlled a number of state governments. Its membership and power began to decline during the Great Depression but experienced a resurgence later.

The Great Depression

The **Great Depression** was the largest economic downturn in the history of the United States. It began in 1929 with the stock market crash and ended around 1939. The Great Depression grew out of several factors that had developed over the previous years, including:

- Growing economic disparity between the rich and middle classes, with the rich amassing wealth much more quickly than the lower classes
- Disparity in economic distribution in industries
- Growing use of credit, leading to an inflated demand for some goods
- Government support of new industries rather than agriculture
- Risky stock market investments, leading to the stock market crash

Additional factors contributing to the Depression also included the **Labor Day Hurricane** in the Florida Keys (1935) and the **Great Hurricane of 1938** in New England, along with the **Dust Bowl** in the Great Plains, which destroyed crops and resulted in the displacement of as many as 2.5 million people.

Review Video: Causes of the Great Depression
Visit mometrix.com/academy and enter code: 635912

The Dust Bowl

The Dust Bowl (1930-1941) was a period of American history characterized by a high incidence of dust storms in the Great Plains region. The instability of the world agriculture market during World War I led to overproduction in the 1920s. Even lands previously considered unsuitable for agricultural use were leveled and developed. This excessive activity devastated the Great Plains, eliminating the natural vegetation that could have prevented the massive soil movement that occurred during the drought and strong winds of the 1930s, and resulted in widespread crop failure. In turn, the Dust Bowl led to millions of people being displaced from their homes and hundreds of thousands migrating to California in search of work and better living conditions. On their journeys, however, these migrants faced poor conditions, starvation, and dehydration. Even when they arrived in California, many of them struggled to find work. The work that was available was often hard labor, like picking cotton. Migrants also faced hostility and even phyisical violence from locals. They were often forced to live in roadside camps, which were sometimes the target of arson.

Franklin D. Roosevelt's Election and New Deal

Franklin D. Roosevelt was elected president in 1932 with his promise of a "**New Deal**" for Americans. His goals were to provide government work programs to provide jobs, wages, and relief to numerous workers throughout the beleaguered US. Congress gave Roosevelt almost free rein to produce relief legislation. The goals of this legislation were:

- **Relief**—creating jobs for the high numbers of unemployed
- **Recovery**—stimulating the economy through the National Recovery Administration
- **Reform**—passing legislation to prevent future, similar economic crashes

The Roosevelt Administration also passed legislation regarding ecological issues, including the Soil Conservation Service, aimed at preventing another Dust Bowl.

Roosevelt's Alphabet Organizations

So-called "alphabet organizations" set up during Roosevelt's administration included:

- **Civilian Conservation Corps** (CCC)—provided jobs in the forestry service
- **Agricultural Adjustment Administration** (AAA)—increased agricultural income by adjusting both production and prices
- **Tennessee Valley Authority** (TVA)—organized projects to build dams in the Tennessee River for flood control and production of electricity, resulting in increased productivity for industries in the area, and easier navigation of the Tennessee River
- **Public Works Administration** (PWA) and Civil Works Administration (CWA)—provided a multitude of jobs, initiating over 34,000 projects
- **Works Progress Administration** (WPA)—helped unemployed persons to secure employment on government work projects or elsewhere

Actions Taken During the Roosevelt Administration to Prevent Future Crashes

The Roosevelt administration passed several laws and established several institutions to initiate the "reform" portion of the New Deal, including:

- **Glass-Steagall Act**—separated investment from commercial banking
- **Securities Exchange Commission (SEC)**—helped regulate Wall Street investment practices, making them less dangerous to the overall economy
- **Wagner Act**—provided worker and union rights to improve relations between employees and employers
- **Social Security Act of 1935**—provided pensions as well as unemployment insurance

Other actions focused on insuring bank deposits and adjusting the value of American currency. Most of these regulatory agencies and government policies and programs still exist today.

Major Regulations Regarding Labor During the Great Depression

Three major regulations regarding labor that were passed after the Great Depression are:

- **Davis-Bacon Act** (1931)—provided fair compensation for contractors and subcontractors.
- The **Wagner Act** (1935)—also known as the National Labor Relations Act, it established that unions were legal, protected members of unions, and required collective bargaining. This act was later amended by the Taft-Hartley Act of 1947 and the Landrum-Griffin Act of 1959, which further clarified certain elements.
- **Walsh-Healey Act** (1936)—established a minimum wage, child labor laws, safety standards, and overtime pay.

World War II

America's Introduction to WWII

After the First World War, the US became obsessed with isolating itself from foreign conflicts. The **Nye Committee** studied the war and determined that it had been fought for financial reasons and could have been avoided. Isolationist parties achieved some popularity during this period, including the **America First Committee**, led by Charles Lindbergh, and **SOS** (Stop Organized Slaughter). The **Neutrality Laws** of 1935-7 declared that the US could not sell weapons to another country in a time of war and that US citizens could not travel on the ships of a nation at war. In 1937, FDR delivered the **Quarantine Speech**, in which he asserted that the Nazi "disease" must be contained. Finally, after conflict in Europe had escalated considerably, FDR declared that the US needed to help Britain and be an "arsenal of democracy in the world." The **Neutrality Act of 1940** made it legal for the US to sell weapons on a cash and carry basis. In August of 1941, FDR and Churchill drew up the **Atlantic Charter**, which vowed to destroy Nazism, protect the right of self-determination, and create a World Peace Organization.

Buildup to the Attack on Pearl Harbor

A number of events had created a stormy relationship between the US and Japan long before the invasion of Pearl Harbor, but the conflict reached a boiling point after President Roosevelt froze all Japanese assets in the US and cut Japan off from US oil and steel. America also had a cordial relationship at this time with Japan's longtime rival, China. The Japanese launched surprise attacks both on the American naval base at **Pearl Harbor** and on the **Philippines**, where they hoped to secure some oil.

US Involvement in WWII Concerning Europe and Africa

After the Japanese attack on Pearl Harbor in 1941, the US declared **war** on Japan, after which Germany declared war on the US. Before going after Japan, however, the US first attacked Germany; this was done because the US underestimated Japan industrially and militarily, and because the US feared Britain was on the verge of defeat. **Operation Overlord**, the Allied invasion of the European continent at Normandy, was led in part by General **Dwight D. Eisenhower**. The American generals Omar Bradley and George Patton took part in the **Allied Operation Torch**, aimed at taking back North Africa. At the **Battle of the Bulge**, in Belgium, the Germans tried to break the Allied lines, but were unsuccessful, in part because of the heroism of American soldiers.

US Involvement in WWII Concerning Asia and the Pacific

The US strategy for controlling the Pacific was known as "island hopping." In the **Coral Sea Battle of 1942**, Americans stopped the Japanese from taking Australia and New Guinea. In the same year, the **Doolittle raids** of Japanese naval bases boosted American morale. In the **Battle of Midway** (1942), the US sunk four Japanese aircraft carriers. In the **Battle of Leyte Gulf**, General Douglas MacArthur took back the Philippines and also took control of Iwo Jima and Okinawa. During this period, a team of American scientists led by Robert Oppenheimer was developing the **atomic bomb** in Los Alamos, New Mexico. Japan was warned several times by President Truman that the bomb would be used if they did not surrender. Surely enough, Americans dropped atomic bombs on **Hiroshima** on August 6, 1945, and on **Nagasaki** three days later. Japanese leaders surrendered aboard the USS Missouri on August 15, 1945.

The Holocaust is the name given to the systematic killing of Jews, Gypsies, homosexuals, and others by the Nazis. **Anti-Semitism** had existed in Europe for a long time, but the Nazis gave it renewed emphasis and, after making numerous false claims about Jews, began persecuting them upon Hitler's rise to power in 1933. Jews were disenfranchised, forced into ghettos, had their property taken, and were finally sent to work and be killed in **concentration camps**. Approximately 6 million Jews were killed during the **Holocaust**. As the situation for the Germans became more dire in the Second World War, Hitler sought to implement what he called the "final solution," in which hundreds of thousands were killed just before the fall of Nazi Germany.

Interventionist and Isolationist Approaches in World War II

When war broke out in Europe in 1939, President Roosevelt stated that the US would remain **neutral**. However, his overall approach was considered "**interventionist**," as he was willing to provide aid to the Allies without actually entering the conflict. Thus, the US supplied a wide variety of war materials to the Allied nations in the early years of the war.

Isolationists believed the US should not provide any aid to the Allies, including supplies. They felt Roosevelt, by assisting the Allies, was leading the US into a war for which it was not prepared. Led by Charles Lindbergh, the Isolationists believed that any involvement in the European conflict endangered the US by weakening its national defense.

Sequence of Events that Led the US to Declare War and Enter World War II

In 1937, Japan invaded China, prompting the US to eventually halt exports to Japan. Roosevelt also did not allow Japanese interests to withdraw money held in US banks. In 1941, **General Tojo** rose to power as the Japanese prime minister. Recognizing America's ability to bring a halt to Japan's expansion, he authorized the bombing of **Pearl Harbor** on December 7. The US responded by declaring war on Japan. Partially because of the **Tripartite Pact** among the Axis Powers, Germany and Italy then declared war on the US, later followed by Bulgaria, Hungary, and other Axis nations.

Review Video: World War II Overview
Visit mometrix.com/academy and enter code: 759402

Occurrences of World War II that Led to the Surrender of Germany

In 1941, **Hitler** violated the non-aggression pact he had signed with Stalin two years earlier by invading the USSR. **Stalin** then joined the **Allies**. Stalin, Roosevelt, and Winston Churchill planned to defeat Germany first, then Japan, bringing the war to an end.

In 1942-1943, the Allies drove **Axis** forces out of Africa. In addition, the Germans were soundly defeated at Stalingrad.

The **Italian Campaign** involved Allied operations in Italy between July 1943 and May 1945, including Italy's liberation. On June 6, 1944, known as **D-Day**, the Allies invaded France at Normandy. Soviet troops moved on the eastern front at the same time, driving German forces back. By April 25, 1945, Berlin was surrounded by Soviet troops. On May 7, Germany surrendered.

Major Events of World War II that Led to the Surrender of Japan

War continued with **Japan** after Germany's surrender. Japanese forces had taken a large portion of Southeast Asia and the Western Pacific, all the way to the Aleutian Islands in Alaska. **General Doolittle** bombed several Japanese cities while American troops scored a victory at Midway. Additional fighting in the Battle of the Coral Sea further weakened Japan's position. As a final blow, the US dropped two **atomic bombs** on Japan, one on Hiroshima and the other on Nagasaki. This was the first time atomic bombs had been used in warfare, and the devastation was horrific and demoralizing. Japan surrendered on September 2, 1945, which became **V-J Day** in the US.

The 442nd Regimental Combat Team, Tuskegee Airmen, and Navajo Code Talkers

The 442nd Regimental Combat Team consisted of Japanese-Americans fighting in Europe for the US. The most highly decorated unit per member in US history, they suffered a 93% casualty rate during the war. The **Tuskegee Airmen** were African American aviators, the first black Americans allowed to fly for the military. In spite of being ineligible to become official navy pilots, they flew over 15,000 missions and were highly decorated. The **Navajo Code Talkers** were native Navajo who used their traditional language to transmit information among Allied forces. Because Navajo is a highly-complex and unwritten language and not simply a code, the Axis powers were never able to translate it. The use of Navajo Code Talkers to transmit information was instrumental in the taking of Iwo Jima and other major victories of the war.

Circumstances and Opportunities for Women During World War II

Women served widely in the military during WWII, working in numerous positions, including the **Flight Nurses Corps**. Women also moved into the workforce while men were overseas, leading to over 19 million women in the US workforce by 1944. **Rosie the Riveter** stood as a symbol of these women and a means of recruiting others to take needed positions. Women, as well as their families left behind during wartime, also grew **Victory Gardens** to help provide food.

Japanese-American Internment During World War II

Following the attack on Pearl Harbor, the American government began to suspect that people of Japanese ancestry in America may be operating as spies for Japan, though there was little evidence for this. Just a couple of months after the attack, President Franklin D. Roosevelt signed Executive Order 9066, which allowed the government to declare Military Exclusion Zones for the purpose of national security. This made it legal for the military to remove people or other perceived threats from these exclusion zones. As a result, over 100,000 people of Japanese ancestry were removed from their homes in these areas and placed into internment camps. These camps were hastily built and offered poor living conditions. Children interned in these camps did not have access to a full education, and many Japanese-Americans lost their businesses and homes as a result of their internment.

In **Korematsu v. US** (1944), the Supreme Court ruled that the internment camps were legal, but in **ex parte Endo** (1944), the Court adjusted its decision to state that the US could only intern those whose disloyalty could be proven. Japanese internment ended in 1945, but the effects of internment on Japanese-Americans endured.

Importance of the Atomic Bomb During World War II

The atomic bomb, developed during WWII, was the most powerful bomb ever invented. A single bomb, carried by a single plane, held enough power to destroy an entire city. This devastating effect was demonstrated with the bombing of **Hiroshima** and **Nagasaki** in 1945 in what later became a controversial move, but ended the war. The bombings resulted in as many as 150,000 immediate deaths and many more as time passed after the bombings, mostly due to **radiation poisoning**.

Whatever the arguments against the use of "The Bomb," the post-WWII era saw many countries develop similar weapons to match the newly expanded military power of the US. The impact of those developments and use of nuclear weapons continues to haunt international relations today.

Importance of the Yalta Conference and the Potsdam Conference

In February 1945, Joseph Stalin, Franklin D. Roosevelt, and Winston Churchill met in Yalta to discuss the post-war treatment of the **Axis nations**, particularly Germany. Though Germany had not yet surrendered, its defeat was imminent. After Germany's official surrender, Joseph Stalin, Harry Truman (Roosevelt's successor), and Clement Attlee (replacing Churchill partway through the conference) met to formalize those plans. This meeting was called the **Potsdam Conference**. Basic provisions of these agreements included:

- Dividing Germany and Berlin into four zones of occupation
- Demilitarization of Germany
- Poland remaining under Soviet control
- Outlawing the Nazi Party
- Trials for Nazi leaders
- Relocation of numerous German citizens
- The USSR joining the United Nations, established in 1945
- Establishment of the United Nations Security Council, consisting of the US, the UK, the USSR, China, and France

Agreements Made with Post-War Japan

General Douglas MacArthur led the American **military occupation of Japan** after the country surrendered. The goals of the US occupation included removing Japan's military and making the country a democracy. A 1947 constitution removed power from the emperor and gave it to the people, as well as granting voting rights to women. Japan was no longer allowed to declare war, and a group of 28 government officials were tried for war crimes. In 1951, the US finally signed a peace treaty with Japan. This treaty allowed Japan to rearm itself for purposes of self-defense but stripped the country of the empire it had built overseas.

US Treatment of Immigrants During and After World War II

In 1940, the US passed the **Alien Registration Act**, which required all aliens older than fourteen to be fingerprinted and registered. They were also required to report changes of address within five days.

Tension between whites and Japanese immigrants in **California**, which had been building since the beginning of the century, came to a head with the bombing of **Pearl Harbor** in 1941. Believing that even those Japanese living in the US were likely to be loyal to their native country, the president ordered numerous Japanese to be arrested on suspicion of subversive action and isolated in exclusion zones known as **War Relocation Camps**. Approximately 120,000 Japanese-Americans, two-thirds of them US citizens, were sent to these camps during the war.

General State of the US After World War II

Following WWII, the US became the strongest political power in the world, becoming a major player in world affairs and foreign policies. The US determined to stop the spread of **communism**, having named itself the "**arsenal of democracy**" during the war. In addition, America emerged with a greater sense of itself as a single, integrated nation, with many regional and economic differences diminished. The government worked for greater equality, and the growth of communications increased contact among different areas of the country. Both the aftermath of the Great Depression and the necessities of WWII had given the government greater **control** over various institutions as well as the economy. This also meant that the American government took on greater responsibility for the well-being of its citizens, both in the domestic arena, such as providing basic needs, and in protecting them from foreign threats. This increased role of providing basic necessities for all Americans has been criticized by some as "**the welfare state**."

Fear of Communism Following World War II

After World War II, America became greatly concerned with the spread of communism, which was being propagated mainly by the Soviet Union and the communist party in China. A series of policies in America, Western Europe, and the Soviet Union brought the anti-communist and communist groups ever closer to open conflict. As these tensions grew in the international community, Americans became increasingly paranoid about the spread of **Communism**. There were numerous investigations aimed at weeding Communist spies out of the government, and two people, Julius and Ethel Rosenberg, were executed for spying. The leader of much of this was Senator **Joseph McCarthy**, who was famous for promoting and prolonging the "**Red Scare**" as the often-termed witch-hunt for communists in the government was known (Soviet communications released after the fall of the Soviet Union confirmed the vast majority of his accusations). The tide of anti-communism extended into a general disapproval of organized labor. The **Taft-Hartley Act** restricted the ability of labor unions markedly. In order to survive, the nation's two largest labor unions combined, forming the **AFL-CIO**.

US Policy Toward Immigrants After World War II

Prior to WWII, the US had been limiting **immigration** for several decades. After WWII, policy shifted slightly to accommodate political refugees from Europe and elsewhere. So many people were displaced by the war that in 1946, the UN formed the **International Refugee Organization** to deal with the problem. In 1948, the US Congress passed the **Displaced Persons Act**, which allowed over 400,000 European refugees to enter the US, most of them concentration camp survivors and refugees from Eastern Europe.

In 1952, the **United States Escapee Program (USEP)** increased the quotas, allowing refugees from communist Europe to enter the US, as did the **Refugee Relief Act**, passed in 1953. At the same time, however, the **Internal Security Act of 1950** allowed deportation of declared communists, and Asians were subjected to a quota based on race, rather than country of origin. Later changes included:

- **Migration and Refugee Assistance Act** (1962)—provided aid for refugees in need
- **Immigration and Nationality Act** (1965)—ended quotas based on nation of origin
- **Immigration Reform and Control Act** (1986)—prohibited the hiring of illegal immigrants but also granted amnesty to about three million illegals already in the country

Accomplishments of Harry S. Truman

Harry S. Truman took over the presidency from Franklin D. Roosevelt near the end of WWII. He made the final decision to drop atomic bombs on Japan and played a major role in the final decisions regarding the treatment of post-war Germany. On the domestic front, Truman initiated a 21-point plan known as the **Fair Deal**. This plan expanded Social Security, provided public housing, and made the Fair Employment Practice Committee permanent. Truman helped support Greece and Turkey (which were under threat from the USSR), supported South Korea against communist North Korea, and helped with recovery in Western Europe. He also participated in the formation of **NATO**, the North Atlantic Treaty Organization.

Events and Importance of the Korean War

The Korean War began in 1950 and ended in 1953. For the first time in history, a world organization—the **United Nations**—played a military role in a war. North Korea sent communist troops into South Korea, seeking to bring the entire country under communist control. The UN sent out a call to member nations, asking them to support South Korea. Truman sent troops, as did many other UN member nations. The war ended three years later with a **truce** rather than a peace treaty, and Korea remains divided at the **38th parallel north**, with communist rule remaining in the North and a democratic government ruling the South.

Effects of US Cold War Foreign Policy Acts on the International Relationships

The following are US Cold War foreign policy acts and how they affected international relationships, especially between the US and the Soviet Union:

- **Marshall Plan**—this sent aid to war-torn Europe after WWII, largely focusing on preventing the spread of communism.
- **Containment Policy**—proposed by George F. Kennan, the containment policy focused on containing the spread of Soviet communism.
- **Truman Doctrine**—Harry S. Truman stated that the US would provide both economic and military support to any country threatened by Soviet takeover.
- **National Security Act**—passed in 1947, this act reorganized the government's military departments into the Department of Defense and created the Central Intelligence Agency and the National Security Council.

The combination of these acts led to the **Cold War**, with Soviet communists attempting to spread their influence and the US and other countries trying to contain or stop this spread.

Accomplishments of Dwight D. Eisenhower

Eisenhower carried out a middle-of-the-road foreign policy and brought the US several steps forward in equal rights. He worked to minimize tensions during the Cold War and negotiated a peace treaty with Russia after the death of Stalin. He enforced desegregation by sending troops to Little Rock Central High School in Arkansas, as well as ordering the desegregation of the military. Organizations formed during his administration included the Department of Health, Education, and Welfare, and the National Aeronautics and Space Administration (NASA).

Effect of the Arms Race on Post WWII International Relations

After World War II, major nations, particularly the US and USSR, rushed to develop highly advanced weapons systems such as the **atomic bomb** and later the **hydrogen bomb**. These countries seemed determined to outpace each other with the development of numerous, deadly weapons. These weapons were expensive and extremely dangerous, and it is possible that the war between US and Soviet interests remained "cold" due to the fear that one side or the other would use these powerful weapons.

Technological Advances that Occurred Throughout the 1900s

Numerous technological advances throughout the 1900s led to more effective treatment of diseases, more efficient communication and transportation, and new means of generating power. Advances in **medicine** increased the human lifespan in developed countries, and near-instantaneous **communication** opened up a myriad of possibilities. Some of these advances include:

- Discovery of penicillin (1928)
- Supersonic air travel (1947)
- Nuclear power plants (1951)
- Orbital satellite leading to manned space flight (Sputnik, 1957)
- First man on the moon (1969)

NATO, Warsaw Pact, and the Berlin Wall

NATO, the **North Atlantic Treaty Organization**, came into being in 1949. It essentially amounted to an agreement among the US and Western European countries that an attack on any one of these countries was to be considered an attack against the entire group. Under the influence of the Soviet Union, the Eastern European countries of the USSR, Bulgaria, East Germany, Poland, Romania, Albania, Hungary, and Czechoslovakia responded with the **Warsaw Pact**, which created a similar agreement among those nations. In 1961, a wall was built to separate communist East Berlin from democratic West Berlin. This was a literal representation of the "**Iron Curtain**" that separated the democratic and communist countries throughout the world.

Presidency of John F. Kennedy

Although his term was cut short by his assassination, **JFK** instituted economic programs that led to a period of continuous expansion in the US unmatched since before WWII. He formed the Alliance for Progress and the Peace Corps, organizations intended to help developing nations. He also oversaw the passage of new civil rights legislation and drafted plans to attack poverty and its causes, along with support of the arts. Kennedy's presidency ended when he was assassinated by **Lee Harvey Oswald** in 1963.

Events of the Cuban Missile Crisis

The Cuban Missile Crisis occurred in 1962, during John F. Kennedy's presidency. Russian Premier **Nikita Khrushchev** decided to place nuclear missiles in **Cuba** to protect the island from invasion by the US. An American U-2 plane flying over the island photographed the missile bases as they were being built. Tensions rose, with the US concerned about nuclear missiles so close to its shores, and the USSR concerned about American missiles that had been placed in **Turkey**. Eventually, the missile sites were removed, and a US naval blockade turned back Soviet ships carrying missiles to Cuba. During negotiations, the US agreed to remove their missiles from Turkey and agreed to sell surplus wheat to the USSR. A telephone hotline between Moscow and Washington was set up to allow instant communication between the two heads of state to prevent similar incidents in the future.

Accomplishments of the Lyndon B. Johnson Presidency

Kennedy's vice president, **Lyndon Johnson**, assumed the presidency after Kennedy's **assassination**. He supported civil rights bills, tax cuts, and other wide-reaching legislation that Kennedy had also supported. Johnson saw America as a "**Great Society**," and enacted legislation to fight disease and poverty, renew urban areas, and support education and environmental conservation. Medicare and Medicaid were instituted under his administration. He continued Kennedy's support of space exploration, and he is also known, although less positively, for his handling of the **Vietnam War**.

Factors That Led to the Growth of the Civil Rights Movement

In the 1950s, post-war America was experiencing a rapid growth in prosperity; however, African Americans found themselves left behind. Racial segregation and discrimination were still legalized at this time and disproportionately affected black Americans and other minority groups. The civil rights movement arose to abolish legalized discrimination and provide equality for all Americans. While there were many different ideologies that made up the civil rights movement, the movement is largely characterized by peaceful protest and civil disobedience.

- **Rosa Parks**—often called the "mother of the Civil Rights Movement," her refusal to give up her seat on the bus to a white man served as a seed from which the movement grew.
- **Martin Luther King, Jr.**—the best-known leader of the movement, King drew on Gandhi's beliefs and encouraged non-violent opposition. He led a march on Washington in 1963, received the Nobel Peace Prize in 1964, and was assassinated in 1968.
- **Malcolm X**—espousing less peaceful means of change, Malcolm X became a Black Muslim and supported black nationalism.

Policies and Legislation Enacted Expanding Minority Rights

Several major acts have been passed, particularly since WWII, to protect the rights of minorities in America. These include:

- Civil Rights Act (1964)
- Voting Rights Act (1965)
- Age Discrimination Act (1967)
- Americans with Disabilities Act (1990)

Other important movements for civil rights included a prisoner's rights movement, movements for immigrant rights, and the women's rights movement. The National Organization for Women (NOW) was established in 1966 and worked to pass the Equal Rights Amendment. The amendment was passed, but not enough states ratified it for it to become part of the US Constitution.

Impact of Stokely Carmichael, Adam Clayton Powell, and Jesse Jackson

- **Stokely Carmichael**—Carmichael originated the term "Black Power" and served as head of the Student Nonviolent Coordinating Committee. He believed in black pride and black culture and felt separate political and social institutions should be developed for blacks.
- **Adam Clayton Powell**—chairman of the Coordinating Committee for Employment, he led rent strikes and other actions, as well as a bus boycott, to increase the hiring of blacks.
- **Jesse Jackson**—Jackson was selected to head the Chicago Operation Breadbasket in 1966, and went on to organize boycotts and other actions. He also had an unsuccessful run for president.

Events of the Civil Rights Movement

Major events of the Civil Rights Movement include:

- **Montgomery Bus Boycott**—in 1955, Rosa Parks refused to give her seat on the bus to a white man. As a result, she was tried and convicted of disorderly conduct and of violating local ordinances. A 381-day bus boycott ensued, protesting segregation on public buses.

- **Desegregation of Little Rock**—in 1957, after the Supreme Court decision on Brown v. Board of Education, which declared "separate but equal" unconstitutional, the Arkansas school board voted to desegregate their schools. Even though Arkansas was considered progressive, its governor brought in the Arkansas National Guard to prevent nine black students from entering Central High School in Little Rock. President Eisenhower responded by federalizing the National Guard and ordering them to stand down.
- **Birmingham Campaign**—protestors organized a variety of actions such as sit-ins and an organized march to launch a voting campaign. When the City of Birmingham declared the protests illegal, the protestors, including Martin Luther King, Jr., persisted and were arrested and jailed.
- **March on Washington**—on August 28, 1963, more than 200,000 people marched on Washington, D.C. to advocate for civil and economic rights for African Americans. Dr. Martin Luther King Jr., positioned near the Lincoln Memorial, gave his famous "I Have a Dream" speech. This march was heavily influential in passing the Civil Rights Act of 1964.

Pieces of Legislation Passed as a Result of the Civil Rights Movement

Other pieces of legislation passed as a result of the Civil Rights movement include:

- **Brown v. Board of Education** (1954)—the Supreme Court declared that "separate but equal" accommodations and services were unconstitutional.
- **Civil Rights Act of 1964**—this declared discrimination illegal in employment, education, or public accommodation.
- **Voting Rights Act of 1965**—this act ended various activities practiced, mostly in the South, to bar blacks from exercising their voting rights. These included poll taxes and literacy tests.
- **Fair Housing Act of 1968**—this act prohibited discrimination in the sale, purchase, and rental of housing.

Other pieces of legislation that expanded minority rights include the Age Discrimination Act (1967) and the Americans with Disabilities Act (1990). Other important movements for civil rights included prisoners' rights movements, movements for immigrant rights, and the women's rights movement. The National Organization for Women (NOW) was established in 1966 and worked to pass the Equal Rights Amendment. The amendment was passed, but not enough states ratified it for it to become part of the US Constitution.

Events of the Richard Nixon Presidency

Richard Nixon is best known for the **Watergate scandal** during his presidency, but other important events marked his tenure as president, including:

- End of the Vietnam War
- Improved diplomatic relations between the US and China, and the US and the USSR
- National Environmental Policy Act passed, providing for environmental protection
- Compulsory draft ended
- Supreme Court legalized abortion in Roe v. Wade (subsequently overturned in 2022)
- Watergate

The Watergate scandal of 1972 ended Nixon's presidency. Rather than face impeachment and removal from office, he **resigned** in 1974.

US Perspective on the Progression of the Vietnam War

After World War II, the US pledged, as part of its foreign policy, to come to the assistance of any country threatened by **communism**. When Vietnam was divided into a communist North and democratic South, much like Korea before it, the eventual attempts by the North to unify the country under Communist rule led to intervention by the US. On the home front, the **Vietnam War** became more and more unpopular politically, with Americans growing increasingly discontent with the inability of the US to achieve the goals it had set for the Asian country. When President **Richard Nixon** took office in 1969, his escalation of the war led to protests at Kent State in Ohio, during which several students were killed by National Guard troops. Protests continued, eventually resulting in the end of the compulsory draft in 1973. In that same year, the US departed Vietnam. In 1975, the South surrendered, and Vietnam became a unified country under communist rule.

Events of the Gerald Ford Presidency

Gerald Ford was appointed to the vice presidency after Nixon's vice president **Spiro Agnew** resigned in 1973 under charges of tax evasion. With Nixon's resignation, Ford became president.

Ford's presidency saw negotiations with Russia to limit nuclear arms, as well as struggles to deal with inflation, economic downturn, and energy shortages. Ford's policies sought to reduce governmental control of various businesses and reduce the role of government overall. He also worked to prevent escalation of conflicts in the Middle East.

End of the Cold War and the Dissolution of the Soviet Union

In the late 1980s, **Mikhail Gorbachev** led the Soviet Union. He introduced a series of reform programs. **Ronald Reagan** famously urged Gorbachev to tear down the **Berlin Wall** as a gesture of growing freedom in the Eastern Bloc, and in 1989 it was demolished, ending the separation of East and West Germany. The Soviet Union relinquished its power over the various republics in Eastern Europe, and they became independent nations with their own individual governments. In 1991, the **USSR** was dissolved and the Cold War also came to an end.

Review Video: The End of the Cold War
Visit mometrix.com/academy and enter code: 278032

Events of the Jimmy Carter Presidency

Jimmy Carter was elected as president in 1976. Faced with a budget deficit, high unemployment, and continued inflation, Carter also dealt with numerous matters of international diplomacy, including:

- **Torrijos-Carter Treaties**—the US gave control of the Panama Canal to Panama.
- **Camp David Accords**—negotiations between Anwar el-Sadat, the president of Egypt, and Menachem Begin, the Israeli Prime Minister, led to a peace treaty between Egypt and Israel.
- **Strategic Arms Limitation Talks (SALT)**—these led to agreements and treaties between the US and the Soviet Union.
- **Iran Hostage Crisis**—after the Shah of Iran was deposed, an Islamic cleric, Ayatollah Khomeini, came to power. The shah came to the US for medical treatment, and Iran demanded his return so he could stand trial. In retaliation, a group of Iranian students stormed the US Embassy in Iran. Fifty-two American hostages were held for 444 days.

Jimmy Carter was awarded the **Nobel Peace Prize** in 2002.

Events of the Ronald Reagan Presidency

Ronald Reagan, at 69, became the oldest American president. The two terms of his administration included notable events such as:

- Reaganomics, also known as supply-side, trickle-down, or free-market economics, involving major tax cuts
- Economic Recovery Tax Act of 1981
- First female justice appointed to the Supreme Court—Sandra Day O'Connor
- Massive increase in the national debt—from $1 trillion to $3 trillion
- Reduction of nuclear weapons via negotiations with Mikhail Gorbachev
- Iran-Contra scandal—cover-up of US involvement in revolutions in El Salvador and Nicaragua

- Deregulation of savings and loan industry
- Loss of the space shuttle *Challenger*

Events of the George H. W. Bush Presidency

Reagan's presidency was followed by a term under his former vice president, **George H. W. Bush**. Bush's run for president included the famous "**thousand points of light**" speech, which was instrumental in increasing his standing in the election polls. During Bush's presidency, numerous international events took place, including:

- Fall of the Berlin wall and Germany's unification
- Panamanian dictator Manuel Noriega captured and tried on drug and racketeering charges
- Dissolution of the Soviet Union
- Gulf War, or Operation Desert Storm, triggered by Iraq's invasion of Kuwait
- Tiananmen Square Massacre in Beijing, China
- Ruby Ridge
- The arrival of the World Wide Web

Events of the William Clinton Presidency

William Jefferson "Bill" Clinton was the second president in US history to be impeached, but he was not convicted, and maintained high approval ratings in spite of the impeachment. Major events during his presidency included:

- Family and Medical Leave Act
- "Don't Ask, Don't Tell," a compromise position regarding homosexuals serving in the military
- North American Free Trade Agreement, or NAFTA
- Defense of Marriage Act
- Oslo Accords
- Siege at Waco, Texas, involving the Branch Davidians led by David Koresh
- Bombing of the Murrah Federal Building in Oklahoma City, Oklahoma
- Troops sent to Haiti, Bosnia, and Somalia to assist with domestic problems in those areas

Events of the George W. Bush Presidency

George W. Bush, son of George H. W. Bush, became president after Clinton. Major events during his presidency included:

- September 11, 2001, al-Qaeda terrorists hijack commercial airliners and fly into the World Trade Center towers and the Pentagon, killing nearly 3,000 Americans
- US troops sent to Afghanistan to hunt down al-Qaeda leaders, including the head of the organization, Osama Bin Laden; beginning of the War on Terror
- US troops sent to Iraq, along with a multinational coalition, to depose Saddam Hussein and prevent his deployment of suspected weapons of mass destruction
- Subprime mortgage crisis and near collapse of the financial industry, leading to the Great Recession; first of multiple government bailouts of the financial industry

Events of the Barack Obama Presidency

In 2008, Barack Obama, a senator from Illinois, became the first African American US president. His administration focused on improving the lot of a country suffering from a major recession. His major initiatives included:

- Economic bailout packages
- Improvements in women's rights

- Moves to broaden LGBT rights
- Health care reform legislation
- Reinforcement of the war in Afghanistan

Events of the Donald Trump Presidency

In 2016, Donald Trump, previously a real estate developer and television personality, was elected 45th president after a tumultuous election in which he won the electoral college but lost the popular vote. Marked by tension between the administration and domestic media, Trump's initiatives included:

- Appointing three Supreme Court Justices: Neil Gorsuch, Brett Kavanaugh, and Amy Coney Barrett
- Passing a major tax reform bill
- Enacting travel and emigration restrictions on eight nations: Iran, Libya, Syria, Yemen, Somalia, Chad, North Korea, and Venezuela
- Recognizing Jerusalem, rather than Tel Aviv, as the capital of Israel
- Responding to the novel coronavirus (SARS-CoV-2) outbreak

Almost completely along party lines, Donald Trump was impeached by the House on charges of abuse of power and obstruction of Congress; he was acquitted by the Senate.

World History

World History Pre-1400

Different Periods of Prehistory

History begins when people started recording their existence with writing systems, but the vast majority of human existence occurred during prehistoric times. Because writing systems were not yet invented, much of our information about prehistory comes from archaeology and anthropology, which use physical remains and environmental evidence to uncover insights into humanity before we developed systems of recording our experiences.

- **Lower Paleolithic or Early Stone Age**— early humans were hunter-gatherers who lived in small groups or tribes and used crude tools like needles, hatchets, awls, and cutting tools made of stone, wood, and other natural materials.
- **Middle Paleolithic or Middle Stone Age**, beginning approximately 300,000 BC—stone tools became more sophisticated, local traditions were developed, and communities became more complex.
- **Upper Paleolithic or Late Stone Age**—Humans began to develop a wider variety of tools. These tools were better made and more specialized. They also began to wear clothes, organize in groups with definite social structures, and practice art. Most lived in caves during this time period.
- **Bronze Age**, beginning approximately 3000 BC—metals are discovered, and the first civilizations emerge as humans become more technologically advanced.
- **Iron Age**, beginning 1200 to 1000 BC—metal tools replace stone tools as humans develop knowledge of smelting.

Anthropology

Anthropology is the study of human culture. Anthropologists study groups of humans, how they relate to each other, and the similarities and differences between these different groups and cultures. Anthropological research takes two approaches: **cross-cultural research** and **comparative research**. Most anthropologists work by living among different cultures and participating in those cultures in order to learn about them.

There are four major **divisions** within anthropology:

- Biological anthropology
- Cultural anthropology
- Linguistic anthropology
- Archaeology

SCIENCE OF ARCHAEOLOGY

Archaeology is the study of past human cultures by evaluating what they leave behind. This can include bones, buildings, art, tools, pottery, graves, and even trash. Archaeologists maintain detailed notes and records of their findings and use special tools to evaluate what they find. Photographs, notes, maps, artifacts, and surveys of the area can all contribute to the evaluation of an archaeological site. By studying all these elements of numerous archeological sites, scientists have been able to theorize that humans or near-humans have existed for about 600,000 years. Before that, more primitive humans are believed to have appeared about one million years ago. These humans eventually developed into **Cro-Magnon man**, and then **Homo sapiens**, or modern man.

NEOLITHIC PERIOD

The Neolithic period, also known as the **New Stone Age**, refers to that stage of human cultural evolution in which man developed stone tools, settled in villages, and began making crafts. In order to begin living in towns, man had to learn how to domesticate animals and sustain agriculture; formerly, in the Paleolithic and Mesolithic periods, man had subsisted through hunting, fishing, and gathering. The **Neolithic period** is said to have ended when urban civilizations began, or when metal tools or writing began. Because the designation of Neolithic depends on these factors, anthropologists date its occurrence differently for different regions and populations. At present, anthropologists believe that the earliest Neolithic culture was in southwest Asia between 8000 and 6000 BC.

REQUIREMENTS FOR EARLY CIVILIZATIONS AND STATES

While historians and archaeologists don't all agree on exactly what makes a civilization, many consider the following features defining characteristics of civilizations:

- Urban centers
- Complex social structures
- Centralized government
- Organized religion
- Monumental architecture
- Writing systems
- Economic systems and trade
- Division of labor

The **earliest civilizations** developed in river valleys where reliable, fertile land was easily found, including:

- The Nile River Valley in Egypt
- Mesopotamia
- The Indus Valley
- Hwang Ho in China

The very earliest civilizations developed in the **Tigris-Euphrates valley** in Mesopotamia, which is now part of Iraq, and in Egypt's **Nile valley**. These civilizations arose between 5000 and 3000 BC. The area where these civilizations grew is known as the Fertile Crescent. Geography and the availability of water made large-scale human habitation possible. The walled city of Uruk, which was built in Sumer (southern Mesopotamia), is often considered the first city ever constructed.

Importance of Rivers and Water to the Growth of Early Civilizations

The earliest civilizations are also referred to as **fluvial civilizations** because they were founded near rivers. Rivers and the water they provide were vital to these early groupings, offering:

- Water for drinking, cultivating crops, and caring for domesticated animals
- A gathering place for wild animals that could be hunted
- Rich soil deposits as a result of regular flooding

Irrigation techniques helped direct water where it was most needed, to sustain herds of domestic animals and to nourish crops of increasing size and quality.

Fertile Crescent

James Breasted, an archaeologist from the University of Chicago, popularized the term "**Fertile Crescent**" to describe the area in Southwest Asia and the Mediterranean basin where the earliest civilizations arose. The region includes modern-day Iraq, Syria, Lebanon, Israel, Palestine, and Jordan. It is bordered on the south by the Syrian and Arabian Deserts, the west by the Mediterranean Sea, and to the north and east by the Taurus and Zagros Mountains, respectively. This area not only provided the raw materials for the development of increasingly advanced civilizations but also saw waves of migration and invasion, leading to the earliest wars and genocides as groups conquered and absorbed each other's cultures and inhabitants.

Ancient Civilizations of Mesopotamia and the Near East

The Near East was home to many distinct cultures and civilizations in the ancient world. These cultures controlled different areas of Mesopotamia and the Near East during various time periods but were similar in that they were **autocratic**: a single ruler served as the head of the government and often was the main religious ruler as well. These rulers were often tyrannical, militaristic leaders who controlled all aspects of life, including law, trade, and religious activity. Portions of the legacies of these civilizations remain in cultures today. These include mythologies, religious systems, mathematical innovations, and even elements of various languages.

The Sumerians

Sumer, located in the southern part of Mesopotamia, consisted of a dozen **city-states**. Each city-state had its own patron gods, and the leader of each city-state also served as the high priest. Cultural legacies of Sumer include:

- The invention of writing
- The invention of the wheel
- The first library—established in Assyria by Ashurbanipal
- The Hanging Gardens of Babylon—one of the Seven Wonders of the Ancient World
- First written laws—Ur-Nammu's Codes and the Codes of Hammurabi
- The *Epic of Gilgamesh*—the first recorded epic story

Review Video: Early Mesopotamia: The Sumerians
Visit mometrix.com/academy and enter code: 939880

The Babylonians

The Babylonians conquered the Sumerians and established a city on the Euphrates River in approximately 1750 BC One of the most famous Babylonian rulers was Hammurabi, an Amorite leader who established the famous Code of Hammurabi, an extremely detailed set of laws. This marked the first time that a set of rules governing every aspect of social life was applied to an entire people.

THE AMORITES

A group of Semitic-speaking people often referred to as the Amorites existed in Mesopotamia for a long time, but the early history of this group is not well known. Some scholars believe the term actually referred to multiple different groups of people from the west. The earliest records of them paint the Amorites as a nomadic, potentially uncivilized, people who made incursions into established territories, oftentimes stealing from communities; however, they eventually assimilated into Mesopotamia and added elements of their own culture. The Amorites are best known for their period of rule over the kingdom of Babylonia.

THE HITTITES

The Hittites conquered the Babylonian civilization but adopted their religion, laws, and literature. Overall, the Hittites tended to tolerate other religions, unlike many other contemporary cultures, and absorbed foreign gods into their own belief systems rather than forcing their religion onto peoples they conquered. The Hittite Empire reached its peak in 1600-1200 BC. After a war with Egypt, which weakened them severely, they were eventually conquered by the Assyrians.

THE ASSYRIANS

The Assyrians developed powerful military technologies, such as horse-drawn chariots and iron weapons, that allowed them to eventually build one of the world's oldest empires. They had a long and complex history, at times being subjects under the rule of other civilizations, like the Babylonians. At their peak (c. 911-612 BC), they were one of the most powerful civilizations in the world, and they were able to maintain their empire for hundreds of years.

THE CHALDEANS

The Chaldeans were a Semitic people who ruled over the Neo-Babylonian Empire. Originally a separate tribal group, they largely assimilated into Babylonian culture. The Neo-Babylonian Empire ultimately fell to the Persian Empire in 539 BC.

THE PERSIAN EMPIRE

The Persian Empire (Achaemenid Empire) were conquerors, but those they conquered were often allowed to keep their own laws, customs, and religious traditions rather than being forced to accept those of their conquerors. They are recognized for their centralized bureaucratic administration and complex infrastructure. They mainly practiced Zoroastrianism, a religion that was heavily influential before it declined after the spread of Islam in the region.

HEBREWS

The Hebrew or ancient Israelite culture emerged in the Levant in the second century BC. They developed the monotheistic religion that eventually developed into modern Judaism and Christianity. The Hebrew history is well-preserved and contains detailed descriptions of conquests against them from Egypt, Assyria, Babylon, Persia, and Rome, many of which can be confirmed from artifacts of other cultures. Despite being conquered by a variety of empires, their cultural identity has survived and still exists today.

EGYPT

Egypt was one of the most powerful and culturally significant civilizations in the ancient world. Its history is often broken up into a few distinct eras: the Old Kingdom, the First Intermediate Period, the Middle Kingdom, the Second Intermediate Period, the New Kingdom, the Third Intermediate Period, and the Late Period. These eras cover a span of around 3,000 years, beginning approximately in the year 3150 BC, when Menes (an Egyptian ruler whose identity is debated) united Upper and Lower Egypt, and ending around 332 BC, when Alexander the Great conquered the region.

Egypt was centered around the Nile River, which had a predictable annual flooding schedule that the Egyptians used to grow large surpluses of crops. The Egyptians traded these surplus crops with nearby civilizations, particularly Mesopotamia. This trade formed one of the chief bases of their wealth and influence.

During its long history, Ancient Egypt contributed many technological and cultural innovations in the fields of religion, art, engineering, astronomy, medicine, and more. They are renowned for their impressive monuments, temples, and tombs, including the Great Pyramids and the Sphinx of Giza. On many of these monuments is a complex script developed by the Egyptians called hieroglyphics. This is a written language that uses pictures and other symbols to represent words, ideas, and sounds. It was often used to record important events, such as battles, and the lives of important people, such as the Pharaoh (the modern title attributed to the king of Egypt).

KUSHITES

Kush, or Cush, was located in Nubia, south of ancient Egypt, and the earliest existing records of this civilization were found in Egyptian texts. At one time, Kush was the largest empire on the Nile River, ruling not only Nubia but Upper and Lower Egypt as well.

In Neolithic times, Kushites lived in villages, with buildings made of mud bricks. They were settled rather than nomadic and practiced hunting and fishing, cultivated grain, and also herded cattle. Kerma, the capital, was a major center of trade.

Kush determined leadership through matrilineal descent of their kings, as did Egypt. Their heads of state, the Kandake or Kentake, were female. Their polytheistic religion included the primary Egyptian gods as well as regional gods, including a lion-headed god, which is commonly found in African cultures. Kush was conquered by the Aksumite Empire in the 4th century AD.

PHOENICIANS

Skilled seafarers and navigators, the Phoenicians were a maritime civilization mostly along the coast of the Levant region. They were highly skilled in trade and developed a purple dye that was in great demand in the ancient world. They were also skilled glass and metal workers. They devised a phonetic alphabet, using symbols to represent individual sounds rather than whole words or syllables.

MINOANS

The Minoans lived on the island of Crete, just off the coast of Greece. This civilization reigned from approximately 4000 to 1400 BC and is considered to be the first advanced civilization in Europe. The Minoans developed writing systems known to linguists as **Linear A** and **Linear B**. Linear A has not yet been translated; Linear B evolved into classical Greek script. "Minoans" is not the name they used for themselves but is instead a variation on the name of King Minos, a king in Greek mythology believed by some to have been a denizen of Crete. The Minoan civilization subsisted on trade, and their way of life was often disrupted by earthquakes and volcanoes. Much is still unknown about the Minoans, and archaeologists continue to study their architecture and archaeological remains. The Minoan culture eventually fell to Greek invaders and was supplanted by the **Mycenaean civilization**.

MYCENAEANS

In contrast to the Minoans, whom they displaced, the **Mycenaeans** relied more on conquest than on trade. Mycenaean states included Sparta, Athens, and Corinth. The history of this civilization, including the **Trojan War**, was recorded by the Greek poet **Homer**. His work was largely considered mythical until archaeologists discovered evidence of the city of **Troy** in Hisarlik, Turkey. Archaeologists continue to add to the body of information about this ancient culture, translating documents written in Linear B, a script derived from the Minoan Linear A. It is theorized that the Mycenaean civilization was eventually destroyed in either a Dorian invasion or an attack by Greek invaders from the north.

DORIAN INVASION

A Dorian invasion does not refer to an invasion by a particular group of people, but rather is a hypothetical theory to explain the end of the **Mycenaean civilization** and the growth of **classical Greece**. Ancient tradition refers to these events as "the return of the Heracleidae," or the sons (descendants) of Hercules. Archaeologists and historians still do not know exactly who conquered the Mycenaeans, but it is believed to have occurred around 1200 BC, contemporaneous with the destruction of the **Hittite civilization** in what is now modern Turkey. The Hittites speak of an attack by people of the Aegean Sea, or the "Sea People." Only Athens was left intact.

Ancient India

The civilizations of ancient India gave rise to both **Hinduism** and **Buddhism**, major world religions that have influenced countries far from their place of origin. Practices such as yoga, increasingly popular in the West, can trace their roots to these earliest Indian civilizations, and the poses are still formally referred to by Sanskrit names. Literature from ancient India includes the *Mahabharata* containing the *Bhagavad Gita*, the *Ramayana*, *Arthashastra*, and the *Vedas*, a collection of sacred texts. Indo-European languages, including English, find their beginnings in these ancient cultures. Ancient Indo-Aryan languages such as Sanskrit are still used in some formal Hindu practices.

Indus Valley Civilization

The Indus Valley Civilization (IVC) was an urban civilization that arose in the Indus Valley, located in between the modern countries of Iran, India, and Pakistan. These ancient humans developed the concept of zero in mathematics, practiced an early form of the Hindu religion, and developed the caste system which is still prevalent in India today. Archeologists are still uncovering information about this highly developed ancient civilization.

Earliest Civilizations in China

Many historians believe **Chinese civilization** is the oldest uninterrupted civilization in the world. The **Neolithic age** in China goes back to 10,000 BC, with agriculture in China beginning as early as 5000 BC. Their system of writing dates to 1500 BC. The Yellow River served as the center for the earliest Chinese settlements. In Ningxia, in northwest China, there are carvings on cliffs that date back to the Paleolithic Period, indicating the extreme antiquity of Chinese culture. Literature from ancient China includes Confucius' *Analects*, the *Tao Te Ching*, and a variety of poetry.

Ancient Cultures in the Americas

Less is known of ancient American civilizations since less was left behind. Some of the more well-known cultures include:

- The **Norte Chico civilization** in Peru, an agricultural society of up to 30 individual communities, existed over 5,000 years ago. This culture is also known as the Caral-Supe civilization, and is the oldest known civilization in the Americas.
- The **Anasazi**, or Ancestral Pueblo People, lived in what is now the southwestern United States. Emerging about 1200 BC, the Anasazi built complex adobe dwellings and were the forerunners of later Pueblo Indian cultures.
- The **Maya** emerged in southern Mexico and northern Central America as early as 2600 BC. They developed a written language and a complex calendar.

Greece

After the fall of Mycenaean civilization came a dark age out of which would spring one of the most influential cultures in the western world: Greece. While much was lost after the fall of the Mycenaeans, including writing, the Ancient Greeks, in the Archaic Period (800-500 BC) and the Classical Period (500-323 BC), went on to make fundamental achievements in politics, philosophy, history, drama, literature, art, mathematics, and science. They colonized areas all across the Mediterranean and spread their culture around the world. Their culture was heavily influential in shaping the Roman Empire and later civilizations, including those that exist today.

Spartans vs. Athenians

Both powerful Greek city-states, Sparta and Athens fought each other in the **Peloponnesian War** (431-404 BC). Despite their proximity, the Spartans and the Athenians nurtured contrasting cultures:

- The **Spartans**, located in Peloponnesus, were ruled by an oligarchic military state. They practiced farming, disallowed trade for Spartan citizens, and valued military arts and strict discipline. They emerged as the strongest military force in the area and maintained this status for many years. In one memorable encounter, a small group of Spartans held off a huge army of Persians at Thermopylae.
- The **Athenians** were centered in Attica, where the land was rocky and unsuitable for farming. Like the Spartans, they descended from invaders who spoke Greek. Their government was very different from Sparta's; it was in Athens that democracy was created by Cleisthenes of Athens in 508 BC. Athenians excelled in art, theater, architecture, and philosophy.

Contributions of Ancient Greece That Still Exist Today

Ancient Greece made numerous major contributions to cultural development, including:

- **Theater**—Aristophanes and other Greek playwrights laid the groundwork for modern theatrical performance.
- **Alphabet**—the Greek alphabet, derived from the Phoenician alphabet, developed into the Roman alphabet, and then into our modern-day alphabet.
- **Geometry**—Pythagoras and Euclid pioneered much of the system of geometry still taught today. Archimedes made various mathematical discoveries, including calculating a very accurate value of pi.
- **Historical writing**—much of ancient history doubles as mythology or religious texts. Herodotus and Thucydides made use of research and interpretation to record historical events.
- **Philosophy**—Socrates, Plato, and Aristotle served as the fathers of Western philosophy. Their work is still required reading for philosophy students.

Review Video: Ancient Greece Timeline
Visit mometrix.com/academy and enter code: 800829

Alexander the Great

Born to Philip II of Macedon and tutored by Aristotle, **Alexander the Great** is considered one of the greatest conquerors in history. He conquered Egypt and the Achaemenid/Persian Empire, a powerful empire founded by Cyrus the Great that spanned three continents, and he traveled as far as India and the Iberian Peninsula. Alexander the Great died at an early age and, though his cause of death is not known for certain, one hypothesis is that he succumbed to malaria at the early age of 32. His conquering efforts spread Greek culture into the east. This cultural diffusion left a greater mark on history than did his empire, which fell apart due to internal conflict not long after his death. Trade between the East and West increased, as did an exchange of ideas and beliefs that influenced both regions greatly. The **Hellenistic traditions** his conquest spread were prevalent in Byzantine culture until as late as the 15th century.

Persian Wars

The Persian Empire, ruled by **Cyrus the Great**, encompassed an area from the Black Sea to Afghanistan and beyond into Central Asia. After the death of Cyrus, **Darius I** became king in 522 BC. The empire reached its zenith during his reign, and Darius attempted to conquer Greece as well. From 499 to 449 BC, the Greeks and Persians fought in the **Persian Wars**. The **Peace of Callias** brought an end to the fighting, after the Greeks were able to repel the invasion.

Battles of the Persian Wars included:

- The **Battle of Marathon**—heavily outnumbered Greek forces managed to achieve victory.
- The **Battle of Thermopylae**—a small band of Spartans held off a throng of Persian troops for several days before Persia defeated the Greeks and captured an evacuated Athens.
- The **Battle of Salamis**—this was a naval battle that again saw outnumbered Greeks achieving victory.
- The **Battle of Plataea**—this was another Greek victory, but one in which they outnumbered the Persians. This ended the invasion of Greece.

Maurya Empire

The Maurya Empire was a large, powerful empire established in India. It was one of the largest ever to rule in the Indian subcontinent and existed from 322 to 185 BC, ruled by **Chandragupta Maurya** after the withdrawal from India of Alexander the Great. The Maurya Empire was highly developed, including a standardized economic system, waterways, and private corporations. Trade to the Greeks and others became common, with goods including silk, exotic foods, and spices. Religious development included the rise of Buddhism and Jainism. The laws of the Maurya Empire protected not only civil and social rights of the citizens, but they also protected animals, establishing protected zones for economically important creatures such as elephants, lions, and tigers. This period of time in Indian history was largely peaceful, perhaps due to the strong Buddhist beliefs of many of its leaders. The empire finally fell after a succession of weak leaders and was taken over by **Demetrius**, a Greco-Bactrian king who took advantage of this lapse in leadership to conquer southern Afghanistan and Pakistan around 180 BC, forming the **Indo-Greek Kingdom**.

Hinduism

Hinduism is the traditional religion of India. It is expressed in an individual's philosophy and behavior, rather than in the performance of any specific rituals. **Hinduism** does not claim a founder but has evolved slowly over thousands of years; the first Hindu writings date back to the third millennium BC. There are a few concepts that are common to all permutations of Hinduism, such as the **Vedas**, which are considered to be the sacred texts of the religion. The chief aim in life for a Hindu is to be liberated from the cycle of suffering and rebirth. Hindus believe in **reincarnation** and that a person's conduct in this life will affect his or her position in the next (**karma**). Although Hinduism is frequently associated with the caste system, the two are actually unrelated.

Buddhism

Buddhism was created by **Gautama Siddhartha** (otherwise known as Buddha) in about 528 B.C. It was in part a response to Hinduism, which Buddha felt had become bloated with worldliness and politics. Traditional Buddhism is based upon the **Four Noble Truths**: existence is suffering, suffering is caused by desire, an end of suffering will come with Nirvana, and Nirvana will come with the practice of the **Eightfold Path**. The steps of the Eightfold Path are as follows: right views, right resolve, right speech, right action, right livelihood, right effort, right mindfulness, and right concentration. Buddhism did not receive any official sanction for a long time but did eventually spread and take hold in India, China, Japan, and elsewhere.

Development and Growth of the Chinese Empires

In China, history was divided into a series of **dynasties**. The most famous of these, the **Han dynasty**, existed from 206 BC to AD 220. Accomplishments of the Chinese empires included:

- Building the Great Wall of China
- Numerous inventions, including paper, paper money, printing, and gunpowder
- High level of artistic development
- Silk production

The Chinese dynasties were comparable to Rome as far as their artistic and intellectual accomplishments, as well as the size and scope of their influence.

Confucianism and Taoism

Confucianism was founded by Confucius (551–479 BC), who lived around the same time as Buddha. This faith was designed to relieve conflict in all arenas, from that which existed among families to that between Heaven and Earth. Confucius defined "appropriate" social roles for people of different ages, sexes, and social ranks; by assuming these roles, Confucians attempt to create a more peaceful world.

Taoism originated in China at approximately the same time as Confucianism. Taoism strives to create harmony between humans and the natural world. Unlike Confucianism, which has a significant political aspect and is largely monistic, Taoism values natural goodness and expressiveness over social order and is largely dualistic.

Roman Empire and Republic

Rome began humbly, in a single town that grew out of Etruscan settlements and traditions, founded, according to legend, by twin brothers Romulus and Remus, who were raised by wolves. Romulus killed Remus, and from his legacy grew Rome. A thousand years later, the **Roman Empire** covered a significant portion of the known world, from what is now Scotland, across Europe, and into the Middle East. **Hellenization**, or the spread of Greek culture throughout the world, served as an inspiration and a model for the spread of Roman culture. Rome brought in belief systems of conquered peoples as well as their technological and scientific accomplishments, melding the disparate parts into a Roman core. Rome began as a **republic** ruled by consuls, but after the assassination of **Julius Caesar**, it became an **empire** led by emperors. Rome's overall government was autocratic, but local officials came from the provinces where they lived. This limited administrative system was probably a major factor in the long life of the empire.

Review Video: Roman Republic Part One
Visit mometrix.com/academy and enter code: 360192

Review Video: Roman Republic Part Two
Visit mometrix.com/academy and enter code: 881514

Development of the Byzantine Empire from the Roman Empire

Constantinople developed as the eastern capital of the Roman Empire and later the Byzantine Empire. Its culture and institutions were primarily shaped by the continuation of Roman political structures, the dominance of Greek language and intellectual traditions, and the growing influence of Christianity as the empire's central religious and cultural force. These three elements together defined Byzantine civilization and distinguished it from other ancient regional traditions.

Early Christianity

Early Christianity was a mass of competing doctrines, including various groups such as the Gnostics and Arians who all sought to have their view legitimized as the truth. Eventually, the **orthodox church**, through an ecumenical council of bishops, created in the 4th century AD the canon of New Testament texts which exists today. The apostles had created a hierarchy of bishops, priests, and deacons who stressed obedience to duly constituted church authority. By the middle of the 2nd century, Christianity began to attract intellectuals in the **Roman Empire**. Although Christians were still liable to be persecuted in the farther reaches of the empire, many turned to the Church as the empire crumbled. For many, the christian church was all that was left of civilization and would rebuild Europe over the next millennium.

Significance of the Nicene Creed

The **Byzantine Empire** was Christian-based but incorporated Greek language, philosophy, and literature and drew its law and government policies from Rome. However, there was as yet no unified doctrine of Christianity, as it was a relatively new religion that had spread rapidly and without a great deal of organization. In 325, the **First Council of Nicaea** addressed this issue. From this conference came the **Nicene Creed**, addressing the Trinity and other basic Christian beliefs. The **Council of Chalcedon** in 451 further defined the view of the Trinity.

Factors That Led to the Fall of the Western Roman Empire

Germanic tribes, including the Visigoths, Ostrogoths, Vandals, Saxons, and Franks, controlled most of Europe. The Roman Empire faced major opposition on that front. The increasing size of the empire also made it harder to manage, leading to dissatisfaction throughout the empire as Roman government became less efficient. Germanic tribes refused to adhere to the Nicene Creed, instead following **Arianism**, which led the Roman Catholic Church to declare them heretics. The **Franks** proved a powerful military force in their defeat of the Muslims in 732. In 768, **Charlemagne** became king of the Franks. These tribes waged several wars against Rome, including the invasion of Britannia by the Angles and Saxons. Far-flung Rome lost control over this area of its empire, and eventually, Rome itself was **invaded**.

Iconoclasm and Conflicts of Roman Catholic and Eastern Orthodox Churches

Emperor Leo III ordered the destruction of all icons throughout the Byzantine Empire. Images of Jesus were replaced with crosses, and images of Jesus, Mary, or other religious figures were considered blasphemy on the grounds of idolatry. **Pope Gregory II** called a synod to discuss the issue. The synod declared that the images were not heretical and that strong disciplinary measures would result for anyone who destroyed them. Leo's response was an attempt to kill Pope Gregory, but this plan ended in failure.

Effect of the Viking Invasions on the Culture of England and Europe

Vikings invaded Northern France in the 10th century, eventually becoming the **Normans**. Originating in Scandinavia, the **Vikings** were accomplished seafarers with advanced knowledge of trade routes. With overpopulation plaguing their native lands, they began to travel. From the 8th to the 11th centuries, they spread throughout Europe, conquering and colonizing. Vikings invaded and colonized England in several waves, including the **Anglo-Saxon invasions** that displaced Roman control. Their influence remained significant in England, affecting everything from the language of the country to place names and even the government and social structure. By 900, Vikings had settled in **Iceland**. They proceeded then to **Greenland** and eventually to **North America**, arriving in the New World even before the Spanish and British who claimed the lands several centuries later. They also traded with the Byzantine Empire until the 11th century, when their significant level of activity came to an end.

West vs. East 10th-Century Events

In **Europe**, the years AD 500-1000 are largely known as the **Dark Ages**. In the 10th century, numerous Viking invasions disrupted societies that had been more settled under Roman rule. Vikings settled in Northern France, eventually becoming the Normans. By the 11th century, Europe would rise again into the **High Middle Ages** with the beginning of the **Crusades**.

In **China**, wars also raged. This led the Chinese to make use of gunpowder for the first time in warfare.

In the **Americas**, the **Mayan Empire** was winding down while the **Toltec** became more prominent. **Pueblo** Indian culture was also at its zenith.

In the **East**, the **Muslims** and the **Byzantine Empire** were experiencing a significant period of growth and development.

World History 1400 to 1914

Feudalism in Europe in the Middle Ages

A major element of the social and economic life of Europe, **feudalism** developed as a way to ensure European rulers would have the wherewithal to quickly raise an army when necessary. **Vassals** swore loyalty and promised to provide military service for lords, who in return offered a **fief**, or a parcel of land, for them to use to generate their livelihood. Vassals could work the land themselves, have it worked by **peasants** or **serfs**—

workers who had few rights and were little more than slaves—or grant the fief to someone else. The king legally owned all the land, but in return, promised to protect the vassals from invasion and war. Vassals returned a certain percentage of their income to the lords, who in turn, passed a portion of their income on to the king. A similar practice was **manorialism**, in which the feudal system was applied to a self-contained manor. These manors were often owned by the lords who ran them but were usually included in the same system of loyalty and promises of protection that drove feudalism.

Review Video: The Middle Ages: Feudalism
Visit mometrix.com/academy and enter code: 165907

EFFECT OF BLACK DEATH ON MEDIEVAL POLITICS AND ECONOMIC CONDITIONS

The Black Death, believed to be **bubonic plague**, most likely came to Europe on fleas carried by rats on sailing vessels. The plague killed more than a third of the entire population of Europe and effectively ended **feudalism** as a political system. Many who had formerly served as peasants or serfs found different work, as a demand for skilled labor grew. Nation-states grew in power, and in the face of the pandemic, many began to turn away from faith in God and toward the ideals of ancient Greece and Rome for government and other beliefs.

Review Video: Black Death (An Overview)
Visit mometrix.com/academy and enter code: 431857

INFLUENCE OF THE ROMAN CATHOLIC CHURCH OVER MEDIEVAL SOCIETY

The Roman Catholic Church extended significant influence both politically and economically throughout medieval society. The church supplied **education**, as there were no established schools or universities. To a large extent, the church had filled a power void left by various invasions throughout the former Roman Empire, leading it to exercise a role that was far more **political** than religious. Kings were heavily influenced by the pope and other church officials, and churches controlled large amounts of land throughout Europe.

PROGRESSION OF THE CRUSADES AND MAJOR FIGURES INVOLVED

The Crusades began in the 11th century and continued into the 15th. The major goal of these various military ventures was to slow the progression of Muslim forces into Europe and to expel them from the **Holy Land**, where they had taken control of Jerusalem and Palestine. Alexius I, the Byzantine emperor, called for help from **Pope Urban** II when Palestine was taken. In 1095, the pope, hoping to reunite Eastern and Western Christianity, encouraged all Christians to help the cause. Amidst great bloodshed, this crusade recaptured **Jerusalem**, but over the next centuries, Jerusalem and other areas of the Holy Land changed hands numerous times. The **Second Crusade** (1147-1149) consisted of an unsuccessful attempt to retake Damascus. The **Third Crusade**, under Pope Gregory VIII, attempted to recapture Jerusalem but failed. The **Fourth Crusade**, under Pope Innocent III, attempted to come into the Holy Land via Egypt. The Crusades led to greater power for the pope and the Catholic Church in general and also opened numerous trading and cultural routes between Europe and the East.

POLITICAL DEVELOPMENTS IN INDIA THROUGH THE 11TH CENTURY

After the Mauryan dynasty, the **Guptas** ruled India, maintaining a long period of peace and prosperity in the area. During this time, the Indian people invented the decimal system and the concept of zero. They produced cotton and calico, as well as other products in high demand in Europe and Asia, and developed a complex system of medicine. The Gupta Dynasty ended in the 6th century. First, the **Huns** invaded, and then the **Hephthalites** (an Asian nomadic tribe) destroyed the weakened empire. In the 14th century, **Tamerlane**, a Muslim who envisioned restoring Genghis Khan's empire, expanded India's borders and founded the **Mogul Empire**. His grandson Akbar promoted freedom of religion and built a widespread number of mosques, forts, and other buildings throughout the country.

Development of Chinese and Japanese Governments Through the 11th Century

After the Mongols, led by Genghis Khan and his grandson Kublai Khan, unified the Mongol Empire, **China** was led by the **Ming Dynasty** (1368-1644) and the **Manchu (also known as Qing) Dynasty** (1644-1912). Both dynasties were isolationist, ending China's interaction with other countries until the 18th century. The Ming Dynasty was known for its porcelain, while the Manchus focused on farming and road construction as the population grew.

Japan developed independently of China but borrowed the Buddhist religion, the Chinese writing system, and other elements of Chinese society. Ruled by the divine emperor, Japan basically functioned on a feudal system led by **daimyo**, or warlords, and soldiers known as **samurai**. Japan remained isolationist, not interacting significantly with the rest of the world until the 1800s.

Ming Dynasty

The Ming dynasty lasted in China from AD 1368 to 1644. This dynasty was established by a Buddhist monk, **Zhu Yuanzhang**, who quickly became obsessed with consolidating power in the central government and was known for the brutality with which he achieved his ends. It was during the **Ming dynasty** that China developed and introduced its famous civil service examinations, rigorous tests on the **Confucian classics**. The future of an ambitious Chinese youth depended on his performance on this exam. The capital was transferred from Nanjing to Beijing during this period, and the **Forbidden City** was constructed inside the new capital. The Ming period, despite its constant expansionary wars, also continued China's artistic resurgence; the porcelain of this period is especially admired.

Developments in Africa Through the 11th Century

Much of Africa was difficult to traverse early on, due to the large amount of desert and other inhospitable terrain. **Egypt** remained important, though most of the northern coast became Muslim as their armies spread through the area. **Ghana** rose as a trade center in the 9th century, lasting into the 12th century, primarily trading in gold, which it exchanged for Saharan salt. **Mali** rose somewhat later, with the trade center Timbuktu becoming an important exporter of goods such as iron, leather, and tin. Mali also dealt in agricultural trade, becoming one of the most significant trading centers in West Africa. The Muslim religion dominated, and technological advancement was sparse.

African culture was largely defined through migration, as Arab merchants and others settled on the continent, particularly along the east coast. Scholars from the Muslim nations gravitated to Timbuktu, which in addition to its importance in trade, had also become a magnet for those seeking Islamic knowledge and education.

History of Islam and Its Role in Bringing Unity to the Middle East

Born in AD 570, **Muhammad** began preaching around 613, leading his followers in a new religion called **Islam**, which means "submission to God's will." Before this time, the Arabian Peninsula was inhabited largely by Bedouins, nomads who battled amongst each other and lived in tribal organizations. But by the time Muhammad died in 632, most of Arabia had become Muslim to some extent.

Muhammad conquered **Mecca**, where a temple called the **Kaaba** had long served as a center of the nomadic religions. He declared this temple the most sacred of Islam, and Mecca as the holy city. His writings became the **Koran**, or **Qur'an**, divine revelations he said had been delivered to him by the angel Gabriel.

Muhammad's teachings gave the formerly tribal Arabian people a sense of unity that had not existed in the area before. After his death, the converted Muslims of Arabia conquered a vast territory, creating an empire and bringing advances in literature, technology, science, and art as Europe was declining under the scourge of the Black Death. Literature from this period includes the *Arabian Nights* and the *Rubaiyat* of Omar Khayyam.

Later in its development, Islam split into two factions; the **Shiite** and the **Sunni** Muslims. Conflict continues today between these groups.

OTTOMAN EMPIRE

By 1400, the Ottomans had grown in power in Anatolia and had begun attempts to take Constantinople. In 1453, they finally conquered the Byzantine capital and renamed it **Istanbul**. The **Ottoman Empire's** major strength, much like Rome before it, lay in its ability to unite widely disparate people through religious tolerance. This tolerance, which stemmed from the idea that Muslims, Christians, and Jews were fundamentally related and could coexist, enabled the Ottomans to develop a widely varied culture. They also believed in just laws and just government, with government centered in a monarch, known as the **sultan**.

RENAISSANCE

The French word "renaissance" means "rebirth." This is the term used to describe a period of history and cultural movement that occurred after the Middle Ages. During this time, interest rose again in the beliefs and politics of ancient Greece and Rome. Art, literature, music, science, and philosophy all burgeoned during the Renaissance and experience rapid progress.

Many of the ideas of the Renaissance began in **Florence, Italy** in the 14th century, spurred by the **Medici** family. Education for the upper classes expanded to include law, math, reading, writing, and classical Greek and Roman works. As the Renaissance progressed, the world was presented through art and literature in a realistic way that had never been explored before. This **realism** drove culture to new heights.

Review Video: The Renaissance
Visit mometrix.com/academy and enter code: 123100

HUMANISM

The term "humanism" was attributed long after the Renaissance but represents a foundational collection of ideas that propelled much of the developments that occurred during the Renaissance in art, politics, education, and many other fields. Humanists believed that the study of classics from Ancient Greece and Rome was essential to understanding humanity, virtues, ethics, and peoples' roles in society. The study of humanity was given precedence over the study of religion, though religion and humanism were not mutually exclusive, and many religious people also held many humanist beliefs. Humanism did not represent a formal school of thought or encompassing philosophy. It was, rather, a general intellectual movement that placed education—specifically of classical texts—at the forefront. Some of the main subjects of Renaissance humanism were:

- Private and civic virtue
- Latin
- Grammar and rhetoric
- Literature and poetry
- Moral philosophy

RENAISSANCE ARTISTS, AUTHORS, AND SCIENTISTS

Artists of the Renaissance included Leonardo da Vinci, also an inventor; Michelangelo, also an architect; and others who focused on realism in their work. In **literature**, major contributions came from humanist authors like Petrarch, Erasmus, Sir Thomas More, and Boccaccio, who believed man should focus on reality rather than on the ethereal. Shakespeare, Cervantes, and Dante followed in their footsteps, and their works found a wide audience thanks to Gutenberg's development of the printing press.

Scientific developments of the Renaissance included the work of Copernicus, Galileo, and Kepler, who challenged the geocentric philosophies of the day by proving that the earth was not the center of the solar system.

TWO PHASES OF THE REFORMATION PERIOD

The Reformation period arose near the later part of the Renaissance and consisted of both the Protestant and the Catholic Reformation. The **Protestant Reformation** rose in Germany when **Martin Luther** protested abuses of the Catholic Church. **John Calvin** led the movement in Switzerland, while in England, King Henry VIII made use of the Reformation's ideas to further his own political goals. The **Catholic Reformation**, or **Counter-Reformation**, occurred in response to the Protestant movement, leading to various changes in the Catholic Church. Some provided wider tolerance of different religious viewpoints, but others actually increased the persecution of those deemed to be heretics.

From a **religious** standpoint, the Reformation occurred due to abuses by the Catholic Church such as indulgences and dispensations, religious offices being offered up for sale, and an increasingly dissolute clergy. **Politically**, the Reformation was driven by increased power of various ruling monarchs, who wished to take all power to themselves rather than allowing power to remain with the church. They also had begun to chafe at papal taxes and the church's increasing wealth. The ideas of the Protestant Revolution removed power from the Catholic Church and the Pope himself, playing nicely into the hands of those monarchs, such as Henry VIII, who wanted out from under the church's control.

Review Video: Martin Luther and the Reformation
Visit mometrix.com/academy and enter code: 691828

Review Video: The Counter-Reformation
Visit mometrix.com/academy and enter code: 950498

Review Video: The Protestants
Visit mometrix.com/academy and enter code: 583582

Developments of the Scientific Revolution

In addition to holding power in the political realm, church doctrine also governed scientific belief. During the **Scientific Revolution**, however, which began during the renaissance, astronomers and other scientists began to amass evidence that challenged the church's scientific doctrines. These scientists employed the scientific method and emergent theories and technologies to make new discoveries about the universe. It was during the Scientific Revolution that many huge scientific discoveries were made, and the very nature of knowledge gathering changed. Major figures of the Scientific Revolution included:

- **Nicolaus Copernicus**—wrote *On the Revolutions of the Celestial Spheres*, arguing that the earth revolved around the sun
- **Tycho Brahe**—cataloged astronomical observations
- **Johannes Kepler**—developed laws of planetary motion
- **Galileo Galilei**—defended the heliocentric theories of Copernicus and Kepler, discovered four moons of Jupiter, and died under house arrest by the church, charged with heresy
- **Isaac Newton**—discovered gravity; studied optics, calculus, and physics; and believed the workings of nature could be studied and proven through observation

Review Video: The Scientific Revolution
Visit mometrix.com/academy and enter code: 974600

Major Ideas of the Enlightenment

The Enlightenment (also called the Age of Reason) began in the late 17th century and lasted until around the late 18th century. It came partially as a result of the reformation, which diminished some of the power of the Christian Church. This allowed more freedom of expression and thought. During this time in Europe and North America, philosophers and scientists began to rely more and more on **observation** and logic to support their ideas rather than building on past beliefs, particularly those held by the church. A focus on **ethics and reason** drove their work. Through reason, they believed, some of the universe's most difficult questions—be them in ethics, politics, or science — could be answered. Major philosophers of the Enlightenment included:

- **Rene Descartes**—while often considered a pre-Enlightenment thinker, Descartes's philosophical work was instrumental to the development of philosophy in the Enlightenment. He believed that in order to know something, everything must first be put into doubt until it could be proved. He believed the senses could not be fully trusted to represent reality, but that reason may be relied upon to understand the foundational aspects of existence. He famously wrote, "I think, therefore I am," which is his assertion that the very fact that he is thinking is evidence that he really exists.
- **David Hume**—he pioneered empiricism and skepticism, believing that truth could only be found through direct experience and that what others said to be true was always suspect.
- **Immanuel Kant**—he believed in self-examination and observation and that the root of morality lay within human beings.
- **Jean-Jacques Rousseau**—he developed the idea of the social contract, that government existed by the agreement of the people, and that the government was obligated to protect the people and their basic rights. His ideas heavily influenced the founding fathers.

Review Video: Age of Enlightenment
Visit mometrix.com/academy and enter code: 143022

American Revolution vs. French Revolution

Both the American and French Revolution came about as a protest against the excesses and overly controlling nature of their respective monarchs. In **America**, the British colonies had been left mostly to self-govern until the British monarchs began to increase control, spurring the colonies to revolt. In **France**, the nobility's excesses had led to increasingly difficult economic conditions, with inflation, heavy taxation, and food shortages creating great burdens on the lower classes. Both revolutions led to the development of republics to replace the monarchies that were displaced. However, the French Revolution eventually led to the rise of the dictator **Napoleon Bonaparte**, while the American Revolution produced a functioning, though imperfect, **republic** from the beginning.

Events and Figures of the French Revolution

In 1789, **King Louis XVI**, faced with a huge national debt, convened parliament. The **Third Estate**, or Commons, a division of the French parliament, then claimed power, and the king's resistance led to the storming of the **Bastille**, the royal prison. The people established a constitutional monarchy. When King Louis XVI and Marie Antoinette attempted to leave the country, they were executed on the guillotine. From 1793 to 1794, **Robespierre** and extreme radicals, the **Jacobins**, instituted a **Reign of Terror**, executing tens of thousands of nobles as well as anyone considered an enemy of the Revolution. Robespierre was then executed as well, and the **Directory** came into power, leading to a temporary return to bourgeois values. This governing body proved incompetent and corrupt, allowing **Napoleon Bonaparte** to come to power in 1799, first as a dictator, then as emperor. While the French Revolution threw off the power of a corrupt monarchy, its immediate results were likely not what the original perpetrators of the revolt had intended.

Review Video: The French Revolution: Napoleon Bonaparte
Visit mometrix.com/academy and enter code: 876330

Industrial Revolution

Effects of the Industrial Revolution on Society

The Industrial Revolution began in Great Britain in the 18th century, bringing coal- and steam-powered machinery into widespread use. Industry began a period of rapid growth with these developments. Goods that had previously been produced in small workshops or even in homes were produced more efficiently and in much larger quantities in **factories**. Where society had been largely agrarian-based, the focus swiftly shifted to an **industrial** outlook. As electricity and internal combustion engines replaced coal and steam as energy sources, even more drastic and rapid changes occurred. Western European countries, in particular, turned to colonialism, taking control of portions of Africa and Asia to ensure access to the raw materials needed to produce factory goods. Specialized labor became very much in demand, and businesses grew rapidly, creating monopolies, increasing world trade, and developing large urban centers. Even agriculture changed fundamentally as the Industrial Revolution led to a second **Agricultural Revolution** with the addition of new technology to advance agricultural production.

> **Review Video: Industrialization**
> Visit mometrix.com/academy and enter code: 893924

First and Second Phases of the Industrial Revolution

The **first phase** of the Industrial Revolution took place from roughly 1750 to 1830. The textile industry experienced major changes as more and more elements of the process became mechanized. Mining benefited from the steam engine. Transportation became easier and more widely available as waterways were improved and the railroad came into prominence. In the **second phase**, from 1830 to 1910, industries further improved in efficiency, and new industries were introduced as photography, various chemical processes, and electricity became more widely available to produce new goods or new, improved versions of old goods. Petroleum and hydroelectricity became major sources of power. During this time, the Industrial Revolution spread out of Western Europe and into the US and Japan.

Political, Social and Economic Side Effects of the Industrial Revolution

The Industrial Revolution led to widespread education, a wider franchise, and the development of mass communication in the political arena. **Economically**, conflicts arose between companies and their employees, as struggles for fair treatment and fair wages increased. Unions gained power and became more active. Government regulation over industries increased, but at the same time, growing businesses fought for the right to free enterprise. In the **social** sphere, populations increased and began to concentrate around centers of industry. Cities became larger and more densely populated. Scientific advancements led to more efficient agriculture, greater supply of goods, and increased knowledge of medicine and sanitation, leading to better overall health.

> **Review Video: The Industrial Revolution**
> Visit mometrix.com/academy and enter code: 372796

Causes and Progression of the Russian Revolution of 1905

In Russia, rule lay in the hands of the **czars**, and the overall structure was **feudalistic**. Beneath the czars was a group of rich nobles, landowners whose lands were worked by peasants and serfs. The **Russo-Japanese War** (1904-1905) made conditions much worse for the lower classes. When peasants demonstrated outside the czar's Winter Palace, the palace guard fired upon the crowd. The demonstration had been organized by a trade union leader, and after the violent response, many unions and political parties blossomed and began to lead numerous strikes. When the economy ground to a halt, Czar Nicholas II signed a document known as the **October Manifesto**, which established a constitutional monarchy and gave legislative power to parliament. However, he violated the manifesto shortly thereafter, disbanding parliament and ignoring the civil liberties granted by the manifesto. This eventually led to the **Bolshevik Revolution**.

World History 1914 to Present

Nationalism and Its Effect on Society Through the 18th and 19th Centuries

Nationalism, put simply, is a strong belief in, identification with, and allegiance to a particular nation and people. **Nationalistic belief** unified various areas that had previously seen themselves as fragmented, which led to **patriotism** and, in some cases, **imperialism**. As nationalism grew, individual nations sought to grow, bringing in other, smaller states that shared similar characteristics such as language and cultural beliefs. Unfortunately, a major side effect of these growing nationalistic beliefs was often conflict and outright **war**.

In Europe, imperialism led countries to spread their influence into Africa and Asia. **Africa** was eventually divided among several European countries that wanted certain raw materials. **Asia** also came under European control, with the exception of China, Japan, and Siam (now Thailand). In the US, **Manifest Destiny** became the rallying cry as the country expanded west. Italy and Germany formed larger nations from a variety of smaller states.

Review Video: Historical Nationalism
Visit mometrix.com/academy and enter code: 510185

Review Video: Nationalism
Visit mometrix.com/academy and enter code: 865693

Events of World War I in the European Theater

WWI began in 1914 with the assassination of **Archduke Franz Ferdinand**, heir to the throne of Austria-Hungary, by a Serbian national. This led to a conflict between Austria-Hungary and Serbia that quickly escalated into the First World War. Europe split into the **Allies**—Britain, France, and Russia, and later Italy, Japan, and the US, against the **Central Powers**—Austria-Hungary, Germany, the Ottoman Empire, and Bulgaria. As the war spread, countries beyond Europe became involved. The war left Europe deeply in debt, and particularly devastated the German economy. The ensuing **Great Depression** made matters worse, and economic devastation opened the door for communist, fascist, and socialist governments to gain power.

Combat in World War I

Despite the fact that almost every nation in Europe had entered into World War I, most Europeans thought the conflict would be brief. Instead, advances in **weapons technology** made the war bloody and excruciatingly slow. Fighting during WWI largely took place in a series of **trenches** built along the Eastern and Western Fronts. These trenches added up to more than 24,000 miles. This produced fronts that stretched over 400 miles, from the coast of Belgium to the border of Switzerland. The Allies made use of straightforward open-air trenches with a front line, supporting lines, and communications lines. By contrast, the German trenches sometimes included well-equipped underground living quarters.

Contributions of the American Public and Public Opinion of the War

The **18th amendment** to the Constitution, otherwise known as the **Volstead Act**, outlawed alcohol in 1920. This amendment was purported to conserve food, though it was really an attempt to influence public morality. Through the **Food Administration**, President Wilson encouraged people to plant "victory gardens," and to skip meat one day a week. The war was also supported through the **Espionage and Sedition Acts of 1917-8**, which made it illegal to say negative things about the war or to interfere with the sale of war bonds. In **Schenck v. US** (1919), the arrest of the Socialist leader Charles Schenck for criticizing the war was upheld by the Supreme Court, which asserted that First Amendment rights were only exercisable when they did not present a clear and present danger to the nation. In **Abrams v. US** (1919), a Russian immigrant critical of the US actions in Russia was also declared to be a clear and present danger.

Treaty of Versailles

As the First World War wound down, a disgruntled German populace ousted the emperor and installed a moderate socialist government. This government, known as the **Weimar Republic**, would last until 1933. At the **Paris Peace Conference**, the victors of the war (the US, Britain, France, and Italy) exacted some revenge on Germany. The **Treaty of Versailles** penalized Germany economically and territorially; Alsace-Lorraine became independent, and the German military was dismantled. The Treaty of Versailles would need to be modified by two subsequent agreements: the **Treaty of Locarno,** which outlined a more reasonable reparations plan for Germany, and the **Kellogg-Briand Pact,** which asserted that diplomacy rather than force would be used to resolve conflicts.

Bolshevik Revolution

Factors Leading to the Bolshevik Revolution of 1917

Throughout its modern history, Russia had lagged behind other countries in development. The continued existence of a feudal system, combined with harsh conditions and the overall size of the country, led to massive food shortages and increasingly harsh conditions for the majority of the population. The tyrannical rule of the czars only made this worse, as did repeated losses in various military conflicts. Increasing poverty, decreasing supplies, and the czar's violation of the **October Manifesto,** which had given some political power and civil rights to the people, finally came to a head with the **Bolshevik Revolution**.

Events of the Bolshevik Revolution

A **workers' strike in Petrograd** in 1917 set the revolutionary wheels in motion when the army sided with the workers. While parliament set up a provisional government made up of nobles, the workers and military joined to form their own governmental system known as **soviets**, which consisted of local councils elected by the people. The ensuing chaos opened the doors for formerly exiled leaders Vladimir Lenin, Joseph Stalin, and Leon Trotsky to move in and gain popular support as well as the support of the Red Guard. Overthrowing parliament, they took power, creating a **communist** state in Russia. This development led to the spread of communism throughout Eastern Europe and elsewhere, greatly affecting diplomatic policies throughout the world for several decades.

Communism vs. Socialism

At their roots, socialism and communism both focus on public ownership and distribution of goods and services. However, **communism** works toward revolution by drawing on what it sees to be inevitable class antagonism, eventually overthrowing the upper classes and the systems of capitalism. **Socialism** makes use of democratic procedures, building on the existing order. This was particularly true of the utopian socialists, who saw industrial capitalism as oppressive, not allowing workers to prosper. While socialism struggled between the World Wars, communism took hold, especially in Eastern Europe. After WWII, **democratic socialism** became more common. Later, **capitalism** took a stronger hold again, and today most industrialized countries in the western world function under an economy that mixes elements of capitalism and socialism.

Review Video: Communism vs. Socialism
Visit mometrix.com/academy and enter code: 917677

Conditions that Led to the Rise of the Nazi Party in Germany

The **Great Depression** had a particularly devastating effect on Germany's economy, especially after the US was no longer able to supply reconstruction loans to help the country regain its footing. With unemployment rising rapidly, dissatisfaction with the government grew. Fascist and Communist parties rose, promising change and improvement.

Led by **Adolf Hitler**, the fascist **Nazi Party** eventually gained power in Parliament based on these promises and the votes of desperate German workers. When Hitler became chancellor, he launched numerous expansionist policies, violating the peace treaties that had ended WWI. His military buildup and conquering of neighboring countries sparked the aggression that soon led to WWII.

Belief System of the Nazi Party

Led by **Adolf Hitler**, the Nazi party championed the **Aryan race** as superior to all others, especially the "insidious" Jews. Hitler suggested that the noble ambitions of the true German people required ***lebensraum***, or living space. In other words, Germany needed more territory. In its early days, the Nazi party was part of the German republican system; Nazi candidates ran for office and served in the **Reichstag** (German parliament). As Germany suffered through a terrible economic depression in the early 1930s, however, the people became impatient. In 1933, the Reichstag was set on fire, and the Nazis used the opportunity to claim total control of the government. Hitler had already been appointed Chancellor in January 1933. He was able to quickly improve the German economy, mostly through the expansion of the weapon-building industry. At the same time, the new government began to quietly round up Jews, Gypsies, and homosexuals.

Beginning and Initial Years of World War II in Europe

Still shell-shocked from the First World War, the nations of western Europe were slow to respond to the growing menace of **Nazi Germany**. In general, they pursued a policy of appeasement and isolation. The British prime minister **Neville Chamberlain** was especially committed to using diplomacy over war. Then, in 1936, Hitler sent troops to occupy the **Rhineland**, a strip of territory on the German border. At around the same time, **Mussolini** invaded Ethiopia; the two aggressors, Germany and Italy, entered into an agreement making them the **Axis Powers**. In 1938, Germany annexed Austria and indicated that it was about to attack Czechoslovakia. In response to these actions, Chamberlain brought together Mussolini and Hitler for the **Munich Conference of 1938**. These talks would only briefly suspend German aggression.

After **Chamberlain** had tried to forestall German aggression at the **Munich Conference of 1938**, Germany nevertheless invaded Czechoslovakia in 1939. It was also during this year that Hitler signed a secret agreement with **Stalin** pledging not to attack Russia so long as Russia stayed out of German affairs. Hitler then declared war on and conquered Poland. At this step, Great Britain and France were finally forced to declare war upon Germany. Germany at this point was a dominating military adversary. The **Axis powers** conquered almost the entire European continent, including France, over the course of 1940.

Importance of the German Blitzkrieg to the Progression of World War II

The blitzkrieg, or "lightning war," consisted of fast, powerful surprise attacks that disrupted communications, made it difficult if not impossible for the victims to retaliate, and demoralized Germany's foes. The "blitz," or the aerial bombing of England in 1940, was one example, with bombings occurring in London and other cities 57 nights in a row. The **Battle of Britain** in 1940 also brought intense raids by Germany's air force, the **Luftwaffe**, mostly targeting ports and British air force bases. Eventually, Britain's Royal Air Force blocked the Luftwaffe, ending Germany's hopes for conquering Britain.

Battle of the Bulge

Following the **D-Day Invasion**, Allied forces gained considerable ground and began a major campaign to push through Europe. In December of 1944, Hitler launched a counteroffensive, attempting to retake Antwerp, an important port. The ensuing battle became the largest land battle on the war's Western Front and was known as the Battle of the Ardennes, or the **Battle of the Bulge**. The battle lasted from December 16, 1944, to January 25, 1945. The Germans pushed forward, making inroads into Allied lines, but in the end, the Allies brought the advance to a halt. The Germans were pushed back, with massive losses on both sides. However, those losses proved crippling to the German army. Surrounded and with the war lost, Hitler committed suicide in his bunker in Berlin in April 1945, and the remaining German forces surrendered shortly afterward.

Holocaust

As Germany sank deeper and deeper into dire economic straits, the tendency was to look for a person or group of people to blame for the problems of the country. With distrust of the Jewish people already ingrained, it was easy for German authorities to set up the **Jews** as scapegoats for Germany's problems. Under the rule of Hitler and the Nazi party, the "Final Solution" for the supposed Jewish problem was devised. Millions of Jews, as well as Gypsies, homosexuals, communists, Catholics, the mentally ill, and others, simply named as criminals, were transported to concentration camps during the course of the war. At least six million were slaughtered in death camps such as **Auschwitz**, where horrible conditions and torture of prisoners were commonplace. The Allies were aware of rumors of mass slaughter throughout the war, but many discounted the reports. Only when troops went in to liberate the prisoners was the true horror of the concentration camps brought to light. The **Holocaust** resulted in massive loss of human life, but also in the loss and destruction of cultures. Because the genocide focused on specific ethnic groups, many traditions, histories, knowledge, and other cultural elements were lost, particularly among the Jewish and Gypsy populations. After World War II, the United Nations recognized **genocide** as a "crime against humanity." The UN passed the **Universal Declaration of Human**

Rights in 1948 in order to further specify what rights the organization protected. Nazi war criminals faced justice during the **Nuremberg Trials**. There, individuals, rather than their governments, were held accountable for war crimes.

Review Video: The Holocaust
Visit mometrix.com/academy and enter code: 350695

Pacific Arena in WWII

The **Japanese**, like the Germans, became seduced by the notion of their own racial superiority during the 1930s. As in Germany, this inevitably led to a lust for territorial expansion. By 1941, Japan had conquered Korea, Manchuria, and parts of China. Japan was also threatening to invade American interests in the Philippines. The United States imposed **economic sanctions** on Japan, making it difficult for the Japanese war industry to function. In response, the Japanese launched a surprise attack on the United States by bombing the US naval base of **Pearl Harbor**. After the attack on Pearl Harbor, the United States declared war upon Japan (and Germany, in turn, declared war on the United States). The Japanese made huge territorial gains before the US turned the tide at the **Battles of Midway and Guadalcanal**. The war in the Pacific would take much longer than the war in Europe due to the island-hopping nature of the fight. The unwillingness of the Japanese to surrender made it almost impossible for America to entirely vanquish them without enormous loss of life. So, the United States decided to drop atomic bombs on **Hiroshima** and **Nagasaki** to force Japan to surrender and finally end the war in the Pacific in August 1945.

India and Pakistan After WWII

In 1947, after years of peaceful protests led by **Mahatma Gandhi**, India was given its independence and partitioned into two states, **India** and **Pakistan**. The following year, Gandhi would be assassinated in India. In 1965, border disputes would flare into the **Indo-Pakistani War**. In 1971, Pakistan would fend off attacks from Bengali rebels, who sought to achieve independence. The next year, however, **Bangladesh** would be established as an independent state. In 1984, India had its own internal problems; after the Indian army occupied the **Golden Temple** sacred to the Sikhs, the Indian leader **Indira Gandhi** was assassinated by her Sikh bodyguards. **Anti-Sikh riots** resulted, and much blood was shed.

World War II and the Ensuing Diplomatic Climate that Led to the Cold War

With millions of military and civilian deaths and over 12 million persons displaced, **WWII** left large regions of Europe and Asia in disarray. **Communist** governments moved in with promises of renewed prosperity and economic stability. The **Soviet Union** backed communist regimes in much of Eastern Europe. In China, **Mao Zedong** led communist forces in the overthrow of the Chinese Nationalist Party and instituted a communist government in 1949. While the new communist governments restored a measure of stability to much of Eastern Europe, it brought its own problems, with dictatorial governments and an oppressive police force. The spread of communism also led to several years of tension between communist countries and the democratic West, as the West fought to slow the spread of oppressive regimes throughout the world. With both sides in possession of nuclear weapons, tensions rose. Each side feared the other would resort to nuclear attack. This standoff lasted until 1989, when the **Berlin Wall** fell. The Soviet Union was dissolved two years later.

Truman Doctrine, Marshall Plan, NATO, and Warsaw Pact

In order to stop the spread of communism in Europe and elsewhere, President Truman asserted his policy of "containment" in the so-called **Truman Doctrine**. This meant that the US would support anticommunist governments throughout the world. The **Marshall Plan** advanced this policy by supplying aid to war-ravaged countries in Western Europe. When the **Eastern Bloc countries** prevented aid from reaching West Berlin, the US, England, and France organized the **Berlin Airlift** to overcome this obstacle. In 1949, the Western European and North American nations entered into a mutual defense treaty, NATO (North Atlantic Treaty Organization). As a response, the Eastern Bloc nations joined with the Soviet Union in the **Warsaw Pact**.

Origins of the United Nations

The United Nations (**UN**) came into being toward the end of World War II. A successor to the less-than-successful League of Nations formed after World War I, the UN built and improved on those ideas. Since its inception, the UN has worked to bring the countries of the world together for **diplomatic solutions** to international problems, including sanctions and other restrictions. It has also initiated military action, calling for peacekeeping troops from member countries to move against countries violating UN policies. The **Korean War** was the first example of UN involvement in an international conflict.

Effects of Decolonization on the Post-War Period

A rise of nationalism among European colonies led to many of them declaring independence. **India** and **Pakistan** became independent of Britain in 1947, and numerous African and Asian colonies declared independence as well. This period of **decolonization** lasted into the 1960s. Some colonies moved successfully into independence, but many, especially in Africa and Asia, struggled to create stable governments and economies and suffered from ethnic and religious conflicts, some of which continue today.

Factors and Shifts in Power that Led to the Korean War

In 1910, Japan annexed Korea and maintained this control until 1945. After WWII, Soviet and US troops occupied Korea, with the **Soviet Union** controlling North Korea and the **US** controlling South Korea. In 1947, the UN ordered elections in Korea to unify the country, but the Soviet Union refused to allow them to take place in North Korea, instead setting up a communist government. In 1950, the US withdrew troops, and the North Korean troops moved to invade South Korea. The **Korean War** was the first war in which the UN—or any international organization—played a major role. The US, Australia, Canada, France, Netherlands, Great Britain, Turkey, China, the USSR, and other countries sent troops at various times, for both sides, throughout the war. In 1953, the war ended in a truce, but no peace agreement was ever achieved, and Korea remains divided.

Events that Led to the Vietnam War

Vietnam had previously been part of a French colony called French Indochina. The **Vietnam War** began with the **First Indochina War** from 1946 to 1954, in which France battled with the Democratic Republic of Vietnam, ruled by Ho Chi Minh.

In 1954, a siege at Dien Bien Phu ended in a Vietnamese victory. Vietnam was then divided into North and South, much like Korea. Communist forces controlled the North, and the South was controlled by South Vietnamese forces, supported by the US. Conflict ensued, leading to another war. US troops eventually led the fight, in support of South Vietnam. The war became a major political issue in the US, with many citizens protesting American involvement. In 1975, South Vietnam surrendered, and Vietnam became the **Socialist Republic of Vietnam**.

Middle East from 1947 to 1977

After WWII, the United Nations announced that **Palestine** would be partitioned in order to make room for a new Jewish state. **Israel** was created in 1948. In 1951, the Iranian leader **Mossadegh** nationalized the oil interests, making his government extremely wealthy and powerful. This move would be emulated by future leaders. In 1967, in the **Six-Day War**, Israel routed a coalition of Arab nations, seizing the West Bank, Sinai, and Jerusalem. In 1972, Palestinian terrorists murdered 12 Israeli athletes at the Olympics in Munich. In 1973, the oil-producing Arab nations placed an embargo on shipments to the West, causing major energy crises in the US and Europe. Also, in 1973, Israelis and Arabs battled again in the **Yom Kippur War**. In 1977, Egyptian leader **Anwar Sadat** became the first Arab leader to visit Israel.

Middle East from 1978 to 1985

In 1978, American President **Jimmy Carter** hosted successful peace talks between Egypt and Israel at **Camp David**. The next year, however, a fundamentalist Islamist regime would take power in Iran, and many Americans would be taken hostage, only released upon the election of **Ronald Reagan**. Between 1980 and

1988, Iran and Iraq engaged in a bloody and brutal war, begun when the Iraqi leader **Saddam Hussein** seized territory in eastern Iran. Also, during this period, Afghan rebels were engaged in a prolonged, ultimately successful fight for independence from the Soviets. In 1982, Israel attacked Lebanon, which was harboring the Palestinian leader **Yasser Arafat**. Lebanon would be forced to oust Arafat the next year. Israel would continue attacking Arafat and the **Palestinian Liberation Organization**, and the PLO would continue to sponsor terrorist activities against Israel.

END OF THE COLD WAR

Over time, the leaders of the Soviet Union and United States began to realize the total annihilation that would ensue if nuclear war was declared, and it was agreed that both sides would **disarm**. The two treaties that were signed during the 1970s are known as the **Strategic Arms Limitation Talks (SALT) I and II**. When **Mikhail Gorbachev** came into power in the USSR in 1985, he established a policy of **glasnost**, or "openness." In response to US President Ronald Reagan's military build-up using the might of the US economy, Gorbachev understood that the Soviet Union could not economically compete militarily under a communist system and overcome the military might of the United States. He thus advocated **perestroika**, a gradual metamorphosis of the Soviet economy. In 1991, these reforms culminated in the disintegration of the ruling Communist party, and the **disbanding of the Soviet Union**. This occurred two years after the **Berlin Wall**, which for more than forty years had separated communist and anticommunist Germany, was finally torn down.

GLOBALISM

In the modern era, globalism has emerged as a popular political ideology. **Globalism** is based on the idea that all people and all nations are **interdependent**. Each nation is dependent on one or more other nations for production of and markets for goods, and for income generation. Today's ease of international travel and communication, including technological advances such as the airplane, has heightened this sense of interdependence. The global economy and the general idea of globalism have shaped many economic and political choices since the beginning of the 20th century. Many of today's issues, including environmental awareness, economic struggles, and continued warfare, often require the cooperation of many countries if they are to be dealt with effectively.

EFFECT OF GLOBALIZATION ON THE WAY COUNTRIES INTERACT WITH EACH OTHER

Countries worldwide often seek the same resources, leading to high demand, particularly for **nonrenewable resources**. This can result in heavy fluctuations in price. One major example is the demand for petroleum products such as oil and natural gas. Increased travel and communication make it possible to deal with diseases in remote locations; however, this also allows diseases to be spread via travelers.

A major factor contributing to increased globalization over the past few decades has been the **internet**. By allowing instantaneous communication with anyone nearly anywhere on the globe, the internet has led to interaction between far-flung individuals and countries, and an ever-increasing awareness of events all over the world.

Review Video: Globalization
Visit mometrix.com/academy and enter code: 551962

ROLE OF THE MIDDLE EAST IN INTERNATIONAL RELATIONS AND ECONOMICS

The location on the globe, with ease of access to Europe and Asia, and its preponderance of oil deposits, makes the **Middle Eastern countries** crucial in many international issues, both diplomatic and economic. Because of its central location, the Middle East has been a hotbed for violence since before the beginning of recorded history. Conflicts over land, resources, and religious and political power continue in the area today, spurred by conflict over control of the area's vast oil fields as well as over territories that have been disputed for thousands of years.

MIDDLE EAST FROM 1987 TO 2003

In 1987, Syrian troops entered Lebanon and stopped the civil war. Also, during this year, 402 pilgrims died during riots in the Saudi Arabian sacred city of Mecca. In 1988, the Palestinian resistance (known as the Intifada) began in earnest against Israel. Iraq invaded Kuwait in 1990, and after UN sanctions were levied, the US invaded in 1991. The Iraqi soldiers set fire to thousands of Kuwaiti oil wells while retreating. In 1992, Arafat and Israeli PM Yitzhak Rabin shook hands in Washington, and Arafat would soon return to Gaza after years of exile. In 1995, the Israelis and Palestinians signed an agreement giving the Palestinians autonomy in the West Bank and Gaza areas. Despite continuing violence, another agreement was reached in 1998, this one stating that the Palestinians would be granted land in exchange for keeping the peace. Violence continued, however, and in 2003, Israel began construction of a barrier between itself and the Palestinian territories.

WAR ON TERROR

Following the terrorist attacks on the United States on September 11, 2001, the United States invaded Afghanistan, marking the start of the Global War on Terrorism. This was a global campaign led by the Americans to oust Islamic extremist terrorist groups mainly situated in the Middle East. On the side of the Americans was a large coalition of other countries, many of whom were members of NATO. American allies that fought in the War on Terror included the United Kingdom, Australia, Canada, Denmark, France, Italy, the Netherlands, New Zealand, and Norway. Major wars occurred in Afghanistan and Iraq against al-Qaeda, the Taliban, and their allies.

While stopping terrorism was the main stated goal of the War on Terror, the American government invaded Iraq under the claims that Saddam Hussein's government had weapons of mass destruction, but these claims were found to be false. The goal of removing extremist groups from the region has also not been entirely successful, as the Taliban took control of Afghanistan in 2021, and militant groups continue to have heavy influence in the region.

NEW EUROPE AFTER 1991 THROUGH 1998

In 1991, **Gorbachev** resigned as the last president of the USSR, and a number of the Soviet provinces, including Lithuania and Latvia, declared independence. The **Maastricht Treaty**, formally announcing the creation of the European Union, was signed in 1992, and the next year a unified European stock market opened. In the **"Velvet" Revolution of 1993**, Slovakia separated from Czechoslovakia, which became the Czech Republic. Meanwhile, the former USSR was enduring civil strife until **Boris Yeltsin** seized power in 1993. In 1994, Russian troops attacked **Chechnya**, which was trying to achieve independence. In 1998, President Clinton helped broker a peace agreement between the **British** and **North Irish rebels**.

NEW EUROPE AFTER 1999

In 1999, the Czech Republic, Poland, and Hungary all joined **NATO**, further eliminating the old divides between western and eastern Europe. The conflict in Chechnya increased during this year, and Yeltsin was succeeded as Russian leader by the former KGB agent Vladimir Putin. An **International Criminal Court** was created in the Hague (Netherlands) in 2002, despite the vehement opposition of the United States. In the late '90s, many of the western European governments had become quasi-socialist, and they spent much of their time debating the immense increase in **immigration**. Meanwhile, the former Soviet states have had a rough transition from command to market economies, and are still somewhat economically depressed.

THE RUSSO-UKRAINIAN WAR

The Russo-Ukrainian war began in February of 2014 when Russia annexed the Crimea region of Ukraine following Ukraine's Revolution of Dignity, in which the pro-Russian president of Ukraine was ousted. This resulted in pro-Russian unrest in the Donbas region of Ukraine. A war eventually broke out between Ukraine and Russian-backed separatists in the region. This conflict is referred to as the Donbas War.

In 2022, the war was escalated by Russia's invasion of Ukraine, sparking the biggest conflict in Europe since WWII. Russia's actions in starting the invasion have been internationally condemned. The Ukrainians have since been fighting a costly war to maintain their independence, with casualties estimated to be in the tens of thousands. Russia has been accused of many war crimes, including deliberately targeting large numbers of civilians throughout the course of the war.

Human-Induced Global Climate Change and Further Climate Change

Today, the climate change debate mostly focuses on whether it is specifically **human activities** that have wrought **changes in our world climate**; in other words, is mankind directly responsible for causing the change in global temperature and thus directly responsible for implementing choices to counteract the impact of its actions. For example, the United Nations Intergovernmental Panel on Climate Change, a multinational group of the world's leading environmental scientists, has documented increases in the average tidal levels, increasing temperatures at ground level, concentrations of greenhouse gases in the atmosphere, glaciers whose ice is melting, explorations of the Arctic ice core, and so forth. Based on this data, this panel has made predictions of variations in patterns of weather and temperatures in the near future. They believe these variations to be directly caused by emissions from human use of fossil fuels. These foremost scientists state that the climate likely will change dramatically within 50-100 years, almost completely due to human actions and their impact on the natural environment.

Major Occurrences of Genocide in Modern History

Five major occurrences of genocide in modern history other than the Holocaust are:

- **Armenian genocide**—from 1914 to 1918, the Young Turks, heirs to the Ottoman Empire, slaughtered between 800,000 and 1.5 million Armenians. This constituted approximately half of the Armenian population at the time.
- **Holodomor**—from 1932 to 1933, the people of Ukraine suffered the effects of a famine created by Joseph Stalin's collectivization of agriculture. Millions of Ukranians starved to death due to a lack of access to food.
- **Cambodian genocide**—from 1975 to 1979, the Khmer Rouge, a communist group, inflicted violence on the people of Cambodia. Between 1.5 million and 3 million Cambodians were killed. The Khmer Rouge were removed from power when the Vietnamese military took the capital of Cambodia.
- **Rwandan genocide**—in 1994, hundreds of thousands of Tutsis and Hutu sympathizers were slaughtered during the Rwandan Civil War. The UN did not act or authorize intervention during these atrocities.
- **Darfur genocide**—In 2003, militias tasked with combating rebel activity in Darfur kept the people of Darfur from accessing food and resources. This resulted in the death of hundreds of thousands of people in Darfur.

Geography

Geography

Geography is the study of Earth. Geographers study **physical characteristics** of Earth as well as man-made borders and boundaries. They also study the **distribution of life** on the planet, such as where certain species of animals can be found or how different forms of life interact. Major elements of the study of geography include:

- Locations
- Regional characteristics
- Spatial relations
- Natural and man-made forces that change elements of Earth

These elements are studied from regional, topical, physical, and human perspectives. Geography also focuses on the origins of Earth, as well as the history and backgrounds of different human populations.

Physical vs. Cultural Geography

Physical geography is the study of the physical characteristics of Earth: how they relate to each other, how they were formed, and how they develop. These characteristics include climate, land, and water, and also how they affect human population in various areas. Different landforms, in combination with various climates and other conditions, determine the characteristics of various cultures.

Cultural geography is the study of how the various aspects of physical geography affect individual cultures. Cultural geography also compares various cultures: how their lifestyles and customs are affected by their geographical location, climate, and other factors, as well as how they interact with their environment.

Review Video: Regional Geography
Visit mometrix.com/academy and enter code: 350378

Divisions of Geographical Study and Tools Used

The four divisions of geographical study and tools used are:

- **Topical**—the study of a single feature of Earth or one specific human activity that occurs worldwide.
- **Physical**—the various physical features of Earth, how they are created, the forces that change them, and how they are related to each other and to various human activities.
- **Regional**—specific characteristics of individual places and regions.
- **Human**—how human activity affects the environment. This includes the study of political, historical, social, and cultural activities.

Tools used in geographical study include special research methods like mapping, field studies, statistics, interviews, mathematics, and the use of various scientific instruments.

Important Ancient Geographers

The following are three important ancient geographers and their contributions to the study of geography:

- **Eratosthenes** lived in ancient Greek times and mathematically calculated the circumference of Earth and the tilt of Earth's axis. He also created the first map of the world.
- **Strabo** wrote a description of the ancient world called *Geographica* in seventeen volumes.
- **Ptolemy**, primarily an astronomer, was an experienced mapmaker. He wrote a treatise entitled *Geography*, which was used by Christopher Columbus in his travels.

Ways Geographers Analyze Areas of Human Population

In cities, towns, or other areas where many people have settled, geographers focus on the **distribution** of populations, neighborhoods, industrial areas, transportation, and other elements important to the society in question. For example, they would map out the locations of hospitals, airports, factories, police stations, schools, and housing groups. They would also make note of how these facilities are distributed in relation to the areas of habitation, such as the number of schools in a certain neighborhood or how many grocery stores are located in a specific suburban area. Another area of study and discussion is the distribution of **towns** themselves, from widely spaced rural towns to large cities that merge into each other to form a megalopolis.

Role of a Cartographer

A cartographer is a mapmaker. Mapmakers produce detailed illustrations of geographic areas to record where various features are located within that area. These illustrations can be compiled into maps, charts, graphs, and even globes. When constructing maps, **cartographers** must take into account the problem of **distortion**. Because Earth is round, a flat map does not accurately represent the correct proportions, especially if a very large geographical area is being depicted. Maps must be designed in such a way as to minimize this distortion and maximize accuracy. Accurately representing Earth's features on a flat surface is achieved through **projection**.

Types of Projection Used in Creating World Maps

The three major types of projection used in creating world maps are:

- **Cylindrical projection**—this is created by wrapping the globe of Earth in a cylindrical piece of paper, then using a light to project the globe onto the paper. The largest distortion occurs at the outermost edges.
- **Conical projection**—the paper is shaped like a cone and contacts the globe only at the cone's base. This type of projection is most useful for middle latitudes.
- **Flat-Plane projections**—also known as a gnomonic projection, this type of map is projected onto a flat piece of paper that only touches the globe at a single point. Flat-plane projections make it possible to map out Great-Circle routes, or the shortest route between one point and another on the globe, as a straight line.

Specific Types of Map Projections

Four specific types of map projections that are commonly used today are:

- **Winkel Tripel projection**—The Winkel Tripel projection balances size and shape, greatly reducing distortion. In 1998, the National Geographic Society accepted the Winkel Tripel projection as a standard, though other map forms have remained popular.
- **Robinson projection**—east and west sections of the map are less distorted, but continental shapes are somewhat inaccurate.
- **Goode homolosine projection**—sizes and shapes are accurate, but distances are not. This projection basically represents a globe that has been cut into connected sections so that it can lie flat.
- **Mercator projection**—though distortion is high, particularly in areas farther from the equator, this cylindrical projection is commonly used by seafarers.

Major Elements of Any Map

The five major elements of any map are:

- **Title**—this tells basic information about the map, such as the area represented.
- **Legend**—also known as the key, the legend explains what symbols used on a particular map represent, such as symbols for major landmarks.
- **Grid**—this most commonly represents the geographic grid system, or latitude and longitude marks used to precisely locate specific locations.
- **Directions**—a compass rose or other symbol is used to indicate the cardinal directions.
- **Scale**—this shows the relation between a certain distance on the map and the actual distance. For example, one inch might represent one mile, or ten miles, or even more, depending on the size of the map.

Review Video: Elements of a Map
Visit mometrix.com/academy and enter code: 437727

Equal-Area Maps vs. Conformal Maps

An equal-area map is designed such that the proportional sizes of various areas are accurate. For example, if one landmass is one-fifth the size of another, the lines on the map will be shifted to accommodate for distortion so that the proportional size is accurate. In many maps, areas farther from the equator are greatly distorted; this type of map compensates for this phenomenon. A **conformal map** focuses on representing the correct shape of geographical areas, with less concern for comparative size.

Consistent Scale Maps and Thematic Maps

With a consistent scale map, the same scale, such as one inch being equal to ten miles, is used throughout the entire map. This is most often used for maps of smaller areas, as maps that cover larger areas, such as the full globe, must make allowances for distortion. Maps of very large areas often make use of more than one scale, with scales closer to the center representing a larger area than those at the edges.

A **thematic map** is constructed to show very specific information about a chosen theme. For example, a thematic map might represent political information, such as how votes were distributed in an election, or could show population distribution or climatic features.

Relief maps

A relief map is constructed to show details of various **elevations** across the area of the map. Higher elevations are represented by different colors than lower elevations. **Relief maps** often also show additional details, such as the overall ruggedness or smoothness of an area. Mountains would be represented as ridged and rugged, while deserts would be shown as smooth.

Elevation in relief maps can also be represented by contour lines, or lines that connect points of the same elevation. Some relief maps even feature textures, reconstructing details in a sort of miniature model.

Geographical Features

- **Mountains** are elevated areas that measure 2,000 feet or more above sea level. Often steep and rugged, they usually occur in groups called chains or ranges. Six of the seven continents on Earth contain at least one range.
- **Hills** are of lower elevation than mountains, at about 500-2,000 feet. Hills are usually more rounded and are found throughout every continent.
- **Plains** are large, flat areas and are usually very fertile. The majority of Earth's population is supported by crops grown on vast plains.
- **Valleys** lie between hills and mountains. Depending on their location, their specific features can vary greatly, from fertile and habitable to rugged and inhospitable.
- **Plateaus** are elevated, but flat on top. Some plateaus are extremely dry, such as the Kenya Plateau, because surrounding mountains prevent them from receiving moisture.
- **Deserts** receive less than ten inches of rain per year. They are usually large areas, such as the Sahara Desert in Africa or the Australian Outback.
- **Deltas** occur at river mouths. Because the rivers carry sediment to the deltas, these areas are often very fertile.
- **Mesas** are flat, steep-sided mountains or hills. The term is sometimes used to refer to plateaus.
- **Basins** are areas of low elevation where rivers drain.
- **Foothills** are the transitional area between plains and mountains, usually consisting of hills that gradually increase in size as they approach a mountain range.
- **Marshes** and **swamps** are also lowlands, but they are very wet and largely covered in vegetation such as reeds and rushes.

Geographical Terms Referring to Bodies of Water

- The **ocean** refers to the salt water that covers about two-thirds of Earth's surface.
- **Ocean basins** are named portions of the ocean. The five major ocean basins are the Atlantic, Pacific, Indian, Southern, and Arctic.
- **Seas** are generally also salt water, but are smaller than ocean basins and surrounded by land. Examples include the Mediterranean Sea, the Caribbean Sea, and the Caspian Sea.
- **Lakes** are bodies of fresh water found inland. Sixty percent of all lakes are located in Canada.

- **Rivers** are moving bodies of water that flow from higher elevations to lower. They usually start as rivulets or streams and grow until they finally empty into a sea or the ocean.
- **Canals**, such as the Panama Canal and the Suez Canal, are man-made waterways connecting two large bodies of water.

How Communities Develop

Communities, or groups of people who settle together in a specific area, typically gather where certain conditions exist. These conditions include:

- Easy access to resources such as food, water, and raw materials
- Ability to easily transport raw materials and goods, such as access to a waterway
- Room to house a sufficient workforce

People also tend to form groups with others who are similar to them. In a typical **community**, people can be found who share values, a common language, and common or similar cultural characteristics and religious beliefs. These factors will determine the overall composition of a community as it develops.

Differences Between Cities in Various Areas of the World

Cities develop and grow as an area develops. Modern statistics show that over half of the world's people live in **cities**. That percentage is even higher in developed areas of the globe. Cities are currently growing more quickly in developing regions, and even established cities continue to experience growth throughout the world. In developing or developed areas, cities often are surrounded by a metropolitan area made up of both urban and suburban sections. In some places, cities have merged into each other and become a **megalopolis**—a single, huge city.

Cities develop differently in different areas of the world. The area available for cities to grow, as well as cultural and economic forces, drives how cities develop. For example, North American cities tend to cover wider areas. European cities tend to have better-developed transportation systems. In Latin America, the richest inhabitants can be found in the city centers, while in North America, wealthier inhabitants tend to live in suburban areas.

In other parts of the world, transportation and communication between cities are less developed. Technological innovations such as the cell phone have increased communication even in these areas. Urban areas must also maintain communication with rural areas in order to procure food, resources, and raw materials that cannot be produced within the city limits.

Weather vs. Climate

Weather and climate are physical systems that affect geography. Though they deal with similar information, the way this information is measured and compiled is different.

Weather involves daily conditions in the atmosphere that affect temperature, precipitation (rain, snow, hail, or sleet), wind speed, air pressure, and other factors. Weather focuses on the short-term—what the conditions will be today, tomorrow, or over the next few days.

In contrast, **climate** aggregates information about daily and seasonal weather conditions in a region over a long period of time. The climate takes into account average monthly and yearly temperatures, average precipitation over long periods of time, and the growing season of an area. Climates are classified according to latitude, or how close they lie to Earth's equator. The three major divisions are:

- **Low Latitudes**, lying from 0 to approximately 23.5 degrees
- **Middle Latitudes**, found from approximately 23.5 to 66.5 degrees
- **High Latitudes**, found from approximately 66.5 degrees to the poles

Review Video: Climates
Visit mometrix.com/academy and enter code: 991320

Climates Found in the Low Latitudes

Rainforests, savannas, and deserts occur in low latitudes:

- **Rainforest** climates, near the equator, experience high average temperatures and humidity, as well as relatively high rainfall.
- **Savannas** are found on either side of the rainforest region. Mostly grasslands, they typically experience dry winters and wet summers.
- Beyond the savannas lie the **desert** regions, with hot, dry climates, sparse rainfall, and temperature fluctuations of up to fifty degrees from day to night.

Climate Regions Found in the Middle Latitudes

The climate regions found in the middle latitudes are:

- **Mediterranean**—the Mediterranean climate occurs between 30- and 40-degrees latitude, both north and south, on the western coasts of continents. Characteristics include a year-long growing season; hot, dry summers followed by mild winters; and sparse rainfall that occurs mostly during the winter months.
- **Humid-subtropical**—humid-subtropical regions are located in southeastern coastal areas. Winds that blow in over warm ocean currents produce long summers, mild winters, and a long growing season. These areas are highly productive and support a larger part of Earth's population than any other climate.
- **Humid-continental**—the humid continental climate produces the familiar four seasons typical of a good portion of the US. Some of the most productive farmlands in the world lie in these climates. Winters are cold, and summers are hot and humid.

Marine, Steppe, and Desert Climates

The climate regions found in the middle latitudes are:

- **Marine**—marine climates are found near water or on islands. Ocean winds help make these areas mild and rainy. Summers are cooler than humid-subtropical summers, but winters also bring milder temperatures due to the warmth of the ocean winds.
- **Steppe**—steppe climates, or prairie climates, are found far inland on large continents. Summers are hot and winters are cold, but rainfall is sparser than in continental climates.
- **Desert**—desert climates occur where steppe climates receive even less rainfall. Examples include the Gobi Desert in Asia as well as desert areas of Australia and the southwestern US.

Climates Found in the High Latitudes

The high latitudes consist of two major climate areas, the tundra and taiga:

- **Tundra** means "marshy plain." The ground is frozen throughout long, cold winters, but there is little snowfall. During the short summers, it becomes wet and marshy. Tundras are not amenable to crops, but many plants and animals have adapted to the conditions.

- **Taigas** lie south of tundra regions and include the largest forest areas in the world, as well as swamps and marshes. Large mineral deposits exist here, as well as many animals valued for their fur. In the winter, taiga regions are colder than the tundra, and summers are hotter. The growing season is short.

A **vertical climate** exists in high mountain ranges. Increasing elevation leads to varying temperatures, growing conditions, types of vegetation and animals, and occurrence of human habitation, often encompassing elements of various other climate regions.

Factors Affecting Climate

Because Earth is tilted, its **rotation** brings about changes in **seasons**. Regions closer to the equator, and those nearest the poles, experience very little change in seasonal temperatures. Mid-range latitudes are most likely to experience distinct seasons. Large bodies of water also affect climate. Ocean currents and wind patterns can change the climate for an area that lies in a typically cold latitude, such as England, to a much more temperate climate. Mountains can affect both short-term weather and long-term climates. Some deserts occur because precipitation is stopped by the wall of a mountain range.

Over time, established **climate patterns** can shift and change. While the issue is hotly debated, it has been theorized that human activity has also led to climate change.

Effect of Human Systems

Human Systems that Geographers Incorporate into the Study of Earth

Human systems affect geography in the way in which they settle, form groups that grow into large-scale habitations, and even create permanent changes in the landscape. **Geographers** study movements of people, how they distribute goods among each other and to other settlements or cultures, and how ideas grow and spread. Migrations, wars, forced relocations, and trade can all spread cultural ideas, language, goods, and other practices to widespread areas. Throughout history, cultures have been changed due to a wide range of events, including major migrations and the conquering of one people by another. In addition, **human systems** can lead to various conflicts or alliances to control access to and the use of natural resources.

Human Systems that Form the Basis of Cultures in North America

North America consists of 23 countries, including (in decreasing population order) the United States of America, Mexico, Canada, Guatemala, Cuba, Haiti, and the Dominican Republic. The US and Canada support similarly diverse cultures, as both were formed from groups of native races and large numbers of immigrants. Many **North American cultures** come from a mixture of indigenous and colonial European influences. Agriculture is important to North American countries, while service industries and technology also play a large part in the economy. On average, North America supports a high standard of living and a high level of development and supports trade with countries throughout the world.

Human Systems that Shape South America

Home to twelve sovereign states, including Brazil (largest in area and population), Colombia, Argentina, Venezuela, and Peru; two independent territories; and one internal territory, **South America** is largely defined by its prevailing languages. The majority of countries in South America speak Spanish or Portuguese. Most of South America has experienced a similar history, having been originally dominated by Native cultures and then conquered by European nations. The countries of South America have since gained independence, but there is a wide disparity between various countries' economic and political factors. Most South American countries rely on only one or two exports, usually agricultural, with suitable lands often controlled by rich families. Most societies in South America feature major separations between classes, both economically and socially. Challenges faced by developing South American countries include geographical limitations, economic issues, and sustainable development, including the need to preserve the existing rainforests.

Human Systems Influencing Europe

Europe contains a wide variety of cultures, ethnic groups, physical geographical features, climates, and resources, all of which have influenced the distribution of its varied population. **Europe**, in general, is industrialized and developed, with cultural differences giving each individual country its own unique characteristics. Greek and Roman influences played a major role in European culture, as did Christianity. European countries spread their beliefs and cultural elements throughout the world by means of migration and colonization. They have had a significant influence on nearly every other continent in the world. While Western Europe has been largely democratic, Eastern Europe functioned under communist rule for many years. The formation of the European Union (EU) in 1993 has increased stability and positive diplomatic relations among European nations. Like other industrialized regions, Europe is now focusing on various environmental issues.

Human Systems that Have Shaped Russia

After numerous conflicts, Russia became a Communist state, known as the **USSR**. With the collapse of the USSR in 1991, the country has struggled in its transition to a market-driven economy. Attempts to build a workable system have led to the destruction of natural resources as well as problems with nuclear power, including accidents such as Chernobyl. To complete the transition to a market economy, Russia would need to improve its transportation and communication systems and find a way to more efficiently use its natural resources.

The population of Russia is not distributed evenly, with three-quarters of the population living west of the Ural Mountains. The people of Russia encompass over a hundred different ethnic groups. Over eighty percent of the population is ethnically Russian, and Russian is the official language of the country.

Human Systems that Have Shaped North Africa and Southwest and Central Asia

The largely desert climate of these areas has led most population centers to rise around sources of **water**, such as the Nile River. This area is the home of the **earliest known civilizations** and the origin of Christianity, Judaism, and Islam. After serving as the site of huge, independent civilizations in ancient times, North Africa and Southwest and Central Asia were largely parceled out as **European colonies** during the 18th and 19th centuries. The beginning of the 20th century saw many of these countries gain their independence. **Islam** has served as a unifying force for large portions of these areas, and many of the inhabitants speak Arabic. In spite of the arid climate, agriculture is a large business, but the most valuable resource is **oil**. Centuries of conflict throughout this area have led to ongoing political problems. These political problems have also contributed to environmental issues.

Human Systems that Shape and Influence the Culture of Sub-Saharan Africa

South of the Sahara Desert, **Africa** is divided into a number of culturally diverse nations. The inhabitants are unevenly distributed due to geographical limitations that prevent settlement in vast areas. **AIDS** has become a major plague throughout this part of Africa, killing millions, largely due to restrictive beliefs that prevent education about the disease, as well as abject poverty and unsettled political situations that make it impossible to manage the pandemic. The population of this area of Africa is widely diverse due to extensive **migration**. Many of the people still rely on **subsistence farming** for their welfare. Starvation and poverty are rampant due to drought and political instability. Some areas are far more stable than others due to the greater availability of resources. These areas have been able to begin the process of **industrialization**.

Human Systems that Determine the Cultural Makeup of South Asia

South Asia is home to one of the first human civilizations, which grew up in the **Indus River Valley**. With a great deal of disparity between rural and urban life, South Asia has much to do to improve the quality of life for its lower classes. Two major religions, **Hinduism** and **Buddhism**, have their origins in this region. Parts of South Asia, most notably India, were subject to **British rule** for several decades and are still working to improve independent governments and social systems. Overall, South Asia is very culturally diverse, with a wide mix of religions and languages throughout. Many individuals are **farmers**, but a growing number have found prosperity in the spread of **high-tech industries**. Industrialization is growing in South Asia but continues to face environmental, social, religious, and economic challenges.

Human Systems Shaping the Culture of East Asia

Governments in East Asia are varied, ranging from communist to democratic governments, with some governments that mix both approaches. **Isolationism** throughout the area limited the countries' contact with other nations until the early 20th century. The unevenly distributed population of East Asia consists of over one and a half billion people with widely diverse ethnic backgrounds, religions, and languages. More residents live in **urban** areas than in **rural** areas, creating shortages of farmworkers at times. Japan, Taiwan, and South Korea are overall more urban, while China and Mongolia are more rural. Japan stands as the most industrial country in East Asia. Some areas of East Asia are suffering from major environmental issues. Japan has dealt with many of these problems and now has some of the strictest environmental laws in the world.

Human Systems that Have Influenced Southeast Asia

Much of Southeast Asia was **colonized** by European countries during the 18th and 19th centuries, with the exception of Siam, now known as Thailand. All Southeast Asian countries are now independent, but the 20th century saw numerous conflicts between **communist** and **democratic** forces.

Southeast Asia has been heavily influenced by both Buddhist and Muslim religions. Industrialization is growing, with the population moving in large numbers from rural to urban areas. Some have moved to avoid conflict, oppression, and poverty.

Natural disasters, including volcanoes, typhoons, and flash flooding, are fairly common in Southeast Asia, creating extensive economic damage and societal disruption.

Human Systems that Affect the Development and Culture of Australia, Oceana, and Antarctica

South Pacific cultures originally migrated from Southeast Asia, creating hunter-gatherer or sometimes settled agricultural communities. **European** countries moved in during later centuries, seeking the plentiful natural resources of the area. Today, some South Pacific islands remain under the control of foreign governments, and culture in these areas mixes modern, industrialized society with indigenous culture. Population is unevenly distributed, largely due to the inhabitability of many parts of the South Pacific, such as the extremely hot desert areas of Australia. **Agriculture** still drives much of the economy, with **tourism** growing. **Antarctica** remains the only continent that has not been claimed by any country. There are no permanent human habitations in Antarctica, but scientists and explorers visit the area on a temporary basis.

Human-Environment Interaction

Geography also studies the ways people interact with, use, and change their **environment**. The effects, reasons, and consequences of these changes are studied, as are the ways the environment limits or influences human behavior. This kind of study can help determine the best course of action when a nation or group of people is considering making changes to the environment, such as building a dam or removing natural landscape to build or expand roads. Study of the **consequences** can help determine if these actions are manageable and how long-term, detrimental results can be mitigated.

Physical Geography and Climates

Physical Geography and Climate of North America

Together, the US and Canada make up the majority of North America and both have a similar distribution of geographical features: mountain ranges in both the east and the west, stretches of fertile plains through the center, and lakes and waterways. Both areas were shaped by **glaciers**, which also deposited highly fertile soil. Because they are so large, Canada and the US experience several varieties of **climate**, including continental climates with four seasons in median areas, tropical climates in the southern part of the US, and arctic climes in the far north. The remaining area of North America includes Mexico, Central America, the Caribbean Isles, and Greenland.

Physical Geography and Climate of South America

South America contains a wide variety of geographical features, including high **mountains** such as the Andes, wide **plains**, and high-altitude **plateaus**. The region contains numerous natural resources, but many of them have remained unused due to various obstacles, including political issues, geographic barriers, and lack of sufficient economic power. Climate zones in South America are largely **tropical**, with rainforests and savannas, but vertical climate zones and grasslands also exist in some places.

Physical Geography and Climate of Europe

Europe spans a wide area with a variety of climate zones. In the east and south are **mountain** ranges, while the north is dominated by a **plains** region. The long coastline and the island nature of some countries, such as Britain, mean the climate is often warmer than other lands at similar latitudes, as the area is warmed by **ocean currents**. Many areas of western Europe have a moderate climate, while areas of the south are dominated by the classic Mediterranean climate. Europe carries a high level of natural resources. Numerous waterways help connect the inner regions with the coastal areas. Much of Europe is **industrialized**, and **agriculture** has been developed for thousands of years.

Physical Geography and Climate of Russia

Russia's area encompasses part of Asia and Europe. From the standpoint of square footage alone, **Russia** is the largest country in the world. Due to its size, Russia encompasses a wide variety of climatic regions, including **plains**, **plateaus**, **mountains**, and **tundra**.

Russia's **climate** can be quite harsh, with rivers that are frozen most of the year, making transportation of the country's rich natural resources more difficult. Siberia, in northern Russia, is dominated by **permafrost**. Native peoples in this area still follow a hunting and gathering lifestyle, living in portable yurts and subsisting largely on herds of reindeer or caribou. Other areas include taiga with extensive, dense woods in north-central Russia and more temperate steppes and grasslands in the southwest.

Physical Geography and Climate of North Africa, Southwest, and Central Asia

This area of the world is complex in its geographical structure and climate, incorporating seas, peninsulas, rivers, mountains, and numerous other features. **Earthquakes** are common, with tectonic plates in the area remaining active. Much of the world's **oil** lies in this area. The tendency of the large rivers of North Africa, especially the Nile, to follow a set pattern of **drought** and extreme **fertility**, led people to settle there from prehistoric times. As technology has advanced, people have tamed this river, making its activity more predictable and the land around it more productive. The extremely arid nature of many other parts of this area has also led to **human intervention** such as irrigation to increase agricultural production.

Physical Geography and Climate of the Southern Portion of Africa

South of the Sahara Desert, the high elevations and other geographical characteristics have made it very difficult for human travel or settlement to occur. The geography of the area is dominated by a series of **plateaus**. There are also mountain ranges and a large rift valley in the eastern part of the country. Contrasting the wide desert areas, sub-Saharan Africa contains numerous lakes, rivers, and world-famous waterfalls. The area has **tropical** climates, including rainforests, savannas, steppes, and desert areas. The main natural resources are minerals, including gems and water.

Physical Geography and Climate of South Asia

The longest **alluvial plain**, a plain caused by shifting floodplains of major rivers and river systems over time, exists in South Asia. South Asia boasts three major **river systems** in the Ganges, Indus, and Brahmaputra. It also has large deposits of **minerals**, including iron ore that is in great demand internationally. South Asia holds mountains, plains, plateaus, and numerous islands. The climates range from tropical to highlands and desert areas. South Asia also experiences monsoon winds that cause a long rainy season. Variations in climate, elevation, and human activity influence agricultural production.

Geography and Climate of East Asia

East Asia includes North and South Korea, Mongolia, China, Japan, and Taiwan. Mineral resources are plentiful but not evenly distributed throughout. The coastlines are long, and while the population is large, farmlands are sparse. As a result, the surrounding ocean has become a major source of sustenance. East Asia is large enough to encompass several climate regions. **Ocean currents** provide milder climates to coastal areas, while **monsoons** provide the majority of the rainfall for the region. **Typhoons** are somewhat common, as are **earthquakes**, **volcanoes**, and **tsunamis**. The latter occur because of the tectonic plates that meet beneath the continent and remain somewhat active.

Geography and Climate of Southeast Asia

Southeast Asia lies largely on the **equator**, and roughly half of the countries of the region are island nations. These countries include Indonesia, the Philippines, Vietnam, Thailand, Myanmar, and Malaysia (which is partially on the mainland and partially an island country). The island nations of Southeast Asia feature mountains that are considered part of the **Ring of Fire**, an area where tectonic plates remain active, leading to extensive volcanic activity as well as earthquakes and tsunamis. Southeast Asia boasts many rivers and abundant natural resources, including gems, fossil fuels, and minerals. There are basically two seasons: wet and dry. The wet season arrives with the **monsoons**. In general, Southeast Asia consists of **tropical rainforest climates**, but there are some mountain areas and tropical savannas.

Geography and Climate of Australia, Oceania, and Antarctica

In the far southern hemisphere of the globe, Australia and Oceania present their own climatic combinations. **Australia**, the only island on Earth that is also a continent, has extensive deserts as well as mountains and lowlands. The economy is driven by agriculture, including ranches and farms, and minerals. While the steppes bordering extremely arid inland areas are suitable for livestock, only the coastal areas receive sufficient rainfall for crops without using irrigation. **Oceania** refers to over 10,000 Pacific islands created by volcanic activity. Most of these have tropical climates with wet and dry seasons. **New Zealand**, Australia's nearest neighbor, boasts rich forests, mountain ranges, and relatively moderate temperatures, including rainfall throughout the year. **Antarctica** is covered with ice. Its major resource consists of scientific information. It supports some wildlife, such as penguins, and little vegetation, primarily mosses or lichens.

Theory of Plate Tectonics

According to the geological theory of plate tectonics, Earth's crust is made up of ten major and several minor **tectonic plates**. These plates are the solid areas of the crust. They float on top of Earth's mantle, which is made up of molten rock. Because the plates float on this liquid component of Earth's crust, they move, creating major changes in Earth's surface. These changes can happen very slowly over a long time period, such as in continental drift, or rapidly, such as when earthquakes occur. **Interaction** between the different continental plates can create mountain ranges, volcanic activity, major earthquakes, and deep rifts.

Types of Plate Boundaries

Plate tectonics defines three types of plate boundaries, determined by how the edges of the plates interact. These **plate boundaries** are:

- **Convergent boundaries**—the bordering plates move toward one another. When they collide directly, this is known as continental collision, which can create very large, high mountain ranges such as the Himalayas and the Andes. If one plate slides under the other, this is called subduction. Subduction can lead to intense volcanic activity. One example is the Ring of Fire that lies along the northern Pacific coastlines.
- **Divergent boundaries**—plates move away from each other. This movement leads to rifts such as the Mid-Atlantic Ridge and East Africa's Great Rift Valley.
- **Transform boundaries**—plate boundaries slide in opposite directions against each other. Intense pressure builds up along transform boundaries as the plates grind along each other's edges, leading to earthquakes. Many major fault lines, including the San Andreas Fault, lie along transform boundaries.

Erosion, Weathering, Transportation, and Deposition

Erosion involves movement of any loose material on Earth's surface. This can include soil, sand, or rock fragments. These loose fragments can be displaced by natural forces such as wind, water, ice, plant cover, and human factors. **Mechanical erosion** occurs due to natural forces. **Chemical erosion** occurs as a result of human intervention and activities. **Weathering** occurs when atmospheric elements affect Earth's surface. Water, heat, ice, and pressure all lead to weathering. **Transportation** refers to loose material being moved by wind, water, or ice. Glacial movement, for example, carries everything from pebbles to boulders, sometimes over long distances. **Deposition** is the result of transportation. When material is transported, it is eventually deposited, and builds up to create formations like moraines and sand dunes.

Effects of Human Interaction and Conflict on Geographical Boundaries

Human societies and their interaction have led to divisions of territories into **countries** and various other subdivisions. While these divisions are at their root artificial, they are important to geographers in discussing various populations' interactions.

Geographical divisions often occur through conflict between different human populations. The reasons behind these divisions include:

- Control of resources
- Control of important trade routes
- Control of populations

Conflict often occurs due to religious, political, language, or race differences. Natural resources are finite and so often lead to conflict over how they are distributed among populations.

State Sovereignty

State sovereignty recognizes the division of geographical areas into areas controlled by various governments or groups of people. These groups control not only the territory but also all its natural resources and the inhabitants of the area. The entire planet Earth is divided into **political** or **administratively sovereign areas** recognized to be controlled by a particular government, with the exception of the continent of Antarctica.

Alliances

Alliances form between different countries based on similar interests, political goals, cultural values, or military issues. Six existing **international alliances** include:

- North Atlantic Treaty Organization (NATO)
- Common Market
- European Union (EU)
- United Nations (UN)
- Caribbean Community
- Council of Arab Economic Unity

In addition, very large **companies** and **multi-national corporations** can create alliances and various kinds of competition based on the need to control resources, production, and the overall marketplace.

Ways Agricultural Revolution Changed Society

The agricultural revolution began approximately 6,000 years ago when the **plow** was invented in **Mesopotamia**. Using a plow drawn by animals, people were able to cultivate crops in large quantities rather than gathering available seeds and grains and planting them by hand. Because large-scale agriculture was labor-intensive, this led to the development of stable communities where people gathered to make farming possible. As **stable farming communities** replaced groups of nomadic hunter-gatherers, human society underwent profound changes. Societies became dependent on limited numbers of crops as well as subject to the vagaries of weather. Trading livestock and surplus agricultural output led to the growth of large-scale **commerce** and **trade routes**.

WAYS HUMAN POPULATIONS MODIFY THEIR SURROUNDING ENVIRONMENT

The agricultural revolution led human societies to begin changing their surroundings to accommodate their needs for shelter and room to cultivate food and to provide for domestic animals. Clearing ground for crops, redirecting waterways for irrigation purposes, and building permanent settlements all create major changes in the **environment**. Large-scale agriculture can lead to loose topsoil and damaging erosion. Building large cities leads to degraded air quality, water pollution from energy consumption, and many other side effects that can severely damage the environment. Recently, many countries have taken action by passing laws to **reduce human impact** on the environment and reduce the potentially damaging side effects. This is called **environmental policy**.

ECOLOGY

Ecology is the study of the way living creatures interact with their environment. **Biogeography** explores the way physical features of Earth affect living creatures.

Ecology bases its studies on three different levels of the environment:

- **Ecosystem**—this is a specific physical environment and all the organisms that live there.
- **Biome**—this is a group of ecosystems, usually consisting of a large area with similar flora and fauna as well as similar climate and soil. Examples of biomes include deserts, tropical rain forests, taigas, and tundra.
- **Habitat**—this is an area in which a specific species usually lives. The habitat includes the necessary soil, water, and resources for that particular species, as well as predators and other species that compete for the same resources.

TYPES OF INTERACTIONS OCCURRING BETWEEN SPECIES IN AN INDIVIDUAL HABITAT

Different interactions occur among species and members of single species within a habitat. These **interactions** fall into three categories:

- **Competition** — competition occurs when different animals, either of the same species or of different species, compete for the same resources. Robins can compete with other robins for available food, but other insectivores also compete for these same resources.
- **Predation**— predation occurs when one species depends on the other species for food, such as a fox who subsists on small mammals.
- **Symbiosis** — symbiosis occurs when two different species exist in the same environment without negatively affecting each other. Some symbiotic relationships are beneficial to one or both organisms without harm occurring to either.

IMPORTANCE OF AN ORGANISM'S ABILITY TO ADAPT

If a species is relocated from one habitat to another, it must **adapt** in order to survive. Some species are more capable of adapting than others. Those that cannot adapt will not survive. There are different ways a creature can adapt, including behavior modification and structural or physiological changes. Adaptation is also vital if an organism's environment changes around it. Although the creature has not been relocated, it finds itself in a new environment that requires changes in order to survive. The more readily an organism can adapt, the more likely it is to survive. The almost infinite ability of **humans** to adapt is a major reason why they are able to survive in almost any habitat in any area of the world.

BIODIVERSITY

Biodiversity refers to the variety of habitats that exist on the planet, as well as the variety of organisms that can exist within these habitats. A greater level of **biodiversity** makes it more likely that an individual habitat will flourish along with the species that depend upon it. Changes in habitat, including climate change, human intervention, or other factors, can reduce biodiversity by causing the extinction of certain species.

Economics

ECONOMICS

Economics is the study of the ways specific societies **allocate** resources to individuals and groups within that society. Also important are the choices society makes regarding what efforts or initiatives are funded and which are not. Since resources in any society are finite, allocation becomes a vivid reflection of that society's values. In general, the economic system that drives an individual society is based on:

- What goods are produced
- How those goods are produced
- Who acquires the goods or benefits from them

Economics consists of two main categories: **macroeconomics**, which studies larger systems, and **microeconomics**, which studies smaller systems.

SCARCITY AND CHOICE

Economics could rightfully be called the study of **scarcity**. Limited resources are available to satisfy the wants and needs of both individuals and states. Economics involves the **choices** made by an economy to satisfy these wants and needs. Every economy must choose what goods and services to produce, how to produce them, and for whom they are intended. Limitations of the factors of production—land, labor, and capital—sometimes make these choices difficult. When an economic choice is made, there is an "**opportunity cost**" implicit in the choice. The opportunity cost is what is given up by making a choice. If a country chooses to manufacture automobiles, it may not have the industrial capacity to produce tanks or aircraft. Thus, the economic choice to make automobiles involves the opportunity cost of not making tanks or aircraft. Individuals and countries continually make economic choices and sacrifice opportunist costs in the process. An individual may choose to attend a film rather than go out to dinner. Choices are driven by what people and countries feel is in their best interest.

MARGINALISM

Marginalism concerns itself with the economic worth of the last (or next) product or service provided. The cost of making the last product, the cost of hiring the last employee, and the cost of selling the last product, determine the **marginal cost** of that next good. Presumably, a company will continue to produce goods and services until it becomes unprofitable. Production will cease when the marginal return of a product does not yield a profit. From the consumer's viewpoint, the **marginal utility** of the purchase is the crucial factor. How much satisfaction does an individual get from each purchase? When this marginal utility decreases too much, the buyer will not buy the next unit. The idea of diminishing returns often determines how many units of a good or service a buyer will purchase. For example, after eating a piece of pie, the want-satisfying power of the next piece of pie is decreased. When this marginal utility reaches a certain point, the consumer will stop buying.

COSTS

Costs and revenues are the two determinants of income, the most common measuring tools for assessing business success. Firms incur **fixed costs**, which are constant and do not depend on that amount of production. Examples would be physical plants and heavy equipment, which must be paid for even if production is zero. **Variable costs** are tied directly to the production of finished goods and services. As more goods are produced, variable costs rise. Examples of variable costs are raw materials used in the production process, extra labor needed in peak production periods, and additional capital if expansion is needed.

EXCHANGE

Economic exchange is the basic activity of economics. The circular cycle of exchange from consumer to suppliers and back are the transactions that move an economy. The field of exchange is the marketplace, and money is the medium through which these transactions move. Building an **infrastructure** for market transactions is necessary to allow an orderly and dependable mechanism for economic exchange.

TRADITIONAL ECONOMY

In a traditional economy, determinations of the types and amounts of goods produced, methods of production, and distribution of goods are based on long-established customs and habits. Such economies are sometimes referred to as subsistence economies because little surplus is produced, which negates the need for markets.

MARKET ECONOMY

A market economy is based on supply and demand. **Demand** has to do with what customers want and need, as well as what quantity those consumers are able to purchase based on other economic factors. **Supply** refers to how much can be produced to meet demand, or how much suppliers are willing and able to sell. Where the needs of consumers meet the needs of suppliers is referred to as a market equilibrium price. This price varies depending on many factors, including the overall health of a society's economy and the overall beliefs and considerations of individuals in society. The following is a list of terms defined in the context of a market economy:

- **Elasticity**—this is based on how the quantity of a particular product responds to the price demanded for that product. If quantity responds quickly to changes in price, the supply/demand for that product is said to be elastic. If it does not respond quickly, then the supply/demand is inelastic.
- **Market efficiency**—this occurs when a market is capable of producing output high enough to meet consumer demand.
- **Comparative advantage**—in the field of international trade, this refers to a country focusing on a specific product that it can produce more efficiently and more cheaply, or at a lower opportunity cost, than another country, thus giving it a comparative advantage in production.

Review Video: Basics of Market Economy
Visit mometrix.com/academy and enter code: 791556

PLANNED ECONOMY VS. MARKET ECONOMY

In a **market economy**, supply and demand are determined by consumers. In a **planned economy**, a public entity or planning authority makes the decisions about what resources will be produced, how they will be produced, and who will be able to benefit from them. The means of production, such as factories, are also owned by a public entity rather than by private interests. In **market socialism**, the economic structure falls somewhere between the market economy and the planned economy. Planning authorities determine the allocation of resources at higher economic levels, while consumer goods are driven by a market economy.

MICROECONOMICS

While economics generally studies how resources are allocated, **microeconomics** focuses on economic factors such as the way consumers behave, how income is distributed, and output and input markets. Studies are limited to the industry or firm level rather than an entire country or society. Among the elements studied in microeconomics are factors of production, costs of production, and factor income. These factors determine production decisions of individual firms, based on resources and costs.

CLASSIFICATION OF VARIOUS MARKETS BY ECONOMISTS

The conditions prevailing in a given market are used to **classify** markets. Conditions considered include:

- Existence of competition
- Number and size of suppliers

- Influence of suppliers over price
- Variety of available products
- Ease of entering the market

Once these questions are answered, an economist can classify a certain market according to its structure and the nature of competition within the market.

Market Failure

When any of the elements for a successfully competitive market are missing, this can lead to a **market failure**. Certain elements are necessary to create what economists call "**perfect competition**." If one of these factors is weak or lacking, the market is classified as having "**imperfect competition**." Worse than imperfect competition, though, is a market failure. There are five major types of market failure:

- Inadequate competition
- Inadequate information
- Immobile resources
- Negative externalities, or side effects
- Failure to provide public goods

Externalities are side effects of a market that affect third parties. These effects can be either negative or positive.

Factors of Production and Costs of Production

Every good and service requires certain resources, or **inputs**. These inputs are referred to as **factors of production**. Every good and service requires four factors of production:

- Labor
- Capital
- Land
- Entrepreneurship

These factors can be fixed or variable and can produce fixed or variable costs. Examples of **fixed costs** include land and equipment. **Variable costs** include labor. The total of fixed and variable costs makes up the cost of production.

Factor Income

Factors of production each have an associated **factor income**. Factors that earn income include:

- **Labor**—earns wages
- **Capital**—earns interest
- **Land**—earns rent
- **Entrepreneurship**—earns profit

Each factor's income is determined by its **contribution**. In a market economy, this income is not guaranteed to be equal. How scarce the factor is and the weight of its contribution to the overall production process determines the final factor income.

KINDS OF MARKET STRUCTURES IN AN OUTPUT MARKET.

The four kinds of market structures in an output market are:

- **Perfect competition**—all existing firms sell an identical product. The firms are not able to control the final price. In addition, there is nothing that makes it difficult to become involved in or leave the industry. Anything that would prevent entering or leaving an industry is called a barrier to entry. An example of this market structure is agriculture.
- **Monopoly**—a single seller controls the product and its price. Barriers to entry, such as prohibitively high fixed cost structures, prevent other sellers from entering the market.
- **Monopolistic competition**—a number of firms sell similar products, but they are not identical, such as different brands of clothes or food. Barriers to entry are low.
- **Oligopoly**—only a few firms control the production and distribution of products, such as automobiles. Barriers to entry are high, preventing large numbers of firms from entering the market.

TYPES OF MONOPOLIES

Four types of monopolies are:

- **Natural monopoly**—a single supplier has a distinct advantage over the others.
- **Geographic monopoly**—only one business offers the product in a certain area.
- **Technological monopoly**—a single company controls the technology necessary to supply the product.
- **Government monopoly**—a government agency is the only provider of a specific good or service.

ACTIONS TAKEN BY THE US GOVERNMENT TO CONTROL MONOPOLIES

The US government has passed several acts to regulate businesses, including:

- **Sherman Antitrust Act (1890)**—this prohibited trusts, monopolies, and any other situations that eliminated competition.
- **Clayton Antitrust Act (1914)**—this prohibited price discrimination.
- **Robinson-Patman Act (1936)**—this strengthened provisions of the Clayton Antitrust Act, requiring businesses to offer the same pricing on products to any customer.

The government has also taken other actions to ensure competition, including requirements for public disclosure. The **Securities and Exchange Commission (SEC)** requires companies that provide public stock to provide financial reports on a regular basis. Because of the nature of their business, banks are further regulated and required to provide various information to the government.

MARKETING AND UTILITY

Marketing consists of all of the activity necessary to convince consumers to acquire goods. One major way to move products into the hands of consumers is to convince them that any single product will satisfy a need. The ability of a product or service to satisfy the need of a consumer is called **utility**. There are four types of utility:

- **Form utility**—a product's desirability lies in its physical characteristics.
- **Place utility**—a product's desirability is connected to its location and convenience.
- **Time utility**—a product's desirability is determined by its availability at a certain time.
- **Ownership utility**—a product's desirability is increased because ownership of the product passes to the consumer.

Marketing behavior will stress any or all of these types of utility when marketing to the consumer.

Producers Determining What Customers Desire for Their Products

Successful marketing depends not only on convincing customers they need the product but also on focusing the marketing towards those who already have a need or desire for the product. Before releasing a product into the general marketplace, many producers will **test** markets to determine which will be the most receptive to the product. There are three steps usually taken to evaluate a product's market:

- **Market research**—this involves researching a market to determine if it will be receptive to the product.
- **Market surveys**—a part of market research, market surveys ask consumers specific questions to help determine the marketability of a product to a specific group.
- **Test marketing**—this includes releasing the product into a small geographical area to see how it sells. Often test marketing is followed by wider marketing if the product does well.

Major Elements of a Marketing Plan

The four major elements of a marketing plan are:

- **Product**—this includes any elements pertaining directly to the product, such as packaging, presentation, or services to include along with it.
- **Price**—this calculates the cost of production, distribution, advertising, etc., as well as the desired profit to determine the final price.
- **Place**—this determines which outlets will be used to sell the product, whether traditional outlets such as brick and mortar stores or through direct mail or internet marketing.
- **Promotion**—this involves ways to let consumers know the product is available, through advertising and other means.

Once these elements have all been determined, the producer can proceed with production and distribution of his product.

Distribution Channels

Distribution channels determine the route a product takes on its journey from producer to consumer, and can also influence the final price and availability of the product. There are two major forms of distributions: wholesale and retail. A **wholesale distributor** buys in large quantities and then resells smaller amounts to other businesses. **Retailers** sell directly to the consumers rather than to businesses. In the modern marketplace, additional distribution channels have grown up with the rise of markets such as club warehouse stores as well as purchasing through catalogs or over the internet. Most of these newer distribution channels bring products more directly to the consumer, eliminating the need for middlemen.

Distribution of Income in a Society

Distribution of income in any society ranges from poorest to richest. In most societies, income is not distributed evenly. To determine **income distribution**, family incomes are ranked from lowest to highest. These rankings are divided into five sections called **quintiles**, which are compared to each other. The uneven distribution of income is often linked to higher levels of education and ability in the upper classes but can also be due to other factors such as discrimination and existing monopolies. The **income gap** in America continues to grow, largely due to growth in the service industry, changes in the American family unit, and reduced influence of labor unions. **Poverty** is defined by comparing incomes to poverty guidelines. Poverty guidelines determine the level of income necessary for a family to function. Those below the poverty line are often eligible for assistance from government agencies.

MACROECONOMICS

Macroeconomics examines economies on a much larger level than microeconomics. While **microeconomics** studies economics on a firm or industry level, **macroeconomics** looks at economic trends and structures on a national level. Variables studied in macroeconomics include:

- Output
- Consumption
- Investment
- Government spending
- Net exports

The overall economic condition of a nation is defined as the **Gross Domestic Product**, or GDP. GDP measures a nation's economic output over a limited time period, such as a year.

Review Video: Microeconomics and Macroeconomics
Visit mometrix.com/academy and enter code: 538837

Review Video: Gross Domestic Product
Visit mometrix.com/academy and enter code: 409020

TAXES

Any assessment or charge to an individual economic unit by a government or quasi-government may be termed a **tax**. Some taxes are **direct**, such as a sales tax on goods and services sold. Other taxes may be **indirect**, property taxes being a prime example. Earlier economic systems received "taxes" as goods and services rendered to a ruling authority. In contemporary economics, we usually think of taxes in terms of legal currency. Taxes have caused revolutions ("No taxation without representation"), have overturned governments, and have become a social and political issue of controversy and debate. Who should pay taxes, how much should be paid, and the use of tax revenue are all critical issues in the fabric of society. The branch of formal economics most concerned with taxes is public finance.

TYPES OF CONSUMER BEHAVIOR

The two major types of consumer behavior as defined in macroeconomics are:

- **Marginal propensity to consume (MPC)** defines the tendency of consumers to increase spending in conjunction with increases in income. In general, individuals with greater income will buy more. As individuals increase their income through job changes or growth of experience, they will also increase spending.
- **Utility** is a term that describes the satisfaction experienced by a consumer in relation to acquiring and using a good or service. Providers of goods and services will stress utility to convince consumers they want the products being presented.

WAYS TO MEASURE THE GROSS DOMESTIC PRODUCT OF A COUNTRY

Gross domestic product (GDP) is the total value of all the goods and services produced within a country during a certain time period. It is often used as a measurement of a country's economic health.

The two major ways to measure the Gross Domestic Product of a country are:

- The **expenditures approach** calculates the GDP based on how much money is spent in each individual sector.
- The **income approach** calculates the GDP based on how much money is earned in each sector.

Both methods yield the same results, and both of these calculation methods are based on four **economic sectors** that make up a country's macro-economy:

- Consumers
- Business
- Government
- Foreign sector

Types of Earnings Generated by an Economy Considered to Calculate GDP

Several factors must be considered in order to accurately calculate the GDP using the incomes approach. **Income factors** are:

- Wages paid to laborers, or compensation of employees (CE)
- Rental income derived from land
- Interest income derived from invested capital
- Entrepreneurial income

Entrepreneurial income consists of two forms. **Proprietor's income** is income that comes back to the entrepreneur himself. **Corporate profit** is income that goes back into the corporation as a whole. Corporate profit is divided by the corporation into corporate profits taxes, dividends, and retained earnings. Two other figures must be subtracted in the incomes approach. These are **indirect business taxes**, including property and sales taxes, and **depreciation**.

Effects of Population of a Country on the Gross Domestic Product

Changes in population can affect the calculation of a nation's **GDP**, particularly since GDP and GNP (Gross National Product) are generally measured per capita. If a country's economic production is low but the population is high, the income per individual will be lower than if the income is high and the population is lower. Also, if the population grows quickly and the income grows slowly, individual income will remain low or even drop drastically.

Population growth can also affect overall **economic growth**. Economic growth requires both that consumers purchase goods and workers produce them. A population that does not grow quickly enough will not supply enough workers to support rapid economic growth.

Problems with Equating GDP Per Capita and Economic Well-Being

Several economic factors may interfere with equating GDP per capita with individual well-being. A significant allocation of assets is used to combat the negative effects of economic growth such as the destruction of natural habitats and air and water pollution. Economic growth increases such **intangibles** as the increase in commuting, which affects quality of life. Perhaps most importantly, GDP does not account for a significant amount of **domestic production,** such as child-raising and homemaking. The money equivalents for these tasks are omitted from the GDP calculation. There are numerous markets that are left out of GDP, including black markets, criminal activity, and alternative economies. There is also no provision in GDP for volunteer activity, "do it yourself" tasks such as home improvements and landscape management. All of these economic activities are omitted from the formal measurement of per capita GDP and fail to give an accurate picture of individual well-being.

Ideal Balance to be Obtained in an Economy

Ideally, an economy functions efficiently, with the **aggregate supply**, or the amount of national output, equal to the **aggregate demand**, or the amount of the output that is purchased. In these cases, the economy is stable and prosperous. However, economies more typically go through **phases**. These phases are:

- **Boom**—GDP is high and the economy prospers
- **Recession**—GDP falls and unemployment rises
- **Trough**—the recession reaches its lowest point
- **Recovery**—unemployment lessens, prices rise, and the economy begins to stabilize again

These phases tend to repeat in cycles that are not necessarily predictable or regular.

Measures of National Income and Output

National income may be defined as the aggregate figure of all consumption, individual, business, and governmental income, plus total investments and the balance of trade accounts for a country. This aggregate number, derived from adding these categories together, is called the **expenditure method** of national income determination. Another calculation to determine the national income is to account for all the goods and services produced in a country during a fixed period. This is called the **production accounting** of national income. Yet another way of computing national income is to total all income received by individuals, businesses, and governments to arrive at total national income. This is the **income approach** to national income accounting. To summarize, there are three ways of calculating national income: total expenditures, total value of production, and the aggregate consumption figures for a country.

Consumer Price Indices

A price index, such as the **Consumer Price Index**, can be used as a measuring tool to compare prices at different times. A fictional "market basket" of commonly consumed staples is measured and charted over a period of time (usually one year). If the price of the representative market basket has gone up, **inflation** has occurred. For example, if a typical basket costs $500 this year as compared to $400 last year for the same basket, inflation has risen over a year. Inflation reduces the buying power of money, and if uncontrolled, can threaten the entire economy.

Unemployment and Inflation

When demand outstrips supply, prices are driven artificially high, or are **inflated**. This occurs when too much spending causes an imbalance in the economy. In general, inflation occurs because an economy is growing too quickly. When there is too little spending, and supply has moved far beyond demand, a **surplus** of product results. Companies cut back on production and reduce the number of employees, and **unemployment** rises as people lose their jobs. This imbalance occurs when an economy becomes sluggish. In general, both these economic instability situations are caused by an imbalance between supply and demand. Government intervention may be necessary to stabilize an economy when either inflation or unemployment becomes too serious.

Different Forms of Unemployment

- **Frictional**—when workers change jobs and are unemployed while waiting for new jobs
- **Structural**—when economic shifts reduce the need for workers
- **Cyclical**—when natural business cycles bring about loss of jobs
- **Seasonal**—when seasonal cycles reduce the need for certain jobs
- **Technological**—when advances in technology result in the elimination of certain jobs

Any of these factors can increase unemployment in certain sectors.

Inflation is classified by the overall rate at which it occurs:

- **Creeping inflation**—this is an inflation rate of about 1%-3% annually.
- **Walking inflation**—this is an inflation rate of 3%-10% annually.
- **Galloping inflation**— a severe inflation rate above 10 percent (to upwards of 100 percent and beyond) annually. Highly detrimental to the economy, this deeply impacts the lower and middle class populus.
- **Hyperinflation**— an inflation rate over 50% monthly or 500+ percent annually. Hyperinflation usually leads to complete monetary collapse in a society. Individuals are unable to have enough income to purchase their needed goods.

Government Intervention Policies That Mitigate Inflation and Unemployment

When an economy becomes too imbalanced, either due to excessive spending or not enough spending, **government intervention** often becomes necessary to put the economy back on track. Government fiscal policy can take several forms, including:

- Contractionary policy
- Expansionary policy
- Monetary policy

Contractionary policies help counteract inflation. These include increasing taxes and decreasing government spending to slow spending in the overall economy. **Expansionary policies** increase government spending and lower taxes in order to reduce unemployment and increase the level of spending in the economy overall. **Monetary policy** can take several forms and affects the amount of funds available to banks for making loans.

Study and Quantification of Populations and Population Growth

Populations are studied by **size**, rates of **growth** due to immigration, the overall **fertility rate**, and **life expectancy**. For example, though the population of the United States is considerably larger than it was two hundred years ago, the rate of population growth has decreased greatly, from about three percent per year to less than one percent per year.

In the US, the fertility rate is fairly low, with most choosing not to have large families, and life expectancy is high, creating a projected imbalance between older and younger people in the near future. In addition, immigration and the mixing of racially diverse cultures are projected to increase the percentages of Asians, Hispanics, and African Americans.

Functions and Types of Money

Money is used in three major ways:

- As an accounting unit
- As a store of value
- As an exchange medium

In general, money must be acceptable throughout a society in exchange for debts or to purchase goods and services. Money should be relatively scarce, its value should remain stable, and it should be easily carried, durable, and easy to divide up. There are three basic types of money: commodity, representative, and fiat. **Commodity money** includes gems or precious metals. **Representative money** can be exchanged for items such as gold or silver that have inherent value. **Fiat money**, or legal tender, has no inherent value but has been declared to function as money by the government. It is often backed by gold or silver but not necessarily on a one-to-one ratio.

Investment and Credit

Investment is committing financial resources to a particular account or asset in order to earn a return at a later time. Each type of **investment** carries a different level of risk and a different potential return, though it can be difficult to determine exactly how profitable a particular endeavor will be in the long run. **Credit** is the process by which a financial institution lends funds to an individual for the purchase of a particular product or service. This means that the financial institution will cover the cost of the product or service in exchange for the individual agreeing to pay back that money, and any interest associated with the loan or credit, at a later time.

Types of Money Available in the US and Economists' Measure of It

Money in the US is not just currency. When economists calculate the amount of money available, they must take into account other factors, such as deposits that have been placed in checking accounts, debit cards, and "near moneys," such as savings accounts, that can be quickly converted into cash. Currency, checkable deposits and traveler's checks, referred to as **M1**, are added up, and then **M2** is calculated by adding savings deposits, CDs, and various other monetary deposits. The final result is the total quantity of available money.

Aspects of Monetary Policy and the Role of the Federal Reserve System

The Federal Reserve System, also known as the **Fed**, implements all monetary policy in the US. Monetary policy regulates the amount of money available in the American banking system. The Fed can decrease or increase the amount of available money for loans, thus helping regulate the national economy. Monetary policies implemented by the Fed are part of expansionary or contractionary monetary policies that help counteract inflation or unemployment. The **discount rate** is an interest rate charged by the Fed when banks borrow money from them. A lower discount rate leads banks to borrow more money, leading to increased spending. A higher discount rate has the opposite effect.

How Banks Function

Banks earn their income by **loaning** out money and charging **interest** on those loans. If less money is available, fewer loans can be made, which affects the amount of spending in the overall economy. While banks function by making loans, they are not allowed to loan out all the money they hold in deposit. The amount of money they must maintain in reserve is known as the **reserve ratio**. If the reserve ratio is raised, less money is available for loans and spending decreases. A lower reserve ratio increases available funds and increases spending. This ratio is determined by the Federal Reserve System.

Central Banks

Central banks of countries are the institutions that control currency (and the money supply) through monetary and fiscal policy. These central banks or other monetary authorities (set up as an agency by the government) control and implement monetary policy and activity. Such authorities differ in their power from country to country. For example, in the United States, the Federal Reserve is a wholly independent agency free of political controls. Although Congress legislated the Federal Reserve into existence, it remains completely independent in its activity.

Open Market Operations

The Federal Reserve System can also expand or contract the overall money supply through **open market operations**. In this case, the Fed can buy or sell **bonds** it has purchased from banks or individuals. When the Fed buys bonds, more money is put into circulation, creating an expansionary situation to stimulate the economy. When the Fed sells bonds, money is withdrawn from the system, creating a **contractionary** situation to slow an economy suffering from inflation. Because of international financial markets, however, American banks often borrow and lend money in markets outside the US. By shifting their attention to international markets, domestic banks and other businesses can circumvent whatever contractionary policies the Fed may have put into place.

MAJOR CHARACTERISTICS OF INTERNATIONAL TRADE

International trade can take advantage of broader markets, bringing a wider variety of products within easy reach. By contrast, it can also allow individual countries to specialize in particular products that they can produce easily, such as those for which they have easy access to raw materials. Other products, more difficult to make domestically, can be acquired through trade with other nations. **International trade** requires efficient use of **native resources** as well as sufficient **disposable income** to purchase native and imported products. Many countries in the world engage extensively in international trade, but others still face major economic challenges.

MAJOR CHARACTERISTICS OF A DEVELOPING NATION

The five major characteristics of a developing nation are:

- Low GDP
- Rapid growth of population
- Economy that depends on subsistence agriculture
- Poor conditions, including high infant mortality rates, high disease rates, poor sanitation, and insufficient housing
- Low literacy rate

Developing nations often function under oppressive governments that do not provide private property rights and withhold education and other rights from women. They also often feature an extreme disparity between upper and lower classes, with little opportunity for the lower classes to improve their position.

STAGES OF ECONOMIC DEVELOPMENT

Economic development occurs in three stages that are defined by the activities that drive the economy:

- Agricultural stage
- Manufacturing stage
- Service sector stage

In developing countries, it is often difficult to acquire the necessary funding to provide equipment and training to move into the advanced stages of economic development. Some can receive help from developed countries via foreign aid and investment or international organizations such as the **International Monetary Fund** or the **World Bank**. Having developed countries provide monetary, technical, or military assistance can help developing countries move forward to the next stage in their development.

CONTROLS

An imposition of wage and price controls is a more drastic way to slow or halt inflation. These measures have many drawbacks, including the possibility of depressing the economy too far. Controls also promote hoarding and artificial shortages and sometimes encourage the creation of alternative marketplaces that impair economic growth.

LABOR DEMAND

The totality of all firms' demand for labor is called the **total market demand for labor**. The market supply of labor depends on the population, level of skill required, prevalent economic condition, and effective wage rate. When the demand and supply curves for labor intersect, the **competitive equilibrium wage rate** is determined. Firms will continue to hire labor until the marginal revenue product of labor, or its demand for labor, reaches the wage rate. **Labor unions** can distort the supply and demand for labor, and thus the wage determination, by increasing productivity, reducing the labor force with excessive union dues, and bargaining with businesses and threatening strikes.

OBSTACLES DEVELOPING NATIONS FACE REGARDING ECONOMIC GROWTH

Developing nations typically struggle to overcome obstacles that prevent or slow economic development. Major **obstacles** can include:

- Rapid, uncontrolled population growth
- Trade restrictions
- Misused resources, often perpetrated by the government
- Traditional beliefs that can slow or reject change

Corrupt, oppressive governments often hamper the economic growth of developing nations, creating huge **economic disparities** and making it impossible for individuals to advance, in turn preventing overall growth. Governments sometimes export currency, called **capital flight**, which is detrimental to a country's economic development. In general, countries are more likely to experience economic growth if their governments encourage entrepreneurship and provide private property rights.

PROBLEMS WHEN INDUSTRIALIZATION OCCURS TOO QUICKLY

Rapid growth throughout the world leaves some nations behind and sometimes spurs their governments to move forward too quickly into **industrialization** and **artificially rapid economic growth**. While slow or nonexistent economic growth causes problems in a country, overly rapid industrialization carries its own issues. Four major problems encountered due to rapid industrialization are:

- Use of technology not suited to the products or services being supplied
- Poor investment of capital
- Lack of time for the population to adapt to new paradigms
- Lack of time to experience all stages of development and adjust to each stage

Economic failures in Indonesia were largely due to rapid growth that was poorly handled.

IMPORTANCE OF E-COMMERCE IN TODAY'S MARKETPLACE

The growth of the internet has brought many changes to our society, not the least of which is the modern way of business. Where supply channels used to move in certain necessary ways, many of these channels are now bypassed as **e-commerce** makes it possible for nearly any individual to set up a direct market to consumers, as well as direct interaction with suppliers. Competition is fierce. In many instances, e-commerce can provide nearly instantaneous gratification, with a wide variety of products. Whoever provides the best product most quickly often rises to the top of a marketplace. How this added element to the marketplace will affect the economy in the future remains to be seen. Many industries are still struggling with the best ways to adapt to the rapid, continuous changes.

KNOWLEDGE ECONOMY AND POSSIBLE EFFECT ON FUTURE ECONOMIC GROWTH

The knowledge economy is a growing sector in the economy of developed countries, and includes the trade and development of:

- Data
- Intellectual property
- Technology, especially in the area of communications

Knowledge as a resource is steadily becoming more and more important. What is now being called the **Information Age** may prove to bring about changes in life and culture as significant as those brought on by the Agricultural and Industrial Revolutions.

Cybernomics

Related to the knowledge economy is what has been dubbed "**cybernomics**," or economics driven by e-commerce and other computer-based markets and products. Marketing has changed drastically with the growth of cyber communication, allowing suppliers to connect one-on-one with their customers. Other issues coming to the fore regarding cybernomics include:

- Secure online trade
- Intellectual property rights
- Rights to privacy
- Bringing developing nations into the fold

As these issues are debated and new laws and policies developed, the face of many industries continues to undergo drastic change. Many of the old ways of doing business no longer work, leaving industries scrambling to function profitably within the new system.

Civics and Government

US Government and Citizenship

Political Science and Its Ties to Other Major Disciplines

Political science focuses on studying different governments and how they compare to each other, general political theory, ways political theory is put into action, how nations and governments interact with each other, and a general study of governmental structure and function. Other elements of **political science** include the study of elections, governmental administration at various levels, development and action of political parties, and how values such as freedom, power, justice, and equality are expressed in different political cultures. Political science also encompasses elements of other disciplines, including:

- **History**—how historical events have shaped political thought and process
- **Sociology**—the effects of various stages of social development on the growth and development of government and politics
- **Anthropology**—the effects of governmental process on the culture of an individual group and its relationships with other groups
- **Economics**—how government policies regulate the distribution of products and how they can control and/or influence the economy in general

General Political Theory

Based on general political theory, the four major purposes of any given government are:

- **Ensuring national security**—the government protects against international, domestic, and terrorist attacks and also ensures ongoing security through negotiating and establishing relationships with other governments.
- **Providing public services**—the government should "promote the general welfare," as stated in the Preamble to the US Constitution, by providing whatever is needed to its citizens.
- **Ensuring social order**—the government supplies means of settling conflicts among citizens as well as making laws to govern the nation, state, or city.
- **Making decisions regarding the economy**—laws help form the economic policy of the country, regarding both domestic and international trade and related issues. The government also has the ability to distribute goods and wealth to some extent among its citizens.

Main Theories Regarding the Origin of the State

There are four main theories regarding the origin of the state:

- **Evolutionary**—the state evolved from the family, with the head of state the equivalent of the family's patriarch or matriarch.
- **Force**—one person or group of people brought everyone in an area under their control, forming the first government.
- **Divine Right**—certain people were chosen by the prevailing deity to be the rulers of the nation, which is itself created by the deity or deities.
- **Social Contract**—there is no natural order. The people allow themselves to be governed to maintain social order, while the state, in turn, promises to protect the people they govern. If the government fails to protect its people, the people have the right to seek new leaders.

Public Policy

Public policy is the study of how the various levels of government formulate and implement policies. **Public policy** also refers to the set of policies that a government adopts and implements, including laws, plans, actions, and behaviors, for the purpose of governing society. Public policy is developed and adapted through the process of **policy analysis.** Public policy analysis is the systematic evaluation of alternative means of reaching social goals. Public policy is divided into various policy areas, including domestic policy, foreign policy, healthcare policy, education policy, criminal policy, national defense policy, and energy policy.

Influences of Philosophers on Political Study

Ancient Greek philosophers **Aristotle** and **Plato** believed political science would lead to order in political matters and that this scientifically organized order would create stable, just societies.

- **Thomas Aquinas** adapted the ideas of Aristotle to a Christian perspective. His ideas stated that individuals should have certain rights but also certain duties, and that these rights and duties should determine the type and extent of government rule. In stating that laws should limit the role of government, he laid the groundwork for ideas that would eventually become modern constitutionalism.
- **Niccolò Machiavelli**, author of *The Prince*, was a proponent of politics based on power. He is often considered the founder of modern political science.
- **Thomas Hobbes**, author of *Leviathan* (1651), believed that individuals' lives were focused solely on a quest for power and that the state must work to control this urge. Hobbes felt that people were completely unable to live harmoniously without the intervention of a powerful, undivided government.

Contributions of John Locke, Montesquieu, and Rousseau to Political Science

John Locke published *Two Treatises of Government* in 1689. This work argued against the ideas of Thomas Hobbes. He put forth the theory of *tabula rasa*—that people are born with minds like blank slates. Individual minds are molded by experience, not innate knowledge or intuition. He also believed that all men should be independent and equal. Many of Locke's ideas found their way into the Constitution of the United States.

The two French philosophers, **Montesquieu** and **Rousseau**, heavily influenced the French Revolution (1789-1799). They believed government policies and ideas should change to alleviate existing problems, an idea referred to as "liberalism." Rousseau, in particular, directly influenced the Revolution with writings such as *The Social Contract* (1762) and *Declaration of the Rights of Man and of the Citizen* (1789). Other ideas Rousseau and Montesquieu espoused included:

- Individual freedom and community welfare are of equal importance
- Man's innate goodness leads to natural harmony
- Reason develops with the rise of civilized society
- Individual citizens carry certain obligations to the existing government

Political Ideologies of Famous Philosophers

David Hume and **Jeremy Bentham** believed politics should have as its main goal maintaining "the greatest happiness for the greatest number." Hume also believed in empiricism, or that ideas should not be believed until the proof has been observed. He was a natural skeptic and always sought out the truth of matters rather than believing what he was told.

John Stuart Mill, a British philosopher and economist, made significant contributions to the fields of social and economic theory. A majorly influential thinker in the realm of classical liberalism, Mill believed in progressive policies such as women's suffrage, emancipation, and the development of labor unions and farming cooperatives. His ideas on free speech and the harm principle were the basis for the "clear and present danger" test outlined by Oliver Wendell Holmes Jr. when determining if speech is protected by the First Amendment of the US Constitution.

Johann Fichte and **Georg Hegel**, German philosophers in the late 18th and early 19th centuries, supported a form of liberalism grounded largely in socialism and a sense of nationalism.

Main Political Orientations

The four main political orientations are:

- **Liberal**—liberals believe that government should work to increase equality, even at the expense of some freedoms. Government should assist those in need, focusing on enforced social justice and free basic services for everyone.
- **Conservative**—a conservative believes that government should be limited in most cases. The government should allow its citizens to help one another and solve their own problems rather than enforcing solutions. Business should not be overregulated, allowing a free market.
- **Moderate**—this ideology incorporates some liberal and some conservative values, generally falling somewhere between in overall belief.
- **Libertarian**—libertarians believe that the government's role should be limited to protecting the life and liberty of citizens. Government should not be involved in any citizen's life unless that citizen is encroaching upon the rights of another.

Major Principles of Government as Outlined in the United States Constitution

The six major principles of government as outlined in the United States Constitution are:

- **Federalism**—the power of the government does not belong entirely to the national government but is divided between federal and state governments.
- **Popular sovereignty**—the government is determined by the people and gains its authority and power from the people.
- **Separation of powers**—the government is divided into three branches (executive, legislative, and judicial) with each having its own set of powers.
- **Judicial review**—courts at all levels of government can declare laws invalid if they contradict the constitutions of individual states, or the US Constitution, with the Supreme Court serving as the final judicial authority on decisions of this kind.
- **Checks and balances**—no single branch can act without input from another, and each branch has the power to "check" any other, as well as balance other branches' powers.
- **Limited government**—governmental powers are limited, and certain individual rights are defined as inviolable by the government.

Types of Powers Delegated to the National Government by the US Constitution

The structure of the US government divides power between national and state governments. Powers delegated to the federal government by the Constitution are:

- **Expressed powers**—powers directly defined in the Constitution, including power to declare war, regulate commerce, make money, and collect taxes
- **Implied powers**—powers the national government must have in order to carry out the expressed powers
- **Inherent powers**—powers inherent to any government, not expressly defined in the Constitution

Some of these powers, such as collection and levying of taxes, are also granted to the individual state governments.

Primary Positions of Federalism and Development Through the Years in the US

The way federalism should be practiced has been the subject of debate since the writing of the Constitution. There were—and still are—two main factions regarding this issue:

- **States' rights**—those favoring the states' rights position feel that the state governments should take the lead in performing local actions to manage various problems.
- **Nationalist**—those favoring a nationalist position feel the national government should take the lead to deal with those same matters.

The flexibility of the Constitution has allowed the US government to shift and adapt as the needs of the country have changed. Power has often shifted from the state governments to the national government and back again, and both levels of government have developed various ways to influence each other.

Effects of Federalism on Policy-Making and the Balance of Politics in the US

Federalism has three major effects on **public policy** in the US:

- Determining whether the local, state, or national government originates policy
- Affecting how policies are made
- Ensuring policy-making functions under a set of limitations

Federalism also influences the **political balance of power** in the US by:

- Making it difficult, if not impossible, for a single political party to seize total power
- Ensuring that individuals can participate in the political system at various levels
- Making it possible for individuals working within the system to be able to affect policy at some level, whether local or more widespread

THREE BRANCHES OF THE US FEDERAL GOVERNMENT

The following are the three branches of the US Federal government and the individuals that belong to each branch:

- **Legislative Branch**—this consists of the two houses of Congress: the House of Representatives and the Senate. All members of the Legislative Branch are elected officials.
- **Executive Branch**—this branch is made up of the president, vice president, presidential advisors, and other various cabinet members. Advisors and cabinet members are appointed by the president, but they must be approved by Congress.
- **Judicial Branch**—the federal court system, headed by the Supreme Court.

Review Video: What Does the Executive Branch Do?
Visit mometrix.com/academy and enter code: 210629

Review Video: What Does the Judicial Branch Do?
Visit mometrix.com/academy and enter code: 278093

Review Video: What Does the Legislative Branch Do?
Visit mometrix.com/academy and enter code: 405303

MAJOR RESPONSIBILITIES OF THE THREE BRANCHES OF THE FEDERAL GOVERNMENT

The three branches of the federal government each have specific roles and responsibilities:

- The **Legislative Branch** is largely concerned with lawmaking. All laws must be approved by Congress before they go into effect. They are also responsible for regulating money and trade, approving presidential appointments, and establishing organizations like the postal service and federal courts. Congress can also propose amendments to the Constitution, and can impeach, or bring charges against, the president. Only Congress can declare war.
- The **Executive Branch** carries out laws, treaties, and war declarations enacted by Congress. The president can also veto bills approved by Congress, and serves as commander in chief of the US military. The president appoints cabinet members, ambassadors to foreign countries, and federal judges.

- The **Judicial Branch** makes decisions on challenges as to whether laws passed by Congress meet the requirements of the US Constitution. The Supreme Court may also choose to review decisions made by lower courts to determine their constitutionality.

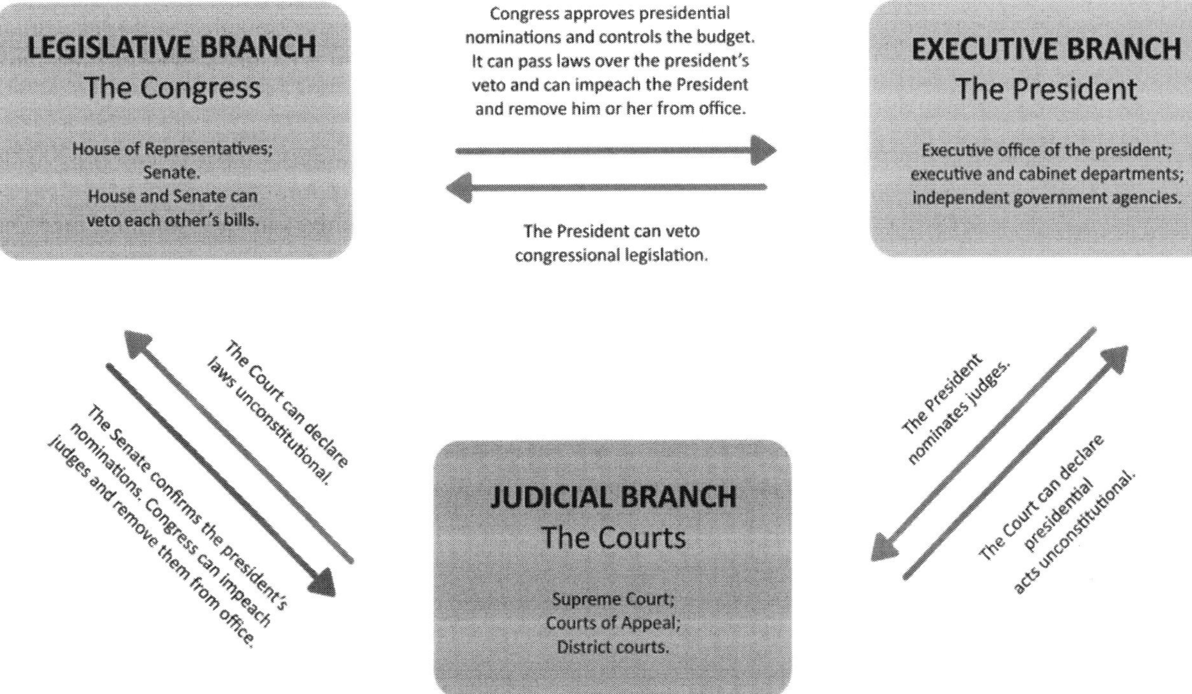

US Citizenship

Qualifications of a US Citizen/How Citizenship May Be Lost

Anyone born in the US, born abroad to a US citizen, or who has gone through a process of naturalization is considered a **citizen** of the United States. It is possible to lose US citizenship as a result of conviction of certain crimes such as treason. Citizenship may also be lost if a citizen pledges an oath to another country or serves in the military of a country engaged in hostilities with the US. A US citizen can also choose to hold dual citizenship, work as an expatriate in another country without losing US citizenship, or even to renounce citizenship if he or she so chooses.

Rights, Duties, and Responsibilities Granted to or Expected from Citizens

Citizens are granted certain rights under the US government. The most important of these are defined in the **Bill of Rights**, and include freedom of speech, religion, assembly, and a variety of other rights the government is not allowed to remove. A US citizen also has a number of **duties**:

- Paying taxes
- Loyalty to the government (though the US does not prosecute those who criticize or seek to change the government)
- Support and defense of the Constitution
- Serving in the Armed Forces when required by law
- Obeying laws as set forth by the various levels of government.

Responsibilities of a US citizen include:

- Voting in elections
- Respecting one another's rights and not infringing on them

- Staying informed about various political and national issues
- Respecting one another's beliefs

Bill of Rights

Importance of the Bill of Rights

The first ten amendments of the US Constitution are known as the **Bill of Rights**. These amendments prevent the government from infringing upon certain freedoms that the Founding Fathers felt were natural rights that already belonged to all people. These rights included freedom of speech, freedom of religion, freedom of assembly, and the right to bear arms. Many of the rights were formulated in direct response to the way the colonists felt they had been mistreated by the British government.

Rights Granted in the Bill of Rights

The first ten amendments were passed by Congress in 1789. Three-fourths of the existing thirteen states had ratified them by December of 1791, making them official additions to the Constitution. The rights granted in the Bill of Rights are:

- **First Amendment**—freedom of religion, speech, freedom of the press, and the right to assemble and to petition the government
- **Second Amendment**—the right to bear arms
- **Third Amendment**—Congress cannot force individuals to house troops
- **Fourth Amendment**—protection from unreasonable search and seizure
- **Fifth Amendment**—no individual is required to testify against himself, and no individual may be tried twice for the same crime
- **Sixth Amendment**—the right to criminal trial by jury and the right to legal counsel
- **Seventh Amendment**—the right to civil trial by jury
- **Eighth Amendment**—protection from excessive bail or cruel and unusual punishment
- **Ninth Amendment**—prevents rights not explicitly named in the Constitution from being taken away because they are not named
- **Tenth Amendment**—any rights not directly delegated to the national government, or not directly prohibited by the government from the states, belong to the states or to the people

Review Video: Bill of Rights
Visit mometrix.com/academy and enter code: 585149

Situations Where the Government Restricts the First Amendment Freedoms

In some cases, the government restricts certain elements of First Amendment rights. Some examples include:

- **Freedom of religion**—when a religion espouses illegal activities, the government often restricts these forms of religious expression. Examples include polygamy, animal sacrifice, and use of illicit drugs or illegal substances.
- **Freedom of speech**—this can be restricted if exercise of free speech endangers other people.
- **Freedom of the press**—laws prevent the press from publishing falsehoods.

In **emergency situations** such as wartime, stricter restrictions are sometimes placed on these rights, especially rights to free speech and assembly, and freedom of the press, in order to protect national security.

Constitution's Address of the Rights of Those Accused of Crimes

The US Constitution makes allowances for the **rights of criminals**, or anyone who has transgressed established laws. There must be laws to protect citizens from criminals, but those accused of crimes must also be protected and their basic rights as individuals preserved. In addition, the Constitution protects individuals from the power of authorities to prevent police forces and other enforcement organizations from becoming oppressive. The fourth, fifth, sixth, and eighth amendments specifically address these rights.

SUPREME COURT'S PROVISION OF EQUAL PROTECTION FOR ALL INDIVIDUALS

When the Founding Fathers wrote in the Declaration of Independence that "all men are created equal," they actually were referring to men, and, in fact, defined citizens as white men who owned land. However, as the country has developed and changed, the definition has expanded to more wholly include all people.

"**Equality**" does not mean all people are inherently the same, but it does mean they all should be granted the same rights and should be treated the same by the government. Amendments to the Constitution have granted citizenship and voting rights to all Americans regardless of race or gender. The Supreme Court evaluates various laws and court decisions to determine if they properly represent the idea of **equal protection**. One sample case was Brown v. Board of Education in 1954, which declared separate-but-equal treatment to be unconstitutional.

PROTESTS

A protest is an expression of opposition to, and sometimes of support of, events or circumstances. **Protests** represent a means for individuals to publicly make their views heard in an effort to influence public opinion or government policy, or as a means to enact **change**. Protests generally result when self-expression of opposing views is restricted by government policy, political or economic circumstances, religion, social structures, or the media, and people react by declaring their views through cultural mechanisms or on the streets. There are numerous forms of protest, including boycotts, civil disobedience, demonstrations, non-violent protests, picketing, protest marches, protest songs, riots, sit-ins, teach-ins, strikes, and others.

CIVIL LIBERTY CHALLENGES ADDRESSED IN CURRENT POLITICAL DISCUSSIONS

The **civil rights movements** of the 1960s and the ongoing struggle for the rights of women and other minorities have sparked **challenges to existing law**. In addition, debate has raged over how much information the government should be required to divulge to the public. Major issues in the 21st century political climate include:

- Continued debate over women's rights, especially regarding equal pay for equal work
- Debate over affirmative action to encourage hiring of minorities
- Debate over civil rights of homosexuals, including marriage and military service
- Decisions as to whether minorities should be compensated for past discriminatory practices
- Balance between the public's right to know and the government's need to maintain national security
- Balance between the public's right to privacy and national security

CIVIL LIBERTIES VS. CIVIL RIGHTS

While the terms *civil liberties* and *civil rights* are often used interchangeably, in actuality, their definitions are slightly different. The two concepts work together, however, to define the basics of a free state:

- **"Civil liberties"** define the constitutional freedoms guaranteed to citizens. Examples include freedoms such as free speech, privacy, or free thought.
- **"Civil rights"** are guarantees of or protections of civil liberties. One comparison can be found in the case of freedom of religion. The civil liberty is that one has the freedom to practice the religion of his or her choice, whereas the civil right would protect that individual from being denied a job on the basis of their religion.

SUFFRAGE, FRANCHISE, AND THE CHANGE OF VOTING RIGHTS OVER AMERICAN HISTORY

Suffrage and franchise both refer to the right to **vote**. As the US developed as a nation, there was much debate over which individuals should hold this right. In the early years, only white male landowners were granted suffrage. By the 19th century, most states had franchised, or granted the right to vote, to all adult white males. The **Fifteenth Amendment** of 1870 granted suffrage to formerly enslaved men. The **Nineteenth Amendment** gave women the right to vote in 1920, and in 1971 the **Twenty-sixth Amendment** expanded voting rights to include any US citizen over the age of eighteen. However, those who have not been granted full citizenship and citizens who have committed certain crimes do not have voting rights.

Ways in Which the Voting Process Has Changed Over the Years

The first elections in the US were held by **public ballot**. However, election abuses soon became common, since public ballot made it easy to intimidate, threaten, or otherwise influence the votes of individuals or groups of individuals. New practices were put into play, including **registering voters** before elections took place and using a **secret or Australian ballot**. In 1892, the introduction of the **voting machine** further privatized the voting process, since it allowed complete privacy for voting. Today, debate continues about the accuracy of various voting methods, including high-tech voting machines and even low-tech punch cards.

Effect of Political Parties on the Functioning of an Individual Government

Different types and numbers of political parties can have a significant effect on how a government is run. If there is a **single party**, or a one-party system, the government is defined by that one party, and all policy is based on that party's beliefs. In a **two-party system**, two parties with different viewpoints compete for power and influence. The US is basically a two-party system, with checks and balances to make it difficult for one party to gain complete power over the other. There are also **multiparty systems**, with three or more parties. In multiparty systems, various parties will often come to agreements in order to form a majority and shift the balance of power.

Development of Political Parties in the US.

George Washington was adamantly against the establishment of **political parties**, based on the abuses perpetrated by such parties in Britain. However, political parties developed in US politics almost from the beginning. Major parties throughout US history have included:

- **Federalists and Democratic-Republicans**—these parties formed in the late 1700s and disagreed on the balance of power between national and state government.
- **Democrats and Whigs**—these developed in the 1830s, and many political topics of the time centered on national economic issues.
- **Democrats and Republicans**—the Republican Party developed before the Civil War, after the collapse of the Whig party, and the two parties debated issues centering on slavery and economic issues, such as taxation.

While third parties sometimes enter the picture in US politics, the government is basically a two-party system, dominated by the Democrats and Republicans.

Functions of Political Parties

Political parties form organizations at all levels of government. Activities of individual parties include:

- Recruiting and backing candidates for offices
- Discussing various issues with the public, increasing public awareness
- Working toward compromise on difficult issues
- Staffing government offices and providing administrative support

At the administrative level, parties work to ensure that viable candidates are available for elections and that offices and staff are in place to support candidates as they run for office and afterward, when they are elected.

Processes of Selecting Political Candidates

Historically, in the quest for political office, a potential candidate has followed one of the following four processes:

- **Nominating convention**—an official meeting of the members of a party for the express purpose of nominating candidates for upcoming elections. The Democratic National Convention and the Republican National Convention, convened to announce candidates for the presidency, are examples of this kind of gathering.
- **Caucus**—a meeting, usually attended by a party's leaders. Some states still use caucuses, but not all.
- **Primary election**—the most common method of choosing candidates today, the primary is a publicly held election to choose candidates.
- **Petition**—signatures gathered to place a candidate on the ballot. Petitions can also be used to place legislation on a ballot.

Ways the Average Citizen Participates in the Political Process

In addition to voting for elected officials, American citizens are able to participate in the political process through several other avenues. These include:

- Participating in local government
- Participating in caucuses for large elections
- Volunteering to help political parties
- Running for election to local, state, or national offices

Individuals can also donate money to political causes or support political groups that focus on specific causes such as abortion, wildlife conservation, or women's rights. These groups often make use of **representatives** who lobby legislators to act in support of their efforts.

Ways in Which Political Campaign Gains Funding

Political campaigns are very expensive. In addition to the basic necessities of a campaign office, including office supplies, office space, etc., a large quantity of the money that funds a political campaign goes toward **advertising**. Money to fund a political campaign can come from several sources, including:

- The candidate's personal funds
- Donations by individuals
- Special interest groups

The most significant source of campaign funding is **special interest groups**. Groups in favor of certain policies will donate money to candidates they believe will support those policies. Special interest groups also do their own advertising in support of candidates they endorse.

Presidential Elections

The President of the United States is elected **indirectly** by members of an **electoral college**. Members of the electoral college nearly always vote along the lines of the popular vote of their respective states. The winner of a presidential election is the candidate with at least 270 **Electoral College votes**. It is possible for a candidate to win the electoral vote and lose the popular vote. Incumbent Presidents and challengers typically prefer a balanced ticket, where the President and Vice President are elected together and generally balance one another with regard to geography, ideology, or experience working in government. The nominated Vice Presidential candidate is referred to as the President's **running mate**.

Importance of Free Press and the Media

The right to free speech guaranteed in the first amendment to the Constitution allows the media to report on **government and political activities** without fear of retribution. Because the media has access to information about the government, the government's policies and actions, and debates and discussions that occur in Congress, it can keep the public informed about the inner workings of the government. The media can also draw attention to injustices, imbalances of power, and other transgressions the government or government officials might commit. However, media outlets may, like special interest groups, align themselves with certain political viewpoints and skew their reports to fit that viewpoint. The rise of the **internet** has made media reporting even more complex, as news can be found from an infinite variety of sources, both reliable and unreliable.

Forms of Government

Anarchism, Communism, and Dictatorship

Anarchists believe that all government should be eliminated and that individuals should rule themselves. Historically, anarchists have used violence and assassination to further their beliefs.

Communism is based on class conflict, revolution, and a one-party state. Ideally, a communist government would involve a single government for the entire world. Communist government controls the production and flow of goods and services rather than leaving this to companies or individuals.

Dictatorship involves rule by a single individual. If rule is enforced by a small group, this is referred to as an oligarchy. Dictators tend to rule with a violent hand, using a highly repressive police force to ensure control over the populace.

Fascism and Monarchy

Fascism centers on a single leader and is, ideologically, an oppositional belief to communism. **Fascism** includes a single-party state and centralized control. The power of the fascist leader lies in the "cult of personality," and the fascist state often focuses on expansion and conquering of other nations. **Monarchy** was the major form of government for Europe through most of its history.

A monarchy is led by a king or a queen. This position is hereditary, and the rulers are not elected. In modern times, constitutional monarchy has developed, where the king and queen still exist, but most of the governmental decisions are made by democratic institutions such as a parliament.

Parliamentary and Democratic Systems

In a parliamentary system, government involves a legislature and a variety of political parties. The head of government, usually a prime minister, is typically the head of the dominant party. A head of state can be elected, or this position can be taken by a monarch, as in Great Britain's constitutional monarchy system.

In a **democratic system** of government, the people elect their government representatives. The word *democracy* is a Greek term that means "rule of the people." There are two forms of democracy: direct and indirect. In a direct democracy, each issue or election is decided by a vote where each individual is counted separately. An indirect democracy employs a legislature that votes on issues that affect large numbers of people whom the legislative members represent. Democracy can exist as a parliamentary system or a presidential system. The US is a presidential, indirect democracy.

Presidential System and Socialism

A presidential system, like a parliamentary system, has a legislature and political parties, but there is no difference between the head of state and the head of government. Instead of separating these functions, an elected president performs both. Election of the president can be direct or indirect, and the president may not necessarily belong to the largest political party. In **socialism**, the state controls the production of goods, though it does not necessarily own all means of production. The state also provides a variety of social services to citizens and helps guide the economy. A democratic form of government often exists in socialist countries.

Review Video: Communism vs. Socialism
Visit mometrix.com/academy and enter code: 917677

Totalitarian and Authoritarian Systems

A totalitarian system believes everything should be under the control of the government—from resource production, to the press, to religion, and other social institutions. All aspects of life under a totalitarian system must conform to the ideals of the government. **Authoritarian** governments practice widespread state authority but do not necessarily dismantle all public institutions. If a church, for example, exists as an organization but poses no threat to the authority of the state, an authoritarian government might leave it as it is. While all totalitarian governments are by definition authoritarian, a government can be authoritarian without becoming totalitarian.

Review Video: Totalitarianism vs. Authoritarianism
Visit mometrix.com/academy and enter code: 104046

Parliamentary and Democratic Systems

In a parliamentary system, government involves a legislature and a variety of political parties. The head of government, usually a prime minister, is typically the head of the dominant party. A head of state can be elected, or this position can be taken by a monarch, as in Great Britain's constitutional monarchy system.

In a **democratic system** of government, the people elect their government representatives. The word *democracy* is a Greek term that means "rule of the people." There are two forms of democracy: direct and indirect. In a direct democracy, each issue or election is decided by a vote where each individual is counted separately. An indirect democracy employs a legislature that votes on issues that affect large numbers of people whom the legislative members represent. Democracy can exist as a parliamentary system or a presidential system. The US is a presidential, indirect democracy.

Realism, Liberalism, Institutionalism, and Constructivism

The theory of realism states that nations are by nature aggressive and work in their own self-interest. Relations between nations are determined by military and economic strength. The nation is seen as the highest authority. **Liberalism** believes states can cooperate and that they act based on capability rather than power. This term was originally coined to describe Woodrow Wilson's theories on international cooperation. In **institutionalism**, institutions provide structure and incentive for cooperation among nations. Institutions are defined as a set of rules used to make international decisions. These institutions also help distribute power and determine how nations will interact. **Constructivism**, like liberalism, is based on international cooperation but recognizes that perceptions countries have of each other can affect their relations.

Effects of Foreign Policy on a Country's Position in World Affairs

Foreign policy is a set of goals, policies, and strategies that determine how an individual nation will interact with other countries. These strategies shift, sometimes quickly and drastically, according to actions or changes occurring in the other countries. However, a nation's **foreign policy** is often based on a certain set of ideals and national needs. Examples of US foreign policy include isolationism versus internationalism. In the 1800s, the US leaned more toward isolationism, exhibiting a reluctance to become involved in foreign affairs. The World Wars led to a period of internationalism, as the US entered these wars in support of other countries and joined the United Nations. Today's foreign policy tends more toward **interdependence**, or **globalism**, recognizing the widespread effects of issues like economic health.

Major Figures Involved in Determining and Enacting US Foreign Policy

US foreign policy is largely determined by Congress and the president, influenced by the secretary of state, secretary of defense, and the national security adviser. Executive officials carry out policies. The main departments in charge of these day-to-day issues are the **US Department of State**, also referred to as the State Department. The Department of State carries out policy, negotiates treaties, maintains diplomatic relations, assists citizens traveling in foreign countries, and ensures that the president is properly informed of any international issues. The **Department of Defense**, the largest executive department in the US, supervises the armed forces and provides assistance to the president in his role as commander-in-chief.

Major Types of International Organizations

Two types of international organizations are:

- **Intergovernmental organizations (IGOs)**. These organizations are made up of members from various national governments. The UN is an example of an intergovernmental organization. Treaties among the member nations determine the functions and powers of these groups.
- **Nongovernmental organizations (NGOs)**. An NGO lies outside the scope of any government and is usually supported through private donations. An example of an NGO is the International Red Cross, which works with governments all over the world when their countries are in crisis but is formally affiliated with no particular country or government.

Role of Diplomats in International Relations

Diplomats are individuals who reside in foreign countries in order to maintain communications between that country and their home country. They help negotiate trade agreements and environmental policies, as well as conveying official information to foreign governments. They also help to resolve conflicts between the countries, often working to sort out issues without making the conflicts official in any way. **Diplomats**, or **ambassadors**, are appointed in the US by the president. Appointments must be approved by Congress.

Role of the United Nations in International Relations and Diplomacy

The United Nations (**UN**) helps form international policies by hosting representatives of various countries who then provide input into policy decisions. Countries that are members of the UN must agree to abide by all final UN resolutions, but this is not always the case in practice, as dissent is not uncommon. If countries do not follow UN resolutions, the UN can decide on sanctions against those countries, often economic sanctions, such as trade restriction. The UN can also send military forces to problem areas, with "peacekeeping" troops brought in from member nations. An example of this function is the Korean War, the first war in which an international organization played a major role.

Landmark Supreme Court Cases and Civil Rights

Marbury v. Madison

Right before President **John Adams** left office after **Thomas Jefferson** won the presidency in the election of 1800, he passed the **Judiciary Act of 1801**. This act eliminated one seat on the Supreme Court, eliminated circuit duties for members of the Supreme Court, and created 16 federal circuit court judgeships. This allowed President John Adams to pack the federal court system with his fellow Federalists before Thomas Jefferson, a Democratic-Republican, took office. **William Marbury** was one of these individuals promised a position by John Adams. However, Adams's Secretary of State, **John Marshall**, did not have time to deliver Marbury's commission (which was the formal job offer for Marbury's position as Justice of the Peace for D.C.) before the Jefferson administration took over. The new Secretary of State, **James Madison**, refused to deliver Marbury's commission after he took office. This led to Marbury suing Madison for his commission, and the issue was brought before the Supreme Court in the case of ***Marbury v. Madison*** (1803).

Although Section XIII of the Judiciary Act of 1789 had a **Writ of Mandamus** which required Madison to honor the appointment, Chief Justice **John Marshall**, whom Adams appointed to the Supreme Court before leaving office, declared this section unconstitutional. This historic act established the doctrine of **judicial review**, which allows the Supreme Court to declare a legislative or executive act unconstitutional. Marshall thereby established an independent judiciary; he is quoted as saying, "The Constitution is the supreme Law of the Land, with the Supreme Court as the final interpreter."

MCCULLOCH V. MARYLAND

When Congress chartered a national bank, the **Second Bank of the United States**, Maryland voted to tax any bank business dealing with banks chartered outside the state, including the federally chartered bank. Andrew McCulloch, an employee of the Second Bank of the US in Baltimore, refused to pay this tax. The resulting lawsuit from the State of Maryland went to the Supreme Court for judgment.

John Marshall, Chief Justice of the Supreme Court, stated that Congress was within its rights to charter a national bank. In addition, the State of Maryland did not have the power to levy a tax on the federal bank or on the federal government in general. In cases where state and federal government collided, precedent was set for the **federal government** to prevail.

THE CIVIL RIGHTS ACT OF 1871

The Civil Rights Act of 1871 was a statute passed following the Civil War. It was comprised of the **1870 Force Act** and the **1871 Ku Klux Klan Act**, and was passed primarily with the intention of protecting Southern black people from the Ku Klux Klan. Since it was passed in 1871, the statute has only undergone small changes. It has, however, been interpreted widely by the courts. In 1882, some parts of the Civil Rights Act of 1871 were found unconstitutional, but the Force Act and the Klan Act continued to be applied in civil rights cases in subsequent years.

PLESSY V. FERGUSON

Plessy v. Ferguson was an 1896 Supreme Court case. The case resulted in the decision that **de jure racial segregation** in **public facilities** was legal in the United States, and permitted states to restrict black people from using public facilities. The case originated when, in 1890, a black man named Homer Plessy decided to challenge a Louisiana law that segregated black and white people on trains by sitting in the white section of a train. Plessy was convicted of breaking the law in a Louisiana court, and the case was appealed to the US Supreme Court, where the Supreme Court upheld the Louisiana decision. The case established the legality of the doctrine of separate but equal, thereby allowing racial segregation. The decision was later overturned by **Brown v. the Board of Education of Topeka**.

THE FAIR EMPLOYMENT ACT

The Fair Employment Act was signed by President Franklin Roosevelt in 1941. The purpose of the act was to **ban racial discrimination** in industries related to **national defense**, and it represented the very first federal law to ban discrimination in employment. The **Fair Employment Act** mandated that all federal government agencies and departments concerned with national defense, as well as private defense contractors, guaranteed that professional training would be conducted without discrimination based on race, creed, color, or national origin. The Fair Employment Act was followed by **Title VII of the 1964 Civil Rights Act**, which banned discrimination by private employers, and by **Executive Order 11246** in 1965, which concerned federal contractors and subcontractors.

BROWN V. BOARD OF EDUCATION

Brown versus the Board of Education of Topeka was a Supreme Court case that was decided in 1954. The case made it illegal for **racial segregation** to exist within **public education facilities**. This decision was based on the finding that separate but equal public educational facilities would not provide black and white students with the same standard of facilities. The case originated in 1951, when a lawsuit was filed by Topeka parents, who were recruited by the NAACP, against the Board of Education of the City of Topeka, Kansas in a US district court. The parents, one of whom was named Oliver Brown, wanted the Topeka Board of Education to eliminate racial segregation. The district court agreed that segregation had negative effects, but did not force the schools to desegregate because it found that black and white school facilities in the District were generally equal in standards. The case was appealed to the Supreme Court, where the finding was that separate educational facilities are unequal.

Bolling v. Sharpe

Bolling v. Sharpe was a 1954 Supreme Court case. Like Brown v. Board of Education, this case addressed issues concerning **segregation in public schools**. The case originated in 1949, when parents from Anacostia, an area in Washington, DC, petitioned the Board of Education of the District of Columbia to allow all races to attend a new school. The request was denied. A lawsuit was brought before the District Court for the District of Columbia on behalf of a student named Bolling and other students to admit them to the all-white school. The case was dismissed by the district court and taken to the Supreme Court. The Supreme Court ruled that the school had to be desegregated based on the Fifth Amendment.

Civil Rights Act of 1964

The Civil Rights Act of 1964 was passed to protect the rights of both **black men** and **women**. It served as part of the foundation for the women's rights movement. The act was a catalyst for change in the United States, as it made it illegal to engage in acts of **discrimination** in public facilities, in government, and in employment. The Civil Rights Act prohibited unequal voter registration, prohibited discrimination in all public facilities involved in interstate commerce, supported desegregating public schools, ensured equal protection for black people in federally funded programs, and banned employment discrimination.

The Pregnancy Discrimination Act

The Pregnancy Discrimination Act was passed in 1978 as an amendment to the sex discrimination clause of the Civil Rights Act of 1964. The **Pregnancy Discrimination Act** stipulated that people cannot be discriminated against due to pregnancy, childbirth, or medical issues related to pregnancy or childbirth. If a person becomes pregnant, gives birth, or has related medical conditions, they must receive treatment that is equivalent to that received by other employees and also receive equal benefits as other employees. The **Family and Medical Leave Act** was passed in 1993 to advance protections under the Pregnancy Discrimination Act.

Civil Rights Act of 1968

The Civil Rights Act of 1968 was passed following the passing of the Civil Rights Act of 1964. The act made it illegal to **discriminate** against individuals during the sale, rental, or financing of **housing**. Therefore, the act is also referred to as the **Fair Housing Act of 1968**. The act made it illegal to refuse to sell or rent housing based on race, color, religion, or national origin. It also made it illegal to advertise housing for sale or rent and to specify a preference to rent or sell the property to an individual of a particular race, color, religion, or national origin. In addition, the act ensured protection for civil rights workers.

Age Discrimination in Employment Act

The Age Discrimination in Employment Act of 1967 made it illegal for employers to discriminate against people who are **forty years old** or greater in age. The act establishes standards for employer-provided pensions and benefits, and mandates that information regarding the needs of older workers be made publicly available. In addition to generally banning age discrimination, the **ADEA** specifies particular actions that are illegal. Employers may not specify that individuals of a certain age are preferred or are conversely restricted from applying to job ads. Age limits are only permitted to be mentioned in job ads if age has been shown to be a bona fide occupational qualification. The act stipulates that it is illegal to discriminate against age through apprenticeship programs and that it is illegal to restrict benefits to older employees. However, employers are permitted to lower the benefits provided to older employees based on age if the expense of providing fewer or lesser benefits is equivalent to the expense of providing benefits to younger employees.

Loving v. Virginia

Loving v. Virginia was a 1967 Supreme Court case that ruled that a particular law in Virginia known as the **Racial Integrity Act of 1924** was unconstitutional, as the law had prohibited interracial marriage. The Supreme Court ruling would put an end to **race-based restrictions on marriage**. The case originated when

Mildred Jeter and Richard Loving, an interracial Virginia couple that was married in Washington, DC due to the Virginia state law prohibiting interracial marriage, returned to Virginia and received charges of violating the interracial marriage ban. After pleading guilty, the couple was forced to move to DC to avoid a jail sentence, where they brought their case to the Supreme Court on the premise that their Fourteenth Amendment rights had been violated. The Supreme Court found that the Virginia law was unconstitutional and overturned the conviction that the couple had been charged with.

Jones v. Mayer

Jones v. Mayer was a 1968 Supreme Court case that ruled that Congress has the authority to **regulate the sale of private property** for the purpose of preventing racial discrimination. This United States Supreme Court ruling was based on a legal statute that stipulates that it is illegal in the United States to commit acts of racial discrimination, both privately and publicly when selling or renting property. The United States Supreme Court ruled that the congressional power to uphold the statute extends from the power of Congress to uphold the Thirteenth Amendment.

Roe v. Wade

Roe v. Wade was a controversial 1973 US Supreme Court case. The case originated in 1970 in Texas, which had an **anti-abortion law**. The plaintiff was an unmarried pregnant woman who was assigned the name "Jane Roe" to protect her identity. Texas anti-abortion law characterized the acts of having or attempting to perform an abortion as crimes, with the exception of cases in which an abortion could save the life of a mother. The lawsuit argued that the Texas law was unconstitutionally vague and was not consistent with the rights guaranteed by the First, Fourth, Fifth, Ninth, and Fourteenth Amendments. While the Texas court ruled in favor of Roe, it did not rule that Texas had to discontinue the enforcement of its anti-abortion law. Roe appealed to the Supreme Court in 1971, and the court's decision in 1973 struck down Texas's abortion laws. The case overturned most state laws prohibiting abortion. In 2022, the supreme court reversed its decision in Roe v Wade, finding no constitutional basis for requiring states to permit abortion, effectively returning the authority to the states to decide.

Regents of the University of California v. Bakke

Regents of the University of California v. Bakke was a 1978 Supreme Court case that banned **quota systems** in the college admissions process but ruled that programs providing **advantages to minorities** are constitutionally sound. The case originated when Allan Bakke, a white male who was a strong student, applied to the University of California at Davis Medical School and was rejected. The school had a program that reserved admissions spots for minority applicants; the program had grown along with the overall size of the school since its opening in 1968. Bakke complained to the school but was still not admitted, and he finally brought his case before the Superior Court of California. The California court ruled in favor of Bakke, who claimed that he had been discriminated against because of his race, and the school appealed to the US Supreme Court. The Supreme Court ruled that race could be used as one factor by discriminatory boards such as college admissions boards; however, quotas were ruled to be **discriminatory**.

Americans with Disabilities Act (ADA)

The ADA was passed by Congress in 1990. This act outlines the rights of individuals with disabilities in society in all ways besides education. It states that they should receive **nondiscriminatory treatment** in jobs, **access** to businesses and other stores, and other services. Due to this law all businesses must be wheelchair accessible, having a ramp that fits the standards of the law, and all doors and bathrooms within those businesses must be able to be used and maneuvered through by someone in a wheelchair. If these rules are not followed, businesses can be subject to large fines until these modifications have been complied with. The ADA also ensures fair treatment when applying for jobs to make sure that there is no unfair discrimination for any person with a disability who is applying to the job.

The Civil Rights Act of 1991

The Civil Rights Act of 1991 is a statute that was passed as a result of a number of Supreme Court decisions that restricted the rights of individuals who had sued their employers on the basis of discrimination. The passing of the **Civil Rights Act of 1991** was the first time since the Civil Rights Act of 1964 was passed that modifications were made to the rights granted under federal laws to individuals in cases involving **employment discrimination**. Specifically, the Civil Rights Act of 1991 granted the right to a trial by jury to individuals involved in cases of employment discrimination, and it also addressed for the first time the potential for emotional distress damages and limited the amount awarded by a jury in such cases.

Planned Parenthood v. Casey

Planned Parenthood of Southeastern Pennsylvania v. Casey was a 1992 Supreme Court case that challenged the constitutionality of Pennsylvania abortion laws. The case was brought before the US District Court for the Eastern District of Pennsylvania by abortion clinics and physicians to challenge four clauses of the **Pennsylvania Abortion Control Act of 1982** as unconstitutional under Roe v. Wade. The district court ruled that all of the clauses of the Pennsylvania act were unconstitutional. The case was then appealed to the Third Circuit Court of Appeals, which ruled to uphold all of the clauses except for one requiring notification of a husband prior to abortion. The case was then appealed to the Supreme Court, which ruled to uphold the constitutional right to have an abortion, thereby upholding Roe v. Wade.

Adarand Constructors, Inc. v. Peña

Adarand Constructors, Inc. v. Peña was a 1995 United States Supreme Court case in which the court ruled that any **racial classifications** that are instituted by representatives of federal, state, or local governments have to be reviewed and analyzed by a court. The court that reviews such racial classifications must abide by a policy of **strict scrutiny**. Strict scrutiny represents the highest standard of Supreme Court review. Racial classifications are deemed constitutional solely under circumstances in which they are being used as specific measures to advance critical and important governmental interests. The ruling of the Supreme Court in this case requiring strict scrutiny as a standard of review for racial classifications overturned the case of **Metro Broadcasting, Inc. v. FCC**, in which the Supreme Court established a two-level method of reviewing and analyzing racial classifications.

The Employment Non-Discrimination Act (ENDA) and the Equality Act

The Employment Non-Discrimination Act was a proposed United States federal law that was introduced various times before Congress but was never passed by both the House and the Senate. The **Employment Non-Discrimination Act** would ban employers from discriminating against their employees based on their **sexual orientation**. A number of states have already passed laws that ban discrimination based on sexual orientation, including California, Connecticut, Hawaii, Maryland, Massachusetts, Minnesota, Nevada, New Hampshire, New Jersey, New Mexico, New York, Rhode Island, Vermont, and Wisconsin. The ENDA has largely been encompassed by a broader resolution known as the Equality Act, which is a bill that would amend the Civil Rights Act of 1964 to further add gender identity and sexual orientation to the list of prohibited categories of discrimination for employment, public accomodations, the jury system, and housing. It has been met with opposition and has not yet been passed by both bodies of Congress.

Miranda v. Arizona

In 1966, the Supreme Court ruled that law enforcement must warn a person of their constitutional rights before interrogating them. If these rights—known as Miranda rights—are not explained to a person, that person's statements cannot be used as evidence against them at trial. The Supreme Court held that interrogating people without informing of them of their rights is in violation of their Constitutional rights.

In this case, Ernesto Miranda was arrested and charged with the kidnapping and rape of an 18-year-old woman. Miranda was not informed of his right to an attorney or to silence before or during the two-hour long interrogation he was subjected to by the police. The interrogation resulted in both oral and written confessions, which were both brought against Miranda in trial. They were initially accepted as evidence, resulting in Miranda being sentenced for 20-30 years in prison. The conviction was reversed after the Supreme Court's decision, though Miranda was later found guilty of the same crime in a later trial.

Grutter v. Bollinger

Grutter v. Bollinger was a 2003 Supreme Court case that upheld an **affirmative action policy** of the University of Michigan Law School admissions process. The case originated in 1996 when Barbara Grutter, a white in-state resident with a strong academic record, applied to the law school and was denied admission. In 1997, she filed a lawsuit claiming that her rejection was based on racial discrimination and violated her Fourteenth Amendment rights, as well as Title VI of the Civil Rights Act of 1964. The case was heard in 2001 in a US District Court, which ruled that the university's admissions policies were unconstitutional. In 2002, the case was appealed to the Sixth Circuit Court of Appeals, which overturned the lower court's decision. The case was then appealed to the US Supreme Court in 2003, which ruled that the school's affirmative action policy could remain in place, upholding the case of Regents of the University of California v. Bakke permitting race to be a factor in admissions but banning quotas.

Chapter Quiz

Ready to see how well you retained what you just read? Scan the QR code to go directly to the chapter quiz interface for this study guide. If you're using a computer, simply visit the online resources page at **mometrix.com/resources719/hiset-27339** and click the Chapter Quizzes link.

HiSET Practice Test #1

Want to take this practice test in an online interactive format?
Check out the online resources page, which includes interactive practice questions and much more: **mometrix.com/resources719/hiset-27339**

Language Arts–Reading

Refer to the following for questions 1–4:

Selection from *Wuthering Heights* by Emily Bronte

1801.—I have just returned from a visit to my landlord—the solitary neighbour that I shall be troubled with. This is certainly a beautiful country! In all England, I do not believe that I could have fixed on a situation so completely removed from the stir of society. A perfect misanthropist's heaven: and Mr. Heathcliff and I are such a suitable pair to divide the desolation between us. A capital fellow! He little imagined how my heart warmed towards him when I beheld his black eyes withdraw so suspiciously under their brows, as I rode up, and when his fingers sheltered themselves, with a jealous resolution, still further in his waistcoat, as I announced my name.

"Mr. Heathcliff?" I said. A nod was the answer.

"Mr. Lockwood, your new tenant, sir. I do myself the honour of calling as soon as possible after my arrival, to express the hope that I have not inconvenienced you by my perseverance in soliciting the occupation of Thrushcross Grange: I heard yesterday you had had some thoughts—"

"Thrushcross Grange is my own, sir," he interrupted, wincing. "I should not allow anyone to inconvenience me, if I could hinder it—walk in!"

The "walk in" was uttered with closed teeth, and expressed the sentiment, "Go to the Deuce:" even the gate over which he leant manifested no sympathizing movement to the words; and I think that circumstance determined me to accept the invitation: I felt interested in a man who seemed more exaggeratedly reserved than myself.

When he saw my horse's breast fairly pushing the barrier, he did put out his hand to unchain it, and then sullenly preceded me up the causeway, calling, as we entered the court—"Joseph, take Mr. Lockwood's horse; and bring up some wine."

"Here we have the whole establishment of domestics, I suppose," was the reflection suggested by this compound order. "No wonder the grass grows up between the flags, and cattle are the only hedge-cutters."

Joseph was an elderly, nay, an old man: very old, perhaps, though hale and sinewy. "The Lord help us!" he soliloquized in an undertone of peevish displeasure, while relieving me of my horse: looking, meantime, in my face so sourly that I charitably conjectured he must have need of divine aid to digest his dinner, and his pious ejaculation had no reference to my unexpected advent.

Wuthering Heights is the name of Mr. Heathcliff's dwelling. "Wuthering" being a significant provincial adjective, descriptive of the atmospheric tumult to which its station is exposed in stormy weather. Pure, bracing ventilation they must have up there at all times, indeed: one may guess the power of the north wind blowing over the edge, by the excessive slant of a few stunted firs at the end of the house; and by a range of gaunt thorns all stretching their limbs one way, as if craving alms of the sun. Happily, the architect had foresight to build it strong: the narrow windows are deeply set in the wall, and the corners defended with large jutting stones.

Before passing the threshold, I paused to admire a quantity of grotesque carving lavished over the front, and especially about the principal door; above which, among a wilderness of crumbling griffins and shameless little boys, I detected the date "1500," and the name "Hareton Earnshaw.'" I would have made a few comments, and requested a short history of the place from the surly owner; but his attitude at the door appeared to demand my speedy entrance, or complete departure, and I had no desire to aggravate his impatience previous to inspecting the penetralium.

1. What is the author's purpose in describing Wuthering Heights in such detail?

a. To explain why Mr. Lockwood is so delighted by the house
b. To prove that Heathcliff is a misanthrope
c. To show how all houses looked in the 1500s
d. To establish a strange and foreboding tone

2. Which line from the excerpt helps establish a somewhat sarcastic tone?

a. "...Mr. Heathcliff and I are such a suitable pair to divide the desolation between us."
b. "...I charitably conjectured he must have need of divine aid to digest his dinner..."
c. "...the narrow windows are deeply set in the wall, and the corners defended with large jutting stones."
d. "...his attitude at the door appeared to demand my speedy entrance..."

3. As it is used in paragraph 9, what does the word *bracing* mean?

a. Supporting
b. Bracketing
c. Staying
d. Invigorating

4. What does Heathcliff mean when he says, "cattle are the only hedge-cutters"?

a. Heathcliff is mad and believes his cattle are capable of gardening.
b. Heathcliff is irritated by how the cattle destroy the vegetation on his property.
c. The only way his property will be landscaped is if cattle decide to eat the hedges.
d. The hedges that grow on Heathcliff's property are particularly delicious to cattle.

Refer to the following for questions 5–12:

Stories have been a part of the world since the beginning of recorded time. For centuries before the invention of the printing press, stories of the world were passed down to generations through oral tradition. With the invention of the printing press, which made written material available to wide ranges of audiences, books were mass-produced and introduced into greater society.

For the last several centuries, books have been at the forefront of education and entertainment. With the invention of the internet, reliance on books for information quickly changed. Soon, almost everything that anyone needed to know could be accessed through the internet. Large, printed volumes of encyclopedias became unnecessary, as all of the information was easily available online.

Despite the progression of the internet, printed media was still very popular in the forms of both fiction and nonfiction books. While waiting for an appointment, enduring a several-hour flight, or relaxing before sleep, books have been a reliable and convenient source of entertainment that society has not been willing to give up.

With the extreme convenience of technology, printed books are likely going to become a thing of the past. Inventions such as the iPad and the Kindle have made the need for any kind of printed media unnecessary. With a rechargeable battery, a large screen, and the ability to have several books saved on file, electronic options will soon take over, and society will no longer utilize printed books.

Although some people may say that the act of reading is not complete without turning a page, sliding a finger across the screen (or pressing a button) is just as satisfying to the reader. The iPad and Kindle are devices that have qualities similar to a computer and can be used for so much more than just reading. Therefore, these devices are better than books because they have multiple uses.

Storytelling is a longstanding societal tradition, and it will always be an important way to communicate ideas and provide information as well as entertainment. Centuries ago, stories could only be remembered and retold through speech. Printed media changed the way the world communicated and was connected, and now, as we move forward with technology, it is only a matter of time before we must say goodbye to the printed past by welcoming in the digital and electronic future.

5. What is the main argument of this essay?

a. iPads and Kindles are easier to read than books.
b. The printing press was a great invention.
c. The internet is how people receive information.
d. Technology will soon replace printed material.

6. What is the main purpose of paragraph 1?

a. To define oral tradition
b. To stress the importance of the printing press
c. To explain the progression of storytelling within society
d. To introduce the essay

7. According to the essay, what was the first way that stories were communicated and passed down?

a. Oral tradition
b. Printed books
c. Technology
d. Hand-written copies

8. Which of the following statements is an opinion?

a. "Despite the progression of the internet, printed media was still very popular in the forms of both fiction and nonfiction books."
b. "Although some people may say that the act of reading is not complete without turning a page, sliding a finger across the screen (or pressing a button) is just as satisfying to the reader."
c. "With the invention of the internet, reliance on books for information quickly changed."
d. "Stories have been a part of the world since the beginning of recorded time."

9. Which of the following reflects a secondary argument made by the author?

a. Devices such as the iPad or Kindle are better than books because they have multiple uses.
b. Books are still important to have while waiting for an appointment or taking a flight.
c. Printed encyclopedias are still used and are more convenient than using the internet.
d. With technology, there will soon be no need for stories.

10. Before the invention of the printing press, what was the main reason books were costly to make?

a. Paper was scarce.
b. Books had to be handwritten.
c. People preferred spoken storytelling.
d. Books were difficult to ship.

11. How are the following two sentences related?

Sentence 1: While waiting for an appointment, enduring a several-hour flight, or relaxing before sleep, books have been a reliable and convenient source of entertainment that society has not been willing to give up.
Sentence 2: With a rechargeable battery, a large screen, and the ability to have several books saved on file, electronic options will soon take over and society will no longer utilize printed books.

a. Sentence 2 clarifies sentence 1.
b. Sentence 1 supports the main idea of sentence 2.
c. They are contradictory of one another.
d. Sentence 2 offers a solution to a problem presented in sentence 1.

12. Which of the following is NOT a reason the author gives for the assertion that electronic devices are better than books?

a. Because they have multiple uses
b. Because they store more than one book at a time
c. Because they can be used to play games online
d. Because they can be used to access information on the internet

Refer to the following for questions 13–18:

In 1906, Elinore Pruitt Stewart moved to Denver for housework to support her daughter, Jerrine. Her employer in Denver was Mrs. Juliet Coney. A few years later, she moved to Wyoming to be a housekeeper for a rancher. The following passage is one of many letters that Stewart wrote to Mrs. Coney on life as a homesteader in Wyoming.

A Letter of Elinore Pruitt Stewart

January 23, 1913

When I read of the hard times among the Denver poor, I feel like urging them every one to get out and file on land. I am very enthusiastic about women homesteading. It really requires less strength and labor to raise plenty to satisfy a large family than it does to go out to wash, with the added satisfaction of knowing that their job will not be lost to them if they care to keep it. Even if improving the place does go slowly, it is that much done to stay done. Whatever is raised is the homesteader's own, and there is no house-rent to pay. This year Jerrine cut and dropped enough potatoes to raise a ton of fine potatoes. She wanted to try, so we let her, and you will remember that she is but six years old.... Any woman strong enough to go out by the day could have done every bit of the work and put in two or three times that much, and it would have been so much more pleasant than to work so hard in the city and be on starvation rations all winter.

To me, homesteading is the solution of all poverty's problems, but I realize that temperament has much to do with success in any undertaking, and persons afraid of coyotes and work and loneliness had better let ranching alone. At the same time, any woman who can stand her own company, can see the beauty of the sunset, loves growing things, and is willing to put in as much time at careful labor as she does over the washtub, will certainly succeed; will have independence, plenty to eat all the time, and a home of her own in the end.

Experimenting need cost the homesteader no more than the work, because by applying to the Department of Agriculture at Washington he can get enough of any seed and as many kinds as he wants to make a thorough trial, and it doesn't even cost postage. Also one can always get bulletins from there and from the Experiment Station of one's own State concerning any problem or as many problems as may come up. I would not, for anything, allow Mr. Stewart to do anything toward improving my place, for I want the fun and the experience myself. And I want to be able to speak from experience when I tell others what they can do. Theories are very beautiful, but facts are what must be had, and what I intend to give some time.

13. The writer of this letter is suggesting that women should own land and farm rather than:

a. Cook in a restaurant.
b. Open a bed and breakfast.
c. Do laundry for others.
d. Teach in a one-room schoolhouse.

14. What do you think Mrs. Coney's reaction to the letter might have been?

a. She was probably glad to be rid of such a lazy worker.
b. She may be glad to know that Mrs. Stewart is enjoying her time with homesteading.
c. She may have been sorry that she too did not homestead.
d. She was likely angry that Mrs. Stewart had written.

15. Which of the following does Stewart NOT give as an advantage of homesteading?

a. It takes less strength and work than doing laundry for others.
b. The worker cannot lose her job if she wants to keep it.
c. No one has to pay rent.
d. One can always find good company.

16. Which of the following is a risk for the poor in Denver?

a. The possibility of losing their jobs
b. The likelihood of a strike
c. The probability of a landslide
d. Losing their homes to fire

17. The tone of the letter is:

a. Complaining and bitter
b. Sad and lonely
c. Positive and encouraging
d. Hopeless and despairing

18. Stewart mentions her daughter's potato crop. She does this to show:

a. That child labor is acceptable
b. That there are no schools in the area
c. That women work just as hard as men do
d. How easy it is to raise crops

Refer to the following for questions 19–23:

The following passage is adapted from Jack London's *The Call of the Wild* (1903).

Buck did not read the newspapers, or he would have known that trouble was brewing, not alone for himself, but for every tide-water dog, strong of muscle and with warm, long hair, from Puget Sound to San Diego. Because men, groping in the Arctic darkness, had found a yellow metal, and because steamship and transportation companies were booming the find, thousands of men were rushing into the Northland. These men wanted dogs, and the dogs they wanted were heavy dogs, with strong muscles by which to toil, and furry coats to protect them from the frost.

Buck lived at a big house in the sun-kissed Santa Clara Valley. Judge Miller's place, it was called. It stood back from the road, half hidden among the trees, through which glimpses could be caught of the wide cool veranda that ran around its four sides. The house was approached by gravelled driveways which wound about through wide-spreading lawns and under the interlacing boughs of tall poplars. At the rear things were on even a more spacious scale than at the front. There were great stables, where a dozen grooms and boys held forth, rows of vine-clad servants' cottages, an endless and orderly array of outhouses, long grape arbors, green pastures, orchards, and berry patches. Then there was the pumping plant for the artesian well, and the big cement tank where Judge Miller's boys took their morning plunge and kept cool in the hot afternoon.

And over this great demesne Buck ruled. Here he was born, and here he had lived the four years of his life. It was true, there were other dogs, there could not but be other dogs on so vast a place, but they did not count. They came and went, resided in the populous kennels, or lived obscurely in the recesses of the house after the fashion of Toots, the Japanese pug, or Ysabel, the Mexican hairless,—strange creatures that rarely put nose out of doors or set foot to ground. On the other hand, there were the fox terriers, a score of them at least, who yelped fearful promises at Toots and Ysabel looking out of the windows at them and protected by a legion of housemaids armed with brooms and mops.

But Buck was neither house-dog nor kennel-dog. The whole realm was his. He plunged into the swimming tank or went hunting with the Judge's sons; he escorted Mollie and Alice, the Judge's daughters, on long twilight or early morning rambles; on wintry nights he lay at the Judge's feet before the roaring library fire; he carried the Judge's grandsons on his back, or rolled them in the grass, and guarded their footsteps through wild adventures down to the fountain in the stable yard, and even beyond, where the paddocks were, and the berry patches. Among the terriers he stalked imperiously, and Toots and Ysabel he utterly ignored, for he was king,—king over all creeping, crawling, flying things of Judge Miller's place, humans included.

His father, Elmo, a huge St. Bernard, had been the Judge's inseparable companion, and Buck bid fair to follow in the way of his father. He was not so large,—he weighed only one hundred and forty pounds,—for his mother, Shep, had been a Scotch shepherd dog. Nevertheless, one hundred and forty pounds, to which was added the dignity that comes of good living and universal respect, enabled him to carry himself in right royal fashion. During the four years since his puppyhood he had lived the life of a sated aristocrat; he had a fine pride in himself, was even a trifle egotistical, as country gentlemen sometimes become because of their insular situation. But he had saved himself by not becoming a mere pampered house-dog. Hunting and kindred outdoor delights had kept down the fat and hardened his muscles; and to him, as to the cold-tubbing races, the love of water had been a tonic and a health preserver.

And this was the manner of dog Buck was in the fall of 1897, when the Klondike strike dragged men from all the world into the frozen North. But Buck did not read the newspapers, and he did not know that Manuel, one of the gardener's helpers, was an undesirable acquaintance. Manuel had one besetting sin. He loved to play Chinese lottery. Also, in his gambling, he had one besetting weakness—faith in a system; and this made his damnation certain. For to play a system requires money, while the wages of a gardener's helper do not lap over the needs of a wife and numerous progenies.

The Judge was at a meeting of the Raisin Growers' Association, and the boys were busy organizing an athletic club, on the memorable night of Manuel's treachery. No one saw him and Buck go off through the orchard on what Buck imagined was merely a stroll. And with the exception of a solitary man, no one saw them arrive at the little flag station known as College Park. This man talked with Manuel, and money chinked between them.

19. What is the most logical explanation for Manuel taking Buck away from Judge Miller's place?

a. Manuel sold the dog to a stranger who is looking for gold in the "frozen North."
b. Buck will be trained to be a service dog for the Judge's daughters.
c. Manuel needs the protection as he meets with the man at College Park.
d. The dog will be used for hunting events.

20. The author uses the details in paragraph 1 to:

a. Describe Buck's life
b. Foreshadow Buck's story
c. Describe the story's setting
d. Introduce the story's villain

21. The author organizes this selection mainly by:

a. Describing Buck's life in the order in which it happened
b. Outlining Buck's history
c. Showing Buck's life and then showing a moment of change
d. Comparing Buck's life at Judge Miller's place to what came afterwards

22. This selection is part of a longer work. Based on the selection, what might be a theme of the larger work?

a. Change
b. Family
c. Hard work
d. Relationships

23. What is the purpose of paragraphs 2–5 (lines 14–89)?

a. To introduce all of the story's characters
b. To show Buck's personality
c. To introduce Buck
d. To show Buck's affection for Toots and Ysabel

Refer to the following for questions 24–28:

In 1603, Queen Elizabeth I of England died. She had never married and had no heir, so the throne passed to a distant relative: James Stuart, the son of Elizabeth's cousin and one-time rival for the throne, Mary, Queen of Scots. James was crowned King James I of England. At the time, he was also King James VI of Scotland, and the combination of roles would create a spirit of conflict that haunted the two nations for generations to come.

The conflict developed as a result of rising tensions among the people within the nations, as well as between them. Scholars in the 21st century are far too hasty in dismissing the role of religion in political disputes, but religion undoubtedly played a role in the problems that faced England and Scotland. By the time of James Stuart's succession to the English throne, the English people had firmly embraced the teachings of Protestant theology. Similarly, the Scottish Lowlands were decisively Protestant. In the Scottish Highlands, however, the clans retained their Catholic faith. James acknowledged the Church of England and still sanctioned the largely Protestant translation of the Bible that still bears his name.

James's son, King Charles I, proved himself to be less committed to the Protestant Church of England. Charles married the Catholic Princess Henrietta Maria of France, and there were suspicions among the English and the Lowland Scots that Charles was quietly a Catholic. Charles's own political troubles extended beyond religion in this case, and he was beheaded in 1649. Eventually, his son, King Charles II, would be crowned, and this Charles is believed to have converted secretly to the Catholic Church. Charles II died without a legitimate heir, and his brother James ascended to the throne as King James II.

James was recognized to be a practicing Catholic, and his commitment to Catholicism would prove to be his downfall. James's wife, Mary Beatrice, lost a number of children during their infancy, and when she became pregnant again in 1687, the public became concerned. If James had a son, that son would undoubtedly be raised a Catholic, and the English people would not stand for this. Mary gave birth to a son, but the story quickly circulated that the royal child had died, and the child named James's heir was a foundling smuggled in. James, his wife, and his infant son were forced to flee; and James's Protestant daughter Mary was crowned the queen.

In spite of a strong resemblance to the king, the young James III was generally rejected among the English and the Lowland Scots, who referred to him as "the Pretender." But in the Highlands, the Catholic princeling was welcomed. He inspired a group known as *Jacobites*, to reflect the Latin version of his name. His own son Charles, known affectionately as Bonnie Prince Charlie, would eventually raise an army and attempt to recapture what he believed to be his throne. The movement was soundly defeated at the Battle of Culloden in 1746, and England and Scotland have remained ostensibly Protestant ever since.

24. Which of the following sentences demonstrate an opinion on the part of the author?

a. "James was recognized to be a practicing Catholic, and his commitment to Catholicism would prove to be his downfall."
b. "James' son King Charles I proved himself to be less committed to the Protestant Church of England."
c. "The movement was soundly defeated at the Battle of Culloden in 1746, and England and Scotland have remained ostensibly Protestant ever since."
d. "Scholars in the 21st century are far too hasty in dismissing the role of religion in political disputes, but religion undoubtedly played a role in the problems that faced England and Scotland."

25. Which of the following is a logical conclusion based on the information that is provided within the passage?

a. Like Elizabeth I, Charles II never married and thus never had children.
b. The English people were relieved each time that James II's wife Mary lost another child, as this prevented the chance of a Catholic monarch.
c. Charles I's beheading had less to do with religion than with other political problems that England was facing.
d. Unlike his son and grandsons, King James I had no Catholic leanings and was a faithful follower of the Protestant Church of England.

26. Based on the information that is provided within the passage, which of the following can be inferred about King James II's son?

a. Considering his resemblance to King James II, James Edward was very likely the legitimate child of the king and the queen.
b. Given the queen's previous inability to produce a healthy child, the English and the Lowland Scots were right in questioning the legitimacy of James Edward.
c. James Edward was not as popular among the Highland clans as his son Bonnie Prince Charlie.
d. James Edward was unable to acquire the resources needed to build the army and plan the invasion that his son succeeded in doing.

27. Which of the following best describes the organization of the information in the passage?

a. Cause-effect
b. Chronological sequence
c. Problem-solution
d. Comparison-contrast

28. Which of the following best describes the author's intent in the passage?

a. To persuade
b. To entertain
c. To express feeling
d. To inform

Refer to the following for questions 29–31:

Prior to her birth, few would have thought that the child born Princess Alexandrina Victoria would eventually become one of Britain's longest reigning monarchs, Queen Victoria. She was born in 1819, the only child of Edward, Duke of Kent, who was the fourth son of King George III. Ahead of Edward were three brothers, two of whom became king but none of whom produced a legitimate, surviving heir. King George's eldest son, who was eventually crowned King George IV, secretly married a Catholic commoner, Maria Fitzherbert, in 1783. The marriage was never officially recognized, and in 1795, George was persuaded to marry a distant cousin, Caroline of Brunswick. The marriage was bitter, and the two had only one daughter, Princess Charlotte Augusta. She was popular in England where her eventual reign was welcomed, but in a tragic event that shocked the nation, the princess and her stillborn son died in childbirth in 1817.

Realizing the precarious position of the British throne, the remaining sons of King George III were motivated to marry and produce an heir. The first in line was Prince Frederick, the Duke of York. Frederick married Princess Frederica Charlotte of Prussia, but the two had no children. After Prince Frederick was Prince William, the Duke of Clarence. William married Princess Adelaide of Saxe-Meiningen, and they had two sickly daughters, neither of whom survived infancy. Finally, Prince Edward, the Duke of Kent, threw his hat into the ring with his marriage to Princess Victoria of Saxe-Coburg-Saalfeld. The Duke of Kent died less than a year after his daughter's birth, but the surviving Duchess of Kent was not unaware of the future possibilities for her daughter. She took every precaution to ensure that the young Princess Victoria was healthy and safe throughout her childhood.

Princess Victoria's uncle, William, succeeded his brother George IV to become King William IV. The new king recognized his niece as his future heir, but he did not necessarily trust her mother. As a result, he was determined to survive until Victoria's 18th birthday to ensure that she could rule in her own right without the regency of the Duchess of Kent. The king's fervent prayers were answered: he died June 20, 1837, less than one month after Victoria turned 18. Though young and inexperienced, the young queen recognized the importance of her position and determined to rule fairly and wisely. The improbable princess who became queen ruled for more than 63 years, and her reign is considered to be one of the most important in British history.

29. Which of the following is a logical conclusion that can be drawn from the information in the passage above?

a. Victoria's long reign provided the opportunity for her to bring balance to England and right the wrongs that had occurred during the reigns of her uncles.
b. It was the death of Princess Charlotte Augusta that motivated the remaining princes to marry and start families.
c. The Duke of Kent had hoped for a son but was delighted with his good fortune in producing the surviving heir that his brothers had failed to produce.
d. King William IV was unreasonably suspicious of the Duchess of Kent's motivations, as she cared only for her daughter's wellbeing.

30. What is the author's likely purpose in writing this passage about Queen Victoria?

a. To persuade the reader to appreciate the accomplishments of Queen Victoria, especially when placed against the failures of her forebears
b. To introduce the historical impact of the Victorian Era by introducing to readers the queen who gave that era its name
c. To explain how small events in history placed an unlikely princess in line to become the queen of England
d. To indicate the role that King George III's many sons played in changing the history of England

31. Based on the context of the passage, the reader can infer that this information is likely to appear in which of the following types of works?

a. A scholarly paper
b. A mystery
c. A fictional story
d. A biography

Refer to the following for questions 32–35:

Poem by Emily Dickinson:

"There's a Certain Slant of Light"

There's a certain slant of light,
On winter afternoons,
That oppresses, like the weight
Of cathedral tunes.
Heavenly hurt it gives us;
We can find no scar,
But internal difference
Where the meanings are.
None may teach it anything,
'Tis the seal, despair,—
An imperial affliction
Sent us of the air.
When it comes, the landscape listens,
Shadows hold their breath;
When it goes, 'tis like the distance
On the look of death.

32. What emotion is Dickinson describing in the poem?

a. Depression
b. Joy
c. Uncertainty
d. Surprise

33. "That oppresses, like the weight / Of cathedral tunes." is an example of the poetic device of:

a. Alliteration
b. Personification
c. Simile
d. Metaphor

34. Which poetic device is used in the following lines?

"When it comes, the landscape listens, / Shadows hold their breath;"

a. Assonance
b. Personification
c. Simile
d. Metaphor

35. The season being described in the poem is:

a. Solstice
b. Summer
c. Autumn
d. Winter

Refer to the following for questions 36–45:

Passage 1 is adapted from John Jay, "Federalist No. 2." Originally published 1787.

Passage 2 is adapted from Patrick Henry's speech before the Virginia Ratifying Convention on June 5, 1788.

Passage 1

Nothing is more certain than the indispensable necessity of government, and it is equally undeniable, that whenever and however it is instituted, the people must cede to it some of their natural rights in order to vest it with requisite powers. It is well worthy of consideration therefore, whether it would conduce more to the interest of the people of America that they should, to all general purposes, be one nation, under one federal government, or that they should divide themselves into separate confederacies, and give to the head of each the same kind of powers which they are advised to place in one national government.

It has until lately been a received and uncontradicted opinion that the prosperity of the people of America depended on their continuing firmly united, and the wishes, prayers, and efforts of our best and wisest citizens have been constantly directed to that object. But politicians now appear, who insist that this opinion is erroneous, and that instead of looking for safety and happiness in union, we ought to seek it in a division of the States into distinct confederacies or sovereignties.

Providence has been pleased to give this one connected country to one united people—a people descended from the same ancestors, speaking the same language, professing the same religion, attached to the same principles of government, very similar in their manners and customs, and who, by their joint counsels, arms, and efforts, fighting side by side throughout a long and bloody war, have nobly established general liberty and independence. To all general purposes we have uniformly been one people each individual citizen everywhere enjoying the same national rights, privileges, and protection. As a nation we have made peace and war; as a nation we have vanquished our common enemies; as a nation we have formed alliances, and made treaties, and entered into various compacts and conventions with foreign states.

Passage 2

The question turns, Sir, on that poor little thing—the expression, *We, the people*, instead of the *States*, of America. I need not take much pains to show that the principles of this system are extremely pernicious, impolitic, and dangerous.

This is not a democracy, wherein the people retain all their rights securely. Had these principles been adhered to, we should not have been brought to this alarming transition, from a Confederacy to a consolidated Government. We have no detail of these great considerations, which, in my opinion, ought to have abounded before we should recur to a government of this kind. Here is a revolution as radical as that which separated us from Great Britain. It is radical in this transition; our rights and privileges are endangered, and the sovereignty of the states will be relinquished: And cannot we plainly see that this is actually the case? The rights of conscience, trial by jury, liberty of the press, all your immunities and franchises, all pretensions to human rights and privileges, are rendered insecure, if not lost, by this change, so loudly talked of by some, and inconsiderately by others. Is this tame relinquishment of rights worthy of freemen? Is it worthy of that manly fortitude that ought to characterize republicans?

You are not to inquire how your trade may be increased, nor how you are to become a great and powerful people, but how your liberties can be secured; for liberty ought to be the direct end of your Government. Will the abandonment of your most sacred rights tend to the security of your liberty? Liberty, the greatest of all earthly blessings—give us that precious jewel, and you may take every thing else.

36. In passage 1, Jay indicates that it is necessary for the American people to do what?

a. Divide the states into separate confederacies.
b. Give up certain rights for their own prosperity.
c. Seek the prosperity of America as a whole rather than as individuals.
d. Remain uniform in language and religion.

37. As used in line 6 of passage 1, *vest* most nearly means:

a. To guard, as a breastplate
b. To grant authority
c. To make an investment
d. To give up

38. As used in line 16 of passage 1, *received* most nearly means:

a. Greeted
b. Acquired from
c. Agreed upon
d. Earned by

39. How would Jay most likely have responded to Henry's statement in line 25 of Passage 2 that American rights "are rendered insecure, if not lost" by consolidated government?

a. He would contend that Americans cannot be secure or prosperous without rescinding some of their rights.
b. He would point out that no one really has rights apart from a unified nation.
c. He would argue that the government actually gives the people more rights, not fewer.
d. He would state that the government is a democracy, so all rights are securely retained by the people.

40. Jay and Henry would most likely agree that:

a. Liberty is the highest gift a person can be given.
b. There must be some kind of central government to avoid chaos.
c. The United States needs to be strong as it conducts global business.
d. The United States has potential to be a land of many privileges.

41. How would Henry most likely have responded to Jay's discussion in lines 24–25 of Passage 1: "looking for safety and happiness in union"?

a. He would argue that personal liberty is actually much safer than protection from the government.
b. He would point out that a collection of separate confederacies gives more safety than a consolidated government.
c. He would contend that invaluable human rights are lost in a powerful government.
d. He would assert that liberty is far more valuable than a sense of safety that the government may provide.

42. Henry objects to Jay's assertion that:

a. Personal liberty is worth more than any wealth or security.
b. America's unity is beneficial because it will lead to the prosperity of her people.
c. Individual rights are lost when a strong government is established.
d. The states should divide into separate confederacies.

43. How could the arguments of each passage be summarized?

a. Passage 1 argues for a strong, unified government, while passage 2 argues for personal liberty.
b. Passage 1 argues for personal liberty, while passage 2 argues for a strong, unified government.
c. Passage 1 argues for separate confederacies, while passage 2 argues for a single democracy.
d. Passage 1 argues for a single democracy, while passage 2 argues for separate confederacies.

44. Which of the following is a concern expressed in both passages about the relationship between government and individual rights?

a. The government must have power to ensure prosperity and security for all individuals.
b. Individuals should retain all of their rights in a democratic society.
c. A strong national government is preferable to separate, smaller entities.
d. The transition to a consolidated government endangers individual liberties.

45. Which of the following choices best represents the relationship between the two passages?

a. Passage 2 provides a different angle to the argument in Passage 1.
b. Passage 2 is a rebuttal to the major claim of Passage 1.
c. Passage 2 mainly agrees with Passage 1 but differs on one point.
d. Passage 2 adds to the claims of Passage 1.

Refer to the following for questions 46–50:

DOCTOR

The Doctor and his wife come onstage quarreling.

Doctor: No, I tell you, I will do nothing of the kind. After all, I am the master.

Martine: And I tell you that I didn't go and marry you to put up with all your freaks.

Doctor: Oh, what an awful trouble it is to have a wife! How right Aristotle was when he said that a woman is worse than the devil!

Martine: Just listen to the clever man, with his fool of an Aristotle.

Doctor: Clever, indeed! You go and find a ditch-digger who can reason like me about everything, who has served for six years a most famous doctor, and who in his youth could say the Latin grammar by heart.

Martine: Plague take the fool!

Doctor: Plague take the wench!

Martine: Cursed be the day when I took it into my head to go and say "Yes!"

Doctor: Cursed be the old idiot who made me sign my ruin!

Martine: It becomes you well to complain of our marriage! You should thank Heaven every moment of your life for having me as a wife. And did you deserve, tell me, to marry a woman like me?

Doctor: True, indeed! You honored me too much, and I had reason to be satisfied on our wedding-day. Gad! Don't make me speak of it, or I might say certain things.

Martine: Well! What is it you'd say?

Doctor: Enough of that. It is sufficient that I know what I know, and that you were very lucky to have me.

Martine: What do you mean by my being lucky to have you? A man who reduces me to beggary; a debauched, deceitful villain, who eats up all I possess.

Doctor: That's a lie; I drink part of it.

Martine: Who sells, bit by bit, all that we have in the house.

Doctor: That is what is called living on one's means.

Martine: Who even sold the bed from under me.

Doctor: You'll get up all the earlier.

Martine: A man who does not leave a single stick of furniture in the house.

Doctor: We move about more easily.

Martine: And who does nothing from morning to night but drink and gamble.

Doctor: That's for fear of depression.

Martine: And what can I do with the children all the time?

Doctor: Anything you like.

Martine: I have four little ones on my hands.

Doctor: Put them down on the ground.

Martine: They do nothing but ask for bread.

Doctor: Whip them. When I have eaten and drunk my fill, I wish everybody to live on the fat of the land.

Martine (threatening, moves toward him): And do you think, drunkard, that things can always go on like this?

Doctor: Now, my wife, gently, if you please.

Martine: That I must endure forever your insolence and excesses.

Doctor (backing away): Do not get in a passion, my dear wife.

Martine: And that I shall not find the means of bringing you to a sense of your duty?

Doctor (standing his ground): My dear wife, you know that I am not very patient, and that I have a good strong arm.

46. This play is an example of a:

a. Tragedy
b. Comedy
c. Drama
d. Soliloquy

47. When the Doctor curses "the old idiot who made me sign my ruin," he is referring to:

a. Someone who loaned him money
b. Someone who sold him his house
c. The clergyman who married him to Martine
d. A government official

48. When Martine criticizes the Doctor's bad habits, such as drinking and gambling, his answers may be described as:

a. Glib
b. Regretful
c. Defensive
d. Apologetic

49. Which of the following best describes the Doctor's personality?

a. Irascible
b. Intolerant
c. Irresponsible
d. Choleric

50. When Martine grows angry and moves toward him, threateningly, what is the Doctor's first response?

a. He grows angry as well.
b. He shows fear.
c. He ignores her.
d. He attempts to placate her.

Language Arts–Writing

Refer to the following for questions 1–3:

(1) I had the same teacher for both third and 4th grades, which were difficult years for me. (2) My teacher and I did not get along, and I don't think she liked me. (3) Every day, I thought she was treating me unfairly and being mean. (4) Because I felt that way, I think I acted out and stopped doing my work. (5) In the middle of fourth grade, my family moved to a new town, and I had Mr. Shanbourne as my new teacher.

(6) From the very first day in Mr. Shanbourne's class, I was on guard. (7) I was expecting to hate my teacher and for him to hate me back when I started his class. (8) Mr. Shanbourne took me by surprise right away when he asked me if I wanted to stand up and introduce myself. (9) I said no, probably in a surly voice, and he just nodded and began teaching the first lesson of the day.

(10) I wasn't sure how to take this. (11) My old teacher forced me to do things and gave me detention if I didn't. (12) She loved detention and gave it to me for anything I did—talking back, working too loudly, forgetting an assignment. (13) He obviously didn't believe in detention, and I tried him! (14) During my first two weeks at my new school I did my best to get in trouble. (15) I zoned out in class, turned work in late, talked during lectures, and handed in assignments after the due date. (16) Mr. Shanbourne just nodded.

(17) Mr. Shanbourne asked me to stay in during recess. (18) *This is it*, I thought. I was going to get in trouble, get the detention my ten-year-old self had practically been begging for. (19) After all of the other kids ran outside, I walked up to Mr. Shanbourne's desk.

(20) "How are you doing, Alberto," he said.

(21) I mumbled something.

(22) He told me he was disappointed in my behavior over the last two weeks. (23) I had expected this and just took it. (24) The detention was coming any second. (25) Than Mr.

Shanbourne took me by surprise. (26) He told me that even though he didn't know me very well, he believed I could be a hard worker and that I could be successful in his class. (27) He asked me how he could help listen better and turn my work in on time.

(28) I told him I had to think about it and rushed out to recess. (29) Even though my answer seemed rude, I was stunned. (30) I hadn't had a teacher in years who seemed to care about me, and said he believed in my abilities.

(31) To be honest, my behavior did not improve right away and I still turned in many of my assignments late. (32) But over the last few months of fourth grade, things changed. (33) Mr. Shanbourne continued to believe in me, encourage me and help me, and I responded by doing my best. (34) I had a different teacher for fifth grade, but whenever I was struggling I walked down to Mr. Shanbourne's classroom to get his advice. (35) I'll never forget how Mr. Shanbourne helped me, and I hope he'll never forget me either.

1. What correction should be made to sentence 1?

a. Change *teacher* to *teachers.*
b. Change *4th* to *fourth.*
c. Delete the comma after *grades.*
d. Change *years* to *year's.*

2. Which phrase, if any, can be deleted from sentence 15 without changing the meaning of the sentence?

a. NO CHANGE
b. "...talked during lectures..."
c. "...handed in assignments after the due date."
d. "...zoned out in class..."

3. What transition should be added to the beginning of sentence 16?

a. Surprisingly
b. Actually
c. Furthermore
d. Instead

Refer to the following for questions 4–9:

How Do You Prepare Your Vehicle for Winter?

A

(1) Anyone who live in a climate which brings snow during the winter knows how important it is to have a working vehicle. (2) Before winter begins, get the car or truck serviced. (3) Consider the following tips. (4) Few things are worst than being unable to see in snow or sleet. (5) Most wiper blades do not last no longer than a year. (6) Be sure that while you are at it, the windshield washer reservoir has fluid. (7) First of all, do the windshield wipers work properly? (8) Do not fill it with water because plain water won't work in the winter since it freezes.

B

(9) Now, you need to check a few things under the hood. (10) Are belts and hoses in good shape is the battery in good working order? (11) When was the last oil change? (12) Make sure you have the right blend of antifreeze and water in the radiator. (13) Add to your vehicle's

emergency kit extra food water and warm clothes or a blanket. (14) In winter, carry an ice scraper and a small shovel. (15) Consider tire chains and salt, sand, or non-clumping kitty litter to give your vehicle traction if needed.

C

(16) Have a plan if you are stranded. (17) You leave only the car because you know exactly where you are and how far you are from help. (18) Following these precautions will help to keep you and your loved ones safe in winter driving.

4. What correction should be made to sentence 6?

a. Move *while you are at it* to the front of the sentence and place a comma after it.
b. Move *Be sure* to the end of the sentence.
c. Place a question mark at the end of the sentence.
d. No correction is necessary.

5. Which revision should be made to sentence 7 to improve the organization of the paragraph?

a. Move sentence 7 to the beginning of paragraph A.
b. Move sentence 7 after sentence 3.
c. Move sentence 7 to the end of paragraph A.
d. Move sentence 7 to the beginning of paragraph B.

6. What correction should be made to sentence 9?

a. NO CHANGE
b. Delete *under the hood* from the sentence.
c. Change *a few* to *one.*
d. Place *have* between *to* and *check.*

7. Consider the following excerpt from the passage.

Sentence 10: "Are belts and hoses in <u>good shape is the</u> battery in good working order?"

Select the best version of the underlined portion.

a. NO CHANGE
b. good shape, is the
c. good shape and is the
d. good shape; is the

8. What correction should be made to sentence 13?

a. Remove the apostrophe from *vehicle's.*
b. Change the spelling of *emergency* to *emergancy.*
c. Place commas after the words *food* and *water.*
d. No correction is necessary.

9. What correction should be made to sentence 17?

a. Move *only* to come between *You* and *leave.*
b. Delete *exactly.*
c. Put a comma before *and.*
d. No correction is necessary.

HiSET Practice Test #1

Refer to the following for questions 10–18:

How Slow Is Your Food?

A

(1) A growing grassroots movement is taking place around the world. (2) Developed nations have spent the past half-century creating fast food products, which are designed more for ease and availability than for taste. (3) Today, people worry more over genetically modified crops, food safety, and the cost of shipping food across the nation. (4) So, slow foods is making a comeback.

B

(5) Slow food puts the emphasize on community and sharing. (6) A major concern is to support local farmers and artisans. (7) Examples are those who are trying to save endangered species of animals, grains, the fruits, and the vegetables. (8) A new interest in heirloom varieties has reawakened palates that were used to food which had lost nutritional appeal and flavor. (9) Slow food also seeks to fully use sustainable agriculture. (10) This way soils can be replenished without the use of chemicals.

C

(11) Slow food usa has taken the program to students in elementary and secondary schools through its Garden to Table program. (12) Focusing on pleasure, tradition, and sustainability, the projects offer young people a chance to be involved in hands-on gardening and cooking. (13) I once had a garden in my backyard. (14) Students learn where their food comes from and they find out who grows it and how to cook it and the need to share with others. (15) A similar program, Slow Food on Campus, is conducted by the college and university students. (16) All programs adhere to the basic ideas of slow food: a good, clean, and fair food system.

10. Consider the following excerpt from the passage.

Sentence 2: "Developed nations have spent the past half-century creating fast food products, which are designed more for ease and availability than for taste."

Select the best version of the underlined portion.

a. NO CHANGE
b. food products which are
c. food product, which are
d. food products, which is

11. What correction should be made to sentence 4?

a. Remove the extra comma.
b. Change *is* to *are.*
c. Capitalize *slow foods.*
d. Put a hyphen between *come* and *back.*

12. Consider the following excerpt from the passage.

Sentence 5: "Slow food <u>puts the emphasize</u> on community and sharing."

Select the best version of the underlined portion.

a. NO CHANGE
b. places the emphasize
c. put the emphasize
d. puts the emphasis

13. Consider the following excerpt from the passage.

Sentence 7: "Examples are those who are trying to save <u>endangered species of animals, grains, the fruits, and the vegetables."</u>

Select the best version of the underlined portion.

a. endangered species of animals, grains, the fruits, and the vegetables
b. endangered specie of animals, grains, the fruits, and the vegetables
c. endangered species of animal, grain, the fruit, and the vegetable
d. endangered species of animals, grains, fruits, and vegetables

14. What correction should be made to sentence 9?

a. Change *seeks* to *seek*.
b. Move *also* to the beginning of the sentence.
c. Delete *fully*.
d. No correction is needed.

15. What correction should be made to sentence 11?

a. Remove capital letters from *Garden* and *Table*.
b. Capitalize *food usa*.
c. Change the spelling of *through* to *thru*.
d. No correction is needed.

16. Which revision should be made to sentence 13 to improve the organization of this paragraph?

a. Move the sentence to the beginning of the paragraph.
b. Use the sentence as the concluding statement of the article.
c. Delete sentence 13.
d. Move the sentence to the previous paragraph.

17. What correction should be made to sentence 14?

a. Add commas.
b. Make the terms parallel.
c. Change *their* to *they're*.
d. Make two sentences.

18. What correction should be made to sentence 15?

a. Make *college and university students* the subject.
b. Remove the commas.
c. Remove the capital letters on *Slow*, *Food*, and *Campus*.
d. Change the spelling of *similar* to *simular*.

Refer to the following for questions 19–21:

(1) Mrs. Conwer, the Jackson High principal, announced last week that Jackson High is considering a student dress code. (2) She is saying that some of the outfits students are wearing to school are being distracting and inappropriate. (3) For example, she says that some of the boys like to wear their pants too low and that some of the girls like to wear very short skirts. (4) I don't see anything wrong with these. (5) This is only Mrs. Conwer's opinion, and I think there are several reasons why it is important that Jackson High does not have a dress code.

(6) High school students are teenagers. (7) The teen years are a time in life when you are exploring new things and learning about yourself. (8) Many teens also like to express themselves. (9) For example, some people I know keep a blog where they write about things that are important to them. (10) Other people play in a band and can express themselves through music. (11) A lot of teens express themselves through fashion. (12) Since many teens start earning their own money, they can buy their own clothes and choose the fashions that they want. (13) If Jackson High adopts a dress code, the students won't be able to express themselves. (14) Self expression are important and is often taught at Jackson High. (15) Ms. Riley, my dance teacher, tells me to express myself through dance. (16) Mr. Hunter, my English teacher, tells me to express myself through writing. (17) Taking away expression through fashion is hypocritical because it goes against what is taught in many classes.

(18) A dress code at Jackson High will never please everyone. (19) Who gets to decide what is appropriate and what is not? (20) What happens if the students disagree with the code? (21) In school, we learn about respecting different opinions and making compromises. (22) However, if Mrs. Conwer or just a couple of teacher's choose the dress code, they will be ignoring them. (23) Jackson High should stop ignoring the lessons that we learn in our classes every day. (24) Teachers should show us, the students, how people are supposed to dress in the real world when they have jobs, explain why certain choices might be inappropriate, and then let us make our own decisions. (25) That's what we learn in all our classes, and that's how it should be for the dress code.

19. Which of the following sentences is unnecessary and could be removed from the passage?

a. Sentence 4
b. Sentence 5
c. Sentence 13
d. Sentence 19

20. Which of the following is the best replacement for the vague *them* in sentence 22?

a. the teachers' wisdom
b. the students' voices
c. the dress code's details
d. the administration's authority

21. Consider the following excerpt from the passage:

Sentence 2: She is saying that some of the outfits students are wearing to school are being distracting and inappropriate.

Select the best version of the sentence.

a. NO CHANGE
b. The outfits are distracting and inappropriate, she says, that students wear to school.
c. She says some of the outfits that students wear to school are distracting and inappropriate.
d. She says that it is distracting and inappropriate that students wear outfits to school.

Refer to the following for questions 22–28:

Are You SAD?

A

(1) For many healthy people, the coming of winter gets them down. (2) Some hibernation tendencies are common. (3) If you notice true depression a sense of hopelessness less energy, or anxiety, you may be suffering from seasonal affective disorder, or SAD. (4) Some people experience SAD during spring and summer for most people, however, winter is the season to be SAD.

B

(5) Researchers are not certainly what causes SAD. (6) One suggestion is that having our regular body rhythms disrupted when less sunlight is available is the culprit. (7) Another study blames increased production of melatonin: a hormone related to sleep. (8) During the dark winter months, the body makes more melatonin. (9) At the same time, it makes less serotonin: the brain chemical that effects our moods. (10) Fewer sunlight means less serotonin. (11) So far, risk factors has not been identified.

C

(12) Most people with SAD just tough it out and waiting for spring. (13) If you have symptoms that last more than two weeks, it is time to see a doctor. (14) People with mild cases of SAD need to spend time outside, exercise regularly, and go to social events or travel. (15) The good news is that spring always comes?

22. Consider the following excerpt from the passage.

Sentence 5: Researchers are not certainly what causes SAD.

What correction should be made to this sentence?

a. NO CHANGE
b. Do not use capital letters for *SAD.*
c. End the sentence with a question mark.
d. Change *certainly* to *certain.*

23. Consider the following excerpt from the passage.

Sentence 8: During the dark winter months, the body makes more melatonin.

What correction should be made to this sentence?

a. NO CHANGE
b. Change *more* to *much.*
c. Capitalize *melatonin.*
d. Put a comma between *dark* and *winter.*

24. Consider the following excerpt from the passage.

Sentence 9: At the same time, it makes less serotonin: the brain chemical that effects our moods.

What correction should be made to this sentence?

a. NO CHANGE
b. Move the first phrase to after *serotonin.*
c. Change *less* to *fewer.*
d. Change *effects* to *affects.*

25. Consider the following excerpt from the passage.

Sentence 10: Fewer sunlight means less serotonin.

What correction should be made to this sentence?

a. Change *means* to *mean*.
b. Capitalize *serotonin*.
c. Change *less* to *fewer*.
d. Change *Fewer* to *Less*.

26. Consider the following excerpt from the passage.

Sentence 11: "<u>So far, risk factors has not</u> been identified."

Select the best version of the underlined portion.

a. NO CHANGE
b. So far, risk factor has not
c. So far, risk factor have not
d. So far, risk factors have not

27. Consider the following excerpt from the passage.

Sentence 12: Most people with SAD just tough it out and waiting for spring.

What correction should be made to this sentence?

a. NO CHANGE
b. Change *tough* to *toughing*.
c. Change *waiting* to *wait*.
d. Write *SAD* as *sad*.

28. Consider the following excerpt from the passage.

Sentence 15: The good news is that spring always comes?

What correction should be made to this sentence?

a. NO CHANGE
b. Change the question mark to a period.
c. Capitalize *spring*.
d. Change *good* to *well*.

Refer to the following for questions 29–36:

Only Temporary

A

(1) Many businesses in the United States regularly hire "temps" or temporary workers. (2) Now known as the staffing industry, temp work employs nearly 3 million people and generating more than $40 billion annually. (3) Because jobs are no longer secure, many people find that moving from job to job is a good way to improve they're skills. (4) They sometimes find the perfect job and are hired as a full-time employee. (5) Businesses love temps, they save the company money because temps do not receive benefits.

B

(6) Would temp work be a good move for you? (7) If you are the kind of worker who bores quickly and needs new challenges, temping may be the way to go. (8) Temp work may offer a more flexible schedule and it gives a changing work environment. (9) On the down side, you will not get benefits like

paid vacations or health insurance. (10) You may not always be treated very well because temp workers come and go.

C

(11) If you're looking for a job, temp work can add valueable experience to your résumé. (12) It also allows you time to look for and interviewing for a new and permanent job. (13) In addition, temp work is a great way to explore different careers. (14) Many temp jobs are temp-to-hire because the company needs to fill a position and is looking among temp workers for a permanant hire. (15) You may be just the employee they are seeking!

29. Consider the following excerpt from the passage.

Sentence 1: Many businesses in the United States regularly hire "temps" or temporary workers.

What correction should be made to this sentence?

a. Remove the quotation marks from *temps.*
b. Remove or *temporary workers* from the sentence.
c. Change the spelling of *temporary* to *temparary.*
d. Place a comma after *temps.*

30. Consider the following excerpt from the passage.

Sentence 2: Now known as the staffing industry, temp work employs nearly 3 million people and generating more than $40 billion annually.

What correction should be made to this sentence?

a. Change *industry* to *industries.*
b. Change *work* to *works.*
c. Change *employs* to *employing.*
d. Change *generating* to *generates.*

31. Consider the following excerpt from the passage.

Sentence 3: Because jobs are no longer secure, many people find that moving from job to job is a good way to improve they're skills.

What correction should be made to this sentence?

a. Change *Because* to *Since.*
b. Remove the comma after *secure.*
c. Change *skills* to *skill.*
d. Change *they're* to *their.*

32. Consider the following excerpt from the passage.

Sentence 4: They sometimes find the perfect job and <u>are hired as a full-time employee.</u>

Select the best version of the underlined portion.

a. NO CHANGE
b. are hired as full-time employees.
c. is hired as a full-time employee.
d. is hired as a fulltime employee.

33. Consider the following excerpt from the passage.

Sentence 5: Businesses love temps, they save the company money because temps do not receive benefits.

Select the best version of the underlined portion.

a. NO CHANGE
b. Businesses love temps, it saves
c. Businesses love temps; they save
d. Businesses love temps, they saves

34. Consider the following excerpt from the passage.

Sentence 8: Temp work may offer a more flexible schedule and it gives a changing work environment.

Select the best version of the underlined portion.

a. NO CHANGE
b. flexible schedule and it give
c. flexible schedules and it gives
d. flexible schedule, and it gives

35. Consider the following excerpt from the passage.

Sentence 11: If you're looking for a job, temp work can add valueable experience to your résumé.

What correction should be made to this sentence?

a. NO CHANGE
b. Change *you're* to *your*.
c. Change *valueable* to *valuable*.
d. Put a hyphen between *temp* and *work*.

36. What correction should be made to sentence 12?

a. NO CHANGE
b. Change *look* to *looking*.
c. Change *interviewing* to *interview*.
d. Change *permanent* to *permanant*.

Refer to the following for questions 37–39:

(1) In Ruth Campbell's book *Exploring the Titanic*, the events of the famous ship's only journey and sinking are brought to life. (2) In 1912, Titanic was built and was the largest passenger steamship at the time. (3) On what would be its first and only journey, the ship departed from Southampton in England and was supposed to arrive in New York City. (4) The ship hit an iceberg late at night on April 14, 1912, and sunked less than three hours later.

(5) Titanic was designed by some of the best engineers and had the latest technology of the time. (6) The ship was made to carry over three and a half thousand passengers and crew members, but had only twenty lifeboats. (7) There was not enough lifeboats for all of the people onboard, and as a result, only seven hundred six people survived.

(8) One interesting thing about Titanic, is that the ship was divided into classes. (9) The most expensive tickets were first class, and first class passengers had the biggest and much luxurious rooms. (10) The first class rooms were the closest to the ship's deck. (11) Because this the majority of survivors came from first class. (12) They were able to reach the deck fastest to get a seat on a lifeboat. (13) The third class rooms were located the farthest below deck, and the majority of the third class passengers did not survive.

(14) Ruth Campbell's book was very interesting but also sad because the story of Titanic is true. (15) However, Campbell ended the book by talking about the positive things that have happened because of this tragedy. (16) Most importantly, experts now recommend that ships' carry enough lifeboats for all passengers onboard. (17) This would have saved a lot of lifes. (18) It was a good book, and it displayed a good message in history that lessons should be learned from mistakes.

37. Which of the following options improves the precision of language in sentence 7 without adding new information?

a. Due to the limited number of lifeboats on board, only seven hundred six individuals were able to survive the sinking of the Titanic.
b. Titanic had insufficient lifeboats to rescue all passengers, causing the death of more than half of those on board.
c. The lifeboats provided were scarce, with the majority of passengers and crew succumbing to the freezing waters.
d. As a result of inadequate safety measures, only seven hundred six people were rescued from the sinking ship, despite having thousands on board.

38. What is the BEST way to revise and combine sentence 11 and sentence 12?

a. Because, the majority of survivors came from first class as they were able to reach the deck fastest to get a seat on a lifeboat.
b. Because of this, the majority of survivors came from first class, as they were able to reach the deck fastest to get a seat on a lifeboat.
c. Because this, the majority of survivors came from first class, they were able to reach the deck fastest to get a seat on a lifeboat.
d. Because of this, the majority of survivors came from first class as they were able to reach the deck fastest to get a seat on a lifeboat.

39. What is the BEST transition that could be added to the beginning of sentence 13?

a. Lastly
b. For example
c. On the other hand
d. Therefore

Refer to the following for questions 40–43:

Picking the Perfect Pet

A

(1) Today's choices for pets go beyond the question of whether to get a cat or a dog? (2) Gerbils, rabbits, and amphibians is all popular options. (3) Before heading to an animal shelter, you need to know what pet makes sense for your home or classroom. (4) An obvious question to answer if you rent is if pets are permitted. (5) Some apartment complex places weight and size limits on pets or charge fees. (6) After gaining permission from the manager, your pet needs to be considered for other issues.

B

(7) If allergies effect someone in your home, be sure to select a pet that will not aggravate the condition. (8) Some dog breeds like the schnauzer and the poodle are acceptable pets for those who are sensitive to fur and dander.

C

(9) Irregardless of the pet you choose, think about other costs such as veterinary care and vaccinations, food costs, licensing, and equipment. (10) Does the pet need a special kind of home? (11) Who will be responsible for feeding and cleaning up after the animal? (12) Taking time to do a little research can save you a lot of heartache and expense later.

40. Consider the following excerpt from the passage.

Sentence 5: "Some apartment complex places weight and size limits on pets or charge fees."

Select the best version of the underlined portion.

a. NO CHANGE
b. Some apartment complex places wait
c. Some apartment complexes places weight
d. Some apartment complexes place weight

41. What correction should be made to sentence 6?

a. Delete the comma.
b. Change *permission* to *permision*.
c. Rewrite the independent clause.
d. No correction is needed.

42. Consider the following excerpt from the passage.

Sentence 7: "If allergies effect someone in your home, be sure to select a pet that will not aggravate the condition."

Select the best version of the underlined portion.

a. NO CHANGE
b. If allergies affect someone
c. If allergies affects someone
d. If allergies effects someone

43. Consider the following excerpt from the passage.

Sentence 9: "Irregardless of the pet you choose, think about other costs such as veterinary care and vaccinations, food costs, licensing and equipment."

What correction should be made to sentence 9?

a. Change *Irregardless* to *Regardless*.
b. Change *licensing* to *lisencing*.
c. Remove the extra commas.
d. No correction is needed.

Refer to the following for questions 44–51:

Madame President (2010)

A

(1) Before they had the right to vote, women have attempted to gain the nations highest executive office. (2) Victoria Woodhull ran as a third party candidate in 1872. (3) Although she did not win, she became the first woman who owned an investment firm on wall street. (4) In 1884 and 1888, the lawyer Belva Lockwood also ran as a third party candidate. (5) Margaret Chase Smith (who served in both houses of Congress) was the first woman nominated by a major party: the Republicans.

B

(6) Nine other women have seeked for the presidency since the 1970s. (7) Five of them were Democrats and one was a Republican and three represented third parties. (8) I think it's about time this country had a woman as president. (9) Only two women have been nominated as vice president: Democrat Geraldine Ferraro in 1984 and Republican Sarah Palin in 2008. (10) Many people believe that soon the United States will join countries such as Britain, India, Germany, Chile, and Liberia, that have women heads of state.

44. What correction should be made to sentence 1?

a. NO CHANGE
b. Change *nations* to *nation's.*
c. Put *finally* between *to* and *gain.*
d. Capitalize *executive office.*

45. What correction should be made to sentence 3?

a. Change *became* to *become.*
b. Capitalize *wall street.*
c. Change *Although* to *Though.*
d. Capitalize *investment firm.*

46. What correction should be made to sentence 5?

a. NO CHANGE
b. Do not capitalize *Republicans.*
c. Change *woman* to *women.*
d. Change the parentheses to commas.

47. Consider the following excerpt from the passage.

Sentence 6: Nine other <u>women have seeked for</u> the presidency since the 1970s.

Select the best version of the underlined portion

a. NO CHANGE
b. woman have seeked for
c. women have seek for
d. women have sought

48. What correction should be made to sentence 7?

a. NO CHANGE
b. Change *them* to *those.*
c. Change *were* to *was.*
d. Add a comma after *Democrats* and delete the *and* after *Democrats.*

49. Which revision would improve the overall organization of this article?

a. Switch paragraphs A and B.
b. Place the final sentence at the beginning of paragraph B.
c. Delete sentence 8.
d. Place sentence 2 at the end of paragraph A.

50. What correction should be made to sentence 9?

a. NO CHANGE
b. Capitalize *vice president.*
c. Remove the colon.
d. Remove *Only* from the sentence.

51. What correction should be made to sentence 10?

a. NO CHANGE
b. Remove the unnecessary commas.
c. Change the spelling of *believe* to *beleive.*
d. Remove the comma after *Liberia.*

Refer to the following for questions 52–60:

(1) Could the future of crops include planting without soil? (2) The concept of hydroponics, or growing plants by directly exposing the roots to water and nutrients, both conserving resources such as water and stimulating extra growth and food production.

(3) While this concept sounds new and innovative—and in fact has being extensively studied by NASA in recent years—the idea is not original to the past decade, or even the past century. (4) Books were published, as early as the 17th century, discussing the idea of growing plants without the traditional concept of planting them in the earth. (5) The term "hydroponics" was first introduced in 1937 by William Gericke, who grew tomatoes in his back yard in a solution of minerals. (6) Since this time, numerous experiments have been conducted and some large hydroponics farms have even been constructed.

(7) Rather than soil, plants are grown in a variety of substitutes; such as rockwool, clay pellets, pumice, wood fiber, or even packing peanuts. (8) These allow the roots easy access to both the nutrient-rich water and to oxygen.

(9) There are many advantages to hydroponic farming. (10) Due to the controlled greenhouse environment, crops can be grown and no pesticides. (11) There is also less waste of water because of no run-off. (12) Furthermore, proponents of hydroponics claim that this method can lead to much greater yields. (13) This is due not only to the better nutrition but additionally to the protection from harsh weather conditions and pests. (14) Additionally, hydroponics farmers are not limited to a single crop during the normal growing season, they can produce year-round.

(15) In addition, hydroponics does have disadvantages. (16) Before beginning, a farmer must have a greenhouse with proper growing stations and temperature control. (17) Soil replacement, nutrients, and specialized lighting must also be purchased. (18) Finally, removing exposure to the outdoor environment means that the farmer must eliminate needs such as pollination. (19) The setup for growing without soil is costly.

(20) Despite the disadvantages, hydroponics is likely to become more popular in coming years. (21) Not only can crops be grown year-round, but plants can also be much closer together, or even grown vertically, allowing for a much greater yield per acre. (22) Additionally, hydroponics may have implications in other areas. (23) For example, NASA has done research with hydroponics to mimic a

Martian environment. (24) So while the work and expense of soil-less gardening is significant, this market, which is already in the hundreds of millions of dollars worldwide, may be a glimpse of the future of farming.

52. Consider the following excerpt from the passage:

Sentence 2: The concept of hydroponics, or growing plants by directly exposing the roots to water and nutrients, both conserving resources such as water and stimulating extra growth and food production.

Select the best version of the underlined portion.

a. NO CHANGE
b. allows farmers to both conserve resources
c. aids in both conserving resources
d. both conserves resources

53. Consider the following excerpt from the passage.

Sentence 3: While this concept sounds new and innovative—and in fact has being extensively studied by NASA in recent years—the idea is not original to the past decade, or even the past century.

Select the best version of the underlined portion.

a. NO CHANGE
b. has been
c. is been
d. having been

54. Consider the following excerpt from the passage.

Sentence 4: Books were published, as early as the 17th century, discussing the idea of growing plants without the traditional concept of planting them in the earth.

Select the best version of the underlined portion.

a. NO CHANGE
b. Books, as early as the 17th century, were published:
c. As early as the 17th century, books were published
d. Books were published as early as the 17th century—

55. Consider the following excerpt from the passage.

Sentence 7: Rather than soil, plants are grown in a variety of substitutes; such as rockwool, clay pellets, pumice, wood fiber, or even packing peanuts.

Select the best version of the underlined portion.

a. NO CHANGE
b. substitutes, such
c. substitutes: like
d. substitutes, like

56. Consider the following excerpt from the passage.

Sentence 13: This is due not only to the better nutrition but additionally to the protection from harsh weather conditions and pests.

Select the best version of the underlined portion.

a. NO CHANGE
b. in addition
c. even to
d. in also to

57. Consider the following excerpt from the passage.

Sentence 15: In addition, hydroponics does have disadvantages.

Select the best version of the underlined portion.

a. NO CHANGE
b. Comparatively
c. Moreover
d. However

58. Consider the following excerpt from the passage.

Sentence 18: Finally, removing exposure to the outdoor environment means that the farmer must eliminate needs such as pollination.

Select the best version of the underlined portion.

a. NO CHANGE
b. track
c. provide for
d. remove

59. Consider the following excerpt from the passage.

Sentence 21: Not only can crops be grown year-round, but plants can also be much closer together, or even grown vertically, allowing for a much greater yield per acre.

Select the best version of the underlined portion.

a. NO CHANGE
b. in a vertical manner
c. vertical
d. horizontal

60. Consider the following excerpt from the passage.

Sentence 22: Additionally, hydroponics farmers are not limited to a single crop during the normal growing season, they can produce year-round.

Select the best version of the underlined portion.

a. NO CHANGE
b. season, or they
c. season, then they
d. season; they

Essay Question

1. On the test, you will have a timed essay portion. Your essay will be graded primarily on the following:

- How well you develop your main idea, using supporting details and examples
- How clearly you organize and explain your points and how cohesively your paragraphs fit together
- How well you exhibit a command of the English language, including grammar and sentence structure

<u>Black History Month</u>

Black History Month began as Negro History Week, established by black historian Carter G. Woodson in 1926. Fifty years later, in 1976, the week was expanded to encompass the month of February. Opinions differ on whether its continued observance is the best way to ensure a shared knowledge, interest, and respect for all that is encompassed in African American history.

Passage 1: "An Outdated Ritual"

Black History Month is unnecessary. In a place and time in which we overwhelmingly elected an African American president, we can and should move to a post-racial approach to education. As *Detroit Free Press* columnist Rochelle Riley wrote in a February 1 column calling for an end to Black History Month, "I propose that, for the first time in American history, this country has reached a point where we can stop celebrating separately, stop learning separately, stop being American separately."

In addition to being unnecessary, the idea that African American history should be focused on in a given month suggests that it belongs in that month alone. It is important to instead incorporate African American history into what is taught every day as American history. It needs to be recreated as part of mainstream thought and not as an optional, often irrelevant, side note. We should focus efforts on pushing schools to diversify and broaden their curricula.

There are a number of other reasons to abolish it: first, it has become a shallow commercial ritual that does not even succeed in its (limited and misguided) goal of focusing for one month on a sophisticated, intelligent appraisal of the contributions and experiences of African Americans throughout history. Second, there is a paternalistic flavor to the mandated bestowing of a month in which to study African American history that is overcome if we instead assert the need for a comprehensive curriculum. Third, the idea of Black History Month suggests that the knowledge imparted in that month is for African Americans only, rather than for all people.

Passage 2: "Let the Celebration Continue"

Black History Month is still an important observance. Despite the important achievement of the election of our first African American president, the need for knowledge and education about African American history is still unmet to a substantial degree. Black History Month is a powerful tool in working towards meeting that need. There is no reason to give up that tool now, and it can easily coexist with an effort to develop a more comprehensive and inclusive yearly curriculum.

Having a month set aside for the study of African American history doesn't limit its study and celebration to that month; it merely focuses complete attention on it for that month. There is absolutely no contradiction between having a set-aside month and having it be present in the curriculum the rest of the year. Equally important is that the debate *itself* about the usefulness of Black History Month can, and should, remind parents that they can't necessarily count on schools to teach African American history as thoroughly as many parents would want.

Although Black History Month has, to an extent, become a shallow ritual, it doesn't have to be. Good teachers and good materials could make the February curriculum deeply informative, thought-provoking, and inspiring. The range of material that can be covered is rich, varied, and full of limitless possibilities.

Finally, it is worthwhile to remind ourselves and our children of the key events that happened during the month of February. In 1926, Woodson organized the first Black History Week to honor the birthdays of essential civil rights activists Abraham Lincoln and Frederick Douglass. W. E. B. DuBois was born on February 23, 1868. The 15th Amendment, which granted African Americans the right to vote, was passed on February 3, 1870. The first black US senator, Hiram R. Revels, took his oath of office on February 25, 1870. The National Association for the Advancement of Colored People (NAACP) was founded on February 12, 1909. Malcolm X was shot on February 21, 1965.

Write an essay to explain your position on the issue of the relevance of Black History Month and what should be done to promote greater understanding of African-American history.

In order to support your position, you will need to use examples from the provided passages and from your own experience. Be sure to acknowledge other viewpoints while you attempt to persuade readers of your own viewpoint. Try to leave time for reviewing your work and making any corrections to spelling, punctuation, or grammar as needed.

Mathematics

1. Jamie had $6.50 in his wallet when he left home. He spent $4.25 on drinks and $2.00 on a magazine. Later, his friend repaid him $2.50 that he had borrowed the previous day. How much money does Jamie have in his wallet now?

a. $2.75
b. $3.25
c. $12.25
d. $14.25

2. Two even integers and one odd integer are multiplied together. Which of the following could be their product?

a. 3.75
b. 9
c. 16.2
d. 24

3. Jerry needs to load 4 pieces of equipment onto a factory elevator that has a weight limit of 800 pounds. Jerry weighs 200 pounds. What would the average weight of each item have to be so that the elevator's weight limit is not exceeded, assuming Jerry accompanies the equipment?

a. 128 pounds
b. 150 pounds
c. 175 pounds
d. 180 pounds

4. Rachel spent $24.15 on produce. She bought 2 pounds of onions, 3 pounds of carrots, and $1\frac{1}{2}$ pounds of mushrooms. If the onions cost $3.69 per pound and the carrots cost $4.29 per pound, what is the price per pound of mushrooms?

a. $2.25
b. $2.60
c. $2.80
d. $3.10

5. In a sequence of prime numbers from least to greatest, which prime number immediately follows 67?

a. 68
b. 69
c. 71
d. 73

6. Dean's Department Store reduces the price of a $30 shirt by 20% but later raises it again by 20% of the sale price. What is the final price of the shirt?

a. $24.40
b. $28.80
c. $30
d. $32

7. In an election in Kimball County, Candidate A obtained 36,800 votes. His opponent, Candidate B, obtained 32,100 votes. Write-in candidates obtained 2,100 votes. What percentage of the vote went to Candidate A?

a. 45.2%
b. 46.8%
c. 51.8%
d. 53.4%

Refer to the following for question 8:

The following diagram of a circle has O as the center, and OA and OC are radii:

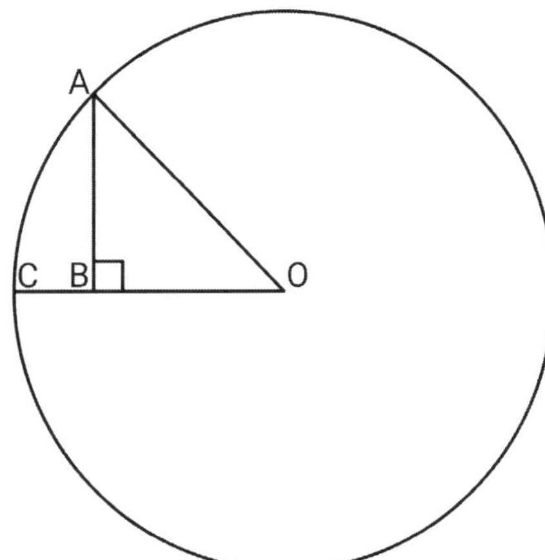

8. If the length of segment $AB = x$, and the length of segment $OB = y$, which of the following expressions describes the radius of the circle?

a. $x + y$
b. $x^2 + y^2$
c. $y + 4$
d. $\sqrt{x^2 + y^2}$

9. If $x = 2y - 3$ and $2x + \frac{1}{2}y = 3$, then what is the value of y?

a. $-\frac{2}{3}$
b. 1
c. 2
d. $\frac{18}{7}$

10. The figure shows an irregular quadrilateral and the lengths of its sides. Which of the following expressions best represents the perimeter of the quadrilateral?

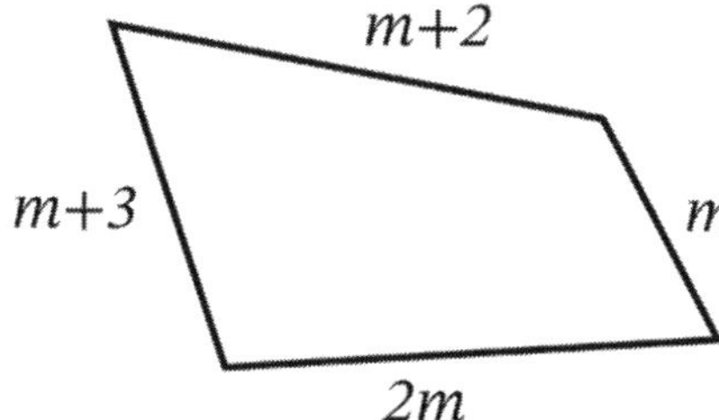

a. $m^4 + 5$
b. $2m^4 + 5$
c. $4m + 5$
d. $5m + 5$

11. A bag contains 14 blue, 6 red, 12 green, and 8 purple buttons. 25 buttons are removed from the bag randomly. How many of the removed buttons were red if the chance of drawing a red button from the bag is now $\frac{1}{3}$?

a. 0 buttons
b. 1 button
c. 3 buttons
d. 5 buttons

12. One method for calculating the area of a circle is to dissect it into a number of wedges. The circle below has a radius *r* and has been evenly dissected into 16 wedges.

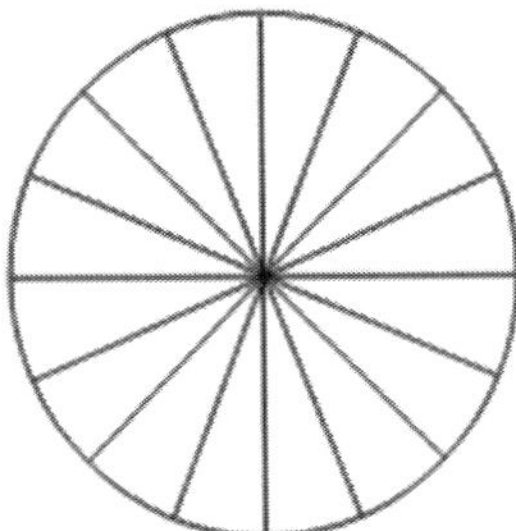

If the wedges are rearranged alternately to create a shape resembling a rectangle, as shown below, what is the approximate length of the rectangle?

a. π
b. πr
c. r
d. πr^2

13. If $\frac{x}{8} = \frac{y}{4} = 4$, what is the value of $x - y$?

a. 8
b. 16
c. 32
d. 48

Refer to the following for question 14:

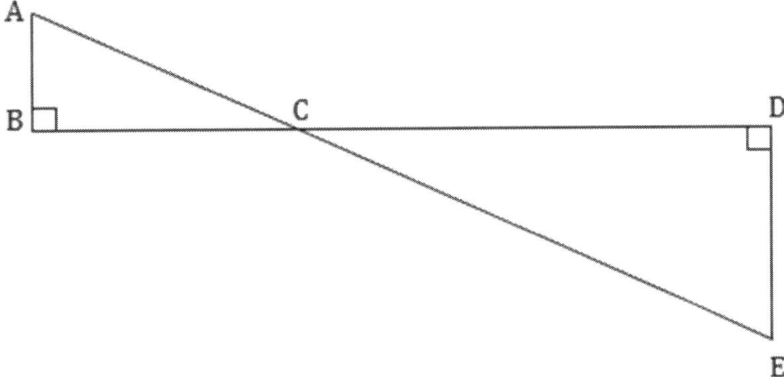

14. In the figure above, $\overline{BC}$ is 4 units long. Segment $\overline{CD}$ is 8 units long. Segment $\overline{DE}$ is 6 units long. What is the length of segment $\overline{AC}$?

a. 7 units
b. 5 units
c. 3 units
d. 2.5 units

15. Which of the following figures shows parallelogram $WXYZ$ being carried onto its image $W'X'Y'Z'$ by a reflection across the x-axis?

a.

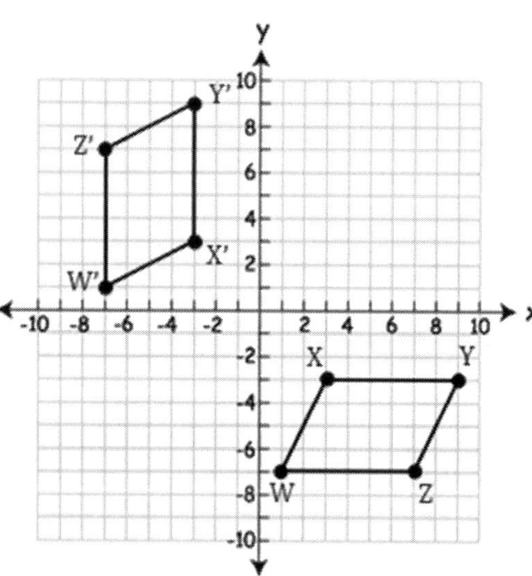

b.

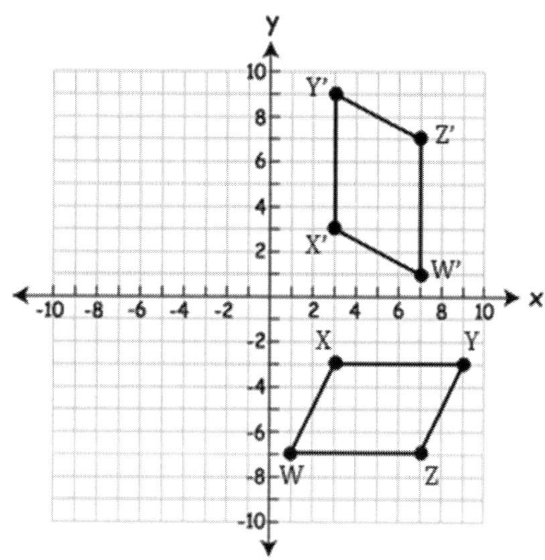

c.

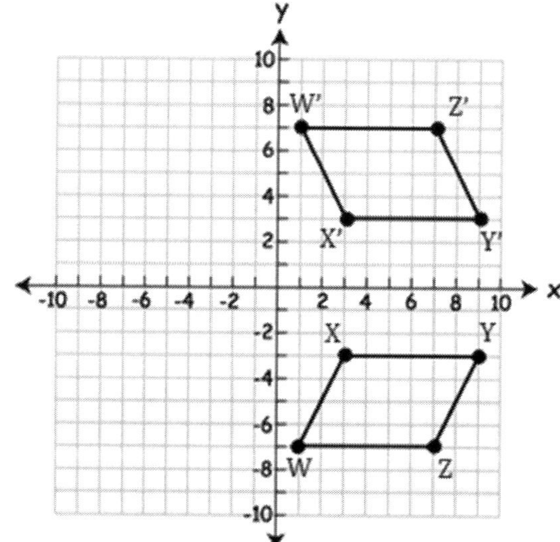

d.

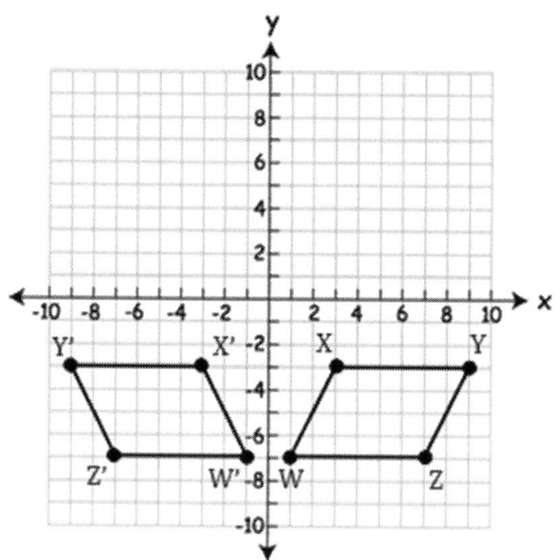

16. The scientific notation for the diameter of a red blood cell is approximately 7.4×10^{-4} centimeters. What is that amount in standard form?

a. 0.00074 cm
b. 0.0074 cm
c. 740 cm
d. 74,000 cm

17. In the figure below, ΔJKL is dilated to the image $\Delta J'\,K'\,L'$.

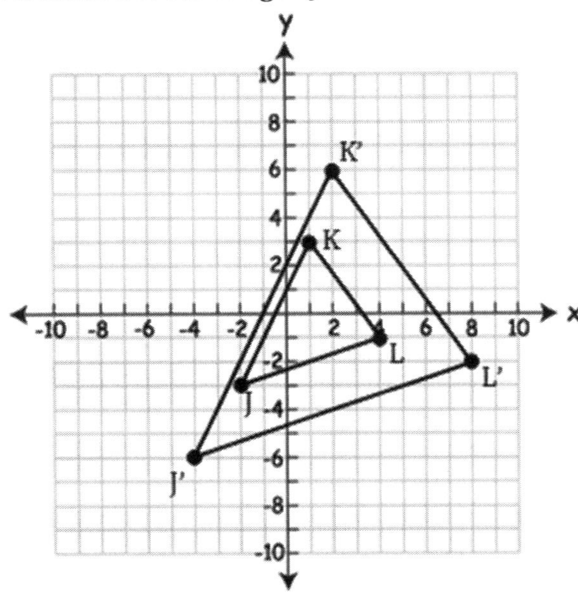

What is the scale factor of the dilation?

a. $\frac{1}{3}$
b. $\frac{1}{2}$
c. 2
d. 3

18. Simplify $(3 \times 10^4) \times (2 \times 10^5)$.

a. 5×10^9
b. 5×10^{20}
c. 6×10^9
d. 6×10^{20}

19. Which of the following represents the factors of the expression $x^2 + 3x - 28$?

a. $(x - 14)(x + 2)$
b. $(x + 6)(x - 3)$
c. $(x + 4)(x - 1)$
d. $(x - 4)(x + 7)$

20. Which of the following is a solution to the inequality $4x - 12 < 4$?

a. 7
b. 6
c. 4
d. 3

21. Which of the following is equivalent to $27x^3 + y^3$?

a. $(3x + y)(3x + y)(3x + y)$
b. $(3x + y)(9x^2 - 3xy + y^2)$
c. $(3x - y)(9x^2 + 3xy + y^2)$
d. $(3x - y)(9x^2 + 9xy + y^2)$

22. Given $x^2 - 7x + 10 \geq 0$, what is the solution set for x?

a. $2 \leq x \leq 5$
b. $x \leq 2$ or $x \geq 5$
c. $7 \leq x \leq 10$
d. $x \leq 7$ or $x \geq 10$

23. A bag contains 8 red marbles, 3 blue marbles, and 4 green marbles. What is the probability Carlos draws a red marble, does not replace it, and then draws another red marble?

a. $\frac{2}{15}$
b. $\frac{4}{15}$
c. $\frac{32}{105}$
d. $\frac{64}{225}$

Refer to the following for question 24:

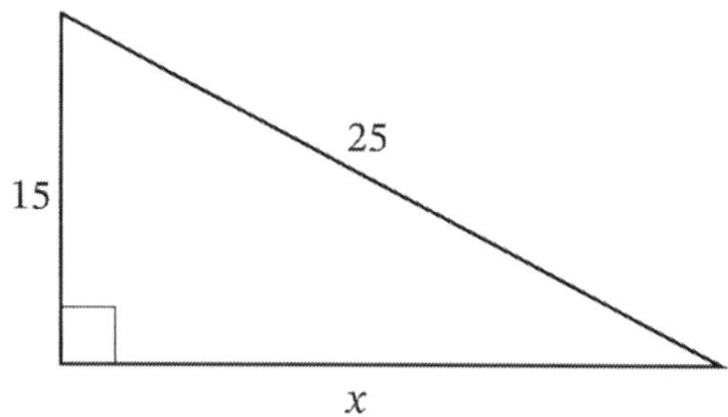

24. What is the length of the side labeled x?

a. 18
b. 20
c. 22
d. 24

25. Matthew has to earn more than 96 points on his high school entrance exam in order to be eligible for varsity sports. Each question is worth 3 points, and the test has a total of 40 questions. Let x represent the number of test questions Matthew does NOT answer correctly. How many questions can Matthew answer incorrectly and still qualify for varsity sports?

a. $x > 32$
b. $x > 8$
c. $0 \leq x < 8$
d. $0 \leq x \leq 8$

26. Under the condition that $x > y$, which of the following CANNOT be true following the inequality $x + y > 0$?

a. $x = 3$ and $y = 0$
b. $x = 6$ and $y = -1$
c. $x = -3$ and $y = 0$
d. $x = 3$ and $y = -3$

27. **If $7\sqrt{x} + 16 = 79$, what is the value of x?**

a. 6
b. 9
c. 27
d. 81

28. **If $\frac{12}{x} = \frac{30}{6}$, what is the value of x?**

a. 3.6
b. 3.0
c. 2.4
d. 2.0

29. **Which of the following could be a graph of the function $y = \frac{1}{x}$?**

a. 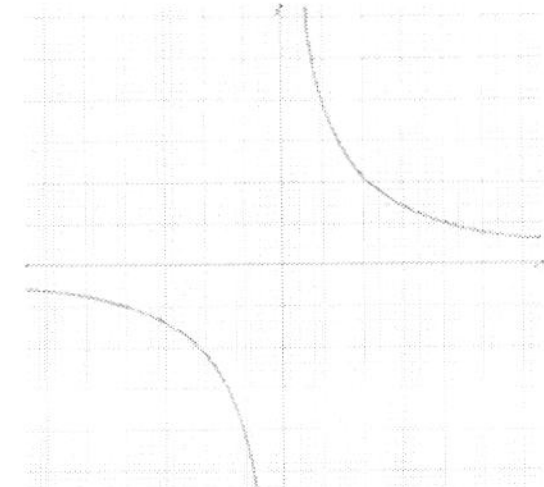

b. 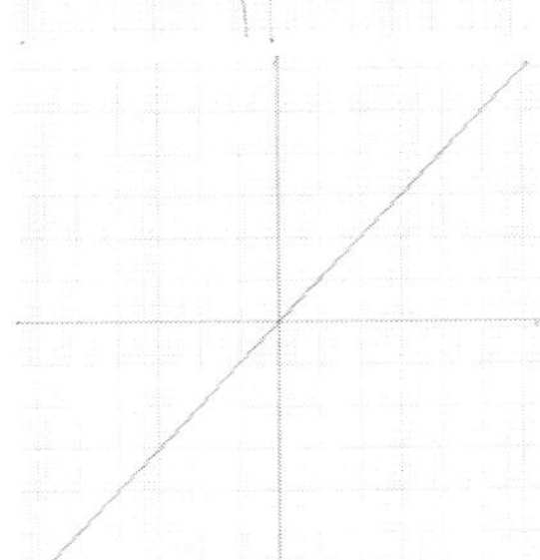

c. 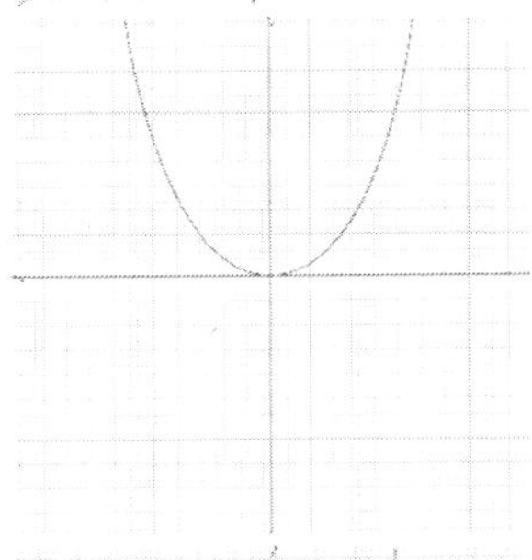

d. 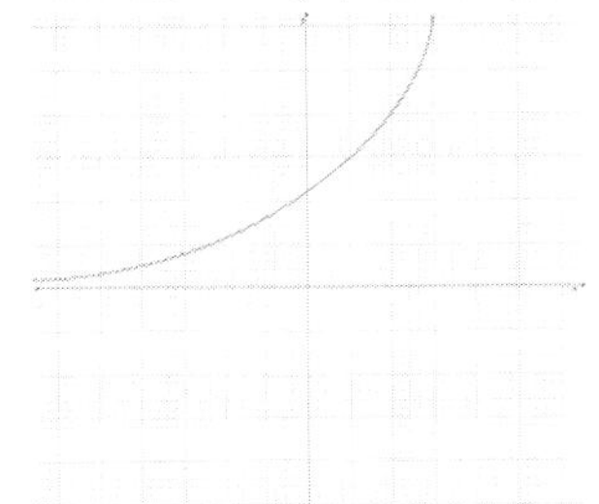

Refer to the following for question 30:

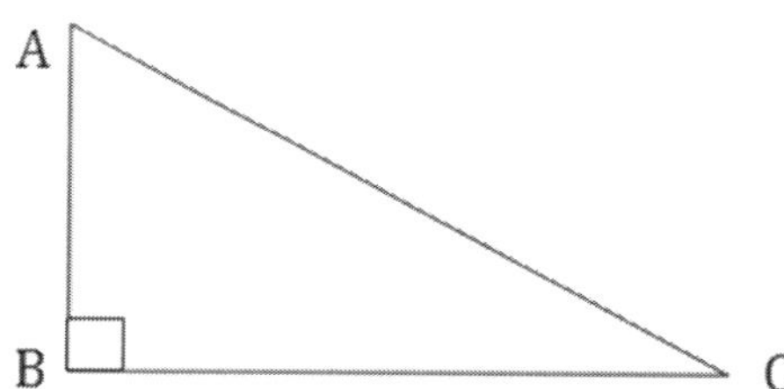

30. ΔABC is a right triangle, and $\angle ACB = 30°$. What is the measure of $\angle BAC$?

a. 40°
b. 45°
c. 50°
d. 60°

31. The table below shows the cost of renting a bicycle for 1, 2, or 3 hours. Which answer choice shows the equation that best represents the data? Let C represent the cost of the rental and h stand for the number of hours of rental time.

Hours	1	2	3
Cost	$3.60	$7.20	$10.80

a. $C = 3.60h$
b. $C = h + 3.60$
c. $C = 3.60h + 10.80$
d. $C = \frac{10.80}{h}$

32. Determine the midpoint of the line shown in the figure.

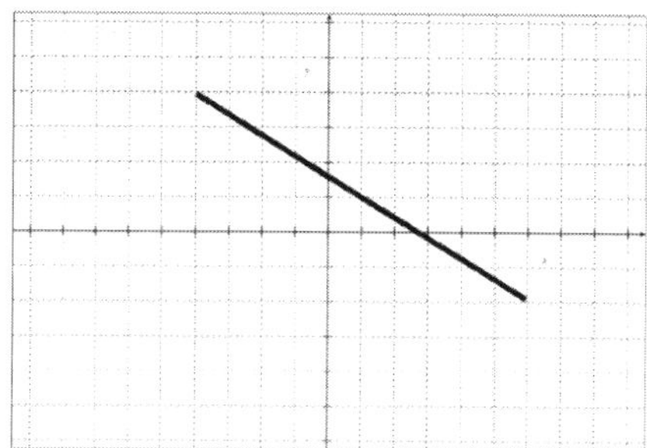

a. (2,2)
b. (6, −2)
c. (1,1)
d. (−4,4)

33. Which of the following statements is true?

a. Perpendicular lines have opposite slopes.
b. Perpendicular lines have the same slopes.
c. Perpendicular lines have reciprocal slopes.
d. Perpendicular lines have opposite reciprocal slopes.

34. Which of the following represents the expected value of the number of tails Adam will get after tossing a coin 6 times?

a. 2
b. 3
c. 6
d. 12

35. Simplify $(8 \times 10^3) + (1 \times 10^3)$.

a. 8×10^3
b. 8×10^6
c. 9×10^3
d. 9×10^6

36. Which function represents the graph?

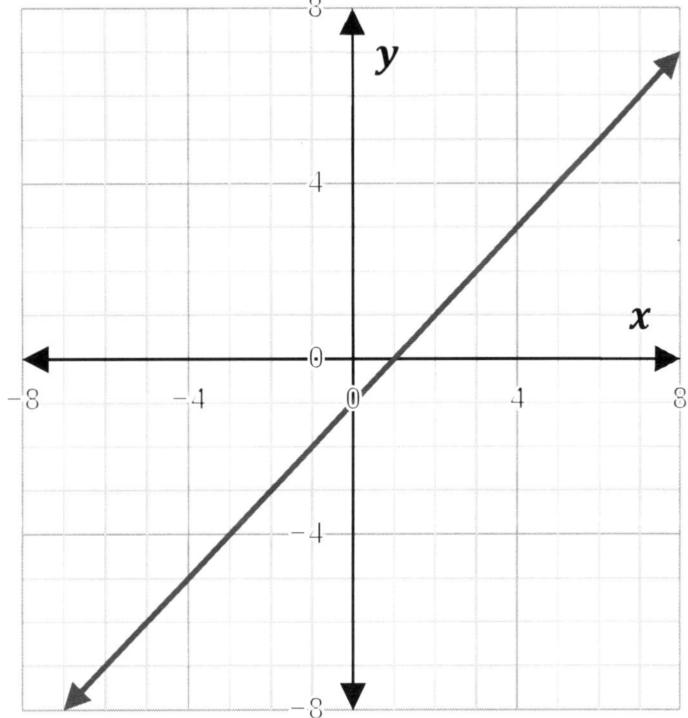

a. $y = x + 1$
b. $y = x - 1$
c. $y = -x + 1$
d. $y = -x - 1$

37. Solve $(3x + 1)(7x + 10)$

a. $12x^2 + 17x + 10$
b. $21x^2 + 37x + 10$
c. $21x^2 + 23x + 10$
d. $21x^2 + 37x + 9$

HiSET Practice Test #1

38. In a game of chance, 3 dice are thrown at the same time. What is the probability that all three will land on a 6?

a. $\frac{1}{6}$
b. $\frac{1}{18}$
c. $\frac{1}{30}$
d. $\frac{1}{216}$

39. Rafael has a business selling computers. He buys computers from the manufacturer for $450 each and sells them for $800. Each month, he must also pay fixed costs of $3,000 for rent and utilities for his store. If he sells n computers in a month, which of the following equations can be used to find his profit?

a. $P = n(\$800 - \$450)$
b. $P = n(\$800 - \$450 - \$3{,}000)$
c. $P = \$3{,}000 \times n(\$800 - \$450)$
d. $P = n(\$800 - \$450) - \$3{,}000$

40. How many solutions does the equation $6x + 1 = 4x + 9$ have?

a. None
b. One
c. Two
d. Infinitely many solutions

41. If $\frac{4}{x-3} - \frac{2}{x} = 1$, then what is the value of x?

a. -6
b. -1
c. -6 or -1
d. -1 or 6

42. Which of the following expressions is equivalent to $\frac{2+3i}{4-2i}$?

a. $\frac{1}{10} + \frac{4}{5}i$
b. $\frac{1}{10}$
c. $\frac{7}{6} + \frac{2}{3}i$
d. $\frac{1}{10} + \frac{3}{10}i$

43. If $a \neq 0$, then $12a^2b \div 3a = ?$

a. $4b$
b. $4ab$
c. $9b^2$
d. $9ab$

44. If $\sqrt{3x-2} = x - 2$, then what is the value of x?

a. 1
b. 6
c. -1 or 6
d. 1 or 6

45. What are the dependent and independent variables in the graph below?

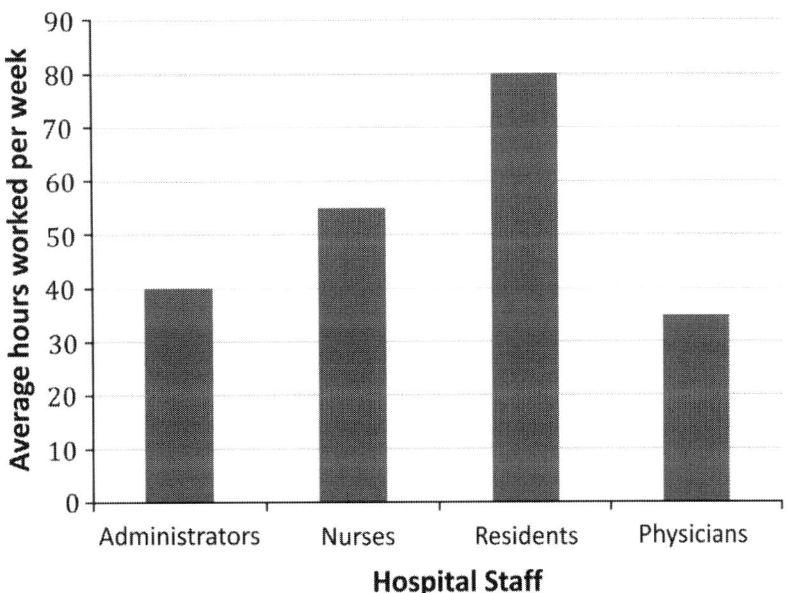

a. The dependent variable is nurses. The independent variable is physicians.
b. The dependent variable is physicians. The independent variable is nurses.
c. The dependent variable is hospital staff. The independent variable is average hours worked per week.
d. The dependent variable is average hours worked per week. The independent variable is hospital staff.

46. Given that $i = \sqrt{-1}$, What is the expression $-2i \times 7i$ equal to?

a. -14
b. 14
c. $14i$
d. $-14i$

47. Which of the following expressions is equivalent to $(a + b)(a - b)$?

a. $a^2 - b^2$
b. $(a + b)^2$
c. $(a - b)^2$
d. $ab(a - b)$

48. If the square of twice the sum of x and three is equal to the product of twenty-four and x, which of these is a possible value of x?

a. $6 + 3\sqrt{2}$
b. $\frac{3}{2}$
c. $-3i$
d. -3

Refer to the following for questions 49–50:

Kyle bats third in the batting order for the Badgers baseball team. The table below shows the number of hits that Kyle had in each of 7 consecutive games played during one week in July.

Day	Monday	Tuesday	Wednesday	Thursday	Friday	Saturday	Sunday
Hits	1	2	3	1	1	4	2

49. What is the mode of the numbers in the distribution shown in the table?

a. 1
b. 2
c. 3
d. 4

50. What is the mean of the numbers in the distribution shown in the table?

a. 1
b. 2
c. 3
d. 4

51. Solve $\frac{x-2}{x-1} = \frac{x-1}{x+1} + \frac{2}{x-1}$.

a. $x = 2$
b. $x = -5$
c. $x = 1$
d. No solution

52. Which of these is NOT a net of a cube?

a. b.  c. d.

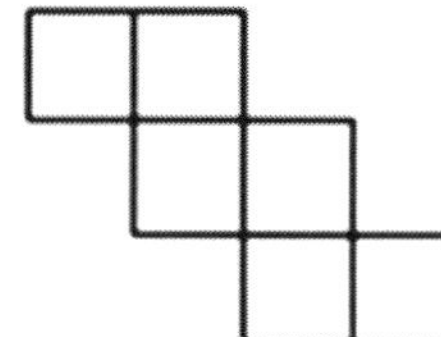
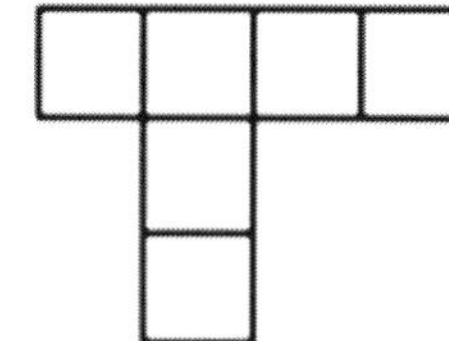
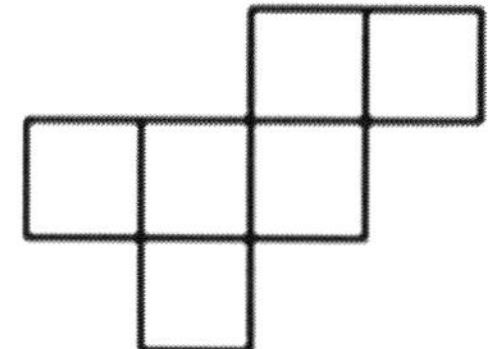
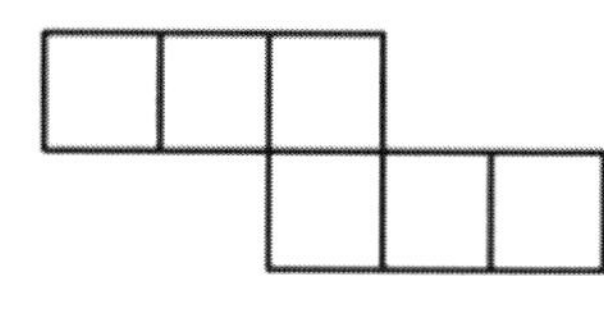

53. A man standing on a flat, level surface casts a shadow that is 6.2 ft in length. The man is 5.8 ft tall. Which of the following best represents the distance from the top of his head to the end of the shadow?

a. 7 ft
b. 7.5 ft
c. 8 ft
d. 8.5 ft

54. If the midpoint of a line segment graphed on the xy-coordinate plane is $(3, -1)$ and the slope of the line segment is -2, which of these is a possible endpoint of the line segment?

a. $(-1,1)$
b. $(0, -5)$
c. $(7,1)$
d. $(5, -5)$

55. $A = \{5, 9, 2, 3, -1, 8\}$ **and** $B = \{2, 0, 4, 5, 6, 8\}$. **What is** $A \cap B$?

a. $\{5, 2, 8\}$
b. $\{-1, 0, 2, 3, 4, 5, 6, 8, 9\}$
c. $\emptyset$
d. $\{5, 8\}$

Science

Refer to the following for questions 1–5:

An *exoplanet* is a planet orbiting a star other than our sun. The technology and techniques to detect and observe exoplanets have only recently been developed, but already thousands of exoplanets have been identified. Most exoplanets that have been discovered so far are gas giants, but the proportion of terrestrial planets closer to the size of Earth may be much larger than represented in these discoveries.

The most widely used method for the detection of extrasolar planets is called transit photometry. As a planet passes in front of the star it orbits, relative to the Earth, it obscures part of the star's light, and to observers on Earth, the star seems to dim slightly. The change in the flux of light detected from the star is called the transit depth. From the transit depth, the size of the planet relative to the size of the star can be determined.

The two graphs below show measurements from observations by transit photometry for two exoplanets around different stars.

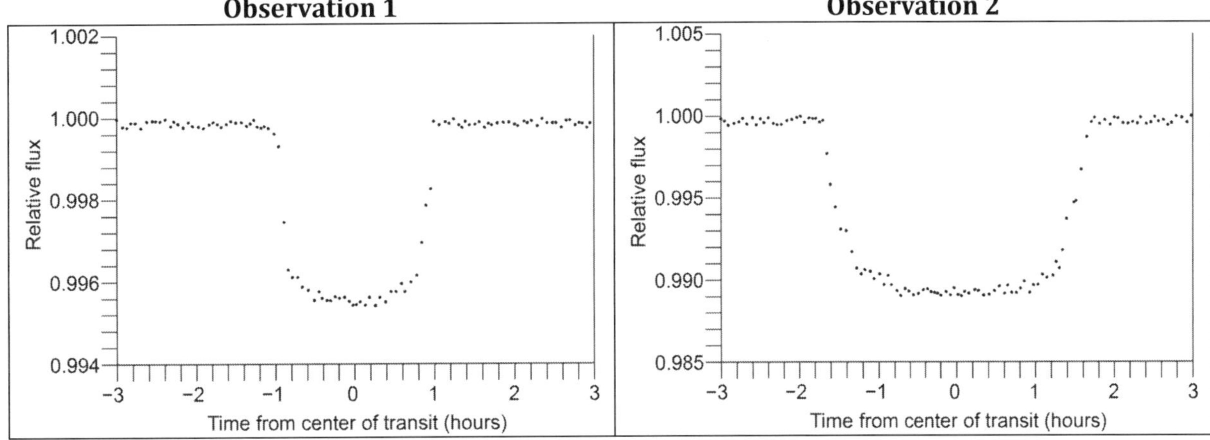

1. Which of the observations corresponds to a planet with a larger radius?

a. Observation 1
b. Observation 2
c. It is impossible to tell from these graphs without knowing the radii of the planets' orbits.
d. It is impossible to tell from these graphs without knowing the radii of the stars the planets are orbiting.

2. About how long did it take the planet in Observation 1 to cross in front of its parent star?

a. One hour
b. Two hours
c. Three hours
d. Six hours

HiSET Practice Test #1

3. The passage says that although most observed exoplanets have been gas giants, the actual proportion of gas giants among exoplanets may be smaller than this suggests. What is the MOST likely reason for this discrepancy?

a. Terrestrial planets are shorter-lived than gas giants.
b. Gas giants are easier to observe than terrestrial planets.
c. Gas giants are disproportionately common in the part of the galaxy near Earth.
d. Astronomers are less interested in terrestrial planets and may fail to record observations of them.

4. Which observation could convince an astronomer that a reduction in the luminosity of a star is caused by an orbiting exoplanet and is NOT a false positive produced by some other object that happens to pass between the star and Earth?

a. The reduction in luminosity repeats at regular intervals.
b. The graph of relative flux over time has a characteristic U shape.
c. The reduction in luminosity is greater than 5% of the average luminosity.
d. The reduction in luminosity is smaller than 1% of the average luminosity.

5. What is a possible limitation of transit photometry as a method for detecting exoplanets?

a. It can only detect exoplanets around stars near the Sun.
b. It can only detect exoplanets around stars near the galactic equator.
c. It can only detect exoplanets with orbits parallel to the line of sight from Earth.
d. It cannot distinguish multiple planets in orbit about a single star.

Refer to the following for questions 6–10:

A new species of frog colonizes a tropical lake, and an ecologist wants to study its population growth over time. To do so, the ecologist counts the number of frogs in a given area of the lake over a series of months. The data are plotted below.

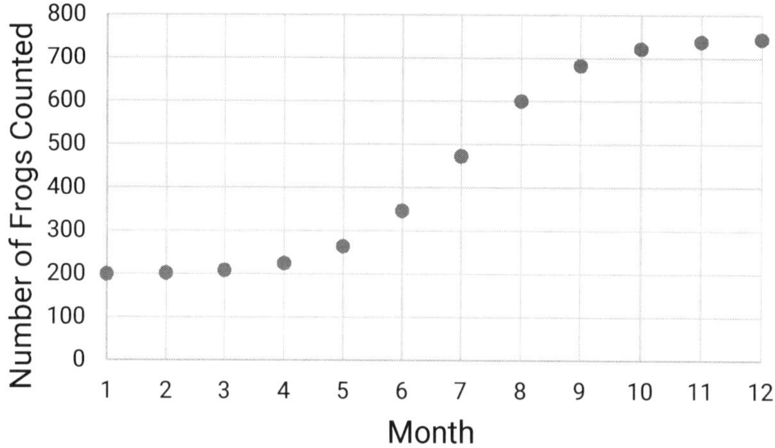

During the third month of observation, the scientist notices that the numbers of another species of frog in the lake are also changing and decides to count its numbers as well. Below is a graph of the data for frog species 2.

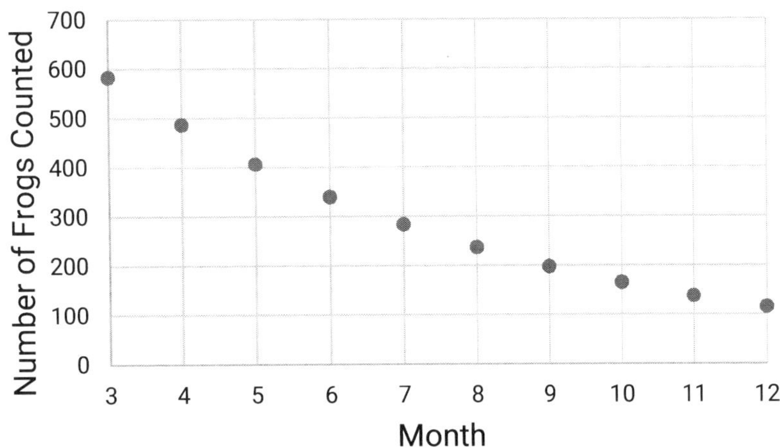

6. Which statement best describes the change in the population of frog species 1?

a. Its numbers grow exponentially.
b. Its numbers grow at a constant rate.
c. Its numbers first grow and then decline.
d. Its numbers first grow rapidly and then level off.

7. In what month were the populations of frog species 1 and 2 closest to equal?

a. Month 2
b. Month 4
c. Month 6
d. Month 8

8. During what month did the numbers of species 1 change most rapidly?

a. Month 1
b. Month 4
c. Month 7
d. Month 10

9. Assuming that the trend shown in the graph continues, how is the population of frog species 1 likely to change after month 12?

a. It will increase rapidly.
b. It will decrease rapidly.
c. It will oscillate between high and low values.
d. It will stay roughly constant.

10. What is a possible explanation for the change in the relative population of the two species of frog, as shown by the ecologist's graphs?

a. The two species of frog cooperate to increase each other's success.
b. Species 1 is outcompeting species 2 for food or other vital resources.
c. Species 2 is outcompeting species 1 for food or other vital resources.
d. Together, the two species overtax the lake's resources, causing both species to decline.

Refer to the following for questions 11–15:

A student interested in rocketry decides to test the relationship of a rocket's mass to the peak velocity it can attain, all else being equal. The student reasons that because the impulse provided by the engine does not depend on the rocket's mass, and because impulse equals mass times change in velocity, the rocket's peak velocity should be inversely proportional to the rocket's mass.

To test the hypothesis, the student acquires six identical model rockets. The student outfits each rocket with a sensor to measure its velocity and attaches weights to increase their mass, distributing the weight as evenly as possible. The student fires each rocket, records its peak velocity, and obtains the following data:

Trial	Mass of rocket	Peak velocity
1	125 g	180 m/s
2	250 g	85 m/s
3	500 g	34 m/s
4	1.0 kg	8 m/s
5	1.5 kg	Rocket failed to launch
6	2.0 kg	Rocket failed to launch

11. Did the data support the student's hypothesis?

a. Yes; the rockets' peak velocities were inversely proportional to their masses.
b. No; the peak velocity did not decrease as the rockets' mass increased.
c. No; the peak velocity did decrease as the rockets' mass increased but not proportionately.
d. The data the student collected was unrelated to the student's hypothesis and neither supported nor contradicted it.

12. What is the most likely reason that the last two rockets failed to launch?

a. They did not have sufficient acceleration to overcome the Earth's gravity.
b. The mass of the rockets prevented the fuel from igniting.
c. Their velocity was canceled by the speed of the Earth's rotation.
d. The rockets did in fact launch, but their velocities were too small to measure with the student's instruments.

13. Which quantity, had the student measured it, probably would have exhibited a similar trend to the peak velocity?

a. Minimum velocity of the rocket
b. Maximum altitude of the rocket
c. Rotation of the rocket
d. Radius of the rocket

14. If the student had done a trial with a rocket with a mass of 750 g, what would have been the most likely result for the peak velocity?

a. 68 m/s
b. 30 m/s
c. 25 m/s
d. 17 m/s

15. After the experiment, the student looks up the expected thrust, impulse, and burn time of the type of rocket used and, with those values, calculates the expected final velocity—which does not match the experimental results. However, reading up further on rocketry after the experiment, the student realizes something that was overlooked in the initial reasoning: the mass of a rocket is not constant but decreases as the fuel is expended. How would the previous calculations have been off if he used the rockets' initial mass and did not take into account the change?

a. The calculated velocities would have been too low.
b. The calculated velocities would have been too high.
c. The calculated velocities would not have been affected by this detail.
d. Some of the calculated velocities would have been too low and others too high, depending on the rockets' masses.

Refer to the following for questions 16–20:

Genetic profiling refers to the analysis of an individual's DNA, either for the purpose of identifying specific genes that might imply a risk of inherited conditions or to compare two DNA samples to see how well they match.

One method of genetic profiling involves first heating the DNA sample to separate the strands. Then, small bits of DNA called primers are added. The primers bind to the selected regions of interest, which are called markers, and then these regions are duplicated with an enzyme called a DNA polymerase. Finally, the replicated DNA samples are subjected to a process called gel electrophoresis: an electric current is used to move the DNA fragments through a gel, and the distance they move depends on the size of the fragment. Finally, the DNA fragments are dyed to form visible bands. If the bands in two DNA samples match, they likely came from the same person. Genetic profiling can also be used to determine paternity—because a person's genes come from his or her parents, each band in the DNA profile must match a band from either the person's mother or father. (There may be exceptions due to mutated genes, but they are rare enough not to play a major role.) Identifying siblings is more difficult because a child may get genes from either parent, and the number of markers shared by two siblings is unpredictable. (In principle, we would expect siblings to share about half their markers on average, but unless a large number of markers are used, there is too much variability for this to be reliable.)

Consider the following DNA profiles. Profile 2 represents the DNA profile of the mother of the individual in DNA profile 1.

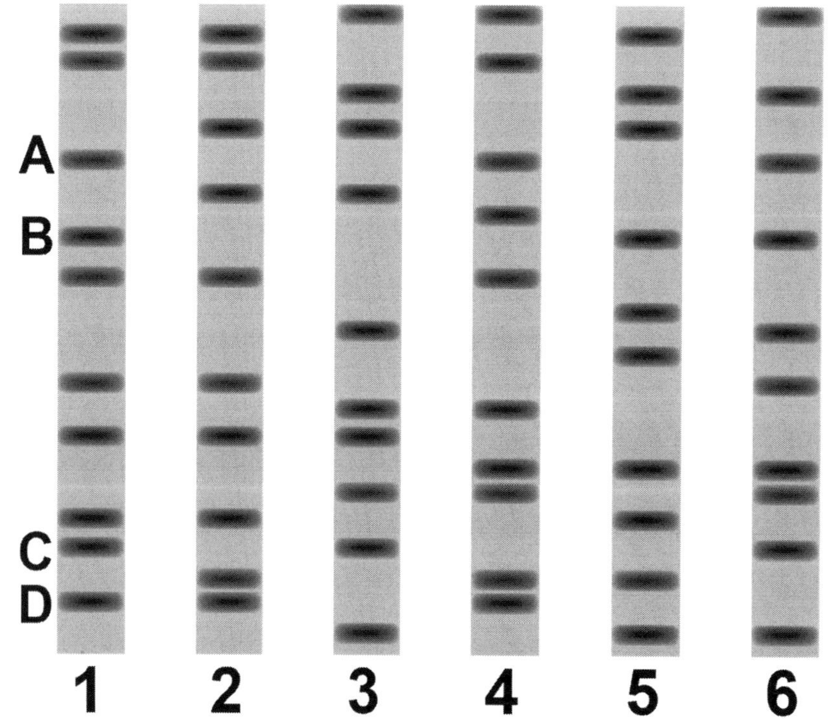

16. Which of the labeled bands in Profile 1 matches a band in Profile 2?

a. Band A
b. Band B
c. Band C
d. Band D

17. How many bands in Profiles 1 and 2 match?

a. 5
b. 6
c. 7
d. 8

18. Which profile likely represents the father of the individual in DNA profile 1?

a. Profile 3
b. Profile 4
c. Profile 5
d. Profile 6

19. Which profile could belong to a child of the individuals in Profiles 3 and 4?

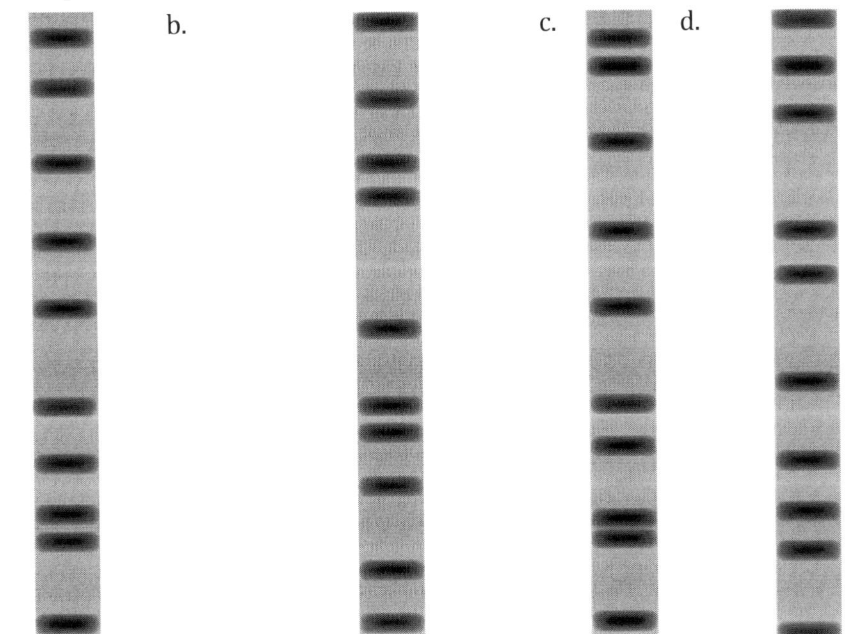

20. Is it possible that Profiles 5 and 6 belong to siblings?

a. Yes; they share more than half their markers.
b. Yes; the number of markers siblings share is unpredictable.
c. No; the two profiles share too few markers to be siblings.
d. No; the two profiles share too many markers to be siblings.

Refer to the following for questions 21–25:

One of the biggest open questions in cosmology involves a phenomenon called dark matter. Among other lines of evidence, calculations on the motion of the stars in a galaxy seem to show that the mass of the stars, gas, and dust in a galaxy is not sufficient to hold the galaxy together; if there's no other force constraining it, a galaxy should fly apart as it rotates. Because of this, most cosmologists have concluded that galaxies must contain a large amount of additional mass not accounted for by the structures we have so far been able to detect. This additional matter is known as "dark matter"— "dark" because it apparently cannot be seen or detected by current means. Not all astronomers, however, agree that dark matter is the best explanation for the phenomena in question. Two scientists express their opinions about dark matter.

Scientist 1

Relativistic gravitational theory has passed every experimental test it has been subjected to and has shown considerable explanatory power. It is far too well established to throw out without a good reason to do so. Cosmological observations do not provide such a reason because they have a much simpler potential explanation: the existence of dark matter. Most likely dark matter comprises some yet undiscovered type of elementary particle. Astrophysicists have named several possible candidates, including the weakly interacting massive particle, or WIMP; the gravitino, a particle related to the graviton but with a different spin; or a light, slow-moving particle called an axion.

HiSET Practice Test #1

Scientist 2

Supposing that 85% of galaxies are made up of some unknown and undetectable type of matter is not the most parsimonious way to explain the observations. Current gravitational theories have only been tested on relatively small scales, from a cosmological point of view. We know they work well within the solar system. But it could be that they break down on galactic scales—as Newtonian mechanics works well for objects moving at everyday velocities but fails for objects moving near the speed of light. It seems more likely that the anomalies in large-scale observations come from the fact that gravity simply behaves differently at those scales.

21. With which statement would both scientists likely agree?

a. Relativistic gravity works well on the scale of the solar system.
b. There is much more mass in galaxies than we can detect by current means.
c. Relativistic gravity will require some modifications when applied to larger scales.
d. There is no way, even in principle, that we would ever be able to detect dark matter.

22. According to Scientist 1, what might dark matter consist of?

a. Stars
b. Gravitons
c. Gravitinos
d. Black holes

23. From the passage, which scientist is more likely to represent the majority view among cosmologists?

a. Scientist 1
b. Scientist 2
c. Neither—both scientists clearly represent idiosyncratic minority views.
d. Scientist 1 and Scientist 2—although they use different words, both scientists fundamentally agree with each other.

24. Some recent observations seem to show that at least two galaxies, NGC-1052-DF2 and NGC-1052-DF4, do have enough visible mass to account for their motion and therefore contain little or no dark matter. If these measurements turn out to be valid, on which scientist's statement would they cast the most doubt?

a. Scientist 1's because Scientist 1 insists that all galaxies must contain dark matter
b. Scientist 1's because they would prove that gravity does not work the same on larger scales
c. Scientist 2's because Scientist 2 assumes that galaxies must follow Newtonian mechanics
d. Scientist 2's because if gravity works differently at a large scale, this should apply to all galaxies

25. With which statement would both scientists likely agree?

a. Gravity works the same at all scales.
b. Galaxies contain large numbers of axions.
c. Galaxies are held together mostly by gravity.
d. Most particles in the universe are unaffected by gravity.

Refer to the following for question 26:

Let B represent the dominant allele for a full head of hair, and let b represent the recessive allele for male-pattern baldness. The following Punnett square represents the offspring of two people with recessive genes for baldness.

	B	b
B	Possibility 1	Possibility 2
b	Possibility 3	Possibility 4

26. According to the Punnett square, which possibility would produce an offspring with male-pattern baldness?

a. Possibility 1
b. Possibility 2
c. Possibility 3
d. Possibility 4

Refer to the following for questions 27–28:

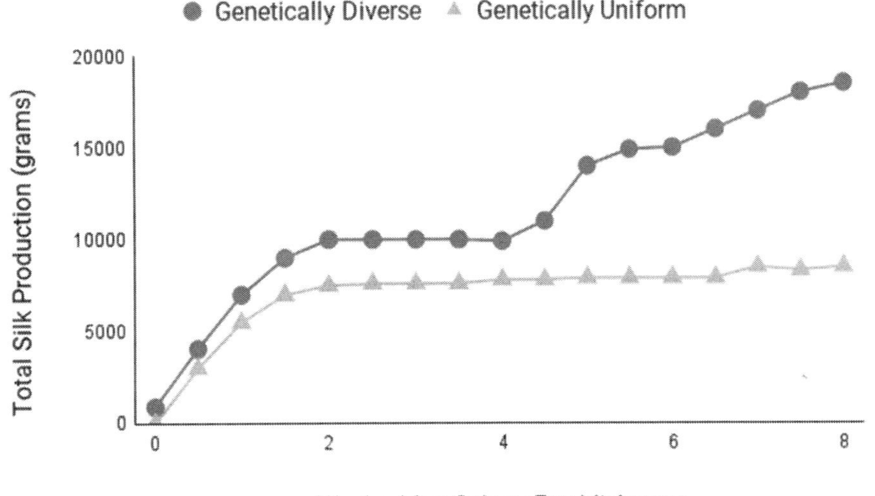

Colonies of silkworms that had the same number of genetically identical or genetically different animals were established. For several weeks after the colonies were created, silk production was estimated by removing small samples of silk from the colonies and weighing them. The results are shown in the graph. The open symbols are for the production of silk by genetically uniform worms. The closed symbols are for the production of silk by genetically diverse worms.

27. Which of the following conclusions can be drawn from the data?

a. Genetically diverse worms produce more silk than genetically uniform worms.
b. Genetically uniform worms produce more silk than genetically diverse worms.
c. Genetically diverse silkworm colonies produce more silk than genetically uniform colonies.
d. Genetically uniform silkworm colonies produce more silk than genetically diverse colonies.

HiSET Practice Test #1

28. If the generation time of a silkworm is about four weeks, which of the following hypotheses offers the best explanation for the difference in silk productivity between the two colonies?

a. Genetically diverse silkworms produce silk longer than genetically uniform worms.
b. Genetically diverse silkworms reproduce more than genetically uniform worms.
c. Genetically diverse silkworms produce heavier silk than genetically uniform worms.
d. Genetically uniform silkworms stop producing silk when they reproduce.

Refer to the following for questions 29–34:

Although only 94 elements occur naturally on Earth, many more have been produced artificially in laboratories. All of these elements are heavier than the natural elements, and many are generally extremely short-lived, lasting only a tiny fraction of a second before decaying into other elements. Still, their presence can be reliably detected, and different labs race to produce new elements first to win naming rights. The latest four elements to be given official names are nihonium, moscovium, tennessine, and oganesson, elements 113, 115, 117, and 118, respectively. There may be a limit to the number of elements that can be discovered, however. Two scientists express their views on the matter.

Scientist 1

Atoms exist because the strong nuclear force causes protons to be attracted to each other, overcoming their electrical repulsion—although not indefinitely for radioactive isotopes. However, the strong nuclear force operates over only short distances. If an atomic nucleus becomes too large, the distance between protons will become too great for the strong nuclear force to hold it together even for a brief period of time. Calculation shows that the threshold occurs at about 173 protons. Therefore, there can never be an element with an atomic number greater than this. There still may remain some fifty-odd elements to be discovered but certainly not much more than 60 at the most.

Scientist 2

Because of the short lifetime of most heavy elements and the difficulty of creating them in the lab, it's not easy to study their properties. It's likely that as the atomic number increases, the configuration of the nucleus changes, possibly in ways that lead to atoms more stable than one might expect—there are sound reasons to expect "islands of stability," perhaps centered around elements 126 and 164, in which certain heavy elements are unusually stable relative to the atoms around them. In any case, we know too little about the arrangement of heavy atoms to confidently name a limit to their size, and I don't think there's any good reason to doubt that the periodic table can be extended indefinitely.

29. What is the main point of disagreement between the two scientists?

a. Scientist 1 thinks there is a limited number of elements; Scientist 2 does not.
b. Scientist 2 thinks there is a limited number of elements; Scientist 1 does not.
c. Scientist 1 thinks there are stable elements that have not yet been discovered; Scientist 2 does not.
d. Scientist 2 thinks there are stable elements that have not yet been discovered; Scientist 1 does not.

30. Which statement would both scientists likely agree on?

a. The higher the atomic number of an element, the less stable it is.
b. There are still new elements remaining to be discovered.
c. The procedure for naming elements needs to be changed.
d. No elements with an atomic number greater than 94 could possibly exist anywhere in nature.

31. What hypothetical piece of evidence would support Scientist 2's view and contradict Scientist 1's?

a. The discovery of element 200
b. The discovery that element 126 is stable
c. The discovery that element 126 is highly unstable
d. The discovery of three elements with atomic numbers between 150 and 160

32. Which statement would be MOST consistent with both scientists' views?

a. Labs investigating heavy elements need better safety precautions.
b. Heavy elements that do not occur in nature can be created in the lab.
c. Elements above number 126 are too short-lived to ever be detectable in a laboratory setting.
d. The arrangement of the particles in an atom changes in predictable ways as the atomic number increases.

33. According to Scientist 1, what force would prevent the formation of elements with an atomic number above 173?

a. The strong nuclear force
b. The weak nuclear force
c. Electromagnetism
d. Gravity

34. If the "islands of stability" exist where Scientist 2 says they might, which element is likely to be the LEAST stable?

a. Element 8
b. Element 126
c. Element 145
d. Element 164

Refer to the following for questions 35–40:

Fossils show that many non-avian dinosaurs had feathers. The prevalence of feathers seems to vary by group of dinosaurs; feathers were particularly common in coelurosaurs, the group of dinosaurs that included the large carnivores like *Allosaurus* and *Megalosaurus*. However, the existing skin impressions of the most famous Mesozoic coelurosaur, *Tyrannosaurus*, show only scales, not feathers. Scientists disagree on the implications of these fossils, as represented by the arguments below.

Scientist 1

Although we have no direct evidence of feathers in *Tyrannosaurus* itself, we do have strong evidence of feathers in its close relatives. Phylogenetic bracketing therefore suggests that *Tyrannosaurus* is likely to also have had feathers. This is not necessarily contradicted by the existing fossils. Feathers are delicate structures that do not fossilize easily, and at least some parts of the *Tyrannosaurus*'s skin may have had both scales *and* feathers in life. We have fossils of other dinosaurs, such as *Kulindadromeus*, that show strong evidence of both scales and feathers on the same parts of the body. They are even known to coexist in some modern birds, such as in the feet of the ruffled grouse.

Scientist 2

We now have scaly skin impressions from locations on the body of the *Tyrannosaurus rex*, enough to say that it was almost certainly scaly all over. Although it's true that some close relatives of *Tyrannosaurus* had feathers, phylogenetic bracketing is not infallible, and in this case, it is superseded by direct evidence. It is likely that ancestors of *Tyrannosaurus* had feathers, but *Tyrannosaurus* apparently lost them. One plausible reason for this is its size; if feathers played a role in thermoregulation, then it makes sense they would be lost in larger organisms—and it's certainly relevant that we also have scaly skin impressions from other large tyrannosaurids such as *Gorgosaurus*.

35. Both scientists mention "phylogenetic bracketing." From the context in the passages, what principle is this likely referring to?

a. Closely related organisms are likely to share similar traits.
b. Traits are gradually lost or gained over time through evolution.
c. Animals can be classified into groups of related organisms called "phyla."
d. How closely related different organisms are can be inferred from their skeletal structures.

36. One possible explanation for scaly *Tyrannosaurus* skin impressions not proposed by either Scientist 1 or Scientist 2 is that *Tyrannosaurus* was scaled over part of its body and feathered over other parts. What information from the passages casts doubt on this idea?

a. Scientist 1 states that some dinosaurs had both feathers and scales on the same parts.
b. Scientist 1 states that feathers do not fossilize easily.
c. Scientist 2 states that we have skin impressions from various parts of the body.
d. Scientist 2 states that feathers may play a role in thermoregulation.

37. With which statement would both Scientist 1 and Scientist 2 MOST likely agree?

a. Feathers are less likely in larger animals.
b. The ancestors of *Tyrannosaurus* probably had feathers.
c. No animals other than dinosaurs and birds had featherlike filaments.
d. The apparent fossils of feathers may actually be leaves that happened to be fossilized with the dinosaurs.

38. Scientist 1 brings up the fact that the ruffled grouse has both feathers and scales on its feet. Why is this relevant to Scientist 1's argument?

a. The ruffled grouse has close relatives that are not feathered.
b. The ruffled grouse is the closest living relative of the *Tyrannosaurus*.
c. Although the ruffled grouse has feathers, its fossils do not show evidence of them.
d. It shows that it is possible for feathers and scales to exist in the same place on an animal.

39. Scientist 2 suggests that large animals may tend to lose feathers, but the largest living bird, the ostrich, is heavily feathered. How might Scientist 2 best explain this?

a. *Tyrannosaurus* was much larger than an ostrich.
b. Unlike *Tyrannosaurus*, the ostrich lives in arid habitats.
c. *Tyrannosaurus* was a carnivore, whereas the ostrich is an herbivore.
d. We have no fossils of the ostrich, so we do not know whether or not its feathers would fossilize.

40. Which of the two scientists is likely to agree with the following statement? Whether an animal has feathers has no correlation with whether animals related to it have feathers.

a. Scientist 1
b. Scientist 2
c. Both
d. Neither

Refer to the following for questions 41–46:

Mass spectrometry is a method used to measure the distribution of masses of particles in a sample. More specifically, it works with charged particles. Rather than measuring mass directly, mass spectrometry determines the ratio of mass to charge. To use mass spectrometry on an ordinary compound, one can ionize the particles of interest before sending them through the mass spectrometer. Because the ions will generally have relatively low charges—at most a few multiples of e (the charge of an electron)—ions of specific masses are easily recognizable.

A mass spectrometer works by sending particles through a magnetic field onto a detector. Neutral particles are not affected by the magnetic field, but charged particles are deflected by some angle depending on their charge and mass. The ions hit the detector at different positions depending on the angle of deflection. The particles that hit the detector at different positions are counted, and their relative numbers are plotted in a mass spectrum. The deflection depends on the ratio of mass to charge, m/Z. In this ratio, m is the mass of the ion in atomic mass units, or the sum of the mass numbers of the atoms. Z is the charge number—the charge of the ion in multiples of the charge of the electron. Generally, when using mass spectrometry on an ionized compound, most molecules will be singly ionized, with $Z = 1$.

A scientist wants to apply mass spectrometry to an unknown solution. The scientist vaporizes the liquid, ionizes its molecules, and sends them through a mass spectrometer, obtaining the following spectrum:

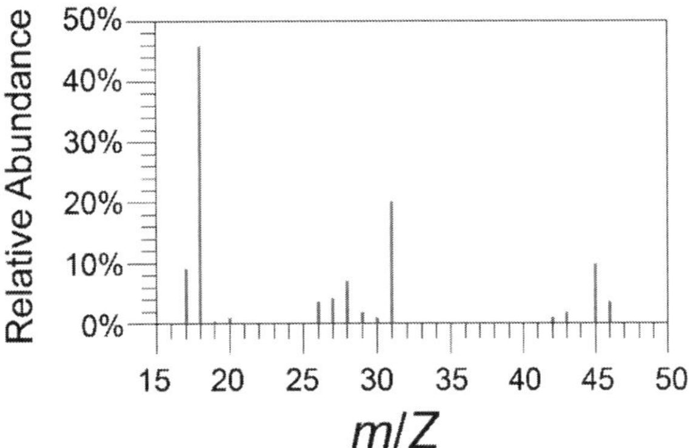

The y-axis on this graph represents relative abundance, or the percentage of the ions detected that had this value of m/Z.

From this spectrum, the scientist recognizes the characteristic peaks of three different compounds: the peaks at $m/Z = 26, 27$, and 28 correspond to ethylene; the peaks at 17 and 18 correspond to water; and the peaks at 31, 45, and 46 correspond to ethanol.

41. Which of the three compounds are MOST and LEAST abundant in the solution?

a. Most: ethanol; least: water
b. Most: water; least: ethanol
c. Most: ethylene; least: water
d. Most: water; least: ethylene

42. The peak at $m/Z = 18$ corresponds to singly ionized water molecules. What would be the value of m/Z for a *doubly* ionized water molecule?

a. 9
b. 16
c. 20
d. 36

HiSET Practice Test #1

43. About what fraction of the mixture is ethanol?

a. $\frac{1}{10}$
b. $\frac{1}{5}$
c. $\frac{1}{3}$
d. $\frac{1}{2}$

44. The most common isotope of oxygen has a mass number of 16. At what value of m/Z would you expect to find the highest peak of the mass spectrum of molecular oxygen, O_2?

a. 4
b. 8
c. 16
d. 32

45. A typical carbon atom has a mass number of 12, and a hydrogen atom has a mass number of 1. What could be the chemical formula of ethylene?

a. C_2H_4
b. C_2H_6
c. C_3H_4
d. C_3H_6

46. Most water molecules have a mass number of 18. What is the MOST likely cause of the peak at $m/Z = 17$ in the mass spectrum of water?

a. Neutral water molecules
b. Water ions that have lost a hydrogen atom (OH^- ions)
c. Water ions that have gained an extra hydrogen atom (H_3O^+ ions)
d. Water ions that include deuterium, a heavier isotope of hydrogen

Refer to the following for questions 47–51:

A scientist wishes to test the effectiveness of an antibiotic. To do this, she takes nine Petri dishes filled with agar, a nutrient substrate on which bacteria grow readily, and labels them with the numbers 1 through 9. She then introduces bacterial cultures into each Petri dish, taking care to spread them evenly along the surfaces.

In dishes 1 through 3, the scientist then places a drop of solution of the antibiotic to be tested at a concentration of 2 parts per thousand. (The rest of the solution is water.) She does the same to dishes 4 through 6 but with a solution at a concentration of one part per thousand. In dishes 7 through 9, the scientist places a drop of a control liquid. The scientist covers the Petri dishes, leaves them in a cool location for five days, and then examines the results. The diagrams below show the growth of bacteria in each dish after five days; the gray areas show where on the Petri dish bacterial cultures have grown, whereas the white areas show parts of the agar that are clear of bacteria.

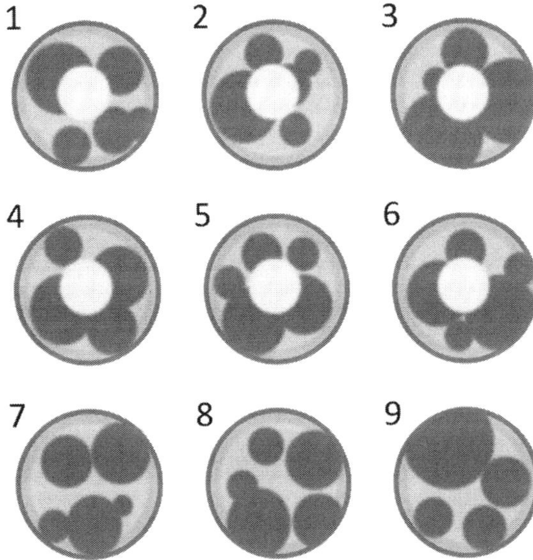

47. The passage says that dishes 7 through 9 are treated with a "control liquid." What would be the best choice as a control liquid?

a. A solution of the antibiotic at an intermediate concentration of 1.5 parts per thousand
b. A solution of the antibiotic at a lower concentration of 0.5 parts per thousand
c. A solution of a different antibiotic
d. Pure distilled water

48. What is the best conclusion that can be drawn from the given data?

a. The antibiotic has no effect on bacterial growth.
b. The antibiotic has an effect on bacterial growth that increases with its concentration.
c. The antibiotic impedes bacterial growth, but increasing the concentration above one part per thousand does not increase the effect.
d. The antibiotic is only effective at concentrations greater than one part per thousand.

49. The scientist discovers that her assistant inadvertently switched the labels on two of the Petri dishes. Although at first upset, she soon realizes that this mistake did not affect her results. Which choice could have been the numbers of the two dishes that were switched?

a. 3 and 9
b. 4 and 6
c. 5 and 7
d. 6 and 7

50. To see how the effectiveness of the antibiotic changes over time, the scientist leaves the Petri dishes for an additional 3 days. Which diagram shows what dish 8 will MOST likely look like after this time?

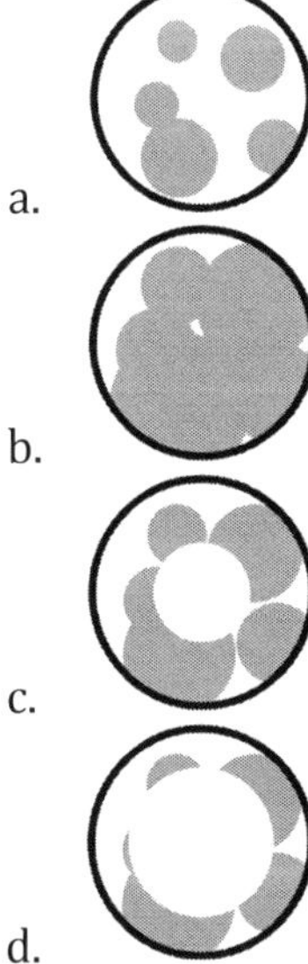

a.
b.
c.
d.

51. Another scientist decides to replicate the first scientist's work, but at a higher temperature, to see if the antibiotic's effectiveness changes at different temperatures. Unlike the first scientist, however, the second scientist neglects to use a control group. The second scientist finds that at this higher temperature, all the Petri dishes treated with the antibiotic are completely free of bacteria and concludes that the antibiotic is more effective at this higher temperature. Given the lack of a control group, what is another possible interpretation of the second scientist's data?

a. The antibiotic is ineffective at the higher temperature.
b. The antibiotic requires a higher concentration to work at the higher temperature.
c. The bacteria are unable to grow in agar.
d. The bacteria are unable to grow at the higher temperature.

Refer to the following for questions 52–55:

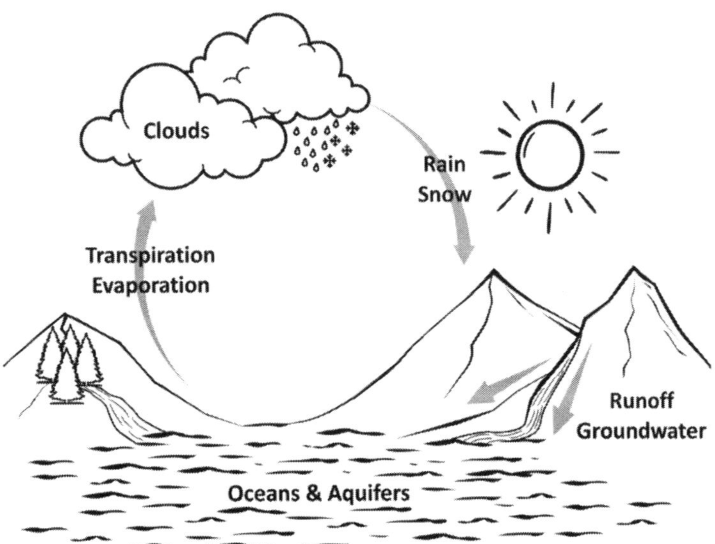

Energy from the Sun heats the water in the oceans and causes it to evaporate. This makes water vapor that rises through the atmosphere. Cooler temperatures at high altitudes cause this vapor to condense and form clouds. Water droplets in the clouds condense and grow, eventually falling to the ground as precipitation. This continuous movement of water above and below ground is called the hydrologic cycle, or water cycle, and it is essential for life on our planet. All the Earth's stores of water, including that found in clouds, oceans, underground, etc., are known as the *hydrosphere*.

Water can be stored in several locations as part of the water cycle. The largest reservoirs are the oceans, which hold about 95% of the world's water, more than 300,000,000 cubic miles. Water is also stored in polar ice caps, mountain snowcaps, lakes and streams, plants, and aquifers below ground. Each of these reservoirs has a characteristic *residence time*, which is the average amount of time a water molecule will spend there before moving on. Some typical residence times are shown in the table.

Average Reservoir Residence Times of Water

Reservoir	Residence Time
Atmosphere	9 days
Oceans	3,000 years
Glaciers and ice caps	100 years
Soil moisture	2 months
Underground aquifers	10,000 years

The water cycle can change over time. During cold climatic periods, more water is stored as ice and snow, and the rate of evaporation is lower. This affects the level of the Earth's oceans. During the last ice age, for instance, oceans were 400 feet lower than today. Human activities that affect the water cycle are agriculture, dam construction, deforestation, and industrial activities.

52. Which of the following is another name for the water cycle?

a. The hydrosphere
b. The atmosphere
c. The residence cycle
d. The hydrologic cycle

53. Water is stored underground. It is also stored in oceans and ice caps. These underground storage reservoirs are called:

a. Storage tanks
b. Aquifers
c. Evaporators
d. Runoff

54. Other than atmospheric water, where do water molecules spend the least time?

a. Aquifers
b. Oceans
c. Glaciers
d. Soil

55. Which of the following statements is NOT true?

a. Cutting down trees affects the water cycle.
b. Ocean levels rise in an ice age.
c. Oceans hold most of the world's water.
d. Clouds are formed because of cold temperatures.

Refer to the following for questions 56–60:

Plants produce energy from sunlight by the process of photosynthesis carried out in organelles called chloroplasts within the plant's cells. During photosynthesis, the plant takes in carbon dioxide and water and uses them to synthesize carbohydrates that store energy for later use. The plants release oxygen as a waste product. The amount of oxygen produced by a plant can be used as a measurement of the rate of photosynthesis.

A student wants to study the rate of photosynthesis in a plant under varying conditions. To do that, the student acquires a sample of an aquatic plant, *Egeria densa*, and places it underneath an inverted funnel, submerged in water. The student then takes a test tube and inverts it, filled with water, over the spout of the funnel. As the plant releases oxygen, the oxygen is directed by the funnel into the test tube, displacing some of the water. After the setup is left undisturbed for 24 hours, the amount of oxygen in the test tube can be measured. A diagram of the experimental apparatus appears below.

A student performs trials with eight different experimental setups. All of the setups are on the same table, but four of the setups are in bright light, and four are in dim light, shaded by an awning. In four of the setups, the student stirs 1 gram of sodium bicarbonate into the water to add some additional carbon dioxide. The table below shows the student's results.

Trial	Light	CO_2 added?	Amount of oxygen produced
1	Bright	No	0.50 mL
2	Bright	No	0.60 mL
3	Bright	Yes	1.10 mL
4	Bright	Yes	1.05 mL
5	Dim	Yes	0.40 mL
6	Dim	Yes	0.35 mL
7	Dim	No	0.20 mL
8	Dim	No	0.20 mL

56. According to the student's data, under which set of conditions did the plants produce the most oxygen?

a. Bright light; CO_2 added
b. Dim light; CO_2 added
c. Bright light; no CO_2 added
d. Dim light; no CO_2 added

57. Which pair of trials involved the same conditions?

a. 4 and 5
b. 5 and 6
c. 6 and 7
d. 4 and 7

58. What is MOST likely to be a significant source of error in the student's experiment?

a. Variation in temperature
b. Variation in the amount of CO_2 added
c. Variation in the amount of oxygen collected
d. Variation in the size of the plants

59. The passage says that during the process of photosynthesis, the plant takes in carbon dioxide and water and synthesizes carbohydrates. As the name implies, carbohydrates contain carbon and hydrogen (as well as oxygen). From where does the plant most likely obtain this carbon and hydrogen?

a. From the water
b. From the carbon dioxide
c. Carbon from the water and hydrogen from the carbon dioxide
d. Hydrogen from the water and carbon from the carbon dioxide

60. Suppose the student wants to do further experiments to study the effects of some of the variables. Which variation on the experiment is MOST likely to yield fruitful results?

a. Varying the size of the test tube
b. Varying the amount of CO_2 added
c. Varying the amount of water in the beaker
d. Varying the amount of oxygen produced

Social Studies

Refer to the following for questions 1–3:

Issues and Compromises in the United States Constitution

Issue	New Jersey Plan	Virginia Plan	Constitution
Legislative branch	A single house with members appointed by state legislatures	Two houses: Upper House with members elected by the people; Lower House elected by Upper House	Two houses: originally Senate members were elected by state legislatures, and representatives were and are still elected by the people.
Executive branch	Congress to choose an executive committee	Congress to choose a single president	President chosen by Electoral College, with electors selected by each of the states.
Judicial branch	Executive committee to appoint national judges	Congress chooses national judges	President appoints and Senate confirms Supreme Court judges.
Representation	Each state receives equal number of representatives	Representation to be based on wealth or population	Two houses created: House of Representatives based on population; Senate has two delegates from each state.

1. Which of the following conclusions can you draw on the issue of representation?

a. Virginia's people were very poor.
b. New Jersey started using the phrase "Liberty, Equality, and Fraternity."
c. Virginia was probably a state with many people.
d. Many wealthy citizens lived in New Jersey.

2. The Virginia Plan for the legislative branch closely mirrors:

a. The Mayflower Compact
b. Britain's Parliament
c. The government of the Sioux
d. France's monarchical system

3. The Electoral College was created to resolve the issue of:

a. How the wealthiest people would be represented
b. Who would appoint the Supreme Court members
c. How to elect senators
d. Who would elect the chief executive

Refer to the following for question 4:

In 1917, Orville Wright wrote of the invention of the airplane: "When my brother and I built and flew the first man-carrying flying machine, we thought that we were introducing into the world an invention which would make further wars practically impossible. That we were not alone in this thought is evidenced by the fact that the French Peace Society presented us with medals on account of our invention. We thought governments would realize the impossibility of winning by surprise attacks, and that no country would enter into war with another when it knew it would have to win by simply wearing out the enemy."

4. Which of the following statements do you think best expresses what the Wright brothers thought of World War I?

a. "Ah, that splendid little war!"
b. "How exciting to see airplanes extending fighting into the air!"
c. "Using airplanes in war is unacceptable."
d. "We can't wait to join the fight."

Refer to the following for question 5:

In 1988, the federal government, as part of the Clean Air Act, began to monitor visibility in national parks and wilderness areas. Eleven years later, the Environmental Protection Agency set forth an attempt to improve the air quality in wilderness areas and national parks.

5. Who of the following historical persons would NOT have agreed with this effort?

a. President Richard M. Nixon, who signed the act in 1970
b. Rachel Carson, environmentalist and author of *Silent Spring*
c. President Theodore Roosevelt, who set aside land for public parks
d. The senator who campaigned in the early 1900s on the promise "Not one penny for scenery!"

Refer to the following for question 6:

Voter Issue from 2008:

ISSUE 3: PROPOSED CONSTITUTIONAL AMENDMENT TO AMEND THE CONSTITUTION TO PROTECT PRIVATE PROPERTY RIGHTS IN GROUND WATER, LAKES AND OTHER WATERCOURSES (Proposed by Joint Resolution of the General Assembly of Ohio) To adopt Section 19b of Article I of the Constitution of the State of Ohio A YES vote means approval of the amendment. A NO vote means disapproval of the amendment. A majority YES vote is required for the amendment to be adopted. If approved, this amendment shall take effect December 1, 2008.

League Explanation of Issue 3: This proposed amendment resulted from the Ohio legislature's passage of the Great Lakes Water Compact this past spring. Some lawmakers feared final approval of the Compact might limit private water rights. The constitutional amendment is intended to recognize that:

- Property owners have a protected right to the "reasonable use" of the ground water flowing under their property and of the water in a lake or watercourse that is on or flows through their property.
- An owner has the right to give or sell these interests to a governmental body.
- The public welfare supersedes individual property owners' rights. The state and political subdivisions may regulate such waters to the extent state law allows.
- The proposed amendment would not affect public use of Lake Erie and the state's other navigable waters.
- The rights confirmed by this amendment may not be limited by sections of the Ohio Constitution addressing home rule, public debt and public works, conservation of natural resources, and the prohibition of the use of "initiative" and "referendum" on property taxes.

6. Which of the following conclusions is correct?

a. The state of Ohio will give up rights to the control of Lake Erie in favor of public rights.
b. People who own property with water on it cannot sell that land to the state.
c. The state considers the public's welfare to be more important than an individual property owner's rights.
d. This issue was created without input from any lawmakers or organizations.

Refer to the following for question 7:

ARTICLE XXVII (Ratified July 1, 1971)

Section 1. The right of citizens of the United States, who are eighteen years of age or older, to vote shall not be denied or abridged by the United States or by any State on account of age.

7. This amendment to the Constitution was ratified in part because of what historic moment?

a. Women gained the right to vote.
b. Suffrage was extended to all African Americans.
c. Young men were being drafted to serve in the Vietnam War.
d. The number of people under 21 years of age increased.

Refer to the following for question 8:

Mother Jones, who was a labor activist, wrote the following about children working in cotton mills in Alabama: "Little girls and boys, barefooted, walked up and down between the endless rows of spindles, reaching thin little hands into the machinery to repair snapped threads. They crawled under machinery to oil it. They replaced spindles all day long; all night through...six-year-olds with faces of sixty did an eight-hour shift for ten cents a day; the machines, built in the North, were built low for the hands of little children."

8. Which of the following do you think happened after this was published?

a. More children signed up to work in the factories.
b. Cotton factories in the South closed.
c. Laws were passed to prevent child labor.
d. The pay scale for these children was increased.

Refer to the following for question 9:

In 1781, a county court in Massachusetts heard the case *Brom & Bett v. Ashley*. What was unusual about the case was that the plaintiffs were both enslaved by John Ashley's family. They had walked out and appealed to a lawyer for help after Mrs. Ashley tried to hit Mum Bett's sister. Mum Bett, whose real name was Elizabeth Freeman, claimed that if all people were free and equal, as she had heard while serving at the Ashley table, slaves too were equal. The court agreed by basing their decision on the Massachusetts constitution of the previous year. The decision, affirmed in subsequent cases, led to the abolishing of slavery in that state.

9. Which of the following statements is most accurate?

a. Mrs. Ashley was probably just having a bad day when she tried to strike another person.
b. Elizabeth Freeman's actions helped to gain women the right to vote.
c. White people in southern states applauded the court's decision.
d. The ideals of the American Revolution reached farther than the founders may have intended.

Refer to the following for questions 10–11:

In 1969, 13 African American members of the House of Representatives gathered to form the Congressional Black Caucus (CBC). They felt that a unified voice for minorities was needed. President Richard Nixon met with the group two years later; his weak response to their list of 60 recommendations increased their efforts. These efforts included ending apartheid in South Africa, reforming welfare, expanding educational opportunities, and developing of businesses by minorities. For nearly 20 years, the CBC has proposed an alternative annual budget; it generally varies widely from the budget that the president submits. In 2008, the organization has 43 members from urban and rural areas. The CBC is sometimes called the conscience of Congress.

10. Which of the following statements is an opinion?

a. The Congressional Black Caucus began in 1969.
b. The CBC is often referred to as Congress's conscience.
c. Every year for two decades, the CBC has proposed a national budget.
d. Apartheid was the worst political system of the 20th century.

11. Which of the following statements is true?

a. The Congressional Black Caucus was started right after the Civil War.
b. The major goal of the CBC is to elect an African American president.
c. Since its beginning, the organization has grown by about 30 members.
d. The president usually implements the budget recommendations of the CBC.

12. As a form of government, what does *oligarchy* mean?

a. Rule by one
b. Rule by a few
c. Rule by law
d. Rule by many

13. To whom was the Declaration of Independence addressed and why?

a. To the British Parliament because the colonists were opposed to being ruled by a king who had only inherited his throne and only considered the popularly elected Parliament to hold any authority over them
b. To the King of England because the colonists were upset that Parliament was passing laws for them even though they did not have the right to elect members of Parliament to represent their interests
c. To the governors of the rebelling colonies so that they would know that they had 30 days to either announce their support of the Revolution or to return to England
d. To the colonial people as a whole because the Declaration of Independence was intended to outline the wrongs that had been inflicted on them by the British military and inspire them to rise up in protest

14. What does *due process* mean?

a. It's important for every citizen to follow the laws of their state and country.
b. Any accused person may confront the accuser and provide a defense.
c. Capital punishment is appropriate if a person is convicted of murder.
d. An accused person is considered guilty until proven to be innocent.

15. A family moves to America from another country with a very different culture. They discard their native cultural practices and adopt American customs. This is an example of:

a. Accommodation
b. Adaptation
c. Acculturation
d. Assimilation

16. Which of the following accurately reflects acculturation vs. assimilation?

a. A nondominant culture giving up all of its traits in favor of the dominant culture is acculturation.
b. A dominant culture absorbing other cultures is assimilation.
c. Assimilation is when cultures adopt traits from other cultures.
d. When two or more cultures adopt some of each other's traits, this is assimilation.

17. How can Congress override the presidential veto of a bill?

a. By a majority vote in the House and a two-thirds majority in the Senate
b. By a two-thirds vote in the House and a majority in the Senate
c. By a majority vote in both the House and the Senate
d. By a two-thirds vote in both the House and the Senate

18. In 1957, President Dwight Eisenhower sent federal troops to Little Rock, Arkansas. They were to enforce integration at Little Rock Central High School, although the governor of the state had tried to prevent integration. Eisenhower's action is an example that illustrates:

a. Showing a governor that he had no real power in state government
b. Trying to keep federal troops out of Vietnam
c. States' rights being more important than federal law
d. Upholding federal law if state or local officials will not

19. Which of the following examples is protected as an expression of free speech?

a. Draftees of the Vietnam War who burned their draft cards
b. A radio personality who states on air that the President should be shot over his most recent budget proposal
c. Pro-life protesters who carry "wanted" signs displaying the photos and home/work addresses of abortion providers during a legally sanctioned protest
d. A high school teacher who allows her students to use profanity when creating poetry

20. Gun control, strong environmental laws, social programs, and opposition to the death penalty are what kind of issues?

a. Compassion issues
b. Activism
c. Regional issues
d. Religious issues

21. Which statement below could be considered an advantage of the United States participating in the United Nations organization?

a. The United Nations does not involve itself in deadly conflicts or civil wars.
b. The United Nations has different foreign policy objectives than the United States has.
c. The United Nations has been a leader in helping to end the humanitarian and military crisis in Darfur.
d. The United Nations does not deal with relief for victims of natural disasters, thereby saving money for the United States.

Refer to the following for questions 22–24:

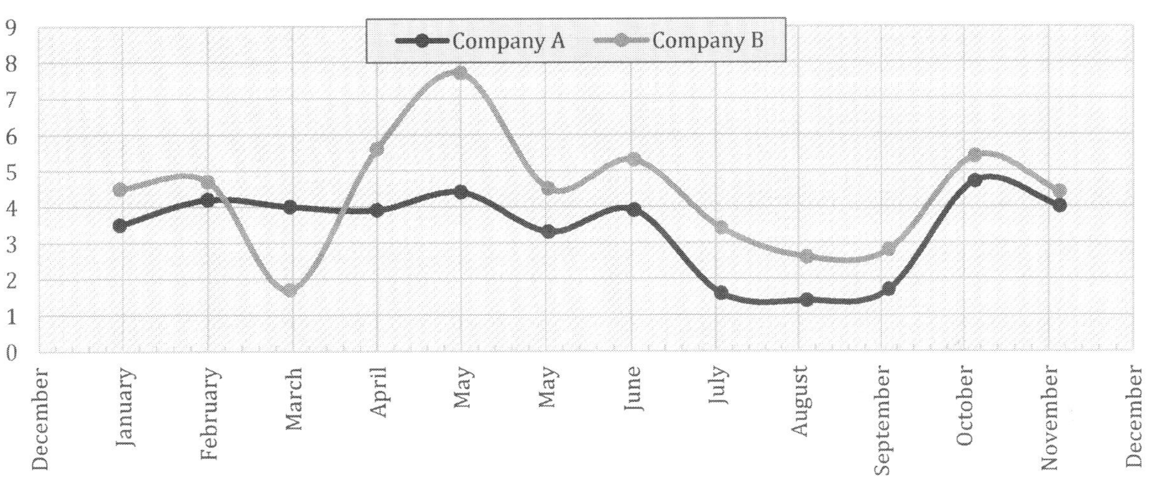

22. Based on the graph, which of the following is TRUE?

a. Company B performed better than Company A in each month.
b. March was a high-performance time for both companies.
c. Sales performance dropped faster for Company A than for Company B from June to July.
d. Company B performed better than Company A during January to May and from July to November.

23. In which month was the difference between the two companies' sales performance greatest?

a. July
b. March
c. May
d. April

24. In which month was the difference between the two companies' sales performance smallest?

a. January
b. February
c. October
d. November

Refer to the following for questions 25–26:

Per Capita National Debt

Year	Historical Context	Amount
1790	Following American Revolution at the beginning of the national government	$19
1816	After the War of 1812	$15
1866	Following the Civil War	$78
1919	After World War I	$240
1948	Three years after World War II ended	$1,720
1975	After the Vietnam War	$2,475
1989	Near the close of Reagan's administration	$11,545

25. Which of the following armed conflicts increased the per capita national debt by the largest *percentage* over the previous conflict listed?

a. War of 1812
b. Civil War
c. World War I
d. World War II

26. Which of the following is a possible explanation for the change of per capita national debt between 1790 and 1816?

a. The United States borrowed more money to pay for the War of 1812.
b. The new nation enacted fiscal policies that focused on paying off debts owed from the Revolutionary War.
c. People did not spend very much money between those wars.
d. More citizens bought Treasury bonds in those days.

Refer to the following for questions 27–28:

Women in the Labor Force, Selected Years

Year	Women in Labor Force (thousands)	Percentage of Total Labor Force
1900	5,114	18.1
1920	8,430	20.4
1940	12,845	24.3
1950	18,412	28.8
1970	31,560	36.7

27. In what year did women first make up more than 25% of the total labor force?

a. 1900
b. 1920
c. 1940
d. 1950

28. How could you express the change in percentage of women as part of the total labor force from 1900 to 1970?

a. The percentage rate declined by half.
b. The percentage rate stayed constant.
c. The percentage rate doubled.
d. The percentage rate fluctuated up and down over the years.

Refer to the following for questions 29–30:

Revenue Sources: 2004

Source	Amount in Millions	Percentage of Budget
Corporation income taxes	$189.3	10.1
Excise [sales] taxes	$69.9	3.7
Individual income taxes	$809.0	43.0
Social insurance and retirement receipts	$733.4	39.0
Other	$78.4	4.2

29. If the government ended the use of offshore tax havens for corporations, how would the above information change?

a. Corporate income taxes would decrease.
b. Retirement receipts would increase.
c. Individuals would pay less in income taxes.
d. The share of corporate income taxes would increase.

30. Which category of taxpayer gives the most to the federal budget?

a. Individuals
b. Corporations
c. Businesses paying Social Security tax
d. Federal government agencies

Refer to the following for questions 31–33:

United States Foreign Trade 1960–1970

(by Category Percentages)

Category	1960		1970	
	Exports	Imports	Exports	Imports
Chemicals	8.7	5.3	9.0	3.6
Crude materials, excluding fuel	13.7	18.3	10.8	8.3
Food and beverages, including tobacco	15.6	22.5	11.8	15.6
Machinery and transport	34.3	9.7	42.0	28.0

31. In 1960, which of the following categories had the greatest disparity between percentage of exports and imports?

a. Chemicals
b. Crude materials
c. Food and beverages
d. Machinery and transport

HiSET Practice Test #1

32. From 1960 to 1970, which of the following categories had the greatest difference between percentage of exports and imports?

a. Chemicals
b. Crude materials
c. Food and beverages
d. Machinery and transport

33. Which category saw the greatest percentage decrease in imports between 1960 and 1970?

a. Chemicals
b. Crude materials
c. Food and beverages
d. Machinery and transport

Refer to the following for question 34:

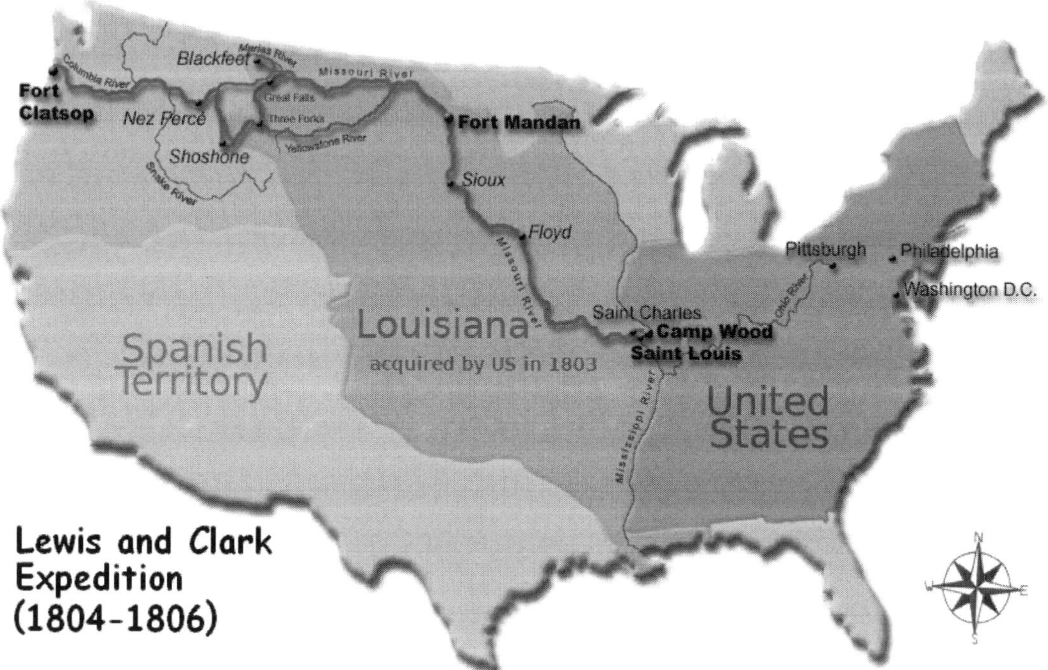

34. The Lewis and Clark expedition of 1803 set out from:

a. Washington, DC
b. The Rocky Mountains
c. Fort Mandan
d. The Mississippi River

35. On a map of Africa, there is a small box around Nairobi. This city is depicted in greater detail in a box at the bottom of the map. What is the name for this box at the bottom of the map?

a. Inset
b. Legend
c. Compass rose
d. Key

Refer to the following for questions 36–38:

36. What major geographical feature is located in Botswana?

a. Zambezi River
b. Lake Tanganyika
c. Kalahari Desert
d. Congo River

37. In Sudan, the Nile River splits into which bodies of water?

a. Gulf of Aden and Red Sea
b. Congo River and Lake Chad
c. Lake Victoria and the White Nile
d. The Blue Nile and the White Nile

38. Which of the following countries are located along the Indian Ocean? (Select all that apply.)

a. Somalia
b. Cameroon
c. Mozambique
d. Chad
e. Kenya
f. Angola

Refer to the following for question 39:

Ethnic Groups in Selected Central American Countries

	Honduras	Nicaragua	El Salvador	Costa Rica	Belize
Mestizo [European and Native American]	90%	69%	90%		49%
Amerindian	7%	5%	1%	1%	
Black	2%	9%		3%	
White	1%	17%	9%	94% [includes Mestizo]	
Chinese				1%	
Creole [African and European]					25%
Mayans					11%

39. To which nation would you go to study the living traditions of the Mayans?

a. Honduras
b. Costa Rica
c. Belize
d. Nicaragua

Refer to the following for questions 40–42:

Important Dates in the History of International Slave Trade

Date	Country	Event
1517	Spain	Begins regular slave trading
1592	British Empire	Begins regular slave trading
1792	Denmark	Abolishes slave trade
1794	France	Abolishes slave trade
1807	British Empire	Abolishes slave trade
1808	United States	Bans Import of Slaves
1811	Spain	Abolishes slave trade
1834	British Empire	Abolishes slavery
1848	Denmark	Abolishes slavery
1848	France	Abolishes slavery
1850	United States	Compromise of 1850
1863	United States	Emancipation Proclamation
1865	United States	Abolishes slavery
1888	Brazil	Abolishes slave trade and slavery

40. According to the information in the table, which of these nations was the first to fully abolish slavery?

a. Denmark
b. United States
c. British Empire
d. France

41. If the United States had not won the Revolutionary War, when would slavery have been outlawed?

a. 1792
b. 1794
c. 1807
d. 1834

42. Which of the following conclusions is true? Use your prior knowledge and the information above.

a. More slaves worked in Brazil than in any other nation.
b. France was more progressive than the United States.
c. Denmark was the largest slave-holding country in Europe.
d. Britain freed enslaved peoples only after losing the Asian nations of the British Empire.

Refer to the following for questions 43–44:

Native Civilizations in Central and South America

Civilization	Location	Conquered by	Date Empires Ended
Maya	Central America	Internal collapse	950
Aztec	Mexico	Spanish under Hernán Cortés	1519
Inca	Peru	Spanish under Francisco Pizarro	1533

43. The Mayan civilization is unlike the Aztec and Incan civilizations because:

a. It collapsed without an outside conqueror.
b. It was the last empire to end.
c. It was located in North America.
d. It was conquered by the Spanish.

44. Which of the following conclusions is supported by the information above?

a. Several nations in South America were conquered by Portugal.
b. The Aztec civilization was the oldest of the three listed.
c. Spain followed an aggressive policy of capturing new lands during the 16th century.
d. Incan warriors tried to assist the Aztec against the Spanish.

Refer to the following for question 45:

- 1978: A Teflon-coated fiberglass used in astronaut spacesuits was reused as a roofing material for buildings and stadiums in the US.
- 1982: Astronauts working on the lunar surface wore liquid-cooled garments under their space suits to protect them from very hot temperatures. The garments became adapted as portable cooling systems for treatment of medical conditions like burning limbs, multiple sclerosis, and spinal injuries.
- 1995: Dr. Michael DeBakey teamed up with Johnson Space Center engineer David Saucier to develop an artificial heart pump based on space shuttle engine fuel pumps. The heart pump they developed can supplement the left ventricle's pumping capacity in a heart.

45. What is the BEST summary of the facts presented in this timeline?

a. Technology used in space explorations can also improve the quality of life on Earth.
b. Architects should study all the technologies used by engineers in space explorations.
c. Doctors should study all the technologies used by engineers for space explorations.
d. Space explorations are too expensive, but they do have some positive benefits also.

Refer to the following for question 46:

Group	Arrived in New World	Settled in
British Catholics	1632	Maryland
British Pilgrims	1620	Plymouth Colony, Massachusetts
British Puritans	1607	Virginia
British Quakers	1681	Pennsylvania
Dutch traders	1625	Manhattan Island
French traders	1608	Quebec

46. Which of the following conclusions can you draw from the information above?

a. Religious influences strongly affected the growth of the North American colonies.
b. The French had large settlements in what became the eastern United States.
c. The Dutch did not get a fair deal for the land they purchased.
d. The Spanish were the first to settle in North America.

Refer to the following for question 47:

Timeline of Events in Puerto Rico's History

1902 The United States declares Puerto Rico a territory.

1904 The Unionist Party of Puerto Rico forms as political opposition against the colonial US government.

1914 Native Puerto Rican islanders form a majority in the government's executive cabinet for the first time in the island's history as a US territory.

1917 President Wilson signs the Jones Act which made Puerto Rico an "organized but unincorporated" territory, gave the island more autonomy in their government, and gave US citizen status to Puerto Ricans.

47. Which conclusion is MOST true based on information in the above timeline?

a. Native Puerto Ricans had a majority in the island's government from the beginning of their time as a US territory
b. Spanish was declared the official language of Puerto Rico, even though the island became a US territory
c. Puerto Rico succumbed to US expansionism but also advocated to get more rights for the island natives
d. Puerto Rico natives formed a violent revolution against US colonialism

Refer to the following for question 48:

Chart—Percentage of African Americans in Certain Military Ranks, 1964-1966

Rank E-6 (Staff Sergeant or Petty Officer, First Class)

	1964	1965	1966
Army	13.9	15.5	18.1
Navy	4.7	5.0	5.6
Marine Corps	5.0	5.3	10.4

Source: Office, Deputy Assistant Secretary of Defense (Civil Rights)

48. In the early 1960s, President Kennedy became more committed to helping civil rights causes, including the cause of desegregation in the military. Based on this chart, what conclusion about African Americans in 1964-66 military ranks can be made?

a. African Americans started making up a larger percentage of Major or Lieutenant Commander Ranks in the Army, Navy, and Marines.
b. African Americans started making up a larger percentage of Staff Sergeant or Petty Officer Ranks in the Army, Navy, and Marines.
c. African Americans started making up a larger percentage of Staff Sergeant or Petty Officer Ranks in the Army and Marines, but not in the Navy.
d. The percentage of African-American Staff Sergeants or Petty Officers grew between 1964 and 1965 but then declined again between 1965 and 1966.

Refer to the following for question 49:

- 1921 - Franklin Roosevelt acquired the disease called polio and lost the use of his legs at age 39.
- 1930s – In the US, polio outbreaks became more frequent, and public desire to help the victims was high.
- 1938 - President Franklin Roosevelt founded the National Foundation for Infantile Paralysis (NFIP), later renamed the March of Dimes Foundation, to help fund research for a polio vaccine.
- 1955 - Dr. Jonas Salk developed and tested the first successful polio vaccine.

49. What is one conclusion that can be made based on this timeline?

a. Historical events and the specific needs of society can contribute to medical inventions.
b. Polio outbreaks were worse in the US than in other countries in the 1920s.
c. A disease outbreak can only be prevented by the development of a vaccine.
d. Franklin Roosevelt developed the first successful polio vaccine.

Refer to the following for questions 50–51:

Westward Migration

Year	Estimated Number of People Headed West
1844	2,000
1849	30,000
1854	10,000
1859	30,000
1864	20,000

50. Given the increase of population, which of the following statements is most likely to be true?

a. More children were being born in 1849 and 1859.
b. Most of the new migrants were women who wanted to open businesses.
c. The Civil War increased the westward migration.
d. Cities and towns in the West grew and supported many businesses.

51. What event caused the increase of westward movement between 1844 and 1849? Use your general knowledge to answer the question.

a. Silver was discovered in Nevada.
b. The Transcontinental Railroad was completed.
c. Roman Catholics developed missions along the California coast.
d. Gold was discovered at Sutter's Mill in California.

Refer to the following for questions 52–53:

NOTE: The years listed represent major milestones in each nation gaining independence.

52. According to the dates provided on the map, which South American nations were the LAST to receive independence?

a. Argentina and Paraguay
b. Ecuador and Venezuela
c. Bolivia and Uruguay
d. Peru and Brazil

53. Which of the following generalizations is valid?

a. The nations of North America were also fighting for independence at the same time as those nations in South America listed above.
b. France lost most of its possessions in the New World as a result of these revolutions.
c. Nations on the west coast received independence first.
d. South America experienced multiple revolutions during the first three decades of the 19th century.

Refer to the following for question 54:

Islam spread to Europe during the medieval period, bringing scientific and technological insights. The Muslim emphasis on knowledge and learning can be traced to an emphasis on both in the Qur'an

HiSET Practice Test #1

[Koran], the holy book of Islam. Because of this emphasis, scholars preserved some of the Greek and Roman texts that were lost to the rest of Europe. The writings of Aristotle, among others, were saved by Muslim translators. Islam scholars modified a Hindu number system. Their modification became the more commonly used Arabic system, which replaced Roman numerals. They also developed algebra. Muslim contributions also include inventing the astrolabe, a device for telling time that also helped sailors to navigate. In medicine, Muslim doctors cleaned wounds with antiseptics. They closed the wounds with gut and silk sutures. They also used sedatives.

54. Based on the information above, which of the following conclusions is likely true?

a. Muslims were braver than others when facing surgery.
b. Fewer Muslim patients died of wound infections than Europeans.
c. The silk market expanded because of the Muslim use of silk sutures.
d. Math classes would be easier without Muslim influence.

Refer to the following for question 55:

In 1949, the National Parks Service added the Effigy Mounds National Monument in northeast Iowa to its list of protected parks. Effigy mounds, which are shaped like animals, were built by Native Americans. Of the more than 200 mounds created by the Mississippian Culture at the park, 31 are in the shape of animals. Most famous are the so-called Marching Bears, clearly visible from an airplane. Other mounds are bird effigies or shaped in cones or lines. The mounds were created over a period of at least 1,500 years. This is just one of the moundbuilders' sites in the eastern third of North America. Historians speculate that the mounds were used for religious purposes and were burial places.

55. Which of the following is NOT accurate?

a. The effigy mounds were built by Native Americans in 1949.
b. Mounds are also found in other states.
c. President Harry S. Truman signed the law that made the mounds a national monument.
d. Effigy mounds are shaped like animals.

56. Which of the following BEST describes the significance of the US Supreme Court's decision in the Dred Scott case?

a. The ruling effectively declared slavery to be a violation of the Constitution.
b. The ruling guaranteed full citizenship rights to freed slaves.
c. The ruling turned many Southerners against the Supreme Court.
d. The ruling furthered the gap between North and South and hastened the Civil War.

Refer to the following for question 57:

During a report on the Industrial Revolution, Mary uses a poster to illustrate cause and effect relationships in the War of 1812.

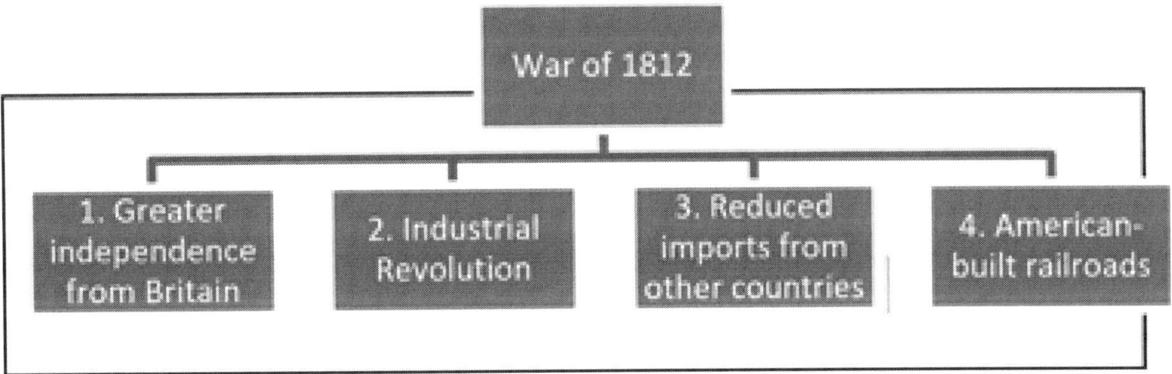

57. Of the following, which should Mary include in her report as more of a cause than an effect of the Industrial Revolution?

a. Emergence of socialism
b. Emergence of capitalism
c. The Romantic movement
d. The Protestant work ethic

58. The Underground Railroad was primarily:

a. A route for abolitionists to smuggle weapons
b. A route for slave owners to traffic slaves
c. A means for slaves to travel to free states
d. A strategy for state control of railway construction

59. Article I of the United States Constitution includes the following paragraph:

No title of nobility shall be granted by the United States: and no person holding any office of profit or trust under them, shall, without the consent of the Congress, accept of any present, emolument, office, or title, of any kind whatever, from any king, prince, or foreign state.

This paragraph most directly reflects the influence of which of the following people?

a. John Locke
b. Baron de Montesquieu
c. Jean-Jacques Rousseau
d. Thomas Paine

60. Which events are correctly paired to show cause and effect?

a. The Spanish-American War → the US annexation of Hawaii
b. The assassination of William McKinley → the decline of US imperialism
c. The Russo-Japanese War → the Boxer Rebellion
d. The Platt Amendment → the establishment of the US naval base at Guantanamo Bay

HiSET Practice Test #1

Answer Key and Explanations for Test #1

Language Arts–Reading

1. D: With its grotesque carvings, excessive slants, and thorny vegetation, Wuthering Heights is a strange and foreboding house. As such, the author's description contributes to the story's strange and foreboding tone. Although Mr. Lockwood seems to like the house, its description alone does not explain why he likes it. Furthermore, although a misanthrope might live in a foreboding house, this fact alone does not prove Heathcliff's misanthropy.

2. B: Although this excerpt is not overly comedic, the narrator, Mr. Lockwood, makes a few sarcastic remarks. Sarcasm combines harshness and humor. When Lockwood remarks that Joseph is so sour that he "must have need of divine aid to digest his dinner," he does not mean that Joseph literally needs God's help to digest. Instead, he is making a sarcastic joke about Joseph's sourness.

3. D: Mr. Lockwood describes the ventilation as bracing. Ventilation allows the flow of cool, fresh air, which can create an invigorating sensation. Although the word *bracing* can mean "supporting," "bracketing," and "staying," this is not how the author uses the word in paragraph 9.

4. C: Heathcliff seems to have little regard for his old home. He does not garden and does not have a gardening staff. As a result, the vegetation on his property will be trimmed and landscaped only if his cattle decide to nibble it. Although the statement is somewhat humorous and possibly eccentric, it does not provide evidence that Heathcliff is mad.

5. D: The main argument is stated in paragraph 4: "With the extreme convenience of technology, printed books are likely going to become a thing of the past." The other choices are either supporting details or extra information not related to the main argument.

6. C: Paragraph 1 explains the progression of storytelling, beginning with oral tradition and going past the invention of the printing press. In context with the rest of the essay, this paragraph is needed to explain how storytelling has evolved and how stories are shared within society.

7. A: In paragraph 1, it is stated that oral tradition was the main medium for storytelling before the invention of the printing press.

8. B: It is not a fact that "sliding a finger across the screen (or pressing a button) is just as satisfying to the reader." Satisfaction is not something universal that can be proven for every reader. This statement is an opinion. All other choices are factual in nature.

9. A: The author makes the argument in paragraph 5 that devices such as the iPad and Kindle are "therefore better than books because they have multiple uses." All other choices reflect either supporting details or misrepresentations of the statements made by the author.

10. B: Based on the information given in paragraph 1, the reader can infer that before the invention of the printing press, books had to be handwritten, making them difficult to create and therefore costly to produce.

11. C: Sentence 1 states that printed materials are still valued and cherished in our society. Sentence 2 asserts that printed materials are a thing of the past. The points contradict one another, making the sentences contradictory.

12. C: The author states that electronic devices can store more than one book at a time and serve many other purposes, such as accessing information on the internet. Because these devices have multiple uses, the author believes they are better than books. While it may be true that electronic devices can be used to play games online, this is not mentioned by the author.

13. C: The question asks which job is less desirable than homesteading according to the writer. Choice C is correct because Stewart speaks of going out to wash as less preferable than homesteading. Choices A, B, and D are incorrect because the letter does not mention cooking in restaurants, opening a bed and breakfast, or teaching.

14. B: Stewart mentions the hard work of laundry, but she does not speak of any enjoyment of it as she does about homesteading. Choice A cannot be correct because Stewart does not seem to be lazy. Choice C is possible, but there is no evidence to support that idea. Choice D cannot be correct because no reason for anger is given.

15. D: Stewart says that homesteading is a lonely task. For example, she mentions that "persons afraid of ...loneliness had better let ranching alone." Stewart explains in the letter that her work uses less strength than washing. So, choice A is wrong. Choice B is also incorrect because it is addressed in the first paragraph of the letter. Choice C is incorrect because it is mentioned as an advantage in the first paragraph.

16. A: Stewart directly states that women would have "the added satisfaction of knowing that their job will not be lost to them if they care to keep it." Although going on strike was common at the time, Stewart does not mention it. So, choice B is incorrect. Denver is in the Rocky Mountains, but landslides are not mentioned as a risk. So, choice C cannot be the correct answer. Fire is always a risk, but Stewart does not bring it up in the letter. So, choice D is not the correct answer.

17. C: The letter is very positive and full of reasons on why homesteading is a good choice. Choice A is incorrect. The reason is that there is no complaint of hard work, weather, or loneliness. Choice B is also incorrect because the letter does not speak of sadness or loneliness. Instead, Stewart rejoices in the good success of the homestead. Also, choice D is incorrect because there is no hopelessness expressed in the letter.

18. D: Growing potatoes is so simple that her six-year-old can do so with little help. The issue is not child labor. So, choice A is incorrect. Stewart does not mention schooling. So, this makes choice B incorrect. Stewart's point has nothing to do with whether women work as hard as men. So, choice C is not the correct response.

19. A: At the beginning of the passage, the author explains that "every tide-water dog, strong of muscle and with warm, long hair, from Puget Sound to San Diego" was being taken to the North to help find the "yellow metal." Since the value of gold is so high, it is the most likely explanation that Manuel took Buck in order for Manuel to pay off his debts from gambling.

20. B: The author uses the details in paragraph 1 to foreshadow what might happen to Buck. Phrases like "trouble was brewing" or "these men wanted dogs" indicate that Buck might be heading for trouble. The paragraph does not give details about Buck's life as a whole; later paragraphs give those details. The first paragraph also does not give details about the setting. Setting details about Buck's current situation are given in later paragraphs. Finally, the first paragraph does not describe any characters other than Buck, and it does not indicate that Buck is the villain.

21. C: Choice C is correct because the first part of the passage mostly describes Buck's life, but the passage ends in a moment of change when the stranger purchases Buck. The passage does not describe a sequence of events as they happen. Instead, the passage gives an overview of how Buck lived before the moment of change. Although part of the passage describes Buck's history, the passage also describes the moment in which his life changes. The passage only describes life at Judge Miller's place but doesn't describe what came afterwards.

22. A: "Change" is correct because the passage begins by setting up Buck's life and then showing a moment where his life is about to change drastically. Only paragraph 5 refers to family; this is not a big enough portion of the passage to imply that the larger selection is about family. Although Buck might need to work hard in the future, the passage does not have many clues about upcoming hard work. The passage does not spend time showing that Buck strongly values relationships. The end of the passage indicates that Buck is about to experience a moment of change.

23. C: Choice C is correct because paragraphs 2–5 introduce Buck and the setting in which he lives. The paragraphs accomplish this introduction by giving many detailed facts, such as the detail in paragraph 4 about the times he escorted Mollie and Alice on walks. Paragraphs 2–5 do not introduce all of the characters, as two new characters, Manuel and the stranger, are introduced in paragraph 6. While aspects of paragraphs 2–4 do show Buck's personality, the paragraphs also give other details about Buck, such as information about his parents and appearance. Toots and Ysabel are only mentioned in paragraphs 3 and 4. Furthermore, paragraph 4 says that he utterly ignored Toots and Ysabel, not that he is affectionate toward them.

24. D: Only the sentence in choice D indicates an unsupported opinion on the part of the author. The author's use of phrases like *far too hasty* and *undoubtedly* make the information in this sentence subjective to the author since it cannot be proven whether the scholars' dismissal is too hasty or whether religion's role in the situation is unable to be doubted. All other sentences in the passage offer support or an explanation that is factual and able to be confirmed.

25. C: The author actually says, "Charles's own political troubles extended beyond religion in this case, and he was beheaded in 1649." This would indicate that religion was less involved in this situation than in other situations. There is not enough information to infer that Charles II never married; the passage only notes that he had no legitimate children. (In fact, he had more than 10 illegitimate children by his mistresses.) While the chance of a Catholic king frightened many in England, it is reaching beyond logical inference to assume that people were relieved when the royal children died. Finally, the author does not provide enough detail for the reader to assume that James I had no Catholic leanings. The author only says that James acknowledged the Church of England and approved a Protestant translation of the Bible.

26. A: The author notes, "In spite of a strong resemblance to the king, the young James III was generally rejected among the English and the Lowland Scots, who referred to him as "the Pretender." This indicates that there *was* a resemblance, and this increases the likelihood that the child was, in fact, that of James and Mary Beatrice. Answer choice B is too much of an opinion statement that does not have enough support in the passage. The passage essentially refutes choice C by pointing out that James "the Pretender" was welcomed in the Highlands, and there is little in the passage to suggest that James was unable to raise an army and mount an attack.

27. B: The passage is composed in a chronological sequence with each king introduced in order of reign, so choice B is correct. While some of the events in the passage may have a cause-and-effect relationship, the organization of the overall passage is not cause and effect. The passage also does not seek to introduce problems and solutions, so choice C is incorrect. While the people mentioned in the passage are compared and contrasted, these comparisons do not dictate the organization of the passage, so choice D is incorrect.

28. D: The passage is largely informative in focus, and the author provides extensive details about this period in English and Scottish history. There is little in the passage to suggest persuasion, and the tone of the passage has no indication of a desire to entertain. Additionally, the passage is historical, so the author avoids expressing feelings and instead focuses on factual information (with the exception of the one opinion statement).

29. B: The passage does not state this outright, but the author indicates that the younger sons of King George III began considering the option of marrying and producing heirs *after* Princess Charlotte Augusta died. Since she was the heir-apparent, her death left the succession undetermined. The author mentions very little about any "wrongs" that Victoria's uncles committed, so this cannot be a logical conclusion. The passage says nothing about the Duke of Kent's preference for a male heir over a female. (In fact, it was likely that he was delighted to have any heir.) The author does not provide enough detail about the relationship between the Duchess of Kent and King William IV to infer logically that his suspicions were "unreasonable" or that the duchess cared only for her daughter's wellbeing.

30. C: The author actually notes in the last paragraph that Victoria was an "improbable princess who became queen," and the rest of the passage demonstrates how it was a series of small events that changed the course of British succession. The passage is largely factual, so it makes little sense as a persuasive argument. The author mentions the Victorian Era, but the passage is more about Queen Victoria's family background than it is about the era to which she gave her name. And the passage is more about how the events affected Victoria (and through her, England) than it is about the direct effect that George III's sons had on English history.

31. D: This passage is most likely to belong in some kind of biographical reference about Queen Victoria. A scholarly paper would include more analysis instead of just fact. The information in the passage does not fit the genre of mystery at all. And since the passage recounts history, it is not a likely candidate for a fictional story.

32. A: Dickinson's words *oppresses, hurt, despair,* and *imperial affliction* confirm that depression is the best answer. The poem certainly does not contain any words that could refer to joy, making choice B incorrect. Likewise, choice C, uncertainty, cannot be supported by the text. There is no sense of surprise in the lines; rather, the certain slant of light can almost be predicted as coming on winter afternoons. Thus, choice D can be eliminated.

33. C: A simile is a comparison of two unlike things using the words *like* or *as*. Dickinson says the slant of light oppresses like "the weight of cathedral tunes." Alliteration is the repetition of sounds used in a sentence, which does not take place in this selection. Personification is the attributing of human qualities to something not human, a device not used here, so choice B is incorrect. A metaphor is a direct comparison, which is not the case in these lines, making choice D wrong.

34. B: Personification is the attributing of human qualities to something not human. Here, the landscape listens and shadows hold their breath, mimicking human or animal behavior. Assonance is the repetition of vowel sounds, which is not evident here, making choice A wrong. A simile is a comparison of two unlike things using the words *like* or *as*. Because that is not the case here, choice C is incorrect. A metaphor is a direct comparison, which is not the case in these lines, making choice D wrong.

35. D: Choice D is correct because the first stanza clearly refers to "winter afternoons." Solstice is not a season but a day on which seasons change, making choice A incorrect. Choice B, summer, is not supported in the text of the poem. Likewise, choice C, autumn, is absent from the text. The reference to the "look of death" in the final line of the poem cannot be construed as anything except winter.

36. B: Lines 4–6 of passage 1 state that "the people must cede to [the government] some of their natural rights in order to vest it with requisite powers." Jay is arguing against dividing the states into separate confederacies. While he would seem to agree with the idea of seeking the overall prosperity of America rather than its individuals, this is not clearly stated in the passage. Jay states in line 31 that the American people speak the same language and profess the same religion but is using this as an illustration of their uniformity, not urging them to retain these characteristics.

37. B: In this case *to vest* means to grant or endow with authority. The answer choice *to guard, as a breastplate* is reminiscent of the noun *vest*, a garment. The answer choice *to make an investment,* also plays on the word *vest*, changing it to *investment*. The answer choice *to give up* means the opposite of the correct answer.

38. C: Jay uses the word *received* to describe how the majority of people have previously accepted or agreed upon this opinion. He is not referring to receiving guests or a gift, nor is he referring to something that is earned.

39. A: Jay claims that "the prosperity of the people of America" (lines 17–18) depends on a united government as well as their "rights, privileges, and protection" (lines 41–43) and that to gain these benefits, "the people must cede to it some of their natural rights" (lines 4–5). The statement that "the government is a democracy, so all rights are securely retained by the people" refers to Henry's definition of a democracy in Passage 2, which is not reflected in Passage 1. The other choices are arguments that are not found in either passage.

40. D: Henry would likely support the statement that liberty is the highest gift a person can be given, as his focus was on the importance of liberty, but Jay might not agree that nothing is more important than liberty, as he encouraged Americans to give up certain freedoms for safety and prosperity. Jay would likely agree with the statement that there must be some kind of central government to avoid chaos, as he advocated for a central government, but Henry might disagree that a central government, rather than individual state governments, is needed. Jay would also probably agree with the statement that the United States needs to be strong as it conducts global business, based on his assertion that "as a nation we have formed alliances, and made treaties, and entered into various compacts and conventions with foreign states" (lines 44–47). However, Henry urges Americans "not to inquire how your trade may be increased, nor how you are to become a great and powerful people" (lines 31–33), so he would likely disagree. Both passages discuss the great potential of America, so Jay and Henry would likely agree that the country could be a land of many privileges.

41. D: Henry states that "the security of your liberty" (line 37) is far more valuable than any benefits that can come from a strong government. He makes no claim that physical safety can be better found without this government. Choice C is an argument he makes, but it does not address the question.

42. B: Jay (Passage 1) claims that "the prosperity of the people of America depended on their continuing firmly united" (lines 17–19). Henry claims that Americans should not "inquire how your trade may be increased, nor how you are to become a great and powerful people, but how your liberties can be secured" (lines 31–34). He holds that these liberties are more valuable than any prosperity a powerful government can bring. Choices A, C, and D are either arguments that Henry, not Jay, makes or something from Jay's article that he is not advocating for.

43. A: John Jay in passage 1 points out the "indispensable necessity of government" (line 2) and that Americans should be "firmly united" (line 19). Patrick Henry declares in passage 2 that "liberty ought to be the direct end of your Government" (lines 34–35). The correct answer choice lines up with these values. The second choice reverses these points. In passage 1, Jay points out that certain politicians, with whom he does not agree, seek separate confederacies. Since he is arguing against this, the third choice, which states he is arguing for separate confederacies, is incorrect. In passage 2, Henry declares that "this is not a democracy" (line 7), much as he seems to wish it were. Passage 1 never clearly discusses a democracy, while Passage 2 never discusses separate confederacies.

44. D: Both passages address the relationship between government and individual rights, expressing concerns about how the government's power may impact personal freedoms. Passage 1 discusses the need for a national government that would require citizens to relinquish some of their natural rights, while passage 2 argues against the abandonment of sacred rights in the transition to a consolidated government. Choices A and C should be ruled out immediately, as they do not address the individual rights issue, while choice B is only a part of the concerns in passage 2. Choice D directly addresses the common concern expressed in both passages about the potential threat to individual liberties in a consolidated government.

45. B: Henry completely disagrees with the premise of Jay's argument that a consolidated government is a necessary and good thing. He is not merely looking at it from a different angle or adding to Jay's claims. He does not, for the most part, agree with Jay.

46. B: The excerpt includes a number of plays on words, exaggerations, and other comic devices that show that it is meant to be funny.

47. C: As part of their argument, the Doctor and Martine are regretting that they are married to one another. As a result, she regrets the day that she said "yes," and, in the very next line, he regrets having signed the marriage papers.

48. A: In this section, Martine levels a series of accusations at the Doctor: drinking, selling the furniture, and gambling. His answers are all flippant one-liners that mock her. He shows no regret, and he does not attempt to defend his actions in any way.

49. C: The Doctor drinks, gambles, sells all that they own, and takes no responsibility for the children. He does not appear to be irascible or choleric (both indicate someone who is easily angered) or intolerant (someone who does not respect other beliefs or opinions).

50. D: In this portion of the excerpt, the Doctor tells Martine to be gentle and, backing away, tells her not to get into a passion, that is, to become emotional. He tries to placate her and then, in the last line, stands his ground and becomes combative as well.

Language Arts–Writing

1. B: The word *fourth* should be written out to match the form of *third*. While the word *teacher* could become plural, choice A is incorrect because the second sentence of the passage shows that Alberto is talking about a single teacher. Choice C is incorrect because the comma correctly separates an independent clause from a phrase that gives extra detail. Choice D is incorrect because Alberto is talking about several years (plural) rather than something belonging to one year (possessive).

2. C: The phrase "handed in assignments after the due date" is redundant with the phrase "turned work in late"; only one of those phrases needs to be in the sentence. Choices B and D are incorrect because both phrases add unique information to the sentence. Choice A is incorrect because the sentence has two redundant phrases, and one of them should be deleted.

3. A: The word *surprisingly* correctly shows that the reaction was unexpected, given Alberto's behavior. Answers B and D are incorrect because *actually* and *instead* imply an alternative reaction was mentioned. Choice C does not work because the second sentence does not further support the first sentence; it is a new idea.

4. A: The sentence has a clarity problem. The dependent clause should come at the beginning of the sentence rather than interrupting the independent clause. Choice B does not make a correction to the sentence. Choice C makes the sentence into a question, which is not necessary. Choice D is incorrect because the sentence needs to be reworded to have clarity.

5. B: This sentence should come after the third sentence because it is the first tip to consider. Choice A is incorrect because this sentence is only one part to a working vehicle. Choice C is incorrect because a sentence that begins with *First of all* should not be the concluding sentence. Choice D is wrong because the sentence belongs with paragraph A. In paragraph B, the focus is on working under the hood and the inside of the vehicle.

6. A: The sentence is written correctly. Choice D is incorrect because splitting the infinitive will be a mistake, not a correction. Choice B is incorrect because you need to know which area of the car needs to be checked. Choice C is incorrect because that would only create a problem in agreement.

7. D: Sentence 10 is a run-on sentence and needs correct punctuation. The use of a semicolon between two sentences that are connected in thought is the only acceptable answer choice. You cannot leave the sentence alone. So, choice A is not the correct choice. Choice C places a conjunction between the two sentences. However, it does not include the necessary comma before the conjunction. So, it is an incorrect choice.

8. C: These words are three items in a series. So, commas are needed to separate them. Choice A is incorrect because the apostrophe shows possession, and it is used correctly. Choice B is also wrong because the word *emergency* is spelled correctly in the sentence. Choice D is incorrect because the sentence needs commas.

9. A: This sentence has a misplaced modifier. Currently, you can read the sentence and think that you should take everything with you except the car. When you move the word, you understand the reason that you are leaving the car is that you know where you are going and what you are doing. Choice B is incorrect because the word is important to the sentence. Choice C is wrong because there is no need for a comma. Choice D is incorrect because there is an error in the sentence.

10. A: There is nothing wrong with the sentence. So, choice A is the correct choice. Everything after the comma could be removed without harming the independent clause at the beginning of the sentence. So, the nonessential adjective clause needs a comma. Choice B is incorrect because it suggests removing the comma. Choice C makes *products* singular. This is incorrect because it creates a problem with subject-verb agreement. The same problem is in choice D; however, the verb is singular.

11. B: This question is about subject-verb agreement. *Slow foods* is plural and needs the plural form of *to be* which is *are*. When you change *is* to *are*, the sentence is corrected. Choice A is incorrect because there is not an extra comma in the sentence. Choice C is also wrong because *slow foods* is not a proper noun. So, it does not need capitalization. Choice D is incorrect because *comeback* is one word.

12. D: The question reviews correct spelling. *Emphasize* is the verb, and *emphasis* is the noun which is needed here. Choice A is incorrect because it does not address the problem. Choice B changes the verb from *puts* to *places*, yet there is no problem with the verb choice. Choice C makes the verb plural, but this only adds to the problem.

13. D: This sentence contains an error related to parallel structure. Placing the definite article *the* in front of the final two terms in the series hurts the structure, so choice A is incorrect. Removing *the* makes all the items parallel. Choice B is also incorrect because *specie* is not the singular form of *species*. Additionally, using a singular noun in place of *species* would be inaccurate, as the author is referring to multiple species. Choice C is incorrect because making all nouns singular does not improve the structure of the sentence.

14. C: The error in this sentence is a split infinitive. The adverb *fully* comes between the words *to* and *use*, and this is incorrect grammar. Choice A is incorrect because the change would cause a subject-verb disagreement. Choice B is incorrect because *also* is correctly placed to indicate an additional benefit of slow food. Choice D is incorrect because there is an error in the sentence.

15. B: *Slow Food USA* is the name of an organization. So, this makes it a proper noun that needs capitalization. Choice A is incorrect because this is the proper name of a specific program. So, the capital letters are correct. Choice C is also wrong because *thru* is a shortcut spelling, but *through* is Standard English. Choice D is incorrect because the sentence has an error.

16. C: Sentence 13 is not important to the article. The writer's garden is not a concern. Choice A is wrong. The reason is that placing the sentence at the beginning of the paragraph makes readers think that the paragraph will be a narrative about the writer's garden. Choice B is incorrect because the last sentence of an essay should be related to the rest of the essay. Choice D is incorrect because the sentence should be removed from this passage.

17. D: The sentence is a run-on. So, the best answer choice is to make two sentences of the run-on sentence. Choice A is incorrect because adding commas does not correct the run-on. For choice C, the original word is the correct word. So, this is incorrect. Choice B is incorrect because it suggests that the terms are not parallel.

18. B: The proper noun *Slow Food on Campus* is an essential appositive. So, the commas can be removed. Now, the sentence is in passive voice. Choice A would help move the sentence to active voice, which is preferred over passive voice. However, this is not the error of the sentence. So, choice A is incorrect. Choice C is wrong because *Slow Food on Campus* is a proper noun that needs capital letters. Choice D is also wrong because *similar* is the correct spelling.

19. A: Sentence 4 makes a statement that doesn't add anything to the argument. It is obvious that the author doesn't agree with Mrs. Conwer's statement, so it is not necessary to write a whole sentence just to say so. Sentence 5 is important to the essay because it sets the essay up for the author's list of arguments. Sentence 13 is necessary because it draws the conclusion from the previous two sentences. Sentence 19 is necessary because it brings up an important point.

20. B: In the original sentence, it is unclear what *them* refers to. Using logic and context, we can reason that the object pronoun must refer to the students, since Mrs. Conwer and the teachers are the subject. It does not make sense to say that the principal and teachers would be ignoring other teachers or the administration, so answer choices A and D are incorrect. Answer choice C does not make sense either, as creating a dress code does not ignore a dress code's details.

21. C: Choice C begins with a subject and verb and is followed by a clause. It is also clear and concise. Choice A is incorrect because the words are out of order and don't logically follow the previous sentence. Sentence 2 should begin with "She says" because it is the school principal's opinion being expressed. This choice is also incorrect because it uses the words *not appropriate* instead of *inappropriate*. Choice B is incorrect because the clause "that students wear to school" should come after the word *outfits*. Choice D is incorrect because the word order changes the meaning of the sentence by stating that any outfits are distracting and inappropriate.

22. D: The sentence does not need an adverb. Instead, it needs a predicate adjective to modify the subject *researchers*. Choice B is incorrect because SAD is an acronym that should have capital letters. The sentence is not a question, so choice C is wrong because it does not need a question mark. Choice A is incorrect because there is a mistake in the sentence.

23. A: The sentence is written correctly, so choice D is incorrect because the adjectives are not coordinate. Choice B is incorrect because the sentence is making a comparison to months that are not during the winter. In other words, the body makes less melatonin in the summer months. Choice C is wrong because *melatonin* does not need to be capitalized.

24. D: The question tests on the use of *effect* and *affect*. In this sentence, you are looking for the verb that means *influence*. So, affect is the correct word in this sentence. Choice B is wrong because the prepositional phrase should not come after *serotonin*. Choice C is incorrect because *less* is for amounts, which is true for this sentence. *Fewer* is for numbers and applies to things that can be counted. So, the correct adverb is being used in this sentence. Choice A is wrong because the sentence has an error.

25. D: The word *fewer* is for numbers and applies to things that can be counted. Sunlight cannot be counted. *Less* is for an amount, which is true for this sentence. Also, making the change brings back the intended parallelism of the sentence. Choice A is incorrect because the subject and verb agree as they are written. Choice B is also incorrect because the word is not a proper noun and does not need capitalization. Because starting the sentence with the word *Less* is correct, choice C would break the desired parallelism and is incorrect.

26. D: The word *factors* is plural and needs a plural verb. The verb *has* is singular. So, this makes a disagreement between subject and verb. The word *have* is the plural form of *has* and needs to be used here. Choice A is incorrect because the sentence has an error with subject-verb agreement. Choice B is wrong because removing the capital letter causes another error. Choice C is incorrect because it just moves the problem in agreement rather than eliminating it.

27. C: The sentence has a problem with parallel structure. The verbs *tough* and *wait* need to be parallel. Choice D is incorrect because SAD is an acronym and needs capital letters. Choice B is also incorrect. There is an attempt to correct the problem of parallelism, but *toughing* needs an auxiliary verb. Choice A is wrong because there is an error that needs to be corrected.

28. B: The sentence is not interrogative; it is declarative. In other words, it needs a period at the end, not a question mark. Choice D is incorrect because *well* is an adverb, and the noun *news* needs an adjective modifier.

Choice C is incorrect because the seasons are not capitalized. Choice A is wrong because there is an error that needs to be corrected.

29. A: Choice A is correct because the word is not being used in a different way from a dictionary definition. Choice B is incorrect because readers need an explanation of the word *temp*. Choice C is wrong because *temporary* is spelled correctly. Choice D is incorrect because a comma is not needed.

30. D: This question is about parallel structure. Both *employs* and *generating* are verbs that need to be changed to be parallel. The best way to make them parallel is by putting both in the present tense. Choice A is incorrect because *the staffing industry* is a single unit, so it does not need the plural form. Choice B is incorrect because the noun is singular and needs a singular verb. Choice C cannot be done without adding more words.

31. D: The sentence uses the wrong homonym. The word *their* is possessive and is needed in this sentence, and *they're* is a contraction of *they are*, so this is the wrong word. In this sentence, *because* is used correctly, so choice A is incorrect. Choice C makes *skills* singular; however, this is not the correct choice. After all, an employer wants a worker who has more than one skill.

32. B: The problem in this question is with antecedent agreement. The pronoun *they* needs a plural noun: *employees*. Choice A is incorrect because of the problem with antecedent agreement. Choice C is incorrect because the subject and verb disagree. Choice D is also wrong. The hyphen in *full-time* does not need to be removed and the subject and verb disagree.

33. C: The problem with the sentence is a comma splice. A semicolon shows that the thoughts of both sentences are related, so the problem is corrected with the semicolon. Choice A cannot be correct because the original has a comma splice. Choice B is also wrong because it has a pronoun-antecedent agreement problem. Choice D is incorrect because it creates a subject-verb agreement problem.

34. D: Adding a comma eliminates the problem of the run-on sentence. Choice A is wrong because there is an error in the sentence. Choice B is also incorrect because it creates a problem with subject-verb agreement. Choice C is incorrect because it creates a subject-verb disagreement in a different part of the sentence.

35. C: The problem in this sentence is a misspelling of *valuable*. Choice D is wrong because a hyphen is not needed to connect the two words. Choice B cannot be correct because *you're* is the right homonym. Choice A is incorrect because there is an error in the sentence.

36. C: This sentence has no parallelism. *To look for* and *interviewing* can be made parallel by making the change suggested in Choice C. Choice D is incorrect because the word *permanent* is spelled correctly. Choice B is incorrect because it tries to correct the problem, but it fails. Choice A cannot be correct because of the error with parallel structure in the sentence.

37. A: Choice A provides a more precise explanation of the reason why only a limited number of people were able to survive the sinking of the Titanic. It replaces the vague phrase *not enough* with *limited*, which is a more specific term that clearly identifies the issue. Additionally, the revised sentence maintains the original meaning and accurately conveys the fact that the insufficient number of lifeboats was the main reason why so many people died. Choice B introduces new information by suggesting that more than half of the passengers on board died, which is not mentioned in the original sentence. The word *insufficient* can also be interpreted in several ways, which does not contribute to a more precise meaning. Choice C uses the improved word *scarce* but also adds new information about the freezing waters, which is not relevant to the sentence. Choice D uses the term *inadequate safety measures*, which is not specifically mentioned in the original sentence and introduces a new idea that may not be entirely accurate.

38. B: Choice B is the simplest way to express the idea in a grammatically correct sentence. *Because of this* refers to the content of the previous sentence.

39. C: Choice C shows the contrast between first-class and third-class passengers. The previous sentences explained why majority of the survivors were a part of the first class passengers. Sentence 13 shifts to explain explains why most of the third class passengers did not survive. "On the other hand" clearly signals this contrast. "Lastly" is not an appropriate transition word, as there was not a series of listed facts. "For example" is not an appropriate transition to use since it is not giving an example. "Therefore" is not an appropriate transition word because the new information does not involve cause and effect with the previous sentences.

40. D: The problem in the sentence as written is one of subject-verb agreement and colloquial or substandard English. *Some* indicates that more than one apartment complex is being discussed. It, therefore, is necessary to change both the subject and verb to plural. Choice A is incorrect; the sentence as written clearly contains an error to be remedied. Choice B is incorrect; choosing an alternative spelling for the homonym does not solve the problem. Choice C is incorrect as well; it creates a different subject-verb agreement problem.

41. C: The problem in this sentence is a dangling modifier. To correct the problem, you can write the independent clause as "you need to consider the other issues about keeping your pet at your apartment." Choice A is wrong because the comma needs to come after the introductory prepositional phrase. Choice B is incorrect because the word is spelled correctly. Choice D cannot be correct because there is an error in the sentence.

42. B: This question is on the use of *affect* and *effect. Affect* is the verb that means to influence, and it is needed here. *Effect* is the noun that points to the influence. Choice A is incorrect because there is a problem in the sentence. Choice C is also incorrect because it creates a subject-verb agreement problem. Choice D is incorrect because it does not address the word choice and creates a subject-verb agreement problem.

43. A: *Irregardless* is used very often in informal communication. However, it is not an acceptable word in Standard English. The correct word is *regardless.* Choice B is incorrect because the word *licensing* is spelled correctly. Choice C is incorrect because the sentence does not have extra commas. The first comma separates the dependent clause. The other commas are needed for the items in a series. Choice D is incorrect as well because the sentence does have an error.

44. B: The apostrophe is needed in *nations* to show possession of the *highest executive office.* Choice D is incorrect because *executive office* is not a proper noun that needs capitalization. Choice C is wrong because you do not want to separate an infinitive. Also, choice A is wrong because there is an error in the sentence.

45. B: *Wall Street* is the name of a street in New York, so it needs to be capitalized. Choice A is wrong because this would make an error in verb tense. Choice C is incorrect because the words *although* and *though* are nearly synonyms, so choosing *although* is not an error. Choice D is incorrect as well because *investment firm* is a common noun. It is not the name of a certain investment firm, so no capitalization is needed.

46. D: The information in the parentheses is not necessary information. However, the information is closely connected to the sentence, so commas should be used instead of parentheses. Choice B is wrong because *Republicans* is the name of a certain political party and needs capitalization. Choice C is incorrect because the sentence needs a singular noun for *Margaret Chase Smith.* Choice A is incorrect because there is a mistake in the sentence.

47. D: The question is about irregular verb forms. The sentence needs the past participle of *seek,* which is *sought.* So, choice A is incorrect. Choice B is also wrong because the singular subject causes a problem with subject-verb agreement. Choice C is incorrect because the problem is not with the verb tense.

48. D: This is a run-on sentence that can be corrected with a comma between the short independent clauses. Choice B is incorrect because the pronoun *them* is correct. Choice C is incorrect. If you made the change, then you would have an error in subject-verb agreement. Choice A is wrong because there is an error in the sentence.

49. C: Sentence 8 is a personal opinion that does not help this passage. Choice A is incorrect. Changing the order of the paragraphs only hurts the chronological order of the passage. Choices B and D are incorrect because moving these sentences upsets the unity and coherence of the piece.

50. A: The sentence is written correctly. So, choice D is incorrect because *Only* does not need to be removed from the sentence. Choice B is incorrect because vice president is capitalized when the name of a vice president follows the title or when the title is used as a substitute for the name of the specific person. An example would be *Vice President William Rufus de Vane King*. Choice C is wrong because the colon needs to stay in the sentence to signal a formal list of names.

51. D: The sentence places a comma after each country correctly because they are items in a series. However, a comma is not needed after *Liberia* because it is the last item in the series. Choice B is incorrect because the commas are necessary for the items in the series. The exception is the comma after *Liberia*. Choice C is incorrect because *believe* is spelled correctly and choice A is incorrect because there is an error in the sentence.

52. C: This clause needs a present-tense verb for the sentence to be complete. Choice A is incorrect because it does not include a present-tense verb (*conserving* and *stimulating* are participles). Choices B and D are incorrect because they change the participle *conserving* to the present-tense verb *conserve(s)* without adjusting *stimulating*, so the parts of speech do not match. Choice C correctly adds a verb (*aids*) and leaves *conserving* to match *stimulating*.

53. B: The correct present perfect phrase is *has been*. To use *being* (A), the verb needs to be *is* instead of *has* (although this would not fit logically with the sentence, referring to past research rather than an ongoing process). The phrase *is been* (C) incorrectly combines present tense and present perfect. The phrase *having been* (D) is a correct pairing but does not flow logically with this clause because of the *and* before the underlined portion.

54. C: Choice C is both straightforward and clear. Choice A places the clauses in a less clear order and adds unnecessary commas. Choice B also creates an awkward order and adds an incorrect colon, since the part of the sentence after the colon does not define the first or give a list. Choice D removes the unnecessary commas but adds an incorrect em-dash, since it does not set off a parenthetical statement or provide a necessary pause.

55. B: The phrase *such as* begins a nonrestrictive clause (a clause that can be removed from the sentence without altering the meaning). Nonrestrictive clauses must be preceded by commas. Using a semicolon (A) is incorrect. Changing *such* to *like* (C, D) is incorrect because this causes the sentence to read "...variety of substitutes; like as rockwool...," which is incorrect.

56. A: This sentence uses a form of *not only ... but also*, substituting *additionally* for *also*. To use *in addition* (B) is incorrect because it lacks the *to*. The phrase *even to* (C) is incorrect because it does not go with *not only*. The phrase *in also to* (D) is incorrect because of the added *in*.

57. D: This paragraph is written in contrast to the previous one, showing the disadvantages rather than the advantages, so the introduction needs to reflect that. Choices A, B, and C each use a term that shows agreement rather than contrast.

58. C: Because the plants are not exposed to the open air, they are not pollinated by insects (unless introduced by the farmer). It is the farmer's responsibility to provide for these needs. The farmer cannot eliminate (A) or remove (D) natural needs, and simply tracking them (B) is not sufficient.

59. A: The term is modifying the verb *grown*, so it must be an adverb. Although *in a vertical manner* (B) is technically correct, it is unnecessarily verbose and therefore not the best answer. Choices C and D are adjectives rather than adverbs.

60. D: Both the part of the sentence before the punctuation and after it are independent clauses (stand-alone sentences). They can either be separated with a period or joined by a semicolon. Joining them with a comma (A) creates a comma-splice sentence. Using a conjunction such as *and* would be grammatically correct with a comma, but *or* (B) does not make sense. Adding *then* (C) creates another independent clause, which would require a semicolon or period rather than a comma.

Essay Question

1. Essay question graders commonly look for the following elements in a strong response: strong content knowledge, clear organization, and effective arguments or examples. Language and usage are not usually strictly graded, but they can make a big impact on the clarity of your ideas.

Please use the provided rubric to make sure your response meets these common criteria. Try to have a friend or family member grade your response for you or take a break after writing your response and return to grade it with fresh eyes.

Constructed Response Rubric

Domain	Description
Content Knowledge	• The response directly addresses every part of the prompt. • The response demonstrates independent knowledge of the topic. • The response discusses the topic at an appropriate depth.
Organization	• The response introduces the topic, usually with a thesis statement or by restating the prompt. • The response directly addresses the prompt by providing a clear and concise answer or solution. • The answer or solution is supported by logical arguments or evidence. • The response restates the main idea in the conclusion.
Arguments and Examples	• The response provides a reasonable answer to the prompt. • The answer is supported by strong reasoning or evidence. • The response develops ideas logically and connects ideas to one another. • The reasoning and evidence provided act to support a unified main idea.
Language and Usage	• The response demonstrates effective use of grammar and uses varied sentence structure throughout the response. • The response demonstrates correct use of spelling, punctuation, and capitalization. • The response demonstrates strong and varied use of vocabulary relevant to the topic and appropriate for the intended audience.

Mathematics

1. A: Jamie had \$6.50 in his wallet. To solve this problem, you subtract \$4.25 and \$2.00 from that amount: $\$6.50 - \$4.25 - \$2.00 = \$0.25$. So, you are left with \$0.25. Then, you add the \$2.50 that your friend had borrowed: $\$0.25 + \$2.50 = \$2.75$. Therefore, Jamie currently has \$2.75 in his wallet.

2. D: Integers consist of all positive and negative whole numbers and the number zero. The product of three integers must be an integer, so you can eliminate any answer choice that is not an integer. The product of two even integers is even. The product of an even and odd integer is even. The only even choice is 24, and we can see that $2 \times 4 \times 3 = 24$.

3. B: To solve, first subtract Jerry's weight from the total permitted weight to find out how much the items can weight together.

$$800 - 200 = 600$$

Since there are 4 pieces of equipment, divide 600 by 4 to find out the average weight of each item.

$$600 \div 4 = 150$$

Each item should weigh about 150 pounds.

4. B: To answer this question, we first determine the total cost of the onions and carrots, since these prices are given. This will equal $2 \times \$3.69 + 3 \times \$4.29 = \$20.25$. Next, this sum is subtracted from the total cost of the produce to determine the cost of the mushrooms: $\$24.15 - \$20.25 = \$3.90$. Finally, the cost of the mushrooms is divided by the quantity in pounds to determine the cost per pound:

$$\text{Cost per lb} = \frac{\$3.90}{1.5} = \$2.60$$

Therefore, the mushrooms cost $2.60 per pound.

5. C: Prime numbers are those that are only evenly divisible by 1 and themselves. 68 is not a prime number because it is divisible by 1, 2, 4, 17, 34, and 68. 69 is not a prime number because it is divisible by 1, 3, 23, and 69. 70 is not a prime number because it is divisible by 1, 2, 5, 7, 10, 14, 35, and 70. 71 is a prime number because it is only divisible by 1 and itself. Therefore, in a sequence of prime numbers from least to greatest, the number 71 immediately follows 67.

6. B: Multiply 30 by 0.2 and subtract this from the original price of the shirt to find the sale price.

$$30 \times 0.2 = 6$$
$$30 - 6 = 24$$

The sale price of the shirt is $24. Then, multiply 24 by 0.2 and add the product to the sale price to find the final price.

$$24 \times 0.2 = 4.8$$
$$24 + 4.8 = 28.8$$

Therefore, the final price of the shirt is $28.80.

7. C: Candidate A's vote percentage is determined by the number of votes that he obtained divided by the total number of votes cast, and then multiplied by 100 to convert the decimal into a percentage.

$$\text{Candidate A's vote percentage} = \frac{36{,}800}{36{,}800 + 32{,}100 + 2{,}100} \times 100 = 51.8\%$$

Therefore, 51.8% of the vote went to Candidate A.

8. D: The radius r of this circle is the line segment OA. Since $\angle ABO$ is a right angle, line segment OA is the hypotenuse of the right triangle. By the Pythagorean theorem, $r^2 = x^2 + y^2$, so $r = \sqrt{x^2 + y^2}$.

9. C: The given equations form a system of linear equations. Since the first equation is already given in terms of x, it will be easier to solve it using the substitution method. Start by substituting $2y - 3$ for x in the second equation.

$$2x + \frac{1}{2}y = 3$$
$$2(2y - 3) + \frac{1}{2}y = 3$$

Next, solve the resulting equation for y. Distribute the 2 and then combine like y-terms in the result.

$$4y - 6 + \frac{1}{2}y = 3$$
$$\frac{9}{2}y - 6 = 3$$

Finally, isolate the variable y by adding 6 to both sides and then dividing both sides by the coefficient of y, which is $\frac{9}{2}$.

$$\frac{9}{2}y = 9$$
$$y = 2$$

Therefore, the value of y is 2.

10. D: The perimeter (P) of the quadrilateral is simply the sum of its sides:

$$P = m + (m + 2) + (m + 3) + 2m$$

Put together like terms by adding the variables (m-terms) together. Then, add the constants. This gives you $P = 5m + 5$.

In this problem, it seems that some of the variables do not have a number in front of them. However, when there is no coefficient, this means multiplication by 1. So, $m = 1m$, $x = 1x$, and so on.

11. B: Add the 14 blue, 6 red, 12 green and 8 purple buttons together to get a total of 40 buttons. If 25 buttons are removed, there are 15 buttons remaining in the bag. The chance of drawing a red button is now $\frac{1}{3}$. So, you divide 15 into thirds to get 5 red buttons remaining in the bag. The original total of red buttons was 6; so $6 - 5 = 1$. One red button was removed, so choice B is correct.

12. B: When the wedges are rearranged into the rectangle, half of the wedge arcs form the top length of the rectangle and the other half of the wedge arcs form the bottom length of the rectangle. Since all of the wedge arcs combine to form the entire circumference of the circle, the length of the rectangle is half of the circumference of the circle. The formula for the circumference of a circle with radius r is $C = 2\pi r$. Half of that circumference is $\left(\frac{1}{2}\right) 2\pi r = \pi r$. Answer C is the width of the rectangle. Answer D is the area of the rectangle.

13. B: $\frac{x}{8}$ and $\frac{y}{4}$ both equal 4, so consequently:

$$\frac{x}{8} = 4 \qquad x = 4 \times 8 \qquad x = 32$$

$$\frac{y}{4} = 4 \qquad y = 4 \times 4 \qquad y = 16$$

$$x - y = 32 - 16 \qquad x - y = 16$$

14. B: The two right triangles are similar because they share a pair of vertical angles. Vertical angles are always congruent (e.g., $\angle ACB$ and $\angle DCE$). Both right angles (e.g., $\angle B$ and $\angle D$) are also congruent. So, $\angle A$ and $\angle E$ are congruent because of the triangular sum theorem.

With similar triangles, corresponding sides will be proportional. $\overline{BC}$ is $\frac{1}{2}$ the length of $\overline{CD}$. So, $\overline{AC}$ will be $\frac{1}{2}$ the length of $\overline{CE}$. The length of $\overline{CE}$ can be computed from the Pythagorean theorem because it is the hypotenuse of a right triangle where the lengths of the other two sides are known.

$$\overline{CE} = \sqrt{6^2 + 8^2} = \sqrt{36 + 64} = \sqrt{100} = 10$$

The length of $\overline{AC}$ will be $\frac{1}{2}$ of this value, or 5 units.

15. C: A reflection is a transformation producing a mirror image. A figure reflected over the x-axis will have its vertices in the form (x, y) transformed to $(x, -y)$. The point W at $(1, -7)$ reflects to W' at $(1,7)$. Only choice C shows $WXYZ$ being carried onto its image $W'X'Y'Z'$ by a reflection across the x-axis. Choice A shows a reflection across the line $y = x$. Choice B shows a 90° counterclockwise rotation about the origin. Choice D shows a reflection across the y-axis.

16. A: To solve, you will need to move the decimal 4 places. Since the scientific notation has a negative power of 10, move the decimal left. If the power of 10 is positive, you need to move it to the right.

$$7.4 \times 10^{-4} = 7.4 \times 0.0001 = 0.00074$$

Therefore, the standard form of the diameter of a red blood cell is 0.00074 centimeters.

17. C: To determine the scale factor of the dilation, compare the coordinates of $\Delta J'K'L'$ to the coordinates of ΔJKL. J is at $(-2, -3)$ and J' is at $(-4, -6)$, which means that the coordinates of J were multiplied by a scale factor of 2 to get the coordinates of J'. K is at $(1,3)$ and K' is at $(2,6)$. L is at $(4, -1)$ and L' is at $(8, -2)$. The coordinates of K and L were also multiplied by a scale factor of 2 to get to the coordinates of K' and L'. Therefore, the scale factor of the dilation is 2.

18. C: Multiply the first numbers in each of the parentheses to get 6, and add the exponents of the tens. $(2 \times 10^5) \times (3 \times 10^4) = 2 \times 3 \times 10^{5+4} = 6 \times 10^9$.

19. D: When the factors $(x - 4)$ and $(x + 7)$ are multiplied, the x-terms sum to $3x$ and the constants produce a product of -28.

20. D: Manipulate the inequality to isolate the variable. Start by adding 12 to each side.

$$4x - 12 < 4$$
$$4x - 12 + 12 < 4 + 12$$
$$4x < 16$$

Then, divide both sides by 4.

$$\frac{4x}{4} < \frac{16}{4}$$
$$x < 4$$

Since x must be less than and not equal to 4, only the last choice works.

21. B: The product given for choice B can be written as $27x^3 - 9x^2y + 3xy^2 + 9x^2y - 3xy^2 + y^3$, which reduces to $27x^3 + y^3$.

22. B: Solve the inequality by changing the inequality sign to an equal sign and factoring the left side of the resulting equation:

$$x^2 - 7x + 10 = 0$$
$$(x - 2)(x - 5) = 0$$
$$x - 2 = 0 \qquad x - 5 = 0$$
$$x = 2 \qquad x = 5$$

Since the original inequality sign was a greater-than or equal-to sign (rather than just a greater-than sign), the solution set will include $x = 2$ and $x = 5$.

These two solutions divide the number line into three distinct regions: $x < 2$, $2 < x < 5$, and $x > 5$. To see which regions are in the solution set, pick one test value from each region and substitute it in the original inequality. If the result is a true inequality, then the whole region is part of the solution set. Otherwise, the whole region is not part in the solution set:

Region	Test Value	$x^2 - 7x + 10 \geq 0$	Conclusion
$x < 2$	0	$(0)^2 - 7(0) + 10 \geq 0$ $10 \geq 0$	Part of the solution set
$2 < x < 5$	3	$(3)^2 - 7(3) + 10 \geq 0$ $9-21 + 10 \geq 0$ $-2 \geq 0$	Not part of the solution set
$x > 5$	6	$(6)^2 - 7(6) + 10 \geq 0$ $36-42 + 10 \geq 0$ $4 \geq 0$	Part of the solution set

Therefore, the solution set is $x \leq 2$ or $x \geq 5$.

23. B: The events are dependent since the first marble was not replaced. The sample space of the second draw will decrease by 1 because there will be one fewer marble to choose from. The number of possible red marbles for the second draw will also decrease by 1. Thus, the probability may be written as $P(A \text{ and } B) = \frac{8}{15} \times \frac{7}{14} = \frac{8}{15} \times \frac{1}{2} = \frac{8}{30} = \frac{4}{15}$. The probability he draws a red marble, does not replace it, and draws another red marble is $\frac{4}{15}$.

24. B: The figure is a right triangle, so the Pythagorean theorem ($c^2 = a^2 + b^2$) can be used. The side that is 25 units long is the hypotenuse (c).

$$25^2 = 15^2 + x^2$$

Solve for x.

$$625 = 225 + x^2$$
$$400 = x^2$$
$$20 = x$$

25. C: The test has 40 questions, and Matthew gets x questions wrong, so he gets $40 - x$ questions right. Each right answer is worth 3 points, so his total score is $3(40 - x)$. Since his total score must be greater than 96, we have:

$$3(40 - x) > 96$$
$$40 - x > 32$$
$$8 - x > 0$$
$$8 > x$$

Because Matthew cannot miss fewer than zero questions, we have $0 \leq x < 8$.

26. D: First, test each expression to see which satisfies the condition $x > y$. This condition is met for all the answer choices except for the third choice, so this doesn't need to be considered further. Next, test the remaining choices to see which satisfy the inequality $x + y > 0$. It can be seen that this inequality holds for the first two choices, but it does not for the last choice, since $x + y = 3 + (-3) = 3 - 3 = 0$. In this case, the sum $x + y$ is not greater than 0.

27. D: Get all of the variables on one side of the equation and solve.

$7\sqrt{x} + 16 = 79$	Subtract 16 from both sides of the equation
$7\sqrt{x} = 63$	Divide both sides by 7
$\sqrt{x} = 9$	Square both sides
$x = 81$	

28. C: Take the cross product of the numerators and denominators from either side of this proportion.

$$\frac{12}{x} = \frac{30}{6}$$

Cross multiply to get $30x = 72$. Then, divide each side by 30. So, you are left with $x = 2.4$.

29. A: This is a typical plot of an inverse variation where the product of the dependent and independent variables, x and y, is always equal to the same value. In this case, the product is always equal to 1. So, the plot is in the first and third quadrants of the coordinate plane. As x increases and goes to infinity, y decreases and goes to zero while keeping the constant product. In contrast, choice B is a linear plot for an equation of the form $y = x$. Choice C is a quadratic plot for the equation $y = x^2$. Choice D is an exponential plot for the equation $y = 2^x$.

30. D: The internal angles of a triangle always add up to 180°. Since ΔABC is a right triangle, then $\angle ABC = 90°$, and $\angle ACB$ is given as 30°. The middle letter is for the vertex. By using the triangle addition theorem, the answer must be: $\angle BAC = 180 - (90 + 30) = 180 - 120 = 60$. Therefore, $\angle BAC = 60°$.

31. A: This equation is a linear relationship that has a slope of 3.60 and passes through the origin. The table shows that for each hour of rental, the cost increases by $3.60. This matches with the slope of the equation. Of course, if the bicycle is not rented at all (0 hours), there will be no charge ($0). If plotted on the Cartesian plane, the line would have a y-intercept of 0. The first choice is the only one that meets these requirements.

32. C: The correct answer is (1,1). The line on the graph extends from a point at the upper left (quadrant IV) with x, y coordinates $(-4,4)$ to a point at the lower right (quadrant II) with coordinates $(6,-2)$. To determine the midpoint, add the x and y coordinates for each point separately and divide by 2. Thus, for x:

$$x_{mid} = \frac{x_1 + x_2}{2} = \frac{(-4) + 6}{2} = \frac{2}{2} = 1$$

Similarly, for y:

$$y_{mid} = \frac{y_1 + y_2}{2} = \frac{4 + (-2)}{2} = \frac{2}{2} = 1$$

33. D: The slopes of perpendicular lines are reciprocals and have the opposite sign. As an example, in the figure below, Line A has a slope of $-\frac{1}{2}$, and Line B has a slope of 2. These lines are perpendicular.

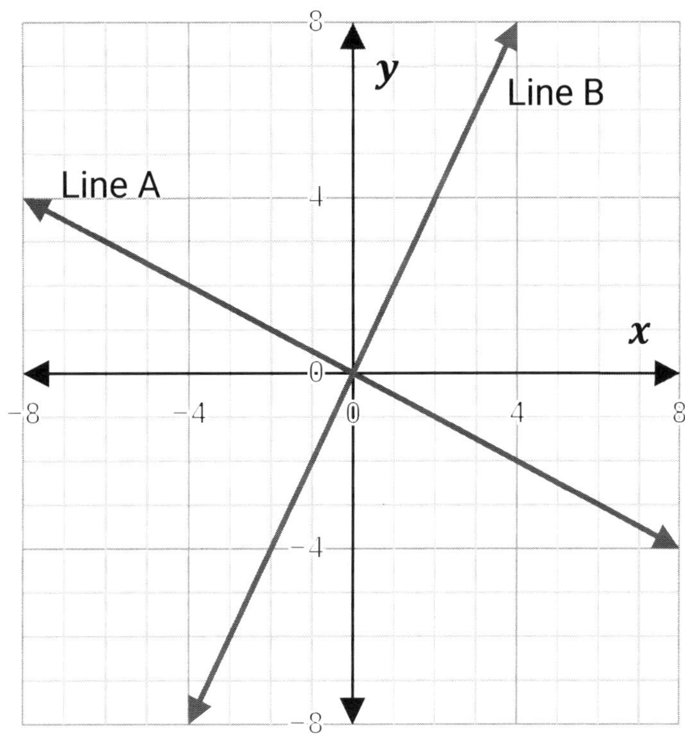

34. B: The number of tails he can expect after 6 coin tosses is equal to the product of the probability of getting tails on one coin toss and the number of coin tosses. Thus, the expected value is $\frac{1}{2} \cdot 6 = 3$.

35. C: Because both expressions share the factor 10^3, we can simply factor and add the ones places. $(8 \times 10^3) + (1 \times 10^3) = (1 + 8)(10^3) = 9 \times 10^3$.

36. B: The y-intercept of the line is $(0,-1)$. Another point on the line is (1,0). Slope is the vertical change over horizontal change, which is $m = \frac{0-(-1)}{1-0} = \frac{1}{1} = 1$. Plugging this information into the slope-intercept form $y = mx + b$, the equation is $y = x - 1$.

37. B: Use the FOIL method (First, Outer, Inner, Last) and then combine like terms to solve this equation:

$$\begin{aligned}(3x+1)(7x+10) &= (3x)(7x)+(3x)(10)+(1)(7x)+(1)(10)\\ &= 21x^2+30x+7x+10\\ &= 21x^2+37x+10\end{aligned}$$

38. D: For each die there is a $\frac{1}{6}$ chance that a 6 will be on top because a die has 6 sides. The probability that a 6 will show for each die is not affected by the results from another roll of the die. In other words, these probabilities are independent. So, the overall probability of throwing 3 sixes is the product of the individual probabilities: $P = \frac{1}{6} \times \frac{1}{6} \times \frac{1}{6} = \frac{1}{6^3} = \frac{1}{216}$. Therefore, the probability that all three dice will land on a 6 is $\frac{1}{216}$.

39. D: Rafael's profit on each computer is given by the difference between the price he pays and the price he charges his customer, or \$800 − \$450. If he sells n computers in a month, his total profit will be n times this difference, or $n(\$800 - \$450)$. However, it is necessary to subtract his fixed costs of \$3,000 from this to compute his final profit per month. This gives the complete equation:

$$P = n(\$800 - \$450) - \$3{,}000$$

40. B: The equation is solved below:

$$\begin{aligned} 6x+1 &= 4x+9 && \text{Subtract } 4x \text{ from both sides of the equation}\\ 2x+1 &= 9 && \text{Subtract 1 from both sides of the equation}\\ 2x &= 8 && \text{Divide by 2 on both sides of the equation}\\ x &= 4 \end{aligned}$$

Therefore, the equation has only one solution.

41. D: To solve the equation, first get rid of the denominators by multiplying both sides of the equation by $x(x-3)$ and simplifying the result.

$$\begin{aligned} \frac{4}{x-3} - \frac{2}{x} &= 1\\ x(x-3)\left[\frac{4}{x-3} - \frac{2}{x}\right] &= x(x-3) \times 1\\ 4x - 2(x-3) &= x(x-3)\\ 4x - 2x + 6 &= x^2 - 3x\\ 2x + 6 &= x^2 - 3x \end{aligned}$$

The result is a quadratic equation. Move everything to one side and then solve for x by factoring the left side and applying the zero-product rule.

$$\begin{aligned} x^2 - 5x - 6 &= 0\\ (x+1)(x-6) &= 0\\ x+1 = 0 \qquad & x-6 = 0\\ x = -1 \qquad & x = 6 \end{aligned}$$

Therefore, the possible solutions are $x = -1$ and $x = 6$. Since neither of these values will cause division by zero when substituted back into the original equation, they are both valid solutions.

42. A: First, multiply the numerator and denominator by the denominator's conjugate, $4 + 2i$. Then, simplify the result and write the answer in the form $a + bi$. Remember, $i^2 = -1$.

$$\begin{aligned} \frac{2+3i}{4-2i} \times \frac{4+2i}{4+2i} &= \frac{8+4i+12i+6i^2}{16-4i^2} \\ &= \frac{8+16i-6}{16+4} \\ &= \frac{2+16i}{20} \\ &= \frac{2}{20} + \frac{16i}{20} \\ &= \frac{1}{10} + \frac{4}{5}i \end{aligned}$$

43. B: To divide expressions that contain variables, divide pairs of like variables (or constants) that appear in both the numerator and denominator. For this problem, first divide the constants: $12 \div 3$, then divide the a's: $a^2 \div a$. Since $a^2 \div a$ is equivalent to $\frac{a^2}{a^1}$, use the quotient rule, $\frac{x^a}{x^b} = x^{a-b}$, to simplify it. There is no change to b, since the divisor does not contain the variable b:

$$\begin{aligned} \frac{12a^2b}{3a} &= \frac{4a^{2-1}b}{1} \\ &= 4ab \end{aligned}$$

44. B: Start by squaring both sides of the equation and simplifying the result.

$$\begin{aligned} \left(\sqrt{3x-2}\right)^2 &= (x-2)^2 \\ 3x - 2 &= x^2 - 4x + 4 \end{aligned}$$

Next, move everything to one side and factor to find solutions for x.

$$\begin{gathered} x^2 - 7x + 6 = 0 \\ (x-1)(x-6) = 0 \\ x - 1 = 0 \qquad x - 6 = 0 \\ x = 1 \qquad\quad x = 6 \end{gathered}$$

Therefore, the possible solutions are $x = 1$ and $x = 6$. Substitute these solutions into the original equation to see if they are valid solutions.

$$\begin{aligned} \sqrt{3(1)-2} &= (1) - 2 \\ \sqrt{1} &= 1 - 2 \\ 1 &= 1 - 2 \\ 1 &= -1 \\ &\text{False} \end{aligned} \qquad \begin{aligned} \sqrt{3(6)-2} &= (6) - 2 \\ \sqrt{16} &= 6 - 2 \\ 4 &= 6 - 2 \\ 4 &= 4 \\ &\text{True} \end{aligned}$$

Since only $x = 6$ leads to a true equality, that is the only solution.

45. D: The variables are the objects the graph measures. In this case, the graph measures the hospital staff and the average hours worked per week. The dependent variable changes with the independent variable. Here, the average hours worked per week depends on the particular type of hospital staff. Therefore, the dependent variable is average hours worked per week and the independent variable is hospital staff.

46. B: Start by multiplying the coefficients and then multiply the i-terms. $-2 \times 7 = -14$ and $i \times i = i^2$. The expression simplifies to $-14i^2$. Remember, $i^2 = \sqrt{-1} \times \sqrt{-1} = -1$, so the expression becomes $-14 \times (-1) = 14$. Therefore, the expression is equal to 14.

47. A: Compute the product using the FOIL method, in which the first terms, the outer terms, the inner terms, and finally the last terms are figured in sequence of multiplication. As a result, $(a + b)(a - b) = a^2 + ba - ab - b^2$. The middle terms, ba and $-ab$, cancel each other out, which leaves $a^2 - b^2$.

48. C: "The square of twice the sum of x and three is equal to the product of twenty-four and x" is represented by the equation $[2(x + 3)]^2 = 24x$. Solve for x.

$$[2x + 6]^2 = 24x$$
$$(2x + 6)(2x + 6) = 24x$$
$$4x^2 + 24x + 36 = 24x$$
$$4x^2 + 36 = 0$$
$$4x^2 = -36$$
$$x^2 = -9$$
$$x = \pm\sqrt{-9}$$
$$x = \pm 3i$$

So, $-3i$ is a possible value of x.

49. A: The mode is the number that appears most often in a set of data. If no item appears most often, then the data set has no mode. In this case, Kyle had 1 hit for a total of 3 times. There were 2 times that he had 2 hits. Also, on 1 day, he had 3 hits. Then, on another day, he had 4 hits. 1 hit happened the most times, so the mode of the data set is 1.

50. B: The mean, or average, is the sum of the numbers in a data set divided by the total number of items in the set. This data set has 7 items (one for each day of the week). The total number of hits that Kyle had during the week is the sum of the numbers in the bottom row. The sum is 14, so the mean is 2 because $14 \div 7 = 2$.

51. B: Notice that $x = 1$ results in a zero in the denominator, so choice C cannot be correct since $x \neq 1$. To solve, subtract $\frac{2}{x-1}$ from both sides, then cross-multiply.

$\frac{x-2}{x-1} = \frac{x-1}{x+1} + \frac{2}{x-1}$	Write out the original equation.
$\frac{x-4}{x-1} = \frac{x-1}{x+1}$	Subtract $\frac{2}{x-1}$ from both sides.
$(x+1)(x-4) = (x-1)(x-1)$	Cross multiply.
$x^2 - 3x - 4 = x^2 - 2x + 1$	Multiply the binomials on both sides.
$-3x - 4 = -2x + 1$	Subtract x^2 from both sides.
$-4 = x + 1$	Add $3x$ to both sides.
$-5 = x$	Subtract 1 from both sides.

52. B: A cube has six square faces. The arrangement of these faces in a two-dimensional figure is a net of a cube if the figure can be folded to form a cube. If choice B is folded, the bottom square in the second column will overlap the fourth square in the top row, so the figure does not represent a net of a cube. The other figures represent three of the eleven possible nets of a cube.

53. D: The Pythagorean theorem may be used to find the diagonal distance from the top of his head to the base of the shadow. Using the following equation, we can determine this distance, c: $5.8^2 + 6.2^2 = c^2$. Thus, $c \approx 8.5$. The distance is approximately 8.5 ft.

54. D: The point $(5, -5)$ lies on the line segment that has a slope of −2 and passes through $(3, -1)$. If $(5, -5)$ is one of the endpoints of the line segment, then the other would be (1,3).

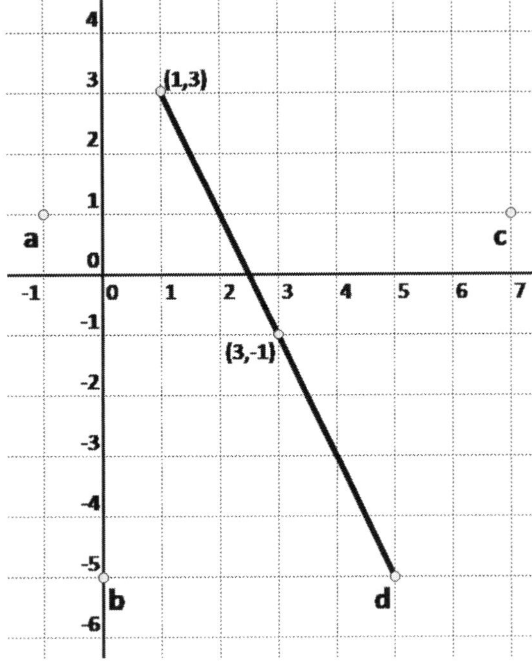

55. A: $A \cap B$ means "*A* intersect *B*," or the elements that are common to both sets. "*A* intersect *B*" represents "*A* and *B*," that is, an element is in the intersection of *A* and *B* if it is in *A* *and* it is in *B*. The elements 2, 5, and 8 are common to both sets.

Science

1. D: The passage specifies that transit photometry can determine the size of the planet relative to the size of the star. It is clear from the graphs that the planet in Observation 2 is larger relative to its parent star than the planet in Observation 1, but that does not mean that the planet in Observation 2 is larger in absolute size; it is possible that the planet in Observation 1 is orbiting a much larger star.

Knowing the planets' orbital radii would enable us to calculate the mass of the star if we knew its orbital period, or vice versa, using Kepler's third law. However, it would in no way allow us to calculate the radii of the planets themselves.

2. B: The transit of the planet in front of the star is represented by the "dip" in the graph—the interval during which the relative flux is significantly smaller than 1. The relative flux first starts to drop precipitously at about $t = -1$ hour and returns to its value of 1 at about $t = 1$ hour. The width of the interval representing the transit is then $1 - (-1) = 2$ hours.

3. B: The passage notes that the transit depth depends on the radius of the planet. It follows that larger planets would lead to a larger transit depth—that is, a more pronounced decrease in the apparent luminosity of the star. The larger the change in the luminosity, the easier it would be to detect.

Although it isn't impossible that gas giants might happen to be more common in the vicinity of the Earth, there is no obvious reason why this should be true, and nothing in the passage suggests this. There is not any clear reason why astronomers would be less interested in terrestrial planets than in gas giants either. Even if it were true that terrestrial planets were shorter-lived than gas giants, this would have no effect on the relative proportion of each type of planet that was observed.

4. A: If a planet passes in front of a star as seen from Earth, then it will do so again in each orbit; the transit will repeat with a regular interval of the planet's orbital period. This will not be the case if some other object not in orbit around the star happens to pass in front of it once. Any transit of a star, whether by a planet or by some other object, is likely to lead to a similarly U-shaped graph, and the magnitude of the transit depth depends on the radius of the transiting object but not on whether or not it is in orbit around the star.

5. C: Transit photometry depends on the planet passing in front of its parent star, relative to the Earth. This means that it requires the planet's orbit to be aligned in such a way that this happens. If the plane of the planet's orbit does not pass near the Earth, then from the vantage point of the Earth, the planet will circle its parent star but will never pass in front of it, and transit photometry cannot be used. (There are other methods of detecting exoplanets that may work in such cases, but they have their own limitations.)

There is nothing in the description of transit photometry that indicates that it should be limited by the location of the parent star of the observed planet. As for systems with multiple planets around a single star, they will each produce their own transits at different intervals and (unless they happen to have the same radii) with different transit depths. Therefore, they can be observationally distinguished—this, in fact, is one of the strengths of transit photometry relative to some other methods of exoplanet detection.

6. D: The slope of the graph is always positive, so the numbers are continually growing. However, the rate of growth is not constant—if it were, the graph would be a straight line. In the beginning, the slope is continually increasing—the rate of population growth is rapidly rising and appears to possibly be exponential. However, at about the 7-month mark, the slope begins decreasing—the population is still increasing but at a smaller or slower rate—and eventually the curve becomes nearly flat and levels off.

7. C: As the population of species 1 increases and species 2 decreases, at some point the two lines cross. This would be easier to see if the two were plotted on the same graph. However, even without that, we can look at the numbers. At month 2, the scientist had not even started counting the frogs of species 2 yet, so month 2 cannot be correct. Before about month 6, the numbers of species 2 are clearly larger than the numbers of species 1—at month 4, for instance, there are about 200 frogs of species 1, and about 500 of species 2. After month 6, the numbers of species 1 are clearly larger—at month 8, for example, there are about 600 frogs of species 1 and about 250 of species 2. At month 6, however, the two numbers are approximately the same; the graphs of both species 1 and species 2 at that point show about 350 frogs.

8. C: The slope of the graph represents the rate of change, so the numbers are changing most rapidly where the slope is steepest. At months 1 and 10, the graph is close to horizontal; the rate of change is low. The graph is steeper at month 4, but it is steeper still at month 7; this is where the graph has its greatest slope and therefore where the rate of change is highest.

We can also look at the difference between the numbers in consecutive months. Here again, the difference between the number of frogs of species 1 in months 6 and 7, or 7 and 8, is significantly larger than the difference between the number of frogs in any other two consecutive months.

9. D: At the right end of the graph, the slope is close to horizontal, indicating a low or zero rate of change. Equivalently, the difference between the number of frogs in consecutive months near the right end of the graph is small. If this trend continues, then we would expect the rate of change to continue to be small, if there is any change at all.

Of course, this could very well not be the case; it could be that the frogs are stricken by disease and die out, or any number of other eventualities could come to pass. We cannot know for sure what is going to happen. But in this case, the question explicitly asks us to assume that the trend shown in the graph continues, so we do not need to worry about taking into consideration possible events that could disrupt this trend.

10. B: Each of the answer choices implies a different prediction about what would happen to the two populations. If the two species of frogs cooperated to increase mutual success, we would expect both populations to increase over time. If the two species overtaxed the lake's resources, we would expect both to decrease.

What we see from the graphs is that the population of species 1 increases and the population of species 2 decreases. Of course, species 1 outcompeting species 2 for resources is not the only possible explanation; it could be, for example, that frogs of species 1 predate on the larvae of species 2 directly. However, the only valid conclusion from the data that is found in the answer choices is that species 1 is outcompeting species 2 for food or other vital resources.

11. C: The peak velocities of the rockets did indeed decrease as the rockets' mass increased; reading the data table from top to bottom, the masses become larger and the velocities become smaller. But for the values to be inversely proportional, it means that as one value increased, the other decreased by the same factor. This was not the case. Consider the third and fourth rows of the table: the rocket's mass is increased by a factor of 2, from 500 g to 1.0 kg. However, the rocket's peak velocity decreases from 34 m/s to 8 m/s, a decrease of more than a factor of 4.

12. A: The rockets, like any object resting on or near the Earth's surface, are subject to the Earth's gravity, which is constantly pulling them toward the Earth. The force of gravity on an object is proportional to the mass of the object (more specifically, it is equal to the mass of the object times the acceleration of gravity, about 9.8 m/s^2 on the Earth's surface). On the other hand, the thrust provided by the rocket engines does not scale with the rockets' mass. (The passage states that the rockets were identical except for the added mass.) Therefore, if the rocket's mass is too great, the force of gravity pulling the rocket toward the Earth would be greater than the thrust provided by the rocket, leaving a net force on the rocket toward the Earth and preventing it from leaving the surface. (The gravitational pull of the Earth is one reason that the student's reasoning behind the hypothesis was incorrect but not the only reason.)

13. B: The faster the rocket is going, the greater the altitude it will reach—and, conversely, the slower the rocket is moving, the less its maximum altitude. This is not simple projectile motion because the rocket's acceleration is not constant, but it is a reasonable assumption that the rockets with the lower maximum velocities also have smaller velocities at other points in their flight and will reach lower maximum altitudes.

The minimum velocity of the rocket is not a useful thing to measure—because the rockets start from rest, they'll all have the same minimum velocity of zero. There is no reason to expect that the rockets will rotate or that their rotational velocity would be correlated with their maximum velocity if they did. Although it is possible that the student adding weights to the rockets might increase their radii (if the weights are attached around the sides of the rockets), we'd expect the radius to increase as more weight is added, not to decrease as the maximum velocity does.

14. D: The maximum speeds of the rockets consistently decrease as the rockets' masses increase. The maximum speed for the 750 g rocket should therefore be between those of the 500 g rocket (34 m/s) and the 1,000 g rocket (8 m/s), eliminating 68 m/s. To decide between the remaining choices, note that the relationship between the rocket's mass and the maximum velocity is not linear—as the rocket's mass increases the rate of change of the maximum velocity decreases; the graph is concave up. (You can see this from the fact that, for example, the change in velocity as the mass changes from 125 g to 250 g is much greater than the change in velocity from 500 g to 1000 g, despite the latter representing a greater change in mass.) We would therefore expect the maximum speed for the 750 g rocket to be closer to the maximum speed of the 1,000 g rocket than to the 500 g rocket—that is, it should be closer to 8 m/s than to 34 m/s. The only option that meets this criterion is 17 m/s.

15. A: If the rocket's mass decreases, the same thrust would give rise to a larger change in velocity. (This is just a matter of Newton's second law, $F = ma$: for the same force, a smaller mass means a greater acceleration.) If the student's calculations did not take this into account, the calculated velocities would have been too low.

Although you do not need to know it to answer this question, there is, in fact, a formula relating the mass of a rocket to its final velocity. In the absence of external forces, the change in velocity is equal to the exhaust velocity of the fuel times the natural logarithm of the ratio between the initial mass of the rocket and its final mass after the fuel is burned: $\Delta v = v_e \ln\left(\frac{m_i}{m_f}\right)$. Because the mass changes as the fuel is being expended, deriving this formula requires calculus—but, again, you do not need to know this formula or to be able to derive it to answer this question qualitatively.

16. D: For the bands to match between the two profiles, a band in Profile 2 must appear in the same position as the band in Profile 1. Only Band D has a match in Profile 2:

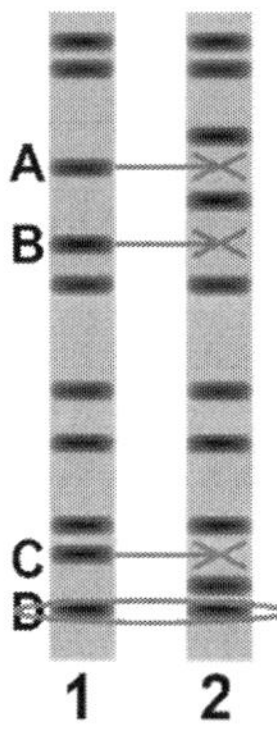

17. C: Seven bands match between Profiles 1 and 2:

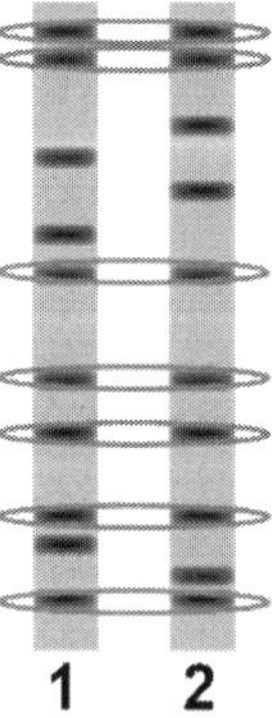

This is slightly more than would be expected by chance; on average, we would expect half the bands to match between a parent and child—so because there are 10 bands, we would expect five matches on average. However, this is only an average, and a slight deviation isn't that surprising; seven matches instead of five is not especially improbable.

18. D: According to the passage, any bands in the child that are not present in one parent must be present in the other. This means that any band in Profile 1 that is not in Profile 2 must be in the profile of the father. These are the bands we should expect to find:

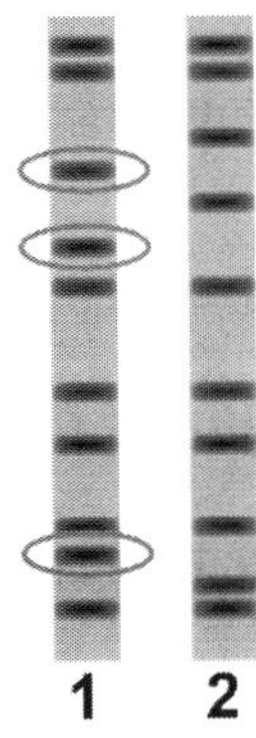

The only profile to have all of these bands is Profile 6:

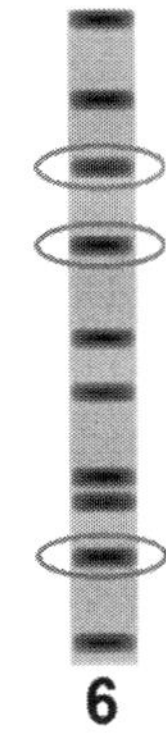

19. B: As stated in the passage, each mark in the genetic profile of a child should also appear in one (or both) of the parents. The profile in the second choice is the only one for which this is true. All the other choices have some marks that do not appear in either Profiles 3 or 4.

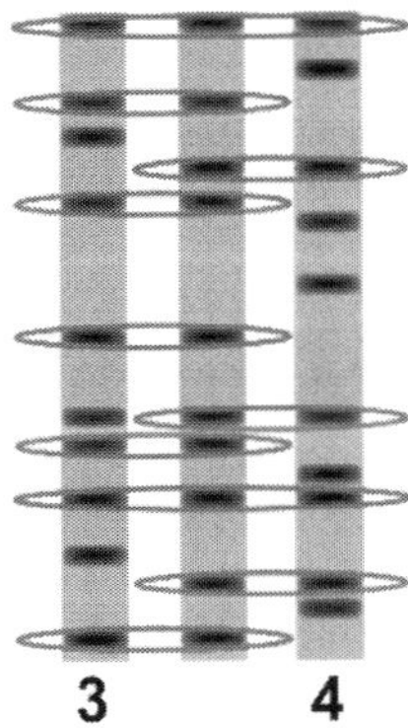

20. B: The passage explicitly says that the number of markers shared by siblings is unpredictable. Therefore, there's no firm reason to conclude that Profiles 5 and 6 could not belong to siblings. However, they do not share more than half of their markers. They do share some markers, but only four of the 10 markers are shared, which is less than half.

21. A: Scientist 1 makes a point of stating how well confirmed relativistic gravitational theory is, and Scientist 2, although arguing that it may need modification on the galactic scale, explicitly acknowledges that it works well on the scale of the solar system. None of the other choices represents the views of both scientists. Scientist 1 opines that galaxies contain a large amount of unseen matter—"dark matter"—but Scientist 2 disagrees. Conversely, only Scientist 2 thinks that the phenomena are better explained by gravitational theory needing modifications at larger scales. Neither scientist says anything about dark matter being in principle undetectable; in fact, Scientist 1's mention of a "yet undiscovered type of elementary particle" strongly implies that Scientist 1 thinks it could be discovered in the future.

22. C: Scientist 1 says that dark matter is likely to consist of some yet undiscovered type of elementary particle and then goes on to name three proposed examples, one of which is gravitinos. (The other two are weakly interacting massive particles [WIMPs] and axions.) None of the other choices are plausible candidates for dark matter. Stars are visible and therefore cannot be dark matter, which is by definition undetectable by current means. We also have ways of detecting black holes, and in any case, they are not mentioned at all by Scientist 1. Scientist 1 does mention gravitons but only in passing in comparing them to gravitinos; even if you do not know what a graviton is, the context implies that they are a known type of particle and therefore not a dark-matter candidate.

23. A: The passage says that "most cosmologists have concluded" that galaxies must contain dark matter. This matches the view of Scientist 1. The two scientists certainly do not fundamentally agree with each other; Scientist 1 believes that dark matter exists, and Scientist 2 believes that it does not and that alterations to relativistic gravitational theory provide a better explanation for the observed phenomena.

24. D: Scientist 2 argues that the apparent anomalies in the behavior of galaxies can be caused by gravity working differently on a larger scale. If this is true, however, one would expect it to apply to all galaxies, and it would then be difficult (although not necessarily impossible) to explain why some galaxies did not exhibit those anomalies.

None of the other choices point to a real difficulty with the scientists' statements. Nowhere does Scientist 1 insist that all galaxies must contain dark matter; there is no reason to think it impossible that some galaxies might contain dark matter and others not. The discovery of some galaxies without dark matter would not prove that gravity works differently on a larger scale—if anything, as already noted, it makes this idea less likely. Finally, Scientist 2 does not assume that galaxies must follow Newtonian mechanics—Scientist 2 does mention Newtonian mechanics but only as an example of a theory that works well only at specific scales—and this has nothing obvious to do with the described discovery.

25. C: Both scientists' arguments start from the basis that galaxies are held together by gravity. They simply have different ways of explaining why the gravity of known matter in the galaxies is insufficient—Scientist 1 thinks it is because there is additional matter we cannot currently detect; Scientist 2 thinks it is because gravity works differently on galactic scales. Scientist 2 would certainly disagree with the statement that gravity works the same at all scales because Scientist 2's entire argument is that the opposite must be the case. Scientist 1 mentions axions as one possible candidate for dark matter, but Scientist 2 gives no indication of even accepting that axions might be a real type of particle, much less that they might exist in large quantities. Finally, neither Scientist 1 nor Scientist 2 says anything about most particles being unaffected by gravity; in fact, this would seem to go against the fact that they are explaining the behavior of galaxies in terms of gravitational attraction.

26. D: The complete Punnett square is shown below.

	B	**b**
B	BB	Bb
b	Bb	bb

Because male-pattern baldness is a recessive gene, the offspring would need the *bb* gene combination in order to inherit this trait. Possibility 4 corresponds to the *bb* gene combination.

27. C: The data indicates that up until about 4 weeks, the silk production from both colonies was similar. This suggests that the worms from each colony produced the same amount of silk and that choices A and B are incorrect. The data does indicate that, over the long term, the silk produced by the entire colony of genetically diverse worms was greater than the silk produced by the entire colony of genetically uniform worms. This might be because the worms produce for a longer time or because of some other mechanism. The experiment does not indicate what that mechanism might be.

28. B: The increase in productivity from the diverse culture occurs at about 4 weeks, coinciding with the time at which new worms are hatched and begin to produce silk.

29. A: Scientist 1 argues that due to the limitations on the range of the strong nuclear force, elements cannot exist with an atomic number greater than about 173. Scientist 2 explicitly says in the last sentence that the periodic table can probably be extended indefinitely. Although Scientist 2 does mention "islands of stability," they do not form a major part of Scientist 2's argument, nor do they contradict Scientist 1's claims; Scientist 1 says only that the number of elements yet to be discovered is limited, not that undiscovered elements cannot be stable.

30. B: Both scientists agree that there are more elements remaining to be discovered, although they disagree as to how many such elements there are—Scientist 1 thinks they will stop around element 173, whereas Scientist 2 thinks the elements could go on indefinitely. Scientist 2's mention of "islands of stability" contradicts the thought that the higher an atomic number, the less stable the element, and neither scientist expresses any opinion on the procedure for naming elements or on which elements might exist in nature. (The passage does state that only 94 elements exist in nature on Earth, but this doesn't preclude heavier elements existing, e.g., inside ultra-dense neutron stars.)

31. A: Scientist 1 argues that no element with an atomic number greater than about 173 could exist. The discovery of an element of atomic number 200 would be a clear contradiction of this and would support Scientist 2's argument that the periodic table continues indefinitely (although it would not prove Scientist 2 correct—e.g., it could still be that the periodic table stops at element 220). The discovery of elements with atomic numbers between 150 and 160 would not damage Scientist 1's argument because those are still less than 173. The stability or instability of element 126 has little to do with either scientist's argument—Scientist 2 does mention the possibility of an "island of stability" there, but it is not important to the overall argument and has no bearing on Scientist 1's argument at all.

32. B: Both scientists make reference to discovering new elements and accept that elements that do not occur in nature can be created in the lab. (Indeed, considering the number of elements that *have* been created in the lab, it would be odd for any chemist not to accept this.) Neither scientist says anything about safety precautions, nor does either rule out the possibility of detecting elements with atomic numbers above 126—indeed, Scientist 2 even mentions a possible "island of stability" around atomic number 164. Although Scientist 1 might accept the idea that the arrangement of the particles in an atom changes in predictable ways as the atomic number increases, Scientist 2 certainly wouldn't, as Scientist 2 explicitly mentions that we "know too little about the arrangement of heavy atoms to confidently name a limit to their size."

33. C: Although Scientist 1 refers to both the strong nuclear force and electromagnetism, Scientist 1 states that the former holds nuclei together. It is the fact that protons repel each other through electromagnetism that, according to Scientist 1, would place a limit on the size of an atomic nucleus. Scientist 1 makes no mention of either the weak nuclear force or gravity—although, as an attractive force, gravity, if anything, would also help hold the nucleus together. (In fact, however, gravity is far too weak a force to have any significant effect at all on the nuclear scale.)

34. C: Scientist 2 speaks of possible "islands of stability" centered on elements 126 and 164. If these islands of stability exist there, then elements 126 and 164 themselves would be relatively stable in comparison to the elements around and between them—and element 145 in particular, lying halfway between these "islands of stability," would not be expected to be as stable. As for element 8, the discussion of "islands of stability" refers to relative stability among the heavy elements that don't exist in nature and have yet to be created in the lab. Element 8 is not such an element—with that low atomic number, it's a light element that exists in nature and is certainly stable. (As a matter of fact, element 8 is oxygen, which is not only abundant in the Earth's atmosphere, lithosphere, and oceans but is by mass the most abundant element in your body!)

35. A: Both scientists mention phylogenetic bracketing as suggesting that the fact that close relatives of *Tyrannosaurus* had feathers makes it more likely that *Tyrannosaurus* itself also had feathers. The most straightforward interpretation, therefore, is that phylogenetic bracketing refers to the principle that closely related organisms have similar traits. Although all the other answer choices may include true statements, none of them seems relevant to how the term is used in the passages. In particular, it's important not to be misled by the fact that one answer choice uses the word *phyla*—it's true that a phylum (plural *phyla*) is a level of taxonomic classification, and *phylum* and the *phylo-* in *phylogenetic* come from the same Greek root, but the two concepts are not directly related.

36. C: All the statements in the answer choices do indeed appear in the passages, but choice C is the only one relevant to the argument. If we have skin patches from many different parts of the body of the *Tyrannosaurus*, that makes it less likely that it was feathered on part of its body. If, for example, we had skin patches from only the tail, its neck or torso could be feathered—or if we had skin patches from only the stomach area, that would leave the possibility of its back being feathered—but the more different parts of the body from which we have scaly patches, the fewer places remain for it to have been only feathered, and the less likely it is that it had feathers in those places.

37. B: Both Scientist 1 and Scientist 2 concede that many relatives of *Tyrannosaurus* had feathers, and it is more likely that this condition existed in their common ancestor than that they each evolved it independently. Indeed, Scientist 2 explicitly states that ancestors of *Tyrannosaurus* probably had feathers.

Although Scientist 2 does contend that large animals are likely to lose feathers, there is nothing to indicate that Scientist 1 would agree with this—if anything, this would cut against Scientist 1's argument. Neither scientist addresses the existence of feathers or featherlike structures in animals aside from dinosaurs and birds, and both scientists accept that the fossil evidence for feathers is genuine.

38. D: Scientist 1 argues that the *Tyrannosaurus* may have had both feathers and scales on the same part of its body. The fact that another animal has this feature strengthens the argument because it shows that it is possible for this feature to be evolved. Answer choice C would support Scientist 1's argument if it were true, but there is nothing in the passage to suggest this. The remaining incorrect answer choices are either not supported in the passage or do not support Scientist 1's argument.

39. A: Although the ostrich is the largest living bird, it is not nearly as large as the *Tyrannosaurus*, so it does not significantly weaken Scientist 2's contention that an animal the size of *Tyrannosaurus* would tend to lose feathers. Scientist 2's argument said nothing about the *Tyrannosaurus*'s diet or habitat, and there is nothing in the passage to indicate that these factors should affect the loss of feathers—if anything, one might expect that in an arid habitat it would be important to prevent heat gain and more likely that coverings like feathers would be lost. Whether or not feathers would fossilize is a separate question not directly related to Scientist 2's argument about feather loss in large animals.

40. D: Scientist 1 would certainly disagree strongly with this statement because the crux of Scientist 1's argument is that since close relatives of *Tyrannosaurus* are known to have feathers, it is more likely that *Tyrannosaurus* had feathers as well. However, whereas Scientist 2 ultimately argues that *Tyrannosaurus* did not have feathers, Scientist 2 still acknowledges the relevance of the fact that its relatives did, while going on to argue that other factors are more significant in its case. Based on the passages, neither scientist is likely to agree with the given statement.

41. D: Because the graph measures the abundance of ions of each value of m/Z, the highest peaks indicate the most abundant ions. By far the highest peak is the one at 18, which according to the passage corresponds to water. Meanwhile, the peaks for ethylene, at 26, 27, and 28, are lower than the peaks for either of the other compounds, so it must be the least abundant.

42. A: "Singly ionized" means that the ion is missing a single electron (or has a single extra electron); $Z = 1$. "Doubly ionized" means that it is missing two electrons (or has two extra electrons); $Z = 2$. Because Z is in the denominator of m/Z, doubling Z from 1 to 2 means multiplying m/Z by 1/2; half of 18 is 9.

43. C: The three peaks for ethanol, at $m/Z = 31, 45$, and 46, have relative abundances of about 20%, 10%, and 4%, respectively. Together, they add to about 34%, which means that about 34% of the solution is ethanol. And 34% is about $\frac{1}{3}$.

44. D: One molecule of O_2 contains two atoms; if each atom has a mass number of 16, then the mass number of the molecule is $2 \times 16 = 32$. The passage says that generally most ions will have $Z = 1$. The most common value of m/Z will therefore be $32/1 = 32$.

45. A: The largest peak in the mass spectrum of ethylene occurs at $m/Z = 28$. Because most of the ions are singly ionized ($Z = 1$), for the largest peaks we can assume $Z = 1$ and hence $m/Z = m$. It's therefore reasonable to assume that a typical ethylene molecule has a molecular mass of 28 atomic mass units.

The molecular mass should be equal to the sum of the atomic masses of the atoms. With two carbon atoms and four hydrogen atoms, C_2H_4 would have a molecular mass of $2(12) + 4(1) = 24 + 4 = 28$. None of the other choices yields a value that matches the position of the peak: C_2H_6 would have a molecular mass of 30, C_4H_4 of 52, and C_4H_6 of 54.

46. B: Water dissociates readily into H^+ and OH^- ions. Because ordinary hydrogen has a mass number of 1, an OH^- ion would have a mass number 1 less than an H_2O molecule (or an H_2O^- ion)—that is, 17 instead of 18. Both an H_3O^+ ion and a water molecule with deuterium would have a *larger* mass number than ordinary H_2O, not smaller. (Besides, deuterium makes up only about 0.02% of all water atoms; it wouldn't be responsible for such a large peak.) Neutral water molecules, as described in the passage, would be unaffected by the magnetic field in the mass spectrometer and would not be deflected at all.

47. D: The purpose of a scientific control is to make sure that any observed effect is solely due to the variable under investigation. In this case, the variable being investigated is the concentration of the antibiotic; we want to make sure that adding a drop of liquid doesn't produce a similar effect—or at least to see what effect it does produce so that it can be taken into account in the analysis. Because we want to investigate the effect of the antibiotic, using different concentrations of the antibiotic would not be a suitable control—nor would using a different antibiotic because our experimental solutions do not contain this other antibiotic. We want something as close as possible to the solution we are investigating but without the presence of the antibiotic, so the best choice is to use pure water.

48. C: All the Petri dishes treated with the antibiotic show a clear circle free of bacterial growth. It is clear that the antibiotic impedes bacterial growth at both tested concentrations. However, there is no obvious significant difference between the dishes treated with the antibiotic solution at a concentration of one part per thousand and those treated with a solution at a concentration of two parts per thousand. This means that the effect does not necessarily scale with increasing concentration.

49. B: For the switch in labels not to affect the scientist's results, they must have been on dishes that had the same concentration of the antibiotic. Petri dishes 4 and 6 were both treated with the antibiotic solution at a concentration of one part per thousand; switching the labels on these two dishes would not have affected the scientist's results. All of the other choices describe pairs of dishes in which one was treated with the antibiotic and the other was treated with the control solution. Switching the labels on any of these pairs of Petri dishes would certainly have affected the results.

50. B: Dish 8 is one of those treated with the control liquid. Because the control liquid should have no effect on bacterial growth, there is no reason why the Petri dish should develop a clear circle in the middle. Furthermore, there is no reason to expect the sizes of the bacterial colonies to decrease. If anything, we would expect the bacterial colonies to grow further.

51. D: If there are no bacteria present at the higher temperature, it could be that the antibiotic was more effective and killed them all, but given the lack of a control, it could also be that the bacteria could not grow at that higher temperature in the first place. If the bacteria did grow at that higher temperature, then if the antibiotic were less effective, we would expect the Petri dishes to contain more bacteria, not for the bacteria to be absent. If the bacteria could not grow in agar, then there would have been no bacteria in the first scientist's experiment either.

52. D: The term *hydrologic cycle* is defined in the first paragraph, where it is described as being equivalent to the *water cycle*. It is derived from the Greek root *hydros*, which means "water."

53. B: The second paragraph gives examples of different storage reservoirs for water in the water cycle. An underground aquifer is one example. An aquifer is any geologic formation that has ground water. The word comes from the Latin root *aqua*, which means "water."

54. D: According to the table, the average residence time of water in soil is only two months. Only its residence time in the atmosphere (9 days) is shorter. Residence time is the average amount of time a water molecule spends in a reservoir before it moves on to another reservoir in the water cycle.

55. B: According to the final paragraph, ocean levels actually fall during an ice age. More water is stored in ice caps and glaciers when the temperatures are very cold, so less water stays in the oceans as liquid.

56. A: According to the data table, the two trials in which the most oxygen was produced were trials 3 and 4. Both of these trials involved bright light and added CO_2.

57. B: According to the data table, trials 5 and 6 both involved dim light and added CO_2. Each of the other pairs of trials named in the choices differ either in the amount of light or in whether or not CO_2 was added.

58. D: Nothing in the passage indicates that the student made any attempts to control for the sizes of the plants; all else being equal, it seems likely that larger plants would produce more oxygen. Because all the plants were on the same table, it is unlikely that there was significant variation in temperature. The passage specifies that the student put 1 gram of sodium bicarbonate in each setup that had added CO_2, so it seems there was no significant variation there. Finally, the amount of oxygen produced was what the student was measuring; any variation in this amount would have been a result of error, not a cause of it.

59. D: The chemical formula of water is H_2O—each molecule of water contains two atoms of hydrogen and one atom of oxygen. Water does not contain carbon, so although the plant could acquire hydrogen from water, the carbon must have come from somewhere else. Conversely, the chemical formula for carbon dioxide is CO_2—each molecule of carbon dioxide contains one atom of carbon and two atoms of oxygen. So, carbon dioxide contains carbon and oxygen (as you might guess from the name, even if you didn't know the chemical formula) but no hydrogen. So, the hydrogen must have come from the water and the carbon from the carbon dioxide.

60. B: Although the student did test whether adding CO_2 to the water (by stirring in sodium bicarbonate) affected the results, the test was purely binary—either the setups had added CO_2 or they didn't, and the student added the same amount of sodium bicarbonate (1 gram) to all the setups that did. It might be interesting to vary the amount of CO_2 added to see if the amount of oxygen produced keeps increasing as more

CO_2 is added or whether a point of diminishing returns is reached. There is no reason to expect that varying the size of the test tube or the amount of water in the beaker should affect the results—the experiment will work only if the funnel is fully submerged, but beyond that, any added water is unlikely to have an additional effect. Finally, the amount of oxygen produced is the dependent variable being measured; the student cannot vary it directly.

Another potentially interesting extension of the experiment could be to vary the amount of light the setup is exposed to (and to find a way to quantify the lighting beyond simply "bright" or "dim"), but this was not one of the choices.

Social Studies

1. C: Virginia's plan called for representation based on population. So, that plan would help states with larger populations. Choice A is incorrect because Virginia would not want representation based on wealth if it were a poor state. Choice B uses the motto of the French Revolution. So, this has nothing to do with the US Constitution. Choice D is incorrect because the New Jersey Plan did not ask for representation to be based on wealth.

2. B: Britain's Parliament has a two-house system. So, this may have been a model for the Virginia Plan. Choice A is incorrect because the Mayflower Compact set up a more theocratic system of government. Choice C is also wrong because some historians believe that the Iroquois system of government influenced the framers' ideas. However, there is no sign that the Sioux system had an influence. Choice D is clearly incorrect because the legislature is not a monarchy.

3. D: The Electoral College was a compromise for a way to elect the president. Choice A is incorrect because wealth has nothing to do with the role of the Electoral College. Choice B is wrong as well. The appointment of Supreme Court justices is not part of the Electoral College. That is a job for the chief executive. Electing senators is also not the responsibility of the Electoral College. So, this makes choice C incorrect.

4. C: The men had expected their invention to end war. Instead, it became a new weapon. Choice A is often cited as a reference to the Spanish-American War of 1898. So, it is incorrect. The Wright brothers hoped that their invention would put an end to war. So, choice B is the opposite idea. Since the Wright brothers wanted peace, they probably would not be interested in fighting. So, choice D is incorrect.

5. D: A politician who did not want to give even a penny for "scenery" would likely not have favored the Clean Air Act. All others would have favored the measures. Choice A is not the right answer because Nixon signed the bill. In 1970, he was still a popular president. So, he did not need to sign it to create goodwill. Rachel Carson sounded an early warning about the effects of DDT. So, she would likely have been excited about the act. Theodore Roosevelt was a strong supporter of environmental causes and would have championed the bill.

6. C: The proposal states that public welfare overrides private rights. Choice A is incorrect. The reason is that the proposal does not suggest that Ohio will lose rights to the control of the lake. Choice B is also incorrect. The property owners are said to have a protected right to their land and to be able to give or sell those rights. Choice D is wrong. The reason is that the amendment clearly refers to the lawmakers' response to passing the Great Lakes Water Compact.

7. C: Young people protested that they were old enough to fight and die for their country, yet they could not vote. Choice A is incorrect because women had the right to vote after the Nineteenth Amendment passed in 1920. Choice B is also wrong. African American males were able to vote after the Civil War. African American females gained the right in 1920. The baby boom ended in 1964. So, choice D is incorrect.

8. C: Mother Jones wanted laws to protect child workers. Legislators finally responded to appeals from her and others. None of the other answer choices would logically follow. The words would not have been an encouragement for children to work in factories. So, choice A is incorrect. Choice B is also not right. The South continued to be a major textile region. Increasing pay for child labor was not the solution to the problem. So, choice D is incorrect.

9. D: Many of the founders were also slaveholders, yet they believed that the practice was wrong. Choice A is an assumption that cannot be supported. Choice B is false. Freeman's actions had no effect on women's suffrage. However, it did have an impact on slavery. Many white southerners wanted slavery to continue. Thus, they were unlikely to applaud the decision of the court. This makes choice C incorrect.

10. D: One key to an opinion statement is the use of superlatives. This sentence states that apartheid was the worst political system. This is an opinion that could be challenged, given Nazism and fascism during World War II. All other statements can be verified as fact.

11. C: In 1969, there were 13 members in the CBC. In 2008, there were 43. So, this is an increase of 30. Choice A is incorrect because the CBC was set up 100 years after the Civil War. Choice B is also incorrect because there is nothing in the passage about a goal of a black president. Choice D is wrong as well. The reason is that the passage clearly says that the alternative budget has many differences from the president's budget.

12. B: Oligarchy is defined as the rule by few. An example is aristocracy, which in ancient Greece, was government by an elite group of citizens as opposed to a monarchy. In later times, it meant government by the class of aristocrats, a privileged group, as opposed to democracy. The rule of one is called autocracy. Examples include monarchy, dictatorship, and many others. The rule by law is called a republic. Some examples are constitutional republics, parliamentary republics, and federal republics. The rule by many could apply to democracy, which governs according to the people's votes, or to the collective leadership form of socialism, where no one individual has too much power.

13. B: The Founding Fathers decided that because the colonies did not have the right to elect members of Parliament, Parliament should not pass laws for them. The Declaration of Independence recognized the British Empire's government as being headed by the King of England, under whom the various local parliaments and legislative bodies served to enact laws for the peoples whom they represented. By addressing their ills to the King, the Founding Fathers sought to prevent the appearance that they acknowledged the British Parliament in London as having any authority over the American colonies.

14. B: Due process refers to the right of a defendant to confront accusers and to provide a defense.

15. D: Assimilation is the process whereby members of one cultural group (voluntarily or involuntarily) give up their own traditions to adopt those of another culture, often one which is dominant. Acculturation (C) can mean gradual cultural modifications to a person or group through adopting some elements of another culture, the merging of cultures via long-term interaction, or a person's acquiring a society's culture from birth. Accommodation (A) as a general vocabulary word means providing a service (as in hospitality services) or adjustment (as in schools) to meet a need. As a term used by Piaget, it means forming a new schema (concept) or altering an existing one to include new input. Piaget also used assimilation (D) to mean fitting new input into an existing schema without changing the schema. Adaptation (B) in general vocabulary means adjustment; for Piaget, it meant the learning process of assimilation and accommodation combined.

16. B: When a dominant culture absorbs other cultures so that they all adopt all the behaviors of the dominant culture, this is called assimilation. The other options represent the opposite of the truth; answer A is an example of assimilation, answer C is acculturation, and option D is acculturation.

17. D: The process of overriding a presidential veto is described in Article I, Section 7 of the Constitution. It requires a two-thirds vote from both the House and the Senate.

18. D: It is the duty of the President to see that federal laws are enforced. National laws are not subject to state laws or interpretations in matters constitutionally delegated to the federal government. Choice A is incorrect, as the governor of a state does have power; he cannot act, however, in defiance of constitutional federal law.

Choice B is incorrect as well, as the conflict in Vietnam had nothing to do with the situation in Arkansas. Choice C is incorrect, as the Constitution outlines powers delegated to both levels of government, with regard to different spheres of influence.

19. B: Despite the constitutional guarantee of free speech, it is not absolute. There are certain restrictions in which laws regulate defamation, slander, libel, conspiracy, and occasions when speech has the potential of causing "imminent harm." During the Vietnam War era, draftees would publicize their displeasure by burning their draft cards—this action actually constituted a federal crime. School employees are required to be socially responsible and are liable to discipline if their actions encourage delinquency or profanity. The laws prohibit threats against the President only when it represents a real threat, not "political hyperbole."

20. A: Compassion issues, such as gun control, strong environmental laws, social programs, and opposition to the death penalty, show a wide gender gap, as women are more likely to support compassion issues.

21. C: The UN has been a leader in helping end the crisis in Darfur, which helps the US and its international image when it participates in the UN. The other choices are all false statements. The UN does get involved in deadly conflicts, civil wars, and aid for victims of natural disasters. The UN also generally does have the same foreign policy objectives as the US.

22. C: Company A outperformed Company B in March, March was not a peak performance for either company, and Company B did not perform better than Company A during all of January to May. The only true statement is that sales performance dropped faster for Company A than Company B from June to July.

23. C: The graphical way to determine the answer is to visually assess the distance of the points. The month with the most visually distant points is May.

24. D: The graphical way to determine the answer is to visually assess the closeness of the points. The month with the visually closest points is November.

25. D: After World War II, the per capita national debt increased by over 600% compared to World War I. Choice A is not an accurate choice; the amount of debt per capita actually decreased after the War of 1812 compared to the American Revolution. After the Civil War, the percentage of debt increased by 420%. So, choice B is also incorrect. The per capita national debt increased after World War I by just over 200%. So, this makes choice C wrong as well.

26. B: The only time that the national debt level fell after a war was after the American Revolution. One conclusion is that the new government felt the need to show fiscal responsibility to the world. Choice A is incorrect. To borrow more money would increase the debt, not lower it. Choice C is incorrect. The amount of money that people spent had nothing to do with the per capita national debt. Purchase of Treasury bonds would show a growing debt. This was the opposite of what was actually happening. So, this makes choice D incorrect.

27. D: By 1950, the number of women in the workforce had climbed to 28.8%. This was the first time that the percentage was above 25%. Choice A is incorrect because women in 1900 made up only 18.1% of the workforce. By 1920, women still made up only 20.4% of the workforce. So, choice B is incorrect. In 1940, 24.3% of women were in the labor force, but the question asks for a percentage higher than 25.

28. C: The percentage of women in the workforce steadily increased through seven decades and beyond. By 1970, it reached 36.7%. This was double the 18.1% of 1900. Choice A is wrong because the rate did not decline. Choice B is also incorrect. The reason is that the rate climbed. Choice D is incorrect because the rate did not go up and down. Instead, it increased steadily.

29. D: Corporate taxes would be paid in greater amounts because businesses would no longer be able to use offshore havens. Choice A suggests the opposite situation. So, it is clearly incorrect. The offshore tax havens have nothing to do with retirement receipts. So, choice B is also incorrect. Again, individual income tax is not related to the problem of offshore tax havens. So, choice C is incorrect as well.

30. A: Individuals give the largest part of the total revenue at 43%. Choice B is incorrect. The reason is that corporations were adding only 10.1% of the revenue in 2004. Social Security is part of the 39% that comes from social insurance and retirement receipts. So, this makes Choice C incorrect. Choice D is also wrong. Government agencies do not pay taxes and do not appear on the chart.

31. D: Machinery and transport had the greatest difference between exports and imports, 34.3% compared to 9.7%. Chemicals exports were 8.7% and imports were 5.3%. Crude material exports were 13.7% and imports were 18.3%. Food and beverages exports were 15.6% and imports were 22.5%.

32. D: Machinery and transport jumped from 34.3% to 42.0% in exports. Also, they went from 9.7% to 28.0% in imports. Chemicals increased exports from 8.7% to 9.0%. Imports declined from 5.3% to 3.6%. So, choice A is incorrect. Crude material exports declined from 13.7% to 10.8%. For imports, they declined from 18.3% to 8.3%. So, this makes choice B incorrect. The decline in exports of food and beverages was just under 4%, and imports declined 7%. So, choice C is incorrect.

33. B: Crude material imports declined by 10 percentage points. All other categories saw imports that declined less than 10 points over the decade. Chemicals decreased in that time by only 1.7%. So, this makes choice A incorrect. Choice C is also incorrect. Food and beverages decreased during those 10 years by just over 7%. Imports of machinery and transport did not decrease during this time; instead, they nearly tripled. This means that choice D is incorrect.

34. D: The route began at the Mississippi River. Choice A is incorrect because the order came from President Jefferson in Washington, D.C. However, the journey did not start from that city. Instead, St. Louis was the starting point. Choice B is also incorrect. The reason is that the group had to cross the Rockies, but they did not start their journey from that area. Fort Mandan was one of the forts built farther west. So, choice C cannot be the correct answer.

35. A: A smaller box in which some part of the larger map is depicted in greater detail is known as an inset. Insets provide a closer look at parts of the map that the cartographer deems to be more important (for instance, cities, national parks, or historical sites). Often, traffic maps will include several insets depicting the roads in the most congested area of the city. Legends, also known as keys, are the boxes in which the symbols used in the map are explained. A legend, or key, might indicate how railroads and boundaries are depicted, for example. A compass rose indicates how the map is oriented along the north-south axis. It is common for cartographers to tilt a map for ease of display, such that up may not be due north.

36. C: The Kalahari Desert is located in the middle western part of Botswana. Answer A is incorrect; the Zambezi River runs through Zambia and Angola, countries that are north of Botswana. Answer B is also wrong; Lake Tanganyika is northeast of Botswana, along Tanzania's western border. The Congo River is in the Democratic Republic of the Congo, also located north of Botswana, making answer D incorrect.

37. D: Khartoum is Sudan's capital. At this point, the Nile splits into the White and Blue Nile rivers. Choice A is incorrect. The Gulf of Aden and the Red Sea are north of Somalia. Choice B is incorrect because the Congo River and Lake Chad are not in Sudan. Also, they do not come from the Nile. Choice C is incorrect because Lake Victoria is not in Sudan at all.

38. A, C, E: Somalia, Mozambique, and Kenya are bordered by the Indian Ocean. The other answer choices are not bordered by the Indian Ocean.

39. C: The Mayan population of Belize stands at about 10%. Choice A, Honduras; Choice B, Costa Rica; and Choice D, Nicaragua are incorrect because they do not have a Mayan presence.

40. C: Of the countries listed, the British Empire was the first to fully abolish slavery in all of its colonies. This was a gradual process that took place from 1834 to 1840. While Denmark and France were the first of these countries to abolish slave trade, they did not fully abolish slavery until 1848. In all of the answer choices, the slave trade was abolished several decades before slavery itself was fully outlawed. This means that people who were enslaved at the time that the slave trade was abolished were not freed at that time, and often their children and grandchildren were also enslaved until slavery was fully abolished. Of all of the countries represented in the table, Brazil was last to abolish slavery and slave trade was also abolished at the same time instead of with a gap in between.

41. D: The United States was a British colony before winning independence and so would have been required to end slavery in 1834, when slavery was abolished in all British colonies. Each of the other options is incorrect. Denmark abolished slavery in 1792, but the colonies did not have a major relationship with that nation. In 1794, France forbade slavery, but most of the colonies were not French possessions by the time of the American Revolution because France ceded land to Britain following the French and Indian War in 1763. In 1807, Britain ended slavery but did not yet extend that rule to its colonies. The final date, 1888, refers to the end of slavery in Brazil.

42. B: The French Revolution began in 1789. Only five years later, the slave trade was abolished. This seems to show an understanding and spreading out of the ideals of independence. The United States Revolution began in 1776. Then, almost a century passed before slavery finally ended in 1865. None of the other conclusions can be supported from the chart. Brazil was a large slave-holding nation, but that information is not given in the chart. It is unlikely that Denmark, a small nation with few colonies, would have been a large slave-holding state. The Asian nations stayed in Britain's empire until the mid-twentieth century.

43. A: The Mayan Empire collapsed internally, whereas the other civilizations were conquered by the Spanish. The Incan Empire was the last to fall, making choice B an incorrect choice. None of the empires were located in North America, as the head of the chart makes clear, so choice C is not valid. The Mayans were not conquered by Spain, unlike the other two empires. Choice D is thus incorrect.

44. C: The Spanish conquistadors were active in both Central and South America during the 16th century. Answer A is incorrect; Portugal was active in Brazil, but that location is not mentioned in the chart. The Mayan empire is older than both Aztec and Incan civilizations, making answer B incorrect. There is no indication that the Incan warriors in Peru tried to assist the Aztecs in Mexico when they battled the Spanish more than a decade before another conquistador would arrive in Peru.

45. A: Choice A is the best summary of the facts presented in the timeline, which is that technologies used in space explorations can also improve the quality of life on Earth. It is a good suggestion that doctors and architects study space technologies, but just naming one of those professions does not summarize the whole timeline. Only one fact deals with architectural use of space technologies, and using the doctor choice as a summary leaves out the architectural use. Choice D may be a true statement, but because there is no mention of the cost of space exploration in the timeline, it is not a good summary of the timeline.

46. A: Catholics, Pilgrims, Puritans, and Quakers were important in developing new colonies. So, this shows you the importance of religion to these people. Choice B is incorrect because the French did not hold much territory in the eastern United States. They did have land in areas west of the Appalachians and in what became Canada. Choice C is incorrect because there is nothing on the chart to confirm this information. Choice D is true. However, that information cannot be known from the chart.

47. C: The timeline shows that Puerto Rico did succumb to US expansionism by becoming a territory, but it also shows that native islanders fought for more political rights. There was no major violent revolution against the US in those years, and no minor ones are mentioned in the timeline, so that conclusion cannot be made. Spanish was not made the official language; English and Spanish were "co-official" for a time, and then English was made official in 1917. Also, languages are not mentioned in the timeline facts. Native Puerto Ricans did not have a majority in the island's government from the beginning of their time as a US territory; that did not occur until 1914 (according to the timeline facts).

48. B: In the years shown in the chart (1964–1966), the percentage of African Americans in E-6 ranks (Staff Sergeant or Petty Officer, First Class) ranks in the Army, Navy, and Marines all grew. In 1964, African Americans made up 13.9% of the E-6 ranked members of the Army, 4.7% of the E-6 ranked members of the Navy, and 5.0% of the E-6 ranked members of the Marine Corps. By 1966, these numbers were 18.1%, 5.6%, and 10.4%, respectively.

49. A: Choice A can best be concluded based on the timeline facts. Historical events and the specific needs of society can contribute to medical inventions, such as how the history of polio outbreaks and the fact that President Roosevelt had the disease contributed to the scientific discovery of a polio vaccine. The other statements cannot be proven true by the timeline facts. Other countries besides the US also had polio outbreaks in the 1920s and 1930s. Disease outbreaks can sometimes be prevented in other ways besides just from vaccines. And it was Jonas Salk, not FDR, who invented the polio vaccine, although FDR helped raise money to fund scientific research.

50. D: With an increasing population, cities and towns sprang up and became sites of hotels, brothels, laundries, and saloons. Answer A is not likely; most of the migration consisted of men coming to seek their fortunes and planning to return east. The key term in answer B is *most.* Although the women who went west often did establish businesses, most of the new migrants were men. The Civil War did not begin until 1860, more than a decade after the Gold Rush. The harsh climate conditions were not the only reason for the deaths that occurred during western migration. In any case, death would not be a contributor to increased population.

51. D: In 1848, gold was discovered in California at John Sutter's mill. This event led to the migration of people known as the Forty-Niners. The silver rush in Nevada came later. So, this makes choice A incorrect. The Transcontinental Railroad was finished in 1869. This date is not included in the chart. So, choice B cannot be correct. Choice C is also incorrect. The reason is that the founding of Spanish missions in California and the Southwest happened several centuries earlier.

52. B: Neither Ecuador nor Venezuela received independence from Spain until 1830. Argentina received independence from Spain in 1810, so answer A cannot be the correct answer. Answer C is also incorrect because Bolivia became independent from Spain in 1825, and Uruguay followed three years later. Peru gained independence from Spain in 1821, and Brazil was free of Portuguese control by 1822. Thus, all the other nations listed had received their independence from Spain or Portugal during the previous two decades.

53. D: Ten nations received independence during the first 30 years of the 19th century. Choice A is incorrect; the American Revolution was fought during the latter 1770s and early 1780s, some decades before independence movements in South America. In fact, the American Revolution inspired some of the movements. France did not have significant possessions in South America, so choice B is wrong. Nations on the west coast were among the last to receive independence, making choice C incorrect.

54. B: Antiseptics kept infections down. By using antiseptics, Muslim doctors prevented infections that often led to loss of limbs or life for Europeans. The other choices are opinions or statements that are not supported by the paragraph. There is no way to compare the bravery of Muslims with the bravery of other faiths when facing surgery. So, choice A can be eliminated. Also, choice C is incorrect. There would not be a noticeable rise in silk use for sutures to explain a larger silk market. Choice D is an opinion, not a fact.

55. A: The mounds were built much earlier. 1949 is the date that they came under the protection of the National Park Service. Mounds are located in other places in the United States. So, choice B is not the right choice. In 1949, Truman was president, and he would have signed the bill into law. So, choice C is not a correct answer. Effigy mounds are shaped like animals. So, choice D is incorrect.

56. D: In the Dred Scott decision of 1857, the Court ruled that no slave or descendant of slaves could ever be a United States citizen. It also declared the Missouri Compromise of 1820 to be unconstitutional, clearing the way for the expansion of slavery in new American territories. This ruling pleased Southerners and outraged the North, further dividing the nation and setting the stage for war.

57. D: The Protestant work ethic is considered by many historians to have contributed to the Industrial Revolution. In Britain, where industrialization started, financial stability encouraged investment in industry, and the eventual dominance of Protestantism is believed to have contributed to a class of entrepreneurs who believed in education, technological progress, and hard work. The other choices are considered effects of industrialization. Mass production enabled the privately owned, for-profit enterprises that characterize capitalist economic systems. Socialism developed as a criticism of capitalism; Karl Marx argued that capitalism polarized societies into owners versus workers. Marx also viewed capitalism as a necessary precursor to socialism within the logical progression of economies. Romanticism also developed in reaction against mechanization and involved using art and literature to contrast nature with the dark side of scientific progress.

58. C: The Underground Railroad was not necessary literally a railroad but a series of clandestine paths to move runaway and freed slaves out of southern states prior to 1865.

59. D: In his extremely influential pamphlet *Common Sense*, Paine argued persuasively against all forms of monarchy and aristocracy. He advocated the formation of a republic that derives its power exclusively from the governed. While the European writers also advocated government that derives its authority from the people, none went as far as Paine in proposing the total abolition of the traditional noble classes.

60. D: The Platt Amendment of 1901 granted the United States the right to intervene in Cuban affairs and maintain a presence on the island. Hawaii was annexed during the Spanish-American War, though the war was not a direct cause of it. US imperialism was accelerated following McKinley's assassination. The Boxer Rebellion took place in China between 1899 and 1901 and preceded the Russo-Japanese War, which began in 1904.

HiSET Practice Tests #2 and #3

To take these additional HiSET practice tests, visit our online resources page:
mometrix.com/resources719/hiset-27339

How to Overcome Test Anxiety

Just the thought of taking a test is enough to make most people a little nervous. A test is an important event that can have a long-term impact on your future, so it's important to take it seriously and it's natural to feel anxious about performing well. But just because anxiety is normal, that doesn't mean that it's helpful in test taking, or that you should simply accept it as part of your life. Anxiety can have a variety of effects. These effects can be mild, like making you feel slightly nervous, or severe, like blocking your ability to focus or remember even a simple detail.

If you experience test anxiety—whether severe or mild—it's important to know how to beat it. To discover this, first you need to understand what causes test anxiety.

Causes of Test Anxiety

While we often think of anxiety as an uncontrollable emotional state, it can actually be caused by simple, practical things. One of the most common causes of test anxiety is that a person does not feel adequately prepared for their test. This feeling can be the result of many different issues such as poor study habits or lack of organization, but the most common culprit is time management. Starting to study too late, failing to organize your study time to cover all of the material, or being distracted while you study will mean that you're not well prepared for the test. This may lead to cramming the night before, which will cause you to be physically and mentally exhausted for the test. Poor time management also contributes to feelings of stress, fear, and hopelessness as you realize you are not well prepared but don't know what to do about it.

Other times, test anxiety is not related to your preparation for the test but comes from unresolved fear. This may be a past failure on a test, or poor performance on tests in general. It may come from comparing yourself to others who seem to be performing better or from the stress of living up to expectations. Anxiety may be driven by fears of the future—how failure on this test would affect your educational and career goals. These fears are often completely irrational, but they can still negatively impact your test performance.

Elements of Test Anxiety

As mentioned earlier, test anxiety is considered to be an emotional state, but it has physical and mental components as well. Sometimes you may not even realize that you are suffering from test anxiety until you notice the physical symptoms. These can include trembling hands, rapid heartbeat, sweating, nausea, and tense muscles. Extreme anxiety may lead to fainting or vomiting. Obviously, any of these symptoms can have a negative impact on testing. It is important to recognize them as soon as they begin to occur so that you can address the problem before it damages your performance.

The mental components of test anxiety include trouble focusing and inability to remember learned information. During a test, your mind is on high alert, which can help you recall information and stay focused for an extended period of time. However, anxiety interferes with your mind's natural processes, causing you to blank out, even on the questions you know well. The strain of testing during anxiety makes it difficult to stay focused, especially on a test that may take several hours. Extreme anxiety can take a huge mental toll, making it difficult not only to recall test information but even to understand the test questions or pull your thoughts together.

Effects of Test Anxiety

Test anxiety is like a disease—if left untreated, it will get progressively worse. Anxiety leads to poor performance, and this reinforces the feelings of fear and failure, which in turn lead to poor performances on subsequent tests. It can grow from a mild nervousness to a crippling condition. If allowed to progress, test anxiety can have a big impact on your schooling, and consequently on your future.

Test anxiety can spread to other parts of your life. Anxiety on tests can become anxiety in any stressful situation, and blanking on a test can turn into panicking in a job situation. But fortunately, you don't have to let anxiety rule your testing and determine your grades. There are a number of relatively simple steps you can take to move past anxiety and function normally on a test and in the rest of life.

Physical Steps for Beating Test Anxiety

While test anxiety is a serious problem, the good news is that it can be overcome. It doesn't have to control your ability to think and remember information. While it may take time, you can begin taking steps today to beat anxiety.

Just as your first hint that you may be struggling with anxiety comes from the physical symptoms, the first step to treating it is also physical. Rest is crucial for having a clear, strong mind. If you are tired, it is much easier to give in to anxiety. But if you establish good sleep habits, your body and mind will be ready to perform optimally, without the strain of exhaustion. Additionally, sleeping well helps you to retain information better, so you're more likely to recall the answers when you see the test questions.

Getting good sleep means more than going to bed on time. It's important to allow your brain time to relax. Take study breaks from time to time so it doesn't get overworked, and don't study right before bed. Take time to rest your mind before trying to rest your body, or you may find it difficult to fall asleep.

Along with sleep, other aspects of physical health are important in preparing for a test. Good nutrition is vital for good brain function. Sugary foods and drinks may give a burst of energy but this burst is followed by a crash, both physically and emotionally. Instead, fuel your body with protein and vitamin-rich foods.

Also, drink plenty of water. Dehydration can lead to headaches and exhaustion, especially if your brain is already under stress from the rigors of the test. Particularly if your test is a long one, drink water during the breaks. And if possible, take an energy-boosting snack to eat between sections.

Along with sleep and diet, a third important part of physical health is exercise. Maintaining a steady workout schedule is helpful, but even taking 5-minute study breaks to walk can help get your blood pumping faster and clear your head. Exercise also releases endorphins, which contribute to a positive feeling and can help combat test anxiety.

When you nurture your physical health, you are also contributing to your mental health. If your body is healthy, your mind is much more likely to be healthy as well. So take time to rest, nourish your body with healthy food and water, and get moving as much as possible. Taking these physical steps will make you stronger and more able to take the mental steps necessary to overcome test anxiety.

Mental Steps for Beating Test Anxiety

Working on the mental side of test anxiety can be more challenging, but as with the physical side, there are clear steps you can take to overcome it. As mentioned earlier, test anxiety often stems from lack of preparation, so the obvious solution is to prepare for the test. Effective studying may be the most important weapon you have for beating test anxiety, but you can and should employ several other mental tools to combat fear.

First, boost your confidence by reminding yourself of past success—tests or projects that you aced. If you're putting as much effort into preparing for this test as you did for those, there's no reason you should expect to fail here. Work hard to prepare; then trust your preparation.

Second, surround yourself with encouraging people. It can be helpful to find a study group, but be sure that the people you're around will encourage a positive attitude. If you spend time with others who are anxious or cynical, this will only contribute to your own anxiety. Look for others who are motivated to study hard from a desire to succeed, not from a fear of failure.

Third, reward yourself. A test is physically and mentally tiring, even without anxiety, and it can be helpful to have something to look forward to. Plan an activity following the test, regardless of the outcome, such as going to a movie or getting ice cream.

When you are taking the test, if you find yourself beginning to feel anxious, remind yourself that you know the material. Visualize successfully completing the test. Then take a few deep, relaxing breaths and return to it. Work through the questions carefully but with confidence, knowing that you are capable of succeeding.

Developing a healthy mental approach to test taking will also aid in other areas of life. Test anxiety affects more than just the actual test—it can be damaging to your mental health and even contribute to depression. It's important to beat test anxiety before it becomes a problem for more than testing.

Study Strategy

Being prepared for the test is necessary to combat anxiety, but what does being prepared look like? You may study for hours on end and still not feel prepared. What you need is a strategy for test prep. The next few pages outline our recommended steps to help you plan out and conquer the challenge of preparation.

Step 1: Scope Out the Test

Learn everything you can about the format (multiple choice, essay, etc.) and what will be on the test. Gather any study materials, course outlines, or sample exams that may be available. Not only will this help you to prepare, but knowing what to expect can help to alleviate test anxiety.

Step 2: Map Out the Material

Look through the textbook or study guide and make note of how many chapters or sections it has. Then divide these over the time you have. For example, if a book has 15 chapters and you have five days to study, you need to cover three chapters each day. Even better, if you have the time, leave an extra day at the end for overall review after you have gone through the material in depth.

If time is limited, you may need to prioritize the material. Look through it and make note of which sections you think you already have a good grasp on, and which need review. While you are studying, skim quickly through the familiar sections and take more time on the challenging parts. Write out your plan so you don't get lost as you go. Having a written plan also helps you feel more in control of the study, so anxiety is less likely to arise from feeling overwhelmed at the amount to cover.

STEP 3: GATHER YOUR TOOLS

Decide what study method works best for you. Do you prefer to highlight in the book as you study and then go back over the highlighted portions? Or do you type out notes of the important information? Or is it helpful to make flashcards that you can carry with you? Assemble the pens, index cards, highlighters, post-it notes, and any other materials you may need so you won't be distracted by getting up to find things while you study.

If you're having a hard time retaining the information or organizing your notes, experiment with different methods. For example, try color-coding by subject with colored pens, highlighters, or post-it notes. If you learn better by hearing, try recording yourself reading your notes so you can listen while in the car, working out, or simply sitting at your desk. Ask a friend to quiz you from your flashcards, or try teaching someone the material to solidify it in your mind.

STEP 4: CREATE YOUR ENVIRONMENT

It's important to avoid distractions while you study. This includes both the obvious distractions like visitors and the subtle distractions like an uncomfortable chair (or a too-comfortable couch that makes you want to fall asleep). Set up the best study environment possible: good lighting and a comfortable work area. If background music helps you focus, you may want to turn it on, but otherwise keep the room quiet. If you are using a computer to take notes, be sure you don't have any other windows open, especially applications like social media, games, or anything else that could distract you. Silence your phone and turn off notifications. Be sure to keep water close by so you stay hydrated while you study (but avoid unhealthy drinks and snacks).

Also, take into account the best time of day to study. Are you freshest first thing in the morning? Try to set aside some time then to work through the material. Is your mind clearer in the afternoon or evening? Schedule your study session then. Another method is to study at the same time of day that you will take the test, so that your brain gets used to working on the material at that time and will be ready to focus at test time.

STEP 5: STUDY!

Once you have done all the study preparation, it's time to settle into the actual studying. Sit down, take a few moments to settle your mind so you can focus, and begin to follow your study plan. Don't give in to distractions or let yourself procrastinate. This is your time to prepare so you'll be ready to fearlessly approach the test. Make the most of the time and stay focused.

Of course, you don't want to burn out. If you study too long you may find that you're not retaining the information very well. Take regular study breaks. For example, taking five minutes out of every hour to walk briskly, breathing deeply and swinging your arms, can help your mind stay fresh.

As you get to the end of each chapter or section, it's a good idea to do a quick review. Remind yourself of what you learned and work on any difficult parts. When you feel that you've mastered the material, move on to the next part. At the end of your study session, briefly skim through your notes again.

But while review is helpful, cramming last minute is NOT. If at all possible, work ahead so that you won't need to fit all your study into the last day. Cramming overloads your brain with more information than it can process and retain, and your tired mind may struggle to recall even previously learned information when it is overwhelmed with last-minute study. Also, the urgent nature of cramming and the stress placed on your brain contribute to anxiety. You'll be more likely to go to the test feeling unprepared and having trouble thinking clearly.

So don't cram, and don't stay up late before the test, even just to review your notes at a leisurely pace. Your brain needs rest more than it needs to go over the information again. In fact, plan to finish your studies by noon or early afternoon the day before the test. Give your brain the rest of the day to relax or focus on other things, and get a good night's sleep. Then you will be fresh for the test and better able to recall what you've studied.

Step 6: Take a Practice Test

Many courses offer sample tests, either online or in the study materials. This is an excellent resource to check whether you have mastered the material, as well as to prepare for the test format and environment.

Check the test format ahead of time: the number of questions, the type (multiple choice, free response, etc.), and the time limit. Then create a plan for working through them. For example, if you have 30 minutes to take a 60-question test, your limit is 30 seconds per question. Spend less time on the questions you know well so that you can take more time on the difficult ones.

If you have time to take several practice tests, take the first one open book, with no time limit. Work through the questions at your own pace and make sure you fully understand them. Gradually work up to taking a test under test conditions: sit at a desk with all study materials put away and set a timer. Pace yourself to make sure you finish the test with time to spare and go back to check your answers if you have time.

After each test, check your answers. On the questions you missed, be sure you understand why you missed them. Did you misread the question (tests can use tricky wording)? Did you forget the information? Or was it something you hadn't learned? Go back and study any shaky areas that the practice tests reveal.

Taking these tests not only helps with your grade, but also aids in combating test anxiety. If you're already used to the test conditions, you're less likely to worry about it, and working through tests until you're scoring well gives you a confidence boost. Go through the practice tests until you feel comfortable, and then you can go into the test knowing that you're ready for it.

Test Tips

On test day, you should be confident, knowing that you've prepared well and are ready to answer the questions. But aside from preparation, there are several test day strategies you can employ to maximize your performance.

First, as stated before, get a good night's sleep the night before the test (and for several nights before that, if possible). Go into the test with a fresh, alert mind rather than staying up late to study.

Try not to change too much about your normal routine on the day of the test. It's important to eat a nutritious breakfast, but if you normally don't eat breakfast at all, consider eating just a protein bar. If you're a coffee drinker, go ahead and have your normal coffee. Just make sure you time it so that the caffeine doesn't wear off right in the middle of your test. Avoid sugary beverages, and drink enough water to stay hydrated but not so much that you need a restroom break 10 minutes into the test. If your test isn't first thing in the morning, consider going for a walk or doing a light workout before the test to get your blood flowing.

Allow yourself enough time to get ready, and leave for the test with plenty of time to spare so you won't have the anxiety of scrambling to arrive in time. Another reason to be early is to select a good seat. It's helpful to sit away from doors and windows, which can be distracting. Find a good seat, get out your supplies, and settle your mind before the test begins.

When the test begins, start by going over the instructions carefully, even if you already know what to expect. Make sure you avoid any careless mistakes by following the directions.

Then begin working through the questions, pacing yourself as you've practiced. If you're not sure on an answer, don't spend too much time on it, and don't let it shake your confidence. Either skip it and come back later, or eliminate as many wrong answers as possible and guess among the remaining ones. Don't dwell on these questions as you continue—put them out of your mind and focus on what lies ahead.

Be sure to read all of the answer choices, even if you're sure the first one is the right answer. Sometimes you'll find a better one if you keep reading. But don't second-guess yourself if you do immediately know the answer. Your gut instinct is usually right. Don't let test anxiety rob you of the information you know.

If you have time at the end of the test (and if the test format allows), go back and review your answers. Be cautious about changing any, since your first instinct tends to be correct, but make sure you didn't misread any of the questions or accidentally mark the wrong answer choice. Look over any you skipped and make an educated guess.

At the end, leave the test feeling confident. You've done your best, so don't waste time worrying about your performance or wishing you could change anything. Instead, celebrate the successful completion of this test. And finally, use this test to learn how to deal with anxiety even better next time.

Review Video: Test Anxiety
Visit mometrix.com/academy and enter code: 100340

Important Qualification

Not all anxiety is created equal. If your test anxiety is causing major issues in your life beyond the classroom or testing center, or if you are experiencing troubling physical symptoms related to your anxiety, it may be a sign of a serious physiological or psychological condition. If this sounds like your situation, we strongly encourage you to seek professional help.

Online Resources

Due to our efforts to try to keep this book to a manageable length, we've created a link that will give you access to all of your online resources:

mometrix.com/resources719/hiset-27339

It's Your Moment, Let's Celebrate It!

Share your story @mometrixtestpreparation